Minnesota Criminal Statutes
&
Study Guide

2021 Revised Edition

Stephen R. Arnott
Gerald P. Krause

ST. CROIX PUBLISHING LLC

Publisher contact information:

ST. CROIX PUBLISHING LLC
1121 Hague Avenue
Suite One
St. Paul, MN 55104
Phone: 651-470-3383
Email: stcroixpublish@gmail.com

ISBN: 978-0-9887842-8-4

INTRODUCTION

This book combines the two major sources of study for Minnesota criminal law, the <u>Learning Objectives for Professional Peace Officer Education</u> promulgated by the Minnesota Board of Peace Officer Standards and Training (POST Board), and their corresponding Minnesota criminal code statutes. These statutes reflect changes enacted by the state legislature and signed into law during the 2021 regular and first special sessions. Hopefully, these materials provide criminal justice and other students with all the material necessary to thoroughly understand Minnesota criminal law. And for those seeking peace officer certification, to successfully perform on this important component of the Minnesota POST License Exam.

In July 1997, the POST Board released a version of the <u>Learning Objectives for Professional Peace Officer Education</u>, updated in May 2011. These objectives were fundamentally reconfigured in April 2015, with minor revisions in July 2017. The 2011 & 2017 iterations provide for more general objectives, requiring law enforcement students to engage in more self-directed study. In 2018, as statutorily required, the POST Board approved learning objectives for training in crisis intervention and mental illness crises, conflict management and mediation and recognizing and valuing community diversity and cultural differences, to include implicit bias.

In 2019, the POST Board released revised learning objectives divided into four categories that are, in turn, divided into numbered sections with objectives assigned to each section. This book has been substantially revised to incorporate the 2019 learning objectives as the organizing framework. In particular, it focuses on Category Two, which groups its learning objectives into three parts - Legal Studies, Human Behavior, and Other – aimed at the foundational goal of providing a specialized body of knowledge for Minnesota's professional peace officer education. In addition to these organizational revisions, a glossary of terms has been appended consistent with various learning objectives that require students to define terms.

New changes to statutes and the addition of any new statutes are indicated by <u>underscoring</u> the new textual changes, and a ~~strikethrough~~ indicating the deletion of prior material. If certain non-essential portions of a subdivision, paragraph or clause have been omitted, such omissions are noted with the symbol "* * *" and other edited and/or omitted material is enclosed with the symbol "[ ]." Where an underscored effective date for a statute is included, that date refers to statutory provisions that are similarly underscored. Changes reflected in the 2020 Supplement distributed for use in the 2021-21 academic year are included in this edition but are not marked as new changes.

These materials have been assembled to serve primarily law enforcement, criminal justice, and other undergraduate students interested in examining criminal law and related concepts in the State of Minnesota. We would encourage the thoughts and comments of students and their instructors if you have suggestions for improvements.

Stephen R. Arnott, J.D., Editor
Associate Professor of Legal Studies, Hamline University
•sarnott01@hamline.edu•

Gerald P. Krause, J.D., Editor
Professor Emeritus of Criminal Justice, Hamline University
•jkrause@hamline.edu•

TABLE OF CONTENTS

TABLE OF STATUTES

LEARNING OBJECTIVES
FOR POST-SECONDARY COURSES IN LAW ENFORCEMENT

MINNESOTA STATUTES

Chapter 1 -- CRIMINAL CODE, CHAPTER 609 -- GENERAL PRINCIPLES

Category 2, Section 5:
2.5.1. Describe the basic organization, purpose, and definitions and principles of the Minnesota Criminal Code.

609.015 SCOPE AND EFFECT.

Subdivision 1. **Common law crimes abolished.** Common law crimes are abolished and no act or omission is a crime unless made so by this chapter or by other applicable statute, but this does not prevent the use of common law rules in the construction or interpretation of the provisions of this chapter or other statute. Crimes committed prior to the effective date of this chapter are not affected thereby.

Subd. 2. **Applicability.** Unless expressly stated otherwise, or the context otherwise requires, the provisions of this chapter also apply to crimes created by statute other than in this chapter.
HIST: 1963 c 753 art 1 s 609.015

Category 2, Sections 1, 5:
2.1.10. Identify the meaning of criminal justice system terms . . .
2.5.2.-.3 Explain the classifications of crimes including felony, misdemeanor, gross misdemeanor and the meaning of the term petty misdemeanor . . . Explain what is meant by elements of a crime and describe the connection between criminal conduct and criminal intent (mens rea).

609.02 DEFINITIONS.

Subdivision 1. **Crime.** "Crime" means conduct which is prohibited by statute and for which the actor may be sentenced to imprisonment, with or without a fine.

Subd. 2. **Felony.** "Felony" means a crime for which a sentence of imprisonment for more than one year may be imposed.

Subd. 3. **Misdemeanor.** "Misdemeanor" means a crime for which a sentence of not more than 90 days or a fine of not more than $1,000, or both, may be imposed.

Subd. 4. **Gross misdemeanor.** "Gross misdemeanor" means any crime which is not a felony or misdemeanor. The maximum fine which may be imposed for a gross misdemeanor is $3,000.

Subd. 4a. **Petty misdemeanor.** "Petty misdemeanor" means a petty offense which is prohibited by statute, which does not constitute a crime and for which a sentence of a fine of not more than $300 may be imposed.

Subd. 5. **Conviction.** "Conviction" means any of the following accepted and recorded by the court:
(1) A plea of guilty; or
(2) A verdict of guilty by a jury or a finding of guilty by the court.

Subd. 6. **Dangerous weapon.** "Dangerous weapon" means any firearm, whether loaded or unloaded, or any device designed as a weapon and capable of producing death or great bodily harm, any combustible or flammable liquid or other device or instrumentality that, in the manner it is used or intended to be used, is calculated or likely to produce death or great bodily harm, or any fire that is used to produce death or great bodily harm.

As used in this subdivision, "flammable liquid" means any liquid having a flash point below 100 degrees Fahrenheit and having a vapor pressure not exceeding 40 pounds per square inch (absolute) at 100 degrees Fahrenheit but does not include intoxicating liquor as defined in section 340A.101. As used in this subdivision, "combustible liquid" is a liquid having a flash point at or above 100 degrees Fahrenheit.

Subd. 7. **Bodily harm.** "Bodily harm" means physical pain or injury, illness, or any impairment of physical condition.

Subd. 7a. **Substantial bodily harm.** "Substantial bodily harm" means bodily injury which involves a temporary but substantial disfigurement, or which causes a temporary but substantial loss or impairment of the function of any bodily member or organ, or which causes a fracture of any bodily member.

Subd. 8. **Great bodily harm.** "Great bodily harm" means bodily injury which creates a high probability of death, or which causes serious permanent disfigurement, or which causes a permanent or protracted loss or impairment of the function of any bodily member or organ or other serious bodily harm.

Subd. 9. **Mental state.** (1) When criminal intent is an element of a crime in this chapter, such intent is indicated by the term "intentionally," the phrase "with intent to," the phrase "with intent that," or some form of the verbs "know" or "believe."

(2) "Know" requires only that the actor believes that the specified fact exists.

(3) "Intentionally" means that the actor either has a purpose to do the thing or cause the result specified or believes that the act performed by the actor, if successful will cause that result. In addition, except as provided in clause (6), the actor must have knowledge of those facts which are necessary to make the actor's conduct criminal and which are set forth after the word "intentionally."

(4) "With intent to" or "with intent that" means that the actor either has a purpose to do the thing or cause the result specified or believes that the act, if successful, will cause that result.

(5) Criminal intent does not require proof of knowledge of the existence or constitutionality of the statute under which the actor is prosecuted or the scope or meaning of the terms used in that statute.

(6) Criminal intent does not require proof of knowledge of the age of a minor even though age is a material element in the crime in question.

Subd. 10. **Assault.** "Assault" is:

(1) An act done with intent to cause fear in another of immediate bodily harm or death; or

(2) The intentional infliction of or attempt to inflict bodily harm upon another.

Subd. 11. **Second or subsequent violation or offense.** "Second or subsequent violation" or "second or subsequent offense" means that prior to the commission of the violation or offense, the actor has been adjudicated guilty of a specified similar violation or offense.

Subd. 12. Repealed, 1993 c 326 art 2 s 34

Subd. 13. Repealed, 1993 c 326 art 2 s 34

Subd. 14. Repealed, 2014 c 263 s 4

Subd. 15. **Probation.** "Probation" means a court-ordered sanction imposed upon an offender for a period of supervision no greater than that set by statute. It is imposed as an alternative to confinement or in conjunction with confinement or intermediate sanctions. The purpose of probation is to deter further criminal behavior, punish the offender, help provide reparation to crime victims and their communities, and provide offenders with opportunities for rehabilitation.

Subd. 16. **Qualified domestic violence-related offense.** "Qualified domestic violence-related offense" includes a violation of or an attempt to violate sections 518B.01, subdivision 14 (violation of domestic abuse order for protection); 518B.01, subdivision 22 (violation of domestic abuse no contact order); 609.185 (first-degree murder); 609.19 (second-degree murder); 609.221 (first-degree assault); 609.222 (second-degree assault); 609.223 (third-degree assault); 609.2231 (fourth-degree assault); 609.224 (fifth-degree assault); 609.2242 (domestic assault); 609.2245 (female genital mutilation); 609.2247 (domestic assault by strangulation); 609.342 (first-degree criminal sexual conduct); 609.343 (second-degree criminal sexual conduct); 609.344 (third-degree criminal sexual conduct); 609.345 (fourth-degree criminal sexual conduct); 609.377 (malicious punishment of a child); 609.713 (terroristic threats); 609.748, subdivision 6 (violation of harassment restraining order); 609.749 (stalking); 609.78, subdivision 2 (interference with an emergency call); 617.261 (nonconsensual dissemination of private sexual images); and 629.75 (violation of domestic abuse no contact order); and similar laws of other states, the United States, the District of Columbia, tribal lands, and United States territories.

Subd. 17. **Ammunition.** "Ammunition" means ammunition or cartridge cases, primers, bullets, or propellent powder designed for use in any firearm. Ammunition does not include ornaments, curiosities, or souvenirs constructed from or resembling ammunition or ammunition components that are not operable as ammunition.
HIST: 1963 c 753 art 1 s 609.02; * * * ; 2016 c 126 s 3

609.27 COERCION.

Subdivision 1. **Acts constituting.** Whoever orally or in writing makes any of the following threats and thereby causes another against the other's will to do any act or forbear doing a lawful act is guilty of coercion and may be sentenced as provided in subdivision 2:

(1) A threat to unlawfully inflict bodily harm upon, or hold in confinement, the person threatened or another, when robbery or attempt to rob is not committed thereby; or

(2) A threat to unlawfully inflict damage to the property of the person threatened or another; or

(3) A threat to unlawfully injure a trade, business, profession, or calling; or

(4) A threat to expose a secret or deformity, publish a defamatory statement, or otherwise to expose any person to disgrace or ridicule;

(5) A threat to make or cause to be made a criminal charge, whether true or false; provided, that a warning of the consequences of a future violation of law given in good faith by a peace officer or prosecuting attorney to any person shall not be deemed a threat for the purposes of this section; or

(6) a threat to commit a violation under section 617.261.
Subd. 2. **Sentence.** Whoever violates subdivision 1 may be sentenced as follows:

(1) To imprisonment for not more than 90 days or to payment of a fine of not more than $1,000, or both if neither the pecuniary gain received by the violator nor the loss suffered by the person threatened or another as a result of the threat exceeds $300, or the benefits received or harm sustained are not susceptible of pecuniary measurement; or

(2) To imprisonment for not more than five years or to payment of a fine of not more than $10,000, or both, if such pecuniary gain or loss is more than $300 but less than $2,500; or

(3) To imprisonment for not more than ten years or to payment of a fine of not more than $20,000, or both, if such pecuniary gain or loss is $2,500, or more.
HIST: 1963 c 753 art 1 s 609.27; * * * ; 2016 c 126 s 4

609.035 CRIME PUNISHABLE UNDER DIFFERENT PROVISIONS.

Subdivision 1. **Conduct; multiple crimes; chargeable for one offense.** Except as provided in subdivisions 2, 3, 4 and 5, and in section 609.251, 609.585, 609.21, subdivision 1b, 609.2691, 609.486, 609.494, and 609.856, if a person's conduct constitutes more than one offense under the laws of this state, the person may be punished for only one of the offenses and a conviction or acquittal of any one of them is a bar to prosecution for any other of them. All the offenses, if prosecuted, shall be included in one prosecution which shall be stated in separate counts.

Subd. 2. **Consecutive sentences.** (a) When a person is being sentenced for a violation of a provision listed in paragraph (e), the court may sentence the person to a consecutive term of imprisonment for a violation of any other provision listed in paragraph (e), notwithstanding the fact that the offenses arose out of the same course of conduct, subject to the limitation on consecutive sentences contained in section 609.15, subdivision 2, and except as provided in paragraphs (b), (c), and f) of this subdivision.

(b) When a person is being sentenced for a violation of section 171.09, 171.20, 171.24, or 171.30, the court may not impose a consecutive sentence for another violation of a provision in chapter 171.

(c) When a person is being sentenced for a violation of section 169.791 or 169.797, the court may not impose a consecutive sentence for another violation of a provision of sections 169.79 to 169.7995.

(d) This subdivision does not limit the authority of the court to impose consecutive sentences for crimes arising on different dates or to impose a consecutive sentence when a person is being sentenced for a crime and is also in violation of the conditions of a stayed or otherwise deferred sentence under section 609.135.

(e) This subdivision applies to misdemeanor and gross misdemeanor violations of the following if the offender has two or more prior impaired driving convictions as defined in section 169A.03 within the past ten years:

(1) section 169A.20, subdivision 1, driving while impaired;

(2) section 169A.20, subdivision 2, test refusal;

(3) section 169.791, failure to provide proof of insurance;

(4) section 169.797, failure to provide vehicle insurance;

(5) section 171.09, violation of condition of restricted license;

(6) section 171.20, subdivision 2, operation after revocation, suspension, cancellation, or disqualification;

(7) section 171.24, driving without valid license; and

(8) section 171.30, violation of condition of limited license.

(f) When a court is sentencing an offender for a violation of section 169A.20 and a violation of an offense listed in paragraph (e), and the offender has five or more qualified prior impaired driving incidents, as defined in section 169A.03, within the past ten years, the court shall sentence the offender to serve consecutive sentences for the offenses, notwithstanding the fact that the offenses arose out of the same course of conduct.

Subd. 3. **Exception; firearms offenses.** Notwithstanding section 609.04, a prosecution for or conviction of a violation of section 609.165 or 624.713, subdivision 1, clause (b), is not a bar to conviction of or punishment for any other crime committed by the defendant as part of the same conduct.

Subd. 4. **Exception; arson offenses.** Notwithstanding section 609.04, a prosecution for or conviction of a violation of sections 609.561 to 609.563 or 609.5641 is not a bar to conviction of or punishment for any other crime committed by the defendant as part of the same conduct when the defendant is shown to have violated sections 609.561 to 609.563 or 609.5641 for the purpose of concealing any other crime.

Subd. 5. **Exception; fleeing a peace officer.** Notwithstanding subdivision 1, a prosecution or conviction for violating section 609.487 is not a bar to conviction of or punishment for any other crime committed by the defendant as part of the same conduct. If an offender is punished for more than one crime as authorized by this subdivision and the court imposes consecutive sentences for the crimes, the consecutive sentences are not a departure from the sentencing guidelines.

Subd. 6. **Exception; criminal sexual conduct offenses.** Notwithstanding subdivision 1, a prosecution or conviction for committing a violation of sections 609.342 to 609.345 with force or violence is not a bar to conviction of or punishment for any other crime committed by the defendant as part of the same conduct. If an offender is punished for more than one crime as authorized by this subdivision and the court imposes consecutive sentences for the crimes, the consecutive sentences are not a departure from the sentencing guidelines.

For purposes of the sentencing guidelines, a violation of sections 609.561 to 609.563 or 609.5641 is a crime against the person.
HIST: 1963 c 753 art 1 s 609.035; * * * ; 2007 c 54 art 4 s 14

609.05 LIABILITY FOR CRIMES OF ANOTHER.

Subdivision 1. Aiding; abetting; liability. A person is criminally liable for a crime committed by another if the person intentionally aids, advises, hires, counsels, or conspires with or otherwise procures the other to commit the crime.

Subd. 2. Expansive liability. A person liable under subdivision 1 is also liable for any other crime committed in pursuance of the intended crime if reasonably foreseeable by the person as a probable consequence of committing or attempting to commit the crime intended.

Subd. 3. Abandonment of criminal purpose. A person who intentionally aids, advises, hires, counsels, or conspires with or otherwise procures another to commit a crime and thereafter abandons that purpose and makes a reasonable effort to prevent the commission of the crime prior to its commission is not liable if the crime is thereafter committed.

Subd. 4. Circumstances of conviction. A person liable under this section may be charged with and convicted of the crime although the person who directly committed it has not been convicted, or has been convicted of some other degree of the crime or of some other crime based on the same act, or if the person is a juvenile who has not been found delinquent for the act.

Subd. 5. Definition. For purposes of this section, a crime also includes an act committed by a juvenile that would be a crime if committed by an adult.
HIST: 1963 c 753 art 1 s 609.05; 1986 c 444; 1991 c 279 s 22, 23

609.055 LIABILITY OF CHILDREN.

Subdivision 1. General rule. Children under the age 14 years are incapable of committing crime.

Subd. 2. Adult prosecution. (a) except as otherwise provided in paragraph (b), children of the age of 14 years or over but under 18 years may be prosecuted for a felony offense if the alleged violation is duly certified for prosecution under the laws and court procedures controlling adult criminal violations or may be designated an extended jurisdiction juvenile in accordance with the provisions of chapter 260. A child who is 16 years of age or older but under 18 years of age is capable of committing a crime and may be prosecuted for a felony if:

(1) the child has been previously certified on a felony charge pursuant to a hearing under section 260.125, subdivision 2, or pursuant to the waiver of the right to such a hearing, or prosecuted pursuant to this subdivision; and

(2) the child was convicted of the felony offense or offenses for which the child was prosecuted or of a lesser included felony offense.

(b) A child who is alleged to have committed murder in the first degree after becoming 16 years of age is capable of committing a crime and may be prosecuted for the felony. This paragraph does not apply to a child alleged to have committed attempted murder in the first degree after becoming 16 years of age.
HIST: 1963 c 753 art 1 s 609.055; * * * ; 1995 c 226 art 3 s 47

Category 2, Section 1:
2.1.8. Explain the functions and jurisdictions of law enforcement agencies including federal, state, county, municipal, tribal, and international.

609.025 JURISDICTION OF STATE.
  A person may be convicted and sentenced under the law of this state if the person:
  (1) Commits an offense in whole or in part within this state; or
  (2) Being without the state, causes, aids or abets another to commit a crime within the state; or
  (3) Being without the state, intentionally causes a result within the state prohibited by the criminal laws of this state.
  It is not a defense that the defendant's conduct is also a criminal offense under the laws of another state or of the United States or of another country.
HIST: 1963 c 753 art 1 s 609.025; Ex1971 c 27 s 44; 1986 c 444

Category 2, Section 8:
2.8.1.-.10 Explain Minnesota statutes and relevant case law related to the application [of] force by peace officers . . .

609.06 AUTHORIZED USE OF FORCE.
  Subdivision 1. **When authorized.** Except as otherwise provided in subdivisions 2 and 3, reasonable force may be used upon or toward the person of another without the other's consent when the following circumstances exist or the actor reasonably believes them to exist:
  (1) when used by a public officer or one assisting a public officer under the public officer's direction:
  (i) in effecting a lawful arrest; or
  (ii) in the execution of legal process; or
  (iii) in enforcing an order of the court; or
  (iv) in executing any other duty imposed upon the public officer by law; or
  (2) when used by a person not a public officer in arresting another in the cases and in the manner provided by law and delivering the other to an officer competent to receive the other into custody; or
  (3) when used by any person in resisting or aiding another to resist an offense against the person; or
  (4) when used by any person in lawful possession of real or personal property, or by another assisting the person in lawful possession, in resisting a trespass upon or other unlawful interference with such property; or
  (5) when used by any person to prevent the escape, or to retake following the escape, of a person lawfully held on a charge or conviction of a crime; or
  (6) when used by a parent, guardian, teacher or other lawful custodian of a child or pupil, in the exercise of lawful authority, to restrain or correct such child or pupil; or
  (7) when used by a school employee or school bus driver, in the exercise of lawful authority, to restrain a child or pupil, or to prevent bodily harm or death to another; or
  (8) when used by a common carrier in expelling a passenger who refuses to obey a lawful requirement for the conduct of passengers and reasonable care is exercised with regard to the passenger's personal safety; or
  (9) when used to restrain a person who has a mental illness or a developmental disability from self-injury or injury to another or when used by one with authority to do so to compel compliance with reasonable requirements for the person's control, conduct or treatment; or
  (10) when used by a public or private institution providing custody or treatment against one lawfully committed to it to compel compliance with reasonable requirements for the control, conduct or treatment of the committed person.
  Subd. 2. **Deadly force used against peace officers.** Deadly force may not be used against peace officers who have announced their presence and are performing official duties at a

location where a person is committing a crime or an act that would be a crime if committed by an adult.

Subd. 3. **Limitations on the use of certain restraints.** (a) A peace officer may not use any of the following restraints unless section 609.066 authorizes the use of deadly force to protect the peace officer or another from death or great bodily harm:

(1) a choke hold;

(2) tying all of a person's limbs together behind the person's back to render the person immobile; or

(3) securing a person in any way that results in transporting the person face down in a vehicle.

(b) For the purposes of this subdivision, "choke hold" means a method by which a person applies sufficient pressure to a person to make breathing difficult or impossible, and includes but is not limited to any pressure to the neck, throat, or windpipe that may prevent or hinder breathing, or reduce intake of air. Choke hold also means applying pressure to a person's neck on either side of the windpipe, but not to the windpipe itself, to stop the flow of blood to the brain via the carotid arteries.

EFFECTIVE DATE. This section is effective the day following final enactment.

HIST: 1963 c 753 art 1 s 609.06; * * *; 2013 c 62 s 28; 2Sp2020 c 1 s 7,8

609.065 JUSTIFIABLE TAKING OF LIFE.

The intentional taking of the life of another is not authorized by section 609.06, except when necessary in resisting or preventing an offense which the actor reasonably believes exposes the actor or another to great bodily harm or death, or preventing the commission of a felony in the actor's place of abode.

HIST: 1963 c 753 art 1 s 609.065; 1978 c 736 s 1; 1986 c 444

609.066 AUTHORIZED USE OF DEADLY FORCE BY PEACE OFFICERS.

Subdivision 1. **Deadly force defined.** For the purposes of this section, "deadly force" means force which the actor uses with the purpose of causing, or which the actor should reasonably know creates a substantial risk of causing, death or great bodily harm. The intentional discharge of a firearm, other than a firearm loaded with less lethal munitions and used by a peace officer within the scope of official duties, in the direction of another person, or at a vehicle in which another person is believed to be, constitutes deadly force. "Less lethal munitions" means projectiles which are designed to stun, temporarily incapacitate, or cause temporary discomfort to a person. "Peace officer" has the meaning given in section 626.84, subdivision 1.

Subd. 1a. **Legislative intent.** The legislature hereby finds and declares the following:

(1) that the authority to use deadly force, conferred on peace officers by this section, is a critical responsibility that shall be exercised judiciously and with respect for human rights and dignity and for the sanctity of every human life. The legislature further finds and declares that every person has a right to be free from excessive use of force by officers acting under color of law;

(2) as set forth below, it is the intent of the legislature that peace officers use deadly force only when necessary in defense of human life or to prevent great bodily harm. In determining whether deadly force is necessary, officers shall evaluate each situation in light of the particular circumstances of each case;

(3) that the decision by a peace officer to use deadly force shall be evaluated from the perspective of a reasonable officer in the same situation, based on the totality of the

circumstances known to or perceived by the officer at the time, rather than with the benefit of hindsight, and that the totality of the circumstances shall account for occasions when officers may be forced to make quick judgments about using deadly force; and

(4) that peace officers should exercise special care when interacting with individuals with known physical, mental health, developmental, or intellectual disabilities as an individual's disability may affect the individual's ability to understand or comply with commands from peace officers.

Subd. 2. Use of deadly force. (a) Notwithstanding the provisions of section 609.06 or 609.065, the use of deadly force by a peace officer in the line of duty is justified only if an objectively reasonable officer would believe, based on the totality of the circumstances known to the officer at the time and without the benefit of hindsight, that such force is necessary:

(1) to protect the peace officer or another from death or great bodily harm, provided that the threat:

(i) can be articulated with specificity by the law enforcement officer;

(ii) is reasonably likely to occur absent action by the law enforcement officer; and

(iii) must be addressed through the use of deadly force without unreasonable delay; or

(2) to effect the arrest or capture, or prevent the escape, of a person whom the peace officer knows or has reasonable grounds to believe has committed or attempted to commit a felony and the officer reasonably believes that the person will cause death or great bodily harm to another person under the threat criteria in clause (1), items (i) to (iii), unless immediately apprehended.

(b) A peace officer shall not use deadly force against a person based on the danger the person poses to self if an objectively reasonable officer would believe, based on the totality of the circumstances known to the officer at the time and without the benefit of hindsight, that the person does not pose a threat of death or great bodily harm to the peace officer or to another under the threat criteria in paragraph (a), clause (1), items (i) to (iii).

Subd. 3. **No defense.** This section and sections 609.06, 609.065 and 629.33 may not be used as a defense in a civil action brought by an innocent third party.

EFFECTIVE DATE. This section is effective March 1, 2021.

HIST: 1978 c 736 s 2; 1986 c 444; 2001 c 127 s 1; 2Sp2020 c 1 s 9,10

Editors' Note: On July 2, 2021, the Minnesota Chiefs of Police Association, the Minnesota Sheriffs' Association, the Minnesota Police and Peace Officers Association, and Law Enforcement Labor Services sued the State of Minnesota in Ramsey County District Court, alleging that the 2020 amendments to Minnesota's use of deadly force statute alleging that the amended statute violates officers' rights to self-defense and unconstitutionally compels officers to forfeit their rights to refuse to testify against themselves in deadly force cases.

═══════════════════════

Category 2, Section 5:
2.5.3. Explain what is meant by elements of a crime and describe the connection between criminal conduct and criminal intent (mens rea).

═══════════════════════

609.075 INTOXICATION AS DEFENSE.
An act committed while in a state of voluntary intoxication is not less criminal by reason thereof, but when a particular intent or other state of mind is a necessary element to constitute a

particular crime, the fact of intoxication may be taken into consideration in determining such intent or state of mind.
HIST: 1963 c 753 art 1 s 609.075

609.08 DURESS.

Except as provided in section 609.20, clause (3), when any crime is committed or participated in by two or more persons, any one of whom participates only under compulsion by another engaged therein, who by threats creates a reasonable apprehension in the mind of such participator that in case of refusal that participator is liable to instant death, such threats and apprehension constitute duress which will excuse such participator from criminal liability.
HIST: 1963 c 753 art 1 s 609.08; 1986 c 444

Category 2, Section 5:
2.5.1. Describe the basic organization, purpose, and definitions and principles of the Minnesota Criminal Code.

609.09 COMPELLING TESTIMONY; IMMUNITY FROM PROSECUTION.

Subdivision 1. **Conditions of immunity.** In any criminal proceeding, including a grand jury proceeding, paternity proceeding, or proceeding in juvenile court, if it appears a person may be entitled to refuse to answer a question or produce evidence of any other kind on the ground that the person may be incriminated thereby, and if the prosecuting attorney, in writing, requests the chief judge of the district or a judge of the court in which the proceeding is pending to order that person to answer the question or produce the evidence, the judge, after notice to the witness and hearing, shall so order if the judge finds that to do so would not be contrary to the public interest and would not be likely to expose the witness to prosecution in another state or in the federal courts.

After complying, and if, but for this section, the witness would have been privileged to withhold the answer given or evidence produced by the witness, no testimony or other information compelled under the order, or any information directly or indirectly derived from such testimony or other information may be used against the witness in any criminal case, but the witness may be prosecuted or subjected to penalty or forfeiture for any perjury, false swearing or contempt committed in answering, or in failing to answer, or in producing, or failing to produce, evidence in accordance with the order.

Subd. 2. **Testimony required; no use of testimony for prosecution.** In every case not provided for in subdivision 1 and in which it is provided by law that a witness shall not be excused from giving testimony tending to be self-incriminating, no person shall be excused from testifying or producing any papers or documents on the ground that doing so may tend to criminate the person or subject the person to a penalty or forfeiture; but no testimony or other information directly or indirectly derived from such testimony or other information may be used against the witness in any criminal case, except for perjury committed in such testimony.
HIST: 1963 c 753 art 1 s 609.09; 1969 c 661 s 1; 1981 c 293 s 1; 1986 c 444

Chapter 2 – SENTENCES AND PREDATORY OFFENDERS

Category 2, Section 2:
2.2.16. Explain the general provisions for sentencing in the Minnesota Criminal Code and the Minnesota Sentencing Guidelines.
2.2.17. Describe crime classifications misdemeanor through felony.
2.2.18. Discuss enhancements that may be applied to repeat offenders, patterned offenders, and career offenders.
2.2.19. Explain the following terms: concurrent and consecutive sentences, imposition and execution of sentence, determinate and indeterminate sentencing.

609.13 CONVICTIONS OF FELONY OR GROSS MISDEMEANOR; WHEN DEEMED MISDEMEANOR OR GROSS MISDEMEANOR.

Subdivision 1. **Felony.** Notwithstanding a conviction is for a felony:

(1) The conviction is deemed to be for a misdemeanor or a gross misdemeanor if the sentence imposed is within the limits provided by law for a misdemeanor or gross misdemeanor as defined in section 609.02; or

(2) The conviction is deemed to be for a misdemeanor if the imposition of the prison sentence is stayed, the defendant is placed on probation, and the defendant is thereafter discharged without a prison sentence.

Subd. 2. **Gross misdemeanor.** Notwithstanding that a conviction is for a gross misdemeanor, the conviction is deemed to be for a misdemeanor if:

(1) The sentence imposed is within the limits provided by law for a misdemeanor as defined in section 609.02; or

(2) If the imposition of the sentence is stayed, the defendant is placed on probation, and the defendant is thereafter discharged without sentence.

Subd. 3. **Misdemeanors.** If a defendant is convicted of a misdemeanor and is sentenced, or if the imposition of sentence is stayed, and the defendant is thereafter discharged without sentence, the conviction is deemed to be for a misdemeanor for purposes of determining the penalty for a subsequent offense.

HIST: 1963 c 753 art 1 s 609.13; * * * 1993 c 326 art 2 s 10

609.135 STAY OF IMPOSITION OR EXECUTION OF SENTENCE.

Subdivision 1. **Terms and conditions.** (a) Except when a sentence of life imprisonment is required by law, or when a mandatory minimum sentence is required by section 609.11, any court may stay imposition or execution of sentence and:

(1) may order intermediate sanctions without placing the defendant on probation; or

(2) may place the defendant on probation with or without supervision and on the terms the court prescribes, including intermediate sanctions when practicable. The court may order the supervision to be under the probation officer of the court, or, if there is none and the conviction is for a felony or gross misdemeanor, by the commissioner of corrections, or in any case by some other suitable and consenting person. Unless the court directs otherwise, state parole and probation agents and probation officers may impose community work service or probation violation sanctions, consistent with section 243.05, subdivision 1; sections 244.196 to 244.199; or 401.02, subdivision 5.

No intermediate sanction may be ordered performed at a location that fails to observe applicable requirements or standards of chapter 181A or 182, or any rule promulgated under them.

(b) For purposes of this subdivision, subdivision 6, and section 609.14, the term "intermediate sanctions" includes but is not limited to incarceration in a local jail or workhouse, home detention, electronic monitoring, intensive probation, sentencing to service, reporting to a day reporting center, chemical dependency or mental health treatment or counseling, restitution, fines, day-fines, community work service, and work in lieu of or to work off fines and, with the victim's consent, work in lieu of or to work off restitution.

(c) A court may not stay the revocation of the driver's license of a person convicted of violating the provisions of section 169A.20.

* * *

Subd. 1a. **Failure to pay restitution.** If the court orders payment of restitution as a condition of probation and if the defendant fails to pay the restitution in accordance with the payment schedule or structure established by the court or the probation officer, the prosecutor or the defendant's probation officer may, on the prosecutor's or the officer's own motion or at the request of the victim, ask the court to hold a hearing to determine whether or not the conditions of probation should be changed or probation should be revoked. The defendant's probation officer shall ask for the hearing if the restitution or fine ordered has not been paid prior to 60 days before the term of probation expires. The court shall schedule and hold this hearing and take appropriate action, including action under subdivision 2, paragraph (g), before the defendant's term of probation expires. * * *

Subd. 2. **Stay of sentence maximum periods.** (a) If the conviction is for a felony other than section 609.2113, subdivision 1 or 2, 609.2114, subdivision 2, <u>or section 609.3451, subdivision 1,</u> or section 609.21, subdivision 1a, paragraph (b) or (c), the stay shall be for not more than four years or the maximum period for which the sentence of imprisonment might have been imposed, whichever is longer.

(b) If the conviction is for a gross misdemeanor violation of section 169A.20, 609.2113, subdivision 3, or 609.3451, or for a felony described in section 609.2113, subdivision 1 or 2, 609.2114, subdivision 2, or 609.21, subdivision 1a, paragraph (d), <u>or 609.3451, subdivision 1,</u> the stay shall be for not more than six years. The court shall provide for unsupervised probation for the last one year of the stay unless the court finds that the defendant needs supervised probation for all or part of the last year.

(c) If the conviction is for a gross misdemeanor not specified in paragraph (b), the stay shall be for not more than two years.

(d) If the conviction is for any misdemeanor under section 169A.20; 609.746, subdivision 1; 609.79; or 617.23; or for a misdemeanor under section 609.2242 or 609.224, subdivision 1, in which the victim of the crime was a family or household member as defined in section 518B.01, the stay shall be for not more than two years. The court shall provide for unsupervised probation for the second year of the stay unless the court finds that the defendant needs supervised probation for all or part of the second year.

(e) If the conviction is for a misdemeanor not specified in paragraph (d), the stay shall be for not more than one year.

(f) The defendant shall be discharged six months after the term of the stay expires, unless the stay has been revoked or extended under paragraph (g), or the defendant has already been discharged.

(g) Notwithstanding the maximum periods specified for stays of sentences under paragraphs (a) to (f), a court may extend a defendant's term of probation for up to one year if it finds, at a hearing conducted under subdivision 1a, that:

(1) the defendant has not paid court-ordered restitution in accordance with the payment schedule or structure; and

(2) the defendant is likely to not pay the restitution the defendant owes before the term of probation expires.

This one-year extension of probation for failure to pay restitution may be extended by the court for up to one additional year if the court finds, at another hearing conducted under subdivision 1a, that the defendant still has not paid the court-ordered restitution that the defendant owes.

* * *

(h) Notwithstanding the maximum periods specified for stays of sentences under paragraphs (a) to (f), a court may extend a defendant's term of probation for up to three years if it finds, at a hearing conducted under subdivision 1c, that:

(1) the defendant has failed to complete court-ordered treatment successfully; and

(2) the defendant is likely not to complete court-ordered treatment before the term of probation expires.

Subd. 3. **Motor vehicle offense report.** The court shall report to the commissioner of public safety any stay of imposition or execution granted in the case of a conviction for an offense in which a motor vehicle, as defined in section 169.01, subdivision 3, is used.

Subd. 4. **Jail as condition of probation.** The court may, as a condition of probation require the defendant to serve up to one year incarceration in a county jail, a county regional jail, a county workfarm, county workhouse or other local correctional facility, or require the defendant to pay a fine, or both. The court may allow the defendant the work release privileges of section 631.425 during the period of incarceration.

Subd. 5. **Assaulting spouse stay conditions.** If a person is convicted of assaulting a spouse or other person with whom the person resides, and the court stays imposition or execution of sentence and places the defendant on probation, the court must condition the stay upon the defendant's participation in counseling or other appropriate programs selected by the court.

Subd. 5a. **Domestic abuse victims; electronic monitoring, pilot project.** (a) Until a judicial district has adopted standards * * * governing electronic monitoring devices used to protect victims of domestic abuse, a court within the judicial district, as a condition of a stay of imposition or execution of a sentence, may not order an offender convicted of a crime described in paragraph (b) to use an electronic monitoring device to protect a victim's safety.

(b) This subdivision applies to the following crimes, if committed by the defendant against a family or household member as defined in section 518B.01, subdivision 2:

(1) violations of orders for protection issued under chapter 518B;

(2) assault in the first, second, third, or fifth degree under section 609.221, 609.222, 609.223, or 609.224; or domestic assault under section 609.2242;

(3) criminal damage to property under section 609.595;

(4) disorderly conduct under section 609.72;

(5) harassing telephone calls under section 609.79;

(6) burglary under section 609.582;

(7) trespass under section 609.605;

(8) criminal sexual conduct in the first, second, third, fourth, or fifth degree under section 609.342, 609.343, 609.344, 609.345, or 609.3451;

(9) terroristic threats under section 609.713;

(10) stalking under section 609.749;

(11) violations of harassment restraining orders under section 609.748;

(12) violations of domestic abuse no contact orders under section 629.75; and

(13) interference with an emergency call under section 609.78, subdivision 2. * * *

(d) A violation of a location restriction by an offender in a situation involving a victim and offender who are both mobile does not automatically constitute a violation of the conditions of the offender's stayed sentence.

Subd. 6. **Preference for intermediate sanctions.** A court staying imposition or execution of a sentence that does not include a term of incarceration as a condition of the stay shall order other intermediate sanctions where practicable.

Subd. 7. **Demand of execution of sentence.** An offender may not demand execution of sentence in lieu of a stay of imposition or execution of sentence if the offender will serve less than nine months at the state institution. This subdivision does not apply to an offender who will be serving the sentence consecutively or concurrently with a previously imposed executed felony sentence. * * *

EFFECTIVE DATE. This section is effective September 15, 2021, and applies to crimes committed on or after that date.

HIST: 1963 c 753 art 1 s 609.135; * * * 2014 c 263 s 1; 2014 c 270 s 1; 1Sp2021 c 11 art 4 s 3

609.15 MULTIPLE SENTENCES.

Subdivision 1. **Concurrent, consecutive sentences; specification requirement.** When separate sentences of imprisonment are imposed on a defendant for two or more crimes, whether charged in a single indictment or information or separately, or when a person who is under sentence of imprisonment in this state is being sentenced to imprisonment for another crime committed prior to or while subject to such former sentence, the court in the later sentences shall specify whether the sentences shall run concurrently or consecutively. If the court does not so specify, the sentences shall run concurrently.

Subd. 2. **Limit on sentences; misdemeanor and gross misdemeanor.** If the court specifies that the sentence shall run consecutively and all of the sentences are for misdemeanors, the total of the sentences shall not exceed one year. If the sentences are for a gross misdemeanor and one or more misdemeanors, the total of the sentences shall not exceed two years. If all of the sentences are for gross misdemeanors, the total of the sentences shall not exceed four years.
HIST: 1963 c 753 art 1 s 609.15; * * * 1999 c 194 s 10

Editors' Note:

SENTENCING GUIDELINES GRID

On the next page is a reproduction of the most-current Minnesota Sentencing Guidelines Grid published by the Minnesota Sentencing Guidelines Commission.

The non-shaded areas of the sentencing guidelines grid (above and to the right of the solid line) indicate a presumptive commitment to state imprisonment. First Degree Murder is excluded from the guidelines by law and continues to have a mandatory life sentence. Pursuant to Minn. Stat. § 609.3455, certain sex offenders are subject to life sentences. Some of these life sentences are life without release, while others are indeterminate life sentences with the minimum term of imprisonment specified by the court and based upon the sentencing guidelines and any applicable mandatory minimums (as a result of aggravating circumstances concerning the then-current sex offense conviction or prior sex offense convictions). The Minnesota Sentencing Guidelines Commission proposed separate sentencing grids specifically for sex offenses and another for drug offenders, similar to the configuration of the grid reproduced on the next page, which became effective on August 1, 2006 and August 1, 2016, respectively.

The shaded areas of the sentencing guidelines grid (below and to the left of the solid line) indicate a presumptive stayed sentence, at the discretion of the court, up to a year in jail and other non-jail sanctions can be imposed as conditions of probation. However, certain offenses in this section of the grid always carry a presumptive commitment to state prison.

Editors' Historical Note: In 2004 and 2005 United States Supreme Court decisions questioned the constitutionality of Minnesota's then-sentencing approach where a sentencing judge (as opposed to a jury) considered aggravating factors, such as a victim's age (very young or elderly) or unusual cruelty by an offender, thereby increasing the offender's sentence in excess of the presumptive sentence that is determined by the severity of the offense and the offender's criminal history. In 2005, a number of legislative changes recommended by the Minnesota Sentencing Guidelines Commission effected changes to Minnesota sentencing procedure in light of these appellate decisions.

SENTENCING GUIDELINES GRID

Presumptive sentence lengths are in months. Italicized numbers within the grid denote the discretionary range within which a court may sentence without the sentence being deemed a departure. Offenders with stayed felony sentences may be subject to local confinement.

CRIMINAL HISTORY SCORE

SEVERITY LEVEL OF CONVICTION OFFENSE (example offenses listed in ...cs)		0	1	2	3	4	5	6 or more
...der, 2nd Degree (...tentional; Drive-By-...ootings)	11	306 *261-367*	326 *278-391*	346 *295-415*	366 *312-439*	386 *329-463*	406 *346-480**	426 *363-480**
...der, 2nd Degree (...ntentional) ...der, 3rd Degree (Depraved ...d)	10	150 *128-180*	165 *141-198*	180 *153-216*	195 *166-234*	210 *179-252*	225 *192-270*	240 *204-288*
...der, 3rd Degree (Controlled ...ances) ...ult, 1st Degree	9	86 *74-103*	98 *84-117*	110 *94-132*	122 *104-146*	134 *114-160*	146 *125-175*	158 *135-189*
Robbery, 1st Degree ...lary, 1st Degree (... Weapon or Assault)	8	48 *41-57*	58 *50-69*	68 *58-81*	78 *67-93*	88 *75-105*	98 *84-117*	108 *92-129*
...ny DWI, Financial ...oitation of a Vulnerable Adult	7	36	42	48	54 *46-64*	60 *51-72*	66 *57-79*	72* *** *62-84*
...ult 2nd Degree ...lary 1st Degree (Occupied ...lling)	6	21	27	33	39 *34-46*	45 *39-54*	51 *44-61*	57 *49-68*
...idential Burglary ...le Robbery	5	18	23	28	33 *29-39*	38 *33-45*	43 *37-51*	48 *41-57*
...esidential Burglary	4	12**	15	18	21	24 *21-28*	27 *23-32*	30 *26-36*
...Crimes (Over $5,000)	3	12**	13	15	17	19 *17-22*	21 *18-25*	23 *20-27*
...t Crimes ($5,000 or less) ...k Forgery ($251-$2,500)	2	12**	12**	13	15	17	19	21 *18-25*
...ult, 4th Degree ...ing a Peace Officer	1	12**	12**	12**	13	15	17	19 *17-22*

...nn. Stat. § 244.09 requires the Sentencing Guidelines provide a range of 15% lower and 20% higher than the fixed ...ation displayed, provided that the minimum sentence is not less than one year and one day and the maximum sentence ...ot more than the statutory maximum.
...e year and one day.

***The statutory maximum for Financial Exploitation of Vulnerable Adult is 240 months, with the standard range of 20% higher than the fixed duration applies at a Criminal History Score of 6 or more (the range is *62-86* months).

Sentencing Guidelines Grid Effective August 1, 2020.

609.1352 [Repealed 1998 c 367 art 6 s 16]

Editors' Note: §§ 609.1352, 609.152 and 609. 184 were recodified in 1998 as §§ 609.108, 609.1095 and 609.106, respectively. The purpose of this recodification was to unify these provisions, thereby facilitating their use, and was not intended to result in any substantive change in these recodified sections. § 609.108 was subsequently repealed in its entirety in 2006.

609.108 MANDATORY INCREASED SENTENCES FOR CERTAIN PATTERNED AND PREDATORY SEX OFFENDERS; NO PRIOR CONVICTION REQUIRED.
Subdivision 1. [Repealed 2006 c 260 art 1 s 48]
Subd. 2. [Repealed 2005 c 136 art 2 s 23]
Subds. 3 to 7. [Repealed 2006 c 260 art 1 s 48]

609.152 Repealed 1998 c 367 art 6 s 16   *Editor's Note: §§ 609.1352, 609.152 and 609. 184 were recodified in 1998 as §§ 609.108, 609.1095 and 609.106, respectively.*

609.1095 INCREASED SENTENCES FOR CERTAIN DANGEROUS AND REPEAT FELONY OFFENDERS.
Subdivision 1. **Definitions.** (a) As used in this section, the following terms have the meanings given.

(b) "Conviction" means any of the following accepted and recorded by the court: a plea of guilty, a verdict of guilty by a jury, or a finding of guilty by the court. The term includes a conviction by any court in Minnesota or another jurisdiction.

(c) "Prior conviction" means a conviction that occurred before the offender committed the next felony resulting in a conviction and before the offense for which the offender is being sentenced under this section.

(d) "Violent crime" means a violation of or an attempt or conspiracy to violate any of the following laws of this state or any similar laws of the United States or any other state: sections 152.137; 609.165; 609.185; 609.19; 609.195; 609.20; 609.205; 609.2112; 609.2113; 609.2114; 609.221; 609.222; 609.223; 609.228; 609.235; 609.24; 609.245; 609.25; 609.255; 609.2661; 609.2662; 609.2663; 609.2664; 609.2665; 609.267; 609.2671; 609.268; 609.322; 609.342; 609.343; 609.344; 609.345; 609.498, subdivision 1; 609.561; 609.562; 609.582, subdivision 1; 609.66, subdivision 1e; 609.687; and 609.855, subdivision 5; any provision of sections 609.229; 609.377; 609.378; 609.749; and 624.713 that is punishable by a felony penalty; or any provision of chapter 152 that is punishable by a maximum sentence of 15 years or more; or . . . section 609.21.

Subd. 2. **Increased sentences for dangerous offender who commits a third violent crime.** Whenever a person is convicted of a violent crime that is a felony, and the judge is imposing an executed sentence based on a sentencing guidelines presumptive imprisonment sentence, the judge may impose an aggravated durational departure from the presumptive imprisonment sentence up to the statutory maximum sentence if the offender was at least 18 years old at the time the felony was committed, and:

(1) the court determines on the record at the time of sentencing that the offender has two or more prior convictions for violent crimes; and

(2) the factfinder determines that the offender is a danger to public safety. The factfinder may base its determination that the offender is a danger to public safety on the following factors:

(i) the offender's past criminal behavior, such as the offender's high frequency rate of criminal activity or juvenile adjudications, or long involvement in criminal activity including juvenile adjudications; or

(ii) the fact that the present offense of conviction involved an aggravating factor that would justify a durational departure under the sentencing guidelines.

Subd. 3. **Mandatory sentence for dangerous offender who commits a third violent felony.** (a) Unless a longer mandatory minimum sentence is otherwise required by law or the court imposes a longer aggravated durational departure under subdivision 2, a person who is convicted of a violent crime that is a felony must be committed to the commissioner of corrections for a mandatory sentence of at least the length of the presumptive sentence under the sentencing guidelines if the court determines on the record at the time of sentencing that the person has two or more prior felony convictions for violent crimes. The court shall impose and execute the prison sentence regardless of whether the guidelines presume an executed prison sentence.

Any person convicted and sentenced as required by this subdivision is not eligible for probation, parole, discharge, or work release, until that person has served the full term of imprisonment imposed by the court, notwithstanding sections 241.26, 242.19, 243.05, 244.04, 609.12, and 609.135.

(b) For purposes of this subdivision, "violent crime" does not include a violation of section 152.023 or 152.024.

Subd. 4. **Increased sentence for offender who commits a sixth felony.** Whenever a person is convicted of a felony, and the judge is imposing an executed sentence based on a sentencing guidelines presumptive imprisonment sentence, the judge may impose an aggravated durational departure from the presumptive sentence up to the statutory maximum sentence if the factfinder determines that the offender has five or more prior felony convictions and that the present offense is a felony that was committed as part of a pattern of criminal conduct.

EFFECTIVE DATE. This section is effective September 15, 2021, and applies to crimes committed on or after that date.

HIST: 1998 c 367 art 6 s 7; 2005 c 136 art 7 s 16; 2005 c 135 art 16 s 11,12; 1Sp2021 c 11 art 2 s 29

Editors' Note: Although the following statute is not specifically described in these learning objectives, it has been included because of its close relationship to other enhanced sentencing provisions above.

609.229 CRIME COMMITTED FOR BENEFIT OF GANG.

Subdivision 1. **Definition.** As used in this section, "criminal gang" means any ongoing organization, association, or group of three or more persons, whether formal or informal, that:

(1) has, as one of its primary activities, the commission of one or more of the offenses listed in section 609.11, subdivision 9;

(2) has a common name or common identifying sign or symbol; and

(3) includes members who individually or collectively engage in or have engaged in a pattern of criminal activity.

Subd. 2. **Crimes.** A person who commits a crime for the benefit of, at the direction of, in association with, or motivated by involvement with a criminal gang, with the intent to promote, further, or assist in criminal conduct by gang members is guilty of a crime and may be sentenced as provided in subdivision 3.

Subd. 3. **Penalty.** (a) If the crime committed in violation of subdivision 2 is a felony, the statutory maximum for the crime is five years longer than the statutory maximum for the underlying crime. If the crime committed in violation of subdivision 2 is a felony, and the victim of the crime is a child under the age of 18 years, the statutory maximum for the crime is ten years longer than the statutory maximum for the underlying crime.

(b) If the crime committed in violation of subdivision 2 is a misdemeanor, the person is guilty of a gross misdemeanor.

(c) If the crime committed in violation of subdivision 2 is a gross misdemeanor, the person is guilty of a felony and may be sentenced to imprisonment for not more than three years or to payment of a fine of not more than $15,000, or both.

Subd. 4. **Mandatory minimum sentence.** (a) Unless a longer mandatory minimum sentence is otherwise required by law, or the court imposes a longer aggravated durational departure, or a longer prison sentence is presumed under the Sentencing Guidelines and imposed by the court, a person convicted of a crime described in subdivision 3, paragraph (a), shall be committed to the custody of the commissioner of corrections for not less than one year plus one day.

(b) Any person convicted and sentenced as required by paragraph (a) is not eligible for probation, parole, discharge, work release, or supervised release until that person has served the full term of imprisonment as provided by law, notwithstanding the provisions of 242.19, 243.05, 244.04, 609.12, and 609.135.
HIST: 1991 c 279 s 30; * * * 2005 c 136 art 17 s 14

609.02 DEFINITIONS.

Subd. 2. **Felony.** "Felony" means a crime for which a sentence of imprisonment for more than one year may be imposed.

Subd. 3. **Misdemeanor.** "Misdemeanor" means a crime for which a sentence of not more than 90 days or a fine of not more than $1,000, or both, may be imposed.

Subd. 4. **Gross misdemeanor.** "Gross misdemeanor" means any crime which is not a felony or misdemeanor. The maximum fine which may be imposed for a gross misdemeanor is $3,000.
HIST: 1963 c 753 art 1 s 609.02; * * * 2015 c 65 art 3 s 16; 2016 c 126 s 3

Category 2, Section 2:
2.2.19. Explain the following terms: concurrent and consecutive sentences, imposition and execution of sentence, determinate and indeterminate sentencing.

Editors' Note: According to Black's Law Dictionary:

"Determinate Sentencing" is a "sentence to confinement for a fixed period of time."

"Indeterminate Sentencing" is a "sentence to imprisonment for the maximum period defined by law, subject to termination by the parole board or other agency at any time after service of the minimum period." (Example: Not less than five years, or more than 10 years.)

Editors' Note: Although the following statutes are not specifically described in these learning objectives, they have been included because of their close relationship to other enhanced repeat offender sentencing provisions in this chapter above.

244.052 PREDATORY OFFENDERS; NOTICE.
Subdivision 1. **Definitions.** As used in this section:
(1) "confinement" means confinement in a state correctional facility or a state treatment facility;
* * *
(3) "law enforcement agency" means the law enforcement agency having primary jurisdiction over the location where the offender expects to reside upon release; [and]
* * *
(5) "predatory offender" and "offender" mean a person who is required to register as a predatory offender under section 243.166. However, the terms do not include persons required to register based solely on a delinquency adjudication.
* * *

Subd. 3. **End-of-confinement review committee.** (a) The commissioner of corrections shall establish and administer end-of-confinement review committees at each state correctional facility and at each state treatment facility where predatory offenders are confined. The committees shall assess on a case-by-case basis the public risk posed by predatory offenders who are about to be released from confinement.
* * *
(d)(i) Except as otherwise provided in items (ii), (iii), and (iv), at least 90 days before a predatory offender is to be released from confinement, the commissioner of corrections shall convene the appropriate end-of-confinement review committee for the purpose of assessing the risk presented by the offender and determining the risk level to which the offender shall be assigned under paragraph (e). The offender and the law enforcement agency that was responsible for the charge resulting in confinement shall be notified of the time and place of the committee's meeting. * * * The law enforcement agency may provide material in writing that is relevant to the offender's risk level to the chair of the committee. * * *
(ii) If an offender is received for confinement in a facility with less than 90 days remaining in the offender's term of confinement, the * * * commissioner shall make reasonable effort to ensure that offender's risk is assessed and a risk level is assigned or reassigned at least 30 days before the offender's release date.
* * *
(iv) If the offender is granted supervised release, the commissioner of corrections * * * shall make reasonable efforts to ensure that the offender's earlier risk level determination is reviewed and the risk level is confirmed or reassigned at least 60 days before the offender's release date. The committee shall give the report to the offender and to the law enforcement agency at least 60 days before an offender is released from confinement.
(e) The committee shall assign to risk level I a predatory offender whose risk assessment score indicates a low risk of re-offense. The committee shall assign to risk level II an offender whose risk assessment score indicates a moderate risk of re-offense. The committee shall assign to risk level III an offender whose risk assessment score indicates a high risk of re-offense.
(f) Before the predatory offender is released from confinement, the committee * * * shall give the report to the offender and to the law enforcement agency at least 60 days before an offender is released from confinement. * * * If the risk assessment is performed under the circumstances described in paragraph (d), item (ii), the report shall be given to the offender and the law enforcement agency as soon as it is available.
* * *
(h) Upon the request of the law enforcement agency or the offender's corrections agent, the commissioner may reconvene the end-of-confinement review committee for the purpose of reassessing the risk level to which an offender has been assigned under paragraph (e). * * * [T]he end-of-confinement review committee may reassign an offender to a different risk level. * * *
(i) An offender may request the end-of-confinement review to reassess the offender's assigned risk level after three years have elapsed since the committee's initial risk assessment and may renew the request once every two years following subsequent denials. * * *
(k) If the committee assigns a predatory offender to risk level III, the committee shall determine whether residency restrictions shall be included in the conditions of the offender's release based on the offender's pattern of offending behavior.
Subd. 3a. **Offenders from other states and offenders released from federal facilities.** (a) Except as provided in paragraph (b), the commissioner shall establish an end-of-confinement review committee to assign a risk level:
(1) to offenders who are released from a federal correctional facility in Minnesota or * * * in another state and who intend to reside in Minnesota;
(2) to offenders who are accepted from another state under [any] authorized interstate agreement; and
(3) to offenders who are referred to the committee by local law enforcement agencies under paragraph (f).

(b) This subdivision does not require the commissioner to convene an end-of-confinement review committee for a person coming into Minnesota who is subject to probation under another state's law. * * *

(d) If a local law enforcement agency learns or suspects that a person who is subject to this section is living in Minnesota and a risk level has not been assigned to the person under this section, the law enforcement agency shall provide this information the Bureau of Criminal Apprehension and the commissioner of corrections within three business days.

(e) If the commissioner receives reliable information from a local law enforcement agency or the bureau that a person subject to this section is living in Minnesota and a local law enforcement agency so requests, the commissioner must determine if the person was assigned a risk level under a law comparable to this section. * * * [The commissioner] shall notify the local law enforcement agency that it may, in consultation with the department, proceed with notification under subdivision 4 based on the person's out-of-state risk level. * * *

(f) If the local law enforcement agency wants to make a broader disclosure than is authorized under paragraph (e), the law enforcement agency may request that an end-of-confinement review committee assign a risk level to the offender. The local law enforcement agency shall provide to the committee all information concerning the offender's criminal history, the risk the offender poses to the community, and other relevant information. The department shall attempt to obtain other information relevant to determining which risk level to assign the offender. The committee shall promptly assign a risk level to an offender referred to the committee under this paragraph.

Subd. 4. **Law enforcement agency; disclosure of information to public.** (a) The law enforcement agency in the area where the predatory offender resides, expects to reside, is employed, or is regularly found, shall disclose to the public any information regarding the offender contained in the report forwarded to the agency under subdivision 3, paragraph (f), that is relevant and necessary to protect the public and to counteract the offender's dangerousness[.] The extent of the information disclosed and the community to whom disclosure is made must relate to the level of danger posed by the offender, to the offender's pattern of offending behavior, and to the need of community members for information to enhance their individual and collective safety.

(b) The law enforcement agency shall employ the following guidelines in determining the scope of disclosure made under this subdivision:

(1) if the offender is assigned to risk level I, the agency may maintain information regarding the offender within the agency and may disclose it to other law enforcement agencies. Additionally, the agency may disclose the information to any victims of or witnesses to the offense committed by the offender. The agency shall disclose the information to victims of the offense committed by the offender who have requested disclosure and to adult members of the offender's immediate household;

(2) if the offender is assigned to risk level II, the agency also may disclose the information to agencies and groups that the offender is likely to encounter for the purpose of securing those institutions and protecting individuals in their care while they are on or near the premises of the institution. These agencies and groups include the staff members of public and private educational institutions, day care establishments, and establishments and organizations that primarily serve individuals [as well as other individuals] likely to be victimized by the offender. * * * The agency's belief shall be based on the offender's pattern of offending or victim preference as documented in the information provided by the department of corrections or human services;

(3) if the offender is assigned to risk level III, the agency shall disclose the information to the persons and entities described in clauses (1) and (2) and to other members of the community whom the offender is likely to encounter, unless the law enforcement agency determines that public safety would be compromised by the disclosure or that a more limited disclosure is necessary to protect the identity of the victim.

Notwithstanding the assignment of a predatory offender to risk level II or III, a law enforcement agency may not make the disclosures permitted or required by clause (2) or (3), if: the offender is placed or resides in a residential facility. However, if an offender is placed or resides in a residential facility, the offender and the head of the facility shall designate the offender's likely residence upon release from the facility and the head of the facility shall notify the commissioner of corrections or the commissioner of human services of the offender's likely residence at least 14 days before the offender's scheduled release date. The commissioner shall give this information to the law enforcement agency having jurisdiction over the offender's likely residence [and] shall give to the appropriate law enforcement agency all relevant information the commissioner has concerning the offender * * *. After receiving this information, the law enforcement agency shall make the disclosures permitted or required by clause (2) or (3), as appropriate.

(c) As used in paragraph (b), clauses (2) and (3), "likely to encounter" means that:

(1) the organizations or community members are in a location or in close proximity to a location where the offender lives or is employed, or which the offender visits or is likely to visit on a regular basis, other than the location of the offender's outpatient treatment program; and

(2) the types of interaction which ordinarily occur at that location and other circumstances indicate that contact with the offender is reasonably certain.

(d) A law enforcement agency or official who discloses information under this subdivision shall make a good faith effort to make the notification within 14 days of receipt of a confirmed address from the Department of Corrections indicating that the offender will be, or has been, released from confinement, or accepted for supervision, or has moved to a new address and will reside at the address indicated. * * *

(e) A law enforcement agency or official who discloses information under this subdivision shall not disclose the identity or any identifying characteristics of the victims of or witnesses to the offender's offenses.

(f) A law enforcement agency shall continue to disclose information on an offender as required by this subdivision for as long as the offender is required to register under section 243.166. This requirement * * * to disclose information also applies to an offender who lacks a primary address and is registering under section 243.166, subdivision 3a.

(g) A law enforcement agency that is disclosing information on an offender assigned to risk level III to the public under this subdivision shall inform the commissioner of corrections what information is being disclosed and forward this information to the commissioner within two days of the agency's determination * * *

(h) A city council may adopt a policy that addresses when information disclosed under this subdivision must be presented in languages in addition to English. * * *

(i) An offender who is the subject of a community notification meeting held pursuant to this section may not attend the meeting.

(j) When a school, day care facility, or other entity or program that primarily educates or serves children receives notice under paragraph (b), clause (3), that a level III predatory offender resides or works in the surrounding community, notice to parents must be made as provided in this paragraph. If the [offender] is participating in programs offered by the facility that require or allow the person to interact with children other than the person's children, the principal or head of the entity must notify parents with children at the facility of the contents of the notice received pursuant to this section. * * *

Subd. 4b. **Level III offenders; mandatory posting of information on Internet.** The commissioner of corrections shall create and maintain an Internet Web site and post * * * the information about offenders assigned to risk level III forwarded by law enforcement agencies under subdivision 4, paragraph (g). * * *

Subd. 4c. **Law enforcement agency; disclosure of information to a health care facility.** (a) The law enforcement agency in the area where a health care facility is located shall disclose the registrant status of any predatory offender registered under section 243.166 to the health care facility if the registered offender is receiving inpatient care in that facility.

(b) As used in this section, "health care facility" means a hospital or other entity licensed under sections 144.50 to 144.58, a nursing home licensed to serve adults * * *, or a [licensed] group residential housing facility or an intermediate care facility for the developmentally disabled * * *.

Subd. 5. **Relevant information provided to law enforcement.** At least 60 days before a predatory offender is released from confinement, the Department of Corrections or the Department of Human Services, in the case of a person who was committed under chapter 253D or Minnesota Statutes 1992, section 526.10, shall give to the law enforcement agency that investigated the offender's crime of conviction or, where relevant, the law enforcement agency having primary jurisdiction where the offender was committed, all relevant information that the departments have concerning the offender, including information on risk factors in the offender's history. * * *
HIST: 1996 c 408 art 5 s 4; * * * 2013 c 49 s 22; 1Sp2019 c 5 art 5 s 9

243.166 REGISTRATION OF PREDATORY OFFENDERS.
* * *

Subdivision 1a. **Definitions.** (a) As used in this section, unless the context clearly indicates otherwise, the following terms have the meanings given them.

(b) "Bureau" means the Bureau of Criminal Apprehension.

(c) "Corrections agent" means a county or state probation agent or other corrections employee. The term also includes United States Probation and Pretrial Services System employees who work with a person subject to this section.

(d) "Dwelling" means the building where the person lives under a formal or informal agreement to do so. However, dwelling does not include a supervised publicly or privately operated shelter or facility designed to provide temporary living accommodations for homeless individuals * * *.

(e) "Incarceration" and "confinement" do not include electronic home monitoring.

(f) "Law enforcement authority" or "authority" means the chief of police of a home rule charter or statutory city and the county sheriff of an unincorporated area in that county. An authority must be located in Minnesota.
* * *

(h) "Primary address" means the mailing address of the person's dwelling. If * * * different from the actual location of the dwelling, primary address also includes the physical location of the dwelling described with as much specificity as possible.

(i) "School" includes any public or private educational institution * * * that the person is enrolled in on a full-time or part-time basis.

(j) "Secondary address" means the mailing address of any place where the person regularly or occasionally stays overnight when not staying at the person's primary address. If * * * different from the actual location of the place, secondary address also includes the physical location of the place described with as much specificity as possible. However, the location of a supervised publicly or privately operated shelter or facility designated to provide temporary living accommodations for homeless individuals * * * does not constitute a secondary address.

(k) "Treatment facility" means a residential facility [, a publicly operated or licensed regional treatment facility, and licensed] residential chemical dependency treatment programs and halfway houses * * *.

(l) "Work" includes employment that is full time or part time for a period of time exceeding 14 days or for an aggregate period of time exceeding 30 days during any calendar year, whether financially compensated, volunteered, or for the purpose of government or educational benefit.

Subd. 1b. **Registration required.** (a) A person shall register under this section if:

(1) the person was charged with or petitioned for a felony violation of or attempt to violate, or aiding, abetting, or conspiracy to commit, any of the following, and convicted of or adjudicated delinquent for that offense or another offense arising out of the same set of circumstances:

(i) murder under section 609.185, paragraph (a), clause (2);

(ii) kidnapping under section 609.25;

(iii) criminal sexual conduct under section 609.342; 609.343; 609.344; 609.345; 609.3451, subdivision 3; or 609.3453;

(iv) indecent exposure under section 617.23, subdivision 3; or

(v) surreptitious intrusion under the circumstances described in section 609.746, subdivision 1, paragraph (f);

(2) the person was charged with or petitioned for a violation of, or attempt to violate, or aiding, abetting, or conspiring to commit any of the following and convicted of or adjudicated delinquent for that offense or another offense arising out of the same set of circumstances:

(i) * * * section 609.2325, subdivision 1, paragraph (b);

(ii) * * * section 609.255, subdivision 2;

(iii) * * * section 609.322;

(iv) * * * section 609.324, subdivision 1, paragraph (a);

(v) * * * section 609.352, subdivision 2 or 2a, clause (1);

(vi) * * * section 617.246; or

(vii)* * * section 617.247;

(3) the person was sentenced as a patterned sex offender under section 609.3455, subdivision 3a; or

(4) the person was charged with or petitioned for, including pursuant to a court martial, violating a law of the United States, including the Uniform Code of Military Justice, similar to the offenses described in clause (1), (2), or (3), and convicted of or adjudicated delinquent for that offense or another offense arising out of the same set of circumstances.

(b) A person also shall register under this section if:

(1) the person was charged with or petitioned for an offense in another state that would be a violation of a law described in paragraph (a) if committed in this state and convicted of or adjudicated delinquent for that offense or another offense arising out of the same set of circumstances;

(2) the person enters this state to reside, work, or attend school, or enters this state and remains for 14 days or longer or for an aggregate period of time exceeding 30 days during any calendar year; and

(3) ten years have not elapsed since the person was released from confinement or, if the person was not confined, since the person was convicted of or adjudicated delinquent for the offense that triggers registration, unless the person is subject to a longer registration period under the laws of another state in which the person has been convicted or adjudicated, or is subject to lifetime registration.

If the person described in this paragraph is subject to a longer registration period in another state or is subject to lifetime registration, the person shall register for that time period regardless of when the person was released from confinement, convicted, or adjudicated delinquent.

(c) A person also shall register under this section if the person was committed pursuant to a court commitment order under Minnesota Statutes 2012, section 253B.185, chapter 253D, Minnesota Statutes 1992, section 526.10, or a similar law of another state or the United States, regardless of whether the person was convicted of any offense.

(d) A person also shall register under this section if:

(1) the person was charged with or petitioned for a felony violation or attempt to violate any of the offenses listed in paragraph (a), clause (1), or a similar law of another state or the United States, or the person was charged with or petitioned for a violation of any of the offenses listed in paragraph (a), clause (2), or a similar law of another state or the United States;

(2) a person was found not guilty by reason mental illness or mental deficiency after a trial for that offense, or found guilty but mentally ill after a trial for that offense, in states with a guilty but mentally ill verdict; and

(3) the person was committed pursuant to a court commitment order under section 253B.18 or a similar law of another state or the United States.

Subd. 2. **Notice.** When a person who is required to register under subdivision 1b, paragraph (a), is sentenced or becomes subject to a juvenile court disposition order, the court * * * shall require the person to read and sign a form stating that the duty of the person to register under this section has been explained. The court shall make available the signed court notification form, the complaint, and the sentencing documents to the bureau. If a person * * * was not notified by the court * * *, the assigned corrections agent shall notify the person of the requirements of this section. When a person * * * is released from commitment, the treatment facility shall notify the person of the requirements of this section. If a person required to register under subdivision 1b, paragraph (a), was not notified by the court of the registration requirement at the time of sentencing or disposition and does not have a corrections agent, the law enforcement authority with jurisdiction over the person's primary address shall notify the person of the requirements.* * *

Subd. 3. **Registration procedure.** (a) Except as provided in subdivision 3a, a person required to register under this section shall register with the corrections agent as soon as the agent is assigned to the person. If the person does not have an assigned corrections or is unable to locate the assigned corrections agent, the person shall register with the law enforcement authority that has jurisdiction in the area of the person's primary address.

(b) Except as provided in subdivision 3a, at least five days before the person starts living at a new primary address, including living in another state, the person shall give written notice of the new primary address to the assigned corrections agent or to the law enforcement authority with which the person currently is registered. If the person will be living in a new state and that state has a registration requirement, the person shall also give written notice of the new address to the designated registration agency in the new state. A person * * * shall also give written notice to the assigned corrections agent or to the law enforcement authority that has jurisdiction in the area of the person's primary address that the person is no longer living or staying at an address, immediately after the person is no longer living or staying at that address. The written notice * * * must be provided in person. The corrections agent or law enforcement authority shall, within two business days after receipt of this information, forward it to the bureau. * * * The person's registration requirements under this section are reactivated if the person resumes living in Minnesota and the registration time period described in subdivision 6 has not expired.

(c) A person required to register under subdivision 1b, paragraph (b), because the person is working or attending school in Minnesota shall register with the law enforcement authority that has jurisdiction in the area where the person works or attends school. In addition to other information required by this section, the person shall provide the address of the school or of the location where the person is employed. A person shall comply with this paragraph within five days of beginning employment or school. A person's obligation to register under this paragraph terminates when the person is no longer working or attending school in Minnesota.

(d) A person * * * who works or attends school outside of Minnesota shall register as a predatory offender in the state where the person works or attends school. The person's corrections agent, or if the person does not have an assigned corrections agent, the law enforcement authority that has jurisdiction in the area of the person's primary address shall notify the person of this requirement.

Subd. 3a. **Registration procedure when person lacks primary address.** (a) If a person leaves a primary address and does not have new primary address, the person shall register with the law enforcement authority that has jurisdiction in the area where the person is staying within 24 hours of the time the person no longer has a primary address.

(b) Notwithstanding the time period for registration in paragraphs (a) and (c), a person with a primary address of a correctional facility who is scheduled to be released from the facility and who does not have a new primary address shall register with the law enforcement authority that has jurisdiction in the area where the person will be staying at least three days before the person is released from the correctional facility.

(c) A person who lacks a primary address shall register with the law enforcement authority that has jurisdiction in the area where the person is staying within 24 hours after entering the jurisdiction. Each time a person who lacks a primary address moves to a new jurisdiction without acquiring a new primary address, the person shall register with the law enforcement authority that has jurisdiction in the area where the person is staying within 24 hours after entering the jurisdiction.

(d) Upon registering under this subdivision, the person shall provide the law enforcement authority with all of the information the individual is required to provide under subdivision 4a. However, instead of reporting the person's primary address, the person shall describe the location of where the person is staying with as much specificity as possible.

(e) Except as otherwise provided in paragraph (f), if a person continues to lack a primary address, the person shall report in person on a weekly basis to the law enforcement authority with jurisdiction in the area where the person is staying. This weekly report shall occur between the hours of 9:00 a.m. and 5:00 p.m. The person is not required to provide the registration information required under subdivision 4a each time the offender reports to an authority, but the person shall inform the authority of changes to any information provided under this subdivision or subdivision 4a and shall otherwise comply with this subdivision.

(f) If the law enforcement authority determines that it is impractical, due to the person's unique circumstances, to require a person lacking a primary address to report weekly and in person as required under paragraph (e), the authority may authorize the person to follow an alternative reporting procedure. The authority shall consult with the person's corrections agent, if the person has one, in establishing the specific criteria of this alternative procedure * * *.

(g) If a person continues to lack a primary address and continues to report to the same law enforcement authority, the person shall provide the authority with all of the information the individual is required to provide under this subdivision and subdivision 4a at least annually, unless the person is required to register under subdivision 1b, paragraph (c), following commitment pursuant to a court commitment under Minnesota Statutes 2012, section 253B.185, chapter 253D, Minnesota Statutes 1992, section 526.10, or a similar law of another state or the United States. If the person is required to register under subdivision 1b, paragraph (c), the person shall provide the law enforcement authority with all of the information the individual is required to report under this subdivision and subdivision 4a at least once every three months.

(h) A law enforcement authority receiving information under the subdivision shall forward registration information and changes to that information to the bureau within two business days of receipt of the information.

(i) For purposes of this subdivision, a person who fails to report a primary address will be deemed to be a person who lacks a primary address, and the person shall comply with the requirement for a person who lacks a primary address.

Subd. 4. **Contents of registration.** (a) The registration provided to the corrections agent or law enforcement authority, must consist of a statement in writing signed by the person, giving information required by the bureau, fingerprints, biological specimen for DNA analysis as defined under section 299C.155, subdivision 1, and photograph of the person taken at the time of the person's release from incarceration or, if the person was not incarcerated, at the time the person initially registered under this section. The registration information also must include a written consent form signed by the person allowing a treatment facility or residential housing unit or shelter to release information to a law enforcement officer about the person's admission to, or residence in, a treatment facility or residential housing unit or shelter. * * *

(b) For persons required to register under subdivision 1b, paragraph (c), following commitment pursuant to a court commitment under Minnesota Statutes 2012, section 253B.185, chapter 253D, Minnesota Statutes 1992, section 526.10, or a similar law of another state or the United States, in addition to other information required by this section, the registration provided to the corrections agent or law enforcement authority must include the person's offense history and documentation of treatment received during the person's commitment. * * *

(c) Within three days of receipt, the corrections agent or law enforcement authority shall forward the registration information to the bureau. * * *

(d) The corrections agent or law enforcement authority may require that a person required to register under this section appear before the agent or authority to be photographed. The agent or authority shall submit the photograph to the bureau.

(1) Except as provided in clause (2), the agent or authority may photograph any offender at a time and frequency chosen by the agent or authority.

(2) The requirements of this paragraph shall not apply during any period where the person to be photographed is: (i) committed to the commissioner of corrections and incarcerated, (ii) incarcerated in a regional jail or county jail, or (iii) committed to the commissioner of human services and receiving treatment in a secure treatment facility.

(e) During the period a person is required to register under this section, the following provisions apply:

(1) Except for persons registering under subdivision 3a, the bureau shall mail a verification form to the person's last reported primary address, [and for those] registered under subdivision 3a, the bureau shall mail [the] verification form to the law enforcement authority where the offender most recently reported. The authority shall provide the verification form to the person at the next weekly meeting and ensure that the person completes and signs the form and returns it to the bureau. * * *

(2) The person shall mail the signed verification form back to the bureau within ten days after receipt of the form, stating on the form the current and last address of the person's residence and the other information required under subdivision 4a.

(3) In addition to the requirements listed in this section, an offender who is no longer under correctional supervision for a registration offense, or a failure to register offense, but who resides, works, or attends school in Minnesota, shall have an in-person contact with a law enforcement authority as provided in this section. If the person resides in Minnesota, the in-person contact shall be with the law enforcement authority that has jurisdiction over the person's primary address or, if the person has no address, the location where the person is staying. If the person does not reside in Minnesota but works or attends school in this state, the person shall have an in-person contact with the law enforcement authority or authorities with jurisdiction over the person's school or workplace. During the month of the person's birth date, the person shall report to the authority to verify the accuracy of the registration information and to be photographed. Within three days of this contact, the authority shall enter information as required by the bureau into the predatory offender registration database and submit an updated photograph of the person to the bureau's predatory offender registration unit.

(4) If the person fails to mail the completed and signed verification form to the bureau within ten days after receipt of the form, or if the person fails to report to the law enforcement authority during the month of the person's birth date, the person is in violation of this section.

(5) For any person who failed to mail the completed and signed verification form to the bureau within ten days after receipt of the form and who has been determined to be subject to community notification * * * or is a risk level III offender under section 244.052, the bureau shall immediately investigate and notify local law enforcement authorities to investigate the person's location and to ensure compliance with this section. The bureau shall immediately give notice of the person's violation of this section to the law enforcement authority having jurisdiction over the person's last registered primary address.
* * *

Subd. 4a. **Information required to be provided.** (a) A person required to register under this section shall provide to the corrections agent or law enforcement authority the following information:

(1) the person's primary address;

(2) all of the person's secondary addresses in Minnesota, including all addresses for residential or recreational purposes;

(3) the addresses of all Minnesota property owned, leased, or rented by the person;

(4) the address of all locations where the person is employed;

(5) the addresses of all schools where the person is enrolled;

(6) the year, model, make, license plate number, and color of all motor vehicles owned or regularly driven by the person;

(7) the expiration year for the motor vehicle license plate tabs of all motor vehicles owned by the person; and

(8) all telephone numbers including work, school, and home and any cellular telephone service.

(b) The person shall report to the agent or authority the information required to be provided under paragraph (a), clauses (2) to (8), within five days of the date the clause becomes applicable. If because of a change in circumstances any information reported under paragraph (a), clauses (1) to (8), no longer applies, the person shall immediately inform the agent or authority that the information is no longer valid. If the person leaves a primary address and does not have new primary address, the person shall register as provided in subdivision 3a.

Subd. 4b. **Health care facility; notice of status.** (a) For purposes of this subdivision:
(1) "health care facility" means a facility:
(i) licensed * * ** as a hospital, boarding care home or supervised living facility * * *, or a nursing home * * *;
(ii) registered by the commissioner of health as a housing with services establishment * * *; or
(iii) licensed * * * residential facility * * * to provide adult foster care, adult mental health treatment, chemical dependency treatment to adults, or residential services to persons with disabilities; and
* * *
(b) Prior to admission to a health care facility or home care services from a home care provider or hospice services from a hospice provider, a person required to register under this section shall disclose to:
(1) the health care facility employee or the home care provider or hospice provider processing the admission the person's status as a registered predatory offender under this section; and
(2) the person's corrections agent, or if the person does not have an assigned corrections agent, the law enforcement authority with whom the person is currently required to register, that admission will occur.
(c) A law enforcement authority or corrections agent who receives notice under paragraph (b) or who knows that a person required to register under this section is planning to be admitted and receive, or has been admitted and is receiving[,] health care at a health care facility or home care services from a home care provider or hospice services from a hospice provider, shall notify the administrator of the facility or the home care provider or the hospice provider and deliver a fact sheet to the administrator or provider containing the following information: (1) name and physical description of the offender; (2) the offender's conviction history, including the dates of conviction; (3) the risk level classification assigned to the offender under section 244.052, if any; and (4) the profile of likely victims. * * *
Subd. 5. **Criminal penalty.** (a) A person required to register under this section who * * *:
(1) knowingly commits an act or fails to fulfill a requirement that violates any provision of this section; or
(2) intentionally provides false information to a corrections agent, law enforcement authority, or the bureau is guilty of a felony and maybe be sentenced to imprisonment for not more than five years or to payment of a fine of not more than $10,000, or both.
* * *
(e) A person convicted and sentenced as required by this subdivision is not eligible for probation, parole, discharge, work release, conditional release, or supervised release, until that person has served the full term of imprisonment as provided by law * * *.
Subd. 5a. **Ten-year conditional release for violations committed by level III offenders.** Notwithstanding the statutory maximum sentence otherwise applicable to the offense or any provision of the sentencing guidelines, when a court commits a person to the custody of the commissioner of corrections for violating subdivision 5 and, at the time of the violation, the person was assigned to risk level III under section 244.052, the court shall provide that after the person has been released from prison, the commissioner shall place the person on conditional release for ten years. * * *
Subd. 6. **Registration period.** (a) Notwithstanding the provisions of section 609.165, subdivision 1, and except as proved in paragraphs (b), (c), and (d), a person required to register under this section shall continue to comply with this section until ten years have elapsed since the person initially registered in connection with the offense, or until the probation, supervised release, or conditional release period expires, whichever occurs later. For a person required to register under this section who is committed under section 253B.18, Minnesota Statutes 2012, section 253B.185, or chapter 253D, the ten-year registration period does not include the period of commitment.

(b) If a person required to register under this section fails to provide the person's primary address as required by subdivision 3, paragraph (b), fails to comply with requirements of subdivision 3a, fails to provide information as required by subdivision 4a, or fails to return the verification form referenced in subdivision 4 within ten days, the commissioner of public safety shall require the person to continue to register for an additional period of five years. This five-year period is added to the end of the offender's registration period.

(c) If a person required to register under this section is incarcerated due to a conviction for a new offense or following revocation of probation, supervised release, or conditional release for any offense, the person shall continue to register until ten years have elapsed since the person was last released from incarceration or until the person's probation, supervised release, or conditional release period expires, whichever occurs later.

(d) A person shall continue to comply with this section for the life of that person:

(1) if the person is convicted of or adjudicated delinquent for any offense for which registration is required under subdivision 1b, or any offense from another state or any federal offense similar to the offenses described in subdivision 1b, and the person has a prior conviction or adjudication for an offense for which registration was or would have been required under subdivision 1b, or an offense from another state or a federal offense similar to an offense described in subdivision 1b;

(2) if the person is required to register based upon a conviction or delinquency adjudication for an offense under section 609.185, paragraph (a), clause (2), or a similar statute from another state or the United States;

(3) if the person is required to register based upon a conviction for an offense under section 609.342, subdivision 1, paragraph (a), (c), (e), (f), or (h); 609.343, subdivision 1, paragraph (a), (c), (e), (f), or (h); 609.344, subdivision 1, paragraph (a), (c), or (g), or a statute from another state or the United States similar to the offenses described in this clause; or

(4) if the person is required to register under subdivision 1b, paragraph (c), following commitment pursuant to a court commitment under Minnesota Statutes 2012, section 253B.185, chapter 253D, Minnesota Statutes 1992, section 526.10, or a similar law of another state or the United States.

(e) A person described in subdivision 1b, paragraph (b), who is required to register under the laws of a state in which the person has been previously convicted or adjudicated delinquent, shall register under this section for the time period required by the state of conviction or adjudication unless a longer time period is required elsewhere in this section.
* * *

Subd. 7a. **Availability of information on offenders who are out of compliance with registration law.** (a) The bureau may make information available to the public about offenders who are 16 years of age or older and who are out of compliance with this section for 30 days or longer for failure to provide the offenders' primary or secondary addresses. * * * The amount and type of information made available is limited to the information necessary for the public to assist law enforcement in locating the offender.
* * *

Subd. 9. **Offenders from other states.** (a) When the state accepts an offender from another state * * *, the acceptance is conditional on the offender agreeing to register under this section when the offender is living in Minnesota.

(b) The [bureau] shall notify the commissioner of corrections:

(1) when the bureau receives notice from a local law enforcement authority that a person from another state who is subject to this section has registered with the authority; [and]

(2) when a registration authority, corrections agent, or law enforcement agency in another state notifies the bureau that a person from another state who is subject to this section is moving to Minnesota[.]

(c) When a local law enforcement agency notifies the bureau of an out-of-state offender's registration, the agency shall provide the bureau with information on whether the person is subject to community notification in another state and the risk level the person was assigned, if any.
* * *

(f) When the bureau learns that a person subject to this section intends to move into Minnesota from another state or has moved into Minnesota from another state, the bureau shall notify the law enforcement authority with jurisdiction in the area of the person's primary address and provide all information concerning the person that is available to the bureau.

(g) * * * If the commissioner determines that a person is subject to parole, supervised release, or conditional release in another state and is not registered in Minnesota under the applicable interstate compact, the commissioner shall inform the local law enforcement agency that the person is in violation of section 243.161. If the person is not subject to supervised release, the commissioner shall notify the bureau and the local law enforcement agency of the person's status.
 * * *

HIST: 1991 c 285 s 3; * * * 2016 c 189 art 4 s 11; 1Sp2019 c 5 art 5 s 2-10; 1Sp2020 c 2 art 8 s 39; 2021 c 20 s 1

243.167 REGISTRATION UNDER PREDATORY OFFENDER REGISTRATION LAW FOR OTHER OFFENSES.

Subdivision 1. **Definitions.** As used in this section, "crime against the person" means a violation of any of the following or a similar law of another state or of the United States: section 609.165; 609.185; 609.19; 609.195; 609.20; 609.205; 609.221; 609.222; 609.223; 609.2231; 609.224, subdivision 2 or 4; 609.2242, subdivision 2 or 4; 609.2247; 609.235; 609.245, subdivision 1; 609.25; 609.255; 609.3451, subdivision 2; 609.498, subdivision 1; 609.582, subdivision 1; or 617.23, subdivision 2; or any felony-level violation of section 609.229; 609.377; 609.749; or 624.713.

Subd. 2. **When required.** (a) In addition to the requirements of section 243.166, a person also shall register under section 243.166 if:

(1) the person is convicted of a crime against the person; and

(2) the person was previously convicted of or adjudicated delinquent for an offense listed in section 243.166, or a comparable offense in another state, but was not required to register for the offense because the registration requirements of that section did not apply to the person at the time the offense was committed or at the time the person was released from imprisonment.

(b) A person who was previously required to register in any state and who has completed the registration requirements of that state shall again register under section 243.166 if the person commits a crime against the person.

HIST: 2000 c 311 art 2 s 11; * * * 2008 c 299 s 8

[This page is left intentionally blank].

[This page is left intentionally blank].

Chapter 3 -- ANTICIPATORY CRIMES

Category 2, Section 5:
2.5.3. Explain what is meant by the elements of a crime and describe the connection between criminal conduct and criminal intent (mens rea).
2.5.5. Given a variety of scenarios, identify indications a particular crime has been committed and identify the elements of that crime.

609.17 ATTEMPTS.

Subdivision 1. **Crime defined.** Whoever, with intent to commit a crime, does an act which is a substantial step toward, and more than preparation for, the commission of the crime is guilty of an attempt to commit that crime, and may be punished as provided subdivision 4.

Subd. 2. **Act defined.** An act may be an attempt notwithstanding the circumstances under which it was performed or the means employed to commit the crime intended or the act itself were such that the commission of the crime was not possible, unless such impossibility would have been clearly evident to a person of normal understanding.

Subd. 3. **Defense.** It is a defense to a charge of attempt that the crime was not committed because the accused desisted voluntarily and in good faith and abandoned the intention to commit the crime.

Subd. 4. **Penalties.** Whoever attempts to commit a crime may be sentenced as follows:

(1) If the maximum sentence provided for the crime is life imprisonment, to not more than 20 years; or

(2) For any other attempt, to not more than one-half of the maximum imprisonment or fine or both provided for the crime attempted, but such maximum in any case shall not be less than imprisonment for 90 days or a fine of $100.

HIST: 1963 c 753 art 1 s 609.17; 1986 c 444

609.175 CONSPIRACY.

Subdivision 1. **To cause arrest or prosecution.** Whoever conspires with another to cause a third person to be arrested or prosecuted on a criminal charge knowing the charge to be false is guilty of a misdemeanor.

Subd. 2. **To commit crime.** Whoever conspires with another to commit a crime and in furtherance of the conspiracy one or more of the parties does some overt act in furtherance of such conspiracy may be sentenced as follows:

(1) If the crime intended is a misdemeanor, by a sentence to imprisonment for not more than 90 days or to payment of a fine of not more than $300, or both; or

(2) If the crime intended is murder in the first degree or treason, to imprisonment for not more than 20 years; or

(3) If the crime intended is any other felony or a gross misdemeanor, to imprisonment or to payment of a fine of not more than one-half the imprisonment or fine provided for that felony or gross misdemeanor or both.

Subd. 3. **Application of section jurisdiction.** This section applies if:

(1) The defendant in this state conspires with another outside of this state; or

(2) The defendant outside of this state conspires with another in this state; or

(3) The defendant outside of this state conspires with another outside of this state and an overt act in furtherance of the conspiracy is committed within this state by either of them; or

(4) The defendant in this state conspires with another in this state.

HIST: 1963 c 753 art 1 s 609.175; 1971 c 23 s 37,38; 1975 c 279 s 1

Chapter 4 -- HOMICIDE AND SUICIDE

Category 2, Section 5:
2.5.3. Explain what is meant by the elements of a crime and describe the connection between criminal conduct and criminal intent (mens rea).
2.5.5. Given a variety of scenarios, identify indications a particular crime has been committed and identify the elements of that crime.

609.184 [Repealed, 1998 c 367 art 6 s 16] *Editor's Note: §§ 609.1352 609.152 and 609. 184 were recodified in 1998 as §§609.108, 609.1095 and 609.106, respectively.*

609.106 HEINOUS CRIMES.
Subdivision 1. **Terms.** (a) As used in this section, "heinous crime" means:
(1) a violation or attempted violation of section 609.185 or 609.19;
(2) a violation of section 609.195 or 609.221; or
(3) a violation of section 609.342, 609.343, or 609.344, if the offense was committed with force or violence.
(b) "Previous conviction" means a conviction in Minnesota for a heinous crime or a conviction elsewhere for conduct that would have been a heinous crime under this chapter if committed in Minnesota. The term includes any conviction that occurred before the commission of the present offense of conviction, but does not include a conviction if 15 years have elapsed since the person was discharged from the sentence imposed for the offense.
Subd. 2. **Life without release.** The court shall sentence a person to life imprisonment without possibility of release under the following circumstances:
(1) the person is convicted of first-degree murder under section 609.185, paragraph (a), clause (1), (2), (4), or (7);
(2) the person is convicted of committing first-degree murder in the course of a kidnapping under section 609.185, paragraph (a), clause (3); or
(3) the person is convicted of first-degree murder under section 609.185, paragraph (a), clause (3), (5), or (6), and the court determines on the record at the time of sentencing that the person has one or more previous convictions for a heinous crime.
HIST: 1998 c 367 art 6 s 3; * * * 2015 c 21 art 1 s 98

609.185 MURDER IN THE FIRST DEGREE.
(a) Whoever does any of the following is guilty of murder in the first degree and shall be sentenced to imprisonment for life:
(1) causes the death of a human being with premeditation and with intent to effect the death of the person or of another:
(2) causes the death of a human being while committing or attempting to commit criminal sexual conduct in the first or second degree with force or violence, either upon or affecting the person or another;
(3) causes the death of a human being with intent to effect the death of the person or another, while committing or attempting to commit burglary, aggravated robbery, kidnapping, arson in the first or second degree, a drive—by shooting, tampering with a witness in the first degree, escape from custody, or any felony violation of chapter 152 involving the unlawful sale of a controlled substance;
(4) causes the death of a peace officer , prosecuting attorney [as defined in section 609.221], judge [as defined in section 609.221], or a guard employed at a Minnesota state

or local correctional facility, with intent to effect the death of that person or another, while the person is engaged in the performance of official duties;

(5) causes the death of a minor while committing child abuse, when the perpetrator has engaged in a past pattern of child abuse upon a child and the death occurs under circumstances manifesting an extreme indifference to human life;

(6) causes the death of a human being while committing domestic abuse, when the perpetrator has engaged in a past pattern of domestic abuse upon the victim or upon another family or household victim and the death occurs under circumstances manifesting an extreme indifference to human life; or

(7) causes the death of a human being while committing, conspiring to commit, or attempting to commit a felony crime to further terrorism and the death occurs under circumstances manifesting an extreme indifference to human life. * * *

(d) For purposes of paragraph (a), clause (5), "child abuse" means an act committed against a minor victim that constitutes a violation of the following laws of this state or any similar laws of the United States or any other state: section 609.221; 609.222; 609.223; 609.224; 609.2242; 609.342; 609.343; 609.344; 609.345; 609.377; 609.378; or 609.713.

(e) For purposes of paragraph (a), clause (6), "domestic abuse" means an act that:

(1) constitutes a violation of section 609.221, 609.222, 609.223, 609.224, 609.2242, 609.342, 609.343, 609.344; 609.345, 609.713, or any similar laws of the United States or any other state; and

(2) is committed against the victim who is a family or household member as defined in section 518B.01, subdivision 2, paragraph (b).

(f) For purposes of paragraph (a), clause (7), "further terrorism" has the meaning given in section 609.714, subdivision 1.

HIST: 1963 c 753 art 1 s 609.185; * * * 2014 c 302 s 1

609.19 MURDER IN THE SECOND DEGREE.

Subdivision 1. **Intentional murder; drive-by shootings.** Whoever does either of the following is guilty of murder in the second degree and may be sentenced to imprisonment for not more than 40 years:

(1) causes the death of a human being with intent to effect the death of that person or another, but without premeditation; or

(2) causes the death of a human being while committing or attempting to commit a drive-by shooting in violation of section 609.66, subdivision 1e, under circumstances other than those described in section 609.185, paragraph (a), clause (3).

Subd. 2. **Unintentional murders.** Whoever does either of the following is guilty of unintentional murder in the second degree and may be sentenced to imprisonment for not more than 40 years;

(1) causes the death of a human being, without intent to effect the death of any person, while committing or attempting to commit a felony offense other than criminal sexual conduct in the first or second degree with force or violence or a drive-by shooting; or

(2) causes the death of a human being without intent to effect the death of any person, while intentionally inflicting or attempting to inflict bodily harm upon the victim, when the perpetrator is restrained under an order for protection and the victim is a person designated to receive protection under the order.

As used in this clause, "order for protection" includes an order for protection issued under chapter 518B; a harassment restraining order issued under section 609.748; a court order setting conditions of pretrial release or conditions of a criminal sentence or juvenile court disposition; a restraining order issued in a marriage dissolution action; and any order issued by a court of another state or of the United States that is similar to any of these orders.

HIST: 1963 c 753 art 1 s 609.19; * * * 2015 c 21 art 1 s 99

609.195 MURDER IN THE THIRD DEGREE.

(a) Whoever, without intent to effect the death of any person, causes the death of another by perpetrating an act eminently dangerous to others and evincing a depraved mind, without regard for human life, is guilty of murder in the third degree and may be sentenced to imprisonment for not more than 25 years.

(b) Whoever, without intent to cause death, proximately causes the death of a human being by, directly or indirectly, unlawfully selling, giving away, bartering, delivering, exchanging, distributing, or administering a controlled substance classified in schedule I or II, is guilty of murder the third degree and may be sentenced to imprisonment for not more than 25 years or to payment of a fine of not more than $40,000, or both.

HIST: 1963 c 753 art 1 s 609.195; 1977 c 130 s 3; 1981 c 227 s 11; 1987 c 176 s 1

Editors' Note: Historically, third-degree murder has been used to prosecute drug dealers who sold deadly products, but who were not planning to kill specific individuals. However, in State v. Noor, 955 N.W.2d 644 (Minn. Ct. App. 2021) (rev. granted March 21, 2021), the Minnesota Court of Appeals upheld a police officer's conviction for third-degree murder where the officer fired across his partner and killed a woman who had reported a possible sexual assault in progress. Subsequently, former Minneapolis police officer, Dennis Chauvin, was convicted of the same charge. The Noor case is now before the Minnesota Supreme Court.

609.20 MANSLAUGHTER IN THE FIRST DEGREE.

Whoever does any of the following is guilty of manslaughter in the first degree and may be sentenced to imprisonment for not more than 15 years or to payment of a fine of not more than $30,000, or both:

(1) intentionally causes the death of another person in the heat of passion provoked by such words or acts of another as would provoke a person of ordinary self-control under like circumstances, provided that the crying of a child does not constitute provocation;

(2) violates section 609.224 and causes the death of another or causes the death of another in committing or attempting to commit a misdemeanor or gross misdemeanor offense with such force and violence that death of or great bodily harm to any person was reasonably foreseeable, and murder in the first or second degree was not committed thereby;

(3) intentionally causes the death of another person because the actor is coerced by threats made by someone other than the actor's coconspirator and which cause the actor reasonably to believe that the act performed by the actor is the only means of preventing imminent death to the actor or another; or

(4) proximately causes the death of another, without intent to cause death by, directly or indirectly, unlawfully selling, giving away, bartering, delivering, exchanging, distributing, or administering a controlled substance classified in schedule III, IV, or V.

(5) causes the death of another in committing or attempting to commit a violation of section 609.377 (malicious punishment of a child), and murder in the first, second, or third degree is not committed thereby.

As used in this section a "person of ordinary self-control" does not include a person under the influence of intoxicants or a controlled substance.

HIST: 1963 c 753 art 1 s 609.20; * * * 1996 c 408 art 3 s 13

609.205 MANSLAUGHTER IN THE SECOND DEGREE.

A person who causes the death of another by any of the following means is guilty of manslaughter in the second degree and may be sentenced to imprisonment for not more than ten years or to payment of a fine of not more than $20,000, or both:

(1) by the person's culpable negligence whereby the person creates an unreasonable risk, and consciously takes chances of causing death or great bodily harm to another; or

(2) by shooting another with a firearm or other dangerous weapon as a result of negligently believing the other to be a deer or other animal; or

(3) by setting a spring gun, pit fall, deadfall, snare, or other like dangerous weapon or device; or

(4) by negligently or intentionally permitting any animal, known by the person to have vicious propensities or to have caused great or substantial bodily harm in the past, to run uncontrolled off the owner's premises, or negligently failing to keep it properly confined.

(5) by committing or attempting to commit a violation of section 609. 378 (neglect or endangerment of a child), and murder in the first, second, or third degree is not committed thereby.

If proven by a preponderance of the evidence, it shall be an affirmative defense to criminal liability under clause (4) that the victim provoked the animal to cause the victim's death.

HIST: 1963 c 753 art 1 s 609.205; * * * 1995 c 244 s 14

609.21 Subdivision 1. [Renumbered 609.2112, subd. 1]
Subd. 1a. [Renumbered 609.2113, subd. 1
Subd. 1b. [Renumbered 609.2114, subd. 3]
Subd. 2. [Repealed, 2007 c 54 art 4 s 15]
Subd. 2a. [Repealed, 2007 c 54 art 4 s 15]
Subd. 2b. [Repealed, 2007 c 54 art 4 s 15]
Subd. 3. [Repealed, 2007 c 54 art 4 s 15]
Subd. 4. [Repealed, 2007 c 54 art 4 s 15]
Subd. 4a. [Renumbered 609.2112, subd. 2]
Subd. 5. [Renumbered 609.2111]

Editors' Note: Portions of §609.21 relating to Criminal Vehicular Homicide were recodified in 2014 as §§609.2111 to .2114 set forth immediately below.

609.2111 DEFINITIONS.
(a) For purposes of sections 609.2111 to 609.2114, the terms defined in this subdivision have the meanings given them.

(b) "Motor vehicle" has the meaning given in section 609.52, subdivision 1, and includes attached trailers.

(c) "Controlled substance" has the meaning given in section 152.01, subdivision 4.

(d) "Intoxicating substance" has the meaning given in section 169A.03, subdivision 11a.

(e) "Qualified prior driving offense" includes a prior conviction [for certain driving while impaired and criminal vehicular homicide offenses].
HIST: 1990 c 602 art 4 s 1; * * * 2018 c 195 art 3 s 18

609.2112 CRIMINAL VEHICULAR HOMICIDE.
Subdivision 1. **Criminal vehicular homicide.** (a) Except as provided in paragraph (b), a person is guilty of criminal vehicular homicide may be sentenced to imprisonment for not more than ten years or to payment of a fine of not more than $20,000, or both, if the person causes the death of a human being not constituting murder or manslaughter as a result of operating a motor vehicle;
(1) in a grossly negligent manner;
(2) in a negligent manner while under the influence of:

(i) alcohol;

(ii) a controlled substance; or

(iii) any combination of those elements;

(3) while having an alcohol concentration of 0.08 or more;

(4) while having an alcohol concentration of 0.08 or more, as measured within two hours of the time of driving;

(5) in a negligent manner while under the influence of an intoxicating substance and the person knows or has reason to know that the substance has the capacity to cause impairment;

(6) in a negligent manner while any amount of a controlled substance listed in Schedule I or II, or its metabolite, other than marijuana or tetrahydrocannabinols, is present in the person's body;

(7) where the driver who causes the collision leaves the scene of the collision in violation of section 169.09, subdivision 1 or 6; or

(8) where the driver had actual knowledge that a peace officer had previously issued a citation or warning that the motor vehicle was defectively maintained, the driver had actual knowledge that the remedial action was not taken, the driver had reason to know that the defect created a present danger to others, and the death was caused by the defective maintenance.

(b) If a person is sentenced under paragraph (a) for a violation under paragraph (a), clauses (2) to (6), occurring within ten years of a qualified prior driving offense, the statutory maximum sentence of imprisonment is 15 years.

Subd. 2. **Affirmative defense.** It shall be an affirmative defense to a charge under subdivision 1, clause (6) that the defendant used the controlled substance according to the terms of a prescription issued for the defendant in accordance with sections 152.11 and 152.12.

HIST: 1963 c 753 art 1 s 609.21; * * * 2018 c 195 art 3 s 19

609.2113 CRIMINAL VEHICULAR OPERATION; BODILY HARM.

Subdivision 1. **Great bodily harm.** A person is guilty of criminal vehicular operation resulting in great bodily harm and may be sentenced to imprisonment for not more than five years or to payment of a fine of not more than $10,000, or both, if the person causes great bodily harm to another as a result of operating a motor vehicle;

(1) in a grossly negligent manner;

(2) in a negligent manner while under the influence of:

(i) alcohol;

(ii) a controlled substance; or

(iii) any combination of those elements;

(3) while having an alcohol concentration of 0.08 or more;

(4) while having an alcohol concentration of 0.08 or more, as measured within two hours of the time of driving;

(5) in a negligent manner while under the influence of an intoxicating substance and the person knows or has reason to know that the substance has the capacity to cause impairment;

(6) in a negligent manner while any amount of a controlled substance listed in Schedule I or II, or its metabolite, other than marijuana or tetrahydrocannabinols, is present in the person's body;

(7) where the driver who causes the accident leaves the scene of the accident in violation of section 169.09, subdivision 1 or 6; or

(8) where the driver had actual knowledge that a peace officer had previously issued a citation or warning that the motor vehicle was defectively maintained, the driver had actual knowledge that the remedial action was not taken, the driver had reason to know that the defect created a present danger to others, and the injury was caused by the defective maintenance.

Subd. 2. **Substantial bodily harm.** A person is guilty of criminal vehicular operation resulting in substantial bodily harm and may be sentenced to imprisonment for not more than three years or to payment of a fine of not more than $10,000, or both, if the person causes substantial bodily harm to another as a result of operating a motor vehicle;
(1) in a grossly negligent manner;
(2) in a negligent manner while under the influence of:
(i) alcohol;
(ii) a controlled substance; or
(iii) any combination of those elements;
(3) while having an alcohol concentration of 0.08 or more;
(4) while having an alcohol concentration of 0.08 or more, as measured within two hours of the time of driving;
(5) in a negligent manner while under the influence of an intoxicating substance and the person knows or has reason to know that the substance has the capacity to cause impairment;
(6) in a negligent manner while any amount of a controlled substance listed in Schedule I or II, or its metabolite, other than marijuana or tetrahydrocannabinols, is present in the person's body;
(7) where the driver who causes the accident leaves the scene of the accident in violation of section 169.09, subdivision 1 or 6; or
(8) where the driver had actual knowledge that a peace officer had previously issued a citation or warning that the motor vehicle was defectively maintained, the driver had actual knowledge that the remedial action was not taken, the driver had reason to know that the defect created a present danger to others, and the injury was caused by the defective maintenance.

Subd. 3. **Bodily harm.** A person is guilty of criminal vehicular operation resulting in bodily harm and may be sentenced to imprisonment for not more than one year or to payment of a fine of not more than $3,000, or both, if the person causes bodily harm to another as a result of operating a motor vehicle;
(1) in a grossly negligent manner;
(2) in a negligent manner while under the influence of:
(i) alcohol;
(ii) a controlled substance; or
(iii) any combination of those elements;
(3) while having an alcohol concentration of 0.08 or more;
(4) while having an alcohol concentration of 0.08 or more, as measured within two hours of the time of driving;
(5) in a negligent manner while under the influence of an intoxicating substance and the person knows or has reason to know that the substance has the capacity to cause impairment;
(6) in a negligent manner while any amount of a controlled substance listed in Schedule I or II, or its metabolite, other than marijuana or tetrahydrocannabinols, is present in the person's body;
(7) where the driver who causes the accident leaves the scene of the accident in violation of section 169.09, subdivision 1 or 6; or
(8) where the driver had actual knowledge that a peace officer had previously issued a citation or warning that the motor vehicle was defectively maintained, the driver had actual knowledge that the remedial action was not taken, the driver had reason to know that the defect created a present danger to others, and the injury was caused by the defective maintenance.

Subd. 4. **Affirmative defense.** It shall be an affirmative defense to a charge under subdivision 1, clause (6); subdivision 2, clause (6); or subdivision 3, clause (6), that the defendant used the controlled substance according to the terms of a prescription issued for the defendant in accordance with sections 152.11 and 152.12.

HIST: 1983 c 12 s 1; * * * 2018 c 195 art 3 s 20-22

609.2114 CRIMINAL VEHICULAR OPERATION; UNBORN CHILD.

Subdivision 1. **Death to an unborn child.** (a) Except as provided in paragraph (b), a person is guilty of criminal vehicular operation resulting in death to an unborn child and may be sentenced to imprisonment for not more than ten years or to payment of a fine of not more than $20,000, or both, if the person causes the death of an unborn child as a result of operating a motor vehicle;

(1) in a grossly negligent manner;

(2) in a negligent manner while under the influence of:

(i) alcohol;

(ii) a controlled substance; or

(iii) any combination of those elements;

(3) while having an alcohol concentration of 0.08 or more;

(4) while having an alcohol concentration of 0.08 or more, as measured within two hours of the time of driving;

(5) in a negligent manner while under the influence of an intoxicating substance and the person knows or has reason to know that the substance has the capacity to cause impairment;

(6) in a negligent manner while any amount of a controlled substance listed in Schedule I or II, or its metabolite, other than marijuana or tetrahydrocannabinols, is present in the person's body;

(7) where the driver who causes the accident leaves the scene of the accident in violation of section 169.09, subdivision 1 or 6; or

(8) where the driver had actual knowledge that a peace officer had previously issued a citation or warning that the motor vehicle was defectively maintained, the driver had actual knowledge that the remedial action was not taken, the driver had reason to know that the defect created a present danger to others, and the injury [sic: death] was caused by the defective maintenance.

(b) If a person is sentenced under paragraph (a) for a violation under paragraph (a), clauses (2) to (6), occurring within ten years of a qualified prior driving offense, the statutory maximum sentence of imprisonment is 15 years.

Subd. 2. **Injury to an unborn child.** A person is guilty of criminal vehicular operation resulting in the injury to an unborn child and may be sentenced to imprisonment for not more than five years or to payment of a fine of not more than $10,000, or both, if the person causes great bodily harm to an unborn child subsequently born alive as a result of operating a motor vehicle;

(1) in a grossly negligent manner;

(2) in a negligent manner while under the influence of:

(i) alcohol;

(ii) a controlled substance; or

(iii) any combination of those elements;

(3) while having an alcohol concentration of 0.08 or more;

(4) while having an alcohol concentration of 0.08 or more, as measured within two hours of the time of driving;

(5) in a negligent manner while under the influence of an intoxicating substance and the person knows or has reason to know that the substance has the capacity to cause impairment;

(6) in a negligent manner while any amount of a controlled substance listed in Schedule I or II, or its metabolite, other than marijuana or tetrahydrocannabinols, is present in the person's body;

(7) where the driver who causes the accident leaves the scene of the accident in violation of section 169.09, subdivision 1 or 6; or

(8) where the driver had actual knowledge that a peace officer had previously issued a citation or warning that the motor vehicle was defectively maintained, the driver had actual knowledge that the remedial action was not taken, the driver had reason to know that the defect created a present danger to others, and the injury was caused by the defective maintenance.

Subd. 3. **Conviction not bar to punishment for other crimes.** A prosecution for or a conviction of a crime under this section relating to causing death or injury to an unborn child is not a bar to conviction of or punishment for any other crime committed by the defendant as part of the same conduct.

Subd. 4. **Affirmative defense.** It shall be an affirmative defense to a charge under subdivision 1, clause (6), and subdivision 2, clause (6), that the defendant used the controlled substance according to the terms of a prescription issued for the defendant in accordance with sections 152.11 and 152.12.

HIST: 1986 c 388 s 3,4; * * * 2018 c 195 art 3 s 23,24

609.215 SUICIDE.

Subdivision 1. **Aiding suicide.** Whoever intentionally advises, encourages, or assists another in taking the other's own life may be sentenced to imprisonment for not more than 15 years or to payment of a fine of not more than $30,000, or both.

Subd. 2. **Aiding attempted suicide.** Whoever intentionally advises, encourages, or assists another who attempts but fails to take the other's own life may be sentenced to imprisonment for not more than seven years or to payment of fine of not more than $14,000, or both.

Subd. 3. **Acts or omissions not considered aiding suicide or aiding attempted suicide.** (a) A health care provider, as defined in section 145B.02, subdivision 6, who administers, prescribes, or dispenses medications or procedures to relieve another person's pain or discomfort, even if the medication or procedure may hasten or increase the risk of death, does not violate this section unless the medications or procedures are knowingly administered, prescribed, or dispensed to cause death.

(b) A health care provider, as defined in section 145B.02, subdivision 6, who withholds or withdraws a life-sustaining procedure in compliance with chapter 145B or 145C or in accordance with reasonable medical practice does not violate this section.

Subd. 4. **Injunctive relief.** A cause of action for injunctive relief may be maintained against any person who is reasonably believed to be about to violate or who is in the course of violating this section by any person who is:

(1) the spouse, parent, child, or sibling of the person who would commit suicide;

(2) an heir or a beneficiary under a life insurance policy of the person who would commit suicide;

(3) a health care provider of the person who would commit suicide;

(4) a person authorized to prosecute or enforce the laws of this state; or

(5) a legally appointed guardian or conservator of the person who would have committed suicide.

Subd. 5. **Civil damages.** A person given standing by subdivision 4, clause (1), (2), or (5), or the person who would have committed suicide, in the case of an attempt, may maintain a cause of action against any person who violates or who attempts to violate subdivision 1 or 2 for compensatory damages and punitive damages as provided in section 549.20. A person described in subdivision 4, clause (4), may maintain a cause of action against a person who violates or attempts to violate subdivision 1 or 2 for a civil penalty of up to $50,000 on behalf of the state. An action under this subdivision may be brought whether or not the plaintiff had prior knowledge of the violation or attempt.

Subd. 6. **Attorney fees.** Reasonable attorney fees shall be awarded to the prevailing plaintiff in a civil action brought under subdivision 4 or 5.

HIST: 1963 c 753 art 1 s 609.215; 1984 c 628 art 3 s 11; 1986 c 444; 1992 c 577 s 6-9; 1998 c 399 s 37

Chapter 5 -- <u>CRIMES AGAINST THE PERSON</u>

Category 2, Section 5:
2.5.3. Explain what is meant by the elements of a crime and describe the connection between criminal conduct and criminal intent (mens rea).
2.5.5. Given a variety of scenarios, identify indications a particular crime has been committed and identify the elements of that crime.

609.221 ASSAULT IN THE FIRST DEGREE.

Subdivision 1. **Great bodily harm.** Whoever assaults another and inflicts great bodily harm may be sentenced to imprisonment for not more than 20 years or to payment of a fine of not more than $30,000, or both.

Subd. 2. **Use of deadly force against peace officer, prosecuting attorney, judge, or correctional employee.** (a) Whoever assaults a peace officer, prosecuting attorney, judge, or correctional employee by using or attempting to use deadly force against the person while the officer, attorney, judge, or employee is engaged in the performance of a duty imposed by law, policy, or rule, may be sentenced to imprisonment for not more than 20 years or to payment of a fine of not more than $30,000, or both.

~~(b) A person convicted of assaulting a peace officer, prosecuting attorney, judge, or correctional employee as described in paragraph (a) shall be committed to the commissioner of corrections for not less than ten years, not more than 20 years. A defendant convicted and sentenced as required by this paragraph is not eligible for probation, parole, discharge, work release, or supervised release, until that person has served the full term of imprisonment as provided by law, notwithstanding the provisions of sections 241.26, 242.19, 243.05, 244.04, 609.12, and 609.135. Notwithstanding section 609.135, the court may not stay the imposition or execution of this sentence.~~

Subd. 3. <u>**Great bodily harm; peace officer, prosecuting attorney, judge, or correctional employee.**</u>

<u>Whoever assaults a peace officer, prosecuting attorney, judge, or correctional employee and inflicts great bodily harm on the officer, attorney, judge, or employee while the person is engaged in the performance of a duty imposed by law, policy, or rule may be sentenced to imprisonment for not more than 25 years or to payment of a fine of not more than $35,000, or both.</u>

Subd. 4. <u>**Use of dangerous weapon or deadly force resulting in great bodily harm against peace officer, prosecuting attorney, judge, or correctional employee.**</u>

<u>Whoever assaults and inflicts great bodily harm upon a peace officer, prosecuting attorney, judge, or correctional employee with a dangerous weapon or by using or attempting to use deadly force against the officer, attorney, judge, or employee while the person is engaged in the performance of a duty imposed by law, policy, or rule may be sentenced to imprisonment for not more than 30 years or to payment of a fine of not more than $40,000, or both.</u>

Subd. 5. <u>**Mandatory sentences for assaults against a peace officer, prosecuting attorney, judge, or correctional employee.**</u>

<u>(a) A person convicted of assaulting a peace officer, prosecuting attorney, judge, or correctional employee shall be committed to the custody of the commissioner of corrections for not less than:</u>

<u>(1) ten years, nor more than 20 years, for a violation of subdivision 2;</u>
<u>(2) 15 years, nor more than 25 years, for a violation of subdivision 3; or</u>
<u>(3) 25 years, nor more than 30 years, for a violation of subdivision 4.</u>

(b) A defendant convicted and sentenced as required by this subdivision is not eligible for probation, parole, discharge, work release, or supervised release, until that person has served the full term of imprisonment as provided by law, notwithstanding the provisions of sections 241.26, 242.19, 243.05, 244.04, 609.12, and 609.135. Notwithstanding section 609.135, the court may not stay the imposition or execution of this sentence.

Subd. 6. **Definitions.**

(c) As used in this ~~subdivision~~ section:

(1) "correctional employee" means an employee of a public or private prison, jail, or workhouse;

(2) "deadly force" has the meaning given in section 609.066, subdivision 1;

(3) "peace officer" has the meaning given in section 626.84, subdivision 1;

(4) "prosecuting attorney" means an attorney, with criminal prosecution or civil responsibilities, who is the attorney general, a political subdivision's elected or appointed county or city attorney, or a deputy, assistant, or special assistant of any of these; and

(5) "judge" means a judge or justice of any court of this state that is established by the Minnesota Constitution.

EFFECTIVE DATE.

This section is effective September 15, 2021, and applies to crimes committed on or after that date.

HIST: 1979 c 258 s 4; * * * 2014 c 302 s 2; 1Sp2021 c 11 art 2 s 31

609.222 ASSAULT IN THE SECOND DEGREE.

Subdivision 1. **Dangerous weapon.** Whoever assaults another with a dangerous weapon may be sentenced to imprisonment for not more than seven years or to payment of a fine of not more than $14,000, or both.

Subd. 2. **Dangerous weapon; substantial bodily harm.** Whoever assaults another with a dangerous weapon and inflicts substantial bodily harm may be sentenced to imprisonment for not more than ten years or to payment of a fine of not more than $20,000, or both.

HIST: 1979 c 258 s 5; * * * 1992 c 571 art 4 s 7

609.223 ASSAULT IN THE THIRD DEGREE.

Subdivision 1. **Substantial bodily harm.** Whoever assaults another and inflicts substantial bodily harm may be sentenced to imprisonment for not more than five years or to payment of a fine of not more than $10,000, or both.

Subd. 2. **Past pattern of child abuse.** Whoever assaults a minor may be sentenced to imprisonment for not more than five years or to payment of a fine of not more than $10,000, or both, if the perpetrator has engaged in a past pattern of child abuse against the minor. As used in this subdivision, "child abuse" has the meaning given it in section 609.185, paragraph (a), clause (5).

Subd. 3. **Felony; victim under four.** Whoever assaults a victim under the age of four, and causes bodily harm to the child's head, eyes, or neck, or otherwise causes multiple bruises to the body, is guilty of a felony and may be sentenced to imprisonment for not more than five years or to payment of a fine of not more than $10,000, or both.

HIST: 1979 c 258 s 6; * * * 2015 c 21 art 1 s 100

609.2231 ASSAULT IN THE FOURTH DEGREE.

Subdivision 1. **Peace officers.** (a) As used in this subdivision, "peace officer" means a person who is licensed under section 626.845, subdivision 1, and effecting a lawful arrest or executing any other duty imposed by law.

(b) Whoever physically assaults a peace officer is guilty of a gross misdemeanor.

(c) Whoever commits either of the following acts against a peace officer is guilty of a felony and may be sentenced to imprisonment for not more than three years or to payment of a fine of not more than $6,000, or both: (1) physically assaults the officer if the assault inflicts demonstrable bodily harm; or (2) intentionally throws or otherwise transfers bodily fluids or feces at or onto the officer.

Subd. 2. **Firefighters and emergency medical personnel.** Whoever assaults any of the following persons and inflicts demonstrable bodily harm is guilty of a felony and may be sentenced to imprisonment for not more than two years or to payment of a fine of not more than $4,000, or both:

(1) a member of a municipal or volunteer fire department or emergency medical services personnel unit in the performance of the member's duties; or

(2) a physician, nurse, or other person providing health care services in a hospital emergency department.

Subd. 2a. **Certain department of natural resources employees.** Whoever assaults and inflicts demonstrable bodily harm on an employee of the department of natural resources who is engaged in forest fire activities is guilty of a gross misdemeanor.

Subd. 3. **Correctional employees; prosecuting attorneys; judges; probation officers.** Whoever commits either of the following acts against an employee of a correctional facility as defined in section 241.021, subdivision 1, paragraph (f), against a prosecuting attorney as defined in section 609.221, subdivision 2, paragraph (c), clause (4), against a judge as defined in section 609.221, subdivision 2, paragraph (c), clause (5), or against a probation officer or other qualified person employed in supervising offenders while the person is engaged in the performance of a duty imposed by law, policy or rule is guilty of a felony and may be sentenced to imprisonment for not more than two years or to payment of a fine of not more than $4,000, or both:

(1) assaults the person and inflicts demonstrable bodily harm; or

(2) intentionally throws or otherwise transfers bodily fluids or feces at or onto the person.

Subd. 3a. **Secure treatment facility personnel.** * * *

(b) Whoever, while committed under chapter 253D, Minnesota Statutes 2012, section 253B.185 or Minnesota Statutes 1992, section 526.10, commits either of the following acts against an employee or other individual who provides care or treatment at a secure treatment facility while the person is engaged in the performance of a duty imposed by law, policy, or rule is guilty of a felony and may be sentenced to imprisonment for not more than two years or to payment of a fine of not more than $4,000, or both:

(1) assaults the person and inflicts demonstrable bodily harm; or

(2) intentionally throws or otherwise transfers bodily fluids or feces at or onto the person.

* * *

(c) Whoever, while committed under section 253B.18, or admitted under the provision of section 253B.10, subdivision 1, commits either of the following acts against an employee or other individual who supervises and works directly with patients at a secure treatment facility while the person is engaged in the performance of a duty imposed by law, policy, or rule, is guilty of a felony and may be sentenced to imprisonment for not more than two years or to payment of a fine of not more than $4,000, or both:

(1) assaults the person and inflicts demonstrable bodily harm; or

(2) intentionally throws or otherwise transfers urine, blood, semen, or feces onto the person.

Subd. 4. **Assaults motivated by bias.** (a) Whoever assaults another because of the victim's or another's actual or perceived race, color, religion, sex, sexual orientation, disability as defined in section 363.01, age, or national origin may be sentenced to imprisonment for not more than one year or to payment of a fine of not more than $3,000, or both.

(b) Whoever violates the provisions of paragraph (a) within five years of a previous conviction under paragraph (a) is guilty of a felony and may be sentenced to imprisonment for not more than one year and a day or to payment of a fine of not more than $3,000, or both.

Subd. 5. **School official.** Whoever assaults a school official while the official is engaged in the performance of the official's duties, and inflicts demonstrable bodily harm, is guilty of a gross misdemeanor. As used in this subdivision, "school official" includes teachers, school administrators, and other employees of a public or private school.

Subd. 6. **Public employees with mandated duties.** A person is guilty of a gross misdemeanor who:

(1) assaults an agricultural inspector, occupational safety and health investigator, child protection worker, public health nurse, animal control officer, or probation or parole officer while the employee is engaged in the performance of a duty mandated by law, court order, or ordinance;

(2) knows that the victim is a public employee engaged in the performance of the official public duties of the office; and

(3) inflicts demonstrable bodily harm.

Subd. 7. **Community crime prevention group members.** (a) A person is guilty of a gross misdemeanor who:

(1) assaults a community crime prevention group member while the member is engaged in neighborhood patrol;

(2) should reasonably know that the victim is a community crime prevention group member engaged in neighborhood patrol; and

(3) inflicts demonstrable bodily harm.

(b) As used in this subdivision, "community crime prevention group" means a community group focused on community safety and crime prevention that:

(1) is organized for the purpose of discussing community safety and patrolling community neighborhoods for criminal activity;

(2) is designated and trained by the local law enforcement agency as a community crime prevention group; or

(3) interacts with local law enforcement regarding community safety issues.

Subd. 8. **Vulnerable adults.** (a) As used in this subdivision, "vulnerable adult" has the meaning given in section 609.232, subdivision 11.

(b) Whoever assaults and inflicts demonstrable bodily harm on a vulnerable adult, knowing or having reason to know that the person is a vulnerable adult, is guilty of a gross misdemeanor.

Subd. 9. **Reserve officer.** A person is guilty of a gross misdemeanor who:

(1) assaults a reserve officer as defined in section 626.84, subdivision 1, paragraph (e), who is engaged in the performance of official public duties at the direction of, under the control of, or on behalf of a peace officer or supervising law enforcement officer or agency; and

(2) should reasonably know that the victim is a reserve officer engaged in the performance of official public duties of the peace officer, or supervising law enforcement officer or agency.

Subd. 10. **Utility and postal service employees and contractors.** (a) A person is guilty of a gross misdemeanor who:

(1) assaults an employee or contractor of a utility or the United States Postal Service while the employee or contractor is engaged in the performance of the employee's or contractor's duties;

(2) should reasonably know that the victim is an employee or contractor of a utility or the postal service who is:

(i) performing duties of the victim's employment; or

(ii) fulfilling the victim's contractual obligations; and

(iii) inflicts demonstrable bodily harm.

(b) As used in this subdivision, "utility" has the meaning given it in section 609.594, subdivision 1, clause (3).

Subd. 11. **Transit operators.** (a) A person is guilty of a gross misdemeanor if (1) the person assaults a transit operator, or intentionally throws or otherwise transfers bodily fluid onto a transit operator; and (2) the transit operator is acting in the course of the operator's duties and is operating a transit vehicle, aboard a transit vehicle, or otherwise responsible for a transit vehicle. A person convicted under this paragraph may be sentenced to imprisonment for not more than one year or to payment of a fine of not more than $3,000, or both.

(b) For purposes of this subdivision, "transit operator" means a driver or operator of a transit vehicle that is used to provide any of the following services:
(1) public transit * * *;
(2) light rail transit service;
(3) special transportation service * * *; or
(4) commuter rail service.
HIST: 1983 c 169 s 1; * * * 2015 c 23 s 1; 2016 c 93 s 1

Editors' Note: Although the following statute is not specifically described in these learning objectives, it has been included because of its close relationship to other assault statutes above.

609.2233 FELONY ASSAULT MOTIVATED BY BIAS; INCREASED STATUTORY MAXIMUM SENTENCE.

A person who violates section 609.221, 609.222, or 609.223 because of the victim's or another person's actual or perceived race, color, religion, sex, sexual orientation, disability * * *, age, or national origin is subject to a statutory maximum penalty of 25 percent longer than the maximum penalty otherwise applicable.
HIST: 2016 c 189 art 4 s 14

609.224 ASSAULT IN THE FIFTH DEGREE.

Subdivision 1. **Misdemeanor.** Whoever does any of the following commits an assault and is guilty of a misdemeanor:
(1) commits an act with intent to cause fear in another of immediate bodily harm or death; or
(2) intentionally inflicts or attempts to inflict bodily harm upon another.

Subd. 2. **Gross misdemeanor.** (a) Whoever violates the provisions of subdivision 1 against the same victim within ten years of a previous qualified domestic violence-related offense conviction or adjudication of delinquency, is guilty of a gross misdemeanor and may be sentenced to imprisonment for not more than one year or to payment of a fine of not more than $3,000, or both.

(b) Whoever violates the provisions of subdivision 1 within three years of a previous qualified domestic violence-related offense conviction or adjudication of delinquency is guilty of a gross misdemeanor and may be sentenced to imprisonment for not more than one year or to payment of a fine or not more than $3,000, or both.

Subd. 3. **Firearms.** (a) When a person is convicted of a violation of this section or section 609.221, 609.222, or 609.223, the court shall determine and make written findings on the record as to whether:
(1) the defendant owns or possesses a firearm; and
(2) the firearm was used in any way during the commission of the assault.

(b) Except as otherwise provided in section 609.2242, subdivision 3, paragraph (c), a person is not entitled to possess a pistol if the person has been convicted after August 1, 1992, of assault in the fifth degree if the offense was committed within three years of a previous conviction under sections 609.221 to 609.224; unless three years have elapsed from the date of conviction and, during that time, the person has not been convicted of any other violation of this section. Property rights may not be abated but access may be restricted by the courts. A person who possesses a pistol in violation of this paragraph is guilty of a gross misdemeanor.

Subd. 4. **Felony.** (a) Whoever violates the provisions of subdivision 1 against the same victim within ten years of the first of any combination of two or more previous qualified domestic violence-related offense convictions or adjudications of delinquency is guilty of a felony and may be sentenced to imprisonment for not more than five years or payment of a fine of not more than $10,000, or both.

(b) Whoever violates the provisions of subdivision 1 within three years of the first of any combination of two or more previous qualified domestic violence-related offense convictions or

adjudications of delinquency is guilty of a felony and may be sentenced to imprisonment for not more than five years or to payment of a fine of not more than $10,000, or both.
HIST: 1979 c 258 s 7; * * * 2011 c 28 s 8; 2020 c 83 art 1 s 91

609.2241 KNOWING TRANSFER OF COMMUNICABLE DISEASE.

Subdivision 1. **Definitions.** As used in this section, the following terms have the meanings given:

(a) "Communicable disease" means a disease or condition that causes serious illness, serious disability, or death; the infectious agent of which may pass or be carried from the body of one person to the body of another through direct transmission.

(b) "Direct transmission" means predominately sexual or blood-borne transmission.

(c) "A person who knowingly harbors an infectious agent" refers to a person who receives from a physician or other health professional:

(1) advice that the person harbors an infectious agent for a communicable disease;

(2) educational information about behavior which might transmit the infectious agent; and

(3) instruction of practical means of preventing such transmission.

(d) "Transfer" means to engage in behavior that has been demonstrated epidemiologically to be a mode of direct transmission of an infectious agent which causes the communicable disease.

(e) "Sexual penetration" means any of the acts listed in section 609.341, subdivision 12, when the acts described are committed without the use of a latex or other effective barrier.

Subd. 2. **Crime.** It is a crime, which may be prosecuted under section 609.17, 609.185, 609.19, 609.221, 609.222, 609.223, 609.2231, or 609.224, for a person who knowingly harbors an infectious agent to transfer, if the crime involved:

(1) sexual penetration with another person without having first informed the other person that the person has a communicable disease;

(2) transfer of blood, sperm, organs, or tissue, except as deemed necessary for medical research or if disclosed on donor screening forms; or

(3) sharing of nonsterile syringes or needles for the purpose of injecting drugs.

Subd. 3. **Affirmative defense.** It is an affirmative defense to prosecution, if it is proven by a preponderance of the evidence, that:

(1) the person who knowingly harbors an infectious agent for a communicable disease took practical means to prevent transmission as advised by a physician or other health professional; or

(2) the person who knowingly harbors an infectious agent for a communicable disease is a health care provider who was following professionally accepted infection control procedures.

Nothing in this section shall be construed to be a defense to a criminal prosecution that does not allege a violation of subdivision 2.

Subd. 4. **Health Department data.** Data protected by section 13.3805, subdivision 1, and information collected as part of a Health Department investigation under sections 144.4171 to 144.4186 may not be accessed or subpoenaed by law enforcement authorities or prosecutors without the consent of the subject of the data.
HIST: 1995 c 226 art 2 s 17; 1999 c 227 s 22

Category 2, Section 5:
2.5.5. Given a variety of scenarios, identify indications a particular crime has been committed and identify the elements of that crime.
2.5.7. Explain special Minnesota peace officer duties associated with specific statutes including: informing crime victims of their rights and assisting victims of violent crime including domestic assault . . .

609.2242 DOMESTIC ASSAULT.

Subdivision 1. **Misdemeanor.** Whoever does any of the following against a family or household member as defined in section 518B.01, subdivision 2, commits an assault and is guilty of a misdemeanor:

(1) commits an act with intent to cause fear in another of immediate bodily harm or death; or

(2) intentionally inflicts or attempts to inflict bodily harm upon another.

Subd. 2. **Gross misdemeanor.** Whoever violates subdivision 1 within ten years of a previous qualified domestic violence-related offense conviction or an adjudication of delinquency is guilty of a gross misdemeanor and may be sentenced to imprisonment for not more than one year or to payment of a fine of not more than $3,000, or both.

Subd. 3. **Domestic assaults; firearms.** (a) When a person is convicted of a violation of this section or section 609.221, 609.222, 609.223, 609.224, or 609.2247, the court shall determine and make written findings on the record as to whether:

(1) the assault was committed against a family or household member, as defined in section 518B.01, subdivision 2;

(2) the defendant owns or possesses a firearm; and

(3) the firearm was used in any way during the commission of the assault.

(b) If the court determines that the assault was of a family or household member, and that the offender owns or possesses a firearm and used it in any way during the commission of the assault, it shall order that the firearm be summarily forfeited under section 609.5316, subdivision 3.

(c) When a person is convicted of assaulting a family or household member and is determined by the court to have used a firearm in any way during commission of the assault, the court may order that the person is prohibited from possessing any type of firearm for any period longer than three years or for the remainder of the person's life. A person who violates this paragraph is guilty of a gross misdemeanor. At the time of the conviction, the court shall inform the defendant for how long the defendant is prohibited from possessing a firearm and that it is a gross misdemeanor to violate this paragraph. The failure of the court to provide this information to a defendant does not affect the applicability of the firearm possession prohibition or the gross misdemeanor penalty to that defendant.

(d) Except as otherwise provided in paragraph (c), when a person is convicted of a violation of this section or section 609.224 and the court determines that the victim was a family or household member, the court shall inform the defendant that the defendant is prohibited from possessing a pistol for three years from the date of conviction and that it is a gross misdemeanor offense to violate this prohibition. The failure of the court to provide this information to a defendant does not affect the applicability of the firearm possession prohibition or the gross misdemeanor penalty to that defendant.

(e) Except as otherwise provided in paragraph (c), a person is not entitled to possess a pistol if the person has been convicted after August 1, 1992, or a firearm if a person has been convicted on or after the effective date of this act, of domestic assault under this section or assault in the fifth degree under section 609.224 and the assault victim was a family or household member as defined in section 518B.01, subdivision 2, unless three years have elapsed from the date of conviction and, during that time, the person has not been convicted of any other violation of this section or section 609.224. Property rights may not be abated but access may be restricted by the courts. A person who possesses a firearm in violation of this paragraph is guilty of a gross misdemeanor.

(f) Except as otherwise provided in paragraphs (b) and (h), when a person is convicted of a violation of this section or section 609.221, 609.222, 609.223, 609.224, or 609.2247 and the court determines that the assault was against a family or household member, the court shall order the defendant to transfer any firearms that the person possesses, within three business days, to a federally licensed firearms dealer, a law enforcement agency, or a third party who may lawfully receive them. * * * [Such transferees] shall return the transferred firearms to the person upon request after the expiration of the prohibiting time period imposed under this subdivision, provided the person is not otherwise prohibited from possessing firearms under state or federal law. * * * The court shall order that the person surrender all permits to carry and purchase firearms to the sheriff.

(g) A defendant who is ordered to transfer firearms under paragraph (f) must file proof of transfer as provided for in this paragraph. If the transfer is made to a third party, the third party must sign an affidavit under oath before a notary public either acknowledging that the defendant permanently transferred the defendant's firearms to the third party or agreeing to temporarily store the defendant's firearms until such time as the defendant is legally permitted to possess firearms. * * * If the transfer is to a law enforcement agency or federally licensed firearms dealer, the law enforcement agency or federally licensed firearms dealer shall provide proof of transfer to the defendant. * * *

(h) When a person is convicted of a violation of this section or section 609.221, 609.222, 609.223, 609.224, or 609.2247, and the court determines that the assault was against a family or household member, the court shall determine by a preponderance of evidence if the person poses an imminent risk of causing another person substantial bodily harm. Upon a finding of imminent risk, the court shall order that the local law enforcement agency take immediate possession of all firearms in the person's possession. * * * [The agency] shall return the firearms to the person upon request after the expiration of the prohibiting time period, provided the person is not otherwise prohibited from possessing firearms under state or federal law. The local law enforcement agency shall, upon written notice from the person, transfer the firearms to a federally licensed firearms dealer or a third party who may lawfully receive them. * * *

Subd. 4. **Felony.** Whoever violates the provisions of this section or section 609.224, subdivision 1, within ten years of the first of any combination of two or more previous qualified domestic violence-related offense convictions or adjudications of delinquency is guilty of a felony and may be sentenced to imprisonment for not more than five years or payment of a fine or not more than $10,000, or both.

HIST: 1995 c 259 art 3 s 15; 2000 c 437 s 8,9; 1Sp2001 c 8 art 10 s 10,11; 2005 c 135 art 17 s 12; 2006 c 260 art 1 s 18,19; 2013 c 47 s 3; 2014 c 213 s 3

609.2247 DOMESTIC ASSAULT BY STRANGULATION.

Subdivision 1. **Definitions.** (a) As used in this section, the following terms have the meanings given.

(b) "Family or household members" has the meaning given in section 518B.01, subdivision 2.

(c) "Strangulation" means intentionally impeding normal breathing or circulation of the blood by applying pressure on the throat or neck or by blocking the nose or mouth of another person.

Subd. 2. **Crime.** Unless a greater penalty is provided elsewhere, whoever assaults a family or household member by strangulation is guilty of a felony and may be sentenced to imprisonment for not more than three years or to payment of a fine of not more than $5,000, or both.

HIST: 2005 c 136 art 17 s 13

Category 2, Section 5:
2.5.3. Explain what is meant by the elements of a crime and describe the connection between criminal conduct and criminal intent (mens rea).
2.5.5. Given a variety of scenarios, identify indications a particular crime has been committed and identify the elements of that crime.

609.23 MISTREATMENT OF PERSONS CONFINED.

Whoever, being in charge of or employed in any institution whether public or private, intentionally abuses or ill-treats any person confined therein who is mentally or physically disabled or who is involuntarily confined therein by order of court or other duly constituted authority may be sentenced to imprisonment for not more than one year or to payment of a fine of not more than $3,000, or both.

HIST: 1963 c 753 art 1 s 609.23; 1984 c 628 art 3 s 11

609.231 MISTREATMENT OF RESIDENTS OR PATIENTS.

Whoever, being in charge of or employed in any facility required to be licensed under the provisions of sections 144.50 to 144.58, or 144A.02, intentionally abuses, ill-treats, or culpably neglects any patient or resident therein to the patient's or resident's physical detriment may be sentenced to imprisonment for not more than one year or to payment of a fine of not more than $3,000, or both.

HIST: 1973 c 688 s 9; 1976 c 173 s 60; 1984 c 628 art 3 s 11; 1986 c 444

609.232 CRIMES AGAINST VULNERABLE ADULTS; DEFINITIONS.

Subdivision 1. **Scope.** As used in sections 609.2325, 609.233, 609.2335, and 609.234, the terms defined in this section have the meanings given.

Subd. 2. **Caregiver.** "Caregiver" means an individual or facility who has responsibility for the care of a vulnerable adult as a result of a family relationship, or who has assumed responsibility for all or a portion of the care of a vulnerable adult voluntarily, by contract, or by agreement.

Subd. 3. **Facility.** (a) "Facility" means a hospital or other entity required to be licensed under sections 144.50 to 144.58; a nursing home required to be licensed to serve adults under section 144A.02; a home care provider licensed or required to be licensed under sections 144A.43 to 144A.482; a residential or nonresidential facility required to be licensed to serve adults under sections 245A.01 to 245A.16; or a person or organization that exclusively offers, provides, or arranges for personal care assistance services under the medical assistance program as authorized under sections 256B.0625, subdivision 19a, 256B.0651, 256B.0653, and 256B.0654.

(b) For home care providers and personal care attendants, the term "facility" refers to the provider or person or organization that exclusively offers, provides, or arranges for personal care services, and does not refer to the client's home or other location at which services are rendered.

Subd. 4. **Immediately.** "Immediately" means as soon as possible, but no longer than 24 hours from the time of initial knowledge that the incident occurred has been received.

Subd. 5. **Legal authority.** "Legal authority" includes, but is not limited to:

(1) a fiduciary obligation recognized elsewhere in law, including pertinent regulations;

(2) a contractual obligation; or

(3) documented consent by a competent person.

Subd. 6. **Maltreatment.** "Maltreatment" means any of the following:

(1) abuse under section 609.2325;

(2) neglect under section 609.233; or

(3) financial exploitation under section 609.2335.

Subd. 7. **Operator.** "Operator" means any person whose duties and responsibilities evidence actual control of administrative activities or authority for the decision making of or by a facility.

Subd. 8. **Person.** "Person" means any individual, corporation, firm, partnership, incorporated and unincorporated association, or any other legal, professional, or commercial entity.

Subd. 9. **Report.** "Report" means a statement concerning all the circumstances surrounding the alleged or suspected maltreatment, as defined in this section, of a vulnerable adult which are known to the reporter at the time the statement is made.

Subd. 10. **Therapeutic conduct.** "Therapeutic conduct" means the provision of program services, health care, or other personal care services done in good faith in the interests of the vulnerable adult by: (1) an individual, facility or employee, or person providing services in a facility under the rights, privileges, and responsibilities conferred by state license, certification, or registration; or (2) a caregiver.

Subd. 11. **Vulnerable adult.** "Vulnerable adult" means any person 18 years of age or older who:

(1) is a resident inpatient of a facility;

(2) receives services at or from a facility required to be licensed to serve adults under sections 245A.01 to 245A.15, except that a person receiving outpatient services for treatment of chemical dependency or mental illness, or one who is committed as a sexual psychopathic personality or as a sexually dangerous person under chapter 253B, is not considered a vulnerable adult unless the person meets the requirements of clause (4);

(3) receives services from a home care provider required to be licensed under sections 144A.43 to 144A.482; or from a person or organization that exclusively offers, provides, or arranges for personal care assistance services under the medical assistance program as authorized under sections 256B.0625, subdivision 19a, 256B.0651 to 256B.0654, and 256B.0659; or

(4) regardless of residence or whether any type of service is received, possesses a physical or mental infirmity or other physical, mental, or emotional dysfunction:

(i) that impairs the individual's ability to provide adequately for the individual's own care without assistance, including the provision of food, shelter, clothing, health care, or supervision; and

(ii) because of the dysfunction or infirmity and the need for assistance, the individual has an impaired ability to protect the individual from maltreatment.

HIST: 1995 c 229 art 2 s 2; 2009 c 79 art 6 s 19; 2014 c 262 art 4 s 9; art 5 s 6; 2016 c 158 art 1 s 202, 203

609.2325 CRIMINAL ABUSE.

Subdivision 1. Crimes. (a) A caregiver who, with intent to produce physical or mental pain or injury to a vulnerable adult, subjects a vulnerable adult to any aversive or deprivation procedure, unreasonable confinement, or involuntary seclusion, is guilty of criminal abuse and may be sentenced as provided in subdivision 3. This ~~paragraph~~ subdivision does not apply to therapeutic conduct.

~~(b) A caregiver, facility staff person, or person providing services in a facility who engages in sexual contact or penetration, as defined in section 609.341, under circumstances other than those described in sections 609.342 to 609.345, with a resident, patient, or client of the facility is guilty of criminal abuse and may be sentenced as provided in subdivision 3.~~

Subd. 2. **Exemptions.** For the purposes of this section, a vulnerable adult is not abused for the sole reason that:

(1) the vulnerable adult or a person with authority to make health care decisions for the vulnerable adult * * *, refuses consent or withdraws consent, consistent with that authority and within the boundary of reasonable medical practice, to any therapeutic conduct, including any care, service, or procedure to diagnose, maintain, or treat the physical or mental condition of the vulnerable adult or, where permitted under law, to provide nutrition and hydration parenterally or through intubation; this paragraph does not enlarge or diminish rights otherwise held under law by:

(i) a vulnerable adult or a person acting on behalf of a vulnerable adult, including an involved family member, to consent to or refuse consent for therapeutic conduct; or

(ii) a caregiver to offer or provide or refuse to offer or provide therapeutic conduct;

(2) the vulnerable adult, a person with authority to make health care decisions for the vulnerable adult, or a caregiver in good faith selects and depends upon spiritual means or prayer for treatment or care of disease or remedial care of the vulnerable adult in lieu of medical care, provided that this is consistent with the prior practice or belief of the vulnerable adult or with the expressed intentions of the vulnerable adult; ~~or~~

(3) the vulnerable adult, who is not impaired in judgment or capacity by mental or emotional dysfunction or undue influence, engages in consensual sexual contact with: (i) a person, including a facility staff person, when a consensual sexual personal relationship existed prior to the caregiving relationship; or (ii) a personal care attendant, regardless of whether the consensual sexual personal relationship existed prior to the caregiving relationship.

Subd. 3. **Penalties.** (a) A person who violates subdivision 1, paragraph (a), may be sentenced as follows:

(1) if the act results in the death of a vulnerable adult, imprisonment for not more than 15 years or payment of a fine of not more than $30,000, or both;

(2) if the act results in great bodily harm, imprisonment for not more than ten years or payment of a fine of not more than $20,000, or both;

(3) if the act results in substantial bodily harm or the risk of death, imprisonment for not more than five years or payment of a fine of not more than $10,000, or both; or

(4) in other cases, imprisonment for not more than one year or payment of a fine of not more than $3,000, or both.

(b) A person who violates subdivision 1, paragraph (b), may be sentenced to imprisonment for not more than one year or to payment of a fine of not more than $3,000, or both.

EFFECTIVE DATE.
This section is effective September 15, 2021, and applies to crimes committed on or after that date.
HIST: 1995 c 229 art 2 s 3; 1996 c 408 art 10 s 11; 2004 c 146 art 3 s 43; 1Sp2021 c 11 art 4 s 4

609.233 CRIMINAL NEGLECT.

Subdivision 1. **Gross misdemeanor crime.** A caregiver or operator who intentionally neglects a vulnerable adult or knowingly permits conditions to exist that result in the abuse or neglect of a vulnerable adult is guilty of a gross misdemeanor. For purposes of this section, "abuse" has the meaning given in section 626.5572, subdivision 2, and "neglect" means a failure to provide a vulnerable adult with necessary food, clothing, shelter, health care, or supervision.

Subd. 1a.Felony deprivation. A caregiver or operator who intentionally deprives a vulnerable adult of necessary food, clothing, shelter, health care, or supervision, when the caregiver or operator is reasonably able to make the necessary provisions, is guilty of a felony and may be sentenced as provided in subdivision 3 if:

(1) the caregiver or operator knows or has reason to know the deprivation could likely result in substantial bodily harm or great bodily harm to the vulnerable adult; or

(2) the deprivation occurred over an extended period of time.

Subd. 2. **Exemptions.** A vulnerable adult is not neglected or deprived under subdivision 1 or 1a for the sole reason that:

(1) the vulnerable adult or a person with authority to make health care decisions for the vulnerable adult * * * refuses consent or withdraws consent, consistent with that authority and within the boundary of reasonable medical practice, to any therapeutic conduct, including any care, service, or procedure to diagnose, maintain, or treat the physical or mental condition of the vulnerable adult or, where permitted under law, to provide nutrition and hydration parenterally or through intubation; this paragraph does not enlarge or diminish rights otherwise held under law by:

(i) a vulnerable adult or a person acting on behalf of a vulnerable adult, including an involved family member, to consent to or refuse consent for therapeutic conduct; or

(ii) a caregiver to offer or provide or refuse to offer or provide therapeutic conduct;

(2) the vulnerable adult, a person with authority to make health care decisions for the vulnerable adult, or a caregiver in good faith selects and depends upon spiritual means or prayer for treatment or care of disease or remedial care of the vulnerable adult in lieu of medical care, provided that this is consistent with the prior practice or belief of the vulnerable adult or with the expressed intentions of the vulnerable adult; or

(3) the vulnerable adult, who is not impaired in judgment or capacity by mental or emotional dysfunction or undue influence, engages in consensual sexual contact with: (i) a person including a facility staff person when a consensual sexual personal relationship existed prior to the caregiving relationship; or (ii) a personal care attendant, regardless of whether the consensual sexual personal relationship existed prior to the caregiving relationship.

Subd. 3. **Penalties.** A person who violates subdivision 1a may be sentenced as follows:

(1) if the conduct results in great bodily harm to the vulnerable adult, imprisonment for not more than ten years or payment of a fine of not more than $10,000, or both; or

(2) if the conduct results in substantial bodily harm to the vulnerable adult, imprisonment for not more than five years or payment of a fine of not more than $5,000, or both.
* * *
HIST: 1995 c 229 art 2 s 4; 2004 c 146 art 3 s 44; 2012 c 175 s 1; 2013 c 125 art 1 s 85

609.228 GREAT BODILY HARM CAUSED BY DISTRIBUTION OF DRUGS.

Whoever proximately causes great bodily harm by, directly or indirectly, unlawfully selling, giving away, bartering, delivering, exchanging, distributing, or administering a controlled substance classified in schedule I or II may be sentenced to imprisonment for not more than ten years or to payment of a fine of not more than $20,000, or both.
HIST: 1987 c 176 s 3

609.235 USE OF DRUGS TO INJURE OR FACILITATE CRIME.

Whoever administers to another or causes another to take any poisonous, stupefying, overpowering, narcotic or anesthetic substance with intent thereby to injure or to facilitate the commission of a crime may be sentenced to imprisonment for not more than five years or to payment of a fine of not more than $10,000, or both.
HIST: 1963 c 753 art 1 s 609.235; 1984 c 628 art 3 s 11

609.24 SIMPLE ROBBERY.

Whoever, having knowledge of not being entitled thereto, takes personal property from the person or in the presence of another and uses or threatens the imminent use of force against any person to overcome the person's resistance or powers of resistance to, or to compel acquiescence in, the taking or carrying away of the property is guilty of robbery and may be sentenced to imprisonment for not more than ten years or to payment of a fine of not more than $20,000, or both.
HIST: 1963 c 753 art 1 s 609.24; 1984 c 628 art 3 s 11; 1986 c 444

609.245 AGGRAVATED ROBBERY.

Subdivision 1. **First degree.** Whoever, while committing a robbery, is armed with a dangerous weapon or any article used or fashioned in a manner to lead the victim to reasonably believe it to be a dangerous weapon, or inflicts bodily harm upon another, is guilty of aggravated robbery in the first degree and may be sentenced to imprisonment for not more than 20 years or to payment of a fine of not more than $35,000, or both.

Subd. 2. **Second degree.** Whoever, while committing a robbery, implies, by word or act, possession of a dangerous weapon, is guilty of aggravated robbery in the second degree and may be sentenced to imprisonment for not more than 15 years or to payment of a fine of not more than $30,000, or both.
HIST: 1963 c 753 art 1 s 609.245; 1984 c 628 art 3 s 11; 1988 c 712 s 5; 1994 c 636 art 2 s 23

Category 2, Sections 1, 5:
2.1.10. Identify the meaning of criminal justice system terms, e.g., . . . double jeopardy . . .
2.5.3. Explain what is meant by the elements of a crime and describe the connection between criminal conduct and criminal intent (mens rea).

2.5.5. Given a variety of scenarios, identify indications a particular crime has been committed and identify the elements of that crime.

609.25 KIDNAPPING.

Subdivision 1. **Acts constituting.** Whoever, for any of the following purposes, confines or removes from one place to another, any person without the person's consent or, if the person is under the age of 16 years, without the consent of the person's parents or other legal custodian, is guilty of kidnapping and may be sentenced as provided in subdivision 2:

(1) To hold for ransom or reward for release, or as shield or hostage; or

(2) To facilitate commission of any felony or flight thereafter; or

(3) To commit great bodily harm or to terrorize the victim or another; or

(4) To hold in involuntary servitude.

Subd. 2. **Sentence.** Whoever violates subdivision 1 may be sentenced as follows:

(1) If the victim is released in a safe place without great bodily harm, to imprisonment for not more than 20 years or to payment of a fine of not more than $35,000, or both; or

(2) If the victim is not released in a safe place or if the victim suffers great bodily harm during the course of the kidnapping, or if the person kidnapped is under the age of 16, to imprisonment for not more than 40 years or to payment of a fine of not more than $50,000, or both.

HIST: 1963 c 753 art 1 s 609.25; * * * 1994 c 636 art 2 s 24

609.251 DOUBLE JEOPARDY; KIDNAPPING.

Notwithstanding section 609.04, a prosecution for or conviction of the crime of kidnapping is not a bar to conviction of or punishment for any other crime committed during the time of the kidnapping.

HIST: 1983 c 139 s 2; 1993 c 326 art 4 s 16

609.255 FALSE IMPRISONMENT.

Subdivision 1. **Definition.** As used in this section, the following term has the meaning given it unless specific content indicates otherwise.

"Caretaker" means an individual who has responsibility for the care of a child as a result of a family relationship, or who has assumed responsibility for all or a portion of the care of a child.

Subd. 2. **Intentional restraint.** Whoever, knowingly lacking lawful authority to do so, intentionally confines or restrains someone else's child under the age of 18 years without consent of the child's parent or legal custodian, or any other person without the person's consent, is guilty of false imprisonment and may be sentenced to imprisonment for not more than three years or to payment of a fine of not more than $5,000, or both.

Subd. 3. **Unreasonable restraint of children.** (a) A parent, legal guardian, or caretaker who intentionally subjects a child under the age of 18 years to unreasonable physical confinement or restraint by means including but not limited to, tying, locking, caging, or chaining for a prolonged period of time and in a cruel manner which is excessive under the circumstances, is guilty of unreasonable restraint of a child , except as provided in paragraph (b) or (c), and may be sentenced to imprisonment for not more than one year or to payment of a fine of not more than $3,000, or both.

(b) If the confinement or restraint results in substantial bodily harm, the person may be sentenced to imprisonment for not more than two years or to payment of a fine of not more than $4,000, or both.

(c) If the confinement or restraint results in substantial bodily harm, the person may be sentenced to imprisonment for not more than five years or to payment of a fine of not more than $10,000, or both.

HIST: 1963 c 753 art 1 s 609.255; * * * 2012 c 175 s 2

609.265 ABDUCTION.

Whoever, for the purpose of marriage, takes a person under the age of 18 years, without the consent of the parents, guardian or other person having legal custody of such person is guilty of abduction and may be sentenced to imprisonment for not more than one year or to payment of a fine of not more than $3,000, or both.

HIST: 1963 c 753 art 1 s 609.265; 1984 c 628 art 3 s 11

Category 2, Section 5:

2.5.3. Explain what is meant by the elements of a crime and describe the connection between criminal conduct and criminal intent (mens rea).

2.5.5. Given a variety of scenarios, identify indications a particular crime has been committed and identify the elements of that crime.

609.26 DEPRIVING ANOTHER OF CUSTODIAL OR PARENTAL RIGHTS.

Subdivision 1. **Prohibited acts.** Whoever intentionally does any of the following acts may be charged with a felony and, upon conviction, may be sentenced as provided in subdivision 6:

(1) conceals a minor child from the child's parent where the action manifests an intent substantially to deprive that parent of parental rights or conceals a minor child from another person having the right to parenting time or custody where the action manifests an intent to substantially deprive that person of rights to parenting time or custody;

(2) takes, obtains, retains, or fails to return a minor child in violation of a court order which has transferred legal custody under chapter 260 to the commissioner of human services, a child placing agency, or the local social services agency;

(3) takes, obtains, retains, or fails to return a minor child from or to the parent in violation of a court order, where the action manifests an intent substantially to deprive that parent of rights to parenting time or custody;

(4) takes, obtains, retains, or fails to return a minor child from or to a parent after commencement of an action relating to child parenting time or custody but prior to the issuance of an order determining custody or parenting time rights, where the action manifests an intent substantially to deprive that parent of parental rights; or

(5) retains a child in this state with the knowledge that the child was removed from another state in violation of any of the above provisions;

(6) refuses to return a minor child to a parent or lawful custodian and is at least 18 years old and more than 24 months older than the child;

(7) causes or contributes to a child being a habitual truant as defined in section 260.015, subdivision 19, and is at least 18 years old and more than 24 months older than the child;

(8) causes or contributes to a child being a runaway as defined in section 260.015, subdivision 20, and is at least 18 years old and more than 24 months older than the child; or

(9) is at least 18 years old and resides with a minor under the age of 16 without the consent of the minor's parent or lawful custodian.

Subd. 2. **Defenses.** It is an affirmative defense if a person charged under subdivision 1 proves that:

(1) the person reasonably believed the action taken was necessary to protect the child from physical or sexual assault or substantial emotional harm;

(2) the person reasonably believed the action taken was necessary to protect the person taking the action from physical or sexual assault;

(3) the action taken is consented to by the parent, stepparent, or legal custodian seeking prosecution, but consent to custody or specific parenting time is not consent to the action of failing to return or concealing a minor child; or

(4) the action taken is otherwise authorized by a court order issued prior to the violation of subdivision 1.

The defenses provided in this subdivision are in addition to and do not limit other defenses available under this chapter or chapter 611.

Subd. 2a. **Original intent clarified.** To the extent that it states that subdivision 2 creates affirmative defenses to a charge under this section, subdivision 2 clarifies the original intent of the legislature in enacting Laws 1984, chapter 484, section 2, and does not change the substance of this section. Subdivision 2 does not modify or alter any convictions entered under this section before August 1, 1988.

Subd. 3. **Venue.** A person who violates this section may be prosecuted and tried either in the county in which the child was taken, concealed, or detained or in the county of lawful residence of the child.

Subd. 4. **Return of child; costs.** A child who has been concealed, obtained, or retained in violation of this section shall be returned to the person having lawful custody of the child or shall be taken into custody pursuant to section 260.165, subdivision 1, paragraph (c), clause (2). In addition to any sentence imposed, the court may assess any expense incurred in returning the child against any person convicted of violating this section. The court may direct the appropriate county welfare agency to provide counseling services to a child who has been returned pursuant to this subdivision.

Subd. 5. **Dismissal of charge.** A felony charge brought under this section shall be dismissed if:

(a) the person voluntarily returns the child within 48 hours after taking, detaining, or failing to return the child in violation of this section: or

(b)(1) the person taking the action and the child have not left the state of Minnesota; and (2) within a period of seven days after taking the action, (i) a motion or proceeding under chapter 518, 518B, 518C, or 518D is commenced by the person taking the action, or (ii) the attorney representing the person taking the action has consented to service of process by the party whose rights are being deprived, for any motion or action pursuant to chapter 518, 518A, 518B, 518C, or 518D.

Clause (a) does not apply if the person returns the child as a result of being located by law enforcement authorities.

This subdivision does not prohibit the filing of felony charges or an offense report before the expiration of the 48 hours.

Subd. 6. **Penalty.** (a) Except as otherwise provided in paragraph (b) and subdivision 5, whoever violates this section may be sentenced as follows:

(1) to imprisonment for not more than two years or to payment of a fine of not more than $4,000, or both; or

(2) to imprisonment for not more than four years or to payment of a fine of not more than $8,000, or both, if the court finds that:

(i) the defendant committed the violation while possessing a dangerous weapon or caused substantial bodily harm to effect the taking;

(ii) the defendant abused or neglected the child during the concealment, detention, or removal of the child;

(iii) the defendant inflicted or threatened to inflict physical harm on a parent or lawful custodian of the child or on the child with intent to cause the parent or lawful custodian to discontinue criminal prosecution;

(iv) the defendant demanded payment in exchange for return of the child or demanded to be relieved of the financial or legal obligation to support the child in exchange for return of the child; or

(v) the defendant has previously been convicted under this section or a similar statute of another jurisdiction.

(b) A violation of subdivision 1, clause (7), is a gross misdemeanor. The county attorney shall prosecute violations of subdivision 1, clause (7).

Subd. 7. **Reporting of deprivation of parental rights.** Any violation of this section shall be reported pursuant to section 626.556, subdivision 3a 260E.11, subdivision 2.
HIST: 1963 c 753 art 1 s 609.26; * * * 2002 c 379 art 1 s 105; 1Sp2020 c 2 art 8 s 137

611A.06 RIGHT TO NOTICE OF RELEASE.

Subdivision 1. **Notice of release required.** The commissioner of corrections or other custodial authority shall make a good faith effort to notify the victim that the offender is to be released from imprisonment or incarceration, including release on extended furlough and for work release; released from a juvenile correctional facility; released from a facility in which the offender was confined due to incompetency, mental illness, or mental deficiency, or commitment under section 253B.18 or chapter 253D; or if the offender's custody status is reduced, if the victim has mailed to the commissioner of corrections or to the head of the facility in which the offender is confined a written request for this notice, or the victim has made a request for this notice to the commissioner of corrections through the Department of Corrections electronic victim notification system. The good faith effort to notify the victim must occur prior to the offender's release or when the offender's custody status is reduced. For a victim of a felony crime against the person for which the offender was sentenced to imprisonment for more than 18 months, the good faith effort to notify the victim must occur 60 days before the offender's release.
* * *

Subd. 2. **Contents of notice.** The notice given to a victim of a crime against a person must include the conditions governing the offender's release, and either the identity of the corrections agent who will be supervising the offender's release or a means to identify the court services agency that will be supervising the offender's release. The commissioner or other custodial authority complies with this section upon mailing the notice of impending release to the victim at the address which the victim has most recently provided to the commissioner or authority in writing, or by providing electronic notice to the victim who requested this notice through the Department of Corrections electronic victim notification system.

Subd. 3. **Notice of escape.** If an offender escapes from imprisonment or incarceration, including from release on extended furlough or work release, or from any facility described in subdivision 1, the commissioner or other custodial authority shall make all reasonable efforts to notify a victim who has requested notice of the offender's release under subdivision 1 within six hours after discovering the escape and shall also make reasonable efforts to notify the victim within 24 hours after the offender is apprehended.

Subd. 3a. **Offender location.** (a) Upon the victim's written or electronic request and if the victim and offender have been household or family members as defined in section 518B.01, subdivision 2, paragraph (b), the commissioner of corrections or the commissioner's designee shall disclose to the victim of an offender convicted of a qualified domestic violence-related offense as defined in section 609.02, subdivision 16, notification of the city and five-digit zip code of the offender's residency upon release from a Department of Corrections facility, unless:

(1) the offender is not under correctional supervision at the time of the victim's request;

(2) the commissioner or the commissioner's designee does not have the city or zip code; or

(3) the commissioner or the commissioner's designee reasonably believes that disclosure of the city or zip code of the offender's residency creates a risk to the victim, offender, or public safety.

(b) All identifying information regarding the victim including, but not limited to, the notification provided by the commissioner or the commissioner's designee is classified as private data on individuals as defined in section 13.02, subdivision 12, and is accessible only to the victim.

(c) This subdivision applies only where the offender is serving a prison term for a qualified domestic violence-related offense committed against the victim seeking notification.

Subd. 4. **Private data.** All identifying information regarding the victim, including the victim's request and the notice provided by the commissioner or custodial authority, is classified as private data on individuals as defined in section 13.02, subdivision 12, and is accessible only to the victim.

Subd. 5. **Definition.** As used in this section, "crime against the person" means a crime listed in section 611A.031.

HIST: 1983 c 262 art 1 s 5; 1986 c 444; 1986 c 445 s 4; 1986 c 463 s 11; 1987 c 224 s 3; 1988 c 649 s 4; 1989 c 190 s 4; 1990 c 579 s 9; 1991 c 170 s 5; 1993 c 326 art 6 s 11; art 13 s 35; 1994 c 636 art 7 s 5; 1Sp1994 c 1 art 2 s 33; 2001 c 209 s 7; 2012 c 155 s 8,9; 2013 c 49 s 22; 2014 c 312 art 6 s 5

Chapter 6 -- CRIMES AGAINST UNBORN CHILDREN

Category 2, Section 5:
2.5.1. Describe the basic organization, purpose, and definitions and principles of the Minnesota Criminal Code.
2.5.5. Given a variety of scenarios, identify indications a particular crime has been committed and identify the elements of that crime.

609.266 DEFINITIONS.

The definitions in this section apply to sections 609.21, subdivision 1a, paragraphs (a) and (b), and 609.2661 to 609.2691:

(a) "Unborn child" means the unborn offspring of a human being conceived, but not yet born.

(b) "Whoever" does not include the pregnant woman.
HIST: 1986 c 388 s 5; 2007 c 54 art 3 s 14; 2015 c 21 art 1 s 101

609.2661 MURDER OF AN UNBORN CHILD IN THE FIRST DEGREE.

Whoever does any of the following is guilty of murder of an unborn child in the first degree and must be sentenced to imprisonment for life:

(1) causes the death of an unborn child with premeditation and with intent to effect the death of the unborn child or of another;

(2) causes the death of an unborn child while committing or attempting to commit criminal sexual conduct in the first or second degree with force or violence, either upon or affecting the mother of the unborn child or another; or

(3) causes the death of an unborn child with intent to effect the death of the unborn child or another while committing or attempting to commit burglary, aggravated robbery, kidnapping, arson in the first or second degree, tampering with a witness in the first degree, or escape from custody.
HIST: 1986 c 388 s 6

609.2662 MURDER OF AN UNBORN CHILD IN THE SECOND DEGREE.

Whoever does either of the following is guilty of murder of an unborn child in the second degree and may be sentenced to imprisonment for not more than 40 years:

(1) causes the death of an unborn child with intent to effect the death of that unborn child or another, but without premeditation; or

(2) causes the death of an unborn child, without intent to effect the death of any unborn child or person, while committing or attempting to commit a felony offense other than criminal sexual conduct in the first or second degree with force or violence.
HIST: 1986 c 388 s 7

609.2663 MURDER OF AN UNBORN CHILD IN THE THIRD DEGREE.
Whoever, without intent to effect the death of any unborn child or person, causes the death of an unborn child by perpetrating an act eminently dangerous to others and evincing a depraved mind, without regard for human or fetal life, is guilty of murder of an unborn child in the third degree and may be sentenced to imprisonment for not more than 25 years.
HIST: 1986 c 388 s 8

609.2664 MANSLAUGHTER OF AN UNBORN CHILD IN THE FIRST DEGREE.
Whoever does any of the following is guilty of manslaughter of an unborn child in the first degree and may be sentenced to imprisonment for not more than 15 years or to payment of a fine of not more than $30,000, or both:
(1) intentionally causes the death of an unborn child in the heat of passion provoked by such words or acts of another as would provoke a person of ordinary self-control under like circumstances;
(2) causes the death of an unborn child in committing or attempting to commit a misdemeanor or gross misdemeanor offense with such force or violence that death of or great bodily harm to any person or unborn child was reasonably foreseeable, and murder of an unborn child in the first or second degree was not committed thereby; or
(3) intentionally causes the death of an unborn child because the actor is coerced by threats made by someone other than the actor's coconspirator and which cause the actor to reasonably believe that the act performed by the actor is the only means of preventing imminent death to the actor or another.
HIST: 1986 c 388 s 9; 1986 c 444

609.2665 MANSLAUGHTER OF AN UNBORN CHILD IN THE SECOND DEGREE.
A person who causes the death of an unborn child by any of the following means is guilty of manslaughter of an unborn child in the second degree and may be sentenced to imprisonment for not more than ten years or to payment of a fine of not more than $20,000, or both:
(1) by the actor's culpable negligence whereby the actor creates an unreasonable risk and consciously takes chances of causing death or great bodily harm to an unborn child or a person;
(2) by shooting the mother of the unborn child with a firearm or other dangerous weapon as a result of negligently believing her to be a deer or other animal;
(3) by setting a spring gun, pit fall, deadfall, snare, or other like dangerous weapon or device; or
(4) by negligently or intentionally permitting any animal, known by the person to have vicious propensities or to have caused great or substantial bodily harm in the past, to run uncontrolled off the owner's premises, or negligently failing to keep it properly confined.
If proven by a preponderance of the evidence, it shall be an affirmative defense to criminal liability under clause (4) that the mother of the unborn child provoked the animal to cause the unborn child's death.
HIST: 1986 c 388 s 10; 1989 c 290 art 6 s 13

609.267 ASSAULT OF AN UNBORN CHILD IN THE FIRST DEGREE.
Whoever assaults a pregnant woman and inflicts great bodily harm on an unborn child who is subsequently born alive may be sentenced to imprisonment for not more than 15 years or to payment of a fine of not more than $30,000, or both.
HIST: 1986 c 388 s 11; 1989 c 290 art 6 s 14

609.2671 ASSAULT OF AN UNBORN CHILD IN THE SECOND DEGREE.
Whoever assaults a pregnant woman and inflicts substantial bodily harm on an unborn child who is subsequently born alive may be sentenced to imprisonment for not more than five years to payment of a fine of not more than $10,000, or both.

As used in this section, "substantial bodily harm" includes the birth of the unborn child prior to 37 weeks gestation if the child weighs 2,500 grams or less at the time of birth. "Substantial bodily harm" does not include the inducement of the unborn child's birth when done for bona fide medical purposes.
HIST: 1986 c 388 s 12; 1989 c 20 s 1

609.2672 ASSAULT OF AN UNBORN CHILD IN THE THIRD DEGREE.
Whoever does any of the following commits an assault of an unborn child in the third degree and is guilty of a misdemeanor:
(1) commits an act with intent to cause fear in a pregnant woman of immediate bodily harm or death to the unborn child; or
(2) intentionally inflicts or attempts to inflict bodily harm on an unborn child who is subsequently born alive.
HIST: 1986 c 388 s 13

609.268 INJURY OR DEATH OF AN UNBORN CHILD IN COMMISSION OF CRIME.
Subdivision 1. **Death of an unborn child.** Whoever, in the commission of a felony or in a violation of section 609.224, 609.2242, 609.23, 609.231, 609.2325, or 609.233, causes the death of an unborn child is guilty of a felony and may be sentenced to imprisonment for not more than 15 years or to payment of a fine not more than $30,000, or both. As used in this subdivision, "felony" does not include a violation of sections 609.185 to 609.21, 609.221 to 609.2231, or 609.2661 to 609.2665.
Subd. 2. **Injury to an unborn child.** Whoever, in the commission of a felony or in a violation of section 609.23, 609.231, 609.2325 or 609.233, causes great or substantial bodily harm to an unborn child who is subsequently born alive, is guilty of a felony and may be sentenced to imprisonment for not more than ten years or to payment of a fine of not more than $20,000, or both. As used in this subdivision, "felony" does not include a violation of sections 609.21, 609.221 to 609.2231, or 609.267 to 609.2672.
HIST: 1986 c 388 s 14; 1995 c 229 art 4 s 17, 18; 1995 c 259 art 3 s 16

Chapter 7 -- SEX CRIMES

Category 2, Section 5:
2.5.1. Describe the basic organization, purpose, and definitions and principles of the Minnesota Criminal Code.
2.5.5. Given a variety of scenarios, identify indications a particular crime has been committed and identify the elements of that crime.

609.293 SODOMY.

Subdivision 1. **Definition.** "Sodomy" means carnally knowing any person by the anus or by or with the mouth.
Subd. 2. Repealed, 1977 c 130 s 10
Subd. 3. Repealed, 1977 c 130 s 10
Subd. 4. Repealed, 1977 c 130 s 10
Subd. 5. **Consensual acts.** Whoever, in cases not coming within the provisions of sections 609.342 or 609.344, voluntarily engages in or submits to an act of sodomy with another may be sentenced to imprisonment for not more than one year or to payment of a fine of not more than $3,000, or both.
HIST: 1967 c 507 s 4; 1977 c 130 s 4; 1984 c 628 art 3 s 11

609.294 BESTIALITY.

Whoever carnally knows a dead body or an animal or bird is guilty of bestiality, which is a misdemeanor. If knowingly done in the presence of another the person may be sentenced to imprisonment for not more than one year or to payment of a fine of not more than $3,000 or both.
HIST: 1967 c 507 s 5; 1971 c 23 s 42; 1984 c 628 art 3 s 11; 1986 c 444

609.321 PROSTITUTION; DEFINITIONS.

Subdivision 1. **Scope.** For the purposes of sections 609.321 to 609.325, the following terms have the meanings given.
Subd. 2. **Business of prostitution.** "Business of prostitution" means any arrangement between or organization of two or more persons, acting other than as prostitutes or patrons, who commit acts punishable under sections 609.321 to 609.324.
Subd. 3. Repealed, 1998 c 367 art 2 s 33
Subd. 4. **Patron.** "Patron" means an individual who engages in prostitution by hiring, offering to hire, or agreeing to hire another individual to engage in sexual penetration or sexual contact.
Subd. 5. **Place of prostitution.** "Place of prostitution" means a house or other place where prostitution is practiced.
Subd. 6. Repealed, 1998 c 367 art 2 s 33
Subd. 7. **Promotes the prostitution of an individual.** "Promotes the prostitution of an individual" means any of the following wherein the person knowingly:
(1) solicits or procures patrons for a prostitute;
(2) provides, leases or otherwise permits premises or facilities owned or controlled by the person to aid the prostitution of an individual;
(3) owns, manages, supervises, controls, keeps or operates, either alone or with others, a place of prostitution to aid the prostitution of an individual;

(4) owns, manages, supervises, controls, operates, institutes, aids or facilitates, either alone or with others, business of prostitution to aid the prostitution of an individual;

(5) admits a patron to a place of prostitution to aid the prostitution of an individual; or

(6) transports an individual from one point within this state to another point either within or without this state, or brings an individual into this state to aid the prostitution of the individual.

Subd. 7a. **Sex trafficking.** "Sex trafficking" means:

(1) receiving, recruiting, enticing, harboring, providing, or obtaining by any means an individual to aid in the prostitution of the individual; or

(2) receiving profit or anything of value, knowing or having reason to know it is derived from an act described in clause (1).

Subd. 7b. **Sex trafficking victim.** "Sex trafficking victim" means a person subjected to the practices in subdivision 7a.

Subd. 8. **Prostitute.** "Prostitute" means an individual who engages in prostitution by being hired, offering to be hired, or agreeing to be hired by another individual to engage in sexual penetration or sexual contact.

Subd. 9. **Prostitution.** "Prostitution" means hiring, offering to hire, or agreeing to hire another individual to engage in sexual penetration or sexual contact, or being hired, offering to be hired, or agreeing to be hired by another individual to engage in sexual penetration or sexual contact.

Subd. 10. **Sexual contact.** "Sexual contact" means any of the following acts, if the acts can reasonably be construed as being for the purpose of satisfying the actor's sexual impulses:

(i) The intentional touching by an individual of a prostitute's intimate parts; or

(ii) The intentional touching by a prostitute of another individual's intimate parts.

Subd. 11. **Sexual penetration.** "Sexual penetration" means any of the following acts, if for the purpose of satisfying sexual impulses: sexual intercourse, cunnilingus, fellatio, anal intercourse, or any intrusion however slight into the genital or anal openings of an individual's body by any part of another individual's body or any object used for the purpose of satisfying sexual impulses. Emission of semen is not necessary.

Subd. 12. **Public place.** A "public place" means a public street or sidewalk, a pedestrian skyway system as defined in section 469.125, subdivision 4, a hotel, motel, steam room, sauna, massage parlor, shopping mall and other public shopping areas, or other place of public accommodation, or a place licensed to sell intoxicating liquor, wine, nonintoxicating malt beverages, or food, or a motor vehicle located on a public street, alley, or parking lot ordinarily used by or available to the public though not used as a matter or right and a driveway connecting such a parking lot with a street or highway.

* * *

Subd. 14. **Prior qualified human trafficking-related offense.** * * * [M]eans a conviction or delinquency adjudication within the ten years from the discharge from probation or parole immediately preceding the current offense for a violation of or an attempt to violate section 609.322, subdivision 1 * * *; section 609.322, subdivision 1a * * *; 609.282 * * *; or 609.283 * * *.

HIST: 1979 c 255 s 1; * * * 1Sp2011 c 1 art 5 s 1-3

Editors' Note: In 2010, the State of Minnesota excluded juveniles under age 16 providing prostitution-based services from being "delinquent" and diverting certain 16 & 17 year olds (who meet criteria as "sexually exploited youth") away from typical juvenile delinquency outcomes.

609.322 SOLICITATION, INDUCEMENT AND PROMOTION OF PROSTITUTION; SEX TRAFFICKING.

Subdivision 1. **Solicitation, inducement, and promotion of prostitution; sex trafficking in the first degree.** (a) Whoever, while acting other than as a prostitute or patron, intentionally does any of the following may be sentenced to imprisonment for not more than ~~20~~ 25 years or to payment of a fine of not more than $50,000, or both:

(1) solicits or induces an individual under the age of 18 years to practice prostitution;

(2) promotes the prostitution of an individual under the age of 18 years;

(3) receives profit, knowing or having reason to know that it is derived from the prostitution, or the promotion of the prostitution, of an individual under the age of 18 years; or engages in the sex trafficking of an individual under the age of 18 years.

(b) Whoever violates paragraph (a) or subdivision 1a may be sentenced to imprisonment for not more than 25 years or to the payment of a fine of not more than $60,000, or both, if one or more of the following aggravating factors are present:

(1) the offender has committed a prior qualified human trafficking-related offense;

(2) the offense involved a sex trafficking victim who suffered bodily harm during the commission of the offense;

(3) the time period that a sex trafficking victim was held in debt bondage or forced labor or services exceeded 180 days; or

(4) the offense involved more than one sex trafficking victim.

Subd. 1a. **Solicitation, inducement, and promotion of prostitution; sex trafficking in the second degree.** Whoever, while acting other than as a prostitute or patron, intentionally does any of the following may be sentenced to imprisonment for not more than ~~15~~ 20 years or to payment of a fine of not more than $40,000, or both:

(1) solicits or induces an individual to practice prostitution;

(2) promotes the prostitution of an individual;

(3) receives profit, knowing or having reason to know that it is derived from the prostitution, or the promotion of the prostitution, of an individual; or

(4) engages in the sex trafficking of an individual.

Subd. 1b. **Exceptions.** Subdivisions 1, clause (3), and 1a, clause (3), do not apply to:

(1) a minor who is dependent on an individual acting as a prostitute and who may have benefited from or been supported by the individual's earnings derived from prostitution; or

(2) a parent over the age of 55 who is dependent on an individual acting as a prostitute, who may have benefited from or been supported by the individual's earnings derived from prostitution, and who did not know that the earnings were derived from prostitution; or

(3) the sale of goods or services to a prostitute in the ordinary course of a lawful business.

Subd. 1c. **Aggregation of cases.** Acts by the defendant in violation of any one or more of the provisions in this section within any six-month period may be aggregated and the defendant charged accordingly in applying the provisions of this section; provided that when two or more offenses are committed by the same person in two or more counties, the accused may be prosecuted in any county in which one of the offenses was committed for all of the offenses aggregated under this paragraph.

Subd. 2. Repealed, 1998 c 367 art 2 s 33

Subd. 3. Repealed, 1998 c 367 art 2 s 33

EFFECTIVE DATE. This section is effective September 15, 2021, and applies to crimes committed on or after that date.

HIST: 1979 c 255 s 2; * * * 2009 c 137 s 7; 1Sp2021 c 11 art 2 s 32, 33

Editors' Note: Many of the changes to §609.322 above were previously found in §609.323 which was repealed by 1998 c 367 art 2 s 33.

609.323 [Repealed, 1998 c 367 art 2 c 33]

609.324 OTHER PROSTITUTION CRIMES; PATRONS, PROSTITUTES, AND INDIVIDUALS HOUSING INDIVIDUALS ENGAGED IN PROSTITUTION; PENALTIES.

Subdivision 1. **Engaging in hiring, or agreeing to hire a minor to engage in prostitution; penalties.** (a) Whoever intentionally does any of the following may be sentenced to imprisonment for not more than 20 years or to payment of a fine of not more than $40,000, or both:

(1) engages in prostitution with an individual under the age of 13 years;

(2) hires or offers or agrees to hire an individual under the age of 13 years to engage in sexual penetration or sexual contact; or

(3) hires or offers or agrees to hire an individual who the actor reasonably believes to be under the age of 13 years to engage in sexual penetration or sexual contact.

(b) Whoever intentionally does any of the following may be sentenced to imprisonment for not more than ten years or to payment of a fine of not more than $20,000, or both:

(1) engages in prostitution with an individual under the age of 16 years but at least 13 years;

(2) hires or offers or agrees to hire an individual under the age of 16 years but at least 13 years to engage in sexual penetration or sexual contact; or

(3) hires or offers or agrees to hire an individual who the actor reasonably believes to be under the age of 16 years but at least 13 years to engage in sexual penetration or sexual contact.

(c) Whoever intentionally does any of the following may be sentenced to imprisonment for not more than five years or to payment of a fine of not more than $10,000, or both:

(1) engages in prostitution with an individual under the age of 18 years but at least 16 years;

(2) hires or offers or agrees to hire an individual under the age of 18 years but at least 16 years to engage in sexual penetration or sexual contact; or

(3) hires or offers or agrees to hire an individual who the actor reasonably believes to be under the age of 18 years but at least 16 years to engage in sexual penetration or sexual contact.

Subd. 1a. **Housing an unrelated minor engaged in prostitution; penalties.** Any person, other than one related by blood, adoption, or marriage to the minor, who permits a minor to reside, temporarily or permanently, in the person's dwelling without the consent of the minor's parents or guardian, knowing or having reason to know that the minor is engaging in prostitution may be sentenced to imprisonment for not more than one year or to payment of a fine of not more than $3,000, or both; except that, this subdivision does not apply to residential placements made, sanctioned, or supervised by a public or private social service agency.

Subd. 2. __Patrons of__ prostitution in public place; penalty for patrons. (a) Whoever, while acting as a patron, intentionally does any of the following while in a public place is guilty of a gross misdemeanor:

(1) engages in prostitution with an individual 18 years of age or older; or

(2) hires, offers to hire, or agrees to hire an individual 18 years of age or older to engage in sexual penetration or sexual contact.

Except as otherwise provided in subdivision 4, a person who is convicted of violating this subdivision must, at a minimum, be sentenced to pay a fine of at least $1,500.

(b) Whoever violates the provisions of this subdivision within ten years of a previous conviction for violating this section or section 609.322 is guilty of a felony and may be sentenced to imprisonment for not more than five years or to payment of a fine of not more than $10,000, or both.

Subd. 3. Repealed, 1Sp2021 c 11, art 2, s 57

Subd. 4. **Community service in lieu of minimum fine.** The court may order a person convicted of violating subdivision 2 or 3 to perform community work service in lieu of all or a portion of the minimum fine required under those subdivisions the court makes specific, written findings that the convicted person is indigent or that payment of the fine would create undue hardship for the convicted person or that person's immediate family. Community work service ordered under this subdivision is in addition to any mandatory community work service ordered under subdivision 3.

Subd. 5. **Use of motor vehicle to patronize prostitutes; driving record notation.** (a) When a court sentences a person convicted of violating this section while acting as a patron, the court shall determine whether the person used a motor vehicle during the commission of the offense and whether the person has previously been convicted of violating this section or section

609.322. If the court finds that the person used a motor vehicle during the commission of the offense, it shall forward its finding along with an indication of whether the person has previously been convicted of a prostitution offense to the commissioner of public safety who shall record the finding on the person's driving record. Except as provided in paragraph (b), the finding is classified as private data on individuals, as defined in section 13.02, subdivision 12, but is accessible for law enforcement purposes.

(b) If the person has previously been convicted of a violation of this section or section 609.322, the finding is public data.

Subd. 6. **Prostitution in public place; penalty for prostitutes.** Whoever, while acting as a prostitute, intentionally does any of the following while in a public place is guilty of a gross misdemeanor:

(1) engages in prostitution with an individual 18 years of age or older; or

(2) is hired, offers to be hired, or agrees to be hired by an individual 18 years of age or older to engage in sexual penetration or sexual contact.

Subd. 7. **General prostitution crimes; penalties for prostitutes.** (a) Whoever, while acting as a prostitute, intentionally does any of the following is guilty of a misdemeanor:

(1) engages in prostitution with an individual 18 years of age or older; or

(2) is hired, offers to be hired, or agrees to be hired by an individual 18 years of age or older to engage in sexual penetration or sexual contact.

(b) Whoever violates the provisions of this subdivision within two years of a previous prostitution conviction for violating this section or section 609.322 is guilty of a gross misdemeanor.

EFFECTIVE DATE. This section is effective September 15, 2021, and applies to crimes committed on or after that date.

HIST: 1979 c 255 s 4; * * * 2015 c 65 art 6 s 11; 2016 c 189 art 4 s 15; 1Sp2021 c 11 art 2, 4, s 5, 34, 35

609.3242 PROSTITUTION CRIMES COMMITTED IN SCHOOL OR PARK ZONES; INCREASED PENALTIES.

Subdivision 1. **Definitions.** As used in this section:

(1) "park zone" has the meaning given in section 152.01, subdivision 12a; and

(2) "school zone" has the meaning given in section 152.01, subdivision 14a, and also includes school bus stops established by a school board under section 123.39, while school children are waiting for the bus.

Subd. 2. **Increased penalties.** Any person who commits a violation of section 609.324 while acting other than as a prostitute while in a school or park zone may be sentenced as follows:

(1) if the crime committed is a felony, the statutory maximum for the crime is three years longer than the statutory maximum for the underlying crime;

(2) if the crime committed is a gross misdemeanor, the person is guilty of a felony and may be sentenced to imprisonment for not more than two years or to payment of a fine of not more than $4,000, or both; and

(3) if the crime committed is a misdemeanor, the person is guilty of a gross misdemeanor.

HIST: 1998 c 367 art 2 s 15

609.3243 LOITERING WITH INTENT TO PARTICIPATE IN PROSTITUTION.

A person who loiters in a public place with intent to participate in prostitution is guilty of a misdemeanor.

HIST: 2005 c 136 art 17 s 24

Editors' Note: The forgoing statute recodifies a portion of § 609.725 Vagrancy that was repealed in 2005.

609.325 DEFENSES.

Subdivision 1. **No defense; solicited; not engaged.** It shall be no defense to a prosecution under section 609.322 that an individual solicited or induced to practice prostitution or whose prostitution was promoted, did not actually engage in prostitution.

Subd. 2. **Consent no defense.** Consent or mistake as to age shall be no defense to prosecutions under section 609.322, 609.323, or 609.324.

Subd. 3. **No defense; prior prostitution.** It shall be no defense to actions under section 609.322 that the individual solicited or induced to practice prostitution, or whose prostitution was promoted, had engaged in prostitution prior to that solicitation, inducement, or promotion.

Subd. 3a. **No defense; undercover operative.** The fact that an undercover operative or law enforcement officer was involved in the detection or investigation of an offense shall not be a defense to a prosecution under section 609.324.

Subd. 4. **Affirmative defense.** It is an affirmative defense to a charge under section 609.324, subdivision 6 or 7, if the defendant proves by a preponderance of the evidence that the defendant is a labor trafficking victim, as defined in section 609.281, or a sex trafficking victim, as defined in section 609.321, and that the defendant committed the acts underlying the charge as a result of being a labor trafficking or sex trafficking victim.

HIST: 1979 c 255 s 5; 1994 c 636 art 2 s 29; 2005 c 136 art 17 s 25; 2015 c 65 art 6 s 12,13

609.326 EVIDENCE.

The marital privilege provided for in section 595.02 shall not apply in any proceeding under section 609.322 or 609.323.

HIST: 1979 c 255 s 6

609.281 DEFINITIONS.

Subdivision 1. **Generally.** As used in sections 609.281 to 609.284, the following terms have the meanings given.

Subd. 2. **Blackmail.** "Blackmail" means a threat to expose any fact or alleged fact tending to cause shame or to subject any person to hatred, contempt, or ridicule.

Subd. 3. **Debt bondage.** "Debt bondage" means the status or condition of a debtor arising from a pledge by the debtor of the debtor's personal services or those of a person under the debtor's control as a security for debt, if the value of those services as reasonably assessed is not applied toward the liquidation of the debt or the length and nature of those services are not respectively limited and defined.

Subd. 4. **Forced labor or services.** "Forced labor or services" means labor or services that are performed or provided by another person and are obtained or maintained through an actor's:

(1) threat, either implicit or explicit, scheme, plan, or pattern, or other action intended to cause a person to believe that, if the person did not perform or provide the labor or services, that person or another person would suffer bodily harm or physical restraint;

(2) physically restraining or threatening to physically restrain a person;

(3) abuse or threatened abuse of the legal process;

(4) knowingly destroying, concealing, removing, confiscating, or possessing any actual or purported passport or other immigration document, or any other actual or purported government identification document, of another person; or

(5) use of blackmail.

Subd. 5. **Labor trafficking.** "Labor trafficking" means:

(1) the recruitment, transportation, transfer, harboring, enticement, provision, obtaining, or receipt of a person by any means, for the purpose of:

(i) debt bondage or forced labor or services;

(ii) slavery or practices similar to slavery; or

(iii) the removal of organs through the use of coercion or intimidation; or

(2) receiving profit or anything of value, knowing or having reason to know it is derived from an act described in clause (1).

Subd. 6. **Labor trafficking victim.** "Labor trafficking victim" means a person subjected to the practices in subdivision 5.
HIST: 2005 c 136 art 17 s 15; 2009 c 137 s 2

609.282 LABOR TRAFFICKING.

Subdivision 1. **Individuals under age 18.** Whoever knowingly engages in the labor trafficking of an individual who is under the age of 18 is guilty of a crime and may be sentenced to imprisonment for not more than 20 years or to payment of a fine of not more than $40,000, or both.

Subd. 2. **Other offenses.** Whoever knowingly engages in the labor trafficking of another is guilty of a crime and may be sentenced to imprisonment for not more than 15 years or to payment of a fine of not more than $30,000, or both. In a prosecution under this section the consent or age of the victim is not a defense.

Subd. 3. **Consent or age of victim not a defense.** In a prosecution under this section the consent or age of the victim is not a defense.
HIST: 2005 c 136 art 17 s 16; 2006 c 260 art 1 s 20

609.283 UNLAWFUL CONDUCT WITH RESPECT TO DOCUMENTS IN FURTHERANCE OF LABOR OR SEX TRAFFICKING.

Subdivision 1. **Crime defined.** Unless the person's conduct constitutes a violation of section 609.282, a person who knowingly destroys, conceals, removes, confiscates, or possesses any actual or purported passport or other immigration document, or any other actual or purported government identification document, of another person:

(1) in the course of a violation section 609.282 or 609.322;

(2) with intent to violate section 609.282 or 609.322; or

(3) to prevent or restrict or to attempt to prevent or restrict, without lawful authority, a person's liberty to move or travel, in order to maintain the labor or services of that person, when the person is or has been a victim of a violation of section 609.282 or 609.322;

is guilty of a crime and may be sentenced as provided in subdivision 2.

Subd. 2. **Penalties.** A person who violates subdivision 1 may be sentenced as follows:

(1) if the crime involves a victim under the age of 18, to imprisonment for not more than ten years or to payment of a fine of $20,000, or both; or

(2) in other cases, to imprisonment for not more than five years or to payment of a fine of not more than $10,000, or both. In a prosecution under this section the consent or age of the victim is not a defense.

Subd. 3. **Consent or age of victim not a defense.** In a prosecution under this section the consent or age of the victim is not a defense.
HIST: 2005 c 136 art 17 s 17; 2006 c 260 art 1 s 21

609.284 LABOR OR SEX TRAFFICKING CRIMES; DEFENSES; CIVIL LIABILITY; CORPORATE LIABILITY.

Subdivision 1. **Consent or age of victim not a defense.** In an action under this section the consent or age of the victim is not a defense.

Subd. 2. **Civil liability.** A labor trafficking victim may bring a cause of action against a person who violates section 609.282 or 609.283. * * *

Subd. 3. **Corporate liability.** If a corporation or other business enterprise is convicted of violating section 609.282, 609.283, or 609.322, in addition to the criminal penalties described in those sections and other remedies provided elsewhere in law, the court may, when appropriate:

(1) order its dissolution or reorganization;

(2) order the suspension or revocation of any license, permit, or prior approval granted to it by a state agency; or

(3) order the surrender of its chart if it is organized under Minnesota law or the revocation of its certificate to conduct business in Minnesota if it is not organized under Minnesota law.

HIST: 2005 c 136 art 17 s 18

609.3232 PROTECTIVE ORDER AUTHORIZED; PROCEDURES; PENALTIES.

Subdivision 1. **Order for protection.** Any parent or guardian who knows or has reason to believe that a person, while acting as other than a prostitute or patron, is inducing, coercing, soliciting, or promoting the prostitution of the parent or guardian's minor child, or is offering or providing food, shelter, or other subsistence for the purpose of enabling the parent or guardian's minor child to engage in prostitution, may seek an order for protection in the manner provided in this section.

Subd. 2. **Court jurisdiction.** An application for relief under this section shall be filed in the juvenile court. Actions under this section shall be given docket priority by the court.

Subd. 3. **Contents of petition.** A petition for relief shall allege the existence of a circumstance or circumstances described in subdivision 1, and shall be accompanied by an affidavit made under oath stating the specific facts and circumstances from which relief is sought. The court shall provide simplified forms and clerical assistance to help with the writing and filing of a petition under this section.

Subd. 4. **Hearing on application; notice.** (a) Upon receipt of the petition, the court shall order a hearing which shall be held no later than 14 days from the date of the order. Personal service shall be made upon the respondent not less than five days before the hearing. In the event that personal service cannot be completed in time to give the respondent the minimum notice required under this paragraph, the court may set a new hearing date.

(b) Notwithstanding the provisions of paragraph (a), service may be made by one week published notice, as provided under section 645.11, provided the petitioner files with the court an affidavit stating that an attempt at personal service made by a sheriff was unsuccessful because the respondent is avoiding service by concealment or otherwise, and that a copy of the petition and notice of hearing has been mailed to the respondent at the respondent's residence or that the residence is not known to the petitioner. Service under this paragraph is complete seven days after publication. The court shall set a new hearing date if necessary to allow the respondent the five-day minimum notice required under paragraph (a).

Subd. 5. **Relief by the court.** Upon notice and hearing, the court may order the respondent to return the minor child to the residence of the child's parents or guardian, and may order that the respondent cease and desist from committing further acts described in subdivision 1 and cease to have further contact with the minor child. Any relief granted by the court in the order for protection shall be for a fixed period of time determined by the court.

Subd. 6. **Service of order.** Any order issued under this section shall be served personally on the respondent. Upon the request of the petitioner, the court shall order the sheriff to assist in the execution or service of the order for protection.

Subd. 7. **Violation of order for protection.** (a) A Violation of an order for protection shall constitute contempt of court and be subject to the penalties provided under chapter 588.(b) Any person who willfully fails to return a minor child as required by an order for protection issued under this section commits an act which manifests an intent substantially to deprive the parent or guardian of custodial rights within the meaning of section 609.26, clause (3).
HIST: 1986 c 448 s 4

609.33 DISORDERLY HOUSE.

Subdivision 1. **Definition.** For the purpose of this section, "disorderly house" means a building, dwelling, place, establishment, or premises in which actions or conduct habitually occur in violation of laws relating to:

(1) the sale of intoxicating liquor or 3.2 percent malt liquor;

(2) gambling;

(3) prostitution as defined in section 609.321, subdivision 9, or acts relating to prostitution; or

(4) the sale or possession of controlled substances as defined in section 152.01, subdivision 4.

Subd. 2. **Prohibiting owning or operating a disorderly house.** No person may own, lease, operate, manage, maintain, or conduct a disorderly house, or invite or attempt to invite others to visit or remain in the disorderly house. A violation of this subdivision is a gross misdemeanor.

Subd. 3. **Mandatory minimum penalties.** (a) If a person is convicted of a first violation of subdivision 2, in addition to any sentence of imprisonment authorized by subdivision 2 which the court may impose, the court shall impose a fine of not less than $300 nor more than $3,000.

(b) If a person is convicted of a second violation of subdivision 2, in addition to any sentence of imprisonment authorized by subdivision 2 which the court may impose, the court shall impose a fine of not less than $500 nor more than $3,000.

(c) If a person is convicted of a third or subsequent violation of subdivision 2, in addition to any sentence of imprisonment authorized by subdivision 2 which the court may impose, the court shall impose a fine of not less than $1,000 nor more than $3,000

Subd. 4. **Evidence.** Evidence of unlawful sales of intoxicating liquor or 3.2 percent malt liquor, of unlawful possession or sale of controlled substances, of prostitution or acts relating to prostitution, or of gambling or acts relating to gambling, is prima facie evidence of the existence of a disorderly house. Evidence of sales of intoxicating liquor or 3.2 percent malt liquor between the hours of 1:00 a.m. and 8:00 a.m., while a person is within a disorderly house, is prima facie evidence that the person knew it to be a disorderly house.

Subd. 5. **Local regulation.** Subdivisions 1 to 4 do not prohibit or restrict a local governmental unit from imposing more restrictive provisions.

Subd. 6. **Pretrial release.** When a person is charged under this section with owning or leasing a disorderly house, the court may require as a condition of pretrial release that the defendant bring an eviction action against a lessee who has violated the covenant not to allow drugs established by section 504B.171.
HIST: 1967 c 507 s 10; * * * 2003 c 2 art 2 s 18

609.341 DEFINITIONS.

Subdivision 1. **Scope.** For the purposes of sections 609.341 to 609.351, the terms in this section have the meanings given them

Subd. 2. **Actor.** "Actor" means a person accused of criminal sexual conduct.

Subd. 3. **Force.** "Force" means either: (1) the infliction, by the actor of bodily harm; or (2) the attempted infliction, or threatened infliction by the actor of bodily harm or commission or threat of any other crime by the actor against the complainant or another, which (a) causes the complainant to reasonably believe that the actor has the present ability to execute the threat and (b) if the actor does not have a significant relationship to the complainant, also causes the complainant to submit.

Subd. 4. **Consent.** (a) "Consent" means words or overt actions by a person indicating a freely given present agreement to perform a particular sexual act with the actor. Consent does not mean the existence of a prior or current social relationship between the actor and the complainant or that the complainant failed to resist a particular act.

(b) A person who is mentally incapacitated or physically helpless as defined by this section cannot consent to a sexual act.

(c) Corroboration of the victim's testimony is not required to show lack of consent.

Subd. 5. **Intimate parts.** "Intimate parts" includes the primary genital area, groin, inner thigh, buttocks, or breast of a human being

Subd. 6. **Mentally impaired.** "Mentally impaired" means that a person, as a result of inadequately developed or impaired intelligence or a substantial psychiatric disorder of thought or mood, lacks the judgment to give a reasoned consent to sexual contact or to sexual penetration.

Subd. 7. **Mentally incapacitated.** "Mentally incapacitated" means:

(1) that a person under the influence of alcohol, a narcotic, anesthetic, or any other substance, administered to that person without the person's agreement, lacks the judgment to give a reasoned consent to sexual contact or sexual penetration; or

(2) that a person is under the influence of any substance or substances to a degree that renders them incapable of consenting or incapable of appreciating, understanding, or controlling the person's conduct.

Subd. 8. **Personal injury.** "Personal injury" means bodily harm as defined in section 609.02, subdivision 7, or severe mental anguish or pregnancy.

Subd. 9. **Physically helpless.** "Physically helpless" means that a person is (a) asleep or not conscious, (b) unable to withhold consent or to withdraw because of a physical condition, or (c) unable to communicate nonconsent and the condition is known or reasonably should have been known to the actor.

Subd. 10. **Current or recent [p]osition of authority.** "Current or recent [p]osition of authority" includes but is not limited to any person who is a parent or acting in the place of a parent and charged with or assumes any of a parent's rights, duties or responsibilities to a child, or a person who is charged with or assumes any duty or responsibility for the health, welfare, or supervision of a child, either independently or through another, no matter how brief, at the time of or within 120 days immediately preceding the act. For the purposes of subdivision 11, "current or recent position of authority" includes a psychotherapist.

Subd. 11. **Sexual contact.** (a) "Sexual contact," for the purposes of sections 609.343, subdivision 1, clauses (a) to (f), and 609.345, subdivision 1, clauses (a) to (e), (d) and (h) to (p) (i), and subdivision 1a, clauses (a) to (e), (h) and (i), includes any of the following acts committed without the complainant's consent, except in those cases where consent is not a defense, and committed with sexual or aggressive intent:

(i) the intentional touching by the actor of the complainant's intimate parts, or

(ii) the touching by the complainant of the actor's, the complainant's, or another's intimate parts effected by a person in a current or recent position of authority, or by coercion or by inducement if the complainant is under 13 14 years of age or mentally impaired, or

(iii) the touching by another of the complainant's intimate parts effected by coercion or by a person in a current or recent position of authority, or

(iv) in any of the cases above, the touching of the clothing covering the immediate area of the intimate parts; or

(v) the intentional touching with seminal fluid or sperm by the actor of the complainant's body or the clothing covering the complainant's body.

(b) "Sexual contact" for the purposes of sections 609.343, subdivision 1 1a, clauses (g) and (h), and 609.345, subdivision 1 1a, clauses (f) and (g), and 609.3458, includes any of the following acts committed with sexual or aggressive intent:

(i) the intentional touching by the actor of the complainant's intimate parts;

(ii) the touching by the complainant of the actor's, the complainant's, or another's intimate parts;

(iii) the touching by another of the complainant's intimate parts;

(iv) in any of the cases listed above, touching of the clothing covering the immediate area of the intimate parts; or

(v) the intentional touching with seminal fluid or sperm by the actor of the complainant's body or the clothing covering the complainant's body.

(c) "Sexual contact with a person under 13 14" means the intentional touching of the complainant's bare genitals or anal opening by the actor's bare genitals or anal opening with sexual or aggressive intent or the touching by the complainant's bare genitals or anal opening of the actor's or another's bare genitals or anal opening with sexual or aggressive intent.

Subd. 12. **Sexual penetration.** "Sexual penetration" means any of the following acts committed without the complainant's consent, except in those cases where consent is not a defense, whether or not emission of semen occurs:

(1) sexual intercourse, cunnilingus, fellatio, or anal intercourse; or

(2) any intrusion however slight into the genital or anal openings:

(i) of the complainant's body by any part of the actor's body or any object used by the actor for this purpose;

(ii) of the complainant's body by any part of the body of the complainant, by any part of the body of another person, or by any object used by the complainant or another person for this purpose, when effected by a person in a current or recent position of authority, or by coercion, or by inducement if the child is under ~~13~~ 14 years of age or mentally impaired; or

(iii) of the body of the actor or another person by any part of the body of the complainant or by any object used by the complainant for this purpose, when effected by a person in a current or recent position of authority, or by coercion, or by inducement if the child is under ~~13~~ 14 years of age or mentally impaired.

Subd. 13. **Complainant.** "Complainant" means a person alleged to have been subjected to criminal sexual conduct, but need not be the person who signs the complaint.

Subd. 14. **Coercion.** "Coercion" means the use by the actor of words or circumstances that cause the complainant reasonably to fear ~~that the actor will inflict~~ the infliction of bodily harm upon the complainant or another, or the use by the actor of confinement, or superior size or strength, against the complainant ~~that causes the complainant to submit to sexual penetration or contact, against the complainant's will~~ to accomplish the act. Proof of coercion does not require proof of a specific act or threat.

Subd. 15. **Significant relationship.** "Significant relationship" means a situation in which the actor is:

(1) the complainant's parent, stepparent, or guardian;

(2) any of the following persons related to the complainant by blood, marriage, or adoption: brother, sister, stepbrother, stepsister, first cousin, aunt, uncle, nephew, niece, grandparent, great-grandparent, great-uncle, great-aunt; ~~or~~

(3) an adult who jointly resides intermittently or regularly in the same dwelling as the complainant and who is not the complainant's spouse; or

(4) an adult who is or was involved in a significant romantic or sexual relationship with the parent of a complainant.

Subd. 16. **Patient.** "Patient" means a person who seeks or obtains psychotherapeutic services.

Subd. 17. **Psychotherapist.** "Psychotherapist" means a person who is or purports to be a physician, psychologist, nurse, chemical dependency counselor, social worker, marriage and family therapist, licensed professional counselor, or other mental health service provider; or any other person, whether or not licensed by the state, who performs or purports to perform psychotherapy.

Subd. 18. **Psychotherapy.** "Psychotherapy" means the professional treatment, assessment, or counseling of a mental or emotional illness, symptom, or condition.

Subd. 19. **Emotionally dependent.** "Emotionally dependent" means that the nature of the former patient's emotional condition and the nature of the treatment provided by the psychotherapist are such that the psychotherapist knows or has reason to know that the former patient is unable to withhold consent to sexual contact or sexual penetration by the psychotherapist.

Subd. 20. **Therapeutic deception.** "Therapeutic deception" means a representation by a psychotherapist that sexual contact or sexual penetration by the psychotherapist is consistent with or part of the patient's treatment.

Subd. 21. **Special transportation.** "Special transportation service" means motor vehicle transportation provided on a regular basis by a public or private entity or person that is intended exclusively or primarily to serve individuals who are vulnerable adults, handicapped, or disabled. Special transportation service includes, but is not limited to, service provided by buses, vans, taxis, and volunteers driving private automobiles.

Subd. 22. **Predatory crime.** "Predatory crime" means a felony violation of section 609.185 (first-degree murder), 609.19 (second-degree murder), 609.195 (third-degree murder), 609.20 (first-degree manslaughter), 609.205 (second-degree manslaughter), 609.221 (first-degree assault), 609.222 (second-degree assault), 609.223 (third-degree assault), 609.24 (simple robbery), 609.245 (aggravated robbery), 609.25 (kidnapping), 609.255 (false imprisonment),

609.498 (tampering with a witness), 609.561 (first-degree arson), or 609.582, subdivision 1 (first-degree burglary).
* * *

Subd. 24. **Prohibited occupational relationship.** A "prohibited occupational relationship" exists when the actor is in one of the following occupations and the act takes place under the specified circumstances:

(1) the actor performed massage or other bodywork for hire, the sexual penetration or sexual contact occurred during or immediately before or after the actor performed or was hired to perform one of those services for the complainant, and the sexual penetration or sexual contact was nonconsensual; or

(2) the actor and the complainant were in one of the following occupational relationships at the time of the act. Consent by the complainant is not a defense:

(i) the actor was a psychotherapist, the complainant was the actor's patient, and the sexual penetration or sexual contact occurred during a psychotherapy session or during a period of time when the psychotherapist-patient relationship was ongoing;

(ii) the actor was a psychotherapist and the complainant was the actor's former patient who was emotionally dependent on the actor;

(iii) the actor was or falsely impersonated a psychotherapist, the complainant was the actor's patient or former patient, and the sexual penetration or sexual contact occurred by means of therapeutic deception;

(iv) the actor was or falsely impersonated a provider of medical services to the complainant and the sexual penetration or sexual contact occurred by means of deception or false representation that the sexual penetration or sexual contact was for a bona fide medical purpose;

(v) the actor was or falsely impersonated a member of the clergy, the complainant was not married to the actor, the complainant met with the actor in private seeking or receiving religious or spiritual advice, aid, or comfort from the actor, and the sexual penetration or sexual contact occurred during the course of the meeting or during a period of time when the meetings were ongoing;

(vi) the actor provided special transportation service to the complainant and the sexual penetration or sexual contact occurred during or immediately before or after the actor transported the complainant;

(vii) the actor was or falsely impersonated a peace officer, as defined in section 626.84, the actor physically or constructively restrained the complainant or the complainant did not reasonably feel free to leave the actor's presence, and the sexual penetration or sexual contact was not pursuant to a lawful search or lawful use of force;

(viii) the actor was an employee, independent contractor, or volunteer of a state, county, city, or privately operated adult or juvenile correctional system, or secure treatment facility, or treatment facility providing services to clients civilly committed as mentally ill and dangerous, sexually dangerous persons, or sexual psychopathic personalities, including but not limited to jails, prisons, detention centers, or work release facilities, and the complainant was a resident of a facility or under supervision of the correctional system;

(ix) the complainant was enrolled in a secondary school and:

(A) the actor was a licensed educator employed or contracted to provide service for the school at which the complainant was a student;

(B) the actor was age 18 or older and at least 48 months older than the complainant and was employed or contracted to provide service for the secondary school at which the complainant was a student; or

(C) the actor was age 18 or older and at least 48 months older than the complainant, and was a licensed educator employed or contracted to provide services for an elementary, middle, or secondary school;

(x) the actor was a caregiver, facility staff person, or person providing services in a facility, and the complainant was a vulnerable adult who was a resident, patient, or client of the facility who was impaired in judgment or capacity by mental or emotional dysfunction or undue influence; or

(xi) the actor was a caregiver, facility staff person, or person providing services in a facility, and the complainant was a resident, patient, or client of the facility. This clause does not apply if a consensual sexual personal relationship existed prior to the caregiving relationship or if the actor was a personal care attendant.

Subd. 25. **Caregiver.** "Caregiver" has the meaning given in section 609.232. subdivision 2.

Subd. 26. **Facility.** "Facility" has the meaning given in section 609.232, subdivision 2.

Subd. 27. **Vulnerable adult.** "Vulnerable adult" has the meaning given in section 609.232, subdivision 11.

EFFECTIVE DATE. This section is effective September 15, 2021, and applies to crimes committed on or after that date.

HIST: 1975 c 374 s 2; * * * 2010 c 270 s 1; 1Sp2019 c 5 art 4 s 2-4; 1Sp2021 c 11 art 4 s 6-15

Editors' Note: In State v. Khalil, 956 N.W. 2d 627 (Minn. 2021), the Minnesota Supreme Court held that section 609.341, subd. 7, as it was drafted, meant that a person under the influence of alcohol was not mentally incapacitated unless the alcohol was administered to the person under its influence without that person's agreement and that if the legislature intended for the definition of mentally incapacitated to include voluntarily intoxicated persons, "it is the Legislature's prerogative to reexamine the . . . statute and amend it accordingly." Id. at 642. In amending the statute, the legislature appears to have taken the Court up on its invitation.

609.342 CRIMINAL SEXUAL CONDUCT IN THE FIRST DEGREE.

Subdivision 1. **Adult victim; crime defined.** A person who engages in sexual penetration with another person, ~~or in sexual contact with a person under 13 years of age as defined in section 609.341, subdivision 11, paragraph (c),~~ is guilty of criminal sexual conduct in the first degree if any of the following circumstances exists:

~~(a) the complainant is under 13 years of age and the actor is more than 36 months older than the complainant. Neither mistake as to the complainant's age nor consent to the act by the complainant is a defense;~~

~~(b) the complainant is at least 13 years of age but less than 16 years of age and the actor is more than 48 months older than the complainant and in a current or recent position of authority over the complainant. Neither mistake as to the complainant's age nor consent to the act by the complainant is a defense;~~

~~(c)~~ (a) circumstances existing at the time of the act cause the complainant to have a reasonable fear of imminent great bodily harm to the complainant or another;

~~(d)~~ (b) the actor is armed with a dangerous weapon or any article used or fashioned in a manner to lead the complainant to reasonably believe it to be a dangerous weapon and uses or threatens to use the weapon or article to cause the complainant to submit;

~~(e)~~ (c) the actor causes personal injury to the complainant, and ~~either~~ any of the following circumstances exist:

(i) the actor uses ~~force or~~ coercion to accomplish the act; ~~or~~

(ii) the actor uses force, as defined in section 609.341, subdivision 3, clause 2; or

~~(ii)~~ (iii) the actor knows or has reason to know that the complainant is mentally impaired, mentally incapacitated, or physically helpless;

(d) the actor uses force as defined in section 609.341, subdivision 3, clause 1; or

~~(f)~~ (e) the actor is aided or abetted by one or more accomplices within the meaning of section 609.05, and either of the following circumstances exists:

(i) the actor or an accomplice uses force or coercion to cause the complainant to submit; or

(ii) the actor or an accomplice is armed with a dangerous weapon or any article used or fashioned in a manner to lead the complainant reasonably to believe it to be a dangerous weapon and uses or threatens to use the weapon or article to cause the complainant to submit;

~~(g) the actor has a significant relationship to the complainant and the complainant was under 16 years of age at the time of the act. Neither mistake as to the complainant's age nor consent to the act by the complainant is a defense; or~~

~~(h) the actor has a significant relationship to the complainant, the complainant was under 16 years of age at the time of the act, and:~~

~~(i) the actor or an accomplice used force or coercion to accomplish the act;~~
~~(ii) the complainant suffered personal injury; or~~
~~(iii) the sexual abuse involved multiple acts committed over an extended period of time.~~
~~Neither mistake as to the complainant's age nor consent to the act by the complainant is a defense.~~

Subd. 1a. **Victim under the age of 18; crime defined.**

A person who engages in penetration with anyone under 18 years of age or sexual contact with a person under 14 years of age as defined in section 609.341, subdivision 11, paragraph (c), is guilty of criminal sexual conduct in the first degree if any of the following circumstances exists:

(a) circumstances existing at the time of the act cause the complainant to have a reasonable fear of imminent great bodily harm to the complainant or another;

(b) the actor is armed with a dangerous weapon or any article used or fashioned in a manner to lead the complainant to reasonably believe it to be a dangerous weapon and uses or threatens to use the weapon or article to cause the complainant to submit;

(c) the actor causes personal injury to the complainant, and any of the following circumstances exist:

(i) the actor uses coercion to accomplish the act;
(ii) the actor uses force, as defined in section 609.341, subdivision 3, clause (2); or
(iii) the actor knows or has reason to know that the complainant is mentally impaired, mentally incapacitated, or physically helpless;

(d) the actor is aided or abetted by one or more accomplices within the meaning of section 609.05, and either of the following circumstances exists:

(i) the actor or an accomplice uses force or coercion to cause the complainant to submit; or

(ii) the actor or an accomplice is armed with a dangerous weapon or any article used or fashioned in a manner to lead the complainant to reasonably believe it to be a dangerous weapon and uses or threatens to use the weapon or article to cause the complainant to submit;

(e) the complainant is under 14 years of age and the actor is more than 36 months older than the complainant. Neither mistake as to the complainant's age nor consent to the act by the complainant is a defense;

(f) the complainant is at least 14 years of age but less than 16 years of age and:
(i) the actor is more than 36 months older than the complainant; and
(ii) the actor is in a current or recent position of authority over the complainant. Neither mistake as to the complainant's age nor consent to the act by the complainant is a defense;

(g) the complainant was under 16 years of age at the time of the act and the actor has a significant relationship to the complainant. Neither mistake as to the complainant's age nor consent to the act by the complainant is a defense;

(h) the complainant was under 16 years of age at the time of the act, and the actor has a significant relationship to the complainant and any of the following circumstances exist:

(i) the actor or an accomplice used force or coercion to accomplish the act;
(ii) the complainant suffered personal injury; or
(iii) the sexual abuse involved multiple acts committed over an extended period of time. Neither mistake as to the complainant's age nor consent to the act by the complainant is a defense; or

(i) the actor uses force, as defined in section 609.341, subdivision 3, clause (1).

Subd. 2. **Penalty.** (a) Except as otherwise provided in section 609.3455; or Minnesota Statutes 2004, section 609.109, a person convicted under subdivision 1 or subdivision 1a may be sentenced to imprisonment for not more than 30 years or to a payment of a fine of not more than $40,000, or both.

(b) Unless a longer mandatory minimum sentence is otherwise required by law or the sentencing guidelines provide for a longer presumptive executed sentence, the court shall presume that an executed sentence of 144 months must be imposed on an offender convicted of violating this section. Sentencing a person in a manner other than that described in this paragraph is a departure from the sentencing guidelines.

(c) A person convicted under this section is also subject to conditional release under section 609.3455.

Subd. 3. **Stay.** Except when imprisonment is required under section 609.3455; or Minnesota Statutes 2004, section 609.109, if a person is convicted under subdivision 1, clause (g), the court may stay imposition or execution of the sentence if it finds that: (a) a stay is in the best interest of the complainant or the family unit; and

(b) a professional assessment indicates that the offender has been accepted by and can respond to a treatment program.

If the court stays imposition or execution of sentence, it shall include the following as conditions of probation:

(1) incarceration in a local jail or workhouse;

(2) a requirement that the offender complete a treatment program; and

(3) a requirement that the offender have no unsupervised contact with the complainant until the offender has successfully completed the treatment program unless approved by the treatment program and the supervising correctional agent.

EFFECTIVE DATE.

This section is effective September 15, 2021, and applies to crimes committed on or after that date.

HIST: 1975 c 374 s 3; * * * 2007 c 13 art 3 s 37; 1Sp2019 c 5 art 4 s 5; 1Sp2021 c 11 art 4 s 16

609.343 CRIMINAL SEXUAL CONDUCT IN THE SECOND DEGREE.

Subdivision 1. **Adult victim; crime defined.** A person who engages in sexual contact with another person is guilty of criminal sexual conduct in the second degree if any of the following circumstances exists:

(a) the complainant is under 13 years of age and the actor is more than 36 months older than the complainant. Neither mistake as to the complainant's age nor consent to the act by the complainant is a defense. In a prosecution under this clause, the state is not required to prove that the sexual contact was coerced;

(b) the complainant is at least 13 but less than 16 years of age and the actor is more than 48 months older than the complainant and in a current or recent position of authority over the complainant. Neither mistake as to the complainant's age nor consent to the act by the complainant is a defense;

(c) (a) circumstances existing at the time of the act cause the complainant to have a reasonable fear of imminent great bodily harm to the complainant or another;

(d) (b) the actor is armed with a dangerous weapon or any article used or fashioned in a manner to lead the complainant to reasonably believe it to be a dangerous weapon and uses or threatens to use the weapon or article to cause the complainant to submit;

(e) (c) the actor causes personal injury to the complainant, and either any of the following circumstances exist:

(i) the actor uses force or coercion to accomplish the sexual contact; or

(ii) the actor uses force as defined section 609.341, subdivision 3, clause 2; or

(ii) (iii) the actor knows or has reason to know that the complainant is mentally impaired, mentally incapacitated, or physically helpless;

(d) the actor uses force as defined section 609.341, subdivision 3, clause 1; or

(f) (e) the actor is aided or abetted by one or more accomplices within the meaning of section 609.05, and either of the following circumstances exists:

(i) <u>the actor or</u> an accomplice uses force or coercion to cause the complainant to submit; or

(ii) <u>the actor or</u> an accomplice is armed with a dangerous weapon or any article used or fashioned in a manner to lead the complainant to reasonably believe it to be a dangerous weapon and uses or threatens to use the weapon or article to cause the complainant to submit;

~~(g) the actor has a significant relationship to the complainant and the complainant was under 16 years of age at the time of the sexual contact. Neither mistake as to the complainant's age nor consent to the act by the complainant is a defense; or~~

~~(h) the actor has a significant relationship to the complainant, the complainant was under 16 years of age at the time of the sexual contact, and:~~

~~(i) the actor or an accomplice used force or coercion to accomplish the contact;~~

~~(ii) the complainant suffered personal injury; or~~

~~(iii) the sexual abuse involved multiple acts committed over an extended period of time.~~

~~Neither mistake as to the complainant's age nor consent to the act by the complainant is a defense.~~

Subd. 1a. **Victim under the age of 18; crime defined.** A person who engages in sexual contact with anyone under 18 years of age is guilty of criminal sexual conduct in the second degree if any of the following circumstances exists:

(a) circumstances existing at the time of the act cause the complainant to have a reasonable fear of imminent great bodily harm to the complainant or another;

(b) the actor is armed with a dangerous weapon or any article used or fashioned in a manner to lead the complainant to reasonably believe it to be a dangerous weapon and uses or threatens to use the dangerous weapon to cause the complainant to submit;

(c) the actor causes personal injury to the complainant, and any of the following circumstances exist:

(i) the actor uses coercion to accomplish the sexual contact;

(ii) the actor uses force, as defined in section 609.341, subdivision 3, clause (2); or

(iii) the actor knows or has reason to know that the complainant is mentally impaired, mentally incapacitated, or physically helpless;

(d) the actor is aided or abetted by one or more accomplices within the meaning of section 609.05, and either of the following circumstances exists:

(i) the actor or an accomplice uses force or coercion to cause the complainant to submit; or

(ii) the actor or an accomplice is armed with a dangerous weapon or any article used or fashioned in a manner to lead the complainant to reasonably believe it to be a dangerous weapon and uses or threatens to use the weapon or article to cause the complainant to submit;

(e) the complainant is under 14 years of age and the actor is more than 36 months older than the complainant. Neither mistake as to the complainant's age nor consent to the act by the complainant is a defense. In a prosecution under this clause, the state is not required to prove that the sexual contact was coerced;

(f) the complainant is at least 14 but less than 16 years of age and the actor is more than 36 months older than the complainant and in a current or recent position of authority over the complainant. Neither mistake as to the complainant's age nor consent to the act by the complainant is a defense;

(g) the complainant was under 16 years of age at the time of the sexual contact and the actor has a significant relationship to the complainant. Neither mistake as to the complainant's age nor consent to the act by the complainant is a defense;

(h) the actor has a significant relationship to the complainant, the complainant was under 16 years of age at the time of the sexual contact, and:

(i) the actor or an accomplice used force or coercion to accomplish the contact;

(ii) the complainant suffered personal injury; or

(iii) the sexual abuse involved multiple acts committed over an extended period of time.

Neither mistake as to the complainant's age nor consent to the act by the complainant is a defense; or
(i) the actor uses force, as defined in section 609.341, subdivision 3, clause (1).
Subd. 2. **Penalty.** (a) Except as otherwise provided in section 609.3455; or Minnesota Statutes 2004, section 609.109, a person convicted under subdivision 1 or subdivision 1a may be sentenced to imprisonment for not more than 25 years or to a payment of a fine of not more than $35,000, or both.
(b) Unless a longer mandatory minimum sentence is otherwise required by law or the sentencing guidelines provide for a longer presumptive executed sentence, the court shall presume that an executed sentence of 90 months must be imposed on an offender convicted of violating subdivision 1, clause (a), (b), (c), (d), or (e), (f), or subdivision 1a, clause (a), (b), (c), or (d), (h), or (i). Sentencing a person in a manner other than that described in this paragraph is a departure from the sentencing guidelines.
(c) A person convicted under this section is also subject to conditional release under section 609.3455.
Subd. 3. **Stay.** Except when imprisonment is required under section 609.3455; or Minnesota Statutes 2004, section 609.109, if a person is convicted under subdivision 1a, clause (g), the court may stay imposition or execution of the sentence if it finds that:
(a) a stay is in the best interest of the complainant or the family unit; and
(b) a professional assessment indicates that the offender has been accepted by and can respond to a treatment program.
If the court stays imposition or execution of sentence, it shall include the following as conditions of probation:
(1) incarceration in a local jail or workhouse;
(2) a requirement that the offender complete a treatment program; and
(3) a requirement that the offender have no unsupervised contact with the complainant until the offender has successfully completed the treatment program unless approved by the treatment program and the supervising correctional agent.
EFFECTIVE DATE.
This section is effective September 15, 2021, and applies to crimes committed on or after that date.
HIST: 1975 c 374 s 4; * * * 2007 c 13 art 3 s 37; 1Sp2019 c 5 art 4 s 6; 1Sp2021 c 11 art 4 s 17

609.344 CRIMINAL SEXUAL CONDUCT IN THE THIRD DEGREE.

Subdivision 1. **Adult victim; crime defined.** A person who engages in sexual penetration with another person is guilty of criminal sexual conduct in the third degree if any of the following circumstances exists:
(a) the complainant is under 13 years of age and the actor is no more than 36 months older than the complainant. Neither mistake as to the complainant's age nor consent to the act by the complainant shall be a defense;
(b) the complainant is at least 13 but less than 16 years of age and the actor is more than 24 months older than the complainant. In any such case if the actor is no more than 120 months older than the complainant, it shall be an affirmative defense, which must be proved by a preponderance of the evidence, that the actor reasonably believes the complainant to be 16 years of age or older. In all other cases, mistake as to the complainant's age shall not be a defense. Consent by the complainant is not a defense;
(c) (a) the actor uses force or coercion to accomplish the penetration;
(d) (b) the actor knows or has reason to know that the complainant is mentally impaired, mentally incapacitated, or physically helpless;
(c) the actor uses force, as defined in section 609.341, subdivision 3, clause 2; or
(d) at the time of the act, the actor is in a prohibited occupational relationship with the complainant.
Subd. 1a. **Victim under the age of 18; crime defined.**

7-17

A person who engages in sexual penetration with anyone under 18 years of age is guilty of criminal sexual conduct in the third degree if any of the following circumstances exists:

(a) the complainant is under 14 years of age and the actor is no more than 36 months older than the complainant. Neither mistake as to the complainant's age nor consent to the act by the complainant shall be a defense;

(b) the complainant is at least 14 but less than 16 years of age and the actor is more than 24 months older than the complainant. In any such case if the actor is no more than 60 months older than the complainant, it shall be an affirmative defense, which must be proved by a preponderance of the evidence, that the actor reasonably believes the complainant to be 16 years of age or older. In all other cases, mistake as to the complainant's age shall not be a defense. Consent by the complainant is not a defense;

(c) the actor uses coercion to accomplish the penetration;

(d) the actor knows or has reason to know that the complainant is mentally impaired, mentally incapacitated, or physically helpless;

(e) the complainant is at least 16 but less than 18 years of age and the actor is more than ~~48~~ 36 months older than the complainant and in a current or recent position of authority over the complainant. Neither mistake as to the complainant's age nor consent to the act by the complainant is a defense;

(f) the actor has a significant relationship to the complainant and the complainant was at least 16 but under 18 years of age at the time of the sexual penetration. Neither mistake as to the complainant's age nor consent to the act by the complainant is a defense;

(g) the actor has a significant relationship to the complainant, the complainant was at least 16 but under 18 years of age at the time of the sexual penetration, and:

(i) the actor or an accomplice used force or coercion to accomplish the penetration;

(ii) the complainant suffered personal injury; or

(iii) the sexual abuse involved multiple acts committed over an extended period of time.

Neither mistake as to the complainant's age nor consent to the act by the complainant is a defense;

(h) ~~the actor is a psychotherapist and the complainant is patient of the psychotherapist and the sexual penetration occurred:~~ the actor uses force, as defined in section 609.341, subdivision 3, clause 2; or

(i) at the time of the act, the actor is in a prohibited occupational relationship with the complainant.

~~(i) during the psychotherapy session; or~~

~~(ii) outside the psychotherapy session if an ongoing psychotherapist-patient relationship exists.~~

~~Consent by the complainant is not a defense.~~

~~(i) the actor is a psychotherapist and the complainant is a former patient of the psychotherapist and the former patient is emotionally dependent upon the psychotherapist;~~

~~(j) the actor is a psychotherapist and the complainant is a patient or former patient and the sexual penetration occurred by means of therapeutic deception. Consent by the complainant is not a defense;~~

~~(k) the actor accomplishes the sexual penetration by means of deception or false representation that the penetration is for a bona fide medical purpose. Consent by the complainant is not a defense;~~

~~(l) the actor is or purports to be a member of the clergy, the complainant is not married to the actor, and:~~

~~(i) the sexual penetration occurred during the course of a meeting in which the complainant sought or received religious or spiritual advice, aid, or comfort from the actor in private; or~~

~~(ii) the sexual penetration occurred during a period of time in which the complainant was meeting on an ongoing basis with the actor to seek or receive religious or spiritual advice, aid, or comfort in private. Consent by the complainant is not a defense;~~

(m) the actor is an employee, independent contractor, or volunteer of a state, county, city, or privately operated adult or juvenile correctional system, or secure treatment facility, or treatment facility providing services to clients civilly committed as mentally ill and dangerous, sexually dangerous persons, or sexual psychopathic personalities, including, but not limited to, jails, prisons, detention centers, or work release facilities, and the complainant is a resident of a facility or under supervision of the correctional system. Consent by the complainant is not a defense;

(n) the actor provides or is an agent of an entity that provides special transportation service, the complainant used the special transportation service, and the sexual penetration occurred during or immediately before or after the actor transported the complainant. Consent by the complainant is not a defense;

(o) the actor performs massage or other bodywork for hire, the complainant was a user of one of those services, and nonconsensual sexual penetration occurred during or immediately before or after the actor performed or was hired to perform one of those services for the complainant; or

(p) the actor is a peace officer, as defined in section 626.84, and the officer physically or constructively restrains the complainant or the complainant does not reasonably feel free to leave the officer's presence. Consent by the complainant is not a defense. This paragraph does not apply to any penetration of the mouth, genitals, or anus during a lawful search.

Subd. 2. **Penalty.** Except as otherwise provided in section 609.3455, a person convicted under subdivision 1 or subdivision 1a may be sentenced:

(1) to imprisonment for not more than 15 years or to a payment of a fine of not more than $30,000, or both; or

(2) if the person was convicted under subdivision 1, paragraph (b), and if the actor was no more than 48 36 months but more than 24 months older than the complainant, to imprisonment for not more than five years or a fine of not more than $30,000, or both.

A person convicted under this section is also subject to conditional release under section 609.3455.

Subd. 3. **Stay.** Except when imprisonment is required under section 609.3455; or Minnesota Statutes 2004, section 609.109, if a person is convicted under subdivision 1 1a, clause (f), the court may stay imposition or execution of the sentence if it finds that:

(a) a stay is in the best interest of the complainant or the family unit; and

(b) a professional assessment indicates that the offender has been accepted by and can respond to a treatment program.

If the court stays imposition or execution of sentence, it shall include the following as conditions of probation:

(1) incarceration in a local jail or workhouse;

(2) a requirement that the offender complete a treatment program; and

(3) a requirement that the offender have no unsupervised contact with the complainant until the offender has successfully completed the treatment program unless approved by the treatment program and the supervising correctional agent.

EFFECTIVE DATE.
This section is effective September 15, 2021, and applies to crimes committed on or after that date.
HIST: 1975 c 374 s 5; * * * 2014 c 259 s 5,6; 1Sp2019 c 5 art 4 s 7; 1Sp2021 c 11 art 4 s 18

609.345 CRIMINAL SEXUAL CONDUCT IN THE FOURTH DEGREE.

Subdivision 1. **Adult victim; crime defined.** A person who engages in sexual contact with another person is guilty of criminal sexual conduct in the fourth degree if any of the following circumstances exists:

(a) the complainant is under 13 years of age and the actor is no more than 36 months older than the complainant. Neither mistake as to the complainant's age or consent to the act by the complainant is a defense. In a prosecution under this clause, the state is not required to prove that the sexual contact was coerced;

~~(b) the complainant is at least 13 but less than 16 years of age and the actor is more than 48 months older than the complainant or in a current or recent position of authority over the complainant. Consent by the complainant to the act is not a defense. In any such case if the actor is no more than 120 months older than the complainant, it shall be an affirmative defense which must be proved by a preponderance of the evidence that the actor reasonably believes the complainant to be 16 years of age or older. In all other cases, mistake as to the complainant's age shall not be a defense;~~

~~(c)~~ (a) the actor uses ~~force or~~ coercion to accomplish the sexual contact;

~~(d)~~ (b) the actor knows or has reason to know that the complainant is mentally impaired, mentally incapacitated, or physically helpless;

(c) the actor uses force, as defined in section 609, subdivision 3, clause 2; or

(d) at the time of the act, the actor is in a prohibited relationship with the complainant.

Subd. 1a. **Victim under the age of 18; crime defined.**

A person who engages in sexual contact with anyone under 18 years of age is guilty of criminal sexual conduct in the fourth degree if any of the following circumstances exists:

(a) the complainant is under 14 years of age and the actor is no more than 36 months older than the complainant. Neither mistake as to the complainant's age or consent to the act by the complainant is a defense. In a prosecution under this clause, the state is not required to prove that the sexual contact was coerced;

(b) the complainant is at least 14 but less than 16 years of age and the actor is more than 36 months older than the complainant or in a current or recent position of authority over the complainant. Consent by the complainant to the act is not a defense.

Mistake of age is not a defense unless actor is less than 60 months older. In any such case, if the actor is no more than 60 months older than the complainant, it shall be an affirmative defense which must be proved by a preponderance of the evidence that the actor reasonably believes the complainant to be 16 years of age or older. In all other cases, mistake as to the complainant's age shall not be a defense;

(c) the actor uses coercion to accomplish the sexual contact;

(d) The actor knows or has reason to know that the complainant is mentally impaired, mentally incapacitated, or physically helpless;

(e) the complainant is at least 16 but less than 18 years of age and the actor is more than ~~48~~ 36 months older than the complainant and in a current or recent position of authority over the complainant. Neither mistake as to the complainant's age nor consent to the act by the complainant is a defense;

(f) the actor has a significant relationship to the complainant and the complainant was at least 16 but under 18 years of age at the time of the sexual contact. Neither mistake as to the complainant's age nor consent to the act by the complainant is a defense;

(g) the actor has a significant relationship to the complainant, the complainant was at least 16 but under 18 of age at the time of the sexual contact, and:

(i) the actor or an accomplice used force or coercion to accomplish the contact;

(ii) the complainant suffered personal injury; or

(iii) the sexual abuse involved multiple acts committed over an extended period of time.

Neither mistake as to the complainant's age nor consent to the act by the complainant is a defense.

(h) ~~the actor is a psychotherapist and the complainant is a patient of the psychotherapist and the sexual contact occurred:~~ the actor uses force, as defined in section 609.341, subdivision 3, clause 2; or

(i) at the time of the act, the actor is in a prohibited occupational relationship with the complainant.

~~(i) during the psychotherapy session; or~~

~~(ii) outside the psychotherapy session if an ongoing psychotherapist-patient relationship exists.~~

~~Consent by the complainant is not a defense.~~

(i) the actor is a psychotherapist and the complainant is a former patient of the psychotherapist and the former patient is emotionally dependent upon the psychotherapist;

(j) the actor is a psychotherapist and the complainant is a patient or former patient and the sexual contact occurred by means of therapeutic deception. Consent by the complainant is not a defense;

(k) the actor accomplishes the sexual contact by means of deception or false representation that the contact is for a bona fide medical purpose. Consent by the complainant is not a defense; or

(l) the actor is or purports to be a member of the clergy, the complainant is not married to the actor, and:

(i) the sexual contact occurred during the course of a meeting in which the complainant sought or received religious or spiritual advice, aid, or comfort from the actor in private; or

(ii) the sexual contact occurred during a period of time in which the complainant was meeting on an ongoing basis with the actor to seek or receive religious or spiritual advice, aid, or comfort in private. Consent by the complainant is not a defense;

(m) the actor is an employee, independent contractor, or volunteer of a state, county, city, or privately operated adult or juvenile correctional system, or secure treatment facility, or treatment facility providing services to clients civilly committed as mentally ill and dangerous, sexually dangerous persons, or sexual psychopathic personalities, including, but not limited to, jails, prisons, detention centers, or work release facilities, and the complainant is a resident of a facility or under supervision of the correctional system. Consent by the complainant is not a defense;

(n) the actor provides or is an agent of an entity that provides special transportation service, the complainant used the special transportation service, and the sexual contact occurred during or immediately before or after the actor transported the complainant. Consent by the complainant is not a defense;

(o) the actor performs massage or other bodywork for hire, the complainant was a user of one of those services, and nonconsensual sexual contact occurred during or immediately before or after the actor performed or was hired to perform one of those services for the complainant, or

(p) the actor is a peace officer, as defined in section 626.84, and the officer physically or constructively restrains the complainant or the complainant does not reasonably feel free to leave the officer's presence. Consent by the complainant is not a defense.

Subd. 2. **Penalty.** Except as otherwise provided in section 609.3455, a person convicted under subdivision 1 or subdivision 1a may be sentenced to imprisonment for not more than ten years or to a payment of a fine of not more than $20,000, or both. A person convicted under this section is also subject to conditional release under section 609.3455.

Subd. 3. **Stay.** Except when imprisonment is required under section 609.3455; or Minnesota Statutes 2004, section 609.109, if a person is convicted under subdivision 1 1a, clause (f), the court may stay imposition or execution of the sentence if it finds that:

(a) a stay is in the best interest of the complainant or the family unit; and

(b) a professional assessment indicates that the offender has been accepted by and can respond to a treatment program.

If the court stays imposition or execution of sentence, it shall include the following as conditions of probation:

(1) incarceration in a local jail or workhouse;

(2) a requirement that the offender complete a treatment program; and

(3) a requirement that the offender have no unsupervised contact with the complainant until the offender has successfully completed the treatment program unless approved by the treatment program and the supervising correctional agent.

EFFECTIVE DATE.
This section is effective September 15, 2021, and applies to crimes committed on or after that date.

HIST: 1975 c 374 s 6; * * * 2010 c 270 s 3; 1Sp2019 c 5 art 4 s 8; 1Sp2021 c 11 art 4 s 19

609.3451 CRIMINAL SEXUAL CONDUCT IN THE FIFTH DEGREE.
     Subdivision 1. <u>**Sexual penetration; crime defined.**</u> A person is guilty of criminal sexual conduct in the fifth degree: <u>if the person engages in nonconsensual sexual penetration.</u>
     <u>Subd. 1a. **Sexual contact; child present; crime defined.**</u>
<u>A person is guilty of criminal sexual conduct in the fifth degree if:</u>
     (1) ~~if~~ the person engages in nonconsensual sexual contact; or (2) the person engages in masturbation or lewd exhibition of the genitals in the presence of a minor under the age of 16, knowing or having reason to know the minor is present. For purposes of this section, "sexual contact" has the meaning given in section 609.341, subdivision 11, paragraph (a), clauses (i), (iv), and (v). Sexual contact also includes the intentional removal or attempted removal of clothing covering the complainant's intimate parts or undergarments, and the nonconsensual touching by the complainant of the actor's intimate parts, effected by the actor, if the action is performed with sexual or aggressive intent.
     Subd. 2. **Gross misdemeanor.** A person convicted under subdivision ~~1~~ <u>1a</u> may be sentenced to imprisonment for not more than one year or to a payment of a fine of not more than $3,000, or both.
     Subd. 3. **Felony.** (a) <u>A person is guilty of a felony and may be sentenced to imprisonment for not more than two years or to payment of a fine of not more than $10,000, or both, if the person violates subdivision 1.</u>
     <u>(b)</u> A person is guilty of a felony and may be sentenced to imprisonment for not more than seven years or to payment of a fine of not more than $14,000, or both, if the person violates ~~this section~~ <u>subdivision 1 or 1a</u> within ~~seven~~ <u>ten</u> years of:
     <u>(1) a conviction under subdivision 1;</u>
     <u>(2)</u> a previous conviction for violating subdivision ~~1~~ <u>1a</u>, clause (2), a crime described in paragraph ~~(b)~~ <u>(c)</u>, or a statute from another state in conformity with any of these offenses; or
     ~~(2)~~ <u>(3)</u> the first of two or more previous convictions for violating subdivision ~~1~~ <u>1a</u>, clause (1), or a statute from another state in conformity with this offense.
     ~~(b)~~ <u>(c)</u> A previous conviction for violating section 609.342, 609.343, 609.344, 609.345, 609.3453, 617.23, subdivision 2, clause (2), or subdivision 3, or 617.247 may be used to enhance a criminal penalty as provided in paragraph ~~(a)~~ <u>(b)</u>.
<u>**EFFECTIVE DATE.**</u>
<u>This section is effective September 15, 2021, and applies to crimes committed on or after that date.</u>
HIST: 1988 c 529 s 2; * * * 2015 c 65 art 6 s 14; 1 Sp2019 c 5 art 8 s 9<u>; 1Sp2021 c 11 art 4 s 20</u>

609.3453 CRIMINAL SEXUAL PREDATORY CONDUCT.
     Subdivision 1. **Crime defined.** A person is guilty of criminal sexual predatory conduct if the person commits a predatory crime that was motivated by the offender's sexual impulses or was part of a predatory pattern of behavior that had criminal sexual conduct as its goal.
     Subd. 2. **Penalty.** (a) Except as provided in section 609.3455, the statutory maximum sentence for a violation of subdivision 1 is: (1) 25 percent longer than for the underlying predatory crime; or (2) 50 percent longer than for the underlying predatory crime, if the violation is committed by a person with a previous sex offense conviction, as defined in section 609.3455, subdivision 1.
HIST: 2005 c 136 art 2 s 20

Editors' Note: Although the following statute is not specifically described in these learning objectives, it has been included because of its close relationship to the criminal sexual conduct statutes described above.

609.3458 SEXUAL EXTORTION.
     <u>Subdivision 1. **Crime defined.** (a) A person who engages in sexual contact with another person and compels the other person to submit to the contact by making any of the following threats, directly or indirectly, is guilty of sexual extortion:</u>

(1) a threat to withhold or harm the complainant's trade, business, profession, position, employment, or calling;

(2) a threat to make or cause to be made a criminal charge against the complainant, whether true or false;

(3) a threat to report the complainant's immigration status to immigration or law enforcement authorities;

(4) a threat to disseminate private sexual images of the complainant as specified in section 617.261, nonconsensual dissemination of private sexual images;

(5) a threat to expose information that the actor knows the complainant wishes to keep confidential; or

(6) a threat to withhold complainant's housing, or to cause complainant a loss or disadvantage in the complainant's housing, or a change in the cost of complainant's housing.

(b) A person who engages in sexual penetration with another person and compels the other person to submit to such penetration by making any of the following threats, directly or indirectly, is guilty of sexual extortion:

(1) a threat to withhold or harm the complainant's trade, business, profession, position, employment, or calling;

(2) a threat to make or cause to be made a criminal charge against the complainant, whether true or false;

(3) a threat to report the complainant's immigration status to immigration or law enforcement authorities;

(4) a threat to disseminate private sexual images of the complainant as specified in section 617.261, nonconsensual dissemination of private sexual images;

(5) a threat to expose information that the actor knows the complainant wishes to keep confidential; or

(6) a threat to withhold complainant's housing, or to cause complainant a loss or disadvantage in the complainant's housing, or a change in the cost of complainant's housing.

Subd. 2. **Penalty.** (a) A person is guilty of a felony and may be sentenced to imprisonment for not more than ten years or to payment of a fine of not more than $20,000, or both, if the person violates subdivision 1, paragraph (a).

(b) A person is guilty of a felony and may be sentenced to imprisonment for not more than 15 years or to payment of a fine of not more than $30,000, or both, if the person violates subdivision 1, paragraph (b).

(c) A person convicted under this section is also subject to conditional release under section 609.3455.

Subd. 3. **No attempt charge.** Notwithstanding section 609.17, no person may be charged with or convicted of an attempt to commit a violation of this section.

EFFECTIVE DATE. This section is effective September 15, 2021, and applies to crimes committed on or after that date.

HIST: 1Sp2021 c 11 art 4 s 22

609.3459 LAW ENFORCEMENT; REPORTS OF SEXUAL ASSAULTS.

(a) A victim of any violation of sections 609.342 to 609.3453 may initiate a law enforcement investigation by contacting any law enforcement agency, regardless of where the crime may have occurred. The agency must prepare a summary of the allegation and provide the person with a copy of it. The agency must begin an investigation of the facts, or, if the suspected crime was committed in a different jurisdiction, refer the matter along with the summary to the law enforcement agency where the suspected crime was committed for an investigation of the facts. If the agency learns that both the victim and the accused are members of the Minnesota National Guard, the agency receiving the report must refer the matter along with the summary to the Bureau of Criminal Apprehension for investigation pursuant to section 299C.80.

(b) If a law enforcement agency refers the matter to a law enforcement agency where the crime was committed, it need not include the allegation as a crime committed in its jurisdiction for purposes of information that the agency is required to provide to the commissioner of public safety pursuant to section 299C.06, but must confirm that the other law enforcement agency has received the referral.

EFFECTIVE DATE.
This section is effective August 1, 2021, for investigations beginning on or after that date.
HIST: 1Sp2019 c 5 art 4 s 10; 1Sp2021 c 11 art 2 s 37

609.3469 VOLUNTARY INTOXICATION DEFENSE.

(a) The "knows or has reason to know" mental state requirement for violations of sections 609.342 to 609.345 involving a complainant who is mentally incapacitated, as defined in section 609.341, subdivision 7, clause 2, involves specific intent for purposes of determining the applicability of the voluntary intoxication defense described in section 609.075. This defense may be raised by a defendant if the defense is otherwise applicable under section 609.075 and related case law.

(b) Nothing in paragraph (a) may be interpreted to change the application of the defense to other crimes.

(c) Nothing in paragraph (a) is intended to change the scope or limitations of the defense or case law interpreting it beyond clarifying that the defense is available to a defendant described in paragraph (a).

EFFECTIVE DATE. This section is effective September 15, 2021, and applies to crimes committed on or after that date.
HIST: 1Sp2021 c 11 art 4 s 23

609.3471 RECORDS PERTAINING TO VICTIM IDENTITY CONFIDENTIAL.

Notwithstanding any provision of law to the contrary, no data contained in records or reports relating to petitions, complaints, or indictments issued pursuant to section 609.322, 609.342, 609.343, 609.344, 609.345, or 609.3453, which specifically identifies a victim who is a minor shall be accessible to the public, except by order of the court. Nothing in this section authorizes denial of access to any other data contained in the records or reports, including the identity of the defendant.
HIST: 1984 c 573 s 9; * * * 2015 c 65 art 6 s 15

609.352 SOLICITATION OF CHILDREN TO ENGAGE IN SEXUAL CONDUCT; COMMUNICATION OF SEXUALLY EXPLICIT MATERIALS TO CHILDREN.

Subdivision 1. **Definitions.** As used in this section:

(a) "child" means a person 15 years of age or younger;

(b) "sexual conduct" means sexual contact of the individual's primary genital area, sexual penetration as defined in section 609.341, or sexual performance as defined in section 617.246; and

(c) "solicit" means commanding, entreating, or attempting to persuade a specific person in person, by telephone, by letter, or by computerized or other electronic means.

Subd. 2. **Prohibited act.** A person 18 years of age or older who solicits a child or someone the person reasonably believes is a child to engage in sexual conduct with intent to engage in sexual conduct is guilty of a felony and may be sentenced as provided in subdivision 4.

Subd. 2a. **Electronic solicitation of children.** A person 18 years of age or older who uses the Internet, a computer, computer program, computer network, computer system, an electronic communications system, or a telecommunications, wire, or radio communications system, or other electronic device capable of electronic data storage or transmission to commit any of the following acts, with the intent to arouse the sexual desire of any person, is guilty of a felony and may be sentenced as provided in subdivision 4:

(1) soliciting a child or someone the person reasonably believes is a child to engage in sexual conduct;

(2) engaging in communication with a child or someone the person reasonably believes is a child, relating to or describing sexual conduct; or

(3) distributing any material, language, or communication, including a photographic or video image, that relates to or describes sexual conduct to a child or someone the person reasonably believes is a child.

Subd. 2b. **Jurisdiction.** A person may be convicted of an offense under subdivision 2a if the transmission that constitutes the offense either originates within this state or is received within this state.

Subd. 3. **Defenses.** (a) Mistake as to age is not a defense to a prosecution under this section.

(b) The fact that an undercover operative or law enforcement officer was involved in the detection or investigation of an offense under this section does not constitute a defense to a prosecution under this section.

Subd. 4. **Penalty.** A person convicted under this subdivision 2 or 2a is guilty of a felony and may be sentenced to imprisonment for not more than ~~three~~ five years, or to payment of a fine of not more than ~~$5,000~~ $10,000, or both.

HIST: 1986 c 445 s 3; * * * 2009 c 59 art 1 s 6; 1Sp2021 c 11 art 2 s 38

609.353 JURISDICTION.

A violation or attempted violation of section 609.342, 609.343, 609.344, 609.345, 609.3451, 609.3453, or 609.352 may be prosecuted in any jurisdiction in which the violation originates or terminates.

HIST: 2000 c 311 art 2 s 5; 2005 c 136 art 4 s 9

609.349 [Repealed, 2019 c 16 s 1]

609.35 COSTS OF MEDICAL EXAMINATION.

(a) Costs incurred by a county, city, or private hospital or other emergency medical facility or by a private physician for the examination of a victim of criminal sexual conduct when the examination is performed for the purpose of gathering evidence shall be paid by the county in which the criminal sexual conduct occurred. These costs include, but are not limited to, full cost of the rape kit examination, associated tests relating to the complainant's sexually transmitted disease status, and pregnancy status.

(b) Nothing in this section shall be construed to limit the duties, responsibilities, or liabilities of any insurer, whether public or private. However, a county may seek insurance reimbursement from the victim's insurer only if authorized by the victim. This authorization may only be sought after the examination is performed. When seeking this authorization, the county shall inform the victim that if the victim does not authorize this, the county is required by law to authorize the reimbursement.

(c) The applicability of this section does not depend upon whether the victim reports the offense to law enforcement or the existence or status of any investigation or prosecution.

HIST: 1975 c 374 s 11; * * * 2003 c 116 s 3

609.347 EVIDENCE IN CRIMINAL SEXUAL CONDUCT CASES.

Subdivision 1. **Victim testimony; corroboration unnecessary.** In a prosecution under sections 609.342 to 609.3451: 609.3453; or Minnesota Statutes 2004, section 609.109, the testimony of a victim need not be corroborated.

Subd. 2. **Showing of resistance unnecessary.** In a prosecution under sections 609.342 to 609.3451: 609.3453; or Minnesota Statutes 2004, section 609.109, there is no need to show that the victim resisted the accused.

Subd. 3. **Previous sexual conduct.** In a prosecution under sections 609.342 to 609.3451; 609.3453; 609.365: or Minnesota Statutes 2004, section 609.109, evidence of the victim's previous sexual conduct shall not be admitted nor shall any reference to such conduct be made in the presence of the jury, except by court order under the procedure provided in subdivision 4. The evidence can be admitted only if the probative value of the evidence is not substantially outweighed by its inflammatory or prejudicial nature and only in the circumstances set out in paragraphs (a) and (b). For the evidence to be admissible under paragraph (a), subsection (i), the judge must find by a preponderance of the evidence that the facts set out in the accused's offer of proof are true. For the evidence to be admissible under paragraph (a), subsection (ii) or paragraph (b), the judge must find that the evidence is sufficient to support a finding that the facts set out in the accused's offer of proof are true, as provided under Rule 901 of the Rules of Evidence.

(a) When consent of the victim is a defense in the case, the following evidence is admissible:

(i) evidence of the victim's previous sexual conduct tending to establish a common scheme or plan of similar sexual conduct under circumstances similar to the case at issue. In order to find a common scheme or plan, the judge must find that the victim made prior allegations of sexual assault which were fabricated; and

(ii) evidence of the victim's previous sexual conduct with the accused.

(b) When the prosecution's case includes evidence of semen, pregnancy, or disease at the time of the incident or, in the case of pregnancy, between the time of the incident and trial evidence of specific instances of the victim's previous sexual conduct is admissible solely to show the source of the semen pregnancy, or disease.

Subd. 4. **Accused offer of evidence.** The accused may not offer evidence described in subdivision 3 except pursuant to the following procedure

(a) A motion shall be made by the accused at least three business days prior to trial, unless later for good cause shown, setting out with particularity the offer of proof of the evidence that the accused intends to offer, relative to the previous sexual conduct of the victim;

(b) If the court deems the offer of proof sufficient, the court shall order a hearing out of the presence of the jury, if any, and in such hearing shall allow the accused to make a full presentation of the offer of proof,

(c) At the conclusion of the hearing, if the court finds that the evidence proposed to be offered by the accused regarding the previous sexual conduct of the victim is admissible under subdivision 3 and that its probative value is not substantially outweighed by its inflammatory or prejudicial, nature, the court shall make an order stating the extent to which evidence is admissible. The accused may then offer evidence pursuant to the order of the court;

(d) If new information is discovered after the date of the hearing or during the course of trial, which may make evidence described in subdivision 3 admissible, the accused may make an offer of proof pursuant to clause (a) and the court shall order an in camera hearing to determine whether the proposed evidence is admissible by the standards herein.

Subd. 5. **Prohibiting instructing jury on certain points.** In a prosecution under sections 609.342 to 609.3451: 609.3453; or Minnesota Statutes 2004, section 609.109, the court shall not instruct the jury to the effect that:

(a) It may be inferred that a victim who has previously consented to sexual intercourse with persons other than the accused would be therefore more likely to consent to sexual intercourse again; or

(b) The victim's previous or subsequent sexual conduct in and of itself may be considered in determining the credibility of the victim; or

(c) Criminal sexual conduct is a crime easily charged by a victim but very difficult to disprove by an accused because of the heinous nature of the crime; or

(d) The jury should scrutinize the testimony of the victim any more closely than it should scrutinize the testimony of any witness in any felony prosecution.

Subd. 6. **Psychotherapy evidence.** (a) In a prosecution under sections 609.342 to 609.3451; 609.3453; or Minnesota Statutes 2004, section 609.109, involving a psychotherapist and patient, evidence of the patient's personal or medical history is not admissible except when:

(1) the accused requests a hearing at least three business days prior to trial and makes an offer of proof of the relevancy of the history; and

(2) the court finds that the history is relevant and that the probative value of the history outweighs its prejudicial value.

(b) The court shall allow the admission only of specific information or examples of conduct of the victim that are determined by the court to be relevant. The court's order shall detail the information or conduct that is admissible and no other evidence of the history may be introduced.

(c) Violation of the terms of the order is grounds for mistrial but does not prevent the retrial of the accused.

* * *

HIST: 1975 c 374 s 8; * * * 2007 c 13 art 3 s 37

609.3775 CHILD TORTURE.

Subdivision 1. **Definition.** As used in this section, "torture" means the intentional infliction of extreme mental anguish, or extreme psychological or physical abuse, when committed in an especially depraved manner.

Subd. 2. **Crime.** A person who tortures a child is guilty of a felony and may be sentenced to imprisonment for not more than 25 years or to payment of a fine of not more than $35,000, or both.

Subd. 3. **Proof; evidence.** (a) Expert testimony as to the existence or extent of mental anguish or psychological abuse is not a requirement for a conviction under this section.

(b) A child's special susceptibility to mental anguish or psychological abuse does not constitute an independent cause of the condition so that a defendant is exonerated from criminal liability.

(c) Proof that a victim suffered pain is not an element of a violation of this section.

EFFECTIVE DATE. This section is effective September 15, 2021, and applies to crimes committed on or after that date.

HIST: 1Sp2021 c 11 art 2 s 39

Editors' Note: Although the following statutes are not specifically described in these learning objectives, they have been included because of their close relationship to the evidentiary statute described above concerning criminal sexual conduct and sex trafficking prosecutions and other statutes above concerning sexual assault.

611A.211 PROGRAMS FOR VICTIMS OF SEXUAL ASSAULT.

Subdivision 1. **Grants.** The commissioner of public safety shall award grants to programs which provide support services to victims of sexual assault. The commissioner shall also award grants for training, technical assistance, and the development and implementation of education programs to increase public awareness of the causes of sexual assault, the solutions to preventing and ending sexual assault, and the problems faced by sexual assault victims.

* * *

Subd. 4. **Sexual assault.** For the purposes of this section, "sexual assault" means any violation of sections 609.342 to 609.3454.

HIST: 2014 c 212 art 1 s 8

611A.26 POLYGRAPH EXAMINATIONS; CRIMINAL SEXUAL CONDUCT COMPLAINTS; LIMITATIONS.

Subdivision 1. **Polygraph prohibition.** No law enforcement agency or prosecutor shall require that a complainant of a criminal sexual conduct offense or sex trafficking submit to a polygraph examination as part of or a condition to proceeding with the investigation, charging, or prosecution of such offense.

Subd. 2. **Law enforcement inquiry.** A law enforcement agency or prosecutor may not ask that a complainant of a criminal sexual conduct offense submit to a polygraph examination as part of the investigation, charging, or prosecution of such offense unless the complainant has been referred to, and had the opportunity to exercise the option of consulting with a sexual assault counselor[.] * * *

Subd. 3. **Informed consent requirement.** At the request of the complainant, a law enforcement agency may conduct a polygraph examination of the complainant only with the complainant's written, informed consent as provided in this subdivision.

Subd. 4. **Informed consent.** To consent to a polygraph, a complainant must be informed in writing that:

(1) the taking of the polygraph examination is voluntary and solely at the victim's request;

(2) a law enforcement agency or prosecutor may not ask or require that the complainant submit to a polygraph examination;

(3) the results of the examination are not admissible in court; and

(4) the complainant's refusal to take a polygraph examination may not be used as a basis by the law enforcement agency or prosecutor not to investigate, charge, or prosecute the offender.

* * *

HIST: 2007 c 54 art 4 s 7; 2015 c 65 art 6 s 18,19

611A.27 VICTIM RIGHTS TO SEXUAL ASSAULT EVIDENCE INFORMATION.

Subdivision 1. **Access to law enforcement data.** (a) Upon written request from the victim or victim's designee as described in subdivision 2, the investigating law enforcement agency shall release the following * * * to a victim of sexual assault about a submitted sexual assault examination kit, as defined in section 299C.106 * * *:

(1) the date that a sexual assault examination kit was submitted to a forensic laboratory * * * and the date that the agency received notice of the results of that testing; and

(2) whether a DNA profile was obtained from the testing.

(b) The agency may refuse the request under paragraph (a) if the release of that data will interfere with the investigation.

Subd. 2. **Responding to a victim request for data.** No later than January 1, 2019, each law enforcement agency shall adopt policies and procedures * * * to provide investigative data under this section that includes but is not limited to the following requirements:

(1) agency identification of a representative or representatives to respond to requests for the data from sexual assault victims and to serve as a liaison between the agency and the forensic laboratory;

(2) agency response to inquiries within 30 days of receipt, unless the agency declines to provide the information under subdivision 1, paragraph (b);

(3) the sexual assault victim can designate another person to request information on the victim's behalf by providing written authorization to the agency * * *; and

(4) agency development of a procedure that allows a sexual assault victim to contact the agency representative to request that a restricted kit as defined in section 299C.106 * * * be reclassified as an unrestricted kit if the restricted kit is in the possession of the agency.

HIST: 2018 c 160 s 3

Chapter 8 -- CRIMES AGAINST THE FAMILY

Category 2, Section 5:
2.5.1. Describe the basic organization, purpose, and definitions and principles of the Minnesota Criminal Code.
2.5.5. Given a variety of scenarios, identify indications a particular crime has been committed and identify the elements of that crime.

609.376 DEFINITIONS.

Subdivision 1. **Terms defined.** For the purposes of sections 609.255 and 609.376 to 609.38, the following terms have the meanings given unless specific content indicates otherwise.

Subd. 2. **Child.** "Child" means any person under the age of 18 years.

Subd. 3. **Caretaker.** "Caretaker" means an individual who has responsibility for the care of a child as a result of a family relationship or who has assumed responsibility for all or a portion of the care of a child.

Subd. 4. **Complainant.** "Complainant" means a person alleged to have been a victim of a violation of section 609.255, subdivision 3, 609.377, or 609.378, but need not be the person who signs the complaint.
HIST: 1983 c 217 s 3

609.377 MALICIOUS PUNISHMENT OF A CHILD.

Subdivision 1. **Malicious punishment.** A parent, legal guardian, or caretaker who, by an intentional act or a series of intentional acts with respect to a child, evidences unreasonable force or cruel discipline that is excessive under the circumstances is guilty of malicious punishment of a child and may be sentenced as provided in subdivisions 2 to 6.

Subd. 2. **Gross misdemeanor.** If the punishment results in less than substantial bodily harm, the person may be sentenced to imprisonment for not more than one year or to payment of a fine of not more than $3,000, or both.

Subd. 3. **Enhancement to a felony.** Whoever violates the provisions of subdivision 2 during the time period between a previous conviction or adjudication for delinquency under this section or sections 609.221 to 609.2231, 609.224, 609.2242, 609.342 to 609.345, or 609.713, and the end of five years following discharge from sentence or disposition for that conviction or adjudication may be sentenced to imprisonment for not more than five years or a fine of $10,000, or both.

Subd. 4. **Felony; child under age four.** If the punishment is to a child under the age of four and causes bodily harm to the head, eyes, neck, or otherwise causes multiple bruises to the body, the person may be sentenced to imprisonment for not more than five years or a fine of $10,000, or both.

Subd. 5. **Felony; substantial bodily harm.** If the punishment results in substantial bodily harm, the person may be sentenced to imprisonment for not more than five years or to payment of a fine of not more than $10,000, or both.

Subd. 6. **Felony; great bodily harm.** If the punishment results in great bodily harm, the person may be sentenced to imprisonment for not more than ten years or to payment of a fine of not more than $20,000, or both.
HIST: 1983 c 217 s 4; 1984 c 628 art 3 s 11; 1988 c 655 s 2; 1989 c 290 art 6 s 16; 1990 c 542 s 18; 1994 c 636 art 2 s 37; 2000 c 437 s 14

609.3775 CHILD TORTURE.

Subdivision 1. **Definition.** As used in this section, "torture" means the intentional infliction of extreme mental anguish, or extreme psychological or physical abuse, when committed in an especially depraved manner.

Subd. 2. **Crime.** A person who tortures a child is guilty of a felony and may be sentenced to imprisonment for not more than 25 years or to payment of a fine of not more than $35,000, or both.

Subd. 3. **Proof; evidence.** (a) Expert testimony as to the existence or extent of mental anguish or psychological abuse is not a requirement for a conviction under this section.

(b) A child's special susceptibility to mental anguish or psychological abuse does not constitute an independent cause of the condition so that a defendant is exonerated from criminal liability.

(c) Proof that a victim suffered pain is not an element of a violation of this section.

EFFECTIVE DATE. This section is effective September 15, 2021, and applies to crimes committed on or after that date.

HIST:1Sp2021 c 11 art 2 s 39

609.378 NEGLECT OR ENDANGERMENT OF A CHILD.

Subdivision 1. **Persons guilty of neglect or endangerment.**

(a) **Neglect.** (1) A parent, legal guardian, or caretaker who willfully deprives a child of necessary food, clothing, shelter, health care, or supervision appropriate to the child's age, when the parent, guardian, or caretaker is reasonably able to make the necessary provisions and the deprivation harms or is likely to substantially harm the child's physical, mental, or emotional health is guilty of neglect of a child and may be sentenced to imprisonment for not more than one year or to payment of a fine of not more than $3,000, or both. If the deprivation results in substantial harm to the child's physical, mental, or emotional health, the person may be sentenced to imprisonment for not more than five years or to payment of a fine of not more than $10,000, or both. If a parent, guardian, or caretaker responsible for the child's care in good faith selects and depends upon spiritual means or prayer for treatment or care of disease or remedial care of the child, this treatment or care is "health care," for purposes of this clause.

(2) A parent, legal guardian, or caretaker who knowingly permits the continuing physical or sexual abuse of a child is guilty of neglect of a child and may be sentenced to imprisonment for not more than one year or to payment of a fine of not more than $3,000, or both.

(b) **Endangerment.** A parent, legal guardian, or caretaker who endangers the child's person or health by:

(1) intentionally or recklessly causing or permitting a child to be placed in a situation likely to substantially harm the child's physical, mental, or emotional health or cause the child's death; or

(2) knowingly causing or permitting the child to be present where any person is selling, manufacturing, possessing immediate precursors or chemical substances with intent to manufacture, or possessing a controlled substance, as defined in section 152.01, subdivision 4, in violation of section 152.021, 152.022, 152.023, or 152.024; is guilty of child endangerment and may be sentenced to imprisonment for not more than one year or to payment of a fine of not more than $3,000, or both.

If the endangerment results in substantial harm to the child's physical, mental, or emotional health, the person may be sentenced to imprisonment for not more than five years or to payment of a fine of not more than $10,000, or both.

This paragraph does not prevent a parent, legal guardian, or caretaker from causing or permitting a child to engage in activities that are appropriate to the child's age, stage of development, and experience, or from selecting health care as defined in subdivision 1, paragraph (a).

(c) **Endangerment by firearm access.** A person who intentionally or recklessly causes a child under 14 years of age to be placed in a situation likely to substantially harm the child's physical health or cause the child's death as a result of the child's access to a loaded firearm is guilty of child endangerment and may be sentenced to imprisonment for not more than one year or to payment of a fine of not more than $3,000, or both.

If the endangerment results in substantial harm to the child's physical health, the person may be sentenced to imprisonment for not more than five years or to a payment of a fine of not more than $10,000, or both.

Subd. 2. **Defenses.** It is a defense to a prosecution under subdivision 1, paragraph (a), clause (2), or paragraph (b), that at the time of the neglect or endangerment there was a reasonable apprehension in the mind of the defendant that acting to stop or prevent the neglect or endangerment would result in substantial bodily harm to the defendant or the child in retaliation.
HIST: 1983 c 217 s 5; 1984 c 628 art 3 s 11; 1989 c 282 art 2 s 199; 1992 c 571 art 4 s 11; 1993 c 326 art 4 s 22; 2002 c 314 s 6

609.3785 UNHARMED NEWBORNS LEFT AT A SAFE PLACE; AVOIDANCE OF PROSECUTION.

A person may leave a newborn with an employee at a safe place, as defined in section 145.902, in this state, pursuant to section 260C217, subdivision 3, without being subjected to prosecution for that act, provided that:

(1) the newborn was born within seven days of being left at the safe place, as determined within a reasonable degree of medical certainty;

(2) the newborn is left in an unharmed condition; and

(3) in cases where the person leaving the newborn is not the newborn's mother, the person has the mother's approval to do so.
HIST: 2000 c 421 s 3; 2012 c 216 art 2 s 3

609.379 PERMITTED ACTIONS.

Subdivision 1. **Reasonable force.** Reasonable force may be used upon or toward the person of a child without the child's consent when the following circumstance exists or the actor reasonably believes it to exist:

(a) when used by a parent, legal guardian, teacher, or other caretaker of a child or pupil, in the exercise of lawful authority, to restrain or correct the child or pupil; or

(b) when used by a teacher or other member of the instructional, support, or supervisory staff of a public or nonpublic school upon or toward a child when necessary to restrain the child from self-injury or injury to any other person or property.

Subd. 2. **Applicability.** This section applies to sections 260.315, 609.255, 609.376, 609.378, and 626.556 and Chapter 260E.
HIST: 1983 c 217 s 6; 1985 c 266 s 4; 1986 c 444; 1990 c 542 s 19; 1Sp2020 c 2 art 8 s 139

Chapter 9 -- CRIMES AFFECTING PUBLIC OFFICER OR EMPLOYEE

Category 2, Section 5:

2.5.1. Describe the basic organization, purpose, and definitions and principles of the Minnesota Criminal Code.

2.5.5. Given a variety of scenarios, identify indications a particular crime has been committed and identify the elements of that crime.

609.415 DEFINITIONS.

Subdivision 1. **Definitions.** As used in sections 609.415 to 609.465, and 609.515,

(1) "Public officer" means:

(a) an executive or administrative officer of the state or of a county, municipality or other subdivision or agency of the state;

(b) a member of the legislature or of a governing board of a county, municipality, or other subdivision of the state, or other governmental instrumentality within the state;

(c) a judicial officer;

(d) a hearing officer;

(e) a law enforcement officer; or

(f) any other person exercising the functions of a public officer.

(2) "Public employee" means a person employed by or acting for the state or a county, municipality, or other subdivision or governmental instrumentality of the state for the purpose of exercising their respective powers and performing their respective duties, and who is not a public officer. Public employee includes a member of a charter commission.

(3) "Judicial officer" means a judge, court commissioner, referee, or any other person appointed by a judge or court to hear or determine a cause or controversy.

(4) "Hearing officer" means any person authorized by law or private agreement to hear or determine a cause or controversy who is not a judicial officer.

(5) "Political subdivision" means a county, town, statutory or home rule charter city, school district, special service district, or other municipal corporation of the state of Minnesota.

Subd. 2. **Deemed officer or employee.** A person who has been elected, appointed, or otherwise designated as a public officer or public employee is deemed such officer or employee although the person has not yet qualified therefore or entered upon the duties thereof.

HIST: 1963 c 753 art 1 s 609.415; 1983 c 359 s 88; 1986 c 444; 1992 c 592 s 16; 2002 c 352 s 13

609.42 BRIBERY.

Subdivision 1. **Acts constituting** Whoever does any of the following is guilty of bribery and may be sentenced to imprisonment for not more than ten years or to payment of a fine of not more than $20,000, or both:

(1) Offers, gives, or promises to give, directly or indirectly, to any person who is a public officer or employee any benefit, reward or consideration to which the person is not legally entitled with intent thereby to influence the person's performance of the powers or duties as such officer or employee; or

(2) Being a public officer or employee, requests, receives or agrees to receive, directly or indirectly, any such benefit, reward or consideration upon the understanding that it will have such an influence; or

(3) Offers, gives, or promises to give, directly or indirectly any such benefit, reward, or consideration to a person who is a witness or about to become a witness in a proceeding before a judicial or hearing officer, with intent that the person's testimony be influenced thereby, or that the person will not appear at the proceeding; or

(4) As a person who is, or is about to become such witness requests, receives, or agrees to receive, directly or indirectly, any such benefit, reward, or consideration upon the understanding that the person's testimony will be so influenced, or that the person will not appear at the proceeding; or

(5) Accepts directly or indirectly a benefit, reward or consideration upon an agreement or understanding, express or implied, that the acceptor will refrain from giving information that may lead to the prosecution of a crime or purported crime or that the acceptor will abstain from, discontinue, or delay prosecution therefor, except in a case where a compromise is allowed by law.

Subd. 2. **Forfeiture of office.** Any public officer who is convicted of violating or attempting to violate subdivision 1 shall forfeit the public officer's office and be forever disqualified from holding public office under the state

HIST: 1963 c 753 art 1 s 609.42; 1976 c 178 s 2; 1984 c 628 art 3 s 11; 1986 c 444

609.425 CORRUPTLY INFLUENCING LEGISLATOR.

Whoever by menace, deception, concealment of facts, or other corrupt means, attempts to influence the vote or other performance of duty of any member of the legislature or person elected thereto may be sentenced to imprisonment for not more than five years or to payment of a fine of not more than $10,000, or both.

HIST: 1963 c 753 art 1 s 609.425; 1984 c 628 art 3 s 11

609.43 MISCONDUCT OF PUBLIC OFFICER OR EMPLOYEE.

A public officer or employee who does any of the following, for which no other sentence is specifically provided by law, may be sentenced to imprisonment for not more than one year or to payment of a fine of not more than $3,000, or both:

(1) Intentionally fails or refuses to perform a known mandatory, nondiscretionary, ministerial duty of the office or employment within the time or in the manner required by law; or

(2) In the capacity of such officer or employee, does an act knowing it is in excess of lawful authority or knowing it is forbidden by law to be done in that capacity; or

(3) Under pretense or color of official authority intentionally and unlawfully injures another in the other's person, property, or rights; or

(4) In the capacity of such officer or employee, makes a return, certificate, official report, or other like document having knowledge it is false in any material respect.

HIST: 1963 c 753 art 1 s 609.43; 1984 c 628 art 3 s 11; 1986 c 444

609.435 OFFICER NOT FILING SECURITY.

Whoever intentionally performs the functions of a public officer without having executed and duly filed the required security is guilty of a misdemeanor.

HIST: 1963 c 753 art 1 s 609.435; 1971 c 23 s 46

609.44 PUBLIC OFFICE; ILLEGALLY ASSUMING; NONSURRENDER.

Whoever intentionally and without lawful right thereto, exercises a function of a public office or, having held such office and the right thereto having ceased, refuses to surrender the office or its seal, books, papers, or other incidents to a successor or other authority entitled thereto may be sentenced to imprisonment for not more than one year or to payment of a fine of not more than $3,000, or both.

HIST: 1963 c 753 art 1 s 609.44; 1984 c 628 art 3 s 11; 1986 c 444

609.445 FAILURE TO PAY OVER STATE FUNDS.

Whoever receives money on behalf of or for the account of the state or any of its agencies or subdivisions and intentionally refuses or omits to pay the same to the state or its agency or subdivision entitled thereto, or to an officer or agent authorized to receive the same, may be sentenced to imprisonment for not more than five years or to payment of a fine of not more than $10,000, or both.

HIST: 1963 c 753 art 1 s 609.445; 1984 c 628 art 3 s 11; 1989 c 290 art 6 s 17

609.45 PUBLIC OFFICER; UNAUTHORIZED COMPENSATION.

Whoever is a public officer or public employee and under color of office or employment intentionally asks, receives or agrees to receive a fee or other compensation in excess of that allowed by law or where no such fee or compensation is allowed, is guilty of a misdemeanor.
HIST: 1963 c 753 art 1 s 609.45; 1971 c 23 s 47; 1986 c 444

609.455 PERMITTING FALSE CLAIMS AGAINST GOVERNMENT.

A public officer or employee who audits, allows, or pays any claim or demand made upon the state or subdivision thereof or other governmental instrumentality within the state which the public officer or employee knows is false or fraudulent in whole or in part, may be sentenced to imprisonment for not more than five years or to payment of a fine of not more than $10,000, or both.
HIST: 1963 c 753 art 1 s 609.455; 1984 c 628 art 3 s 11; 1986 c 444

609.465 PRESENTING FALSE CLAIMS TO PUBLIC OFFICER OR BODY.

Whoever, with intent to defraud, presents a claim or demand, with knowledge that it is false in whole or in part, for audit, allowance or payment to a public officer or body authorized to make such audit, allowance or payment is guilty of an attempt to commit theft of public funds and may be sentenced accordingly.
HIST: 1963 c 753 art 1 s 609.465; 1986 c 444

609.47 INTERFERENCE WITH PROPERTY IN OFFICIAL CUSTODY.

Whoever intentionally takes, damages, or destroys any personal property held in custody by an officer or other person under process of law may be sentenced to imprisonment for not more than one year or to payment of a fine of not more than $3,000, or both.
HIST: 1963 c 753 art 1 s 609.47; 1984 c 628 art 3 s 11

609.475 IMPERSONATING A MILITARY SERVICE MEMBER, VETERAN, OR PUBLIC OFFICIAL.

Whoever falsely impersonates an active or reserve component military service member, veteran, or public official with intent to wrongfully obtain money, property, or any other tangible benefit is guilty of a misdemeanor.
HIST: 1963 c 753 art 1 s 609.475; * * * 2017 c 95 art 3 s 13

Editors' Note: Section 609.475 above has been amended to address the impersonation of a broader set of persons. The following statute has been added to address specifically matters relating to the impersonation of a peace officer, some of which were previously found in the statute above.

609.4751 IMPERSONATING A PEACE OFFICER.

Subdivision 1. **Misdemeanor.** Whoever falsely impersonates a peace officer with intent to mislead another into believing that the impersonator is actually an officer is guilty of a misdemeanor.

Subd. 2. **Gross misdemeanor.** Whoever violates subdivision 1 while committing any of the following acts is guilty of a gross misdemeanor:

(1) gaining access to a public building or government facility that is not open to the public;

(2) without legal authority, directing or ordering another person to act or refrain from acting;

(3) violating section 169.64, subdivision 2, 3, or 4, or the siren provisions of section 169.68; or

(4) operating a motor vehicle marked:

(i) with the word or words "police," "patrolman," "sheriff," "deputy," "trooper," "state patrol," "conservation officer," "agent," or "marshal"; or

(ii) with any lettering, marking, or insignia, or colorable imitation thereof, including, but not limited to, stars, badges, or shields identifying the vehicle as a law enforcement vehicle, and which a reasonable person would believe is a law enforcement vehicle[.]

Subd. 3. **Felony.** Whoever violates this section within five years of a previous violation of this section is guilty of a felony and may be sentenced to imprisonment for not more than two years or to payment of a fine of not more than $4,000, or both.

HIST: 2017 c 95 art 3 s 14

Chapter 10 -- CRIMES AGAINST THE ADMINISTRATION OF JUSTICE

Category 2, Section 5:
2.5.1. Describe the basic organization, purpose, and definitions and principles of the Minnesota Criminal Code.
2.5.5. Given a variety of scenarios, identify indications a particular crime has been committed and identify the elements of that crime.

609.48 PERJURY.

Subdivision 1. **Acts constituting.** Whoever makes a false material statement not believing it to be true in any of the following cases is guilty of perjury and may be sentenced as provided in subdivision 4:

(1) in or for an action, hearing or proceeding of any kind in which the statement is required or authorized by law to be made under oath or affirmation; or

(2) in any writing which is required or authorized by law to be under oath or affirmation;

(3) in any writing made in accordance with section 358.115;

(4) in any writing made according to section 358.116; or

(5) in any other case in which the penalties for perjury are imposed by law and no specific sentence is otherwise provided.

Subd. 2. **Defenses not available.** It is not a defense to a violation of this section that:

(1) The oath or affirmation was taken or administered in an irregular manner; or

(2) The declarant was not competent to give the statement; or

(3) The declarant did not know that the statement was material or believed it to be immaterial; or

(4) The statement was not used or, if used, did not affect the proceeding for which it was made; or

(5) The statement was inadmissible under the law of evidence.

Subd. 3. **Inconsistent statements.** When the declarant has made two inconsistent statements under such circumstances that one or the other must be false and not believed by the declarant when made, it shall be sufficient for conviction under this section to charge and the jury to find that, without determining which, one or the other of such statements was false and not believed by the declarant. The period of limitations for prosecution under this subdivision runs from the first such statement.

Subd. 4. **Sentence.** Whoever violates this section may be sentenced as follows:

(1) If the false statement was made upon the trial of a felony charge, or upon an application for an explosives license or use permit, to imprisonment for not more than seven years or to payment of a fine of not more than $14,000, or both; or

(2) In all other cases, to imprisonment for not more than five years or to payment of a fine of not more than $10,000, or both. * * *

HIST: 1963 c 753 art 1 s 609.48; * * * 2014 c 204 s 9; 2017 c 95 art 2 s 15

609.485 ESCAPE FROM CUSTODY.

Subdivision 1. **Definition.** "Escape" includes departure without lawful authority and failure to return to custody following temporary leave granted for a specific purpose or limited period.

Subd. 2. **Acts prohibited.** Whoever does any of the following may be sentenced as provided in subdivision 4:

(1) escapes while held pursuant to a lawful arrest, in lawful custody on a charge or conviction of a crime, or while held in lawful custody on an allegation or adjudication of a delinquent act;

(2) transfers to another, who is in lawful custody on a charge or conviction of a crime, or introduces into an institution in which the latter is confined, anything usable in making such escape, with intent that it shall be so used;

(3) having another in lawful custody on a charge or conviction of a crime, intentionally permits the other to escape;

(4) escapes while in a facility designated under section 253B.18, subdivision 1, pursuant to a court commitment order after a finding of not guilty by reason of mental illness or mental deficiency of a crime against the person, as defined in section 253B.02, subdivision 4a. Notwithstanding section 609.17, no person may be charged with or convicted of an attempt to commit a violation of this clause;

(5) escapes while in or under the supervision of a facility designated under section 246B.01, subdivision 2a; 246B.02; 253B.18, subdivision 1; 253B.185, subdivision 1, paragraph (d); or Minnesota Statutes 1992, section 526.106;

(6) escapes while on pass status or provisional discharge according to section 253B.18 or 253B.185; or

(7) escapes while a civilly committed sex offender of the Minnesota sex offender program as defined in section 246B.01, subdivision 1a, or subject to a court hold order under section 253B.185.

For purposes of clauses (1) and (7), "escapes while held in lawful custody" or "escapes while a civilly committed sex offender of the Minnesota sex offender program" includes absconding from electronic monitoring or removing an electronic monitoring device from the person's body.

Subd. 3. **Exceptions.** This section does not apply to a person who is free on bail or who is on parole or probation, or subject to a stayed sentence or stayed execution of sentence, unless the person (1) has been taken into actual custody upon revocation of the parole, probation, or stay of the sentence or execution of sentence, (2) is in custody in a county jail or workhouse as a condition of a stayed sentence, or (3) is subject to electronic monitoring as a condition of parole, probation, or supervised release.

Subd. 3a. **Dismissal of charge.** A felony charge brought under subdivision 2, clause (4) shall be dismissed if the person charged voluntarily returns to the facility within 30 days after a reasonable effort has been made to provide written notice to the person that failure to return within 30 days may result in felony charges being filed.

Subd. 4. **Sentence.** (a) Except as otherwise provided in subdivision 3a, whoever violates this section may be sentenced as follows:

(1) if the person who escapes is in lawful custody for a felony, to imprisonment for not more than five years or to payment of a fine of not more than $10,000, or both.

(2) if the person who escapes is in lawful custody after a finding of not guilty by reason of mental illness or mental deficiency of a crime against the person, as defined in section 253B.02, subdivision 4a, to imprisonment for not more than one year and one day or to payment of a fine of not more than $3,000, or both;

(3) if the person who escapes is in lawful custody for a gross misdemeanor or misdemeanor, or if the person who escapes is in lawful custody on an allegation or adjudication of a delinquent act, to imprisonment for not more than one year or to payment of a fine of not more than $3,000, or both;

(4) if the person who escapes is under civil commitment under section 253B.18, to imprisonment for not more than one year and one day or to payment of a fine of not more than $3,000, or both ; or

(5) if the person who escapes is under a court hold, civil commitment, or supervision under section 253B.185 or Minnesota Statutes 1992, section 526.10, to imprisonment for not more than five years or to payment of a fine of not more than $10,000, or both.

(b) If the escape was a violation of subdivision 2, clause (1), (2), or (3), and was effected by violence or threat of violence against a person, the sentence may be increased to not more than twice those permitted in paragraph (a), clauses (1) and (3).

(c) Unless a concurrent term is specified by the court, a sentence under this section shall be consecutive to any sentence previously imposed or which may be imposed for any crime or offense for which the person was in custody when the person escaped.

(d) Notwithstanding clause (c), if a person who was committed to the commissioner of corrections under section 260.185 escapes from the custody of the commissioner while 18 years of age, the person's sentence under this section shall commence on the person's 19th birthday or on the person's date of discharge by the commissioner of corrections, whichever occurs first. However, if the person described in this clause is convicted under this section after becoming 19 years old and after having been discharged by the commissioner, the person's sentence shall commence upon imposition by the sentencing court.

(e) Notwithstanding clause (c), if a person who is in lawful custody on an allegation or adjudication of a delinquent act while 18 years of age escapes from a local juvenile correctional facility, the person's sentence under this section begins on the person's 19th birthday or on the person's date of discharge from the jurisdiction of the juvenile court, whichever occurs first. However, if the person described in this clause is convicted after becoming 19 years old and after discharge from the jurisdiction of the juvenile court, the person's sentence begins upon imposition by the sentencing court.

(f) Notwithstanding paragraph (a), any person who escapes or absconds from electronic monitoring or removes an electric monitoring device from the person's body is guilty of a crime and shall be sentenced to imprisonment for not more than one year or to a payment of a fine of not more than $3,000, or both. A person in lawful custody for a violation of sections 609.185, 609.19, 609.195, 609.20, 609.205, 609.21, 609.221, 609.222, 609.223, 609.2231, 609.342, 609.343, 609.344, 609.345, 609.3451 or civil commitment under section 253B.185, and who escapes or absconds from electronic monitoring or removes an electronic monitoring device while under sentence may be sentenced to imprisonment for not more than five years or to a payment of a fine of not more than $10,000, or both.
HIST: 1963 c 753 art 1 s 609.485; * * * 2011 c 102 art 2 s 3

609.486 COMMISSION OF CRIME WHILE WEARING OR POSSESSING A BULLET-RESISTANT VEST.

A person who commits or attempts to commit a gross misdemeanor or felony while wearing or possessing a bullet-resistant vest is guilty of a felony and, upon conviction, shall be sentenced to imprisonment for not more than five years or to payment of a fine of not more than $10,000, or both. Notwithstanding section 609.04, a prosecution for or conviction under this section is not a bar to conviction of or punishment for any other crime committed by the defendant as part of the same conduct.

As used in this section, "bullet-resistant vest" means a bullet-resistant garment that provides ballistic and trauma protection.
HIST: 1990 c 439 s 1

609.487 FLEEING A PEACE OFFICER IN A MOTOR VEHICLE.

Subdivision 1. **Flee; definition.** For purposes of this section, the term "flee" means to increase speed, extinguish motor vehicle headlights or taillights, refuse to stop the vehicle, or use other means with intent to attempt to elude a peace officer following a signal given by any peace officer to the driver motor vehicle.

Subd. 2. **Peace officer; definition.** For purposes of this section, "peace officer" means:

(1) an employee of a political subdivision or state law enforcement agency who is licensed by the Minnesota board of peace officer standards and training, charged with the prevention and detection of crime and the enforcement of the general criminal laws of the state and who has the full power of arrest, and shall also include the Minnesota state patrol and Minnesota conservation officers;

(2) an employee of a law enforcement agency of a federally recognized tribe, as defined in United States Code, title 25, section 450b(e), who is licensed by the Minnesota board of peace officer standards and training; or

(3) A member of a duly organized state, county, or municipal law enforcement unit of another state charged with the duty to prevent and detect crime and generally enforce criminal laws, and granted full powers of arrest.

Subd. 2a **Motor vehicle; definition.** "Motor vehicle" has the meaning given in section 169.01, subdivision 3, and includes off-road recreational vehicles as defined in section 169A.03, subdivision 16, and motorboats as defined in section 169A.03, subdivision 13.

Subd. 3. **Fleeing an officer.** Whoever by means of a motor vehicle flees or attempts to flee a peace officer who is acting in the lawful discharge of an official duty, and the perpetrator knows or should reasonably know the same to be a peace officer, is guilty of a felony and may be sentenced to imprisonment for not more than three years and one day or to payment of a fine of not more than $5,000, or both.

Subd. 4. **Fleeing an officer; death; bodily injury.** Whoever flees or attempts to flee by means of a motor vehicle a peace officer who is acting in the lawful discharge of an official duty, and the perpetrator knows or should reasonably know the same to be a peace officer, and who in the course of fleeing in a motor vehicle or subsequently by other means causes the death of a human being not constituting murder or manslaughter or any bodily injury to any person other than the perpetrator may be sentenced to imprisonment as follows:

(a) If the course of fleeing results in death, to imprisonment for not more than 40 years or to payment of a fine of not more than $80,000, or both; or

(b) If the course of fleeing results in great bodily harm, to imprisonment for not more than seven years or to payment of a fine of not more than $14,000, or both; or

(c) If the course of fleeing results in substantial bodily harm, to imprisonment for not more than five years or to payment of a fine of not more than $10,000, or both.

Subd. 5. **Revocation; fleeing peace officer offense.** When a person is convicted of operating a motor vehicle in violation of subdivision 3 or 4, or an ordinance in conformity with those subdivisions, the court shall notify the commissioner of public safety and order the commissioner to revoke the driver's license of the person.

Subd. 6. **Fleeing, other than vehicle.** Whoever, for the purpose of avoiding arrest, detention, or investigation, or in order to conceal or destroy potential evidence related to the commission of a crime, attempts to evade or elude a peace officer, who is acting in the lawful discharge of an official duty, by means of running, hiding, or by any other means except fleeing in a motor vehicle, is guilty of a misdemeanor.

HIST: 1981 c 37 s 2; * * * 2011 c 32 s 1

609.49 RELEASE, FAILURE TO APPEAR.

Subdivision 1. **Felony offenders.** (a) A person charged with or convicted of a felony and released from custody, with or without bail or recognizance, who intentionally fails to appear when required after having been notified that a failure to appear for a court appearance is a criminal offense, or after having been released on an order or condition that the releasee personally appear for trial when required with respect to the charge, is guilty of a crime for failure to appear and may be sentenced to not more than one-half of the maximum term of imprisonment or fine, or both, provided for the underlying crime for which the person failed to appear, but this maximum sentence shall, in no case, be less than a term of imprisonment of one year and one day or a fine of $1,500, or both.

(b) A felony charge under this subdivision may be filed upon the person's nonappearance. However, the charge must be dismissed if the person who fails to appear voluntarily surrenders within 48 hours after the time required for appearance. This paragraph does not apply if the offender appears as a result of being apprehended by law enforcement authorities.

Subd. 1a. **Juvenile offenders.** (a) A person who intentionally fails to appear for a juvenile court disposition is guilty of a felony if:

(1) the person was prosecuted in juvenile court for an offense that would have been a felony if committed by an adult;

(2) the juvenile court made findings pursuant to an admission in court or after trial;

(3) the person was released from custody on condition that the person appear in the juvenile court for a disposition in connection with the offense; and

(4) the person was notified that failure to appear is a criminal offense.

(b) A person who violates the provisions of this subdivision is guilty of a felony and may be sentenced to imprisonment for not more than five years or to payment of a fine of not more than $10,000, or both.

Subd. 2. **Gross misdemeanor and misdemeanor offenders.** A person charged with a gross misdemeanor or misdemeanor who intentionally fails to appear in court for trial on the charge after having been notified that a failure to appear for a court appearance is a criminal offense, or after having been released on an order or condition that the releasee personally appear for trial when required with respect to the charge, is guilty of a misdemeanor.

Subd. 3. **Affirmative defense.** If proven by a preponderance of the evidence, it is an affirmative defense to a violation of subdivision 1, 1a, or 2 that the person's failure to appear in court as required was due to circumstances beyond the person's control.

Subd. 4. **Prosecution.** A violation of this section is prosecuted by the prosecuting authority who was responsible for prosecuting the offense in connection with which the person failed to appear in court.

Subd. 5. **Reimbursement for costs.** Upon conviction of a defendant for a violation of subdivision 1 or 2, the court may order as part of the sentence that the defendant pay the costs incurred by the prosecuting authority or governmental agency due to the defendant's failure to appear. The court may order this payment in addition to any other penalty authorized by law which it may impose. A defendant shall pay the entire amount of any restitution ordered and fine imposed before paying costs ordered under this subdivision. The order for payment of these costs may be enforced in the same manner as the sentence, or by execution against property. When collected, the costs must be paid into the treasury of the county of conviction.
HIST: 1963 c 753 art 1 s 609.49; * * * 1999 c 28 s 1-3

609.495 AIDING AN OFFENDER.

Subdivision 1. **Definition of crime.** (a) Whoever harbors, conceals, aids, or assists by word or acts another whom the actor knows or has reason to know has committed a crime under the laws of this or another state or of the United States with intent that such offender shall avoid or escape from arrest, trial, conviction, or punishment, may be sentenced to imprisonment for not more than three years or to payment of a fine of not more than $5,000, or both if the crime committed or attempted by the other person is a felony.

(b) Whoever knowingly harbors, conceals, or aids a person who is on probation, parole, or supervised release because of a felony level conviction and for whom an arrest and detention order has been issued, with intent that the person evade or escape being taken into custody under the order, may be sentenced to imprisonment for not more than three years or to payment of a fine of not more than $5,000, or both. As used in this paragraph, "arrest and detention order" means a written order to take and detain a probationer, parolee, or supervised releasee * * *.

Subd. 2. [Repealed 1996 c 408 art 3 s 40]

Subd. 3. **Obstructing investigation.** Whoever intentionally aids another person whom the actor knows or has reason to know has committed a criminal act, by destroying or concealing evidence of that crime, providing false or misleading information about that crime, receiving the proceeds of that crime, or otherwise obstructing the investigation or prosecution of that crime is an accomplice after the fact and may be sentenced to not more than one-half of the statutory maximum sentence of imprisonment or to payment of a fine of not more than one-half of the maximum fine that could be imposed on the principal offender for the crime of violence. For purposes of this subdivision, "criminal act" means an act that is a crime listed in section 609.11, subdivision 9, under the laws of this or another state, or of the United States, and also includes an act that would be a criminal act if committed by an adult.

Subd. 4. **Taking responsibility for criminal acts.** (a) Unless the person is convicted of the underlying crime, a person who assumes responsibility for a criminal act with the intent to obstruct, impede, or prevent a criminal investigation may be sentenced to not more than one-half of the statutory maximum sentence of imprisonment or to payment of a fine of not more than one-half of the maximum fine that could be imposed on the principal offender for the criminal act.

(b) Nothing in this subdivision shall be construed to impair the right of any individual or group to engage in speech protected by the United States Constitution or the Minnesota Constitution.

Subd. 5. **Venue.** An offense committed under subdivision 1 or 3 may be prosecuted in:

(1) the county where the aiding or obstructing behavior occurred; or

(2) the county where the underlying criminal act occurred.

HIST: 1963 c 753 art 1 s 609.495; * * * 2006 c 260 art 1 s 26; 2016 c 158 art 1 s 204

609.496 CONCEALING CRIMINAL PROCEEDS.

Subdivision 1. **Crime.** A person is guilty of a felony and may be sentenced under subdivision 2 if the person:

(1) conducts a transaction involving a monetary instrument or instruments with a value exceeding $5,000; and

(2) knows or has reason to know that the monetary instrument or instruments represent the proceeds of, or are derived from the proceeds of, the commission of a felony under this chapter or chapter 152 or an offense in another jurisdiction that would be a felony under this chapter or chapter 152 if committed in Minnesota.

Subd. 2. **Penalty.** A person convicted under subdivision 1 may be sentenced to imprisonment for not more than ten years, or to payment of a fine of not more than $100,000, or both.

Subd. 3. **Monetary instrument.** For purposes of this section, "monetary instrument" means United States currency and coin; the currency and coin of a foreign country; a bank check, cashier's check, traveler's check, money order, stock, investment security, or negotiable instrument in bearer form or otherwise in the form by which title to the instrument passes upon delivery; gold, silver, or platinum bullion or coins; and diamonds, emeralds, rubies, or sapphires.

Subd. 4. **Payment of reasonable attorney fees.** Subdivision 1 does not preclude the payment or receipt of reasonable attorney fees.

HIST: 1989 c 286 s 3

609.497 ENGAGING IN A BUSINESS OF CONCEALING CRIMINAL PROCEEDS.

Subdivision 1. **Crime.** A person is guilty of a felony and may be sentenced under subdivision 2 if the person knowingly initiates, organizes, plans, finances, directs, manages, supervises, or otherwise engages in a business that has as a primary or secondary purpose concealing money or property that was gained as a direct result of the commission of a felony under this chapter or chapter 152, or of an offense committed in another jurisdiction that would be a felony under this chapter or chapter 152 if committed in Minnesota.

Subd. 2. **Penalty.** A person convicted under subdivision 1 may be sentenced to imprisonment for not more than 20 years, or to payment of a fine or not more than $1,000,000, or both.

HIST: 1989 c 286 s 4

609.4971 WARNING SUBJECT OF INVESTIGATION.

Whoever, having knowledge that a subpoena has been issued under sections 8.16 and 388.23, and with intent to obstruct, impede, or prevent the investigation for which the subpoena was issued, gives notice or attempts to give notice of the issuance of the subpoena or the production of the documents to a person, may be sentenced to imprisonment for not more than five years or to payment of a fine of not more than $10,000, or both.

HIST: 1989 c 336 art 2 s 4

609.4975 WARNING SUBJECT OF SURVEILLANCE OR SEARCH.

Subdivision 1. **Electronic communication.** Whoever, having knowledge that an investigative or law enforcement officer has been authorized or has applied for authorization under chapter 626A to intercept a wire, oral, or electronic communication, and with intent to obstruct, impede, or prevent interception, gives notice or attempts to give notice of the possible interception to a person, may be sentenced to imprisonment for not more than five years or to payment fine of not more than $10,000, or both.

Subd. 2. **Pen register.** Whoever, having knowledge that an investigative or law enforcement officer has been authorized or has applied for authorization under chapter 626A to install and use a pen register or a trap and trace device and with intent to obstruct, impede, or prevent the purposes for which the installation and use is being made, gives notice or attempts to give notice of the installation or use to any person, may be sentenced to imprisonment for not more than five years or to payment of a fine of not more than $10,000, or both.

Subd. 3. **Search warrant.** Whoever, having knowledge that a peace officer has been issued or has applied for the issuance of a search warrant, and with intent to obstruct, impede, or prevent the search, gives notice or attempts to give notice of the search or search warrant to any person, may be sentenced to imprisonment for not more than five years or to payment of a fine of not more than $10,000, or both.

HIST: 1989 c 336 art 2 s 3; 1990 c 426 art 2 s 1

609.498 TAMPERING WITH A WITNESS.

Subdivision 1. **Tampering with a witness in the first degree.** Whoever does any of the following is guilty of tampering with a witness in the first degree and may be sentenced as provided in subdivision 1a:

(a) intentionally prevents or dissuades or intentionally attempts to prevent or dissuade by means of force or threats of injury to any person or property, a person who is or may become a witness from attending or testifying at any trial, proceeding, or inquiry authorized by law;

(b) by means of force or threats of injury to any person or property, intentionally coerces or attempts to coerce a person who is or may become a witness to testify falsely at any trial, proceeding, or inquiry authorized by law;

(c) intentionally causes injury or threatens to cause injury to any person or property in retaliation against a person who was summoned as a witness at any trial, proceeding, or inquiry authorized by law, within a year following that trial, proceeding, or inquiry or within a year following the actor's release from incarceration, whichever is later;

(d) intentionally prevents or dissuades or attempts to prevent or dissuade, by means of force or threats of injury to any person or property, a person from providing information to law enforcement authorities concerning a crime;

(e) by means of force or threats of injury to any person or property, intentionally coerces or attempts to coerce a person to provide false information concerning a crime to law enforcement authorities; or

(f) intentionally causes injury or threatens to cause injury to any person or property in retaliation against a person who has provided information to law enforcement authorities concerning a crime within a year of that person providing the information or within a year of the actor's release from incarceration, whichever is later.

Subd. 1a. **Penalty.** Whoever violates subdivision 1 may be sentenced to imprisonment for not more than five years or to payment of a fine not to exceed $10,000.

Subd. 1b. **Aggravated first-degree witness tampering.** (a) A person is guilty of aggravated first-degree witness tampering if the person causes or, by means of an implicit or explicit credible threat, threatens to cause great bodily harm or death to another in the course of committing any of the following acts intentionally:

(1) preventing or dissuading or attempting to prevent or dissuade a person who is or may become a witness from attending or testifying at any criminal trial or proceeding;

(2) coercing or attempting to coerce a person who is or may become a witness to testify falsely at any criminal trial or proceeding;

(3) retaliating against a person who was summoned as a witness at any criminal trial or proceeding within a year following that trial or proceeding or within a year following the actor's release from incarceration, whichever is later;

(4) preventing or dissuading or attempting to prevent or dissuade a person from providing information to law enforcement authorities concerning a crime;

(5) coercing or attempting to coerce a person to provide false information concerning a crime to law enforcement authorities; or

(6) retaliating against any person who has provided information to law enforcement authorities concerning a crime within a year of that person providing the information or within a year of the actor's release from incarceration, whichever is later.

(b) A person convicted of committing any act prohibited by paragraph (a) may be sentenced to imprisonment for not more than 20 years or to payment of a fine of not more than $30,000, or both.

Subd. 2. **Tampering with a witness in the second degree.** Whoever does any of the following is guilty of tampering with a witness in the second degree and may be sentenced as provided in subdivision 3:

(a) intentionally prevents or dissuades or intentionally attempts to prevent or dissuade by means of any act described in section 609.27, subdivision 1, clause (3), (4), or (5), a person who is or may become a witness from attending or testifying at any trial, proceeding, or inquiry authorized by law;

(b) by means of any act described in section 609.27, subdivision 1, clause (3), (4), or (5), intentionally coerces or attempts to coerce a person who is or may become a witness to testify falsely at any trial, proceeding, or inquiry authorized by law;

(c) intentionally prevents or dissuades or attempts to prevent or dissuade by means of any act described in section 609.27, subdivision 1, clause (3), (4), or (5), a person from providing information to law enforcement authorities concerning a crime; or

(d) by means of any act described in section 609.27, subdivision 1, clause (3), (4), or (5), intentionally coerces or attempts to coerce a person to provide false information concerning a crime to law enforcement authorities.

Subd. 2a. **Tampering with a witness in the third degree.** (a) Unless a greater penalty is applicable under subdivision 1, 1b, or 2, whoever does any of the following is guilty of tampering with a witness in the third degree and may be sentenced as provided in subdivision 3:

(1) intentionally prevents or dissuades or intentionally attempts to prevent or dissuade by means of intimidation, a person who is or may become a witness from attending or testifying at any trial, proceeding, or inquiry authorized by law;

(2) by means of intimidation, intentionally influences or attempts to influence a person who is or may become a witness to testify falsely at any trial, proceeding, or inquiry authorized by law;

(3) intentionally prevents or dissuades or attempts to prevent or dissuade by means of intimidation, a person from providing information to law enforcement authorities concerning a crime; or

(4) by means of intimidation, intentionally influences or attempts to influence a person to provide false information concerning a crime to law enforcement authorities.

(b) In a prosecution under this subdivision, proof of intimidation may be based on a specific act or on the totality of the circumstances.

Subd. 3. **Sentence.** (a) Whoever violates subdivision 2 is guilty of a gross misdemeanor.

(b) Whoever violates subdivision 2a is guilty of a misdemeanor.

Subd. 4. **No bar to conviction.** Notwithstanding sections 609.035 or 609.04, a prosecution for or conviction of the crime of aggravated first-degree witness tampering is not a bar to conviction of or punishment for any other crime.

HIST: 1976 c 178 s 1; * * * 2010 c 299 s 6,7

609.50 OBSTRUCTING LEGAL PROCESS, ARREST, OR FIREFIGHTING.

Subdivision 1. **Crime.** Whoever intentionally does any of the following may be sentenced as provided in subdivision 2:

(1) obstructs, hinders, or prevents the lawful execution of any legal process, civil or criminal, or apprehension of another on a charge or conviction of a criminal offense;

(2) obstructs, resists, or interferes with a peace officer while the officer is engaged in the performance of official duties;

(3) interferes with or obstructs a firefighter while the firefighter is engaged in the performance of official duties;

(4) interferes with or obstructs a member of an ambulance service personnel crew * * * who is providing, or attempting to provide, emergency care; or

(5) by force or threat of force endeavors to obstruct any employee of the department of revenue while the employee is lawfully engaged in the performance of official duties for the purpose of deterring or interfering with the performance of those duties.

Subd. 2. **Penalty.** A person convicted of violating subdivision 1 may be sentenced as follows:

(1) if (i) the person knew or had reason to know that the act created a risk of death, substantial bodily harm, or serious property damage; or (ii) the act caused death, substantial bodily harm, or serious property damage; or to imprisonment for not more than five years or to payment of a fine of not more than $10,000, or both;

(2) if the act was accompanied by force or violence or the threat thereof, and is not otherwise covered by clause (1), to imprisonment for not more than one year or to payment of a fine of not more than $3,000, or both; or

(3) in other cases to imprisonment for not more than 90 days or to payment of a fine of not more than $1,000, or both.

HIST: 1963 c 753 art 1 s 609.50; * * * 2008 c 304 s 1

609.502 INTERFERENCE WITH DEAD BODY; REPORTING.

Subdivision 1. **Concealing evidence.** A person is guilty of a crime and may be sentenced under subdivision 1a if the person interferes with the body or scene of death with intent to:

(1) conceal the body;

(2) conceal evidence; or

(3) otherwise mislead the coroner or medical examiner.

Subd. 1a. **Penalty.** A person convicted under subdivision 1, clause (2) or (3), is guilty of a gross misdemeanor. A person convicted under subdivision 1, clause (1), may be sentenced to imprisonment for not more than three years or to a payment of a fine of not more than $5,000 or both. * * *

Subd. 2. **Failure to report.** (a) A person in charge of a cemetery who has knowledge that the body of a deceased person interred in the cemetery has been unlawfully removed shall:

(1) immediately report the occurrence to local law enforcement authorities; and

(2) inform the next of kin of the deceased person, if known, within three business days of the discovery of the body's removal unless the person making the report has been instructed in writing by law enforcement authorities that informing the next of kin would compromise an active law enforcement investigation.

(b) A person who violates either clause (1) or (2) is guilty of a misdemeanor.

HIST: 1976 c 257 s 2; 1990 c 402 s 2; 2016 c 175 s 1,2

609.504 DISARMING A PEACE OFFICER.

Subdivision 1. **Definition.** As used in this section, "defensive device" includes a firearm; a dangerous weapon; an authorized tear gas compound * * * ; an electronic incapacitation device * * * ; a club or baton; and any item issued by a peace officer's employer to the officer to assist in the officer's protection.

Subd. 2. **Crime described.** Whoever intentionally takes possession of a defensive device being carried by a peace officer or from the area within the officer's immediate control, without the officer's consent while the officer is engaged in the performance of official duties, is guilty of a crime and may be sentenced as provided in subdivision 3.

Subd. 3. **Penalty.** A person who violates this section is guilty of a felony and may be sentenced to imprisonment of not more than five years, payment of a fine of not more than $10,000, or both.

HIST: 2008 c 304 s 2

609.505 FALSELY REPORTING CRIME.

Subdivision 1. **False reporting.** Whoever informs a law enforcement officer that a crime has been committed or otherwise provides information to an on-duty peace officer, knowing that the person is a peace officer, regarding the conduct of others, knowing that it is false and intending that the officer shall act in reliance upon it, is guilty of a misdemeanor. A person who is convicted a second or subsequent time under this section is guilty of a gross misdemeanor.

Subd. 2. **Reporting police misconduct.** (a) Whoever informs, or causes information to communicated to, a peace officer, whose responsibilities include investigating or reporting police misconduct, that a peace officer * * * has committed an act of police misconduct, knowing that the information is false, is guilty of a crime and may sentenced as follows:

(1) up to the maximum provided for a misdemeanor if the false information does not allege a criminal act; or

(2) up to the maximum provided for a gross misdemeanor if the false information alleges a criminal act.

(b) The court shall order any person convicted of a violation of this subdivision to make full restitution of all reasonable expenses incurred in the investigation of the false allegation unless the court makes a specific written finding that restitution would be inappropriate under the circumstances. A restitution award may not exceed $3,000.

HIST: 1963 c 753 art 1 s 609.505; * * * 2005 c 136 art 17 s 30

609.506 PROHIBITING GIVING PEACE OFFICER FALSE NAME.

Subdivision 1. **Misdemeanor.** Whoever with intent to obstruct justice gives a fictitious name other than a nickname, or gives a false date of birth, or false or fraudulently altered identification card to a peace officer, as defined in section 626.84, subdivision 1, paragraph (c), when that officer makes inquiries incident to a lawful investigatory stop or lawful arrest, or inquiries incident to executing any other duty imposed by law, is guilty of a misdemeanor.

Subd. 2. **Gross misdemeanor.** Whoever with intent to obstruct justice gives the name and date of birth of another person to a peace officer, as defined in subdivision 1, when the officer makes inquiries incident to a lawful investigatory stop or lawful arrest, or inquiries incident to executing any other duty imposed by law, is guilty of a gross misdemeanor.

Subd. 3. **Gross misdemeanor.** Whoever in any criminal proceeding with intent to obstruct justice gives a fictitious name, other than a nickname, or gives a false date of birth to a court official is guilty of a misdemeanor. Whoever in any criminal proceeding with intent to obstruct justice gives the name and date of birth of another person to a court official is guilty of a gross misdemeanor. "Court official" includes a judge, referee, court administrator, or any employee of the court.

HIST: 1987 c 127 s 1; 1988 c 681 s 17; 1989 c 209 art 1 s 45

609.507 FALSELY REPORTING CHILD ABUSE.

A person is guilty of a misdemeanor who:

(1) informs another person that a person has committed sexual abuse, physical abuse, or neglect of a child, as defined in section 626.556, subdivision 2 260E.03;

(2) knows that the allegation is false or is without reason to believe that the alleged abuser committed the abuse or neglect; and

(3) has the intent that the information influence a custody hearing.

HIST: 1988 c 662 s 3; 1Sp2020 c 2 art 8 s 140

609.508 FALSE INFORMATION TO FINANCIAL INSTITUTION.

A person is guilty of a misdemeanor if the person informs a financial institution, orally or in writing, that one or more of the person's blank checks or debit cards have been lost or stolen, knowing or having reason to know that the information is false.
HIST: 2000 c 354 s 2

609.51 SIMULATING LEGAL PROCESS.

Subdivision 1. **Acts prohibited.** Whoever does any of the following is guilty of a misdemeanor:

(1) Sends or delivers to another any document which simulates a summons, complaint, or court process with intent thereby to induce payment of a claim; or

(2) Prints, distributes, or offers for sale any such document knowing or intending that it shall be so used.

Subd. 2. **Exceptions.** This section does not prohibit the printing, distribution or sale of blank forms of legal documents for use in judicial proceedings.
HIST: 1963 c 753 art 1 s 609.51; 1971 c 23 s 53

609.42 BRIBERY.

Subdivision 1. **Acts constituting** Whoever does any of the following is guilty of bribery and may be sentenced to imprisonment for not more than ten years or to payment of a fine of not more than $20,000, or both:

(1) Offers, gives, or promises to give, directly or indirectly, to any person who is a public officer or employee any benefit, reward or consideration to which the person is not legally entitled with intent thereby to influence the person's performance of the powers or duties as such officer or employee; or

(2) Being a public officer or employee, requests, receives or agrees to receive, directly or indirectly, any such benefit, reward or consideration upon the understanding that it will have such an influence; or

(3) Offers, gives, or promises to give, directly or indirectly any such benefit, reward, or consideration to a person who is a witness or about to become a witness in a proceeding before a judicial or hearing officer, with intent that the person's testimony be influenced thereby, or that the person will not appear at the proceeding; or

(4) As a person who is, or is about to become such witness requests, receives, or agrees to receive, directly or indirectly, any such benefit, reward, or consideration upon the understanding that the person's testimony will be so influenced, or that the person will not appear at the proceeding; or

(5) Accepts directly or indirectly a benefit, reward or consideration upon an agreement or understanding, express or implied, that the acceptor will refrain from giving information that may lead to the prosecution of a crime or purported crime or that the acceptor will abstain from, discontinue, or delay prosecution therefor, except in a case where a compromise is allowed by law.

Subd. 2. **Forfeiture of office.** Any public officer who is convicted of violating or attempting to violate subdivision 1 shall forfeit the public officer's office and be forever disqualified from holding public office under the state.
HIST: 1963 c 753 art 1 s 609.42; 1976 c 178 s 2; 1984 c 628 art 3 s 11; 1986 c 444

609.515 MISCONDUCT OF JUDICIAL OR HEARING OFFICER.

Whoever does any of the following, when the act is not in violation of section 609.42, is guilty of a misdemeanor:

(1) Being a judicial or hearing officer, does either of the following:

(a) Agrees with or promises another to determine a cause or controversy or issue pending or to be brought before the office for or against any party; or

(b) Intentionally obtains or receives and uses information relating thereto contrary to the regular course of the proceeding.

(2) Induces a judicial or hearing officer to act contrary to the provisions of this section.
HIST: 1963 c 753 art 1 s 609.515; 1971 c 23 s 54; 1986 c 444

609.5151 DISSEMINATION OF PERSONAL INFORMATION ABOUT LAW ENFORCEMENT PROHIBITED; PENALTY

Subdivision 1. **Definitions.** As used in this section:

(1) "family or household member" has the meaning given in section 518B.01, subdivision 2;

(2) "law enforcement official" means both peace officers as defined in section 626.84, subdivision 1, and persons employed by a law enforcement agency; and

(3) "personal information" means a home address, directions to a home, or photographs of a home.

Subd. 2. **Crime described.** (a) It is a misdemeanor for a person to knowingly and without consent make publicly available, including but not limited to through the Internet, personal information about a law enforcement official or an official's family or household member, if:

(1) the dissemination poses an imminent and serious threat to the official's safety or the safety of an official's family or household member; and

(2) the person making the information publicly available knows or reasonably should know of the imminent and serious threat.

(b) A person is guilty of a gross misdemeanor if the person violates paragraph (a) and a law enforcement official or an official's family or household member suffers great bodily harm or death as a result of the violation.

(c) A person who is convicted of a second or subsequent violation of this section is guilty of a gross misdemeanor.

EFFECTIVE DATE. This section is effective September 15, 2021, and applies to crimes committed on or after that date.
HIST: 1Sp2021 c 11 art 2 s 40

Chapter 11 -- THEFT AND RELATED CRIMES

Category 2, Section 5:
2.5.1. Describe the basic organization, purpose, and definitions and principles of the Minnesota Criminal Code.
2.5.5. Given a variety of scenarios, identify indications a particular crime has been committed and identify the elements of that crime.

609.52 THEFT
Subdivision 1. **Definitions.** In this section:

(1) "Property" means all forms of tangible property, whether real or personal, without limitation including documents of value, electricity, gas, water, corpses, domestic animals, dogs, pets, fowl, and heat supplied by pipe or conduit by municipalities or public utility companies and articles, as defined in clause (4), representing trade secrets, which articles shall be deemed for the purposes of Extra Session Laws 1967, chapter 15 to include any trade secret represented by the article.

(2) "Movable property" is property whose physical location can be changed, including without limitation things growing on, affixed to, or found in land.

(3) "Value" means the retail market value at the time of the theft, or if the retail market value cannot be ascertained, the cost of replacement of the property within a reasonable time after the theft, or in the case of a theft or the making of a copy of an article representing a trade secret, where the retail market value or replacement cost cannot be ascertained, any reasonable value representing the damage to the owner which the owner has suffered by reason of losing an advantage over those who do not know of or use the trade secret. For a check, draft, or other order for the payment of money, "value" means the amount of money promised or ordered to be paid under the terms of the check, draft, or other order. For a theft committed within the meaning of subdivision 2, paragraph (a), clause (5), items (i) and (ii), if the property has been restored to the owner, "value" means the value of the use of the property or the damage which it sustained, whichever is greater, while the owner was deprived of its possession, but not exceeding the value otherwise provided herein. For a theft committed within the meaning of subdivision 2, clause (9), if the property has been restored to the owner, "value" means the rental value of the property, determined at the rental rate contracted by the defendant or, if no rental rate was contracted, the rental rate customarily charged by the owner for use of the property, plus any damage that occurred to the property while the owner was deprived of its possession, but not exceeding the total retail value of the property at the time of rental. For a theft committed within the meaning of subdivision 2, clause (19), "value" means the difference between wages legally required to be reported or paid to an employee and the amount actually reported or paid to the employee.

(4) "Article" means any object, material, device or substance, including any writing, record, recording, drawing, sample specimen, prototype, model, photograph, microorganism, blueprint or map, or any copy of any of the foregoing.

(5) "Representing" means describing, depicting, containing, constituting, reflecting or recording.

(6) "Trade secret" means information, including a formula, pattern, compilation, program, device, method, technique, or process, that:

(i) derives independent economic value, actual or potential, from not being generally known to, and not being readily ascertainable by proper means by, other persons who can obtain economic value from its disclosure or use, and

(ii) is the subject of efforts that are reasonable under the circumstances to maintain its secrecy.

(7) "Copy" means any facsimile, replica, photograph or other reproduction of an article, and any note, drawing, or sketch made of or from an article while in the presence of the article.

(8) "Property of another" includes property in which the actor is co-owner or has a lien, pledge, bailment, or lease or other subordinate interest, property transferred by the actor in circumstances which are known to the actor and which make the transfer fraudulent as defined in section 513.44, property possessed pursuant to a short-term rental contract, and property of a partnership of which the actor is a member, unless the actor and the victim are husband and wife. It does not include property in which the actor asserts in good faith a claim as a collection fee or commission out of property or funds recovered, or by virtue of a lien, setoff, or counterclaim.

(9) "Services" include but are not limited to labor, professional services, transportation services, electronic computer services, the supplying of hotel accommodations, restaurant services, entertainment services, advertising services, telecommunication services, and the supplying of equipment for use including rental of personal property or equipment.

(10) "Motor vehicle" means a self-propelled device for moving persons or property or pulling implements from one place to another, whether the device is operated on land, rails, water, or in the air.

(11) "Motor fuel" has the meaning given in section 604.15, subdivision 1.

(12) "Retailer" has the meaning given in section 604.15, subdivision 1.

(13) "Wage theft" occurs when an employer with intent to defraud:

(i) fails to pay an employee all wages, salary, gratuities, earnings, or commissions at the employee's rate or rates of pay or at the rate or rates required by law, including any applicable statute, regulation, rule, ordinance, government resolution or policy, contract, or other legal authority, whichever rate of pay is greater;

(ii) directly or indirectly causes any employee to give a receipt for wages for a greater amount than that actually paid to the employee for services rendered;

(iii) directly or indirectly demands or receives from any employee any rebate or refund from the wages owed the employee under contract of employment with the employer; or

(iv) makes or attempts to make it appear in any manner that the wages paid to any employee were greater than the amount actually paid to the employee.

(14) "Employer" means any individual, partnership, association, corporation, business trust, or any person or group of persons acting directly or indirectly in the interest of an employer in relation to an employee.

(15) "Employee" means any individual employed by an employer.

Subd. 2. **Acts constituting theft.** Whoever does any of the following commits theft and may be sentenced as provided in subdivision 3:

(1) intentionally and without claim of right takes, uses, transfers, conceals or retains possession of movable property of another without the other's consent and with intent to deprive the owner permanently of possession of the property; or

(2) with or without having a legal interest in movable property, intentionally and without consent, takes the property out of the possession of a pledgee or other person having a superior right of possession, with intent thereby to deprive the pledgee or other person permanently of the possession of the property; or

(3) obtains for the actor or another the possession, custody, or title to property of or performance of services by a third person by intentionally deceiving the third person with a false representation which is known to be false, made with intent to defraud, and which does defraud the person to whom it is made. "False representation" includes without limitation:

(i) the issuance of a check, draft, or order for the payment of money, except a forged check as defined in section 609.631, or the delivery of property knowing that the actor is not entitled to draw upon the drawee therefor or to order the payment or delivery thereof; or

(ii) a promise made with intent not to perform. Failure to perform is not evidence of intent not to perform unless corroborated by other substantial evidence; or

(iii) the preparation or filing of a claim for reimbursement, a rate application, or a cost report used to establish a rate or claim for payment for medical care provided to a recipient of medical assistance under chapter 256B, which intentionally and falsely states the costs of or actual services provided by a vendor of medical care; or

(iv) the preparation or filing of a claim for reimbursement for providing treatment or supplies required to be furnished to an employee under section 176.135 which intentionally and falsely states the costs of or actual treatment or supplies provided; or

(v) the preparation or filing of a claim for reimbursement for providing treatment or supplies required to be furnished to an employee under section 176.135 for treatment or supplies that the provider knew were medically unnecessary, inappropriate, or excessive; or

(4) by swindling, whether by artifice, trick, device, or any other means, obtains property or services from another person; or

(5) intentionally commits any of the acts listed in this subdivision but with intent to exercise temporary control only and:

(i) the control exercised manifests an indifference to the rights of the owner or the restoration of the property to the owner; or

(ii) the actor pledges or otherwise attempts to subject the property to an adverse claim; or

(iii) the actor intends to restore the property only on condition that the owner pay a reward or buy back or make other compensation; or

(6) finds lost property and, knowing or having reasonable means of ascertaining the true owner, appropriates it to the finder's own use or to that of another not entitled thereto without first having made reasonable effort to find the owner and offer and surrender the property to the owner; or

(7) intentionally obtains property or services, offered upon the deposit of a sum of money or tokens in a coin or token operated machine or other receptacle, without making the required deposit or otherwise obtaining the consent of the owner; or

(8) intentionally and without claim of right converts any article representing a trade secret, knowing it to be such, to the actor's own use or that of another person or makes a copy of an article representing a trade secret, knowing it to be such, and intentionally and without claim of right converts the same to the actor's own use or that of another person. It shall be a complete defense to any prosecution under this clause for the defendant to show that information comprising the trade secret was rightfully known or available to the defendant from a source other than the owner of the trade secret; or

(9) leases or rents personal property under a written instrument and who:

(i) with intent to place the property beyond the control of the lessor conceals or aids or abets the concealment of the property or any part thereof;

(ii) who sells, conveys, or encumbers the property or any part thereof without the written consent of the lessor, without informing the person to whom the lessee sells, conveys, or encumbers that the same is subject to such lease with intent to deprive the lessor of possession thereof; or

(iii) does not return the property to the lessor at the end of the lease or rental term, plus agreed upon extensions, with intent to wrongfully deprive the lessor of possession of the property; or

(iv) returns the property to the lessor at the end of the lease or rental term, plus agreed upon extensions, but does not pay the lease or rental charges agreed upon in the written instrument, with intent to wrongfully deprive the lessor of the agreed upon charges.

For the purposes of items (iii) and (iv), the value of the property must be at least $100.

Evidence that a lessee used a false, fictitious, or not current name, address, or place of employment in obtaining the property or fails or refuses to return the property or pay the rental contract charges to lessor within five days after written demand for the return has been served personally in the manner provided for service of process of a civil action or sent by certified mail to the last known address of the lessee, whichever shall occur later, shall be evidence of intent to violate this clause. Service by certified mail shall be deemed to be complete upon deposit in the United States mail of such demand, postpaid and addressed to the person at the address for the person set forth in the lease or rental agreement, or, in the absence of the address, to the person's last known place of residence; or

(10) alters, removes, or obliterates numbers or symbols placed on movable property for purpose of identification by the owner or person who has legal custody or right to possession thereof with the intent to prevent identification, if the person who alters, removes, or obliterates the numbers or symbols is not the owner and does not have the permission of the owner to make the alteration, removal, or obliteration; or

(11) with the intent to prevent the identification of property involved, so as to deprive the rightful owner of possession thereof, alters or removes any permanent serial number, permanent distinguishing number or manufacturer's identification number on personal property or possesses, sells or buys any personal property knowing or having reason to know that the permanent serial number, permanent distinguishing number or manufacturer's identification number has been removed or altered; or

(12) intentionally deprives another of a lawful charge for cable television service by:

(i) making or using or attempting to make or use an unauthorized external connection outside the individual dwelling unit whether physical, electrical, acoustical, inductive, or other connection, or by

(ii) attaching any unauthorized device to any cable, wire, microwave, or other component of a licensed cable communications system as defined in chapter 238. Nothing herein shall be construed to prohibit the electronic video rerecording of program material transmitted on the cable communications system by a subscriber for fair use as defined by Public Law Number 94-553, section 107; or

(13) except as provided in paragraphs (12) and (14), obtains the services of another with the intention of receiving those services without making the agreed or reasonably expected payment of money or other consideration; or

(14) intentionally deprives another of a lawful charge for telecommunications service by:

(i) making, using, or attempting to make or use an unauthorized connection whether physical, electrical, by wire, microwave, radio, or other means to a component of a local telecommunication system as provided in chapter 237; or

(ii) attaching an unauthorized device to a cable, wire, microwave, radio, or other component of a local telecommunication system as provided in chapter 237.

The existence of an unauthorized connection is prima facie evidence that the occupier of the premises:

(i) made or was aware of the connection; and

(ii) was aware that the connection was unauthorized; or

(15) with intent to defraud, diverts corporate property other than in accordance with general business purposes or for purposes other than those specified in the corporation's articles of incorporation; or

(16) with intent to defraud, authorizes or causes a corporation to make a distribution in violation of section 302A.551, or any other state law in conformity with it; or

(17) takes or drives a motor vehicle without the consent of the owner or an authorized agent of the owner, knowing or having reason to know that the owner or an authorized agent of the owner did not give consent; or

(18) intentionally, and without claim of right, takes motor fuel from a retailer without the retailer's consent and with intent to deprive the retailer permanently of possession of the fuel by driving a motor vehicle from the premises of the retailer without having paid for the fuel dispensed into the vehicle; or

(19) commits wage theft under subdivision 1, clause (13).

Proof that the driver of a motor vehicle into which motor fuel was dispensed drove the vehicle from the premises of the retailer without having paid for the fuel permits the factfinder to infer that the driver acted intentionally and without claim of right, and the driver intended to deprive the retailer permanently of possession of the fuel. This paragraph does not apply if: (1) payment has been made to the retailer within 30 days of the receipt of notice of nonpayment under section 604.15; or (2) a written notice as described in section 604.15, subdivision 4, disputing the retailer's claim, has been sent. This paragraph does not apply to the owner of a motor vehicle if the vehicle or the vehicle's license plate has been reported stolen before the theft of the fuel.

Subd. 3. **Sentence.** Whoever commits theft may be sentenced as follows:

(1) to imprisonment for not more than 20 years or to payment of a fine of not more than $100,000, or both, if the property is a firearm, or the value of the property or services stolen is more than $35,000 and the conviction is for a violation of subdivision 2, clause (3), (4), (15), (16), or (19) or section 609.2335, subdivision 1, clause (1) or (2), item (i); or

(2) to imprisonment for not more than ten years or to payment of a fine of not more than $20,000, or both, if the value of the property or services stolen exceeds $5,000, or if the property stolen was an article representing a trade secret, an explosive or incendiary device, or a controlled substance listed in schedule I or II pursuant to section 152.02 with the exception of marijuana; or

(3) to imprisonment for not more than five years or to payment of a fine of not more than $10,000, or both, if any of the following circumstances exist:

(a) the value of the property or services stolen is more than $1,000 but not more than $5,000; or

(b) the property stolen was a controlled substance listed in schedule III, IV, or V pursuant to section 152.02; or

(c) the value of the property or services stolen is more than $500 but not more than $1,000 and the person has been convicted within the preceding five years for an offense under this section, section 256.98; 268.18, subdivision 3; 609.24; 609.245; 609.53; 609.582, subdivision 1, 2, or 3; 609.625; 609.63; 609.631; or 609.821, or a statute from another state, the United States, or a foreign jurisdiction, in conformity with any of those sections, and the person received a felony or gross misdemeanor sentence for the offense, or a sentence that was stayed under section 609.135 if the offense to which a plea was entered would allow imposition of a felony or gross misdemeanor sentence; or

(d) the value of the property or services stolen is not more than $1,000, and any of the following circumstances exist:

(i) the property is taken from the person of another or from a corpse, or grave or coffin containing a corpse; or

(ii) the property is a record of a court or officer, or a writing, instrument or record kept, filed or deposited according to law with or in the keeping of any public officer or office; or

(iii) the property is taken from a burning building, abandoned, or vacant building or upon its removal therefrom, or from an area of destruction caused by civil disaster, riot, bombing, or the proximity of battle; or

(iv) the property consists of public funds belonging to the state or to any political subdivision or agency thereof; or

(v) the property stolen is a motor vehicle; or

(4) to imprisonment for not more than one year or to payment of a fine of not more than $3,000, or both, if the value of the property or services stolen is more than $500 but not more than $1,000; or

(5) in all other cases where the value of the property or services stolen is $500 or less, to imprisonment for not more than 90 days or to payment of a fine of not more than $1,000, or both, provided, however, in any prosecution under subdivision 2, clauses (1), (2), (3), (4), (13), and (19), the value of the money or property or services received by the defendant in violation of any one or more of the above provisions within any six-month period may be aggregated and the defendant charged accordingly in applying the provisions of this subdivision; provided that when two or more offenses are committed by the same person in two or more counties, the accused may be prosecuted in any county in which one of the offenses was committed for all of the offenses aggregated under this paragraph.

Subd. 3a. **Enhanced penalty.** If a violation of this section creates a reasonably foreseeable risk of bodily harm to another, the penalties described in subdivision 3 are enhanced as follows:

(1) if the penalty is a misdemeanor or a gross misdemeanor, the person is guilty of a felony and may be sentenced to imprisonment for not more than three years or to payment of a fine of not more than $5,000, or both; and

(2) if the penalty is a felony, the statutory maximum sentence for the offense is 50 percent longer than for the underlying crime.

Subd. 4. **Wrongfully obtained public assistance; consideration of disqualification.** When determining the sentence for a person convicted of theft by wrongfully obtaining public assistance, as defined in section 256.98, subdivision 1, the court shall consider the fact that, under section 256.98, subdivision 8, the person will be disqualified from receiving public assistance as a result of the person's conviction.

HIST: 1963 c 753 art 1 s 609.52; * * * 2012 c 173 s 5,6; 1Sp2019 c 7 art 3 s 14-16; 2020 c 83 art 1 s 92

609.521 POSSESSION OF SHOPLIFTING GEAR.

(a) As used in this section, an "electronic article surveillance system" means any electronic device or devices that are designed to detect the unauthorized removal of marked merchandise from a store.

(b) Whoever has in possession any device, gear, or instrument designed to assist in shoplifting or defeating an electronic article surveillance system with intent to use the same to shoplift and thereby commit theft may be sentenced to imprisonment for not more than three years or to payment of a fine of not more than $5,000, or both.

HIST: 1975 c 314 s 1; * * * 1Sp2001 c 8 art 8 s 26

609.523 RETURN OF STOLEN PROPERTY TO OWNERS.

Subdivision 1. **Photographic record.** Photographs of property, as defined in section 609.52, subdivision 1, over which a person is alleged to have exerted unauthorized control or to have otherwise obtained unlawfully, are competent evidence if the photographs are admissible into evidence under all rules of law governing the admissibility of photographs into evidence. The photographic record, when satisfactorily identified, is as admissible in evidence as the property itself.
* * *

Subd. 3. **Return of property.** A law enforcement agency which is holding property over which a person is alleged to have exerted unauthorized control or to have otherwise obtained unlawfully may return that property to its owner[.]
* * *

HIST: 1982 c 539 s 1

609.525 BRINGING STOLEN GOODS INTO STATE.

Subdivision 1. **Crime.** Whoever brings property into the state which the actor has stolen outside the state, or received outside of the state knowing it to have been stolen, may be sentenced in accordance with the provisions of section 609.52, subdivision 3. The actor may be charged, indicted, and tried in any county, but not more than one county, into or through which the actor has brought such property.

Subd. 2. **Defining stolen property.** Property is stolen within the meaning of this section if the act by which the owner was deprived of property was a criminal offense under the laws of the state in which the act was committed and would constitute a theft under this chapter if the act had been committed in this state.

HIST: 1963 c 753 art 1 s 609.525; 1986 c 444

609.526 PRECIOUS METAL OR SCRAP METAL DEALERS; RECEIVING STOLEN PROPERTY.
* * *

Subd. 2. **Crime defined.** Any precious metal dealer or scrap metal dealer or any person employed by a dealer, who receives, possesses, transfers, buys, or conceals any stolen property or property obtained by robbery, knowing or having reason to know the property was stolen or obtained by robbery, may be sentenced as follows:

(1) if the value of the property received, bought, or concealed is $1,000 or more, to imprisonment for not more than ten years or to payment of a fine of not more than $50,000, or both;

(2) if the value of the property received, bought, or concealed is less than $1,000 but more than $500, to imprisonment for not more than three years or to payment of a fine of not more than $25,000, or both;

(3) if the value of the property received, bought, or concealed is $500 or less, to imprisonment for not more than 90 days or to payment of a fine of not more than $1,000, or both.

Any person convicted of violating this section a second or subsequent time within a period of one year may be sentenced as provided in clause (1).
HIST: 1989 c 290 art 7 s 6; 2004 c 228 art 1 s 72; 2007 c 54 art 2 s 10

609.527 IDENTITY THEFT.

Subdivision 1. **Definitions.** (a) As used in this section, the following terms have the meanings given them in this subdivision.

(b) "Direct victim" means any person or entity described in section 611A.01, paragraph (b), whose identity has been transferred, used, or possessed in violation of this section.

(c) "False pretense" means any false, fictitious, misleading, or fraudulent information or pretense or pretext depicting or including or deceptively similar to the name, logo, Web site address, e-mail address, postal address, telephone number, or and other identifying information of a for-profit or not-for-profit business or organization or of a government agency, to which the user has no legitimate claim of right.

(d) "Identity" means any name, number, or data transmission that may be used, alone or in conjunction with any other information, to identify a specific individual or entity, including any of the following:

(1) a name, social security number, date of birth, official government-issued driver's license or identification number, government passport number, or employer or taxpayer identification number;

(2) unique electronic identification number, address, account number, or routing code; or

(3) telecommunication identification information or access device.

(e) "Indirect victim" means any person or entity described in section 611A.01, paragraph (b), other than a direct victim.

(f) "Loss" means value obtained, as defined in section 609.52, subdivision 1, clause (3), and expenses incurred by a direct or indirect victim as a result of a violation of this section.

(g) "Unlawful activity" means:

(1) any felony violation of the laws of this state or any felony violation of a similar law of another state or the United States; and

(2) any non-felony violation of the laws of this state involving theft, theft by swindle, forgery, fraud, or giving false information to a public official, or any non-felony violation of a similar law of another state or the United States.

(h) "Scanning device" means a scanner, reader, or any other electronic device that is used to access, read, scan, obtain, memorize, or store, temporarily or permanently, information encoded on a computer chip or magnetic strip or stripe of a payment card, driver's license, or state-issued identification card.

(i) "Reencoder" means an electronic device that places encoded information from the computer chip or magnetic strip or stripe of a payment card, driver's license, or state-issued identification card, onto the computer chip or magnetic strip or stripe of a different payment card, driver's license, or state-issued identification card, or any electronic medium that allows an authorized transaction to occur.

(j) "Payment card" means a credit card, charge card, debit card, or any other card that:

(1) is issued to an authorized card user; and

(2) allows the user to obtain, purchase, or receive credit, money, a good, a service, or anything of value.

Subd. 2. **Crime.** A person who transfers, possesses, or uses an identity that is not the person's own, with the intent to commit, aid, or abet any unlawful activity is guilty of identity theft and may be punished as provided in subdivision 3.

Subd. 3. **Penalties.** A person who violates subdivision 2 may be sentenced as follows:

(1) if the offense involves a single direct victim and the total, combined loss to the direct victim and any indirect victims is $250 or less, the person may be sentenced as provided in section 609.52, subdivision 3, clause (5);

(2) if the offense involves a single direct victim and the total, combined loss to the direct victim and any indirect victims is more than $250 but not more than $500, the person may be sentenced as provided in section 609.52, subdivision 3, clause (4);

(3) if the offense involves two or three direct victims or the total, combined loss to the direct and indirect victims is more than $500 but not more than $2,500, the person may be sentenced as provided in section 609.52, subdivision 3, clause (3);

(4) if the offense involves more than three but not more than seven direct victims or the total, combined loss to the direct and indirect victims is more than $2,500, the person may be sentenced as provided in section 609.52, subdivision 3, clause (2); and

(5) if the offense involves eight or more direct victims; or if the total, combined loss to the direct and indirect victims is more than $35,000; or, the person may be sentenced as provided in section 609.52, subdivision 3, clause (1);

(6) if the offense is related to possession or distribution of pornographic work in violation of section 617.246 or 617.247; the person may be sentenced as provided in section 609.52, subdivision 3, clause (1).

Subd. 4. **Restitution; items provided to victim.** (a) A direct or indirect victim of an identity theft crime shall be considered a victim for all purposes, including any rights that accrue under chapter 611A and rights to court-ordered restitution. * * *

Subd. 5. **Reporting.** (a) A person who has learned or reasonably suspects that a person is a direct victim of a crime under subdivision 2 may initiate a law enforcement investigation by contacting the local law enforcement agency that has jurisdiction where the person resides, regardless of where the crime may have occurred. The agency must prepare a police report of the matter, provide the complainant with a copy of that report, and may begin an investigation of the facts, or, if the suspected crime was committed in a different jurisdiction, refer the matter to the law enforcement agency where the suspected crime was committed for an investigation of the facts.

(b) If a law enforcement agency refers a report to the law enforcement agency where the crime was committed, it need not include the report as a crime committed in its jurisdiction for purposes of information that the agency is required to provide to the commissioner of public safety pursuant to section 299C.06.

Subd. 5a. **Crime of electronic use of false pretense to obtain identity.** (a) A person who, with intent to obtain the identity of another, uses a false pretense in an e-mail to another person or in a Web page, electronic communication, advertisement, or any other communication on the Internet, is guilty of a crime.

Subd. 5b. **Unlawful possession or use of scanning device or reencoder.** (a) A person who uses a scanning device or reencoder without permission of the cardholder of the card from which the information is being scanned or reencoded, with the intent to commit, aid, or abet any unlawful activity, is guilty of a crime.

(b) A person who possesses, with the intent to commit, aid, or abet any unlawful activity, any device, apparatus, equipment, software, material, good, property, or supply that is designed or adapted for use as a scanning device or a reencoder is guilty of a crime.

(c) Whoever commits an offense under paragraph (a) or (b) may be sentenced to imprisonment for not more than five years or to the payment of a fine of not more than $10,000, or both.

(b) Whoever commits such offense may sentenced to imprisonment for not more than five years or to payment of a fine of not more than $10,000, or both.

(c) In a prosecution under this subdivision, it is not a defense that:

(1) the person committing the offense did not obtain the identity of another;

(2) the person committing the offense did not use the identity; or

(3) the offense did not result in financial loss or any other loss to any person.

Subd. 6. **Venue.** Notwithstanding anything to the contrary in section 627.01, an offense committed under subdivision 2, 5a or 5b may be prosecuted in:

(1) the county where the offense occurred;

(2) the county of residence or place of business of the direct victim or indirect victim; or

(3) in the case of a violation of subdivision 5a or 5b, the county of residence of the person whose identity was obtained or sought.

Subd. 7. **Aggregation.** In any prosecution under subdivision 2, the value of the money or property or services the defendant receives or the number of direct or indirect victims within any six-month period may be aggregated and the defendant charged accordingly in applying the provisions of subdivision 3; * * *

EFFECTIVE DATE. This section is effective August 1, 2021, and applies to crimes committed on or after that date.

HIST: 1999 c 244 s 2; * * * 2010 c 293 s 2-4; 2021 art 25 s 1

609.528 POSSESSION OR SALE OF STOLEN OR COUNTERFEIT CHECK; PENALTIES.

Subdivision 1. **Definition.** (a) As used in this section, the following terms have the meanings given them in this subdivision.

(b) "Direct victim" means any person or entity described in section 611A.01, paragraph (b), from whom a check is stolen or whose name or other identifying information is contained in a counterfeit check.

(c) "Indirect victim" means any person or entity described in section 611A.01, paragraph (b), other than a direct victim.

(d) "Loss" means value obtained, as defined in section 609.52, subdivision 1, clause (3), and expenses incurred by a direct or indirect victim as a result of a violation of this section.

Subd. 2. **Crime.** A person who sells, possesses, receives, or transfers a check that is stolen or counterfeit, knowing or having reason to know the check is stolen or counterfeit, is guilty of a crime and may be punished as provided in subdivision 3.

Subd. 3. **Penalties.** A person who violates subdivision 2 may be sentenced as follows:

(1) if the offense involves a single direct victim and the total, combined loss to the direct victim and any indirect victims is $250 or less, the person may be sentenced as provided in section 609.52, subdivision 3, clause (5);

(2) if the offense involves a single direct victim and the total, combined loss to the direct victim and any indirect victims is more than $250 but not more than $500, the person may be sentenced as provided in section 609.52, subdivision 3, clause (4);

(3) if the offense involves two or three direct victims or the total, combined loss to the direct and indirect victims is more than $500 but not more than $2,500, the person may be sentenced as provided in section 609.52, subdivision 3, clause (3); and

(4) if the offense involves four or more direct victims, or if the total, combined loss to the direct and indirect victims is more than $2,500, the person may be sentenced as provided in section 609.52, subdivision 3, clause (2).

HIST: 2000 c 354 s 4

609.529 MAIL THEFT.

Subdivision 1. **Definitions.** (a) As used in this section, the following terms have the meanings given them in this subdivision.

(b) "Mail" means a letter, postal card, package, bag, or other sealed article addressed to another.

(c) "Mail depository" means a mail box, letter box, or mail receptacle; a post office or station of a post office; a mail route; or a postal service vehicle.

Subd. 2. **Crime.** Whoever does any of the following is guilty of mail theft and may be sentenced as provided in subdivision 3:

(1) intentionally and without claim of right removes mail from a mail depository;

(2) intentionally and without claim of right takes mail from a mail carrier;

(3) obtains custody of mail by intentionally deceiving a mail carrier, or other person who rightfully possesses or controls the mail, with a false representation which is known to be false, made with intent to deceive and which does deceive a mail carrier or other person who possesses or controls the mail;

(4) intentionally and without claim of right removes the contents of mail addressed to another;

(5) intentionally and without claim of right takes mail, or the contents of mail, that has been left for collection on or near a mail depository; or

(6) receives, possesses, transfers, buys, or conceals mail obtained by acts described in clauses (1) to (5), knowing or having reason to know the mail was obtained illegally.

Subd. 3. **Penalties.** A person convicted under subdivision 2 may be sentenced to imprisonment for not more than three years or to a payment of a fine of not more than $5,000, or both. * * *

HIST: 2003 c 106 s 4

609.53 RECEIVING STOLEN PROPERTY.

Subdivision 1. **Penalty.** Except as otherwise provided in section 609.526, any person who receives, possesses, transfers, buys or conceals any stolen property or property obtained by robbery, knowing or having reason to know the property was stolen or obtained by robbery, may be sentenced in accordance with the provisions of section 609.52, subdivision 3. * * *

Subd. 5. **Value.** In this section, "value" has the meaning defined in section 609.52, subdivision 1, clause (3).

HIST: 1963 c 753 art 1 s 609.53; * * * 1989 c 290 art 7 s 7,8

609.535 ISSUANCE OF DISHONORED CHECKS.

Subdivision 1. **Definitions.** For the purpose of this section, the following terms have the meanings given them.

(a) "Check" means a check, draft, order of withdrawal, or similar negotiable or nonnegotiable instrument.

(b) "Credit" means an arrangement or understanding with the drawee for the payment of a check.

Subd. 2. **Acts constituting.** Whoever issues a check which, at the time of issuance, the issuer intends shall not be paid, is guilty of issuing a dishonored check and may be sentenced as provided in subdivision 2a. In addition, restitution may be ordered by the court.

Subd. 2a. **Penalties.** (a) A person who is convicted of issuing a dishonored check under subdivision 2 may be sentenced as follows:

(1) to imprisonment for not more than five years or to payment of a fine of not more than $10,000, or both, if the value of the dishonored check, or checks aggregated under paragraph (b), is more than $500;

(2) to imprisonment for not more than one year or to payment of a fine of not more than $3,000, or both, if the value of the dishonored check, or checks aggregated under paragraph (b), is more than $250 but not more than $500; or

(3) to imprisonment for not more than 90 days or to payment of a fine of not more than $1,000, or both, if the value of the dishonored check, or checks aggregated under paragraph (b), is not more than $250.

(b) In a prosecution under this subdivision, the value of dishonored checks issued by the defendant in violation of this subdivision within any six-month period may be aggregated and the defendant charged accordingly in applying this section. When two or more offenses are committed by the same person in two or more counties, the accused may be prosecuted in any county in which one of the dishonored checks was issued for all of the offenses aggregated under this paragraph.

Subd. 3. **Proof of intent.** Any of the following is evidence sufficient to sustain a finding that the person at the time the person issued the check intended it should not be paid;

(1) proof that, at the time of issuance, the issuer did not have an account with the drawee;

(2) proof that, at the time of issuance, the issuer did not have sufficient funds or credit with the drawee and that the issuer failed to pay the check within five business days after mailing of notice of nonpayment or dishonor as provided in this subdivision; or

(3) proof that, when presentment was made within a reasonable time, the issuer did not have sufficient funds or credit with the drawee and that the issuer failed to pay the check within five business days after mailing of notice of nonpayment or dishonor as provided in this subdivision. * * *

Subd. 4. **Proof of lack of funds or credit.** If the check has been protested, the notice of protest is admissible as proof of presentation, nonpayment, and protest, and is evidence sufficient to sustain a finding that there was a lack of funds or credit with the drawee.

Subd. 5. **Exceptions.** This section does not apply to a postdated check or to a check given for a past consideration, except a payroll check or a check issued to a fund for employee benefits. * * *

HIST: 1963 c 753 art 1 s 609.535; * * * 2004 c 228 art 1 s 72

609.54 EMBEZZLEMENT OF PUBLIC FUNDS.

Whoever does an act which constitutes embezzlement under the provisions of Minnesota Constitution, article XI, section 13 may be sentenced as follows:

(1) If the value of the funds so embezzled is $2,500 or less, to imprisonment for not more than five years or to payment of a fine of not more than $10,000, or both; or

(2) If such value is more than $2,500, to imprisonment for not more than ten years or to payment of a fine of not more than $20,000, or both.

HIST: 1963 c 753 art 1 s 609.54; 1976 c 2 s 172; 1984 c 628 art 3 s 11

Minnesota Constitution, Article XI

Sec. 13. Safekeeping state funds; security; deposit of funds; embezzlement. All officers and other persons charged with the safekeeping of state funds shall be required to give ample security for funds received by them and to keep an accurate entry of each sum received and of each payment and transfer. If any person converts to his own use in any manner or form, or shall loan, with or without interest, or shall deposit in his own name, or otherwise than in the name of the state of Minnesota; or shall deposit in banks or with any person or persons or exchange for other funds or property, any portion of the funds of the state or the school funds aforesaid, except in the manner prescribed by law, every such act shall be and constitute an embezzlement of so much of the aforesaid state and school funds, or either of the same, as shall thus be taken, or loaned, or deposited or exchanged, and shall be a felony. * * *

609.545 MISUSING CREDIT CARD TO SECURE SERVICES.

Whoever obtains the services of another by the intentional unauthorized use of a credit card issued or purporting to be issued by an organization for use as identification in purchasing services is guilty of a misdemeanor.

HIST: 1963 c 753 art 1 s 609.545; 1971 c 23 s 57

609.546 MOTOR VEHICLE TAMPERING.

A person is guilty of a misdemeanor who intentionally:

(1) rides in or on a motor vehicle knowing that the vehicle was taken and is being driven by another without the owner's permission; or

(2) tampers with or enters into or on a motor vehicle without the owner's permission.

HIST: 1989 c 290 art 7 s 9

609.551 RUSTLING AND LIVESTOCK THEFT; PENALTIES.
Subdivision 1. **Crime defined, stealing cattle; penalties.** Whoever intentionally and without claim of right shoots, kills, takes, uses, transfers, conceals or retains possession of live cattle, swine or sheep or the carcasses thereof belonging to another without the other's consent and with the intent to permanently deprive the owner thereof may be sentenced as follows:
(a) If the value of the animals which are shot, killed, taken, used, transferred, concealed or retained exceeds $2,500, the defendant may be sentenced to imprisonment for not more than ten years, and may be fined up to $20,000;
(b) If the value of the animals which are shot, killed, taken, used, transferred, concealed or retained exceeds $300 but is less than $2,500, the defendant may be sentenced to imprisonment for not more than five years, and may be fined up to $10,000;
(c) If the value of the animals which are shot, killed, taken, used, transferred, concealed, or retained is $300 or less, the defendant may be sentenced to imprisonment for not more than 90 days or to payment of a fine of not more than $300 or both.
Subd. 2. **Crime defined; selling stolen cattle.** Whoever knowingly buys, sells, transports or otherwise handles cattle, swine or sheep illegally acquired under subdivision 1 or knowingly aids or abets another in the violation of subdivision 1 shall be sentenced as in subdivision 1, clauses (a), (b), and (c).
Subd. 3. **Aggregation.** In any prosecution under this section the value of the animals which are shot, killed, taken, used, transferred, concealed, or retained within any six-month period may be aggregated and the defendant charged accordingly in applying the provisions of this section. * * *
HIST: 1975 c 314 s 2; 1977 c 355 s 8; 1984 c 628 art 3 s 11; 1986 c 444

609.531 FORFEITURES.
Subdivision 1. **Definitions.** For the purpose of sections 609.531 to 609.5318, the following terms have the meanings given them.
(a) "Conveyance device" means a device used for transportation and includes, but is not limited to, a motor vehicle, trailer, snowmobile, airplane, and vessel and any equipment attached to it. The term "conveyance device" does not include property which is, in fact, itself stolen or taken in violation of the law.
(b) "Weapon used" means a dangerous weapon as defined under section 609.02, subdivision 6, that the actor used or had in possession in furtherance of a crime.
(c) "Property" means property as defined in section 609.52, subdivision 1, clause (1).
(d) "Contraband" means property which is illegal to possess under Minnesota law.
(e) "Appropriate agency" means the Bureau of Criminal Apprehension, the Department of Commerce Division of Insurance Fraud Prevention, the Minnesota Division of Driver and Vehicle Services, the Minnesota State Patrol, a county sheriff's department, the Three Rivers Regional Park District ~~park rangers~~ Department of Public Safety, the Department of Natural Resources Division of Enforcement, the University of Minnesota Police Department, the Department of Corrections' Fugitive Apprehension Unit, or a city, metropolitan transit, or airport police department, or a multijurisdictional entity established under section 299A.642 or 299A.681.
(f) "Designated offense" includes:
(1) for weapons used: any violation of this chapter, chapter 152, or chapter 624;
(2) for driver's license or identification card transactions: any violation of section 171.22; and
(3) for all other purposes: a felony violation of, or a felony-level attempt or conspiracy to violate, section 325E.17; 325E.18; 609.185; 609.19; 609.195; 609.2112; 609.2113; 609.2114; 609.221; 609.222; 609.223; 609.2231; 609.2335; 609.24; 609.245; 609.25; 609.255; 609.282; 609.283; 609.322; 609.342, subdivision 1, clauses (a) to (f); 609.343, subdivision 1, clauses (a) to (f); 609.344, subdivision 1, clauses (a) to (e), and (h) to (j); 609.352; 609.345, subdivision 1,

clauses (a) to (e), and (h) to (j); 609.42; 609.425; 609.466; 609.485; 609.487; 609.52; 609.525; 609.527; 609.528; 609.53; 609.54; 609.551; 609.561; 609.562; 609.563; 609.582; 609.59; 609.595; 609.611; 609.631; 609.66, subdivision 1e; 609.671, subdivisions 3, 4, 5, 8, and 12; 609.687; 609.821; 609.825; 609.86; 609.88; 609.893; 609.895; 609.895; 617.246; 617.247; or a gross misdemeanor or felony violation of section 609.891 or 624.7181; or any violation of section 609.324; or a felony violation of, or a felony-level attempt or conspiracy to violate, Minnesota Statutes 2012, section 609.21.

(g) "Controlled substance" has the meaning given in section 152.01, subdivision 4.

(h) "Prosecuting authority" means the attorney who is responsible for prosecuting an offense that is the basis for a forfeiture under sections 609.531 to 609.5318.

(i) "Asserting person" means a person other than the driver alleged to have used a vehicle in the transportation or exchange of a controlled substance intended for distribution or sale, claiming an ownership interest in a vehicle that has been seized or restrained under this section.

Subd. 1a. **Construction.** Sections 609.531 to 609.5318 must be liberally construed to carry out the following remedial purposes:

(1) to enforce the law;

(2) to deter crime;

(3) to reduce the economic incentive to engage in criminal enterprise;

(4) to increase the pecuniary loss resulting from the detection of criminal activity; and

(5) to forfeit property unlawfully used or acquired and divert the property to law enforcement purposes. * * *

Subd. 4. **Seizure.** (a) Property subject to forfeiture under sections 609.531 to 609.5318 may be seized * * * upon process issued by any court having jurisdiction over the property. Property may be seized without process if:

(1) the seizure is incident to a lawful arrest or a lawful search;

(2) the property subject to seizure has been the subject of a prior judgment in favor of the state in a criminal injunction or forfeiture proceeding under this chapter; or

(3) the appropriate agency has probable cause to believe that the delay occasioned by the necessity to obtain process would result in the removal or destruction of the property and that:

(i) the property was used or is intended to be used in commission of a felony; or

(ii) the property is dangerous to health or safety.

* * *

(b) When property is seized, the officer must provide a receipt to the person found in possession of the property; or in the absence of any person, the officer must leave a receipt in the place where the property was found, if reasonably possible.

Subd. 5. **Right to possession vests immediately; custody of seized property.** All right, title, and interest in property subject to forfeiture under sections 609.531 to 609.531e vests in the appropriate agency upon commission of the act or omission giving rise to the forfeiture. Any property seized under sections 609.531 to 609.5318 is not subject to replevin, but is deemed to be in the custody of the appropriate agency subject to the orders and decrees of the court having jurisdiction over the forfeiture proceedings.

* * *

Subd. 5a. **Bond by owner for possession.** (a) If the owner of property that has been seized under sections 609.531 to 609.5318 seeks possession of the property before the forfeiture action is determined, the owner may give security or post bond payable to the appropriate agency in an amount equal to the retail value of the seized property. On posting the security or bond, the seized property must be returned to the owner and the forfeiture action shall proceed against the security as if it were the seized property. This subdivision does not apply to contraband property or property being held for investigatory purposes.

(b) If the owner of a motor vehicle that has been seized under this section seeks possession of the vehicle before the forfeiture action is determined, the owner may surrender the vehicle's certificate of title in exchange for the vehicle. The motor vehicle must be returned to the owner within 24 hours if the owner surrenders the motor vehicle's certificate of title to the appropriate agency, pending resolution of the forfeiture action. If the certificate is surrendered, the owner may not be ordered to post security or bond as a condition of release of the vehicle. When a certificate of title is surrendered under this provision, the agency shall notify the department of public safety and any secured party noted on the certificate. The agency shall also notify the department and the secured party when it returns a surrendered title to the motor vehicle owner. * * *

Subd. 6a. **Forfeiture a civil procedure; conviction required.** (a) An action for forfeiture is a civil in rem action and is independent of any criminal prosecution, except as provided in this subdivision.

(b) An asset is subject to forfeiture by judicial determination under sections 609.531 to 609.5318 only if:

(1) a person is convicted of the criminal offense related to the action for forfeiture; or

(2) a person is not charged with a criminal offense under chapter 152 related to the action for forfeiture based in whole or in part on the person's agreement to provide information regarding the criminal activity of another person. * * *

(c) The appropriate agency handling the judicial forfeiture may introduce into evidence in the judicial forfeiture case in civil court the agreement in paragraph (b), clause (2).

(d) The appropriate agency handling the judicial forfeiture bears the burden of proving by clear and convincing evidence that the property is an instrument or represents the proceeds of the underlying offense.

Subd. 7. **Petition for remission or mitigation.** Prior to the entry of a court order disposing with the forfeiture action, any person who has an interest in forfeited property may file with the prosecuting authority a petition for remission or mitigation of the forfeiture. The prosecuting authority may remit or mitigate the forfeiture upon terms and conditions the prosecuting authority deems reasonable * * * [.] * * *

Subd. 9. **Transfer of forfeitable property to federal government.** The appropriate agency shall not directly or indirectly transfer property subject to forfeiture under sections 609.531 to 609.5318 to a federal agency for adoption if the forfeiture would be prohibited under state law.

EFFECTIVE DATE. This section is effective January 1, 2022.

HIST: 1984 c 625 s 1; * * * 2015 c 21 art 1 s 102; 2105 c 65 art 6 s 16; 1Sp c 11 art 5 s 9, 10

609.5311 FORFEITURE OF PROPERTY ASSOCIATED WITH CONTROLLED SUBSTANCES.

Subdivision 1. **Controlled substances.** All controlled substances that were manufactured, distributed, dispensed, or acquired in violation of chapter 152 are subject to forfeiture under this section, except as provided in subdivision 3 and section 609.5316.

Subd. 2. **Associated property.** (a) All personal property, and real and personal, other than homestead property exempt from seizure under section 510.01, that has been used, or is intended for use, or has in any way facilitated, in whole or in part, the manufacturing, compounding, processing, delivering, importing, cultivating, exporting, transporting, or exchanging of contraband or a controlled substance that has not been lawfully manufactured, distributed, dispensed, and acquired is an instrument or represents the proceeds of a controlled substance offense is subject to forfeiture under this section, except as provided in subdivision 3. * * *

Subd. 3. **Limitations on forfeiture of certain property associated with controlled substances.** (a) A conveyance device is subject to forfeiture under this section only if the retail value of the controlled substance is $75 $100 or more and the conveyance device is associated with a felony-level controlled substance crime was used in the transportation or exchange of a controlled substance intended for distribution or sale.

(b) Real property is subject to forfeiture under this section only if the retail value of the controlled substance or contraband is $2,000 or more.

(c) Property used by any person as a common carrier in the transaction of business as a common carrier is subject to forfeiture under this section only if the owner of the property is a consenting party to, or is privy to, the use or intended use of the property as described in subdivision 2.

(d) Property is subject to forfeiture under this section only if its owner was privy to the use or intended use described in subdivision 2, or the unlawful use or intended use of the property otherwise occurred with the owner's knowledge or consent.

(e) Forfeiture under this section of a conveyance device or real property encumbered by a bona fide security interest is subject to the interest of the secured party unless the secured party had knowledge of or consented to the act or omission upon which the forfeiture is based. A person claiming a security interest bears the burden of establishing that interest by clear and convincing evidence.

(f) Forfeiture under this section of real property is subject to the interests of a good faith purchaser for value unless the purchaser had knowledge of or consented to the act or omission upon which the forfeiture is based.

(g) Notwithstanding paragraphs (d), (e), and (f), property is not subject to forfeiture based solely on the owner's or secured party's knowledge of the unlawful use or intended use of the property if: (1) the owner or secured party took reasonable steps to terminate use of the property by the offender; or (2) the property is real property owned by the parent of the offender, unless the parent actively participated in, or knowingly acquiesced to, a violation of chapter 152, or the real property constitutes proceeds derived from or traceable to a use described in subdivision 2.
* * *

Subd. 4. **Records; proceeds.** (a) All books, records, and research products and materials, including formulas, microfilm, tapes, and data that are used, or intended for use in the manner described in subdivision 2 are subject to forfeiture.

(b) All property, real and personal, that represents proceeds derived from or traceable to a use described in subdivision 2 is subject to forfeiture.

EFFECTIVE DATE. This section is effective January 1, 2022, and applies to seizures that take place on or after that date.

HIST: 1988 c 665 s 11; * * * 2010 c 391 s 12; 1Sp2021 c 11 art 5 s 11-13

609.5312 FORFEITURE OF PROPERTY ASSOCIATED WITH DESIGNATED OFFENSES.

Subdivision 1. **Property subject to forfeiture.** (a) All personal property is subject to forfeiture if it was used or intended for use to commit or facilitate the commission of a designated offense. All money and other property, real and personal, that represent proceeds of a designated offense, and all contraband property, are subject to forfeiture, except as provided in this section.

(b) All money used or intended to be used to facilitate the commission of a violation of section 609.322 or 609.324 or a violation of a local ordinance substantially similar to section 609.322 or 609.324 is subject to forfeiture. * * *

Subd. 1a. **Computers and related property subject of forfeiture.** (a) As used in this subdivision, "property" has the meaning given in section 609.87, subdivision 6.

(b) When a computer or a component part of a computer is used or intended for use to commit or facilitate the commission of a designated offense, the computer and all software, data, and other property contained in the computer are subject to forfeiture[.]
* * *

Subd. 2. **Limitations on forfeiture of property associated with designated offenses.**

(a) Property used by a person as a common carrier in the transaction of business as a common carrier is subject to forfeiture under this section only if the owner of the property is a consenting party to, or is privy to, the commission of a designated offense.

(b) Property is subject to forfeiture under this section only if the owner was privy to the act or omission upon which the forfeiture is based, or the act or omission occurred with the owner's knowledge or consent.

(c) Property encumbered by a bona fide security interest is subject to the interest of the secured party unless the party had knowledge of or consented to the act or omission upon which the forfeiture is based. A person claiming a security interest bears the burden of establishing that interest by clear and convincing evidence.

(d) Notwithstanding paragraphs (b) and (c), property is not subject to forfeiture based solely on the owner's or secured party's knowledge of the act or omission upon which the forfeiture is based if the owner or secured party took reasonable steps to terminate use of the property by the offender.

Subd. 3. **Vehicle forfeiture for prostitution offenses**. (a) A motor vehicle is subject to forfeiture under this subdivision if it was used to commit or facilitate, or used during the commission of, a violation of section 609.324 or a violation of a local ordinance substantially similar to section 609.324. A motor vehicle is subject to forfeiture under this subdivision only if the offense is established by proof of a criminal conviction for the offense. * * *

(b) When a motor vehicle subject to forfeiture under this subdivision is seized in advance of a judicial forfeiture order, a hearing before a judge or referee must be held * * *. The prosecuting authority shall certify to the court * * * that it has filed or intends to file charges against the alleged violator * * *. [T]he court shall order that the motor vehicle be returned to the owner if:

(1) the prosecutor has failed to make the certification required by paragraph (b);

(2) the owner of the motor vehicle has demonstrated to the court's satisfaction that the owner has a defense to the forfeiture * * *; or

(3) the court determines that seizure of the vehicle creates or would create an undue hardship for members of the owner's family.

(c) If the defendant is acquitted or prostitution charges against the defendant are dismissed, neither the owner nor the defendant is responsible for paying any costs associated with the seizure or storage of the vehicle.

(d) A vehicle leased or rented * * * for a period of 180 days or less is not subject to forfeiture[.] * * *

Subd. 4. **Vehicle forfeiture for fleeing a peace officer.** (a) A motor vehicle is subject to forfeiture under this subdivision if it was used to commit a violation of section 609.487 and endanger life or property. A motor vehicle is subject to forfeiture under this subdivision only if the offense is established by proof of a criminal conviction for the offense. Except as otherwise provided in this subdivision, a forfeiture under this subdivision is governed by sections 609.531, 609.5312, 609.5313, and 609.5315, subdivision 6.

(b) When a motor vehicle subject to forfeiture under this subdivision is seized in advance of a judicial forfeiture order, a hearing before a judge or referee must be held * * *. The prosecuting authority shall certify to the court * * * that it has filed or intends to file charges against the alleged violator for violating section 609.487. After conducting the hearing, the court shall order that the motor vehicle be returned to the owner if:

(1) the prosecutor has failed to make the certification required by this paragraph;

(2) the owner of the motor vehicle has demonstrated to the court's satisfaction that the owner has a defense to the forfeiture, including but not limited to the defenses contained in subdivision 2; or

(3) the court determines that seizure of the vehicle creates or would create an undue hardship for members of the owner's family.

(c) If the defendant is acquitted or the charges against the defendant are dismissed, neither the owner nor the defendant is responsible for paying any costs associated with the seizure or storage of the vehicle.

(d) A vehicle leased or rented under section 168.27, subdivision 4, for a period of 180 days or less is not subject to forfeiture under this subdivision. * * *

HIST: 1988 c 665 s 12; * * * 2013 c 80 s 1

609.5314 ADMINISTRATIVE FORFEITURE OF CERTAIN PROPERTY SEIZED IN CONNECTION WITH A CONTROLLED SUBSTANCES SEIZURE.

Subdivision 1. **Property subject to administrative forfeiture; presumption.** (a) The following are presumed to be subject to administrative forfeiture under this section:

(1) all money totaling $1,500 or more, precious metals, and precious stones found in

~~proximity to:~~ that there is probable cause to believe represent the proceeds of a controlled substance offense;

~~(i) controlled substances;~~

~~(ii) forfeitable drug manufacturing or distributing equipment or devices; or~~

~~(iii) forfeitable records of manufacture or distribution of controlled substances;~~

(2) all money found in proximity to controlled substances when there is probable cause to believe that the money was exchanged for the purchase of a controlled substance;

~~(2)~~ (3) all conveyance devices containing controlled substances with a retail value of $100 or more if ~~possession or sale of the controlled substance would be a felony under chapter 152~~ there is probable cause to believe that the conveyance device was used in the transportation or exchange of a controlled substance intended for distribution or sale; and

~~(3)~~ (4) all firearms, ammunition, and firearm accessories found:

(i) in a conveyance device used or intended for use to commit or facilitate the commission of a felony offense involving a controlled substance;

(ii) on or in proximity to a person from whom a felony amount of controlled substance is seized; or

(iii) on the premises where a controlled substance is seized and in proximity to the controlled substance, if possession or sale of the controlled substance would be a felony under chapter 152. * * *

(c) ~~A claimant of the property bears the burden to rebut this presumption.~~ * * *

Subd. 1a. **Innocent owner.** (a) Any person, other than the defendant driver, alleged to have used a vehicle in the transportation or exchange of a controlled substance intended for distribution or sale, claiming an ownership interest in a vehicle that has been seized or restrained under this section may assert that right by notifying the prosecuting authority in writing and within 60 days of the service of the notice of seizure.

(b) Upon receipt of notice pursuant to paragraph (a), the prosecuting authority may release the vehicle to the asserting person. If the prosecuting authority proceeds with the forfeiture, the prosecuting authority must, within 30 days, file a separate complaint in the name of the jurisdiction pursuing the forfeiture against the vehicle, describing the vehicle, specifying that the vehicle was used in the transportation or exchange of a controlled substance intended for distribution or sale, and specifying the time and place of the vehicle's unlawful use. The complaint may be filed in district court or conciliation court and the filing fee is waived.

(c) A complaint filed by the prosecuting authority must be served on the asserting person and on any other registered owners. Service may be made by certified mail at the address listed in the Department of Public Safety's computerized motor vehicle registration records or by any means permitted by court rules.

(d) The hearing on the complaint shall, to the extent practicable, be held within 30 days of the filing of the petition. The court may consolidate the hearing on the complaint with a hearing on any other complaint involving a claim of an ownership interest in the same vehicle.

(e) At a hearing held pursuant to this subdivision, the state must prove by a preponderance of the evidence that:

(1) the seizure was incident to a lawful arrest or a lawful search; and

(2) the vehicle was used in the transportation or exchange of a controlled substance intended for distribution or sale.

(f) At a hearing held pursuant to this subdivision, the asserting person must prove by a preponderance of the evidence that the asserting person:

(1) has an actual ownership interest in the vehicle; and

(2) did not have actual or constructive knowledge that the vehicle would be used or operated in any manner contrary to law or that the asserting person took reasonable steps to prevent use of the vehicle by the alleged offender.

(g) If the court determines that the state met both burdens under paragraph (e) and the asserting person failed to meet any burden under paragraph (f), the court shall order that the vehicle remains subject to forfeiture under this section.

(h) The court shall order that the vehicle is not subject to forfeiture under this section and shall order the vehicle returned to the asserting person if it determines that:

(1) the state failed to meet any burden under paragraph (e);

(2) the asserting person proved both elements under paragraph (f); or

(3) clauses (1) and (2) apply.

(i) If the court determines that the asserting person is an innocent owner and orders the vehicle returned to the innocent owner, an entity in possession of the vehicle is not required to release the vehicle until the innocent owner pays:

(1) the reasonable costs of the towing, seizure, and storage of the vehicle incurred before the innocent owner provided the notice required under paragraph (a); and

(2) any reasonable costs of storage of the vehicle incurred more than two weeks after an order issued under paragraph (h).

Subd. 2. **Administrative forfeiture procedure.** (a) Forfeiture of property described in subdivision 1 that does not exceed $50,000 in value is governed by this subdivision. Within 60 days from when seizure occurs, all persons known to have an ownership, possessory, or security interest in seized property must be notified of the seizure and the intent to forfeit the property. * * *

(b) Notice may otherwise be given in the manner provided by law for service of a summons in a civil action. The notice must be in writing and contain:

(1) a description of the property seized;

(2) the date of seizure; and

(3) notice of the right to obtain judicial review of the forfeiture and of the procedure for obtaining that judicial review, printed in English. * * *

(c) If notice is not sent in accordance with this paragraph (a), and no time extension is granted or the extension period has expired, the appropriate agency shall return the property to the person from whom the property was seized, if known. An agency's return of property due to lack of proper notice does not restrict the agency's authority to commence a forfeiture proceeding at a later time. The agency shall not be required to return contraband or other property that the person from whom the property was seized may not legally possess.

Subd. 3. **Judicial determination.** (a) Within 60 days following service of a notice of seizure and forfeiture under this section, a claimant may file a demand for a judicial determination of the forfeiture. * * * If the value of the seized property is $15,000 or less, the claimant may file an action in conciliation court for recovery of the seized property. If the value of the seized property is less than $500, the claimant does not have to pay the conciliation court filing fee. No responsive pleading is required of the prosecuting authority[.] * * * The district court administrator shall schedule the hearing as soon as practicable after, and in any event no later than 90 days following, the conclusion of the criminal prosecution. * * *

(c) If the claimant makes a timely demand for judicial determination under this subdivision, the appropriate agency must conduct the forfeiture under section 609.531, subdivision 6a. The limitations and defenses set forth in section 609.5311, subdivision 3, apply to the judicial determination. * * *

EFFECTIVE DATE. This section is effective January 1, 2022, and applies to seizures that take place on or after that date.

HIST: 1988 c 665 s 14; * * * 2014 c 201 s 2; 1Sp2021 c 11 art 5 s 14-17

609.5315 DISPOSITION OF FORFEITED PROPERTY.

Subdivision 1. **Disposition.** (a) Subject to paragraph (b), if the court finds under section 609.5313, 609.5314, or 609.5318 that the property is subject to forfeiture, it shall order the appropriate agency to do one of the following:

(1) unless a different disposition is provided under clause (3) or (4), either destroy firearms, ammunition, and firearm accessories that the agency decides not to use for law enforcement purposes under clause (8), or sell them to federally licensed firearms dealers, as defined in section 624.7161, subdivision 1, and distribute the proceeds under subdivision 5 or 5b;

(2) sell property that is not required to be destroyed by law and is not harmful to the public and distribute the proceeds under subdivision 5 or 5b;

(3) sell antique firearms, as defined in section 624.712, subdivision 3, to the public and distribute the proceeds under subdivision 5 or 5b;

(4) destroy or use for law enforcement purposes semiautomatic military-style assault weapons, as defined in section 624.712, subdivision 7;

(5) take custody of the property and remove it for disposition in accordance with law;

(6) forward the property to the federal drug enforcement administration;

(7) disburse money as provided under subdivision 5, 5b, or 5c; or

(8) keep property other than money for official use by the agency and the prosecuting agency. * * *

(c) If property is sold under paragraph (a), the appropriate agency shall not sell property to (1) an officer or employee of the agency that seized the property or to a person related to the officer or employee by blood or marriage; or (2) the prosecuting authority or any individual working in the same office or a person related to the authority or individual by blood or marriage. * * *

Subd. 3. **Use by law enforcement.** (a) Property kept under this section may be used only in the performance of official duties of the appropriate agency or prosecuting agency and may not be used for any other purpose. If an appropriate agency keeps a forfeited motor vehicle for official use, it shall make reasonable efforts to ensure that the motor vehicle is available for use and adaptation by the agency's officers who participate in the drug abuse resistance education program. * * *

Subd. 6. **Reporting requirement.** (a) For each forfeiture occurring in the state regardless of the authority for it and including forfeitures pursued under federal law, the appropriate agency and the prosecutor shall provide a written record of the forfeiture incident to the state auditor. * * *

Subd. 7. **Firearms.** The agency shall make best efforts for a period of 90 days after the seizure of an abandoned or stolen firearm to protect the firearm from harm and return it to the lawful owner.

HIST: 1988 c 665 s 15; * * * 2013 c 80 s 2-4; 1Sp2017 c 6 art 10 s 137; 1Sp2021 c 11 art 5 s 20

609.5316 SUMMARY FORFEITURES.

Subdivision 1. **Contraband.** Except as otherwise provided in this subdivision, if the property is contraband, the property must be summarily forfeited and either destroyed or used by the appropriate agency for law enforcement purposes. Upon summary forfeiture, weapons used must be destroyed by the appropriate agency unless the agency decides to use the weapons for law enforcement purposes or sell the weapons in a commercially reasonable manner to federally licensed firearms dealers[.]

Subd. 2. **Controlled substances.** * * *

(b) Species of plants from which controlled substances in schedules I and II may be derived that have been planted or cultivated in violation of chapter 152 or of which the owners or cultivators are unknown, or that are wild growths, may be seized and summarily forfeited to the state. The appropriate agency or its authorized agent may seize the plants if the person in occupancy or in control of land or premises where the plants are growing or being stored fails to produce an appropriate registration or proof that the person is the holder of appropriate registration.

Subd. 3. **Weapons, telephone cloning paraphernalia, automated sales suppression devices, and bullet-resistant vests.** Weapons used are contraband and must be summarily forfeited to the appropriate agency upon conviction of the weapon's owner or possessor for a controlled substance crime or for any offense of this chapter or chapter 624, or for a violation of an order for protection under section 518B.01, subdivision 14. Bullet-resistant vests, as defined in section 609.486, worn or possessed during the commission or attempted commission of a crime are contraband and must be summarily forfeited to the appropriate agency upon conviction of the owner or possessor for a controlled substance crime or for any offense of this chapter.

Telephone cloning paraphernalia used in a violation of section 609.894, and automated sales suppression devices [or] phantom-ware * * * are contraband and must be summarily forfeited to the appropriate agency upon a conviction.
HIST: 1988 c 665 s 16; * * * 2014 c 201 s 3; 1Sp2017 c 1 art 1 s 4

609.532 ATTACHMENT OF DEPOSITED FUNDS.
Subdivision 1. **Attachment.** Upon application by the prosecuting authority, a court may issue an attachment order directing a financial institution to freeze some or all of the funds or assets deposited with or held by the financial institution by or on behalf of an account holder charged with the commission of a felony.
* * *
Subd. 3. **Issuance of a court order.** * * * [The] court may order the financial institution to freeze all or part of the account holder's deposited funds or assets so that the funds or assets may not be withdrawn or disposed of until further order of the court.
* * *
Subd. 5. **Release of funds.** (a) The account holder may, upon notice and motion, have a hearing to contest the freezing of funds or assets and to seek the release of all or part of them.
(b) The account holder is entitled to an order releasing the freeze by showing:
(1) that the account holder has posted a bond or other adequate surety, guaranteeing that, upon conviction, adequate funds or assets will be available to pay complete restitution to victims of the alleged offense;
(2) that there is no probable cause to believe that the account holder was involved in the alleged offense;
(3) that the amount of funds or assets frozen is more than is necessary to pay complete restitution to all victims of the alleged offense;
(4) that a joint account holder who is not involved in the alleged criminal activity has deposited all or part of the funds or assets; or
(5) that the funds or assets should be returned in the interests of justice.
(c) It is not grounds for the release of funds or assets that the particular accounts frozen do not contain funds or assets that were proceeds from or used in the commission of the alleged offense.
Subd. 6. **Disposition of funds.** * * *
(b) If the account holder is acquitted or the charges are dismissed, the court must issue an order releasing the freeze on the funds or assets.
Subd. 7. **Time limit.** The freeze permitted by this section expires 24 months after the date of the court's initial attachment order unless the time limit is extended by the court[.]
* * *
HIST: 1987 c 217 s 1

629.361 PEACE OFFICERS RESPONSIBLE FOR CUSTODY OF STOLEN PROPERTY.
A peace officer arresting a person charged with committing or aiding in the committing of a robbery, aggravated robbery, or theft shall use reasonable diligence to secure the property alleged to have been stolen. After seizure of the property, the officer shall be answerable for it while it remains in the officer's custody. The officer shall annex a schedule of the property to the return of the warrant. Upon request of the county attorney, the law enforcement agency that has custody of the property alleged to have been stolen shall deliver the property to the custody of the county attorney for use as evidence at an omnibus hearing or at trial. The county attorney shall make a receipt for the property and be responsible for the property while it is in the county attorney's custody. When the offender is convicted, whoever has custody of the property shall turn it over to the owner.
HIST: (10376) RL s 5095; 1965 c 35 s 11; 1985 c 265 art 10 s 1; 1986 c 444

Chapter 12 -- DAMAGE OR TRESPASS TO PROPERTY

Category 2, Section 5:
2.5.1. Describe the basic organization, purpose, and definitions and principles of the Minnesota Criminal Code.
2.5.5. Given a variety of scenarios, identify indications a particular crime has been committed and identify the elements of that crime.

609.556 DEFINITIONS.

Subdivision 1. Scope. For the purposes of section 609.556 to 609.576 and 609.611, the terms defined in this section have the meanings given them.

Subd. 2. Property of another. "Property of another" means a building or other property, whether real or personal, in which a person other than the accused has an interest which the accused has no authority to defeat or impair even though the accused may also have an interest in the building or property.

Subd. 3. Building. "Building" in addition to its ordinary meaning includes any tent, watercraft, structure or vehicle that is customarily used for overnight lodging of a person or persons. If a building consists of two or more units separately secured or occupied, each unit shall be deemed a separate building.
HIST: 1976 c 124 s 3; 1977 c 347 s 63

609.561 ARSON IN THE FIRST DEGREE.

Subdivision 1. First degree; dwelling. Whoever unlawfully by means of fire or explosives, intentionally destroys or damages any building that is used as a dwelling at the time the act is committed, whether the inhabitant is present therein at the time of the act or not, or any building appurtenant to or connected with a dwelling whether the property of the actor or of another, commits arson in the first degree and may be sentenced to imprisonment for not more than 20 years or to a fine of not more than $20,000, or both.

Subd. 2. First degree; other buildings. Whoever unlawfully by means of fire or explosives, intentionally destroys or damages any building not included in subdivision 1, whether the property of the actor or another commits arson in the first degree and may be sentenced to imprisonment for not more than 20 years or to a fine of not more than $35,000, or both if:

(a) Another person who is not a participant in the crime is present in the building at the time and the defendant knows that; or

(b) The circumstances are such as to render the presence of such a person therein a reasonable possibility.

Subd. 3. First degree; flammable material. (a) Whoever unlawfully by means of fire or explosives, intentionally destroys or damages any building not included in subdivision 1, whether the property of the actor or another, commits arson in the first degree if a flammable material is used to start or accelerate the fire. A person who violates this paragraph may be sentenced to imprisonment for not more than 20 years or a fine of not more than $20,000, or both.

(b) As used in this subdivision:

(1) "combustible liquid" means a liquid having a flash point at or above 100 degrees Fahrenheit;

(2) "flammable gas" means any material which is a gas at 68 degrees Fahrenheit or less and 14.7 psi of pressure and which: (i) is ignitable when in a mixture of 13 percent or less by volume with air at atmospheric pressure; or (ii) has a flammable range with air at atmospheric pressure of at least 12 percent, regardless of the lower flammable limit;

(3) "flammable liquid" means any liquid having a flash point below 100 degrees Fahrenheit and having a vapor pressure not exceeding 40 pounds per square inch (absolute) at 100 degrees Fahrenheit, but does not include intoxicating liquor as defined in section 340A.101;

(4) "flammable material" means a flammable or combustible liquid, a flammable gas, or a flammable solid; and

(5) "flammable solid" means any of the following three types of materials: (i) wetted explosives; (ii) self-reactive materials that are liable to undergo heat-producing decomposition; or (iii) readily combustible solids that may cause a fire through friction or that have a rapid burning rate as determined by specific flammability tests.

HIST: 1976 c 124 s 4; * * * 1999 c 176 s 1

609.562 ARSON IN THE SECOND DEGREE.

Whoever unlawfully by means of fire or explosives, intentionally destroys or damages any building not covered by section 609.561, no matter what its value, or any other real or personal property valued at more than $1,000, whether the property of the actor or another, may be sentenced to imprisonment for not more than ten years or to payment of a fine of not more than $20,000, or both.

HIST: 1976 c 124 s 5; * * * 1993 c 326 art 5 s 7

609.563 ARSON IN THE THIRD DEGREE.

Subdivision 1. **Crime.** Whoever unlawfully by means of fire or explosives, intentionally destroys or damages any real or personal property may be sentenced to imprisonment for not more than five years or to payment of a fine of $10,000, or both, if:

(a) the property intended by the accused to be damaged or destroyed had a value of more than $300 but less than $1,000; or

(b) property of the value of $300 or more was unintentionally damaged or destroyed but such damage or destruction could reasonably have been foreseen; or

(c) the property specified in clauses (a) and (b) in the aggregate had a value of $300 or more.

Subd. 2. Repealed, 1998 c 367 art 2 s 33

HIST: 1976 c 124 s 6; * * * 1998 c 367 art 2 s 33

609.5631 ARSON IN THE FOURTH DEGREE.

Subdivision 1. **Definitions.** (a) For purposes of this section, the following terms have the meanings given.

(b) "Multiple unit residential building" means a building containing two or more apartments.

(c) "Public building" means a building such as a hotel, hospital, motel, dormitory, sanitarium, nursing home, theater, stadium, gymnasium, amusement park building, school or other building used for educational purposes, museum, restaurant, bar, correctional institution, place of worship, or other building of public assembly.

Subd. 2. **Crime described.** Whoever intentionally by means of fire or explosives sets fire to or burns or causes to be burned any personal property in a multiple unit residential building or public building and arson in the first, second or third degree was not committed is guilty of a gross misdemeanor and may be sentenced to imprisonment for not more than one year or to payment of a fine of not more than $3,000, or both.
HIST: 1998 c 367 art 2 s 19; 1999 c 176 s 2

609.5632 ARSON IN THE FIFTH DEGREE.

Whoever intentionally by means of fire or explosives sets fire to or burns or causes to be burned any real or personal property of value is guilty of a misdemeanor and may be sentenced to imprisonment for not more than 90 days or to payment of a fine of not more than $1,000, or both.
HIST: 1998 c 367 art 2 s 20; 2004 c 228 art 1 s 72; 2004 c 228 art 1 s 72

609.5633 USE OF IGNITION DEVICES; PETTY MISDEMEANOR.

A student who uses an ignition device, including a butane or disposable lighter or matches, inside an educational building and under circumstances where there is an obvious risk of fire, and arson in the first, second, third, or fourth degree was not committed, is guilty of a petty misdemeanor. This section does not apply if the student uses the device in a manner authorized by the school.

For purposes of this section, "student' has the meaning given in section 123B.41, subdivision 11.
HIST: 1999 c 176 s 3

609.564 EXCLUDED FIRES.

A person does not violate section 609.561, 609.562, 609.563, or 609.5641 if the person sets a fire pursuant to a validly issued license or permit or with written permission from the fire department of the jurisdiction where the fire occurs.
HIST: 1985 c 141 s 4; 1990 c 478 s 1

609.5641 WILDFIRE ARSON.

Subdivision 1. **Setting wildfires.** A person who intentionally sets a fire to burn out of control on land of another containing timber, underbrush, grass, or other vegetative combustible material is guilty of a felony[.]

Subd. 1a. **Penalty; felonies.** (a) Except as provided in paragraphs (b), (c), and (d), a person who violates subdivision 1 may be sentenced to imprisonment for not more than five years or to payment of a fine of not more than $10,000, or both.

(b) A person who violates subdivision 1 where the fire threatens to damage or damages in excess of five buildings or dwellings, burns 500 acres or more, or damages crops in excess of $100,000, may be sentenced to imprisonment for not more than ten years or to payment of a fine of not more than $15,000, or both.

(c) A person who violates subdivision 1 where the fire threatens to damage or damages in excess of 100 buildings or dwellings, burns 1,500 acres or more, or damages crops in excess of

$250,000, may be sentenced to imprisonment for not more than 20 years or to payment of a fine of not more than $25,000, or both.

(d) A person who violates subdivision 1 where the fire causes another person to suffer demonstrable bodily harm may be sentenced to imprisonment for not more than ten years or to payment of a fine of $15,000, or both.

(e) For purposes of this section, a building or dwelling is threatened where there is a probability of damage to the building or dwelling requiring evacuation for safety of life.

Subd. 2. **Possession of flammables to set wildfires.** A person is guilty of a gross misdemeanor who possesses a flammable, explosive, or incendiary device, substance, or material with intent to use the device, substance, or material to violate subdivision 1.

Subd. 3. **Restitution.** In addition to the sentence otherwise authorized, the court may order a person who is convicted of violating this section to pay fire suppression costs, damages to the owner of the damaged land, costs associated with injuries sustained by a member of a municipal or volunteer fire department in the performance of the member's duties, and any other restitution costs allowed under section 611A.04.
HIST: 1990 c 478 s 2; 2013 c139 s 1-3

609.576 NEGLIGENT FIRES RESULTING IN INJURY OR PROPERTY DAMAGE.

Subdivision 1. **Negligent fire resulting in injury or property damage.** Whoever is grossly negligent in causing a fire to burn or get out of control thereby causing damage or injury to another, and as a result of this:

(1) a human being is injured and great bodily harm incurred, is guilty of a crime and may be sentenced to imprisonment of not more than five years or to payment of a fine of not more than $10,000, or both;

(2) a human being is injured and bodily harm incurred, is guilty of a crime and may be sentenced to imprisonment for not more than one year or to payment of a fine of not more than $3,000, or both; or

(3) property of another is injured, thereby, is guilty of a crime and may be sentenced as follows:

(i) to imprisonment for not more than 90 days or to payment of a fine of not more than $1,000, or both, if the value of the property damage is under $300;

(ii) to imprisonment for not more than one year, or to payment of a fine of not more than $3,000, or both, if the value of the property damaged is at least $300 but is less than $2,500; or

(iii) to imprisonment for not more than three years, or to payment of a fine of not more than $5,000, or both, if the value of the property damaged is $2,500 or more.

Subd. 2. **Dangerous smoking.** A person is guilty of a misdemeanor if the person smokes in the presence of explosives or inflammable materials. If a person violates this subdivision and knows that doing so creates a risk of death or bodily harm or serious property damage, the person is guilty of a felony and may be sentenced to imprisonment for not more than five years or to payment of a fine of not more than $10,000, or both.
HIST: 1976 c 124 s 7; * * * 2003 c 82 s 1

609.581 DEFINITIONS.

Subdivision 1. **Terms defined.** For purpose of sections 609.582 and 609.583 the terms defined in this section have the meanings given them.

Subd. 2. **Building.** "Building" means a structure suitable for affording shelter for human beings including any appurtenant or connected structure.

Subd. 3. **Dwelling.** "Dwelling" means a building used as a permanent or temporary residence.

Subd 4. **Enters a building without consent.** "Enters a building without consent" means:

(a) to enter a building without the consent of the person in lawful possession;

(b) to enter a building by using artifice, trick, or misrepresentation to obtain consent to enter from the person in lawful possession; or

(c) to remain within a building without the consent of the person in lawful possession.

Whoever enters a building while open to the general public does so with consent except when consent was expressly withdrawn before entry.

Subd. 5. **Government building.** "Government building" means a building that is owned, leased, controlled, or operated by a governmental entity for a governmental purpose.

Subd. 6. **Religious establishment.** "Religious establishment" means a building used for worship services by a religious organization and clearly identified as such by a posted sign or other means.

Subd. 7. **School building.** "School building" means a public or private preschool, elementary school, middle school, secondary school, or postsecondary school building.

Subd. 8. **Historic property.** "Historic property" means any property identified as a historic site or historic place by section 138.661 to 138.664 and clearly identified as such by a posted sign or other means.
HIST: 1983 c 321 s 1; 2007 c 54 art 2 s 11-14

609.582 BURGLARY.

Subdivision 1. **Burglary in the first degree.** Whoever enters a building without consent and with intent to commit a crime, or enters a building without consent and commits a crime while in the building, either directly or as an accomplice, commits burglary in the first degree and may be sentenced to imprisonment for not more than 20 years or to payment of a fine of not more than $35,000, or both if:

(a) the building is a dwelling and another person not an accomplice is present in it when the burglar enters or at any time while the burglar is in the building;

(b) the burglar possesses, when entering or at any time while in the building, any of the following: a dangerous weapon, any article used or fashioned in a manner to lead the victim to reasonably believe it to be a dangerous weapon, or an explosive; or

(c) the burglar assaults a person within the building or on the building's appurtenant property.

Subd. 1a. **Mandatory minimum sentence for burglary of occupied dwelling.** A person convicted of committing burglary of an occupied dwelling, as defined in subdivision 1, clause (a), must be committed to the commissioner of corrections or county workhouse for not less than six months.

Subd. 2. **Burglary in the second degree.** (a) Whoever enters a building without consent and with intent to commit a crime, or enters a building without consent and commits a crime while in the building, either directly or as an accomplice, commits burglary in the second degree and may be sentenced to imprisonment for not more than ten years or to payment of a fine of not more than $20,000, or both, if:

(1) the building is a dwelling;

(2) the portion of the building entered contains a banking business or other business of receiving securities or other valuable papers for deposit or safekeeping and the entry is with force or threat of force;

(3) the portion of the building entered contains a pharmacy or other lawful business or practice in which controlled substances are routinely held or stored, and the entry is forcible; or

(4) when entering or while in the building, the burglar possesses a tool to gain access to money or property.

(b) Whoever enters a government building, religious establishment, historic property, or school building without consent and with intent to commit a crime under section 609.52 or 609.595, or enters a government building, religious establishment, historic property, or school building without consent and commits a crime under section 609.52 or 609.595 while in the building, either directly or as an accomplice, commits burglary in the second degree and may be sentenced to imprisonment for not more than ten years or to payment of a fine of not more than $20,000, or both.

Subd. 3. **Burglary in the third degree.** Whoever enters a building without consent and with intent to steal or commit any felony or gross misdemeanor while in the building, or enters a building without consent and steals or commits a felony or gross misdemeanor while in the building, either directly or as an accomplice, commits burglary in the third degree and may be sentenced to imprisonment for not more than five years or to payment of a fine of not more than $10,000, or both.

Subd. 4. **Burglary in the fourth degree.** Whoever enters a building without consent and with intent to commit a misdemeanor other than to steal, or enters a building without consent and commits a misdemeanor other than to steal while in the building, either directly or as an accomplice, commits burglary in the fourth degree and may be sentenced to imprisonment for not more than one year or to payment of a fine of not more than $3,000, or both.
HIST: 1983 c 321 s 2; * * * 2007 c 54 art 2 s 15

609.583 SENTENCING; FIRST BURGLARY OF A DWELLING.
Except as provided in section 609.582, subdivision 1a, in determining an appropriate disposition for a first offense of burglary of a dwelling, the court shall presume that a stay of execution with at least a 90-day period of incarceration as a condition of probation shall be imposed unless the defendant's criminal history score determined according to the sentencing guidelines indicates a presumptive executed sentence, in which case the presumptive executed sentence shall be imposed unless the court departs from the sentencing guidelines pursuant to section 244.10. A stay of imposition of sentence may be granted only if accompanied by a statement on the record of the reasons for it. The presumptive period of incarceration may be waived in whole or in part by the court if the defendant provides restitution or performs community work service.
HIST: 1983 c 321 s 3; * * * 1996 c 408 art 3 s 33

Category 2, Section 1:
2.1.10. Identify the meaning of criminal justice system terms, e.g., . . . double jeopardy . . .

609.585 DOUBLE JEOPARDY.
Notwithstanding section 609.04, a prosecution for or conviction of the crime of burglary is not a bar to conviction of or punishment for any other crime committed on entering or while in the building entered.
HIST: 1963 c 753 art 1 s 609.585; 1993 c 326 art 4 s 31

Category 2, Section 5:
2.5.1. Describe the basic organization, purpose, and definitions and principles of the Minnesota Criminal Code.
2.5.5. Given a variety of scenarios, identify indications a particular crime has been committed and identify the elements of that crime.

609.59 POSSESSION OF BURGLARY OR THEFT TOOLS.
Whoever has in possession any device, explosive, or other instrumentality with intent to use or permit the use of the same to commit burglary or theft may be sentenced to imprisonment for not more than three years or to payment of a fine of not more than $5,000, or both.
HIST: 1963 c 753 art 1 s 609.59; 1984 c 628 art 3 s 11; 1986 c 444; 1988 c 712 s 13

609.595 DAMAGE TO PROPERTY.
Subdivision 1. **Criminal damage to property in the first degree.** Whoever intentionally causes damage to physical property of another without the latter's consent may be sentenced to imprisonment for not more than five years or to payment of a fine of not more than $10,000, or both if:
(1) the damage to the property caused a reasonably foreseeable risk of bodily harm; or
(2) the property damaged was a public safety motor vehicle, the defendant knew the vehicle was a public safety motor vehicle, and the damage to the vehicle caused a substantial interruption or impairment of public safety service or a reasonably foreseeable risk of bodily harm; or

(3) the property damaged belongs to a common carrier and the damage impairs the service to the public rendered by the carrier; or

(4) the damage reduces the value of the property by more than $1,000 measured by the cost of repair and replacement; or

(5) the damage reduces the value of the property by more than $500 measured by the cost of repair and replacement and the defendant has been convicted within the preceding three years of an offense under this subdivision or subdivision 2.

In any prosecution under clause (4), the value of any property damaged by the defendant in violation of that paragraph within any six-month period may be aggregated and the defendant charged accordingly in applying this section. When two or more offenses are committed by the same person in two or more counties, the accused may be prosecuted in any county in which one of the offenses was committed for all of the offenses aggregated under this paragraph.

Subd. 1a. **Criminal damage to property in the second degree.** (a) Whoever intentionally causes damage described in subdivision 2, paragraph (a), because of the property owner's or another's actual or perceived race, color, religion, sex, sexual orientation, disability as defined in section 363.01, age, or national origin is guilty of a felony and may be sentenced to imprisonment for not more than one year and a day or to payment of a fine of not more than $3,000, or both.

(b) In any prosecution under paragraph (a), the value of property damaged by the defendant in violation of that paragraph within any six-month period may be aggregated and the defendant charged accordingly in applying this section. When two or more offenses are committed by the same person in two or more counties, the accused may be prosecuted in any county in which one of the offenses was committed for all of the offenses aggregated under this paragraph.

Subd. 2. **Criminal damage to property in the third degree.** (a) Except as otherwise provided in subdivision 1a, whoever intentionally causes damage to another person's physical property without the other person's consent may be sentenced to imprisonment for not more than one year or to payment of a fine of not more than $3,000, or both, if: (1) the damage reduces the value of the property by more than $500 but not more than $1,000 as measured by the cost of repair and replacement; or (2) the damage was to a public safety motor vehicle and the defendant knew the vehicle was a public safety motor vehicle.

(b) Whoever intentionally causes damage to another person's physical property without the other person's consent because of the property owner's or another's actual or perceived race, color, religion, sex, sexual orientation, disability as defined in section 363.01, age, or national origin may be sentenced to imprisonment for not more than one year or to payment of a fine of not more than $3,000, or both, if the damage reduces the value of the property by not more than $500.

(c) In any prosecution under paragraph (a), clause (1), the value of property damaged by the defendant in violation of that paragraph within any six-month period may be aggregated and the defendant charged accordingly in applying this section. When two or more offenses are committed by the same person in two or more counties, the accused may be prosecuted in any county in which one of the offenses was committed for all of the offenses aggregated under this paragraph.

Subd. 3. **Criminal damage to property in the fourth degree.** Whoever intentionally causes damage described in subdivision 2 under any other circumstances is guilty of a misdemeanor.

Subd. 4. **Definitions.** (a) As used in this section, "public safety motor vehicle" includes [marked and specially marked vehicles used by law enforcement, fire apparatuses and fire-suppression support vehicles, ambulances, and marked vehicles used by conservation officers.]

(b) As used in subdivision 1, clause (2), and subdivision 2, paragraph (a), clause (2), "damage" includes tampering with a public safety motor vehicle and acts that obstruct or interfere with the vehicle's use.

HIST: 1963 c 753 art 1 s 609.595; * * * 2007 c 54 art 2 s 17,18; 2017 c 95 art 3 s 15-17

Editors' Note: Although the following statutes are not specifically described in these learning objectives, they have been included because of their close relationship to the general criminal damage to property statute described above.

609.593 DAMAGE OR THEFT TO ENERGY TRANSMISSION OR TELECOMMUNICATIONS EQUIPMENT.

Subdivision 1. **Crime.** Whoever intentionally and without consent from one authorized to give consent causes any damage to or takes, removes, severs, or breaks:

(1) any line erected or maintained for the purpose of transmitting electricity for light, heat, or power, or any insulator or cross—arm, appurtenance or apparatus connected to the line, or any wire, cable, or current of the line or any component * * *;

(2) any pipe or main or hazardous liquid pipeline erected, operated, or maintained for the purpose of transporting, conveying, or distributing gas or other hazardous liquids for light, heat, power, or any other purpose, or any part of the pipe, main, or pipeline, or any valve, meter, holder, compressor, machinery, appurtenance, equipment, or apparatus connected with any main or pipeline; or

(3) any machinery, equipment, or fixtures used in receiving, initiating, amplifying, processing, transmitting, retransmitting, recording, switching, or monitoring telecommunications services, such as computers, transformers, amplifiers, routers, repeaters, multiplexers, and other items performing comparable functions; and machinery, equipment, and fixtures used in the transportation of telecommunications services, radio transmitters and receivers, satellite equipment, microwave equipment, and other transporting media including wire, cable, fiber, poles, and conduit;

is guilty of a crime and may be sentenced as provided in subdivision 2.

Subd. 2. **Penalty.** Whoever violates subdivision 1 is guilty of a felony and may be sentenced to imprisonment for not more than five years or to payment of a fine of not more than $10,000, or both.

HIST: 2007 c 54 art 2 s 16; 2016 c 152 s 1

609.594 DAMAGE TO PROPERTY OF CRITICAL PUBLIC SERVICE FACILITIES, UTILITIES, AND PIPELINES.

Subdivision 1. **Definitions.** As used in this section:

(1) "critical public service facility" includes railroad yards and stations, bus stations, airports, and other mass transit facilities; oil refineries; storage areas or facilities for hazardous materials, hazardous substances, or hazardous wastes; and bridges;

(2) "pipeline" has the meaning given in section 609.6055, subdivision 1; and

(3) "utility" includes: (i) any organization defined as a utility in section 216C.06, subdivision 18; (ii) any telecommunications carrier or telephone company regulated under chapter 237; and (iii) any local utility or enterprise formed for the purpose of providing electrical or gas heating and power, telephone, water, sewage, wastewater, or other related utility service * * *.

Subd. 2. **Prohibited conduct; penalty.** Whoever causes damage to the physical property of a critical public service facility, utility, or pipeline with the intent to significantly disrupt the operation of or the provision of services by the facility, utility, or pipeline and without the consent of one authorized to give consent, is guilty of a felony and may be sentenced to imprisonment for not more than ten years or to payment of a fine of not more than $20,000, or both.

Subd. 3. **Detention authority; immunity.** An employee or other person designated by a critical public service facility, utility, or pipeline to ensure the provision of services by the critical public service facility or the safe operation of the equipment or facility of the utility or pipeline who has reasonable cause to believe that a person is violating this section may detain the person as provided in this subdivision. The person detained must be promptly informed of the purpose of the detention and may not be subjected to unnecessary or unreasonable force or interrogation. The employee or other designated person must notify a peace officer promptly of the detention and may only detain the person for a reasonable period of time. No employee or other designated person is criminally or civilly liable for any detention that the employee or person reasonably believed was authorized by and conducted in conformity with this subdivision.

HIST: 2002 c 401 art 1 s 16

609.596 KILLING OR HARMING A PUBLIC SAFETY DOG.

Subdivision 1. **Felony.** It is a felony for any person to intentionally and without justification cause the death of or great or substantial bodily harm to a police dog, a search and rescue dog, or an arson dog when the dog is involved in law enforcement, fire, or correctional investigation or apprehension, search and rescue duties, or the dog is in the custody of or under the control of a peace officer, a trained handler, or an employee of a correctional facility. A person convicted under this subdivision may be sentenced to imprisonment for not more than two years or to payment of a fine of not more than $5,000, or both.

Subd. 2. **Gross misdemeanor.** It is a gross misdemeanor for any person to intentionally and without justification cause demonstrable harm to a police dog, search and rescue dog, or an arson dog when the dog is involved in law enforcement, fire, or correctional investigation or apprehension, search and rescue duties, or the dog is in the custody of or under the control of a peace officer, a trained handler, or an employee of a correctional facility.

Subd. 2a. **Misdemeanor.** It is a misdemeanor for any person to intentionally and without justification assault a police dog, search and rescue dog, or an arson dog when the dog is involved in law enforcement, fire, or correctional investigation or apprehension, search and rescue duties, or the dog is in the custody of or under the control of a peace officer, a trained handler, or an employee of a correctional facility.

Subd. 2b. **Mandatory restitution.** The court shall order a person convicted of violating this section to pay restitution for the costs and expenses resulting from the crime. Costs and expenses include, but are not limited to, the purchase and training of a replacement dog and veterinary services for the injured dog. If the court finds that the convicted person is indigent, the court may reduce the amount of restitution to a reasonable level or order it paid in installments.

Subd. 3. **Definitions.** As used in this section:

(1) "arson dog" means a dog that has been certified as an arson dog by a state fire or police agency or by an independent testing laboratory;

(2) "correctional facility" has the meaning given in section 241.021, subdivision 1, clause (5);

(3) "peace officer" has the meaning given in section 626.84, subdivision 1, paragraph (c); and

(4) "search and rescue dog" means a dog that is trained to locate lost or missing persons, victims of natural or other disasters, and human bodies.

HIST: 1987 c 167 s 1; * * * 2011 c 9 s 1

609.605 TRESPASS.

Subdivision 1. **Misdemeanor.** (a) The following terms have the meanings given them for purposes of this section.

(1) "Premises" means real property and any appurtenant building or structure.

(2) "Dwelling" means the building or part of a building used by an individual as a place of residence on either a full-time or a part-time basis. A dwelling may be part of a multidwelling or multipurpose building, or a manufactured home as defined in section 168.011, subdivision 8.

(3) "Construction site" means the site of the construction, alteration, painting, or repair of a building or structure.

(4) "Owner or lawful possessor," as used in paragraph (b), clause (9), means the person on whose behalf a building or dwelling is being constructed, altered, painted, or repaired and the general contractor or subcontractor engaged in that work.

(5) "Posted," as used:

(i) in paragraph (b), clause (4), means the placement of a sign at least 8-1/2 inches by 11 inches in a conspicuous place on the exterior of the building, or in a conspicuous place within the property on which the building is located. The sign must carry a general notice warning against trespass.

(ii) in paragraph (b), clause (9), means the placement of a sign at least 8-1/2 inches by 11 inches in a conspicuous place on the exterior of the building that is under construction, alteration, or repair, or in a conspicuous place within the area being protected. If the area being protected is less than three acres, one additional sign must be conspicuously placed within that area. If the area being protected is three acres but less than ten acres, two additional signs must be conspicuously placed within that area. For each additional full ten acres of area being protected beyond the first ten acres of the area, two additional signs must be conspicuously placed within the area being protected. The sign must carry a general notice warning against trespass; and

(iii) in paragraph (b), clause (10), means the placement of signs that:

(A) carry a general notice warning against trespass;

(B) display letters at least two inches high;

(C) state that Minnesota law prohibits trespassing on the property; and

(D) are posted in a conspicuous place and at intervals of 500 feet or less.

(6) "Business licensee," as used in paragraph (b), clause (9), includes a representative of a building trades labor or management organization.

(7) "Building" has the meaning given in section 609.581, subdivision 2.

(b) A person is guilty of a misdemeanor if the person intentionally:

(1) permits domestic animals or fowls under the actor's control to go on the land of another within a city;

(2) interferes unlawfully with a monument, sign, or pointer erected or marked to designate a point of a boundary, line or a political subdivision, or of a tract of land;

(3) trespasses on the premises of another and, without claim of right, refuses to depart from the premises on demand of the lawful possessor;

(4) occupies or enters the dwelling or locked or posted building of another, without claim of right or consent of the owner or the consent of one who has the right to give consent, except in an emergency situation;

(5) enters the premises of another with intent to take or injure any fruit, fruit trees, or vegetables growing on the premises, without the permission of the owner or occupant;

(6) enters or is found on the premises of a public or private cemetery without authorization during hours the cemetery is posted as closed to the public;

(7) returns to the property of another with the intent to abuse, disturb, or cause distress in or threaten another, after being told to leave the property and not to return, if the actor is without claim of right to the property or consent of one with authority to consent;

(8) returns to the property of another within one year after being told to leave the property and not to return, if the actor is without claim of right to the property or consent of one with authority to consent;

(9) enters the locked or posted construction site of another without the consent of the owner or lawful possessor, unless the person is a business licensee;

(10) enters the locked or posted aggregate mining site of another without the consent of the owner or lawful possessor, unless the person is a business licensee; or

(11) crosses into or enters any public or private area lawfully cordoned off by or at the direction of a peace officer engaged in the performance of official duties. * * * [A]n area may be "cordoned off" through the use of tape, barriers, or other means conspicuously placed and identifying the areas as being restricted by a peace officer and identifying the responsible authority * * *. It is an affirmative defense to a charge under this clause that a peace officer permitted entry into the restricted area.

Subd. 2. **Gross misdemeanor.** Whoever trespasses upon the grounds of a facility providing emergency shelter services for battered women, as defined under section 611A.31, subdivision 3, or providing comparable services for sex trafficking victims, as defined under section 609.321, subdivision 7b, or of a facility providing transitional housing for battered women and their children or sex trafficking victims and their children, without claim of right or consent of one who has right to give consent, and refuses to depart from the grounds of the facility on demand of one who has right to give consent, is guilty of a gross misdemeanor. * * *

Subd. 4. **Trespasses on school property.** (a) It is a misdemeanor for a person to enter or be found in a public or nonpublic elementary, middle, or secondary school building unless the person:

(1) is an enrolled student in, a parent or guardian of an enrolled student in, or an employee of the school or school district;

(2) has permission or an invitation from a school official to be in the building;

(3) is attending a school event, class, or meeting to which the person, the public, or a student's family is invited; or

(4) has reported the person's presence in the school building in the manner required for visitors to the school.

(b) It is a misdemeanor for a person to be on the roof of a public or nonpublic elementary, middle, or secondary school building unless the person has permission from a school official to be on the roof of the building.

(c) It is a gross misdemeanor for a group of three or more persons to enter or be found in a public or nonpublic elementary, middle, or secondary school building unless one of the persons:

(1) is an enrolled student in, a parent or guardian of an enrolled student in, or an employee of the school or school district;

(2) has permission or an invitation from a school official to be in the building;

(3) is attending a school event, class, or meeting to which the person, the public, or a student's family is invited; or

(4) has reported the person's presence in the school building in the manner required for visitors to the school.

(d) It is a misdemeanor for a person to enter or be found on school property within one year after being told by the school principal or the principal's designee to leave the property and not to return, unless the principal or the principal's designee has given the person permission to return to the property. As used in this paragraph, "school property" has the meaning given in section 152.01, subdivision 14a, clauses (1) and (3).

(e) A school principal or a school employee designated by the school principal to maintain order on school property, who has reasonable cause to believe that a person is violating this subdivision may detain the person in a reasonable manner for a reasonable period of time pending the arrival of a peace officer. A school principal or designated school employee is not civilly or criminally liable for any action authorized under this paragraph if the person's action is based on reasonable cause.

(f) A peace officer may arrest a person without a warrant if the officer has probable cause to believe the person violated this subdivision within the preceding four hours. The arrest may be made even though the violation did not occur in the peace officer's presence.

Subd. 4a. **Trespass on a school bus.** * * * (c) A person who boards a school bus when the bus is on its route or otherwise in operation, or while it has pupils (persons in grades prekindergarten through grade 12) on it, and who refuses to leave the bus on demand of the bus operator, is guilty of a misdemeanor.

Subd. 5. **Certain trespass on agricultural land.** (a) A person is guilty of a gross misdemeanor if the person enters the posted premises of another on which cattle, bison, sheep, goats, swine, horses, poultry, farmed cervidae, farmed ratitae, aquaculture stock, or other species of domestic animals for commercial production are kept, without the consent of the owner or lawful occupant of the land. * * *

(c) "Posted," as used in paragraph (a), means the placement of a sign at least 11 inches square in a conspicuous place at each roadway entry to the premises. The sign must provide notice of a bio-security area and wording such as: "Bio-security measures are in force. No entrance beyond this point without authorization." * * *

(d) The provisions of this subdivision do not apply to employees or agents of the state or county when serving in a regulatory capacity and conducting an inspection on posted premises where domestic animals are kept.

EFFECTIVE DATE. This section is effective September 15, 2021, and applies to crimes committed on or after that date.

HIST: 1963 c 753 art 1 s 609.605; * * * 2009 c 123 s 14; 2017 c 95 art 3 s 18; 1Sp2021 c 11 art 2 s 41

Editors' Note: Although the following statutes are not specifically described in these learning objectives, they have been included because of their close relationship to the general trespass statute described above.

609.6055 TRESPASS ON CRITICAL PUBLIC SERVICE FACILITY; UTILITY; OR PIPELINE.

Subdivision 1. **Definitions.** (a) As used in this section, the following terms have the meanings given.

(b) "Critical public service facility" includes buildings and other physical structures, and fenced in or otherwise enclosed property, of railroad yards and stations, bus stations, airports, and other mass transit facilities; oil refineries; and storage areas or facilities for hazardous materials, hazardous substances, or hazardous wastes. The term also includes nonpublic portions of bridges. The term does not include railroad tracks extending beyond a critical public service facility.

(c) "Pipeline" includes an aboveground pipeline, a below ground pipeline housed in an underground structure, and any equipment, facility, or building located in this state that is used to transport natural or synthetic gas, crude petroleum or petroleum fuels or oil or their derivatives, or hazardous liquids, to or within a distribution, refining, manufacturing, or storage facility that is located inside or outside of this state. Pipeline does not include service lines.

(d) "Utility" includes:

(1) any organization defined as a utility in section 216C.06, subdivision 18;

(2) any telecommunications carrier or telephone company regulated under chapter 237; and

(3) any local utility or enterprise formed for the purpose of providing electrical or gas heating and power, telephone, water, sewage, wastewater, or other related utility service[.]

The term does not include property located above buried power or telecommunications lines or property located below suspended power or telecommunications lines, unless the property is fenced in or otherwise enclosed.

(e) "Utility line" includes power, telecommunications, and transmissions lines as well as related equipment owned or controlled by a utility.

Subd. 2. **Prohibited conduct; penalty.** (a) Whoever enters or is found upon property containing a critical public service facility, utility, or pipeline, without claim of right or consent of one who has the right to give consent to be on the property, is guilty of a gross misdemeanor, if:

(1) the person refuses to depart from the property on the demand of one who has the right to give consent;

(2) within the past six months, the person had been told by one who had the right to give consent to leave the property and not to return, unless a person with the right to give consent has given the person permission to return; or

(3) the property is posted.

(b) Whoever enters an underground structure that (1) contains a utility line or pipeline and (2) is not open to the public for pedestrian use, without claim of right or consent of one who has the right to give consent to be in the underground structure, is guilty of a gross misdemeanor. The underground structure does not need to be posted for this paragraph to apply.

Subd. 3. **Posting.** For purposes of this section, a critical public service facility, utility, or pipeline is posted if there are signs that:

(1) state "no trespassing" or similar terms;

(2) display letters at least two inches high;

(3) state that Minnesota law prohibits trespassing on the property; and

(4) are posted in a conspicuous place and at intervals of 500 feet or less.

Subd. 4. **Detention authority; immunity.** An employee or other person designated by a critical public service facility, utility, or pipeline to ensure the provision of services by the critical public service facility or the safe operation of the equipment or facility of the utility or pipeline who has reasonable cause to believe that a person is violating this section may detain the person as provided in this subdivision. The person detained must be promptly informed of the purpose of the detention and may not be subjected to unnecessary or unreasonable force or interrogation. The employee or other designated person must notify a peace officer promptly of the detention and may only detain the person for a reasonable period of time. No employee or other designated person is criminally or civilly liable for any detention that the employee or person reasonably believed was authorized by and conducted in conformity with this subdivision.

Subd. 5. **Arrest authority.** A peace officer may arrest a person without a warrant if the officer has probable cause to believe the person violated this section within the preceding four hours. The arrest may be made even though the violation did not occur in the presence of the peace officer.

HIST: 2002 c 401 art 1 s 18; 2008 c 217 s 1,2

609.6057 GEOGRAPHIC RESTRICTION.

Subdivision 1. **Definition.** As used in this section, "geographic restriction" means a limitation prohibiting a defendant in a criminal proceeding or a juvenile offender in a delinquency proceeding from entering a designated property or geographic area.

Subd. 2. **Prohibited conduct; penalty.** A person who knows of a geographic restriction order issued against the person and intentionally enters or remains in the restricted area is guilty of a misdemeanor.

Subd. 3. **Notice.** (a) A geographic restriction may be issued as a pretrial order before final disposition of the underlying criminal case, as a postconviction probationary order, or both. [The] order is independent of any condition of pretrial release or probation imposed on the defendant [and] may be issued in addition to a similar restriction imposed as a condition of pretrial release or probation.

(b) A court may issue a geographic restriction upon a finding that its issuance will serve the interests of protecting public safety or property. * * *

(c) A court may grant any exceptions to a geographic restriction that it deems necessary in order to avoid the imposition of a significant hardship upon a defendant. * * *

(e) A court issuing a geographic restriction order under this section shall notify a defendant:

(1) of the area subject to a geographic restriction; and

(2) that violation of the geographic restriction order is a crime.

Subd. 4. **Cancellation.** (a) A court shall cancel a pretrial geographic restriction order at the final disposition of the underlying criminal case, and a postconviction [order] when an offender completes a period of probationary supervision or is committed to the commissioner of corrections. The court may cancel a postconviction [order] at any time during which an offender is under probationary supervision.

HIST: 2017 c 95 art 3 s 19

609.611 INSURANCE FRAUD.

Subdivision 1. **Insurance fraud prohibited.** Whoever with the intent to defraud for the purpose of depriving another of property or for pecuniary gain, commits, or permits its employees or its agents to commit any of the following acts, is guilty of insurance fraud and may be sentenced as provided in subdivision 3:

(a) Presents, causes to be presented, or prepares with knowledge or reason to believe that it will be presented, by or on behalf of an insured, claimant, or applicant to an insurer, insurance professional, or premium finance company in connection with an insurance transaction or premium finance transaction, any information that contains a false representation as to any material fact, or that conceals a material fact concerning any of the following:

(1) an application for, rating of, or renewal of, an insurance policy;

(2) a claim for payment or benefit under an insurance policy;

(3) a payment made according to the terms of an insurance policy;

(4) an application used in a premium finance transaction;

(b) Presents, causes to be presented, or prepares with knowledge or reason to believe that it will be presented, to or by an insurer, insurance professional, or a premium finance company in connection with an insurance transaction or premium finance transaction, any information that contains a false representation as to any material fact, or that conceals a material fact, concerning any of the following:

(1) a solicitation for sale of an insurance policy or purported insurance policy;

(2) an application for certificate of authority;

(3) the financial condition of an insurer; or

(4) the acquisition, formation, merger, affiliation, or dissolution of an insurer;

(c) Solicits or accepts new or renewal insurance risks by or for an insolvent insurer;

(d) Removes the assets or any record of assets, transactions, and affairs or any material part thereof, from the home office or other place of business of an insurer, or from the place of safekeeping of an insurer, or destroys or sequesters the same from the department of commerce.

(e) Diverts, misappropriates, converts, or embezzles funds of an insurer, insured, claimant, or applicant for insurance in connection with:

(1) an insurance transaction;

(2) the conducting of business activities by an insurer or insurance professional; or

(3) the acquisition, formation, merger, affiliation, or dissolution of any insurer.
* * *

Subd. 3. **Sentence.** Whoever violates this provision may be sentenced as provided in section 609.52, subdivision 3, based on the greater of (i) the value of property, services, or other benefit wrongfully obtained or attempted to obtain, or (ii) the aggregate economic loss suffered by any person as a result of the violation. A person convicted of a violation of this section must be ordered to pay restitution to persons aggrieved by the violation. Restitution must be ordered in addition to a fine or imprisonment but not in lieu of a fine or imprisonment.

Subd. 4. **Definitions.** (a) "Insurance policy" means the written instrument in which are set forth the terms of any certificate of insurance, binder of coverage, or contract of insurance (including a certificate, binder, or contract issued by a state-assigned risk plan); benefit plan; nonprofit hospital service plan; motor club service plan; or surety bond, cash bond, or any other alternative to insurance authorized by a state's financial responsibility act.

(b) "Insurance professional" means sales agents, agencies, managing general agents, brokers, producers, claims representatives, adjusters, and third-party administrators.

(c) "Insurance transaction" means a transaction by, between or among: (1) an insurance or a person who acts on behalf of an insurer; and (2) an insured, claimant, applicant for insurance, public adjuster, insurance professional, practitioner, or any person who acts on behalf of any of the foregoing, for the purpose of obtaining insurance or reinsurance, calculating insurance premiums, submitting a claim, negotiating or adjusting a claim, or otherwise obtaining insurance, self-insurance, or reinsurance or obtaining the benefits thereof or therefrom.

(d) "Insurer" means a person purporting to engage in the business of insurance or authorized to do business in the state or subject to regulation by the state, who undertakes to indemnify another against loss, damage or liability arising from a contingent or unknown event. Insurer includes, but is not limited to, an insurance company; self-insurer; reinsurer; reciprocal exchange; interinsurer; risk retention group; Lloyd's insurer; fraternal benefit society; surety; medical service, dental, optometric, or any other similar health service plan; and any other legal entity engaged or purportedly engaged in the business of insurance * * *.

(e) "Premium" means consideration paid or payable for coverage under an insurance policy. * * *

(f) "Premium finance company" means a person engaged or purporting to engage in the business of advancing money, directly or indirectly, to an insurer or producer as the request of an insured under the terms of a premium finance agreement[.]

(g) "Premium finance transaction" means a transaction by, between, or among an insured, a producer or other party claiming to act on behalf of an insured and a third-party premium finance company, for the purposes or purportedly or actually advancing money directly or indirectly to an insurer or producer at the request of an insured under the terms of a premium finance agreement[.]
HIST: 1976 c 124 s 8; * * * 1996 c 408 art 3 s 36

609.615 DEFEATING SECURITY ON REALTY.
Whoever removes or damages real property which is subject to a mortgage, mechanic's lien, or contract for deed, including during the period of time allowed for redemption, with intent to impair the value of the property, without the consent of the security holder, may be sentenced as follows:

(1) if the value of the property is impaired by $300 or less, to imprisonment for not more than 90 days or to payment of a fine of not more than $1,000, or both; or

(2) if the value of the property is impaired by more than $300, to imprisonment for not more than five years or to payment of a fine of not more than $10,000, or both.
HIST: 1963 c 753 art 1 s 609.615; * * * 2004 c 228 art 1 s 72

609.62 DEFEATING SECURITY ON PERSONALTY.

Subdivision 1. **Definition.** In this section "security interest" means an interest in property which secure payment or other performance of an obligation.

Subd. 2. **Acts constituting.** Whoever, with intent to defraud, does any of the following may be sentenced to imprisonment for not more than three years or to payment of a fine of not more than $6,000, or both:

(1) conceals, removes, or transfers any personal property in which the actor knows that another has a security interest; or

(2) being an obligor and knowing the location of the property refuses to disclose the same to an obligee entitled to possession thereof.

HIST: 1963 c 753 art 1 s 609.62, * * * 1989 c 290 art 6 s 21

609.621 PROOF OF CONCEALMENT OF PROPERTY BY OBLIGOR OF SECURED PROPERTY.

Subdivision 1. **Crime defined; obligor conceals property.** When in any prosecution under section 609.62, it appears that there is a default in the payment of the debts secured and it further appears that the obligor has failed or refused to reveal the location of the security, this shall be considered sufficient evidence to sustain a finding that the obligor has removed, concealed, or disposed of the property.

Subd. 2. **Allegation.** In any prosecution under section 609.62, it is a sufficient allegation and description of the security and the property secured to state generally that such property was duly mortgaged or sold under a conditional sales contract, or as the case may be, giving the date thereof and the names of the obligor and obligee.

HIST: 1963 c 753 art 2 s 15

Chapter 13 -- FORGERY AND RELATED CRIMES

▬▬▬▬▬▬▬▬▬▬▬▬▬▬▬▬▬▬▬▬▬▬▬▬▬▬▬▬▬▬▬▬

Category 2, Section 5:
2.5.1. Describe the basic organization, purpose, and definitions and principles of the Minnesota Criminal Code.
2.5.5. Given a variety of scenarios, identify indications a particular crime has been committed and identify the elements of that crime.

▬▬▬▬▬▬▬▬▬▬▬▬▬▬▬▬▬▬▬▬▬▬▬▬▬▬▬▬▬▬▬▬

609.625 AGGRAVATED FORGERY.

Subdivision 1. **Making or altering writing or object.** Whoever, with intent to defraud, falsely makes or alters a writing or object of any of the following kinds so that it purports to have been made by another or by the maker or alterer under an assumed or fictitious name, or at another time, or with different provisions, or by authority of one who did not give such authority, is guilty of aggravated forgery and may be sentenced to imprisonment for not more than ten years or to payment of a fine of not more than $20,000, or both:

(1) a writing or object whereby, when genuine, legal rights, privileges, or obligations are created, terminated, transferred, or evidenced, or any writing normally relied upon as evidence of debt or property rights, other than a check as defined in section 609.631 or a financial transaction card as defined in section 609.821; or

(2) an official seal or the seal of a corporation; or

(3) a public record or an official authentication or certification of a copy thereof; or

(4) an official return or certificate entitled to be received as evidence of its contents; or

(5) a court order, judgment, decree, or process; or

(6) the records or accounts of a public body, office, or officer; or

(7) the records or accounts of a bank or person, with whom funds of the state or any of its agencies or subdivisions are deposited or entrusted, relating to such funds.

Subd. 2. **Means for false reproduction.** Whoever, with intent to defraud, makes, engraves, possesses or transfers a plate or instrument for the false reproduction of a writing or object mentioned in subdivision 1, a check as defined in section 609.631, or a financial transaction card as defined in section 609.821, may be sentenced as provided in subdivision 1.

Subd. 3. **Uttering or possessing.** Whoever, with intent to defraud, utters or possesses with intent to utter any forged writing or object mentioned in subdivision 1, not including a check as defined in section 609.631 or a financial transaction card as defined in section 609.821, knowing it to have been so forged, may be sentenced as provided in subdivision 1.
HIST: 1963 c 753 art 1 s 609.625; * * * 1987 c 329 s 12

609.63 FORGERY.

Subdivision 1. **Crime defined; intent to defraud.** Whoever, with intent to injure or defraud, does any of the following is guilty of forgery and may be sentenced to imprisonment for not more than three years or to payment of a fine of not more than $5,000, or both:

(1) Uses a false writing, knowing it to be false, for the purpose of identification or recommendation; or

(2) Without consent, places, or possesses with intent to place, upon any merchandise an identifying label or stamp which is or purports to be that of another craftsperson, tradesperson, packer, or manufacturer, or disposes or possesses with intent to dispose of any merchandise so labeled or stamped; or

(3) Falsely makes or alters a membership card purporting to be that of a fraternal, business, professional, or other association, or of any labor union, or possesses any such card knowing it to have been thus falsely made or altered; or

(4) Falsely makes or alters a writing, or possesses a falsely made or altered writing, evidencing a right to transportation on a common carrier; or

(5) Destroys, mutilates, or by alteration, false entry or omission, falsifies any record, account, or other document relating to a private business; or

(6) Without authority of law, destroys, mutilates, or by alteration, false entry, or omission, falsifies any record, account, or other document relating to a person, corporation, or business, or filed in the office of, or deposited with, any public office or officer, or

(7) Destroys a writing or object to prevent it from being produced at a trial, hearing, or other proceeding authorized by law.

Subd. 2. **Crime defined; forged document at trial.** Whoever, with knowledge that it is forged, offers in evidence in any trial, hearing or other proceedings authorized by law, as genuine, any forged writing or object may be sentenced as follows:

(1) If the writing or object is offered in evidence in the trial of a felony charge, to imprisonment for not more than five years or to payment of a fine of not more than $10,000, or both; or

(2) In all other cases, to imprisonment for not more than three years or to payment of a fine of not more than $5,000, or both.

HIST: 1963 c 753 art 1 s 609.63; 1984 c 628 art 3 s 11; 1986 c 444

609.631 CHECK FORGERY; OFFERING A FORGED CHECK.

Subdivision 1. **Definitions.** (a) The definitions in this subdivision apply to this section.

(b) "Check" means a check, draft, order of withdrawal, or similar negotiable or nonnegotiable instrument.

(c) "Property" and "services" have the meanings given in section 609.52.

Subd. 2. **Check forgery; elements.** A person is guilty of check forgery and may be sentenced under subdivision 4 if the person, with intent to defraud, does any of the following:

(1) falsely makes or alters a check so that it purports to have been made by another or by the maker under an assumed or fictitious name, or at another time, or with different provisions, or by the authority of one who did not give authority; or

(2) falsely endorses or alters a check so that it purports to have been endorsed by another.

Subd. 3. **Offering a forged check; elements.** A person who, with intent to defraud, offers, or possesses with intent to offer, a forged check, whether or not it is accepted, is guilty of offering a forged check and may be sentenced as provided in subdivision 4.

Subd. 4. **Sentencing.** A person who is convicted under subdivision 2 or 3 may be sentenced as follows:

(1) to imprisonment for not more than 20 years or to payment of a fine of not more than $100,000, or both, if the forged check or checks are used to obtain or in an attempt to obtain, property or services of more than $35,000 or the aggregate amount of the forged check or checks is more than $35,000;

(2) to imprisonment for not more than ten years or to payment of a fine of not more than $20,000, or both, if the forged check or checks are used to obtain or in an attempt to obtain, property or services of more than $2,500 or the aggregate amount of the forged check or checks is more than $2,500;

(3) to imprisonment for not more than five years or to payment of a fine of not more than $10,000, or both, if:

(a) the forged check or checks are used to obtain or in an attempt to obtain, property or services of more than $250 but not more than $2,500, or the aggregate face amount of the forged check or checks is more than $250 but not more than $2,500; or

(b) the forged check or checks are used to obtain or in an attempt to obtain, property or services of no more than $250, or have an aggregate face value of no more than $250, and the person has been convicted within the preceding five years for an offense under this section, section 609.24; 609.245; 609.52; 609.53; 609.582, subdivision 1, 2, or 3; 609.625; 609.63; or 609.821, or a statute from another state in conformity with any of those sections, and the person received a felony or gross misdemeanor sentence for the offense, or a sentence that was stayed under section 609.135 if the offense to which a plea was entered would allow imposition of a felony or gross misdemeanor sentence; and

(4) to imprisonment for not more than one year or to payment of a fine of not more than $3,000, or both, if the forged check or checks are used to obtain or in an attempt to obtain, property or services of no more than $250, or the aggregate face amount of the forged check or checks is no more than $250.

In any prosecution under this subdivision, the value of the checks forged or offered by the defendant in violation of this subdivision within any six-month period may be aggregated and the defendant charged accordingly in applying the provisions of this section. When two or more offenses are committed by the same person in two or more counties, the accused may be prosecuted in any county in which one of the checks was forged or offered for all of the offenses aggregated under this paragraph.

HIST: 1987 c 329 s 13; 1988 c 712 s 14: 1989 c 290 art 7 s 10; 1999 c 218 s 4

609.635 OBTAINING SIGNATURE BY FALSE PRETENSE.

Whoever, by false pretense, obtains the signature of another to a writing which is a subject of forgery under section 609.625, subdivision 1, may be punished as therein provided.

HIST: 1963 c 753 art 1 s 609.635

Editors' Note: Although the following statute is not specifically described in these learning objectives, it has been included because of its close relationship to the public disturbance statutes of unlawful assembly and riot described above.

609.632 COUNTERFEITING OF CURRENCY.

Subdivision 1. **Manufacturing; printing.** Whoever, with the intent to defraud, falsely makes, alters, prints, scans, images, or copies any United States postal money order, United States currency, Federal Reserve note, or other obligation or security of the United States so that it purports to be genuine or has different terms or provisions than that of the United States Postal Service or United States Treasury is guilty of counterfeiting and may be sentenced as provided in subdivision 4.

Subd. 2. **Means for false reproduction.** Whoever, with the intent to defraud, makes, engraves, possesses, or transfers a plate or instrument, computer, printer, camera, software, paper, cloth, fabric, ink, or other material for the false reproduction of any United States postal money order, United States currency, Federal Reserve note, or other obligation or security of the United States is guilty of counterfeiting and may be sentenced as provided in subdivision 4.

Subd. 3. **Uttering or possessing.** Whoever with the intent to defraud, utters or possesses with the intent to utter any counterfeit United States postal money order, United States currency, Federal Reserve note, or other obligation or security of the United States, having reason to know that the money order, currency, note, or obligation or security is forged, counterfeited, falsely made, altered, or printed, is guilty of offering counterfeited currency and may be sentenced as provided in subdivision 4.

Subd. 4. **Penalty.** [The penalties for violations of the above subdivisions range from imprisonment for not more than one year or to payment of a fine of not more than $3,000, or both, to imprisonment for not more than 20 years or to payment of a fine of not more than $100,000, or both.] * * *

Subd. 5. **Aggregation; venue.** In any prosecution under this section, the value of the counterfeited United States postal money orders, United States currency, Federal Reserve notes, or other obligations or securities of the United States, offered by the defendant in violation of this section within any six-month period may be aggregated and the defendant charged accordingly in applying the provisions of this section. When two or more offenses are committed by the same person in two or more counties, the accused may be prosecuted in any county in which one of the counterfeited items was forged, offered, or possessed, for all of the offenses aggregated under this subdivision.

HIST: 2006 c 260 art 1 s 27

609.64 RECORDING, FILING OF FORGED INSTRUMENT.

Whoever intentionally presents for filing, registering, or recording, or files, registers or records a false or forged instrument relating to or affecting real or personal property a public office entitled to file, register, or record such instrument when genuine may be sentenced to imprisonment for not more than three years or to payment of a fine of not more than $5,000, or both.

HIST: 1963 c 753 art 1 s 609.64; 1984 c 628 art 3 s 11

609.645 FRAUDULENT STATEMENTS.

Whoever, with intent to injure or defraud, does any of the following may be sentenced to imprisonment for not more than three years or to payment of a fine of not more than $5,000, or both:

(1) circulates or publishes a false statement, oral or written, relating to a corporation, association, or individual, intending thereby to give a false apparent value to securities issued or to be issued by, or to the property of, such corporation, association, or individual; or

(2) makes a false ship's or airplane's manifest, invoice, register, or protest.

HIST: 1963 c 753 art 1 s 609.645; 1984 c 628 art 3 s 11

609.65 FALSE CERTIFICATION BY NOTARY PUBLIC.

Whoever, when acting or purporting to act as a notary public or other public officer, certifies falsely that an instrument has been acknowledged or that any other act was performed by a party appearing before the actor or that as such notary public or other public officer the actor performed any other official act may be sentenced as follows:

(1) If the actor so certifies with intent to injure or defraud, to imprisonment for not more than three years or to payment of a fine of not more than $5,000, or both; or

(2) In any other case, to imprisonment for not more than 90 days or to payment of a fine of not more than $1,000, or both.

HIST: 1963 c 753 art 1 s 609.65; * * * 2004 c 228 art 1 s 72

609.651 STATE LOTTERY FRAUD.

Subdivision 1. **Felony.** A person is guilty of a felony and may be sentenced under subdivision 4 if the person does any of the following with intent to defraud the state lottery:

(1) alters or counterfeits a state lottery ticket;

(2) knowingly presents an altered or counterfeited state lottery ticket for payment;

(3) knowingly transfers an altered or counterfeited state lottery ticket to another person; or

(4) otherwise claims a lottery prize by means of fraud, deceit, or misrepresentation.

Subd. 2. **Computer access.** A person is guilty of a felony and may be sentenced under subdivision 4 if the person:

(1) obtains access to a computer data base maintained by the director without the specific authorization of the director;

(2) obtains access to a computer data base maintained by a person under contract with the director to maintain the data base without the specific authorization of the director and the person maintaining the data base.

Subd. 3. **False statements.** A person is guilty of a felony and may be sentenced under subdivision 4 if the person:

(1) makes a materially false or misleading statement, or a material omission, in a record required to be submitted under chapter 349A; or

(2) makes a materially false or misleading statement, or a material omission, in information submitted to the director of the state lottery in a lottery retailer's application or a document related to a bid.

Subd. 4. **Penalty.** (a) A person who violates subdivision 1 or 2 may be sentenced to imprisonment for not more than ten years or to payment of a fine of not more than $100,000, or both.

(b) A person who violates subdivision 1 or 2 and defrauds the state lottery of $35,000 or more may be sentenced to imprisonment for not more than 20 years or to payment of a fine of not more than $100,000, or both.

(c) A person who violates subdivision 3 may be sentenced to imprisonment for not more than three years or to payment of a fine of not more than $25,000, or both.

HIST: 1989 c 334 art 3 s 16; 1989 c 356 s 36

609.652 FRAUDULENT DRIVERS' LICENSES AND IDENTIFICATION CARDS; PENALTY.

Subdivision 1. **Definitions.** For purposes of this section:

(1) "driver's license or identification card" means a driver's license or identification card issued by the driver and vehicle services division of the department of public safety or receipts issued by its authorized agents or those of any state as defined in section 171.01 that issues licenses recognized in this state for the operation of a motor vehicle or that issues identification cards recognized in this state for the purpose of indicating a person's legal name and age;

(2) "fraudulent driver's license or identification card" means a document purporting to be a driver's license or identification card, but that is not authentic; and

(3) "sell" means to sell, barter, deliver, exchange, distribute, or dispose of to another.

Subd. 2. **Criminal acts.** (a) A person who does any of the following for consideration and with intent to manufacture, sell, issue, publish, or pass more than one fraudulent driver's license or identification card or to cause or permit any of the items listed in clauses (1) to (5) to be used in forging or making more than one false or counterfeit driver's license or identification card is guilty of a crime:

(1) has in control, custody, or possession any plate, block, press, stone, digital image, computer software program, encoding equipment, computer optical scanning equipment, or digital photo printer, or other implement, or any part of such an item, designed to assist in making a fraudulent driver's license or identification card;

(2) engraves, makes, or amends, or begins to engrave, make, or amend, any plate, block, press, stone, or other implement for the purpose of producing a fraudulent driver's license or identification card;

(3) uses a photocopier, digital camera, photographic image, or computer software to generate a fraudulent driver's license or identification card;

(4) has in control, custody, or possession or makes or provides paper or other material adapted and designed for the making of a fraudulent driver's license or identification card; or

(5) prints, photographs, or in any manner makes or executes an engraved photograph, print, or impression purporting to be a driver's license or identification card.

(b) Notwithstanding section 171.22, a person who manufactures or possesses more than one fraudulent driver's license or identification card with intent to sell is guilty of a crime.

Subd. 3. **Penalties.** A person who commits any act described in subdivision 2 is guilty of a gross misdemeanor. A person convicted of a second or subsequent offense of this subdivision may be sentenced to imprisonment for not more than five years or to payment of a fine of not more than $10,000, or both.

HIST: 1Sp2001 c 8 art 8 s 27; 2006 c 212 art 1 s 19

Chapter 14 -- CRIMES AGAINST PUBLIC SAFETY AND HEALTH

Category 2, Section 5:
2.5.1. Describe the basic organization, purpose, and definitions and principles of the Minnesota Criminal Code.
2.5.5. Given a variety of scenarios, identify indications a particular crime has been committed and identify the elements of that crime.

609.66 DANGEROUS WEAPONS.

Subdivision 1. **Misdemeanor and gross misdemeanor crimes.** (a) Whoever does any of the following is guilty of a crime and may be sentenced as provided in paragraph (b):

(1) recklessly handles or uses a gun or other dangerous weapon or explosive so as to endanger the safety of another; or

(2) intentionally points a gun of any kind, capable of injuring or killing a human being and whether loaded or unloaded, at or toward another; or

(3) manufactures or sells for any unlawful purpose any weapon known as a slungshot or sand club; or

(4) manufactures, transfers, or possesses metal knuckles or a switch blade knife opening automatically; or

(5) possesses any other dangerous article or substance for the purpose of being used unlawfully as a weapon against another; or

(6) outside of a municipality and without the parent's or guardian's consent, furnishes a child under 14 years of age, or as a parent or guardian permits the child to handle or use, outside of the parent's or guardian's presence, a firearm or airgun of any kind, or any ammunition or explosive.

Possession of written evidence of prior consent signed by the minor's parent or guardian is a complete defense to a charge under clause (6).

(b) A person convicted under paragraph (a) may be sentenced as follows:

(1) if the act was committed in a public housing zone, as defined in section 152.01, subdivision 19, a school zone, as defined in section 152.01, subdivision 14a, or a park zone, as defined in section 152.01, subdivision 12a, to imprisonment for not more than one year or to payment of a fine of not more than $3,000, or both; or

(2) otherwise, including where the act was committed on residential premises within a zone described in clause (1) if the offender was at the time an owner, tenant, or invitee for a lawful purpose with respect to those residential premises, to imprisonment for not more than 90 days or to payment of a fine of not more than $1,000, or both.

Subd. 1a. **Felony crimes; suppressors; reckless discharge.** (a) Whoever does any of the following is guilty of a felony and may be sentenced as provided in paragraph (b):

(1) sells or has in possession a suppressor that is not lawfully possessed under federal law;

(2) intentionally discharges a firearm under circumstances that endanger the safety of another; or

(3) recklessly discharges a firearm within a municipality.

(b) A person convicted under paragraph (a) may be sentenced as follows:

(1) if the act was a violation of paragraph (a), clause (2), or if the act was a violation of paragraph (a), clause (1) or (3) and was committed in a public housing zone, as defined in section 152.01, subdivision 19, a school zone, as defined in section 152.01, subdivision 14a, or a park zone, as defined in section 152.01, subdivision 12a, to imprisonment for not more than five years or to payments of a fine of not more than $10,000, or both; or

(2) otherwise, to imprisonment for not more than two years or to payment of a fine of not more than $5,000, or both.

(c) As used in the subdivision, "suppressor" means any device for silencing, muffling, or diminishing the report of a portable firearm, including any combination of parts[.]

Subd. 1b. **Felony; furnishing to minors.** Whoever, in any municipality of this state, furnishes a minor under 18 years of age with a firearm, airgun, ammunition, or explosive without the prior consent of the minor's parent or guardian or of the police department of the municipality is guilty of a felony and may be sentenced to imprisonment for not more than ten years or to payment of a fine of not more than $20,000, or both. Possession of written evidence of prior consent signed by the minor's parent or guardian is a complete defense to a charge under this subdivision.

Subd. 1c. **Felony; furnishing a dangerous weapon.** Whoever recklessly furnishes a person with a dangerous weapon in conscious disregard of a known substantial risk that the object will be possessed or used in furtherance of a felony crime of violence is guilty of a felony and may be sentenced to imprisonment for not more than ten years or to payment of a fine of not more than $20,000, or both.

Subd. 1d. **Possession on school property; penalty.** (a) Except as provided under paragraphs (d) and (f), whoever possesses, stores, or keeps a dangerous weapon while knowingly on school property is guilty of a felony and may be sentenced to imprisonment for not more than five years or to payment of a fine of not more than $10,000, or both.

(b) Whoever uses or brandishes a replica firearm or a BB gun while knowingly on school property is guilty of a gross misdemeanor.

(c) Whoever possesses, stores, or keeps a replica firearm or a BB gun while knowingly on school property is guilty of a misdemeanor.

(d) Notwithstanding paragraph (a), (b) or (c), it is a misdemeanor for a person authorized to carry a firearm under the provisions of a permit or otherwise to carry a firearm on or about the person's clothes or person in a location the person knows is school property. Notwithstanding section 609.531, a firearm carried in violation of this paragraph is not subject to forfeiture.

(e) As used in this subdivision:

(1) "BB gun" means a device that fires or ejects a shot measuring .18 of an inch or less in diameter;

(2) "dangerous weapon" has the meaning given it in section 609.02, subdivision 6;

(3) "replica firearm" has the meaning given it in section 609.713; and

(4) "school property" means:

(i) a public or private elementary, middle, or secondary school building and its improved grounds, whether leased or owned by the school;

(ii) a child care center licensed under chapter 245A during the period children are present and participating in a child care program;

(iii) the area within a school bus when that bus is being used by a school to transport one or more elementary, middle, or secondary school students to and from school-related activities, including curricular, cocurricular, noncurricular, extracurricular, and supplementary activities; and

(iv) that portion of a building or facility under the temporary, exclusive control of a public or private school, a school district, or an association of such entities where conspicuous signs are prominently posted at each entrance that give actual notice to persons of the school-related use.

(f) This subdivision does not apply to:

(1) active licensed peace officers;

(2) military personnel, or students participating in military training, who are on-duty, performing official duties;

(3) persons authorized to carry a pistol under section 624.714 while in a motor vehicle or outside of a motor vehicle to directly place a firearm in, or retrieve it from, the trunk or rear area of the vehicle;

(4) persons who keep or store in a motor vehicle pistols in accordance with section 624.714 or 624.715 or other firearms in accordance with section 97B.045;

(5) firearm safety or marksmanship courses or activities conducted on school property;

(6) possession of dangerous weapons, BB guns, or replica firearms by a ceremonial color guard;

(7) a gun or knife show held on school property;

(8) possession of dangerous weapons, BB guns, or replica firearms with written permission of the principal or other person having general control and supervision of the school or the director of a child care center; or

(9) persons who are on unimproved property owned or leased by a child care center, school, or school district unless the person knows that a student is currently present on the land for a school-related activity.

(g) Notwithstanding section 471.634, a school district or other entity composed exclusively of school districts may not regulate firearms, ammunition, or their respective components, when possessed or carried by nonstudents or nonemployees, in a manner that is inconsistent with this subdivision.

Subd. 1e. **Felony; drive-by shooting.** (a) Whoever, A person is guilty of a felony who, while in or having just exited from a motor vehicle, recklessly discharges a firearm at or toward another

(1) an unoccupied motor vehicle, or a building; is guilty of a felony and may be sentenced to imprisonment for not more than three years or to payment of a fine of not more than $6,000, or both.

(2) an occupied motor vehicle or building; or

(3) a person.

(b) Any person who violates this subdivision by firing at or toward a person, or an occupied building or motor vehicle, may be sentenced A person convicted under paragraph (a), clause (1) may be sentenced to imprisonment for not more than three years or to payment of a fine of not more than $6,000, or both. A person convicted under paragraph (a), clause (2) or (3), may be sentenced to imprisonment for not more than ten years or to payment of a fine of not more than $20,000, or both.

(c) For purposes of this subdivision, "motor vehicle" has the meaning given in section 609.52, subdivision 1, and "building" has the meaning given in section 609.581, subdivision 2.

Subd. 1f. **Gross misdemeanor; transferring a firearm without background check.** A person, other than a federally licensed firearms dealer, who transfers a pistol or semiautomatic military-style assault weapon to another without complying with the transfer requirements of section 624.7132, is guilty of a gross misdemeanor if the transferee possesses or uses the weapon within one year after the transfer in furtherance of a felony crime of violence, and if:

(1) the transferee was prohibited from possessing the weapon under section 624.713 at the time of the transfer; or

(2) it was reasonably foreseeable at the time of the transfer that the transferee was likely to use or possess the weapon in furtherance of a felony crime of violence.

Subd. 1g. **Felony; possession in courthouse or certain state buildings.** (a) A person who commits either of the following acts is guilty of a felony and may be sentenced to imprisonment for not more than five years or to payment of a fine of not more than $10,000, or both:

(1) possesses a dangerous weapon, ammunition, or explosive within any courthouse complex; or

(2) possesses a dangerous weapon, ammunition, or explosive in any state building within the capitol area described in section 15.50, other than the National Guard Armory.

(b) Unless a person is otherwise prohibited or restricted by other law to possess a dangerous weapon, this subdivision does not apply to:

(1) licensed peace officers or military personnel who are performing official duties;

(2) persons who carry pistols according to the terms of a permit issued under section 624.714 and who so notify the sheriff or the commissioner of public safety, as appropriate;

(3) persons who possess dangerous weapons for the purpose of display as demonstrative evidence during testimony at a trial or hearing or exhibition in compliance with advance notice and safety guidelines set by the sheriff or the commissioner of public safety; or

(4) persons who possess dangerous weapons in a courthouse complex with the express consent of the county sheriff or who possess dangerous weapons in a state building with the express consent of the commissioner of public safety.

(c) For purposes of this subdivision, the issuance of a permit to carry under section 624.714 constitutes notification of the commissioner of public safety as required under paragraph (b), clause (2).

Subd. 1h. [Repealed, 2015 c 65 art 3 s 38]

Subd. 2. **Exceptions.** Nothing in this section prohibits the possession of the articles mentioned by museums or collectors of art or for other lawful purposes of public exhibition.

EFFECTIVE DATE. This section is effective September 15, 2021, and applies to crimes committed on or after that date.

HIST: 1963 c 753 art 1 s 609.66; * * * 2012 c 194 s 1; 1Sp2021 c 11 art 2 s 42

609.67 MACHINE GUNS AND SHORT-BARRELED SHOTGUNS.

Subdivision 1. **Definitions.** (a) "Machine gun" means any firearm designed to discharge, or capable of discharging automatically more than once by a single function of the trigger.

(b) "Shotgun" means a weapon designed, redesigned, made or remade which is intended to be fired from the shoulder and uses the energy of the explosive in a fixed shotgun shell to fire through a smooth bore either a number of ball shot or a single projectile for each single pull of the trigger.

(c) "Short-barreled shotgun" means a shotgun having one or more barrels less than 18 inches in length and any weapon made from a shotgun if such weapon as modified has an overall length less than 26 inches.

(d) "Trigger activator" means a removable manual or power driven trigger activating device constructed and designed so that, when attached to a firearm, the rate at which the trigger may be pulled increases and the rate of fire of the firearm increases to that of a machine gun.

(e) "Machine gun conversion kit" means any part or combination of parts designed and intended for use in converting a weapon into a machine gun, and any combination of parts from which a machine gun can be assembled, but does not include a spare or replacement part for a machine gun that is possessed lawfully under section 609.67, subdivision 3.

Subd. 2. **Acts prohibited.** Except as otherwise provided herein, whoever owns, possesses, or operates a machine gun, any trigger activator or machine gun conversion kit, or a short-barreled shotgun may be sentenced to imprisonment for not more than five years or to payment of a fine of not more than $10,000, or both.

Subd. 3. **Uses permitted.** The following persons may own or possess a machine gun or short-barreled shotgun provided the provisions of subdivision 4 are complied with:

(1) law enforcement officers for use in the course of their duties;

(2) chief executive officers of correctional facilities and other personnel thereof authorized by them and persons in charge of other institutions for the retention of persons convicted or accused of crime, for use in the course of their duties;

(3) persons possessing machine guns or short-barreled shotguns which, although designed as weapons, have been determined by the superintendent of the bureau of criminal apprehension or the superintendent's delegate by reason of the date of manufacture, value, design or other characteristics to be primarily collector's items, relics, museum pieces or objects of curiosity, ornaments or keepsakes, and are not likely to be used as weapons;

(4) manufacturers of ammunition who possess and use machine guns for the sole purpose of testing ammunition manufactured for sale to federal and state agencies or political subdivisions;

(5) dealers and manufacturers who are federally licensed to buy and sell, or manufacture machine guns or short-barreled shotguns and who either use the machine guns or short-barreled shotguns in peace officer training under courses approved by the board of peace officer standards

and training, or are engaged in the sale of machine guns or short-barreled shotguns to federal and state agencies or political subdivisions; and

(6) persons employed by the Minnesota National Guard as security guards, for use in accordance with applicable federal military regulations.

Subd. 4. **Report required.** (a) A person owning or possessing a machine gun or short-barreled shotgun as authorized by subdivision 3, clause (1), (2), (3), or (4) shall, within ten days after acquiring such ownership or possession, file a written report with the bureau of criminal apprehension, showing the person's name and address; the person's official title and position, if any; a description of the machine gun or short-barreled shotgun sufficient to enable identification thereof; the purpose for which it is owned or possessed; and such further information as the bureau may reasonably require.

(b) A dealer or manufacturer owning or having a machine gun or short-barreled shotgun as authorized by subdivision 3, clause (5) shall, by the tenth day of each month, file a written report with the bureau of criminal apprehension showing the name and address of the dealer or manufacturer and the serial number of each machine gun or short-barreled shotgun acquired or manufactured during the previous month.

Subd. 5. **Exceptions.** This section does not apply to members of the armed services of either the United States or the state of Minnesota for use in the course of their duties or to security guards employed by the Minnesota National Guard for use in accordance with applicable federal military regulations.

Subd. 6. **Preemption.** Laws 1977, chapter 255, supersedes all local ordinances, rules and regulations.
HIST: 1963 c 753 art 1 s 609.67; * * * 2006 c 273 s 11,12

Category 2, Section 5:
2.5.1. Describe the basic organization, purpose, and definitions and principles of the Minnesota Criminal Code.
2.5.3. Explain what is meant by elements of a crime and describe the connection between criminal conduct and criminal intent (mens rea).
2.5.5. Given a variety of scenarios, identify indications a particular crime has been committed and identify the elements of that crime.

609.671 ENVIRONMENT; CRIMINAL PENALTIES.
Subdivision 1. **Definitions.** The definitions in this subdivision apply to this section.

(a) "Agency" means the pollution control agency.

(b) "Deliver" or "delivery" means the transfer of possession of hazardous waste, with or without consideration.

(c) "Dispose" or "disposal" has the meaning given it in section 115A.03, subdivision 9.

(d) "Hazardous air pollutant" means an air pollutant listed under [federal law].

(e) "Hazardous waste" means any waste identified as hazardous under the authority of section 116.07, subdivision 4, except for those wastes exempted under Minnesota Rules, part 7045.0120, wastes generated under Minnesota Rules, part 7045.0213, and household appliances.

(f) "Permit" means a permit issued by the pollution control agency under chapter 115 or 116 or the rules promulgated under those chapters including interim status for hazardous waste facilities.

(g) "Solid waste" has the meaning given in section 116.06, subdivision 22.

(h) "Toxic pollutant" means a toxic pollutant on the list established under [federal law].

Subd. 2. **Definition of knowing.** (a) For purposes of this section, an act is committed knowingly if it is done voluntarily and is not the result of negligence, mistake, accident, or circumstances that are beyond the control of the defendant. Whether an act was knowing may be

inferred from the person's conduct, from the person's familiarity with the subject matter in question, or from all of the facts and circumstances connected with the case. Knowledge may also be established by evidence that the person took affirmative steps to shield the person from relevant information. Proof of knowledge does not require that a person knew a particular act or failure to act was a violation of law or that the person had specific knowledge of the regulatory limits or testing procedures involved in a case.
   * * *
   Subd. 3. **Knowing endangerment.** (a) A person is guilty of a felony if the person:
   (1) commits an act described in subdivision 4, 5, 8, paragraph (a), or 12; and
   (2) at the time of the violation knowingly places another person in imminent danger of death, great bodily harm, or substantial bodily harm.
   (b) A person convicted under this subdivision may be sentenced to imprisonment for not more than ten years, or to payment of a fine of not more than $100,000, or both, except that a defendant that is an organization may be sentenced to payment of a fine of not more than $1,000,000.
   Subd. 4. **Hazardous waste; unlawful disposal or abandonment.** A person who knowingly disposes of or abandons hazardous waste or arranges for the disposal of hazardous waste at a location other than one authorized by the pollution control agency or the United States Environmental Protection Agency, or in violation of any material term or condition of a hazardous in violation of any material term or condition of a hazardous waste facility permit, is guilty of a felony and may be sentenced to imprisonment for not more than five years or to payment of a fine of not more than $50,000, or both.
   Subd. 5. **Hazardous waste; unlawful treatment, storage, transportation, or delivery.** (a) A person is guilty of a felony who knowingly does any of the following:
   (1) delivers hazardous waste to any person other than a person who is authorized to receive the waste * * *:
   (2) treats or stores hazardous waste without a permit if a permit is required, or in violation of a material term or condition of a permit held by the person, unless:
   (i) the person notifies the agency prior to the time a permit would be required that the person will be treating or storing waste without a permit; or
   (ii) for a violation of a material term or condition of a permit, the person immediately notifies the agency issuing the permit of the circumstances of the violation as soon as the person becomes aware of the violation;
   (3) transports hazardous waste to any location other than a facility that is authorized to receive, treat, store, or dispose of the hazardous waste * * *;
   (4) transports hazardous waste without a manifest * * *; or
   (5) transports hazardous waste without a license required for the transportation of hazardous waste * * *.
   (b) A person convicted under this subdivision may be sentenced to imprisonment for not more than three years, or to payment of a fine of not more than $25,000, or both. A person convicted for a second or subsequent offense may be sentenced to imprisonment for not more than five years, or to payment of a fine of not more than $50,000, or both.
   Subd. 6. **Negligent violation as gross misdemeanor.** A person who commits any of the acts set forth in subdivision 4, 5, or 12 as a result of the person's gross negligence is guilty of a gross misdemeanor and may be sentenced to imprisonment for not more than one year, or to payment of a fine of not more than $15,000, or both.
   Subd. 7. **Prosecution.** When two or more offenses in violation of this section are committed by the same person in two or more counties within a two-year period. The accused may be prosecuted in any county in which one of the offenses was committed.
   Subd. 8. **Water pollution.** (a) A person is guilty of a felony who knowingly:
   (1) causes the violation of an effluent standard or limitation for a toxic pollutant in a national pollutant discharge elimination system permit or state disposal system permit;

(2) introduces into a sewer system or into a publicly owned treatment works a hazardous substance that the person knew or reasonably should have known is likely to cause personal injury or property damage; or

(3) except in compliance with all applicable federal, state, and local requirements and permits, introduces into a sewer system or into a publicly owned treatment works a hazardous substance that causes the treatment works to violate an effluent limitation or condition of the treatment works' national pollutant discharge elimination system permit.

(b) For purposes of paragraph (a), "hazardous substance" means a substance on the list established under United States Code, title 33, section 1321(b).

(c) A person convicted under paragraph (a) may be sentenced to imprisonment for not more than three years, or to payment of a fine of not more than $50,000 per day of violation, or both.

(d) A person is guilty of a crime who knowingly:

(1) violates any effluent standard or limitation, or any water quality standard adopted by the agency;

(2) violates any material term or condition of a national pollutant discharge elimination system permit or state disposal system permit;

(3) fails to carry out any recording, reporting, monitoring, sampling, or information gathering requirement * * *; or

(4) fails to file a discharge monitoring report or other document required for compliance with a national pollutant discharge elimination system or state disposal system permit.

(e) A person convicted under paragraph (d) may be sentenced to imprisonment for not more than one year, or to payment of a fine of not less than $2,500 and not more than $25,000 per day of violation, or both. A person convicted for a second or subsequent offense may be sentenced to imprisonment for not more than two years, or to payment of a fine of not more than $50,000 per day of violation, or both.

Subd. 9. **False statements; tampering.** (a) A person is guilty of a felony who knowingly:

(1) makes any false material statement, representation, or certification in; omits material information from: or alters, conceals, or fails to file or maintain a notice, application, record, report, plan, manifest, permit, license, or other document required * * *; or

(2) falsifies, tampers with, renders inaccurate, or fails to install any monitoring device or method required to be maintained or followed * * *.

(b) Except as provided in paragraph (c), a person convicted under this subdivision may be sentenced to imprisonment for not more than two years, or to payment of a fine of not more than $10,000, or both.

(c) A person convicted under this subdivision for a violation related to a notice or report required by an air permit issued by the agency * * * may be sentenced to payment of a fine of not more than $10,000 per day of violation.

Subd. 10. **Failure to report a release of a hazardous substance or an extremely hazardous substance.** (a) A person is, upon conviction, subject to a fine of up to $25,000 or imprisonment for up to two years, or both, who:

(1) is required to report the release of a hazardous [or an extremely hazardous] substance * * *;

(2) knows that a hazardous substance or an extremely hazardous substance has been released; and

(3) fails to provide immediate notification of the release of a reportable quantity of a hazardous substance or an extremely hazardous substance to the state emergency response center and if directed by the center, to notify a local 911 emergency dispatch center.

For purposes of clause (3), the state emergency response center shall direct a caller to notify a local 911 emergency dispatch center if the situation requires an immediate response or the area is unknown to the center. * * *

(b) For a second or subsequent conviction under this subdivision, the violator is subject to a fine of up to $50,000 or imprisonment for not more than five years, or both.

(c) For purposes of this subdivision, a "hazardous substance" means a substance on the list established under [federal law].

(d) For purposes of this subdivision, an "extremely hazardous substance" means a substance on the list established under [federal law].

(e) For purposes of this subdivision, a "reportable quantity" means a quantity that must be reported under [federal law.]

Subd. 11. **Infectious waste.** A person who knowingly disposes of or arranges for the disposal of infectious waste as defined in section 116.76 at a location or in a manner that is prohibited by section 116.78 is guilty of a gross misdemeanor and may be sentenced to imprisonment for not more than one year, or to payment of a fine of not more than $10,000, or both. A person convicted a second or subsequent time under this subdivision is guilty of a felony and may be sentenced to imprisonment for not more than two years, or to payment of a fine of not more than $25,000, or both.

Subd. 12. **Air pollution.** (a) A person is guilty of a felony who knowingly:

(1) causes a violation of a national emission standard for a hazardous air pollutant adopted under [federal law]; or

(2) causes a violation of an emission standard, limitation, or operational limitation for a hazardous air pollutant established in a permit issued by the pollution control agency.

A person convicted under this paragraph may be sentenced to imprisonment for not more than three years, or to payment of a fine of not more than $50,000 per day of violation, or both.

(b) A person is guilty of a misdemeanor who knowingly violates:

(1) a requirement of chapter 116, or a rule adopted under that chapter, that is an applicable requirement of the federal Clean Air Act * * *;

(2) a condition of an air emission permit issued by the agency under chapter 116 or a rule adopted under that chapter; or

(3) a requirement to pay a fee based on air emissions under chapter 116 or a rule adopted under that chapter.

A person convicted under this paragraph may be sentenced to imprisonment for not more than 90 days, or to payment of a fine of not more than $10,000 per day of violation, or both.

Subd. 13. **Solid waste disposal.** (a) A person is guilty of a gross misdemeanor who:

(1) knowingly disposes of solid waste at, transports solid waste to, or arranges for disposal of solid waste at a location that does not have a required permit for the disposal of solid waste; and

(2) does so in exchange for or in expectation of money or other consideration.

(b) A person convicted under this subdivision may be sentenced to imprisonment for not more than one year, or to payment of a fine of not more than $15,000, or both.

Subd. 14. **Defense.** Except for intentional violations, a person is not guilty of a crime for air quality violations under subdivision 6 or 12, or for water quality violations under subdivision 8, if the person notified the pollution control agency of the violation as soon as the person discovered the violation and took steps to promptly remedy the violation.

HIST: 1987 c 267 s 3; * * * 2013 c 92 s 1

609.661 PENALTY FOR SET GUNS; SWIVEL GUNS.

A person who violates a provision relating to set guns or swivel guns is guilty of a gross misdemeanor.

HIST: 1986 c 386 art 4 s 31

609.665 SPRING GUNS.

Whoever sets a spring gun, pitfall, deadfall, snare, or other like dangerous weapon or device, may be sentenced to imprisonment for not more than six months or to payment of a fine of not more than $1,000, or both.

HIST: 1963 c 753 art 1 s 609.665; * * * 2004 c 228 art 1 s 72

609.675 EXPOSURE OF UNUSED REFRIGERATOR OR CONTAINER TO CHILDREN.

Whoever, being the owner or in possession or control, permits an unused refrigerator or other container, sufficiently large to retain any child and with doors which fasten automatically when closed, to be exposed and accessible to children, without removing the doors, lids, hinges, or latches, is guilty of a misdemeanor.
HIST: 1963 c 753 art 1 s 609.675; 1971 c 23 s 67

609.68 UNLAWFUL DEPOSIT OF GARBAGE, LITTER, OR LIKE.

Whoever unlawfully deposits garbage, rubbish, cigarette filters, debris from fireworks, offal, or the body of a dead animal, or other litter in or upon any public highway, public waters or the ice thereon, shoreland areas adjacent to rivers or streams as defined by section 103F.205, public lands, or, without the consent of the owner, private lands or water or ice thereon, is guilty of a petty misdemeanor.
HIST: 1963 c 753 art 1 s 609.68; * * * 1Sp2003 c 2 art 8 s 12

609.681 UNLAWFUL SMOKING.

A person is guilty of a petty misdemeanor if the person intentionally smokes in a building, area, or common carrier in which "no smoking" notices have been prominently posted, or when requested not to by the operator of the common carrier.
HIST: 1989 c 5 s 10; 1Sp2003 c 2 art 8 s 13

609.685 SALE OF TOBACCO TO CHILDREN.

Subdivision 1. **Definitions.** For the purposes of this section, the following terms shall have the meanings respectively ascribed to them in this section.

(a) "Tobacco" means cigarettes and any product containing, made, or derived from tobacco that is intended for human consumption, whether chewed, smoked, absorbed, dissolved, inhaled, snorted, sniffed, or ingested by any other means, or any component, part, or accessory of a tobacco product including but not limited to cigars; cheroots; stogies; perique; granulated, plug cut, crimp cut, ready rubbed, and other smoking tobacco; snuff; snuff flour; cavendish; plug and twist tobacco; fine cut and other chewing tobaccos; shorts; refuse scraps, clippings, cuttings and sweepings of tobacco; and other kinds and forms of tobacco. Tobacco excludes any drugs, devices, or combination products, as those terms are defined in the Federal Food, Drug, and Cosmetic Act, that are authorized for sale by the United States Food and Drug Administration.

(b) "Tobacco-related devices" means cigarette papers or pipes for smoking or other devices intentionally designed or intended to be used in a manner which enables the chewing, sniffing, smoking, or inhalation of aerosol or vapor of tobacco or tobacco products. Tobacco-related devices include components of tobacco-related devices which may be marketed or sold separately.

(c) "Electronic delivery device" means any product containing or delivering nicotine, lobelia, or any other substance, whether natural or synthetic, intended for human consumption through inhalation of aerosol or vapor from the product. Electronic delivery device includes but is not limited to devices manufactured, marketed, or sold as electronic cigarettes, electronic cigars, electronic pipe, vape pens, modes, tank systems, or under any other product name or descriptor. Electronic delivery device includes any component part of a product, whether or not marketed or sold separately. Electronic delivery device excludes drugs, devices, or combination products, as those terms are defined in the Federal Food, Drug, and Cosmetic Act, that are authorized for sale by the United States Food and Drug Administration.

Subd. 1a. **Penalty to sell or furnish.** (a) Any person 21 years of age or older who sells, gives, or otherwise furnishes tobacco, tobacco-related devices, or electronic delivery devices to a person under the age of 21 years is guilty of a petty misdemeanor for the first violation. Whoever violates this subdivision a subsequent time within five years of a previous conviction under this subdivision is guilty of a misdemeanor.

(b) It is an affirmative defense to a charge under this subdivision if the defendant proves by a preponderance of the evidence that the defendant reasonably and in good faith relied on proof of age as described in section 340A.503, subdivision 6.

Subd. 2. **Use of false identification.** A person under the age of 21 years who purchases or attempts to purchase tobacco, tobacco-related devices, or electronic delivery devices and who uses a driver's license, permit, Minnesota identification card, or any type of false identification to misrepresent the person's age, shall only be subject to an alternative civil penalty, in accordance with subdivision 2a.

Subd. 2a. **Alternative penalties.** Law enforcement and court system representatives shall consult, as applicable, with interested persons, including but not limited to parents, guardians, educators, and persons under the age of 21 years, to develop alternative civil penalties for persons under the age of 21 years who violate this section. Consulting participants shall consider a variety of alternative civil penalties including but not limited to tobacco-free education programs, community service, court diversion programs, and tobacco cessation programs, and for persons under the age of 18 years, notice to schools and to parents or guardians. Alternative civil penalties developed under this subdivision shall not include fines or monetary penalties.

Subd. 3. MS 2018 [Repealed by amendment, 2020 c 88 s 11]

Subd. 4. **Effect on local ordinances.** Nothing in subdivisions 1 to 2a shall supersede or preclude the continuation or adoption of any local ordinance which provides for more stringent regulation of the subject matter in subdivisions 1 to 2a.

Subd. 5. **Exceptions.** (a) Notwithstanding subdivision 1a, an Indian may furnish tobacco to an Indian under the age of 21 years if the tobacco is furnished as part of a traditional Indian spiritual or cultural ceremony. For purposes of this paragraph, an Indian is a person who is a member of an Indian tribe as defined in section 260.755, subdivision 12.

(b) The penalties in this section do not apply to a person under the age of 21 years who purchases or attempts to purchase tobacco, tobacco-related devices, or electronic delivery devices while under the direct supervision of a responsible adult for training, education, research, or enforcement purposes.

Subd. 6. **Seizure of false identification.** A licensee may seize a form of identification listed in section 340A.503, subdivision 6, if the licensee has reasonable grounds to believe that the form of identification has been altered or falsified or is being used to violate any law. A licensee that seizes a form of identification as authorized under this subdivision shall deliver it to a law enforcement agency within 24 hours of seizing it.

HIST: 1963 c 753 art 1 s 609.685; * * * 2014 c 292 art 6 s 33; 2020 c 88 s 11

609.6855 SALE OF NICOTINE DELIVERY PRODUCTS TO PERSONS UNDER AGE 21.

Subdivision 1. **Penalty to sell or furnish.** (a) Any person 21 years of age or older who sells, gives, or otherwise furnishes to a person under the age of 21 years a product containing or delivering nicotine or lobelia, whether natural or synthetic, intended for human consumption, or any part of such a product, that is not tobacco or an electronic delivery device as defined by section 609.685, is guilty of a petty misdemeanor for the first violation. Whoever violates this subdivision a subsequent time within five years of a previous conviction under this subdivision is guilty of a misdemeanor.

(b) It is an affirmative defense to a charge under this subdivision if the defendant proves by a preponderance of the evidence that the defendant reasonably and in good faith relied on proof of age as described in section 340A.503, subdivision 6.

(c) Notwithstanding paragraph (a), a product containing or delivering nicotine or lobelia intended for human consumption, whether natural or synthetic, or any part of such a product, that is not tobacco or an electronic delivery device as defined by section 609.685, may be sold to persons under the age of 21 if the product is a drug, device, or combination product, as those terms are defined in the Federal Food, Drug, and Cosmetic Act, that is authorized for sale by the United States Food and Drug Administration.

Subd. 2. **Use of false identification.** A person under the age of 21 years who purchases or attempts to purchase a product containing or delivering nicotine or lobelia intended for human consumption, or any part of such a product, that is not tobacco or an electronic delivery device as defined by section 609.685, and who uses a driver's license, permit, Minnesota identification card, or any type of false identification to misrepresent the person's age, shall only be subject to an alternative civil penalty in accordance with subdivision 3. No penalty shall apply to a person under the age of 21 years who purchases or attempts to purchase these products while under the direct supervision of a responsible adult for training, education, research, or enforcement purposes.

Subd. 3. **Alternative penalties.** Law enforcement and court system representatives shall consult, as applicable, with interested persons, including but not limited to parents, guardians, educators, and persons under the age of 21 years, to develop alternative civil penalties for persons under the age of 21 years who violate this section. Consulting participants shall consider a variety of alternative civil penalties including but not limited to tobacco-free education programs, community service, court diversion programs, and tobacco cessation programs, and for persons under the age of 18 years, notice to schools and to parents or guardians. Alternative civil penalties developed under this subdivision shall not include fines or monetary penalties.
HIST: 2010 c 305 s 12; 2014 c 291 art 6 s 34; 2020 c 88 s 12

609.686 FALSE FIRE ALARMS; TAMPERING WITH OR INJURING A FIRE ALARM SYSTEM.

Subdivision 1. **Misdemeanor.** Whoever intentionally gives a false alarm of fire, or unlawfully tampers or interfere with any fire alarm system, fire protection device, or the station or signal box of any fire alarm system or any auxiliary fire appliance, or unlawfully breaks, injures, defaces, or removes any such system, device, box or station, or unlawfully breaks, injures, destroys, disables, renders inoperable, or disturbs any of the wires, poles, or other supports and appliances connected with or forming a part of any fire alarm system or fire protection device or any auxiliary fire appliance is guilty of a misdemeanor.

Subd. 2. **Felony.** Whoever violates subdivision 1 by tampering and knows or has reason to know that the tampering creates the potential for bodily harm or the tampering results in bodily harm is guilty of a felony and may be sentenced to imprisonment for not more than five years or to payment of a fine of not more than $10,000, or both.

Subd. 3. **Tampering.** For purpose of this section, tampering means to intentionally disable, alter, or change the fire alarm system, fire protective device, or the station or signal box of any fire alarm system of any auxiliary fire appliance, with knowledge that it will be disabled or rendered inoperable.
HIST: 1971 c 77 s 1; 1993 c 326 art 5 s 10

Chapter 15 -- PUBLIC MISCONDUCT OR NUISANCE

Category 2, Section 5:
2.5.1. Describe the basic organization, purpose, and definitions and principles of the Minnesota Criminal Code.
2.5.5. Given a variety of scenarios, identify indications a particular crime has been committed and identify the elements of that crime.

609.687 ADULTERATION.

Subdivision 1. **Definition.** "Adulteration" is the intentional adding of any substance, which has the capacity to cause death, bodily harm or illness by ingestion, injection, inhalation or absorption, to a substance having a customary or reasonably foreseeable human use.

Subd. 2. **Acts constituting.** (a) Whoever, knowing or having reason to know that the adulteration will cause or is capable of causing death, bodily harm or illness, adulterates any substance with the intent to cause death, bodily harm or illness is guilty of a crime and may be sentenced as provided in subdivision 3; or

(b) Whoever, knowing or having reason to know that a substance has been adulterated as defined in subdivision 1, distributes, disseminates, gives, sells, or otherwise transfers an adulterated substance with the intent to cause death, bodily harm or illness is guilty of a crime and may be sentenced as provided in subdivision 3.

Subd. 3. **Sentence.** Whoever violates subdivision 2 may be sentenced as follows:

(1) if the adulteration causes death, to imprisonment for not more than 40 years or to payment of a fine of not more than $100,000, or both;

(2) if the adulteration causes any illness, pain, or other bodily harm, to imprisonment for not more than ten years or to payment of a fine of not more than $20,000, or both;

(3) otherwise, to imprisonment for not more than five years or to payment of a fine of not more than $10,000, or both.

Subd. 4. **Charging discretion.** Criminal proceedings may be instituted under this section, notwithstanding the provisions of section 29.24, 31.02, 31.601, 34.01, 151.34, 340A.508, subdivision 2, or other law proscribing adulteration of substances intended for use by persons.
HIST: 1983 c 8 s 1; * * * 1Sp2001 c 2 s 148

Editors' Note: Although the following statute is not specifically described in these learning objectives, it has been included because of its close relationship to the adulteration statute described above.

609.688 ADULTERATION BY BODILY FLUID.

Subdivision 1. **Definition.** (a) As used in this section, the following terms have the meanings given.

(b) "Adulterates" is the intentional adding of a bodily fluid to a substance.

(c) "Bodily fluid" means the blood, seminal fluid, vaginal fluid, urine, or feces of a human.

Subd. 2. **Crime.** (a) Whoever adulterates any substance that the person knows or should know is intended for human consumption is guilty of a misdemeanor.

(b) Whoever violates paragraph (a) and another person ingests the adulterated substance without knowledge of the adulteration is guilty of a gross misdemeanor.
HIST: 2015 c 65 art 6 s 17

609.705 UNLAWFUL ASSEMBLY.
When three or more persons assemble, each participant is guilty of unlawful assembly, which is a misdemeanor, if the assembly is:
(1) With intent to commit any unlawful act by force; or
(2) With intent to carry out any purpose in such manner as will disturb or threaten the public peace: or
(3) Without unlawful purpose, but the participants so conduct themselves in a disorderly manner as to disturb or threaten the public peace.
HIST: 1963 c 753 art 1 s 609.705; 1971 c 23 s 69

609.71 RIOT.
Subdivision 1. **Riot first degree.** When three or more persons assembled disturb the public peace by an intentional act or threat of unlawful force or violence to person or property and a death results, and one of the persons is armed with a dangerous weapon, that person is guilty of riot first degree and may be sentenced to imprisonment for not more than 20 years or to payment of a fine of not more than $35,000, or both.
Subd. 2. **Riot second degree.** When three or more persons assembled disturb the public peace by an intentional act or threat of unlawful force or violence to person or property, each participant who is armed with a dangerous weapon or knows that any other participant is armed with a dangerous weapon is guilty of riot second degree and may be sentenced to imprisonment for not more than five years or to payment of a fine of not more than $10,000, or both.
Subd. 3. **Riot third degree.** When three or more persons assembled disturb the public peace by an intentional act or threat of unlawful force or violence to person or property, each participant therein is guilty of riot third degree and may be sentenced to imprisonment for not more than one year or to payment of a fine of not more than $1,000, or both.
HIST: 1963 c 753 art 1 s 609.71; * * * 1993 c 326 art 4 s 33

Editors' Note: Although the following statute is not specifically described in these learning objectives, it has been included because of its close relationship to the public disturbance statutes of unlawful assembly and riot described above.

609.712 REAL AND SIMULATED WEAPONS OF MASS DESTRUCTION.
Subdivision 1. **Definitions.** (a) As used in this section, the following terms have the meanings given.
(b) "Biological agent" means any microorganism, virus, infectious substance, or biological product that may be engineered as a result of biotechnology, or any naturally occurring or bioengineered component of a microorganism, virus, infectious substance, or biological product, that is capable of causing:
(1) death, disease, or other biological malfunction in a human, an animal, a plant, or another living organism;
(2) deterioration of food, water, equipment, supplies, or material of any kind; or
(3) deleterious alteration of the environment.
(c) "Simulated weapon of mass destruction" means any device, substance, or object that by its design, construction, content, or characteristics, appears to be or to contain, or is represented to be, constitute, or contain, a weapon of mass destruction, but that is, in fact, an inoperative facsimile, imitation, counterfeit, or representation of a weapon of mass destruction that does not meet the definition of a weapon of mass destruction or that does not actually contain or constitute a weapon, biological agent, toxin, vector, or delivery system prohibited by this section.
(d) "Toxin" means the toxic material of plants, animals, microorganisms, viruses, fungi, or infectious substances, or a recombinant molecule, whatever its origin or method of production[.]

(f) "Weapon of mass destruction" includes weapons, substances, devices, vectors, or delivery systems that:

(1) are designed or have the capacity to cause death or great bodily harm to a considerable number of people through the release, dissemination, or impact of toxic or poisonous chemicals, or their precursors, disease organisms, biological agents, or toxins; or

(2) are designed to release radiation or radioactivity at a level dangerous to human life.

Subd. 2. **Weapons of mass destruction.** (a) Whoever manufactures, acquires, possesses, or makes readily accessible to another a weapon of mass destruction with the intent to cause injury to another is guilty of a crime and may be sentenced to imprisonment for not more than 20 years or to payment of a fine of not more than $100,000, or both.

(b) It is an affirmative defense to criminal liability under this subdivision if the defendant proves by a preponderance of the evidence that the conduct engaged in:

(1) was specifically authorized under state or federal law and conducted in accordance with that law; or

(2) was part of a legitimate scientific or medical research project, or constituted legitimate medical treatment.

Subd. 3. **Prohibited substances.** (a) Whoever knowingly manufactures, acquires, possesses, or makes readily accessible to another the following, or substances that are substantially similar in chemical makeup to the following, in levels dangerous to human life, is guilty of a crime:

(1) variola major (smallpox);

(2) bacillus anthracis (anthrax);

(3) yersinia pestis (plague);

(4) botulinum toxin (botulism);

(5) francisella tularensis (tularemia);

(6) viral hemorrhagic fevers;

(7) a mustard agent;

(8) lewisite;

(9) hydrogen cyanide;

(10) GA (tabun);

(11) GB (Sarin);

(12) GD (Soman);

(13) GF (cyclohexymethyl phosphonofluoridate);

(14) VX (0-ethyl, supdiisopropylaminomethyl methylphosphonothiolate);

(15) radioactive materials; or

(16) any combination of the above.

(b) A person who violates this subdivision may be sentenced to imprisonment for not more than 20 years or to payment of a fine of not more than $100,000, or both. * * *

Subd. 4. **Simulated weapons of mass destruction; penalty.** Whoever manufactures, acquires, possesses, or makes readily accessible to another a simulated weapon of mass destruction with the intent of terrorizing another may be sentenced to imprisonment for not more than ten years or to payment of a fine of not more than $20,000, or both.

Subd. 5. **Threats involving real or simulated weapons of mass destruction.** Whoever does the following with intent to terrorize another or cause evacuation of a place, whether a building or not, or disruption of another's activities, or with reckless disregard of the risk of causing terror, evacuation, or disruption, may be sentenced to imprisonment for not more than ten years or to payment of a fine of not more than $20,000, or both:

(1) displays a weapon of mass destruction or a simulated weapon of mass destruction;

(2) threatens to use a weapon of mass destruction; or

(3) communicates, whether directly or indirectly, that a weapon of mass destruction is or will be present or introduced at a place or location, or will be used to cause death, disease, or injury to another or to another's property, whether or not the same is in fact present or introduced.

Subd. 6. **Civil action to recover.** A person who violates this section is liable in a civil action[.]

HIST: 2002 c 401 art 1 s 19

609.713 THREATS OF VIOLENCE.

Subdivision 1. **Threaten violence; intent to terrorize.** Whoever threatens, directly or indirectly, to commit any crime of violence with purpose to terrorize another or to cause evacuation of a building, place of assembly, vehicle or facility of public transportation or otherwise to cause serious public inconvenience, or in a reckless disregard of the risk of causing such terror or inconvenience may be sentenced to imprisonment for not more than five years or to payment of a fine of not more than $10,000, or both. As used in this subdivision, "crime of violence" has the meaning given "violent crime" in section 609.1095, subdivision 1, paragraph (d).

Subd. 2. **Communicates to terrorize.** Whoever communicates to another with purpose to terrorize another or in reckless disregard of the risk of causing such terror, that explosives or an explosive device or any incendiary device is present at a named place or location, whether or not the same is in fact present, may be sentenced to imprisonment for not more than three years or to payment of a fine of not more than $3,000, or both.

Subd. 3. **Display of replica firearm.** (a) Whoever displays, exhibits, brandishes, or otherwise employs a replica firearm or a BB gun in a threatening manner, may be sentenced to imprisonment for not more than one year and one day or to payment of a fine of not more than $3,000, or both, if, in doing so, the person either:

(1) causes or attempts to cause terror in another person; or

(2) acts in reckless disregard of the risk of causing terror in another person.

(b) For purposes of this subdivision:

(1) "BB gun" means a device that fires or ejects a shot measuring .18 of an inch or less in diameter; and

(2) "replica firearm" means a device or object that is not defined as a dangerous weapon, and that is a facsimile or toy version of, and reasonably appears to be a pistol, revolver, shotgun, sawed-off shotgun, rifle, machine gun, rocket launcher, or any other firearm. The term replica firearm includes, but is not limited to, devices or objects that are designed to fire only blanks.

HIST: 1971 c 845 s 19; * * * 2015 c 21 art 1 s 109

Editors' Note: Although the following statute is not specifically described in these learning objectives, it has been included because of its close relationship to the terroristic threats statute described above.

609.714 CRIMES COMMITTED IN FURTHERANCE OF TERRORISM.

Subdivision 1. **Definition.** As used in this section, a crime is committed to "further terrorism" if the crime is a felony and is a premeditated act involving violence to persons or property that is intended to:

(1) terrorize, intimidate, or coerce a considerable number of members of the public in addition to the direct victims of the act; and

(2) significantly disrupt or interfere with the lawful exercise, operation, or conduct of government, lawful commerce, or the right of lawful assembly.

Subd. 2. **Furtherance of terrorism; crime described; penalty.** A person who commits a felony crime to further terrorism is guilty of a crime. The statutory maximum for the crime is 50 percent longer than the statutory maximum for the underlying crime.

HIST: 2002 c 401 art 1 s 20

609.72 DISORDERLY CONDUCT.

Subdivision 1. **Crime.** Whoever does any of the following in a public or private place, including on a school bus, knowing, or having reasonable grounds to know that it will, or will tend to, alarm, anger or disturb others or provoke an assault or breach of the peace, is guilty of disorderly conduct, which is a misdemeanor:

(1) Engages in brawling or fighting; or

(2) Disturbs an assembly or meeting, not unlawful in its character; or

(3) Engages in offensive, obscene, abusive, boisterous, or noisy conduct or in offensive, obscene, or abusive language tending reasonably to arouse alarm, anger, or resentment in others.

A person does not violate this section if the person's disorderly conduct was caused by an epileptic seizure.

Subd. 2. Repealed, 1969 c 226 s 1

Subd. 3. **Caregiver; penalty for disorderly conduct.** A caregiver, as defined in section 609.232, who violates the provisions of subdivision 1 against a vulnerable adult, as defined in section 609.232, may be sentenced to imprisonment for not more than one year or to payment of a fine of not more than $3,000, or both.

HIST: 1963 c 753 art 1 s 609.72; * * * 1995 c 229 art 2 s 7

Editors' Note: Although the following statute is not specifically described in these learning objectives, it has been included because of its close relationship to the disorderly conduct statute described above.

609.501 FUNERAL OR BURIAL SERVICE; PROHIBITED ACTS.

Subdivision 1. **Definitions.** (a) For purposes of this section, the following terms have the meanings given. * * *

(g) "Targeted residential picketing" has the meaning given in section 609.748, subdivision 1, paragraph (c), but does not require more than one act or that acts be committed on more than one occasion.

Subd. 2. **Crime to disrupt.** (a) Whoever does any of the following is guilty of a misdemeanor:

(1) with intent to disrupt a funeral ceremony, graveside service, or memorial service, protests or pickets within 500 feet of the burial site or the entrance to a facility or location being used for the service or ceremony, within one hour prior to, during, or one hour following the service or ceremony;

(2) with intent to disrupt a funeral procession, impedes or attempts to impede a vehicle that is part of the procession;

(3) intentionally blocks or attempts to block access to a funeral ceremony, graveside service, or memorial service; or

(4) knowingly engages in targeted residential picketing at the home or domicile of any surviving member of the deceased person's family or household on the date of the funeral ceremony, graveside service, or memorial service.

(b) Whoever is convicted of a violation of paragraph (a) following a previous conviction for a violation of paragraph (a) or a similar statute from another state or the United States is guilty of a gross misdemeanor.

Subd. 3. **Civil remedy.** A person who violates subdivision 2 is liable to a surviving member of the deceased person's family or household for damages[.]

HIST: 2006 c 195 s 1

609.74 PUBLIC NUISANCE.

Whoever by an act or failure to perform a legal duty intentionally does any of the following is guilty of maintaining a public nuisance, which is a misdemeanor:

(1) maintains or permits a condition which unreasonably annoys, injures or endangers the safety, health, morals, comfort, or repose of any considerable number of members of the public; or

(2) interferes with, obstructs, or renders dangerous for passage, any public highway or right-of-way, or waters used by the public; or

(3) is guilty of any other act or omission declared by law to be a public nuisance and for which no sentence is specifically provided.
HIST: 1963 c 753 art 1 s 609.74; 1971 c 23 s 74; 1986 c 444

609.715 PRESENCE AT UNLAWFUL ASSEMBLY.

Whoever without lawful purpose is present at the place of an unlawful assembly and refuses to leave when so directed by a law enforcement officer is guilty of a misdemeanor.
HIST: 1963 c 753 art 1 s 609.715; 1971 c 23 s 70

609.735 CONCEALING IDENTITY.

A person whose identity is concealed by the person in a public place by means of a robe, mask, or other disguise, unless based on religious beliefs, or incidental to amusement, entertainment, protection from weather, or medical treatment, is guilty of a misdemeanor.
HIST: 1963 c 753 art 1 s 609.735; 1971 c 23 s 73; 1986 c 444; 1995 c 30 s 1

Editors' Note: Governor Walz issued Emergency Executive Order 20-81 on July 22, 2020. Paragraph 19 of Order 20-81 provided that ". . . [w]earing a face covering in compliance with this Executive Order or local ordinances, rules, or orders is not a violation of . . . [this statute]."

609.745 PERMITTING PUBLIC NUISANCE.

Whoever having control of real property permits it to be used to maintain a public nuisance or lets the same knowing it will be so used is guilty of a misdemeanor.
HIST: 1963 c 753 art 1 s 609.745; 1971 c 23 s 75; 1986 c 444

609.746 INTERFERENCE WITH PRIVACY.

Subdivision 1. **Surreptitious intrusion; observation device.** (a) A person is guilty of a gross misdemeanor who:

(1) enters upon another's property;

(2) surreptitiously gazes, stares, or peeps in the window or any other aperture of a house or place of dwelling of another; and

(3) does so with intent to intrude upon or interfere with the privacy of a member of the household.

(b) A person is guilty of a gross misdemeanor who:

(1) enters upon another's property;

(2) surreptitiously installs or uses any device for observing, photographing, recording, amplifying, or broadcasting sounds or events through the window or any other aperture of a house or place of dwelling of another; and

(3) does so with intent to intrude upon or interfere with the privacy of a member of the household.

(c) A person is guilty of a gross misdemeanor who:

(1) surreptitiously gazes, stares, or peeps in the window or other aperture of a sleeping room in a hotel, as defined in section 327.70, subdivision 3, a tanning booth, or other place where a reasonable person would have an expectation of privacy and has exposed or is likely to expose their intimate parts, as defined in section 609.341, subdivision 5, or the clothing covering the immediate area of the intimate parts; and

(2) does so with intent to intrude upon or interfere with the privacy of the occupant.

(d) A person is guilty of a gross misdemeanor who:

(1) surreptitiously installs or uses any device for observing, photographing, recording, amplifying, or broadcasting sounds or events through the window or other aperture of a sleeping

room in a hotel, as defined in section 327.70, subdivision 3, a tanning booth, or other place where a reasonable person would have an expectation of privacy and has exposed or is likely to expose their intimate parts, as defined in section 609.341, subdivision 5, or the clothing covering the immediate area of the intimate parts; and

(2) does so with intent to intrude upon or interfere with the privacy of the occupant.

(e) A person is guilty of a felony and may be sentenced to imprisonment for not more than two years or to payment of a fine of not more than $5,000, or both, if the person:

(1) violates this subdivision after a previous conviction under this subdivision or section 609.749; or

(2) violates this subdivision against a minor under the age of 18, knowing or having reason to know that the minor is present.

(f) A person is guilty of a felony and may be sentenced to imprisonment for not more than four years or to payment of a fine of not more than $5,000, or both, if: (1) the person violates paragraph (b) or (d) against a minor victim under the age of 18; (2) knows the person is more than 36 months older than the minor victim; (3) the person knows or has reason to know that the minor victim is present; and (4) the violation is committed with sexual intent.

(g) Paragraphs (b) and (d) do not apply to law enforcement officers or corrections investigators, or to those acting under their direction, while engaged in the performance of their lawful duties. Paragraphs (c) and (d) do not apply to conduct in (1) a medical facility; or (2) a commercial establishment if the owner of the establishment has posted conspicuous signs warning that the premises are under surveillance by the owner or the owner's employees.

Subd. 2. [Repealed, 1993 c 326 art 2 s 34]
Subd. 3. [Repealed, 1993 c 326 art 2 s 34]
HIST: 1979 c 258 s 19; * * * 2005 c 136 art 17 s 43; 1Sp2019 c 5 art 4 s 11

Category 2, Section 5:
2.5.1. Describe the basic organization, purpose, and definitions and principles of the Minnesota Criminal Code.
2.5.5. Given a variety of scenarios, identify indications a particular crime has been committed and identify the elements of that crime.
2.5.7 Explain special Minnesota peace officer duties associated with specific statutes including: . . . restraining orders and orders for protection . . .

609.747 Repealed, 1993 c 326 art 2 s 34

609.748 HARASSMENT; RESTRAINING ORDER.
Subdivision 1. **Definition.** For the purposes of this section, the following terms have the meanings given them in this subdivision.

(a) "Harassment" includes:

(1) a single incident of physical or sexual assault, a single incident of harassment under section 609.749, subdivision 2, clause (8), a single incident of nonconsensual dissemination of private sexual images under section 617.261, or repeated incidents of intrusive or unwanted acts, words, or gestures that have a substantial adverse effect or are intended to have a substantial adverse effect on the safety, security, or privacy of another, regardless of the relationship between the actor and the intended target;

(2) targeted residential picketing; and

(3) a pattern of attending public events after being notified that the actor's presence at the event is harassing to another.

(b) "Respondent" includes any adults or juveniles alleged to have engaged in harassment or organizations alleged to have sponsored or promoted harassment.

(c) "Targeted residential picketing" includes the following acts when committed on more than one occasion:

(1) marching, standing, or patrolling by one or more persons directed solely at a particular residential building in a manner that adversely affects the safety, security, or privacy of an occupant of the building; or

(2) marching, standing, or patrolling by one or more persons which prevents an occupant of a residential building from gaining access to or exiting from the property on which the residential building is located.

Subd. 2. **Restraining order; court jurisdiction.** A person who is a victim of harassment or the victim's guardian or conservator may seek a restraining order from the district court in the manner provided in this section. The parent, guardian or conservator, or stepparent of a minor who is a victim of harassment may seek a restraining order from the district court on behalf of the minor. An application for relief under this section may be filed in the county of residence of either party or in the county in which the alleged harassment occurred. There are no residency requirements that apply to a petition for a harassment restraining order.

Subd. 3.Contents of petition; hearing; notice. (a) A petition for relief must allege facts sufficient to show the following:

(1) the name of the alleged harassment victim;

(2) the name of the respondent; and

(3) that the respondent has engaged in harassment.

A petition for relief must state whether the petitioner has had a previous restraining order in effect against the respondent. The petition shall be accompanied by an affidavit made under oath stating the specific facts and circumstances from which relief is sought. The court shall provide simplified forms and clerical assistance to help with the writing and filing of a petition under this section and shall advise the petitioner of the right to sue in forma pauperis under section 563.01. The court shall advise the petitioner of the right to request a hearing. If the petitioner does not request a hearing, the court shall advise the petitioner that the respondent may request a hearing and that notice of the hearing date and time will be provided to the petitioner by mail at least five days before the hearing. Upon receipt of the petition and a request for a hearing by the petitioner, the court shall order a hearing. Personal service must be made upon the respondent not less than five days before the hearing. If personal service cannot be completed in time to give the respondent the minimum notice required under this paragraph, the court may set a new hearing date. Nothing in this section shall be construed as requiring a hearing on a matter that has no merit.

(b) Notwithstanding paragraph (a), the order for a hearing and a temporary order issued under subdivision 4 may be served on the respondent by means of a one-week published notice under section 645.11, if:

(1) the petitioner files an affidavit with the court stating that an attempt at personal service made by a peace officer was unsuccessful because the respondent is avoiding service by concealment or otherwise; and

(2) a copy of the petition and order for hearing and any temporary restraining order has been mailed to the respondent at the respondent's residence or place of business, if the respondent is an organization, or the respondent's residence or place of business is not known to the petitioner.

(c) Regardless of the method of service, if the respondent is a juvenile, whenever possible, the court also shall have notice of the pendency of the case and of the time and place of the hearing served by mail at the last known address upon any parent or guardian of the juvenile respondent who is not the petitioner.

(d) A request for a hearing under this subdivision must be made within 20 days of service of the petition.

Subd. 3a. **Filing fee; cost of service.** The filing fees for a restraining order under this section are waived for the petitioner and the respondent if the petition alleges acts that would constitute a violation of section 609.749, subdivision 2, 3, 4, or 5, or sections 609.342 to 609.3451. The court administrator and any peace officer in this state shall perform their duties rclating to service of process without charge to the petitioner. The court shall direct payment of the reasonable costs of service of process if served by a private process server when a peace officer is unavailable or if service is made by publication.

Subd. 4. **Temporary restraining order; relief by court.** (a) The court may issue a temporary restraining order that provides any or all of the following:

(1) orders the respondent to cease or avoid the harassment of another person; or

(2) orders the respondent to have no contact with another person.

(b) The court may issue an order under paragraph (a) if the petitioner files a petition in compliance with subdivision 3 and if the court finds reasonable grounds to believe that the respondent has engaged in harassment. When a petition alleges harassment as defined by subdivision 1, paragraph (a), clause (1), the petition must further allege an immediate and present danger of harassment before the court may issue a temporary restraining order under this section. When signed by a referee, the temporary order becomes effective upon the referee's signature.

(c) Notice need not be given to the respondent before the court issues a temporary restraining order under this subdivision. A copy of the restraining order must be served on the respondent along with the order for hearing and petition, as provided in subdivision 3. If the respondent is a juvenile, whenever possible, a copy of the restraining order, along with notice of the pendency of the case and the time and place of the hearing, shall also be served by mail at the last known address upon any parent or guardian of the juvenile respondent who is not the petitioner. A temporary restraining order may be entered only against the respondent named in the petition.

(d) The temporary restraining order is in effect until a hearing is held on the issuance of a restraining order under subdivision 5. The court shall hold the hearing on the issuance of a restraining order if the petitioner requests a hearing. The hearing may be continued by the court upon a showing that the respondent has not been served with a copy of the temporary restraining order despite the exercise of due diligence or if service is made by published notice under subdivision 3 and the petitioner files the affidavit required under that subdivision.

(e) If the temporary restraining order has been issued and the respondent requests a hearing, the hearing shall be scheduled by the court upon receipt of the respondent's request. Service of the notice of hearing must be made upon the petitioner not less than five days prior to the hearing. The court shall serve the notice of the hearing upon the petitioner by mail in the manner provided in the Rules of Civil Procedure for pleadings subsequent to a complaint and motions and shall also mail notice of the date and time of the hearing to the respondent. In the event that service cannot be completed in time to give the respondent or petitioner the minimum notice required under this subdivision, the court may set a new hearing date.

(f) A request for a hearing under this subdivision must be made within 20 days of the date of completed service of the petition.

Subd. 5. **Restraining order.** (a) The court may issue a restraining order that provides any or all of the following:

(1) orders the respondent to cease or avoid the harassment of another person; or

(2) orders the respondent to have no contact with another person.

(b) The court may issue an order under paragraph (a) if all of the following occur:

(1) the petitioner has filed a petition under subdivision 3;

(2) a peace officer has served respondent with a copy of the temporary restraining order obtained under subdivision 4, and with notice of the right to request a hearing, or service has been made by publication under subdivision 3, paragraph (b); and

(3) the court finds at the hearing that there are reasonable grounds to believe that the respondent has engaged in harassment.

A restraining order may be issued only against the respondent named in the petition; except that if the respondent is an organization, the order may be issued against and apply to all of the members of the organization. If the court finds that the petitioner has had two or more previous restraining orders in effect against the same respondent or the respondent has violated a prior or existing restraining order on two or more occasions, relief granted by the restraining order may be for a period of up to 50 years. In all other cases, relief granted by the restraining order must be for a fixed period of not more than two years. When a referee presides at the hearing on the petition, the restraining order becomes effective upon the referee's signature.

(c) An order issued under this subdivision must be personally served upon the respondent.

(d) If the court orders relief for a period of up to 50 years under paragraph (a), the respondent named in the restraining order may request to have the restraining order vacated or modified if the order has been in effect for at least five years and the respondent has not violated the order. Application for relief under this paragraph must be made in the county in which the restraining order was issued. Upon receipt of the request, the court shall set a hearing date. Personal service must be made upon the petitioner named in the restraining order not less than 30 days before the date of the hearing. At the hearing, the respondent named in the restraining order has the burden of proving by a preponderance of the evidence that there has been a material change in circumstances and that the reasons upon which the court relied in granting the restraining order no longer apply and are unlikely to occur. If the court finds that the respondent named in the restraining order has met the burden of proof, the court may vacate or modify the order. If the court finds that the respondent named in the restraining order has not met the burden of proof, the court shall deny the request and no request may be made to vacate or modify the restraining order until five years have elapsed from the date of denial. An order vacated or modified under this paragraph must be personally served on the petitioner named in the restraining order.

Subd. 5a. **Short-form notification.** (a) In lieu of personal service of a harassment restraining order, a peace officer may serve a person with a short-form notification. The short-form notification must include the following clauses: the respondent's name; the respondent's date of birth, if known; the petitioner's name; the names of other protected parties; the date and county in which the temporary restraining order or restraining order was filed; the court file number; the hearing date and time, if known; the conditions that apply to the respondent, either in checklist form or handwritten; and the name of the judge who signed the order.

The short-form notification must be in bold print in the following form:

"The restraining order is now enforceable. You must report to your nearest sheriff's office or county court to obtain a copy of the restraining order. You are subject to arrest and may be charged with a misdemeanor, gross misdemeanor, or felony if you violate any of the terms of the restraining order or this short-form notification."

(b) Upon verification of the identity of the respondent and the existence of an unserved harassment restraining order against the respondent, a law enforcement officer may detain the respondent for a reasonable time necessary to complete and serve the short-form notification.

(c) When service is made by short-form notification, it may be proved by the affidavit of the law enforcement officer making the service.

(d) For service under this section only, service upon an individual may occur at any time, including Sundays and legal holidays.

(e) The superintendent of the Bureau of Criminal Apprehension shall provide the short form to law enforcement agencies.
* * *

Subd. 5b. **Service by others.** In addition to peace officers, corrections officers, including but not limited to probation officers, court services officers, parole officers, and employees of jails or correctional facilities, may serve a temporary restraining order or restraining order.

Subd. 6. **Violation of restraining order.** (a) A person who violates a restraining order issued under this section is subject to the penalties provided in paragraphs (b) to (d).

(b) Except as otherwise provided in paragraphs (c) and (d), when a temporary restraining order or a restraining order is granted under this section and the respondent knows of the order, violation of the order is a misdemeanor.

(c) A person is guilty of a gross misdemeanor who violates the order within ten years of a previous qualified domestic violence-related offense conviction or adjudication of delinquency.

(d) A person is guilty of a felony and may be sentenced to imprisonment for not more than five years or to payment of a fine of not more than $10,000, or both, if the person violates the order:

(1) within ten years of the first of two or more previous qualified domestic violence-related offense convictions or adjudications of delinquency;

(2) because of the victim's or another's actual or perceived race, color, religion, sex, sexual orientation, disability as defined in section 363A.03, age, or national origin;

(3) by falsely impersonating another;

(4) while possessing a dangerous weapon;

(5) with an intent to influence or otherwise tamper with a juror or a judicial proceeding or with intent to retaliate against a judicial officer, as defined in section 609.415, or a prosecutor, defense attorney, or officer of the court, because of that person's performance of official duties in connection with a judicial proceeding; or

(6) against a victim under the age of 18, if the respondent is more than 36 months older than the victim.

(e) A person who commits violations in two or more counties may be prosecuted in any county in which one of the acts was committed for all acts in violation of this section.

(f) A person may be prosecuted at the place where any call is made or received or, in the case of wireless or electronic communication or any communication made through any available technologies, where the actor or victim resides, or in the jurisdiction of the victim's designated address if the victim participates in the address confidentiality program established under chapter 5B.

(g) A peace officer shall arrest without a warrant and take into custody a person whom the peace officer has probable cause to believe has violated an order issued under subdivision 4 or 5 if the existence of the order can be verified by the officer.

(h) A violation of a temporary restraining order or restraining order shall also constitute contempt of court.

(i) Upon the filing of an affidavit by the petitioner, any peace officer, or an interested party designated by the court, alleging that the respondent has violated an order issued under subdivision 4 or 5, the court may issue an order to the respondent requiring the respondent to appear within 14 days and show cause why the respondent should not be held in contempt of court. The court also shall refer the violation of the order to the appropriate prosecuting authority for possible prosecution under paragraph (b), (c), or (d).

Subd. 7. **Copy to law enforcement agency.** An order granted under this section shall be forwarded by the court administrator within 24 hours to the local law enforcement agency with jurisdiction over the residence of the applicant. Each appropriate law enforcement agency shall make available to other law enforcement officers through a system for verification, information as to the existence and status of any order issued under this section.

Subd. 8.Notice. (a) An order granted under this section must contain a conspicuous notice to the respondent:

(1) of the specific conduct that will constitute a violation of the order;

(2) that violation of an order is either (i) a misdemeanor punishable by imprisonment for up to 90 days or a fine of up to $1,000, or both, (ii) a gross misdemeanor punishable by imprisonment for up to one year or a fine of up to $3,000, or both, or (iii) a felony punishable by imprisonment for up to five years or a fine of up to $10,000, or both; and

(3) that a peace officer must arrest without warrant and take into custody a person if the peace officer has probable cause to believe the person has violated a restraining order.

(b) If the court grants relief for a period of up to 50 years under subdivision 5, the order must also contain a conspicuous notice to the respondent that the respondent must wait five years to seek a modification of the order.

Subd. 9. **Effect on local ordinances.** Nothing in this section shall supersede or preclude the continuation or adoption of any local ordinance which applies to a broader scope of targeted residential picketing conduct than that described in subdivision 1.

Subd. 10. **Prohibition against employer retaliation.** (a) An employer shall not discharge, discipline, threaten, otherwise discriminate against, or penalize an employee regarding the employee's compensation, terms, conditions, location, or privileges of employment, because the employee took reasonable time off from work to obtain or attempt to obtain relief under this section. Except in cases of imminent danger to the health or safety of the employee or the employee's child, or unless impracticable, an employee who is absent from the workplace shall give 48 hours' advance notice to the employer. Upon request of the employer, the employee shall provide verification that supports the employee's reason for being absent from the workplace. All information related to the employee's leave pursuant to this section shall be kept confidential by the employer.

(b) An employer who violates paragraph (a) is guilty of a misdemeanor and may be punished for contempt of court. In addition, the court shall order the employer to pay back wages and offer job reinstatement to any employee discharged from employment in violation of paragraph (a).

(c) In addition to any remedies otherwise provided by law, an employee injured by a violation of paragraph (a) may bring a civil action for recovery of damages, together with costs and disbursements, including reasonable attorneys fees, and may receive such injunctive and other equitable relief, including reinstatement, as determined by the court.

HIST: 1990 c 461 s 5; * * * 2017 c 95 art 2 s 16; 2017 c 95 art 3 s 20-24; 2017 c 95 art 4 s 2; 2020 c 86 art 1 s 39

609.749 HARASSMENT; STALKING; PENALTIES.

Subdivision 1. Repealed, 2020 c 96 s 6

Subd. 1a. Repealed, 2020 c 96 s 6

* * *

Subd. 1c. **Arrest.** For all violations under this section, except a violation of subdivision 2, clause (7), a peace officer may make an arrest under the provisions of section 629.34. A peace officer may not make a warrantless, custodial arrest of any person for a violation of subdivision 2, clause (7).

Subd. 2. **Harassment crimes.** (a) As used in this subdivision, the following terms have the meanings given:

(1) "family or household members" has the meaning given in section 518B.01, subdivision 2, paragraph (b);

(2) "personal information" has the meaning given in section 617.261, subdivision 7, paragraph (f);

(3) "sexual act" has the meaning given in section 617, subdivision 7, paragraph (g); and

(4) "substantial emotional distress" means mental distress, mental suffering, or mental anguish as demonstrated by a victim's response to an act including but not limited to seeking psychotherapy as defined in section 604.20, losing sleep or appetite, being diagnosed with a mental-health condition, experiencing suicidal ideation, or having difficulty concentrating on tasks resulting in lack of productivity.

(b) A person who harasses another by committing commits any of the following acts listed in paragraph (c) is guilty of a gross misdemeanor if the person, with the intent to kill, injure, harass, or intimidate another person:

(1) places the other person in reasonable fear of substantial bodily harm;

(2) places the person in reasonable fear that the person's family or household members will be subject to substantial bodily harm; or

(3) causes or would reasonably be expected to cause substantial emotional distress to the other person:

(c) A person commits harassment under this section if the person:

(1) directly or indirectly, or through third parties, manifests a purpose or intent to injure the person, property, or rights of another by the commission of an unlawful act;

(2) follows, monitors, or pursues another, whether in person or through any available technological or other means;

(3) returns to the property of another if the actor is without claim of right to the property or consent of one with authority to consent;

(4) repeatedly makes telephone calls, sends text messages, or induces a victim to make telephone calls to the actor, whether or not conversation ensues;

(5) makes or causes the telephone of another repeatedly or continuously to ring;

(6) repeatedly mails or delivers or causes the delivery by any means, including, electronically, of letters, telegrams, messages, packages, through assistive devices for people with vision impairments or hearing loss, or any communication made through any available technologies or other objects;

(7) knowingly makes false allegations against a peace officer concerning the officer's performance of official duties with intent to influence or tamper with the officer's performance of official duties; or

(8) uses another's personal information, without consent, to invite, encourage, or solicit a third party to engage in a sexual act with the person.

For purposes of this clause, "personal information" and "sexual act" have the meanings given in section 617.261, subdivision 7.

Subd. 3. **Aggravated violations.** (a) A person who commits any of the following acts is guilty of a felony and may be sentenced to imprisonment for not more than five years or to payment of a fine of not more than $10,000, or both:

(1) commits any offense described in subdivision 2 because of the victim's or another's actual or perceived race, color, religion, sex, sexual orientation, disability as defined in section 363.01, age, or national origin;

(2) commits any offense described in subdivision 2 by falsely impersonating another;

(3) commits any offense described in subdivision 2 and possesses a dangerous weapon at the time was used in any way in the commission of the offense;

(4) harasses another, as defined in subdivision 1, commits any offense described in subdivision 2 with intent to influence or otherwise tamper with a juror or a judicial proceeding or with intent to retaliate against a judicial officer, as defined in section 609.415, or a prosecutor, defense attorney, or officer of the court, because of that person's performance of official duties in connection with a judicial proceeding; or

(5) commits any offense described in subdivision 2 against a victim under the age of 18, if the actor is more than 36 months older than the victim.

(b) A person who commits any offense described in subdivision 2 against a victim under the age of 18, if the actor is more than 36 months older than the victim, and the act is committed with sexual or aggressive intent, is guilty of a felony and may be sentenced to imprisonment for not more than ten years or to payment of a fine of not more than $20,000, or both.

Subd. 4. **Second or subsequent violations; felony.** (a) A person is guilty of a felony who violates any provision of subdivision 2 within ten years of a previous qualified domestic violence-related offense conviction or adjudication of delinquency, and may be sentenced to imprisonment for not more than five years or to payment of a fine of not more than $10,000, or both.

(b) A person is guilty of a felony who violates any provision of subdivision 2 within ten years of the first of two or more previous qualified domestic violence-related offense convictions or adjudications of delinquency, and may be sentenced to imprisonment for not more than ten years or to payment of a fine of not more than $20,000, or both.

Subd. 5. **Stalking.** (a) A person who engages in stalking with respect to a single victim or one or more members of a single household which the actor knows or has reason to know would cause the victim under the circumstances to feel terrorized or to fear bodily harm and which does cause this reaction on the part of the victim, is guilty of a felony and may be sentenced to imprisonment for not more than ten years or to payment of a fine of not more than $20,000, or both.

(b) For purposes of this subdivision, "stalking " means two or more acts within a five-year period that violate or attempt to violate the provisions of any of the following or a similar law of another state, the United States, the District of Columbia, tribe, or United States territories:

(1) this section;

(2) sections 609.185 to 609.205 (first- to third-degree murder and first- and second-degree manslaughter);

(3) section 609.713 (terroristic threats);

(4) section 609.224 (fifth-degree assault);

(5) section 609.2242 (domestic assault);

(6) section 518B.01, subdivision 14 (violations of domestic abuse orders for protection);

(7) section 609.748, subdivision 6 (violations of harassment restraining orders);

(8) section 609.605, subdivision 1, paragraph (b), clauses (3), (4), and (7) (certain trespass offenses);

(9) sections 609.78, subdivision 2 (interference with an emergency call);

(10) section 609.79 (obscene or harassing telephone calls);

(11) section 609.795 (letter, telegram, or package; opening; harassment);

(12) section 609.582 (burglary);

(13) section 609.595 (damage to property);

(14) section 609.765 (criminal defamation);

(15) sections 609.342 to 609.3451 (first- to fifth-degree criminal sexual conduct); or

(16) section 629.75, subdivision 2 (violations of domestic abuse no contact orders).

* * *

Subd. 6. **Mental health assessment and treatment.** (a) When a person is convicted of a felony offense under this section, or another felony offense arising out of a charge based on this section, the court shall order an independent professional mental health assessment of the offender's need for mental health treatment. The court may waive the assessment if an adequate assessment was conducted prior to the conviction.

(b) Notwithstanding section 13.42, 13.85, 144.335, or 260.161, the assessor has access to the following private or confidential data on the person if access is relevant and necessary for the assessment:

(1) medical data under section 13.42;

(2) welfare data under section 13.46;

(3) corrections and detention data under section 13.85;

(4) health records under section 144.335; and

(5) juvenile court records under section 260.161.

Data disclosed under this section may be used only for purposes of the assessment and may not be further disclosed to any other person, except as authorized by law.

(c) If the assessment indicates that the offender is in need of and amenable to mental health treatment, the court shall include in the sentence a requirement that the offender undergo treatment.

(d) The court shall order the offender to pay the costs of assessment under this subdivision unless the offender is indigent under section 563.01.

Subd. 7. **Exception.** Conduct is not a crime under this section if it is performed under terms of a valid license, to ensure compliance with a court order, or to carry out a specific lawful commercial purpose or employment duty, is authorized or required by a valid contract, or is authorized, required, or protected by state, federal, or tribal law or the state, federal, or tribal constitutions. Subdivision 2, clause (2), does not impair the right of any individual or group to engage in speech protected by the federal, state, or tribal constitutions, or federal, state, or tribal law, including peaceful and lawful handbilling and picketing.

Subd. 8. **Harassment; stalking; firearms.** (a) When a person is convicted of harassment or stalking under this section and the court determines that the person used a firearm in any way during commission of the crime, the court may order that the person is prohibited from possessing any type of firearm for any period longer than three years or for the remainder of the person's life. A person who violates this paragraph is guilty of a gross misdemeanor. At the time of the conviction, the court shall inform the defendant for how long the defendant is prohibited from possessing a firearm and that it is a gross misdemeanor to violate this paragraph. The failure of the court to provide this information to a defendant does not affect the applicability of the firearm possession prohibition or the gross misdemeanor penalty to that defendant.

(b) Except as otherwise provided in paragraph (a), when a person in convicted of harassment or stalking under this section, the court shall inform the defendant that the defendant is prohibited from possessing a firearm from three years from the date of conviction and that it is a gross misdemeanor offense to violate this prohibition. The failure of the court to provide this information to a defendant does not affect the applicability of the firearm possession prohibition or the gross misdemeanor penalty to that defendant.

(c) Except as otherwise provided in paragraph (a), a person is not entitled to possess a pistol if the person has been convicted after August 1, 1996, of harassment or stalking under this section, or to possess a firearm if the person has been convicted on or after the effective of a stalking crime under this section, unless three years have elapsed from the date of conviction and, during that time, the person has not been convicted of any other violation of this section. Property rights may not be abated but access may be restricted by the courts. A person who possesses a firearm in violation of this paragraph is guilty of a gross misdemeanor.

(d) If the court determines that a person convicted of harassment or stalking under this section owns or possesses a firearm and used it in any way during the commission of the crime, it shall order that the firearm be summarily forfeited under section 609.5316, subdivision 3.

(e) Except as otherwise provided in paragraphs (d) and (g), when a person is convicted of harassment or stalking under this section, the court shall order the defendant to transfer any firearms that the person possesses, within three business days, to a federally licensed firearms dealer, a law enforcement agency, or a third party who may lawfully receive them. * * * [Such transferees] shall return the transferred firearms to the person upon request after the expiration of the prohibiting time period imposed under this subdivision, provided the person is not otherwise prohibited from possessing firearms under state or federal law. * * * The court shall order that the person surrender all permits to carry and purchase firearms to the sheriff.

(f) A defendant who is ordered to transfer firearms under paragraph (e) must file proof of transfer as provided for in this paragraph. If the transfer is made to a third party, the third party must sign an affidavit under oath before a notary public either acknowledging that the defendant permanently transferred the defendant's firearms to the third party or agreeing to temporarily store the defendant's firearms until such time as the defendant is legally permitted to possess firearms. * * * If the transfer is to a law enforcement agency or federally licensed firearms dealer, the law enforcement agency or federally licensed firearms dealer shall provide proof of transfer to the defendant. * * *

(g) When a person is convicted of harassment or stalking under this section, the court shall determine by a preponderance of evidence if the person poses an imminent risk of causing another person substantial bodily harm [, and] shall order that the local law enforcement agency take immediate possession of all firearms in the person's possession. * * * [The agency] shall return the firearms to the person upon request after the expiration of the prohibiting time period, provided the person is not otherwise prohibited from possessing firearms under state or federal law. The local law enforcement agency shall, upon written notice from the person, transfer the firearms to a federally licensed firearms dealer or a third party who may lawfully receive them. * * *

HIST: 1993 c 326 art 2 s 22; * * * 1Sp2019 c 5 art 2 s 17-21; 2020 c 96 s 2-3

Chapter 16 -- GAMBLING

Editors' Note: Selected portions of Chapter 16 concerning the Gambling have been edited to eliminate those provisions that have less importance to the duties of peace officers.

Category 2, Section 5:

2.5.1. Describe the basic organization, purpose, and definitions and principles of the Minnesota Criminal Code.

2.5.5. Given a variety of scenarios, identify indications a particular crime has been committed and identify the elements of that crime.

609.75 GAMBLING; DEFINITIONS.

Subdivision 1. **Lottery.** (a) A lottery is a plan which provides for the distribution of money, property or other reward or benefit to persons selected by chance from among participants some or all of whom have given a consideration for the chance of being selected.
* * *

(b) An in-package chance promotion is not a lottery if all of the following are met:

(1) participation is available, free and without purchase of the package, from the retailer or by mail or toll-free telephone request to the sponsor for entry or for a game piece; * * *

(4) the sponsor does not misrepresent a participant's chances of winning any prize; [and]

(5) the sponsor randomly distributes all game pieces and maintains records of random distribution for at least one year after the termination date of the promotion[.] * * *

Subd. 2. **Bet.** A bet is a bargain whereby the parties mutually agree to a gain or loss by one to the other of specified money, property or benefit dependent upon chance although the chance is accompanied by some element of skill.

Subd. 3. **What are not bets.** The following are not bets:

(1) A contract to insure, indemnify, guarantee or otherwise compensate another for a harm or loss sustained, even though the loss depends upon chance.

(2) A contract for the purchase or sale at a future date of securities or other commodities.

(3) Offers of purses, prizes or premiums to the actual contestants in any bona fide contest for the determination of skill, speed, strength, endurance, or quality or to the bona fide owners of animals or other property entered in such a contest.

(4) The game of bingo when conducted in compliance with sections 349.11 to 349.23.

(5) A private social bet not part of or incidental to organized, commercialized, or systematic gambling.

(6) The operation of equipment or the conduct of a raffle under sections 349.11 to 349.22, by an organization licensed the gambling control board or an organization exempt from licensing under section 349.166.

(7) Pari-mutuel betting on horse racing when the betting is conducted under chapter 240.

(8) The purchase and sale of state lottery tickets under chapter 349A.

Subd. 4. **Gambling device.** A gambling device is a contrivance the purpose of which is that for a consideration a player is afforded an opportunity to obtain something of value, other than free plays, automatically from the machine or otherwise, the award of which is determined principally by chance, whether or not the contrivance is actually played. "Gambling device" also includes a video game of chance, as defined in subdivision 8.

Subd. 4a. **Associated equipment.** Associated equipment means any equipment used in connection with gambling that would not be classified as a gambling device, including but not limited to: cards, dice, computerized systems of betting at a race book or sports pool, computerized systems for monitoring slot machines or games of chance, devices for weighing or counting money, and links which connect progressive slot machines.

Subd. 5. **Gambling place.** A gambling place is a location or structure, stationary or movable, or any part thereof, wherein, as one of its uses, betting is permitted or promoted, a lottery is conducted or assisted or a gambling device is operated.

Subd. 6. **Bucket shop.** A bucket shop is a place wherein the operator is engaged in making bets in the form of purchases or sales on public exchanges of securities, commodities or other personal property for future delivery to be settled at prices dependent on the chance of those prevailing at the public exchanges without a bona fide purchase or sale being in fact made on a board of trade or exchange.

Subd. 7. **Sports bookmaking.** Sports bookmaking is the activity of intentionally receiving, recording or forwarding within any 30-day period more than five bets, or offers to bet, that total more than $2,500 on any one or more sporting events.

Subd. 8. **Video game of chance.** A video game of chance is a game or device that simulates one or more games commonly referred to as poker, blackjack, craps, hi-lo, roulette, or other common gambling forms, though not offering any type of pecuniary award or gain to players. The term also includes any video game having one or more of the following characteristics:

(1) it is primarily a game of chance, and has no substantial elements of skill involved;

(2) it awards game credits or replays and contains a meter or device that records unplayed credits or replays. A video game that simulates horse racing that does not involve a prize payout is not a video game of chance. * * *

Subd. 10. **Game.** A game means any game played with cards, dice, equipment, or any mechanical or electronic device or machine for money or other value, whether or not approved by law, and includes, but is not limited to: card and dice games of chance, slot machines, banking or percentage games, video games of chance, sports pools, pari-mutuel betting, and race book. "Game" does not include any private social bet.

Subd. 11. **Authorized gambling activity.** An authorized gambling activity means any form of gambling authorized by and operated in conformance with law.

Subd. 12. **Authorized gambling establishment.** An authorized gambling establishment means any premises where gambling authorized by law is occurring. * * *

Subd. 17. **Applicability of definitions.** For the purposes of sections 609.75 to 609.762, the terms defined in this section have the meanings given, unless the context clearly indicates otherwise.

HIST: 1963 c 753 art 1 s 609.75; * * * 2015 c 29 s 4-7,9

609.755 ACTS OF OR RELATING TO GAMBLING.

Whoever does any of the following is guilty of a misdemeanor:

(1) makes a bet;

(2) sells or transfers a chance to participate in a lottery;

(3) disseminates information about a lottery, except a lottery conducted by an adjoining state, with intent to encourage participation therein;

(4) permits a structure or location owned or occupied by the actor or under the actor's control to be used as a gambling place; or

(5) except where authorized by statute, possesses a gambling device.

Clause (5) does not prohibit operation of a gambling device in a person's dwelling for amusement purposes in a manner that does not afford players an opportunity to obtain anything of value.

HIST: 1963 c 753 art 1 s 609.755; * * * 1994 c 633 art 4 s 10

609.76 OTHER ACTS RELATING TO GAMBLING.

Subdivision 1. **Gross misdemeanors.** Whoever does any of the following may be sentenced to imprisonment for not more than one year or to payment of a fine of not more than $3,000, or both:

(1) maintains or operates a gambling place or operates a bucket shop;

(2) intentionally participates in the income of a gambling place or bucket shop;

(3) conducts a lottery, or, with intent to conduct a lottery, possesses facilities for doing so;

(4) sets up for use for the purpose of gambling, or collects the proceeds of, any gambling device or bucket shop;

(5) except as provided in section 299L.07, manufactures, sells, offers for sale, or otherwise provides, in whole or any part thereof, any gambling device including those defined in section 349.30, subdivision 2;

(6) with intent that it be so used, manufactures, sells, or offers for sale any facility for conducting a lottery, except as provided by section 299L.07; or

(7) receives, records, or forwards bets or offers to bet or, with intent to receive, record, or forward bets or offers to bet, possesses facilities to do so.

Subd. 2. **Sports bookmaking.** Whoever engages in sports bookmaking is guilty of a felony.

Subd. 3. **Cheating.** Whoever cheats in a game, as described in this subdivision, is subject to the following penalties:

(i) if the person holds a license related to gambling or is an employee of the licensee, the person is guilty of a felony; and

(ii) any other person is guilty of a gross misdemeanor. Any person who is a repeat offender is guilty of a felony.

A person cheats in a game by intentionally:

(1) altering or misrepresenting the outcome of a game or event on which wagers have been made, after the outcome is determined, but before the outcome is revealed to the players;

(2) placing, canceling, increasing, or decreasing a bet after acquiring knowledge, not available to other players, of the outcome of the game or subject of the bet, or of events affecting the outcome of the game or subject of the bet;

(3) claiming or collecting money or anything of value from a game or authorized gambling establishment not won or earned from the game or authorized gambling establishment;

(4) manipulating a gambling device or associated equipment to affect the outcome of the game or the number of plays or credits available on the game; or

(5) otherwise altering the elements of chance or methods of selection or criteria which determine the result of the game or amount or frequency of payment of the game.

Subd. 4. **Certain devices prohibited.** (a) Whoever uses or possesses a probability-calculating or outcome-affecting device at an authorized gambling establishment is guilty of a felony. For purposes of this subdivision, a "probability-calculating" or "outcome-affecting" device is any device to assist in:

(1) projecting the outcome of a game other than pari-mutuel betting authorized by chapter 240;

(2) keeping track of or counting cards used in a game;

(3) analyzing the probability of the occurrence of an event relating to a game other than pari-mutuel betting authorized by chapter 240; or

(4) analyzing the strategy for playing or betting in a game other than pari-mutuel betting authorized by chapter 240.

For purposes of this section, a book, graph, periodical, chart, or pamphlet is not a "probability-calculating" or "outcome-affecting" device.

(b) Whoever uses, or possesses with intent to use, a key or other instrument for the purpose of opening, entering, and affecting the operation of any game or gambling device or for removing money, chips, tokens, or other contents from therein, is guilty of a felony. This paragraph does not apply to an agent or employee of an authorized gambling establishment acting within the scope of employment.

Subd. 5. **Counterfeit chips prohibited.** Whoever intentionally uses counterfeit chips or tokens to play a game at an authorized gambling establishment as defined in section 609.75, subdivision 5, designed to be played with or operated by chips or tokens is guilty of a felony. For purposes of the subdivision, counterfeit chips or tokens are chips or tokens not approved the government regulatory agency for use in an authorized gambling activity.

Subd. 6. **Manufacture, sale, and modification prohibited.** (a) Whoever manufactures, sells, distributes, or otherwise provides cards, chips, tokens, dice, or other equipment or devices intended to be used to violate this section, is guilty of a felony.

(b) Whoever intentionally marks, alters, or otherwise modifies lawful associated equipment or gambling devices for the purpose of violating this section is guilty of a felony.

Subd. 7. **Instruction.** Whoever instructs another person to violate the provisions of this section, with the intent that the information or knowledge conveyed be used to violate this section, is guilty of a felony.

Subd. 8. **Value of chips or tokens.** The value of chips or tokens approved for use in a game designed to be played with or operated by chips or tokens, as the term "value" is used in section 609.52, is the amount or denomination shown on the face of the chip or token representing United States currency. Chips used in tournament play at a card club at a class A facility have no United States currency value.

HIST: 1963 c 753 art 1 s 609.76; * * * 2009 c 86 art 1 s 83

609.763 LAWFUL GAMBLING FRAUD.

Subdivision 1. **Crime.** A person is guilty of a crime and may be sentenced as provided in subdivision 2 if the person does any of the following:

(1) knowingly claims a lawful gambling prize using altered or counterfeited gambling equipment;

(2) knowingly claims a lawful gambling prize by means of fraud, deceit, or misrepresentation;

(3) manipulates any form of lawful gambling or tampers with any gambling equipment with intent to influence the outcome of a game or the receipt of a prize;

(4) knowingly tampers with or attempts to alter any component or device used in the conduct or play of electronic pull-tabs or electronic linked bingo * * * or attempts to convert legal gambling into illegal gambling at [a licensed] establishment * * *;

(5) has unauthorized possession of an electronic pull-tab device, an electronic linked bingo device, or other component used in the conduct of electronic pull-tabs or electronic linked bingo * * *; or

(6) knowingly places or uses false information on a prize receipt or on any other form approved for use by the gambling control board or the alcohol and gambling enforcement division of the department of public safety.

Subd. 2. **Penalty.** A person who violates subdivision 1 may be sentenced as follows:

(1) if the dollar amount involved is $500 or less, the person is guilty of a misdemeanor;

(2) if the dollar amount involved is more than $500 but not more than $2,500, the person is guilty of a gross misdemeanor; and

(3) if the dollar amount involved is more than $2,500, the person is guilty of a felony and may be sentenced to imprisonment for not more than three years or to payment of a fine of not more than $6,000, or both.

Subd. 3. **Aggregation; jurisdiction.** In a prosecution under this section, the dollar amounts involved in violation of subdivision 1 within any 12-month period may be aggregated

and the defendant charged accordingly. When two or more offenses are committed by the same person in two or more counties, the defendant may be prosecuted in any county in which one of the offenses was committed for all of the offenses aggregated under this subdivision.
HIST: 2000 c 318 s 1; 2005 c 136 art 17 s 47; 2014 c 240 s 20

609.761 OPERATIONS PERMITTED.

Subdivision 1. **Lawful gambling.** Notwithstanding sections 609.755 and 609.76, an organization may conduct lawful gambling as defined in section 349.12, if authorized under chapter 349, and a person may manufacture, sell, or offer for sale a gambling device to an organization authorized under chapter 349 to conduct lawful gambling, and pari-mutuel betting on horse racing may be conducted under chapter 240.

Subd. 2. **State lottery.** Sections 609.755 and 609.76 do not prohibit the operation of the state lottery or the sale, possession, or purchase of tickets for the state lottery under chapter 349A.

Subd. 3. **Social skill game.** Sections 609.755 and 609.76 do not prohibit tournaments or contests that satisfy all of the following requirements:

(1) the tournament or contest consists of the card games of chance commonly known as cribbage, skat, sheephead, bridge, euchre, pinochle, gin, 500, smear, Texas hold'em, or whist;

(2) the tournament or contest does not provide any direct financial benefit to the promoter or organizer; (3) the value of all prizes awarded for each tournament or contest does not exceed $200; and

(4) for a tournament or contest involving Texas hold'em:

(i) no person under 18 years of age may participate;

(ii) the payment of an entry fee or other consideration for participating is prohibited; [and]

(iii) the value of all prizes awarded to an individual winner of a tournament or contest at a single location may not exceed $200 each day[.] * * *

Subd. 4. **Social dice games.** Sections 609.755 and 609.76 do not prohibit dice games conducted on the premises and adjoining rooms of a retail establishment licensed to sell alcoholic beverages if the following requirements are satisfied:

(1) the games consist of board games played with dice or commonly known dice games such as "shake-a-day," "3-2-1," "who buys," "last chance," "liar's poker," "6-5-4," "horse," and "aces";

(2) wagers or prizes for the games are limited to food or beverages; and

(3) the retail establishment does not organize or participate financially in the games.

Subd. 5. **High school raffles.** Sections 609.755 and 609.76 do not prohibit a raffle, as defined in section 349.12, subdivision 33, conducted by a school district or a nonprofit organization organized primarily to support programs of a school district, if the following conditions are complied with:

(1) tickets for the raffle may only be sold and the drawing conducted at a high school event sponsored by a school district. * * *

(4) one-half of the gross receipts from the sale of tickets must be awarded as prizes for the raffle, and the remaining one-half may only be expended to defray the school district's costs of sending event participants to high school activities held at other locations[.] * * *
HIST: 1978 c 507 s 6; * * * 2015 c 29 s 8

609.762 FORFEITURE OF GAMBLING DEVICES, PRIZES AND PROCEEDS.

Subdivision 1. **Forfeiture.** The following are subject to forfeiture:

(a) Devices used or intended for use, including those defined in section 349.30, subdivision 2, as a gambling device, except as authorized in sections 299L.07 and 349.23;

(b) All moneys, materials, and other property used or intended for use as payment to participate in gambling or a prize or receipt for gambling;

(c) Books, records, and research products and materials, including formulas, microfilm, tapes, and data used or intended for use in gambling; and

(d) Property used or intended to be used to illegally influence the outcome of a horse race.

Subd. 2. **Seizure.** Property subject to forfeiture under subdivision 1 may be seized by any law enforcement agency upon process issued by any court having jurisdiction over the property. Seizure without process may be made if:

(a) the seizure is incident to an arrest or a search under a search warrant;

(b) the property subject to seizure has been the subject of a prior judgment in favor of the state in a criminal injunction or forfeiture proceeding; or

(c) the law enforcement agency has probable cause to believe that the property was used or is intended to be used in a gambling violation and the delay occasioned by the necessity to obtain process would result in the removal, loss, or destruction of the property.

Subd. 3. **Not subject to replevin.** Property taken or detained under subdivision 2 is not subject to a replevin action, but is considered to be in the custody of the law enforcement agency subject only to the orders and decrees of the court having jurisdiction over the forfeiture proceedings.

Subd. 4. **Procedures.** Property must be forfeited after a conviction for a gambling violation according to the following procedure:

(a) a separate complaint must be filed against the property describing it, charging its use in the specified violation, and specifying the time and place of its unlawful use;

(b) if the person charged with a gambling offense is acquitted, the court shall dismiss the complaint and order the property returned to the persons legally entitled to it; and

(c) if after conviction the court finds the property, or any part of it, was used in violation as specified in the complaint, it shall order that the property be sold or retained by the law enforcement agency for official use. Proceeds from the sale of forfeited property may be retained for official use and shared equally between the law enforcement agency investigating the offense involved in the forfeiture and the prosecuting agency that prosecuted the offense involved in the forfeiture and handled the forfeiture proceedings.

Subd. 5. **Exception.** Property may not be seized or forfeited under this section if the owner shows to the satisfaction of the court that the owner had no notice or knowledge or reason to believe that the property was used or intended to be used in violation of this section.

Subd. 6. **Reporting.** The law enforcement and prosecuting agencies shall report on forfeitures occurring under this section as described in section 609.5315, subdivision 6.
HIST: 1983 c 214 s 39; * * * 2010 c 391 s 19

349.12 DEFINITIONS.

Subdivision 1. **Scope.** As used in sections 349.11 to 349.23 the terms in this section have the meanings given them. * * *

Subd. 4. **Bingo.** "Bingo" means a game where each player has a bingo hard card or bingo paper sheet, or a facsimile of a bingo paper sheet when used in conjunction with an electronic bingo device, for which a consideration has been paid, and played in accordance with this chapter and with rules of the board for the conduct of bingo. * * *

Subd. 5. **Bingo occasion.** "Bingo occasion" means a single gathering or session at which a series of one or more successive bingo games is played. There is no limit on the number of games conducted during a bingo occasion but a bingo occasion must not last longer than eight consecutive hours[.] * * *

Subd. 24. **Lawful gambling.** "Lawful gambling" is the operation, conduct or sale of bingo, raffles, paddlewheels, tipboards, and pull-tabs. * * *

Subd. 29. **Paddlewheel.** "Paddlewheel" means a vertical wheel marked off into sections containing one or more numbers, and which, after being turned or spun, uses a pointer or marker to indicate winning chances[.] * * *

Subd. 32. **Pull-tab.** "Pull-tab" means a single folded or banded paper ticket, multi-ply card with perforated break-open tabs, or a facsimile of a paper pull-tab ticket used in conjunction with an electronic pull-tab device, the face of which is initially covered to conceal one or more numbers or symbols, and where one or more of each set of tickets, cards, or facsimiles has been designated in advance as a winner. * * *

Subd. 33. **Raffle.** "Raffle" means a game in which a participant buys a ticket or other certificate of participation in an event where the prize determination is based on a method of random selection and all entries have an equal chance of selection. * * *

Subd. 34. **Tipboard.** "Tipboard" means a board, placard or other device containing a seal that conceals the winning number or symbol, and that serves as the game flare for a tipboard game. * * *

HIST: 1976 c 261 s 2; * * * 2019 c 50 art 1 s 105; 1Sp2019 c 10 art 7 s1

349.13 LAWFUL GAMBLING.

Lawful gambling is not a lottery or gambling within the meaning of sections 609.75 to 609.76 if it is conducted under this chapter. A pull-tab dispensing device, electronic bingo device, and electronic pull-tab device permitted under this chapter and by board rule is not a gambling device within the meaning of sections 609.75 to 609.76 and chapter 299L. * * *

HIST: 1976 c 261 s 3; * * * 2012 c 299 art 4 s 32

Chapter 17 -- CRIMES AGAINST REPUTATION

Category 2, Section 5:
2.5.1. Describe the basic organization, purpose, and definitions and principles of the Minnesota Criminal Code.
2.5.5. Given a variety of scenarios, identify indications a particular crime has been committed and identify the elements of that crime.

609.765 CRIMINAL DEFAMATION.

Subdivision 1. **Definition.** Defamatory matter is anything which exposes a person or a group, class or association to hatred, contempt, ridicule, degradation or disgrace in society, or injury to business or occupation.

Subd. 2. **Acts constituting.** Whoever with knowledge of its false and defamatory character orally, in writing or by any other means, communicates any false and defamatory matter to a third person without the consent of the person defamed is guilty of criminal defamation and may be sentenced to imprisonment for not more than one year or to payment of a fine of not more than $3,000, or both.

Subd. 3. **Justification.** Violation of subdivision 2 is justified if:

(1) the communication is absolutely privileged; or

(2) the communication consists of fair comment made in good faith with respect to persons participating in matters of public concern; or

(3) the communication consists of a fair and true report or a fair summary of any judicial, legislative or other public or official proceedings; or

(4) the communication is between persons each having an interest or duty with respect to the subject matter of the communication and is made with intent to further such interest or duty.

Subd. 4. **Testimony required.** No person shall be convicted on the basis of an oral communication of defamatory matter except upon the testimony of at least two other persons that they heard and understood the oral statement as defamatory or upon a plea of guilty.

HIST: 1963 c 753 art 1 s 609.765; 1984 c 628 art 3 s 11; 1986 c 444; 2016 c 126 s 8

609.77 FALSE INFORMATION TO NEWS MEDIA.

Whoever, with intent that it be published or disseminated and that it defame another person, communicates to any newspaper, magazine or other news media, any statement, knowing it to be false, is guilty of a misdemeanor.

HIST: 1963 c 753 art 1 s 609.77; 1971 c 23 s 77

Chapter 18 -- CRIMES RELATING TO COMMUNICATIONS

Category 2, Section 5:
2.5.1. Describe the basic organization, purpose, and definitions and principles of the Minnesota Criminal Code.
2.5.5. Given a variety of scenarios, identify indications a particular crime has been committed and identify the elements of that crime.

609.774 EMERGENCY COMMUNICATIONS; KIDNAPPINGS.

Subdivision 1. **Definitions.** For the purposes of this section, "supervising peace officer" means a person licensed pursuant to chapter 626, who has probable cause to believe that a person is being unlawfully confined, and who has lawful jurisdiction in the geographical area where the violation is believed to be occurring.

Subd. 2. **Authority.** A supervising peace officer may order a telephone company to cut, reroute, or divert telephone lines for the purpose of establishing and controlling communications with a violator.

Subd. 3. **Designation.** Each telephone company shall designate an employee to serve as a security official and to provide assistance as required by the supervising peace officer to carry out the purposes of this section.

Subd. 4. **Unauthorized communication prohibited.** Whoever initiates telephone communications with a violator with knowledge of an order issued pursuant to subdivision 2 and without prior police authorization, is guilty of a misdemeanor.

Subd. 5. **Defense.** Good faith reliance by telephone employees on an order issued pursuant to subdivision 2 shall constitute a complete defense to any legal action brought for an interruption of telephone communications occurring by reason of this section.
HIST: 1979 c 63 s 1; 1979 c 289 s 2

609.775 DIVULGING TELEPHONE OR TELEGRAPH MESSAGE; NONDELIVERY.

Whoever does any of the following is guilty of a misdemeanor:

(1) Being entrusted as an employee of a telephone or telegraph company with the transmission or delivery of a telephonic or telegraphic message, intentionally or through culpable negligence discloses the contents or meaning thereof to a person other than the intended receiver; or

(2) Having knowledge of not being the intended receiver, obtains such disclosure from such employee; or

(3) Being such employee, intentionally or negligently fails duly to deliver such message.
HIST: 1963 c 753 art 1 s 609.775; 1971 c 23 s 78; 1986 c 444

609.776 INTERFERENCE WITH EMERGENCY COMMUNICATIONS.

Whoever, without prior authorization, broadcasts or transmits on, interferes with, blocks, or cross-patches another frequency onto a law enforcement, firefighting, emergency medical services, emergency radio frequency or channel, any assigned or alternate emergency frequency or channel, or an official cellular telephone communication of a law enforcement agency, a fire department, or emergency medical services provider, knowing, or having reason to know that the act creates a risk of obstructing, preventing, or misdirecting official law enforcement, firefighting, or emergency medical services communications, is guilty of a felony and may be sentenced to imprisonment for not more than three years or to payment of a fine of not more than $10,000, or both.
HIST: 1Sp2003 c 2 art 4 s 27

609.78 EMERGENCY TELEPHONE CALLS AND COMMUNICATIONS.
  Subdivision 1. **Misdemeanor offenses.** Whoever does the following is guilty of a misdemeanor:
  (1) Refuses to relinquish immediately a coin-operated telephone or a telephone line consisting of two or more stations when informed that the line is needed to make an emergency call;
  (2) secures a relinquishment of a coin-operated telephone or a telephone line consisting of two or more stations by falsely stating that the line is needed for an emergency;
  (3) publishes telephone directories to be used for telephones or telephone lines and the directories do not contain a copy of this section;
  (4) makes a call for emergency police, fire, medical, or ambulance service, knowing that no police, fire, or medical emergency exists;
  (5) interrupts, disrupts, impedes, or otherwise interferes with the transmission of a citizen's band radio channel communication the purpose of which is to inform or inquire about a medical emergency or an emergency in which property is or is reasonably believed to be in imminent danger of damage or destruction; or
  (6) makes or initiates an emergency call, knowing that no emergency exists, and with the intent to disrupt, interfere with, or reduce the provision of emergency services or the emergency call center's resources, remains silent, or makes abusive or harassing statements to the call recipient.
  Subd. 2. **Gross misdemeanor offenses.** Whoever does the following is guilty of a gross misdemeanor:
  (1) intentionally interrupts, disrupts, impedes, or interferes with an emergency call or who intentionally prevents or hinders another from placing an emergency call, and whose conduct does not result in a violation of section 609.498;
  (2) places an emergency call and reports a fictitious emergency with the intent of prompting an emergency response by law enforcement, fire, or emergency medical services personnel; or
  (3) violates subdivision 1, clause (6), after having been previously convicted or adjudicated delinquent for violating that clause.
  Subd. 2a. **Felony offense; reporting fictitious emergency resulting in serious injury.** Whoever violates subdivision 2, clause (2), is guilty of a felony and may be sentenced to imprisonment for not more than ten years or to payment of a fine of not more than $20,000, or both, if the call triggers an emergency response and, as a result of the response, someone suffers great bodily harm or death.
  Subd. 2b. **Other felony offenses.** Whoever does the following is guilty of a felony and may be sentenced to imprisonment for not more than five years or to payment of a fine of not more than $10,000, or both:
  (1) violates subdivision 1, clause (6), after having been previously convicted or adjudicated delinquent for violating that clause on more than one occasion; or
  (2) intentionally uses multiple communications devices or electronic means to block, interfere with, overload, or otherwise prevent the emergency call center's system from functioning properly, and these actions make the system unavailable to someone needing emergency assistance.
  Subd. 3. **Definition.** (a) Except as provided in paragraph (b), for purposes of this section, "emergency call" means:
  (1) a 911 call;
  (2) any call for emergency medical or ambulance service; or
  (3) any call for assistance from a police or fire department or for other assistance needed in an emergency to avoid serious harm to person or property, and an emergency exists.
  (b) As used in subdivisions 1 clause (6), 2, clause (2); and 2a:
  (1) "call" includes the use of any method of communication including, but not limit to: telephones, facsimiles, Voice over Internet Protocols, e-mail messages, text messages, and electronic transmissions of an image or video; and

(2) "emergency call" has the meaning given in paragraph (a) but does not require the existence of an emergency.
HIST: 1963 c 753 art 1 s 609.78; * * * 2013 c 20 s 1

609.79 OBSCENE OR HARASSING TELEPHONE CALLS.

Subdivision 1. **Crime defined; obscene call.** Whoever,

(1) by means of a telephone,

(i) makes any comment, request, suggestion or proposal which is obscene, lewd, or lascivious,

(ii) with the intent to harass or intimidate another person, repeatedly makes telephone calls, whether or not conversation ensues, and thereby places the other person in reasonable fear of substantial bodily harm; places the person in reasonable fear that the person's family or household members will be subject to substantial bodily harm; or causes or would reasonably be expected to cause substantial emotional distress to the other person, or

(iii) with the intent to harass or intimidate any person at the called or notified number, makes or causes the telephone of another to repeatedly or continuously ring or receive electronic notifications and thereby places the other person in reasonable fear of substantial bodily harm; places the person in reasonable fear that the person's family or household members will be subject to substantial bodily harm; or causes or would reasonably be expected to cause substantial emotional distress as defined in section 609.749, subdivision 2, paragraph (a), clause (4), to the other person, or

(2) having control of a telephone, knowingly permits it to be used for any purpose prohibited by this section, shall be guilty of a misdemeanor.

Subd. 1a. [Repealed, 1993 c 326 art 2 s 34]

Subd. 2. **Venue.** The offense may be prosecuted either at the place where the call is made or where it is received or, additionally in the case of wireless or electronic communication, where the sender or receiver resides.
HIST: 1963 c 753 art 1 s 609.79; * * *2005 c 136 art 17 s 48; 2020 c 96 s 4

609.795 LETTER, TELEGRAM, OR PACKAGE; OPENING; HARASSMENT.

Subdivision 1. **Misdemeanors.** Whoever does any of the following is guilty of a misdemeanor:

(1) knowing that the actor does not have the consent of either the sender or the addressee, intentionally opens any sealed letter, telegram, or package addressed to another; or

(2) knowing that a sealed letter, telegram, or package has been opened without the consent of either the sender or addressee, intentionally publishes any of the contents thereof; or

(3) with the intent to harass or intimidate another person, repeatedly mails or delivers or causes the delivery by any means, including electronically, of letters, telegrams, or packages and thereby places the other person in reasonable fear of substantial bodily harm; places the person in reasonable fear that the person's family or household members will be subject to substantial bodily harm; or causes or would reasonably be expected to cause substantial emotional distress as defined in section 609.749, subdivision 2, paragraph (a), clause (4), to the other person.

Subd. 2. [Repealed, 1993 c 326 art 2 s 34]

Subd. 3. **Venue.** The offense may be prosecuted either at the place where the letter, telegram, or package is sent or received or, alternatively in the case of wireless electronic communication, where the sender or receiver resides.
HIST: 1963 c 753 art 1 s 609.795; * * * 2005 c 136 art 17 s 49; 2020 c 96 s 5

609.80 INTERFERING WITH CABLE COMMUNICATIONS SYSTEMS.

Subdivision 1. **Misdemeanor.** Whoever does any of the following is guilty of a misdemeanor:

(1) intentionally and with the purpose of making or aiding in an unauthorized connection as prohibited by section 609.52, subdivision 2, paragraph (a), clause (12), to a licensed cable communications system as defined in chapter 238 lends, offers, or gives to another any

instrument, apparatus, equipment, or device designed to make an unauthorized connection, or plan, specification or instruction for making an unauthorized connection, without receiving or seeking to receive money or any other thing of value in exchange; or

(2) intentionally tampers with, removes or injures any cable, wire, or other component of a licensed cable communications system as defined in chapter 238; or

(3) intentionally and without claim of right interrupts a service of a licensed cable communications system as defined in chapter 238.

Subd. 2.Commercial activity; felony. Whoever sells or rents, or offers or advertises for sale or rental, any instrument, apparatus, equipment, or device designed to make an unauthorized connection as prohibited by section 609.52, subdivision 2, paragraph (a), clause (12), to a licensed cable communications system as defined in chapter 238, or a plan, specification, or instructions for making an unauthorized connection, is guilty of a felony and may be sentenced to not more than three years of imprisonment or a fine of not more than $5,000, or both.
HIST: 1977 c 396 s 2; 1988 c 410 s 1; 2020 c 83 art 1 s 94

609.896 CRIMINAL USE OF REAL PROPERTY.

Subdivision 1. **Definitions.** For the purposes of this section, the following terms have the meanings given to them.

(a) "Audiovisual recording function" means the capability of a device to record or transmit a motion picture or any part of a motion picture by means of any technology now known or later developed.
    * * *

Subd. 2. **Crime.** (a) Any person in a motion picture theater while a motion picture is being exhibited who knowingly operates an audiovisual recording function of a device without the consent of the owner or lessee of the motion picture theater is guilty of criminal use of real property.

(b) If a person is convicted of a first offense, it is a misdemeanor.

(c) If a person is convicted of a second offense, it is a gross misdemeanor.

(d) If a person is convicted of a third or subsequent offense, it is a felony and the person may be sentenced to imprisonment for not more than two years or to payment of a fine of not more than $4,000, or both.

Subd. 3. **Detaining suspects.** An owner or lessee of a motion picture theater is a merchant for purposes of section 629.366.
HIST: 2005 c 136 art 17 s 51

Chapter 19 -- CRIMES RELATING TO A BUSINESS

Category 2, Section 5:
2.5.1. Describe the basic organization, purpose, and definitions and principles of the Minnesota Criminal Code.
2.5.5. Given a variety of scenarios, identify indications a particular crime has been committed and identify the elements of that crime.

609.2336 DECEPTIVE OR UNFAIR TRADE PRACTICES; ELDERLY OR DISABLED VICTIMS.

Subdivision 1. **Definitions.** As used in this section:
(1) "charitable solicitation law violation" means a violation of sections 309.50 to 309.61;
(2) "consumer fraud law violation" means a violation of sections 325F.68 to 325F.70;
(3) "deceptive trade practices law violation" means a violation of sections 325D.43 to 325D.48;
(4) "false advertising law violation" means a violation of section 325F.67;
(5) "disabled person" means a person who has an impairment of physical or mental function or emotional status that substantially limits one or more major life activities;
(6) "major life activities" means functions such as caring for oneself, performing manual tasks, walking, seeing, hearing, speaking, breathing, learning, and working; and
(7) "senior citizen" means a person who is 65 years of age or older.
Subd. 2. **Crime.** It is a gross misdemeanor for any person to commit a charitable solicitation law violation, a consumer fraud law violation, a deceptive trade practices law violation, or a false advertising law violation if the person knows or has reason to know that the person's conduct:
(1) is directed at one or more disabled persons or senior citizens; and
(2) will cause or is likely to cause a disabled person or a senior citizen to suffer loss or encumbrance of a primary residence, principal employment or other major source of income, substantial loss of property set aside for retirement or for personal or family care and maintenance, substantial loss of pension, retirement plan, or government benefits, or substantial loss of other assets essential to the victim's health or welfare.
* * *
HIST: 1997 c 239 art 3 s 12; 2005 c 56 s 1

609.815 MISCONDUCT OF JUNK OR SECONDHAND DEALER.

Whoever is a junk dealer or secondhand dealer and does any of the following is guilty of a misdemeanor:
(1) Has stolen goods in possession and refuses to permit a law enforcement officer to examine them during usual business hours; or
(2) Purchases property from a person under lawful age, without the written consent of the person's parent or guardian.
HIST: 1963 c 753 art 1 s 609.815; 1971 c 23 s 84; 1986 c 444

609.82 FRAUD IN OBTAINING CREDIT.

A person who, with intent to defraud, obtains personal credit or credit for another from a bank, trust company, savings or savings association, or credit union, by means of a present or past false representation as to the person's or another's financial ability may be sentenced as follows:

(1) If no money or property is obtained by the defendant by means of such credit, to imprisonment for not more than 90 days or to payment of a fine of not more than $300, or both; or

(2) If money or property is so obtained, the value thereof shall be determined as provided in section 609.52, subdivision 1, clause (3) and the person obtaining the credit may be sentenced as provided in section 609.52, subdivision 3.

HIST: 1963 c 753 art 1 s 609.82; 1971 c 23 s 85; 1986 c 444; 1995 c 202 art 1 s 25

609.821 FINANCIAL TRANSACTION CARD FRAUD.

Subdivision 1. **Definitions.** For the purposes of this section, the following terms have the meanings given them:

(a) "Financial transaction card" means any instrument or device, whether known as a credit card, credit plate, charge plate, courtesy card, bank services card, banking card, check guarantee card, debit card, electronic benefit system (EBS) card, electronic benefit transfer (EBT) card, assistance transaction card, or by any other name[.]

(b) "Cardholder" means a person in whose name a card is issued.

(c) "Issuer" means a person, firm, or governmental agency * * * that issues a financial transaction card.

(d) "Property" includes money, goods, services, public assistance benefit, or anything else of value.

(e) "Public assistance benefit" means any money, goods or services, or anything else of value, issued under chapters 256, 256B, 256D, or section 393.07, subdivision 10.

(f) "Trafficking of SNAP benefits" means:

(1) the buying, selling, stealing, or otherwise effecting an exchange of Supplemental Nutrition Assistance Program (SNAP) benefits issued and accessed via an [EBT] card, card number and personal identification number (PIN), or manual voucher and signature, for cash or consideration other than eligible food * * *;

(2) the exchange of one of the following for SNAP benefits: firearms, ammunition, explosives, or controlled substances as defined [by federal law];

(3) purchasing a product with SNAP benefits that has a container requiring a return deposit with the intent of obtaining cash by discarding the product and returning the container for the deposit amount, intentionally discarding the product, and intentionally returning the container for the deposit amount;

(4) purchasing a product with SNAP benefits with the intent of obtaining cash or consideration other than eligible food by reselling the product, and intentionally reselling the product purchased * * * in exchange for cash or consideration other than eligible food;

(5) intentionally purchasing products originally purchased with SNAP benefits in exchange for cash or consideration other than eligible food; or

(6) attempting to buy, sell, steal, or otherwise effect an exchange of SNAP benefits * * * for cash or consideration other than eligible food[.]

Subd. 2. **Violations; penalties.** A person who does any of the following commits financial transaction card fraud:

(1) without the consent of the cardholder, and knowing that the cardholder has not given consent, uses or attempts to use a card to obtain the property of another, or a public assistance benefit issued for the use of another;

(2) uses or attempts to use a card knowing it to be forged, false, fictitious, or obtained in violation of clause (6);

(3) sells or transfers a card knowing that the cardholder and issuer have not authorized the person to whom the card is sold or transferred to use the card, or that the card is forged, false, fictitious, or was obtained in violation of clause (6);

(4) without a legitimate business purpose, and without the consent of the cardholders, receives or possesses, with intent to use, or with intent to sell or transfer in violation of clause (3), two or more cards issued in the name of another, or two or more cards knowing the cards to be forged, false, fictitious, or obtained in violation of clause (6);

(5) being authorized by an issuer to furnish money, goods, services, or anything else of value, knowingly and with an intent to defraud the issuer or the cardholder:

(i) furnishes money, goods, services, or anything else of value upon presentation of a financial transaction card knowing it to be forged, expired, or revoked, or knowing that it is presented by a person without authority to use the card; or

(ii) represents in writing to the issuer that the person has furnished money, goods, services, or anything else of value which has not in fact been furnished;

(6) upon applying for a financial transaction card to an issuer, or for a public assistance benefit which is distributed by means of a financial transaction card:

(i) knowingly gives a false name or occupation;

(ii) knowingly and substantially overvalues assets or substantially undervalues indebtedness for the purpose of inducing the issuer to issue a financial transaction card; or

(iii) knowingly makes a false statement or representation for the purpose of inducing an issuer to issue a financial transaction card used to obtain a public assistance benefit;

(7) with intent to defraud, falsely notifies the issuer or any other person of a theft, loss, disappearance, or nonreceipt of a financial transaction card;

(8) without the consent of the cardholder and knowing that the cardholder has not given consent, falsely alters, makes, or signs any written document pertaining to a card transaction to obtain or attempt to obtain the property of another; or

(9) engages in trafficking of SNAP benefits.

Subd. 3. **Sentence.** (a) A person who commits financial transaction card fraud may be sentenced as follows:

(1) for a violation of subdivision 2, clause (1), (2), (5), (8), or 9:

(i) to imprisonment for not more than 20 years or to payment of a fine of not more than $100,000, or both, if the value of the property the person obtained or attempted to obtain was more than $35,000, or the aggregate amount of the transactions under this subdivision was more than $35,000, or

(ii) to imprisonment for not more than ten years or to payment of a fine of not more than $20,000, or both, if the value of the property the person obtained or attempted to obtain was more than $2,500, or the aggregate amount of the transactions under this subdivision was more than $2,500; or

(iii) to imprisonment for not more than five years or to payment of a fine of not more than $10,000, or both, if the value of the property the person obtained or attempted to obtain was more than $250 but not more than $2,500, or the aggregate amount of the transactions under this subdivision was more than $250 but not more than $2,500; or

(iv) to imprisonment for not more than five years or to payment of a fine of not more than $10,000, or both, if the value of the property the person obtained or attempted to obtain was not more than $250, or the aggregate amount of the transactions under this subdivision was not more than $250, and the person has previously been convicted within the preceding five years for an offense under this section, section 609.24; 609.245; 609.52; 609.53; 609.582, subdivision 1, 2, or 3; 609.625; 609.63; or 609.631, or a statute from another state in conformity with any of those sections, and the person received a felony or gross misdemeanor sentence for the offense, or a sentence that was stayed under section 609.135 if the offense to which a plea was entered would allow imposition of a felony or gross misdemeanor sentence; or

(v) to imprisonment for not more than one year or to payment of a fine of not more than $3,000, or both, if the value of the property the person obtained or attempted to obtain was not more than $250, or the aggregate amount of the transactions under this subdivision was not more than $250;

(2) for a violation of subdivision 2, clause (3) or (4), to imprisonment for not more than three years or to payment of a fine of not more than $5,000, or both; or

(3) for a violation of subdivision 2, clause (6) or (7):

(i) if no property, other than a financial transaction card, has been obtained by the defendant by means of the false statement or false report, to imprisonment for not more than one year or to payment of a fine of not more than $3,000, or both; or

(ii) if property, other than a financial transaction card, is so obtained, in the manner provided in clause (1).

(b) In any prosecution under paragraph (a), clause (1), the value of the transactions made or attempted within any six-month period may be aggregated and the defendant charged accordingly in applying the provisions of this section. * * *

HIST: 1985 c 243 s 10; * * * 2015 c 78 art 4 s 60

Chapter 20 -- MISCELLANEOUS CRIMES

Category 2, Section 5:
2.5.1. Describe the basic organization, purpose, and definitions and principles of the Minnesota Criminal Code.
2.5.5. Given a variety of scenarios, identify indications a particular crime has been committed and identify the elements of that crime.

609.825 BRIBERY OF PARTICIPANT OR OFFICIAL IN CONTEST.

Subdivision 1. **Definition.** As used in this section, "official" means one who umpires, referees, judges, officiates or is otherwise designated to render decisions concerning the conduct or outcome of any contest included herein.

Subd. 2. **Acts prohibited.** Whoever does any of the following may be sentenced to imprisonment for not more than five years or to payment of a fine of not more than $10,000, or both:

(1) Offers, gives, or agrees to give, directly or indirectly, any benefit, reward or consideration to a participant, manager, director, or other official, or to one who intends to become such participant or official, in any sporting event, race or other contest of any kind whatsoever with intent thereby to influence such participant not to use the participant's best effort to win or enable the participant's team to win or to attain a maximum score or margin of victory, or to influence such official in decisions with respect to such contest; or

(2) Requests, receives, or agrees to receive, directly or indirectly, any benefit, reward or consideration upon the understanding that the actor will be so influenced as such participant or official.

Subd. 3. **Duty to report.** Whoever is offered or promised such benefit, reward or consideration upon the understanding to be so influenced as such participant or official and fails promptly to report the same to the offeree's or promisee's employer, manager, coach, or director, or to a county attorney may be punished by imprisonment for not more than one year or to payment of a fine of not more than $3,000, or both.
HIST: 1963 c 753 art 1 s 609.825; 1984 c 628 art 3 s 11; 1986 c 444

609.83 FALSELY IMPERSONATING ANOTHER.

Whoever does either of the following may be sentenced to imprisonment for not more than five years or to payment of a fine of not more than $10,000, or both:

(1) Assumes to enter into a marriage relationship with another by falsely impersonating a third person; or

(2) By falsely impersonating another with intent to defraud the other or a third person, appears, participates, or executes an instrument to be used in a judicial proceeding.
HIST: 1963 c 753 art 1 s 609.83; 1984 c 628 art 3 s 11; 1986 c 444

609.85 CRIMES AGAINST RAILROAD EMPLOYEES AND PROPERTY; PENALTY.

Subdivision 1. **Intent to cause derailment.** Whoever throws or deposits any type of debris, waste material, or other obstruction on any railroad track or whoever causes damage or causes another person to damage, tamper, change or destroy any railroad track, switch, bridge, trestle, tunnel, signal or moving equipment used in providing rail services, with intention to cause injury, accident or derailment, is guilty of a felony.

Subd. 2. **Foreseeable risk.** Whoever intentionally throws or deposits any type of debris, waste material, or other obstruction on any railroad track or whoever intentionally causes damage or causes another person to damage, tamper, change or destroy any railroad track, switch, bridge, trestle, tunnel, signal or moving equipment used in providing rail services, which creates a reasonably foreseeable risk of any injury, accident or derailment, is guilty of a gross misdemeanor.

        Subd. 3. **Shooting at train.** Whoever intentionally shoots a firearm at any portion of a railroad train, car, caboose, engine or moving equipment so as to endanger the safety of another is guilty of a gross misdemeanor.

        Subd. 4. **Throwing objects at train.** Whoever intentionally throws, shoots or propels any stone, brick or other missile at any railroad train, car, caboose, engine or moving equipment, so as to endanger the safety of another is guilty of a gross misdemeanor.

        Subd. 5. **Placing obstruction on track.** Whoever places an obstruction on a railroad track is guilty of a misdemeanor.

        Subd. 6. **Trespass; allowing animals on track exception.** Whoever intentionally trespasses, or who permits animals under the person's control to trespass on a railroad track, yard, or bridge is guilty of a misdemeanor. * * *

HIST: 1977 c 179 s 1; 1989 c 5 s 11; 2008 c 350 art 2 s 3

609.851 FALSE TRAFFIC SIGNAL.

        Subdivision 1. **Misdemeanor.** A person is guilty of a misdemeanor if the person exhibits a false light or signal or interferes with a light, signal, or sign controlling or guiding traffic on a highway, railroad track, navigable waters, or in the air.

        Subd. 2. **Felony.** A person who violates subdivision 1 and knows that doing so creates a risk of death or bodily harm or serious property damage is guilty of a felony and may be sentenced to imprisonment for not more than five years or to payment of a fine of not more than $10,000, or both.

HIST: 1989 c 5 s 12

609.855 CRIMES INVOLVING TRANSIT; SHOOTING AT TRANSIT VEHICLE.

        Subdivision 1. **Unlawfully obtaining services; misdemeanor.** A person is guilty of a misdemeanor who intentionally obtains or attempts to obtain service for himself, herself, or another person from a provider of public transit or from a public conveyance, by doing any of the following:

        (1) occupies or rides in any public transit vehicle without paying the applicable fare or otherwise obtaining the consent of the transit provider including:

        (i) the use of a reduced fare when a person is not eligible for the fare; or

        (ii) the use of a fare medium issued solely for the use of a particular individual by another individual;

        (2) presents a falsified, counterfeit, photocopied, or other deceptively manipulated fare medium as fare payment or proof of fare payment;

        (3) sells, provides, copies, reproduces, or creates any version of any fare medium without the consent of the transit provider; or

        (4) puts or attempts to put any of the following into any fare box, pass reader, ticket vending machine, or other fare collection equipment of a transit provider:

        (i) papers, articles, instruments, or items other than fare media or currency; or

        (ii) a fare medium that is not valid for the place or time at, or the manner in, which it is used.

        Where self-service barrier-free fare collection is utilized by a public transit provider, it is a violation of this subdivision to intentionally fail to exhibit proof of fare payment upon the request of an authorized transit representative when entering, riding upon, or leaving a transit vehicle or when present in a designated paid fare zone located in a transit facility.

        Subd. 2. **Unlawful interference with transit operator.** (a) Whoever intentionally commits an act that interferes with or obstructs, or tends to interfere with or obstruct, the operation of a transit vehicle is guilty of unlawful interference with a transit operator and may be sentenced as provided in paragraph (c).

(b) An act that is committed on a transit vehicle that distracts the driver from the safe operation of the vehicle or that endangers passengers is a violation of this subdivision if an authorized transit representative has clearly warned the person once to stop the act.

(c) A person who violates this subdivision may be sentenced as follows:

(1) to imprisonment for not more than three years or to payment of a fine of not more than $5,000, or both, if the violation was accompanied by force or violence or a communication of a threat of force or violence; or

(2) to imprisonment for not more than 90 days or to payment of a fine of not more than $1,000, or both, if the violation was not accompanied by force or violence or a communication of a threat of force or violence.

Subd. 3. **Prohibited activities; misdemeanor.** (a) A person is guilty of a misdemeanor who, while riding in a vehicle providing public transit service:

(1) operates a radio, television, tape player, electronic musical instrument, or other electronic device, other than a watch, which amplifies music, unless the sound emanates only from earphones or headphones and except that vehicle operators may operate electronic equipment for official business;

(2) smokes or carries lighted smoking paraphernalia;

(3) consumes food or beverages, except when authorized by the operator or other official of the transit system;

(4) throws or deposits litter; or

(5) carries or is in control of an animal without the operator's consent.

(b) A person is guilty of a violation of this subdivision only if the person continues to act in violation of this subdivision after being warned once by an authorized transit representative to stop the conduct.

Subd. 4. Repealed, 1994 c 636 art 2 s 69

Subd. 5. **Shooting at or in public transit vehicle or facility.** Whoever recklessly discharges a firearm at or in any portion of a public transit vehicle or facility is guilty of a felony and may be sentenced to imprisonment for not more than three years or to payment of a fine of not more than $6,000, or both. If the transit vehicle or facility is occupied by any person other than the offender, the person may be sentenced to imprisonment for not more than five years or to payment of a fine of not more than $10,000, or both.

Subd. 6. **Restraining orders.** (a) At the sentencing on a violation of this section, the district court shall consider the extent to which the person's conduct has negatively disrupted the delivery of transit services or has affected the utilization of public transit services by others. The district court may, in its discretion, include as part of any sentence for a violation of this section, an order restraining the person from using public transit vehicles and facilities for a fixed period, not to exceed two years or any term of probation, whichever is longer.

(b) The district court administrator shall forward copies of any orders, and any subsequent orders of the court rescinding or modifying the original order, promptly to the operator of the transit system on which the offense took place.

(c) A person who violates an order issued under this subdivision is guilty of a gross misdemeanor.

Subd. 7. **Definitions.** (a) The definitions in this subdivision apply in this section.
* * *

(e) "Fare medium" means a ticket, smart card, pass, coupon, token, transfer, or other medium sold or distributed by a public transit provider, or its authorized agents, for use in gaining entry to or use of the public transit facilities or vehicles of the provider.

(f) "Proof of fare payment" means a fare medium valid for the place or time at, or the manner in, which it is used. If using a reduced-fare medium, proof of fare payment also includes proper identification demonstrating a person's eligibility for the reduced fare. If using a fare medium issued solely for the use of a particular individual, proof of fare payment also includes an identification document bearing a photographic likeness of the individual and demonstrating that the individual is the person to whom the fare medium is issued.

(g) "Authorized transit representative" means the person authorized by the transit provider to operate the transit vehicle, a peace officer, or any other person designated by the transit provider as an authorized transit provider under this section.
HIST: 1983 c 189 s 1; * * * 2004 c 228 art 1 s 72

609.856 USE OF POLICE RADIOS DURING COMMISSION OF CRIME; PENALTIES.
Subdivision 1. **Acts constituting.** Whoever has in possession or uses a radio or device capable of receiving or transmitting a police radio signal, message, or transmission of information used for law enforcement purposes, while in the commission of a felony or violation of section 609.487 or the attempt to commit a felony or violation of section 609.487, is guilty of a felony and may be sentenced to imprisonment for not more than three years or to payment of a fine of not more than $5,000, or both. Notwithstanding section 609.04, a prosecution for or conviction under this section is not a bar to conviction of or punishment for any other crime committed by the defendant as part of the same conduct.

Subd. 2. **Forfeiture.** A radio or device defined in subdivision 1 that is used in the commission of a felony or violation of section 609.487 or attempt to commit a felony or violation of section 609.487 is contraband property and subject to the forfeiture provisions of section 609.531.
HIST: 1987 c 111 s 2; 1993 c 326 art 4 s 35

609.857 DISCHARGING A LASER AT AN AIRCRAFT.
Section 1. **Definitions.** (a) As used in this section, the following terms have the meanings given:

(b) "Aircraft" means any contrivance now known or hereafter invented, used, or designed for navigation of or flight in the air, but excluding parachutes.
* * *

Subd. 2. **Crime.** Whoever knowingly aims and discharges a laser or other device that creates visible light into the cockpit of an aircraft that is in the process of taking off or landing or is in flight is guilty of a gross misdemeanor.

Subd. 3. **Exceptions.** This section does not apply to the following individuals who aim and discharge a laser or other device at an aircraft:

(a) an authorized individual in the conduct of research and development or flight test operations * * *; or

(b) members or elements of the Department of Defense or Department of Homeland Security acting in an official capacity for the purpose of research, development, operations, testing, or training.

Subd. 4. **Defenses.** It is an affirmative defense to a charge under this section if the defendant proves by a preponderance of the evidence that the defendant intended to send an emergency distress signal.
HIST: 2009 c 73 s 1

Chapter 21 -- CRIMES AGAINST COMMERCE

Category 2, Section 5:
2.5.1. Describe the basic organization, purpose, and definitions and principles of the Minnesota Criminal Code.
2.5.5. Given a variety of scenarios, identify indications a particular crime has been committed and identify the elements of that crime.

609.86 COMMERCIAL BRIBERY.

Subdivision 1. **Definition.** "Corruptly" means that the actor intends the action to injure or defraud:

(1) The actor's employer or principal: or

(2) The employer or principal of the person to whom the actor offers, gives or agrees to give the bribe or from whom the actor requests, receives or agrees to receive the bribe.

Subd. 2. **Acts constituting.** Whoever does any of the following, when not consistent with usually accepted business practices, is guilty of commercial bribery and may be sentenced as provided in subdivision 3:

(1) Corruptly offers, gives, or agrees to give, directly or indirectly, any benefit, consideration, compensation, or reward to any employee, agent or fiduciary of a person with the intent to influence the person's performance of duties as an employee, agent, or fiduciary in relation to the person's employer's or principal's business; or

(2) Being an employee, agent or fiduciary of a person, corruptly requests, receives or agrees to receive, directly or indirectly, from another person any benefit, consideration, compensation, or reward with the understanding or agreement to be influenced in the performance of duties as an employee, agent, or fiduciary in relation to the employer's or principal's business.

Subd. 3. **Sentence.** Whoever commits commercial bribery may be sentenced as follows:

(1) to imprisonment for not more than five years or to payment of a fine of not more than $10,000, or both, if the value of the benefit, consideration, compensation or reward is greater than $500;

(2) in all other cases where the value of the benefit, consideration, compensation or reward is $500 or less, to imprisonment for not more than 90 days or to payment of a fine of not more than $1,000; provided, however, in any prosecution of the value of the benefit, consideration, compensation or reward received by the defendant within any six-month period may be aggregated and the defendant charged accordingly in applying the provisions of this subdivision; provided that when two or more offenses are committed by the same person in two or more counties, the accused may be prosecuted in any county in which one of the offenses was committed, or all of the offenses aggregated under this clause.

HIST: 1982 c 442 s 1; * * * 2004 c 228 art 1 s 72

609.87 COMPUTER CRIME; DEFINITIONS.

Subdivision 1. **Applicability.** For purposes of sections 609.87 to 609.891 and 609.8912 to 609.8913, the terms defined in this section have the meanings given them.

Subd. 2. **Access.** "Access" means to instruct, communicate with, store data in, or retrieve data from a computer, computer system, or computer network.

Subd. 2a. **Authorization.** (a) "Authorization" means:

(1) with the permission of the owner of the computer, computer system, computer network, computer software, or other property;

(2) access by employees of the Department of Commerce * * *;

(3) access by registrants in the voluntary placing in service program and registered liquefied petroleum gas (LPG) meter inspectors * * *; or

(4) access by other people who have the express permission of the device owner or operator or the device owner's or operator's designated representative but only at times as approved by the device owner or operator and only for purposes approved by the device owner or operator.

(b) Authorization may be limited by the owner by:

(1) giving the user actual notice orally or in writing;

(2) posting a written notice in a prominent location adjacent to the computer being used; or

(3) using a notice displayed on or announced by the computer being used.

Subd. 3. **Computer.** "Computer" means an electronic device which performs logical, arithmetic or memory functions by the manipulations of signals, including but not limited to electronic or magnetic impulses.

Subd. 4. **Computer system.** "Computer system" means related, connected or unconnected, computers and peripheral equipment.

Subd. 5. **Computer network.** "Computer network" means the interconnection of a communication system with a computer through a remote terminal, or with two or more interconnected computers or computer systems, and includes private and public telecommunications networks.

Subd. 6. **Property.** "Property" includes, but is not limited to, electronically processed or produced data and information contained in a computer or computer software in either machine or human readable form.

Subd. 7. **Services.** "Services" includes but is not limited to, computer time, data processing, and storage functions.

Subd. 8. **Computer program.** "Computer program" means an instruction or statement or a series of instructions or statements, in a form acceptable to a computer, which directs the functioning of a computer system in a manner designed to provide appropriate products from the computer.

Subd. 9. **Computer software.** "Computer software" means a computer program or procedures, or associated documentation concerned with the operation of a computer.

Subd. 10. **Loss.** "Loss" means the greatest of the following:

(a) the retail market value of the property or services involved;

(b) the reasonable repair or replacement cost, whichever is less; or

(c) the reasonable value of the damage created by the unavailability or lack of utility of the property or services involved until repair or replacement can be effected.

Subd. 11. **Computer security system.** "Computer security system" means a software program or computer device that is intended to protect the confidentiality and secrecy of data and information stored in or accessible through the computer system.

Subd. 12. **Destructive computer program.** "Destructive computer program" means a computer program that performs a destructive function or produces a destructive product. A program performs a destructive function if it degrades performance of the affected computer, associated peripherals or a computer program; disables the computer, associated peripherals or a computer program; or destroys or alters computer programs or data. A program produces a destructive product if it produces unauthorized data, including data that make computer memory space unavailable, results in the unauthorized alteration of data or computer programs; or produces a destructive computer program, including a self-replicating computer program.

Subd. 13. **Encryption.** "Encryption" means any protective or disruptive measure, including but not limited to, cryptography, enciphering, or encoding that:

(1) causes or makes any data, information, image, program, signal, or sound unintelligible or unusable; or

(2) prevents, impedes, delays, or disrupts access to any data, information, image, program, signal, or sound.

Subd. 14. **Personal data.** "Personal data" means any computer property or computer program which contains records of the employment, salary, credit, or other financial or personal information relating to another person.

Subd. 15. **Electronic terminal.** "Electronic terminal" means an electronic device, other than a telephone operated by a consumer, through which an individual or company may initiate an electronic fund transfer. The term includes, but is not limited to, point-of-sale terminals, automated teller machines, cash dispensing machines, and gas pump dispensers.

* * *

HIST: 1982 c 534 s 1; * * * 2018 c 123 s 1-3

609.88 COMPUTER DAMAGE.

Subdivision 1. **Acts.** Whoever does any of the following is guilty of computer damage and may be sentenced as provided in subdivision 2:

(a) Intentionally and without authorization damages or destroys any computer, computer system, computer network, computer software, or any other property specifically defined in section 609.87, subdivision 6;

(b) Intentionally and without authorization and with intent to injure or defraud alters any computer, computer system, computer network, computer software, or any other property specifically defined in section 609.87, subdivision 6; or

(c) Distributes a destructive computer program, without authorization and with intent to damage or destroy any computer, computer system, computer network, computer software, or any other property specifically defined in section 609.87, subdivision 6.

Subd. 2. **Penalty.** Whoever commits computer damage may be sentenced as follows:

(a) To imprisonment for not more than ten years or to payment of a fine of not more than $50,000, or both, if the damage, destruction or alteration results in a loss in excess of $2,500, to the owner, or the owner's agent, or lessee;

(b) To imprisonment for not more than five years or to payment of a fine of not more than $10,000, or both, if the damage, destruction or alteration results in a loss of more than $500, but not more than $2,500; to the owner, or the owner's agent or lessee; or

(c) In all other cases to imprisonment for not more than 90 days or to payment of a fine of not more than $1,000, or both.

HIST: 1982 c 534 s 2; * * * 2004 c 228 art 1 s 72

609.89 COMPUTER THEFT.

Subdivision 1. **Acts.** Whoever does any of the following is guilty of computer theft and may be sentenced as provided in subdivision 2:

(a) Intentionally and without authorization or claim of right accesses or causes to be accessed any computer, computer system, computer network or any part thereof for the purpose of obtaining services or property; or

(b) Intentionally and without claim of right, and with intent to permanently deprive the owner of use or possession, takes, transfers, conceals or retains possession of any computer, computer system, or any computer software or data contained in a computer, computer system, or computer network.

Subd. 2. **Penalty.** Anyone who commits computer theft may be sentenced as follows:

(a) To imprisonment for not more than ten years or to payment of a fine of not more than $50,000, or both, if the loss to the owner, or the owner's agent, or lessee is in excess of $2,500; or

(b) To imprisonment for not more than five years or to payment of a fine of not more than $10,000, or both, if the loss to the owner, or the owner's agent, or lessee is more than $500 but not more than $2,500; or

(c) In all other cases to imprisonment for not more than 90 days or to payment of a fine of not more than $1,000, or both.

HIST: 1982 c 534 s 3; * * * 2004 c 228 art 1 s 72

609.891 UNAUTHORIZED COMPUTER ACCESS.

Subdivision 1. **Crime.** A person is guilty of unauthorized computer access if the person intentionally and without authorization attempts to or does penetrate a computer security system.

Subd. 2. **Felony.** (a) A person who violates subdivision 1 in a manner that creates a grave risk of causing the death of a person is guilty of a felony and may be sentenced to imprisonment for not more than ten years or to payment of a fine of not more than $20,000, or both.

(b) A person who is convicted of a second or subsequent gross misdemeanor violation of subdivision 1 is guilty of a felony and may be sentenced under paragraph (a).

(c) A person who violates subdivision 1 by accessing, or attempting to access, an electronic terminal through opening any panel or access door without authorization and placing or attaching, or attempting to place or attach, an electronic device to capture, store, or communicate access device information is guilty of a felony.

Subd. 3. **Gross misdemeanor.** (a) A person who violates subdivision 1 in a manner that creates a risk to public health and safety is guilty of a gross misdemeanor and may be sentenced to imprisonment for a term of not more than one year or to payment of a fine of not more than $3,000, or both.

(b) A person who violates subdivision 1 in a manner that compromises the security of data that are protected under section 609.52, subdivision 2, clause (8), or are not public data as defined in section 13.02, subdivision 8a, is guilty of a gross misdemeanor and may be sentenced under paragraph (a).

(c) A person who violates subdivision 1 and gains access to personal data is guilty of a gross misdemeanor and may be sentenced under paragraph (a).

(d) A person who is convicted of a second or subsequent misdemeanor violation of subdivision 1 within five years is guilty of a gross misdemeanor and may be sentenced under paragraph (a).

(e) A person who violates subdivision 1 by accessing, or attempting to access, an electronic terminal through opening, or attempting to open, any panel or access door without authorization is guilty of a gross misdemeanor and may be sentenced under paragraph (a).

Subd. 4. **Misdemeanor.** A person who violates subdivision 1 is guilty of a misdemeanor and may be sentenced to imprisonment for a term of not more than 90 days or to payment of a fine of not more than $1,000, or both.

HIST: 1989 c 95 s 4; * * * 2018 c 123 art 1 s 5,6

609.8912 CRIMINAL USE OF ENCRYPTION.

Subdivision 1. **Crime.** Whoever intentionally uses or attempts to use encryption to do any of the following is guilty of criminal use of encryption and may be sentenced as provided in subdivision 2.

(1) to commit, further, or facilitate conduct constituting a crime;

(2) to conceal the commission of any crime;

(3) to conceal or protect the identity of a person who has committed any crime; or

(4) to prevent, impede, delay, or disrupt the normal operation or use of another's computer, computer program, or computer system.

Subd. 2. **Penalties.** (a) A person who violates subdivision 1 may be sentenced to imprisonment for not more than five years or to payment of a fine of not more than $10,000, or both, if:

(1) the crime referenced in subdivision 1, clause (1), (2), or (3), is a felony; or

(2) the person has two or more prior convictions for an offense under this section, section 609.88, 609.89, 609.891, or 609.8913, or similar laws of other states, the United States, the District of Columbia, tribal lands, and United States territories.

(b) A person who violates subdivision 1, under circumstances not described in paragraph (a), is guilty of a gross misdemeanor and may be sentenced to imprisonment for not more than one year or to payment of a fine of not more than $3,000, or both.
HIST: 2006 c 260 art 1 s 36

609.8913 FACILITATING ACCESS TO A COMPUTER SECURITY SYSTEM.

A person is guilty of a gross misdemeanor if the person knows or has reason to know that by facilitating access to a computer security system the person is aiding another who intends to commit a crime and in fact commits a crime. For purposes of this section, "facilitating access" includes the intentional disclosure of a computer password, identifying code, personal information number, or other confidential information about a computer security system which provides a person with the means or opportunity for the commission of a crime.
HIST: 2006 c 260 art 1 s 37

609.892 DEFINITIONS.

Subdivision 1. **Applicability.** The definitions in this section apply to sections 237.73, 609.892, and 609.893.

Subd. 2. **Access device.** "Access device" means a card, plate, code, account number, or other means of account access that can be used, alone or in conjunction with another access device, to obtain telecommunications service.

Subd. 3. **Credit card number.** "Credit card number" means the card number appearing on a credit card that is an identification card or plate issued to a person by a supplier of telecommunications service that permits the person to whom the card has been issued to obtain telecommunications service on credit. The term includes the number or description of the card or plate even if the card or plate itself is not produced when obtaining telecommunications service.

Subd. 4. **Telecommunications device.** "Telecommunications device" means an instrument, apparatus, equipment mechanism, operating procedure, or code designed or adapted for a particular use and that is intended or can be used in violation of section 609.893. The term includes but is not limited to computer hardware, software, programs, electronic mail system, voice mail system, identification validation system, private branch exchange, or any other means of facilitating telecommunications service.

Subd. 5. **Telecommunications provider.** "Telecommunications provider" means a person, firm, association, or a corporation, private or municipal, owning, operating, or managing facilities used to provide telecommunications service.

Subd. 6. **Telecommunications service.** "Telecommunications service" means a service that, in exchange for a pecuniary consideration, provides or offers to provide transmission of messages, signals, facsimiles, or other communication between persons who are physically separated from each other by telephone, telegraph, cable, wire, fiber optic cable, or the projection of energy without physical connection. This term applies when the telecommunications service originates or ends or both originates and ends in this state.

Subd. 7. **Telephone company.** "Telephone company" means a telecommunications provider that provides local exchange telecommunications service.
HIST: 1990 c 494 s 5; 1991 c 199 art 1 s 86

609.893 TELECOMMUNICATIONS AND INFORMATION SERVICES FRAUD; CRIME DEFINED.

Subdivision 1. **Obtaining services by fraud.** A person commits telecommunications and information services fraud and may be sentenced as provided in subdivision 3 if the person, with intent to evade a lawful charge, obtains telecommunications service for the person's own use by any fraudulent means.

Subd. 2. **Facilitation of telecommunications fraud.** A person commits a felony and may be sentenced as provided in subdivision 4 who:

(1) makes available to another, or offers or advertises to make available, a tele-communications device or information in order to facilitate violation of subdivision 1 by another; or

(2) makes, assembles, or possesses a telecommunications device that is designed or adapted to violate subdivision 1 or to conceal from a provider of telecommunications service or from a lawful authority, the existence or place of origin or destination of telecommunications service.

Subd. 3. **Fraud.** (a) Whoever commits telecommunications and information services fraud in violation of subdivision 1 may be sentenced as follows:

(1) to imprisonment for not more than ten years or to payment of a fine of not more than $20,000, or both, if the value of the services is in excess of $2,500;

(2) to imprisonment for not more than five years or to payment of a fine of not more than $10,000, or both, if the value of the services is more than $500 but not more than $2,500; or

(3) in all other cases, to imprisonment for not more than 90 days or to payment of a fine of not more than $1,000, or both.

(b) Amounts involved in a violation of paragraph (a) under one scheme or course of conduct, whether from the same credit card number or several credit card numbers, may be aggregated in determining the classification of the offense.

Subd. 4. **Facilitation of fraud.** Whoever violates subdivision 2 is guilty of a felony and may be sentenced to imprisonment for not more than five years or to payment of a fine of not more than $10,000, or both.

HIST: 1990 c 494 s 6; 2004 c 228 art 1 s 72

609.895 COUNTERFEITED INTELLECTUAL PROPERTY; PENALTIES.

Subdivision 1. **Definitions.** (a) As used in this section, the following terms have the meanings given them.

(b) "Counterfeit mark" means:

(1) any unauthorized reproduction or copy of intellectual property; or

(2) intellectual property affixed to any item without the authority of the owner of the intellectual property.

(c) "Counterfeited item or service" means an item or service bearing or identified by a counterfeit mark.

(d) "Intellectual property" means any trademark, service mark, or trade name.

(e) "Retail value" means:

(1) the usual selling price of the article or service bearing or identified by the counterfeit mark; or

(2) the usual selling price of a finished product on or in which components bearing or identified by a counterfeit mark are used.

(f) "Service mark" means a mark used by a person to identify services and to distinguish them from the services of others.

(g) "Trademark" means a mark used by a person to identify goods and to distinguish them from the goods of others.

(h) "Trade name" means a word, name, symbol, device, or any combination of the foregoing in any form or arrangement, used by a person to identify the person's business, vocation, or occupation and to distinguish it from the business, vocation, or occupation of others.

Subd. 2. **Crime.** A person who intentionally manufactures, produces, distributes, offers for sale, sells, or possesses with intent to sell or distribute any counterfeited item or service, knowing or having reason to know that the item or service is counterfeit, is guilty of counterfeiting intellectual property and may be punished as provided in subdivision 3.

Subd. 3. **Penalties.** (a) A person who is convicted of violating subdivision 2 may be sentenced to imprisonment for not more than five years or to payment of a fine of not more than $100,000, or both, if:

(1) the violation involves the manufacture or production of a counterfeited item or items;

(2) the violation involves the distribution, offer for sale, sale, or possession with intent to sell or distribute 1,000 or more counterfeited items;

(3) the violation involves the distribution, offer for sale, sale, or possession with intent to sell or distribute counterfeited items or services having a retail value of more than $10,000; or

(4) the defendant has two or more prior convictions for violating this section or a law of another state or the United States that provides criminal penalties for counterfeiting intellectual property.

(b) Except as otherwise provided in paragraph (a), a person who is convicted of violating subdivision 2 may be sentenced to imprisonment for not more than three years or to payment of a fine of not more than $50,000, or both, if:

(1) the violation involves more than 100 but fewer than 1,000 counterfeited items;

(2) the violation involves counterfeited items or services having a retail value of more than $1,000 but not more than $10,000; or

(3) the defendant has one prior conviction for violating this section or a law of another state or the United States that provides criminal penalties for counterfeiting intellectual property.

(c) A person may be sentenced to imprisonment for not more than one year or to payment of a fine of not more than $3,000, or both, if the person is convicted of violating subdivision 2, under circumstances not described in paragraph (a) or (b).

(d) If the defendant distributes, sells, offers for sale, or possesses with intent to sell or distribute more than one item or service bearing or identified by more than one counterfeit mark, the quantity or retail value of these items and services may be aggregated for purposes of determining penalties under this subdivision.

Subd. 4. **Alternative fine.** In lieu of the fine authorized by subdivision 3, a person convicted of violating this section who received economic gain from the act or caused economic loss during the act may be sentenced to pay a fine calculated in the manner provided in section 609.904, subdivision 2.

Subd. 5. **Forfeiture.** Property used to commit or facilitate the commission of a violation of this section, and all money and property representing proceeds of a violation of this section, shall be forfeited in accordance with sections 609.531 to 609.5316. Notwithstanding any provision of section 609.5315 to the contrary, forfeited items bearing or identified by a counterfeit mark must be destroyed unless the intellectual property owner consents to another disposition.

Subd. 6. **Prima facie evidence.** A Minnesota or federal certificate of registration of an intellectual property is prima facie evidence of the registrant's ownership and exclusive right to use the intellectual property in connection with the goods or services described in the certificate.
HIST: 1999 c 142 s 2

609.901 CONSTRUCTION OF RACKETEERING PROVISIONS.

Sections 609.902 to 609.912 shall be liberally construed to achieve their remedial purposes of curtailing racketeering activity and controlled substance crime and lessening their economic and political power in Minnesota.
HIST: 1989 c 286 s 5

609.902 DEFINITIONS.

Subdivision 1. **Definitions.** As used in sections 609.901 to 609.912, the following terms have the meanings given them.

Subd. 2. **Criminal proceeding.** "Criminal proceeding" means a criminal proceeding begun under section 609.903.

Subd. 3. **Enterprise.** "Enterprise" means a sole proprietorship, partnership, corporation, trust, or other legal entity, or a union, governmental entity, association, or group of persons, associated in fact although not a legal entity, and includes illicit as well as legitimate enterprises.

Subd. 4. **Criminal act.** "Criminal act" means conduct constituting, or a conspiracy or attempt to commit, a felony violation of chapter 152, or a felony violation of section 297D.09; 299F.79; 299F.80; 299F.82; 609.185; 609.19; 609.195; 609.20; 609.205; 609.221; 609.222;

Chapter 21

609.223: 609.2231; 609.228; 609.235; 609.245; 609.25; 609.27; 609.322; 609.323; 609.342; 609.343; 609.344; 609.345; 609.42; 609.48; 609.485; 609.495; 609.496; 609.497; 609.498; 609.52, subdivision 2, if the offense is punishable under subdivision 3, clause (1), if the property is a firearm, clause (3)(b) or clause 3(d)(v); section 609.52, subdivision 2, paragraph (a), clause (1) or (4); 609.527, if the crime is punishable under subdivision 3, clause (4); 609.528, if the crime is punishable under subdivision 3, clause (4); 609.53; 609.561; 609.562; 609.582, subdivision 1 or 2; 609.668, subdivision 6, paragraph (a); 609.67; 609.687; 609.713; 609.86; 609.894, subdivision 3 or 4; 609.895; 624.713; 624.74; or 626A.02, subdivision 1, if the offense is punishable under section 626A.02, subdivision 4, paragraph (a). "Criminal act" also includes conduct constituting, or a conspiracy or attempt to commit, a felony violation of section 609.52, subdivision 2, clause (3), (4), (15), or (16) if the violation involves an insurance company as defined in section 60A.02, subdivision 4, a nonprofit health service plan corporation regulated under chapter 62C, a health maintenance organization regulated under chapter 62D, or a fraternal benefit society regulated under chapter 64B.

Subd. 5. **Participation in a pattern of criminal activity.** A person "participates in a pattern of criminal activity" when the person is a principal with respect to conduct constituting at least three of the criminal acts included in the pattern and two of the acts constitute felonies other than conspiracy.

Subd. 6. **Pattern of criminal activity.** "Pattern of criminal activity" means conduct constituting three or more criminal acts that:

(1) were committed within ten years of the commencement of the criminal proceeding;

(2) are neither isolated incidents, nor so closely related and connected in point of time or circumstance of commission as to constitute a single criminal offense; and

(3) were either: (i) related to one another through a common scheme or plan or a shared criminal purpose or (ii) committed, solicited, requested, importuned, or intentionally aided by persons acting with the mental culpability required for the commission of the criminal acts and associated with or in an enterprise involved in those activities.

Subd. 7. **Personal property.** "Personal property" includes personal property, an interest in personal property, or a right, including a bank account, debt, corporate stock, patent, or copyright. Personal property and a beneficial interest in personal property are deemed to be located where the trustee is, the personal property is, or the instrument evidencing the right is.

Subd. 8. **Principal.** "Principal" means a person who personally engages in conduct constituting a violation or who is criminally liable under section 609.05 for the conduct of another constituting a violation.

Subd. 9. **Prosecuting authority.** "Prosecuting authority" means the office of a county attorney or office of the attorney general.

Subd. 10. **Real property.** "Real property" means any real property or an interest in real property, including a lease of, or mortgage on, real property. A beneficial interest in real property is deemed to be located where the real property is located.

HIST: 1989 c 286 s 6; * * * 2011 c 76 art 1 s 68; 2011 c 81 s 1; 2020 c 83 art 1 s 96

609.903 RACKETEERING.

Subdivision 1. **Crime.** A person is guilty of racketeering if the person:

(1) is employed by or associated with an enterprise and intentionally conducts or participates in the affairs of the enterprise by participating in a pattern of criminal activity;

(2) acquires or maintains an interest in or control of an enterprise, or an interest in real property, by participating in a pattern of criminal activity; or

(3) participates in a pattern of criminal activity and knowingly invests any proceeds derived from that conduct, or any proceeds derived from the investment or use of those proceeds, in an enterprise or in real property.

Subd. 2. **Permitted activities.** For purposes of this section, it is not unlawful to:

(1) purchase securities on the open market with intent to make an investment, and without the intent of controlling or participating in the control of the issuer, or of assisting another to do so, if the securities of the issuer held by the purchaser, the members of the

purchaser's immediate family, and the purchaser's accomplices in a pattern of criminal activity do not amount in the aggregate to five percent of the outstanding securities of any one class and do not confer, either in the law or in fact, the power to elect one or more directors of the issuer;

(2) make a deposit in an account maintained in a savings association, or a deposit in any other financial institution, that creates an ownership interest in that association or institution; or

(3) purchase nonvoting shares in a limited partnership, with intent to make an investment, and without the intent of controlling or participating in the control of the partnership.
HIST: 1989 c 286 s 7; 1995 c 202 art 1 s 25

609.904 CRIMINAL PENALTIES.

Subdivision 1. **Penalty.** A person convicted of violating section 609.903 may be sentenced to imprisonment for not more than 20 years or to payment of a fine of not more than $1,000,000, or both.

Subd. 2. **Fine.** In lieu of the fine authorized by subdivision 1, a person convicted of violating section 609.903, who received economic gain from the act or caused economic loss or personal injury during the act, may be sentenced to pay a fine calculated under this subdivision. The maximum fine is three times the gross value gained or three times the gross loss caused, whichever is greater, plus court costs and the costs of investigation and prosecution reasonably incurred, less the value of any property forfeited under section 609.905.
* * *

Subd. 5. **Restitution.** In a settlement discussion or before the imposition of a sentence under this section, the prosecuting authority shall vigorously advocate full and complete restitution to an aggrieved person. * * *
HIST: 1989 c 286 s 8

609.905 CRIMINAL FORFEITURE.

Subdivision 1. **Forfeiture.** When a person is convicted of violating section 609.903, the court may order the person to forfeit to the prosecuting authority any real or personal property subject to forfeiture under this section. Property subject to forfeiture is real and personal property that was used in the course of, intended for use in the course of, derived from, or realized through conduct in violation of section 609.903. A court may not order the forfeiture of property that has been used to pay reasonable attorney fees in connection with a criminal proceeding under section 609.903. The term includes property constituting an interest in or means of control or influence over the enterprise involved in the violation of section 609.902 and any property constituting proceeds derived from the violation of section 609.902, including:

(1) a position, office, appointment, tenure, commission, or employment contract that was acquired or maintained in violation of section 609.903 or through which the person conducted or participated in the conduct of the affairs of an enterprise in violation of section 609.903 or that afforded the person a source of influence or control over the affairs of an enterprise that the person exercised in violation of section 609.903;

(2) any compensation, right, or benefit derived from a position, office, appointment, tenure, commission, or employment contract described in this section that accrued to the person during the period of conduct in violation of section 609.903;

(3) any interest in, security of, claim against, or property or contractual right affording the person a source of influence or control over the affairs of an enterprise that the person exercised in violation of section 609.903; and

(4) any amount payable or paid under any contract for goods or services that was awarded or performed in violation of section 609.903.

Subd. 2. **Other property of defendant.** The district court may order criminal forfeiture of any other property of the defendant up to the value of the property that is unreachable if any property subject to criminal forfeiture under subdivision 1:

(1) cannot be located;

(2) has been sold to a bona fide purchaser for value;

(3) has been placed beyond the jurisdiction of the court;

(4) has been substantially diminished in value by the conduct of the defendant;

(5) has been commingled with other property that cannot be divided without difficulty or undue injury to innocent persons; or

(6) is otherwise unreachable without undue injury to an innocent person.
* * *
HIST: 1989 c 286 s 9; 2010 c 391 s 20

609.907 PRESERVATION OF PROPERTY SUBJECT TO FORFEITURE.

Subdivision 1. **Temporary restraining order.** (a) When an indictment or complaint is filed under section 609.903, the district court may take any of the following actions if the prosecuting authority shows by a preponderance of the evidence that the action is necessary to preserve the reachability of property subject to criminal forfeiture:

(1) enter a restraining order or injunction;

(2) require the execution of a satisfactory performance bond; or

(3) take any other reasonable action, including the appointment of a receiver.

(b) Before granting the remedies provided by this subdivision, the court shall hold a hearing, after notice to all affected persons, giving them a reasonable opportunity to respond. At the hearing, the rules of evidence do not apply.

Subd. 2. **Preindictment order.** (a) If no indictment or complaint has been filed, the district court may take actions provided in subdivision 1 if the prosecuting authority makes the showing required by subdivision 1 and also shows that:

(1) there is probable cause to believe that the property with respect to which the order is sought would, in the event of a conviction, be subject to criminal forfeiture under section 609.904; and

(2) the requested order would not result in substantial and irreparable harm or injury to the party against whom the order is to be entered, or to other affected persons, that outweighs the need to preserve the reachability of the property.
* * *
Subd. 3. **Restraining order without notice.** (a) On application by the prosecuting authority, the district court may grant, without notice to any party, a temporary restraining order to preserve the reachability of property subject to criminal forfeiture under section 609.905[.]
HIST: 1989 c 286 s 10

609.908 DISPOSITION OF FORFEITURE PROCEEDS.

Subdivision 1. **Disposition alternatives.** After making due provisions for the rights of innocent persons, the prosecuting authority shall, as soon as feasible, dispose of all property ordered forfeited under section 609.905[.]

Subd. 2. **No reversion to defendant.** An interest in personal or real property not exercisable by or transferable for value by the prosecuting authority expires and does not revert to the defendant. Forfeited property may not be purchased by the defendant, relative of the defendant, or any person acting in concert with the defendant or on the defendant's behalf. * * *
HIST: 1989 c 286 s 11

609.909 ADDITIONAL RELIEF AVAILABLE.

With respect to property ordered forfeited, fine imposed, or civil penalty imposed in a criminal proceeding under section 609.903 or civil proceeding under section 609.911, the district court may * * * take any other action to protect the rights of innocent persons that is in the interest of justice and is consistent with the purposes of sections 609.901 to 609.912.
HIST: 1989 c 286 s 12

609.910 RELATION TO OTHER SANCTIONS.

Subdivision 1. **Remedy not exclusive.** Except as provided in this section, a criminal penalty, forfeiture, or fine imposed under section 609.903, 609.904, 609.905, or 609.911 does

not preclude the application of any other criminal penalty or civil remedy for the separate criminal acts. * * *
HIST: 1989 c 286 s 13

609.911 CIVIL REMEDIES.

Subdivision 1. **Relief available.** The prosecuting authority may institute civil proceedings in district court against a person seeking relief from conduct constituting a violation of section 609.903 or to prevent or restrain future violations. * * *

Subd. 2. **Injunctive relief.** In a proceeding under this section, the court may grant injunctive relief.

Subd. 3. **Civil penalty.** The prosecuting authority may institute proceedings against an enterprise or an individual to recover a civil penalty. The penalty may be imposed in the discretion of the district court for conduct constituting a violation of section 609.903. The civil penalty may not exceed $1,000,000 less a fine imposed under section 609.903. * * *
HIST: 1989 c 286 s 14

Chapter 22 -- SELECTED STATUTES FOR PEACE OFFICERS

Editors' Note: During the 2003 legislative session, significant and well-publicized changes to the issuance of permits to carry certain firearms ("Conceal & Carry" legislation) were passed. In early 2005, the Minnesota Court of Appeals declared this legislation unconstitutional. Thereafter, during the 2005 legislative session substantially all aspects of the 2003 "Conceal & Carry" legislation were reenacted again. Thus, the 2003 version of §624.712, Subd. 5 previously reprinted in Chapter 22A (removed in the 2006 edition) has been relocated immediately below in substitution of the pre-2003 version of this subdivision. In addition, §624.714 previously reprinted in Chapter 22A has been relocated below (with new changes and editorial modification) in Performance Objective # 4 in substitution of the pre-2003 version of this section. §§624.7142 and 624.7143 (concerning alcohol and controlled substance testing of persons carrying a firearm) previously reprinted in Chapter 22A immediately follow §624.714.

Category 2, Section 5:
2.5.1. Describe the basic organization, purpose, and definitions and principles of the Minnesota Criminal Code.
2.5.5. Given a variety of scenarios, identify indications a particular crime has been committed and identify the elements of that crime.
2.5.7. Explain special Minnesota peace officer duties associated with specific statutes . . .

518.131 TEMPORARY ORDERS AND RESTRAINING ORDERS.

Subdivision 1. Permissible orders. In a proceeding brought for custody, dissolution, or legal separation, or for disposition of property, maintenance, or child support following the dissolution of a marriage, either party may, by motion, request from the court and the court may grant a temporary order pending the final disposition of the proceeding to or for:

(a) Temporary custody and parenting time regarding the minor children of the parties;

(b) Temporary maintenance of either spouse;

(c) Temporary child support for the children of the parties;

(d) Temporary costs and reasonable attorney fees;

(e) Award the temporary use and possession, exclusive or otherwise, of the family home, furniture, household goods, automobiles, and other property of the parties;

(f) Restrain one or both parties from transferring, encumbering, concealing, or disposing of property except in the usual course of business or for the necessities of life, and to account to the court for all such transfers, encumbrances, dispositions, and expenditures made after the order is served or communicated to the party restrained in open court;

(g) Restrain one or both parties from harassing, vilifying, mistreating, molesting, disturbing the peace, or restraining the liberty of the other party or the children of the parties;

(h) Restrain one or both parties from removing any minor child of the parties from the jurisdiction of the court;

(i) Exclude a party from the family home of the parties or from the home of the other party; and

(j) Require one or both of the parties to perform or to not perform such additional acts as will facilitate the just and speedy disposition of the proceeding, or will protect the parties or their children from physical or emotional harm.

Subd. 2. Impermissible orders. No temporary order shall:

(a) Deny parenting time to a parent unless the court finds that the parenting time is likely to cause physical or emotional harm to the child;

(b) Exclude a party from the family home of the parties unless the court finds that physical or emotional harm to one of the parties or to the children of the parties is likely to result, or that the exclusion is reasonable in the circumstances; or

(c) Vacate or modify an order granted under section 518B.01, subdivision 6, paragraph (a), clause (1), restraining an abusing party from committing acts of domestic abuse, except that the court may hear a motion for modification of an order for protection concurrently with a proceeding for dissolution of marriage upon notice of motion and motion. The notice required by court rule shall not be waived. If the proceedings are consolidated and the motion to modify is granted, a separate order for modification of an order for protection shall be issued.

Subd. 3. Ex parte restraining order; limitations. A party may request and the court may make an ex parte restraining order which may include any matter that may be included in a temporary order except:

(a) A restraining order may not exclude either party from the family home of the parties except upon a finding by the court of immediate danger of physical harm to the other party or the children of either party; and

(b) A restraining order may not deny parenting time to either party or grant custody of the minor children to either party except upon a finding by the court of immediate danger of physical harm to the minor children of the parties.

Subd. 4. Hearing on restraining order; duration. Restraining orders shall be personally served upon the party to be restrained and shall be accompanied with a notice of the time and place of hearing for disposition of the matters contained in the restraining order at a hearing for a temporary order. When a restraining order has been issued, a hearing on the temporary order shall be held at the earliest practicable date. The restrained party may upon written notice to the other party advance the hearing date to a time earlier than that noticed by the other party. The restraining order shall continue in full force and effect only until the hearing time noticed, unless the court, for good cause and upon notice extends the time for hearing.

Subd. 5. Duration of temporary order. A temporary order shall continue in full force and effect until the earlier of its amendment or vacation, dismissal of the main action or entry of a final decree of dissolution or legal separation.

Subd. 6. Effect of dismissal of main action. If a proceeding for dissolution or legal separation is dismissed, a temporary custody order is vacated unless one of the parties or the child's custodian moves that the proceeding continue as a custody proceeding and the court finds, after a hearing, that the circumstances of the parties and the best interests of the child require that a custody order be issued.

Subd. 7. Guiding factors. The court shall be guided by the factors set forth in sections 518.551 (concerning child support), 518.552 (concerning maintenance), 518.17 to 518.175 (concerning custody and parenting time), and 518.14 (concerning costs and attorney fees) in making temporary orders and restraining orders.

Subd. 8. Basis for order. Temporary orders shall be made solely on the basis of affidavits and argument of counsel except upon demand by either party in a motion or responsive motion made within the time limit for making and filing a responsive motion that the matter be heard on oral testimony before the court, or if the court in its discretion orders the taking of oral testimony.

Subd. 9. Prejudicial effect; revocation; modification. A temporary order or restraining order:

(a) Shall not prejudice the rights of the parties or the child which are to be adjudicated at subsequent hearings in the proceeding; and

(b) May be revoked or modified by the court before the final disposition of the proceeding upon the same grounds and subject to the same requirements as the initial granting of the order.

Subd. 10. Misdemeanor. In addition to being punishable by contempt, a violation of a provision of a temporary order or restraining order granting the relief authorized in subdivision 1, clauses (g), (h) or (i) is a misdemeanor.

Subd. 11. **Temporary support and maintenance.** Temporary support and maintenance may be ordered during the time a parenting plan is being developed under section 518.1705.
HIST: 1979 c 259 s 11; * * * 2001 c 51 s 1

624.712 DEFINITIONS.

Subdivision 1. **Scope.** As used in sections 624.711 to 624.717, the terms defined in this section shall have the meanings given them.

Subd. 2. **Pistol.** "Pistol" includes a weapon designed to be fired by the use of a single hand and with an overall length less than 26 inches, or having a barrel or barrels of a length less than 18 inches in the case of a shotgun or having a barrel of a length less than 16 inches in the case of a rifle (a) from which may be fired or ejected one or more solid projectiles by means of a cartridge or shell or by the action of an explosive or the igniting of flammable or explosive substances; or (b) for which the propelling force is a spring, elastic band, carbon dioxide, air or other gas, or vapor.

"Pistol" does not include a device firing or ejecting a shot measuring .18 of an inch, or less, in diameter and commonly known as a "BB gun," a scuba gun, a stud gun or nail gun used in the construction industry or children's pop guns or toys.

Subd. 3. **Antique firearm.** "Antique firearm" means any firearm, including any pistol, with a matchlock, flintlock, percussion cap, or similar type of ignition system, manufactured before 1899 and any replica of any firearm described herein if such replica is not designed or redesigned, made or remade, or intended to fire conventional rimfire or conventional centerfire ammunition, or uses conventional rimfire or conventional centerfire ammunition which is not readily available in the ordinary channels of commercial trade.

Subd. 4. **Saturday night special pistol.** "Saturday night special pistol" means a pistol other than an antique firearm or a pistol for which the propelling force is carbon dioxide, air or other vapor, or children's pop guns or toys, having a frame, barrel, cylinder, slide or breechblock:

(a) of any material having a melting point (liquidus) of less than 1,000 degrees Fahrenheit, or

(b) of any material having an ultimate tensile strength of less than 55,000 pounds per square inch, or

(c) of any powdered metal having a density of less than 7.5 grams per cubic centimeter.

Subd. 5. **Crime of violence.** "Crime of violence" means: felony convictions of the following offenses: sections 609.185 (murder in the first degree); 609.19 (murder in the second degree); 609.195 (murder in the third degree); 609.20 (manslaughter in the first degree); 609.205 (manslaughter in the second degree); 609.215 (aiding suicide and aiding attempted suicide); 609.221 (assault in the first degree); 609.222 (assault in the second degree); 609.223 (assault in the third degree); 609.2231 (assault in the fourth degree); 609.224 (assault in the fifth degree); 609.2242 (domestic assault); 609.2247 (domestic assault by strangulation); 609.229 (crimes committed for the benefit of a gang); 609.235 (use of drugs to injure or facilitate crime); 609.24 (simple robbery); 609.245 (aggravated robbery); 609.25 (kidnapping); 609.255 (false imprisonment); 609.322 (solicitation, inducement, and promotion of prostitution; sex trafficking); 609.342 (criminal sexual conduct in the first degree); 609.343 (criminal sexual conduct in the second degree); 609.344 (criminal sexual conduct in the third degree); 609.345 (criminal sexual conduct in the fourth degree); 609.377 (malicious punishment of a child); 609.378 (neglect or endangerment of a child); 609.486 (commission of crime while wearing or possessing a bullet-resistant vest); 609.52 (involving theft of a firearm and theft involving the theft of a controlled substance, an explosive, or an incendiary device); 609.561 (arson in the first degree); 609.562 (arson in the second degree); 609.582, subdivision 1 or 2 (burglary in the first and second degrees); 609.66, subdivision 1e (drive-by shooting); 609.67 (unlawfully owning, possessing, operating a machine gun or short-barreled shotgun); 609.71 (riot); 609.713 (terroristic threats); 609.749 (harassment); 609.855, subdivision 5 (shooting at a public transit vehicle or facility); and chapter 152 (drugs, controlled substances); and an attempt to commit any of these offenses.

Subd. 6. **Transfer.** "Transfer" means a sale, gift, loan, assignment or other delivery to another, whether or not for consideration, of a pistol or semiautomatic military-style assault weapon or the frame or receiver of a pistol or semiautomatic military-style assault weapon.

Subd. 11. **Commissioner.** "Commissioner" means the commissioner of public safety unless otherwise indicated.

Subd. 12. **Ammunition.** "Ammunition" has the meaning given in section 609.02, subdivision 17.

HIST: 1975 c 378 s 2; * * * 2015 c 65 art 3 s 25; 1Sp2019 c 5 art 2 s 26

Editors' Note: The Minnesota Supreme Court recently interpreted the following statute to mean that a device must be a weapon to be a "firearm". State v. Glover, 2020 WL 7636412 (Minn. Dec. 23, 2020) (holding that a distress flare launcher was not a weapon and, therefore, was not a firearm).

624.713 CERTAIN PERSONS NOT TO POSSESS FIREARMS.

Subdivision 1. **Ineligible persons.** The following persons shall not be entitled to possess a pistol or semiautomatic military-style assault weapon or, except for clause (1), any other firearm:

(1) a person under the age of 18 years except that a person under 18 may possess ammunition designed for use in a firearm that the person may lawfully possess and may carry or possess a pistol or semiautomatic military-style assault weapon (i) in the actual presence or under the direct supervision of the person's parent or guardian, (ii) for the purpose of military drill under the auspices of a legally recognized military organization and under competent supervision, (iii) for the purpose of instruction, competition, or target practice on a firing range approved by the chief of police or county sheriff in whose jurisdiction the range is located and under direct supervision; or (iv) if the person has successfully completed a course designed to teach marksmanship and safety with a pistol or semiautomatic military-style assault weapon and approved by the commissioner of natural resources;

(2) except as otherwise provided in clause (i), a person who has been convicted of, or adjudicated delinquent or convicted as an extended jurisdiction juvenile for committing, in this state or elsewhere, a crime of violence. For purposes of this section, crime of violence includes crimes in other states or jurisdictions which would have been crimes of violence as herein defined if they had been committed in this state;

(3) a person who is or has ever been committed in Minnesota or elsewhere by a judicial determination that the person is mentally ill, mentally retarded, or mentally ill and dangerous to the public as defined in section 253B.02, to a treatment facility, or who has ever been found incompetent to stand trial or not guilty by reason of mental illness, unless person's ability to possess a firearm and ammunition has been restored under subdivision 4;

(4) a person who has been convicted in Minnesota or elsewhere of a misdemeanor or gross misdemeanor violation of chapter 152, unless three years have elapsed since the date of conviction and, during that time, the person has not been convicted of any other such violation of chapter 152 or a similar law of another state; or a person who is or has ever been committed by a judicial determination for treatment for the habitual use of a controlled substance or marijuana, as defined in sections 152.01 and 152.02, unless the person's ability to possess a firearm and ammunition has been restored under subdivision 4;

(5) a person who has been committed to a treatment facility in Minnesota or elsewhere by a judicial determination that the person is chemically dependent as defined in section 253B.02, unless the person has completed treatment or the person's ability to possess a firearm and ammunition has been restored under subdivision 4. Property rights may not be abated but access may be restricted by the courts;

(6) a peace officer who is informally admitted to a treatment facility pursuant to section 253B.04 for chemical dependency, unless the officer possesses a certificate from the head of the treatment facility discharging or provisionally discharging the officer from the treatment facility. Property rights may not be abated but access may be restricted by the courts;

(7) a person, including a person under the jurisdiction of the juvenile court, who has been charged with committing a crime of violence and has been placed in a pretrial diversion program by the court before disposition, until the person has completed the diversion program and the charge of committing the crime of violence has been dismissed;

(8) except as otherwise provided in clause (i), a person who has been convicted in another state of committing an offense similar to the offense described in section 609.224, subdivision 3, against a family or household member or section 609.2242, subdivision 3, unless three years have elapsed since the date of conviction and, during that time, the person has not been convicted of any other violation of section 609.224, subdivision 3, or 609.2242, subdivision 3, or a similar law of another state;

(9) a person who has been convicted in this state or elsewhere of assaulting a family or household member and who was found by the court to have used a firearm in any way during commission of the assault is prohibited from possessing any type of firearm or ammunition for the period determined by the sentencing court; or

(10) a person who:

(i) has been convicted in any court of a crime punishable by imprisonment for a term exceeding one year;

(ii) is a fugitive from justice as a result of having fled from any state to avoid prosecution for a crime or to avoid giving testimony in any criminal proceeding;

(iii) is an unlawful user of any controlled substance as defined in chapter 152;

(iv) has been judicially committed to a treatment facility in Minnesota or elsewhere as a "mentally ill," "mentally retarded," or "mentally ill and dangerous to the public" person as defined in section 253B.02;

(v) is an alien who is illegally or unlawfully in the United States;

(vi) has been discharged from the armed forces of the United States under dishonorable conditions;

(vii) has renounced the person's citizenship having been a citizen of the United States; or

(viii) is disqualified from possessing a firearm under [federal law];

(11) a person who has been convicted of the following offenses at the gross misdemeanor level, unless three years have elapsed since the date of conviction and, during that time, the person has not been convicted of any other violation of these sections: section 609.229 (crimes committed for the benefit of a gang); 609.2231, subdivision 4 (assaults motivated by bias); 609.255 (false imprisonment); 609.378 (neglect or endangerment of a child); 609.582, subdivision 4 (burglary in the fourth degree); 609.665 (setting a spring gun); 609.71 (riot); or 609.749 (harassment and stalking). For purposes of this paragraph, the specified gross misdemeanor convictions include crimes committed in other states or jurisdictions which would have been gross misdemeanors if conviction occurred in this state;

(12) a person who has been convicted of a violation of section 609.224 if the court determined that the assault was against a family or household member in accordance with section 609.2242, subdivision 3 (domestic assault), unless three years have elapsed since the date of conviction and, during that time, the person has not been convicted of another violation of section 609.224 or a violation of a section listed in clause (11); or

(13) a person who is subject to an order for protection as described in section 260C.201, subdivision 3, paragraph (d), or section 518B.01, subdivision 6, paragraph (g). * * *

The lifetime prohibition on possessing, receiving, shipping, or transporting firearms and ammunition for persons convicted or adjudicated delinquent of a crime of violence in clause (b), applies only to offenders who are discharged from sentence or court supervision for a crime of violence on or after August 1, 1993.

Subd. 2. **Penalties.** (a) A person named in subdivision 1, clause (1), who possesses ammunition or a pistol or semiautomatic military-style assault weapon in violation of that clause is guilty of a felony and may be sentenced to imprisonment for not more than five years or to payment of a fine of not more than $10,000, or both.

(b) A person named in subdivision 1, clause (2), who possesses any type of firearm or ammunition is guilty of a felony and may be sentenced to imprisonment for not more than 15 years or to payment of a fine of not more than $30,000, or both. * * *

(c) A person named in any other clause of subdivision 1 who possesses any type of firearm or ammunition is guilty of a gross misdemeanor.

HIST: 1975 c 378 s 3; * * * 2015 c 65 art 3 s 26-30; 2016 c 158 art 1 s 208

624.7133 PURCHASING FIREARM ON BEHALF OF INELIGIBLE PERSON.

Any person who purchases or otherwise obtains a firearm on behalf of or for transfer to a person known to be ineligible to possess or purchase a firearm pursuant to federal or state law is guilty of a gross misdemeanor.

HIST: 2015 c 65 art 3 s 31

624.714 CARRYING OF WEAPONS WITHOUT PERMIT; PENALTIES.

Subdivision 1. [Repealed, 2003 c 28 art 2 s 35]

Subd. 1a. **Permit required; penalty.** A person, other than a peace officer, as defined in section 626.84, subdivision 1, who carries, holds, or possesses a pistol in a motor vehicle, snowmobile, or boat, or on or about the person's clothes or the person, or otherwise in possession or control in a public place, as defined in section 624.7181, subdivision 1, paragraph (c), without first having obtained a permit to carry the pistol is guilty of a gross misdemeanor. A person who is convicted a second or subsequent time is guilty of a felony.

Subd. 1b. **Display of permit; penalty.** (a) The holder of a permit to carry must have the permit card and a driver's license, state identification card, or other government-issued photo identification in immediate possession at all times when carrying a pistol and must display the permit card and identification document upon lawful demand by a peace officer, as defined in section 626.84, subdivision 1. A violation of this paragraph is a petty misdemeanor. The fine for a first offense must not exceed $25. Notwithstanding section 609.531, a firearm carried in violation of this paragraph is not subject to forfeiture.

(b) A citation issued for violating paragraph (a) must be dismissed if the person demonstrates, in court or in the office of the arresting officer, that the person was authorized to carry the pistol at the time of the alleged violation.

(c) Upon the request of a peace officer, a permit holder must write a sample signature in the officer's presence to aid in verifying the person's identity.

(d) Upon the request of a peace officer, a permit holder shall disclose to the officer whether or not the permit holder is currently carrying a firearm.

Subd. 2. **Where application made; authority to issue permit; criteria; scope.** (a) Applications by Minnesota residents for permits to carry shall be made to the county sheriff where the applicant resides. Nonresidents, as defined in section 171.01, subdivision 42, may apply to any sheriff.

(b) Unless a sheriff denies a permit under the exception set forth in subdivision 6, paragraph (a), clause (3), a sheriff must issue a permit to an applicant if the person:

(1) has training in the safe use of a pistol;

(2) is at least 21 years old and a citizen or a permanent resident of the United States;

(3) completes an application for a permit;

(4) is not prohibited from possessing a firearm under the following sections:

(i) 518B.01, subdivision 14;

(ii) 609.224, subdivision 3;

(iii) 609.2242, subdivision 3;

(iv) 609.749, subdivision 8;

(v) 624.713;

(vi) 624.719;

(vii) 629.715, subdivision 2;

(viii) 629.72, subdivision 2; or

(ix) any federal law; and

(5) is not listed in the criminal gang investigative data system under section 299C.091.

(c) A permit to carry a pistol issued or recognized under this section is a state permit and is effective throughout the state.

(d) A sheriff may contract with a police chief to process permit applications under this section. If a sheriff contracts with a police chief, the sheriff remains the issuing authority and the police chief acts as the sheriff's agent. If a sheriff contracts with a police chief, all of the provisions of this section will apply.

Subd. 2a. **Training in the safe use of a pistol.** (a) An applicant must present evidence that the applicant received training in the safe use of a pistol within one year of the date of an original or renewal application. Training may be demonstrated by:

(1) employment as a peace officer in the state of Minnesota within the past year; or

(2) completion of a firearms safety or training course providing basic training in the safe use of a pistol and conducted by a certified instructor.

(b) Basic training must include:

(1) instruction in the fundamentals of pistol use;

(2) successful completion of an actual shooting qualification exercise; and

(3) instruction in the fundamental legal aspects of pistol possession, carry, and use, including self-defense and the restrictions on the use of deadly force.

* * *

(e) A sheriff must accept the training described in this subdivision as meeting the requirement in subdivision 2, paragraph (b), for training in the safe use of a pistol. A sheriff may also accept other satisfactory evidence of training in the safe use of a pistol.

Subd. 3. **Form and contents of application.** (a) Applications for permits to carry must be an official, standardized application form[.] * * *

(c) An applicant must submit to the sheriff an application packet consisting only of the following items:

(1) a completed application form, signed and dated by the applicant;

(2) * * * the applicant's evidence of training in the safe use of a pistol; and

(3) an accurate photocopy of the applicant's current driver's license, state identification card, or the photo page of the applicant's passport. * * *

(h) Forms for new and renewal applications must be available at all sheriffs' offices and the commissioner must make the forms available on the Internet.

(i) Application forms must clearly display a notice that a permit, if granted, is void and must be immediately returned to the sheriff if the permit holder is or becomes prohibited by law from possessing a firearm. The notice must list the applicable state criminal offenses and civil categories that prohibit a person from possessing a firearm.

(j) Upon receipt of an application packet and any require fee, the sheriff must provide a signed receipt indicating the date of submission.

Subd. 4. **Investigation.** (a) The sheriff must check, by means of electronic data transfer, criminal records, histories, and warrant information on each applicant through the Minnesota Crime Information System and the National Instant Criminal Background Check System. The sheriff shall also make a reasonable effort to check other available and relevant federal, state, or local record-keeping systems. The sheriff must obtain commitment information from the commissioner of human services as provided in section 245.041 or, if the information is reasonably available, as provided by a similar statute from another state.

(b) When an application for a permit is filed under this section, the sheriff must notify the chief of police, if any, of the municipality where the applicant resides. The police chief may provide the sheriff with any information relevant to the issuance of the permit.

(c) The sheriff must conduct a background check by means of electronic data transfer on a permit holder through the Minnesota Crime Information System and the National Instant Criminal Background Check System at least yearly to ensure continuing eligibility. The sheriff may also conduct additional background checks by means of electronic data transfer on a permit holder at any time during the period that a permit is in effect. * * *

Subd. 6. **Granting and denial of permits.** (a) The sheriff must, within 30 days after the date of receipt of the application packet described in subdivision 3:

(1) issue the permit to carry;

(2) deny the application for a permit to carry solely on the grounds that the applicant failed to qualify under the criteria described in subdivision 2, paragraph (b); or

(3) deny the application on the grounds that there exists a substantial likelihood that the applicant is a danger to self or the public if authorized to carry a pistol under a permit.

(b) Failure of the sheriff to notify the applicant of the denial of the application within 30 days after the date of receipt of the application packet constitutes issuance of the permit to carry and the sheriff must promptly fulfill the requirements under paragraph (c). To deny the application, the sheriff must provide the applicant with written notification and the specific factual basis justifying the denial under paragraph (a), clause (2) or (3), including the source of the factual basis. The sheriff must inform the applicant of the applicant's right to submit, within 20 business days, any additional documentation relating to the propriety of the denial. Upon receiving any additional documentation, the sheriff must reconsider the denial and inform the applicant within 15 business days of the result of the reconsideration. Any denial after reconsideration must be in the same form and substance as the original denial and must specifically address any continued deficiencies in light of the additional documentation submitted by the applicant. The applicant must be informed of the right to seek de novo review of the denial as provided in subdivision 12.

(c) Upon issuing a permit to carry, the sheriff must provide a laminated permit card to the applicant * * *. Within five business days, the sheriff must submit the information specified in subdivision 7, paragraph (a), to the commissioner for inclusion solely in the database required under subdivision 15, paragraph (a). * * *

(d) Within five business days of learning that a permit to carry has been suspended or revoked[.] * * *

(e) Notwithstanding paragraphs (a) and (b), the sheriff may suspend the application process if a charge is pending against the applicant that, if resulting in conviction, will prohibit the applicant from possessing a firearm.

Subd. 7. **Permit card contents; expiration; renewal.** (a) Permits to carry must be on an official, standardized permit card adopted by the commissioner, containing only the name, residence, and driver's license number or state identification card number of the permit holder, if any.

(b) The permit card must also identify the issuing sheriff and state the expiration date of the permit. * * *

(c) A permit to carry a pistol issued under this section expires five years after the date of issue. It may be renewed in the same manner and under the same criteria which the original permit was obtained[.] * * *

Subd. 7a. **Change of address; loss or destruction of permit.** (a) Within 30 days after changing permanent address, or within 30 days of having lost or destroyed the permit card, the permit holder must notify the issuing sheriff of the change, loss, or destruction. Failure to provide notification as required by this subdivision is a petty misdemeanor. The fine for a first offense must not exceed $25. Notwithstanding section 609.531, a firearm carried in violation of this paragraph is not subject to forfeiture.

(b) After notice is given under paragraph (a), a permit holder may obtain a replacement permit card[.] * * *

Subd. 8. **Permit to carry voided.** (a) The permit to carry is void at the time that the holder becomes prohibited by law from possessing a firearm, in which event the holder must return the permit card to the issuing sheriff within five business days after the holder knows or should know that the holder is a prohibited person. If the sheriff has knowledge that a permit is void under this paragraph, the sheriff must give notice to the permit holder in writing in the same manner as a denial. Failure of the holder to return the permit within the five days is a gross misdemeanor unless the court finds that the circumstances or the physical or mental condition of the permit holder prevented the holder from complying with the return requirement.

(b) When a permit holder is convicted of an offense that prohibits the permit holder from possessing a firearm, the court must take possession of the permit, if it is available, and send it to the issuing sheriff. * * *

(d) A permit revocation must be promptly reported to the issuing sheriff. * * *

Subd. 9. **Carrying pistols about one's premises or for purposes of repair, target practice.** A permit to carry is not required of a person:

(a) to keep or carry about the person's place of business, dwelling house, premises or on land possessed by the person a pistol;

(b) to carry a pistol from a place of purchase to the person's dwelling house or place of business, or from the person's dwelling house or place of business to or from a place where repairing is done, to have the pistol repaired;

(c) to carry a pistol between the person's dwelling house and place of business;

(d) to carry a pistol in the woods or fields or upon the waters of this state for the purpose of hunting or of target shooting in a safe area; or

(e) to transport a pistol in a motor vehicle, snowmobile or boat if the pistol is unloaded, contained in a closed and fastened case, gunbox, or securely tied package.

Subd. 10. **False representations.** A person who gives or causes to be given any false material information in applying for a permit to carry, knowing or having reason to know the information is false, is guilty of a gross misdemeanor.

Subd. 11. **No limit on number of pistols.** A person shall not be restricted as to the number of pistols the person may carry.

Subd. 11a. **Emergency issuance of permits.** A sheriff may immediately issue an emergency permit to a person if the sheriff determines that the person is in an emergency situation that may constitute an immediate risk to the safety of the person or someone residing in the person's household. A person seeking an emergency permit must complete an application form and must sign an affidavit describing the emergency situation. An emergency permit applicant does not need to provide evidence of training. An emergency permit is valid for 30 days, may not be renewed, and may be revoked without a hearing. * * *

Subd. 12. **Hearing upon denial or revocation.** (a) Any person aggrieved by denial or revocation of a permit to carry may appeal by petition to the district court having jurisdiction over the county or municipality where the application was submitted. * * *

Subd. 12a. **Suspension as condition of release.** The district court may order suspension of the application process for a permit or suspend the permit of a permit holder as a condition of release[.] * * *

Subd. 13. **Exemptions; adult correctional facility officers.** A permit to carry a pistol is not required of any officer of a state adult correctional facility when on guard duty or otherwise engaged in an assigned duty.

Subd. 14. **Records.** (a) A sheriff must not maintain records or data collected, made, or held under this section concerning any applicant or permit holder that are not necessary under this section to support a permit that is outstanding or eligible for renewal under subdivision 7, paragraph (b). Notwithstanding section 138.163, sheriffs must completely purge all files and databases by March 1 of each year to delete all information collected under this section concerning all persons who are no longer current permit holders or currently eligible to renew their permit.

(b) Paragraph (a) does not apply to records or data concerning an applicant or permit holder who has had a permit denied or revoked under the criteria established in subdivision 2, paragraph (b), clause (1), or subdivision 6, paragraph (a), clause (3), for a period of six years from the date of the denial or revocation.

Subd. 15. **Commissioner; contracts; database.** (a) The commissioner must maintain an automated database of persons authorized to carry pistols under this section that is available 24 hours a day, seven days a week, only to law enforcement agencies[.] * * *

Subd. 16. **Recognition of permits from other states.** (a) The commissioner must annually establish and publish a list of other states that have laws governing the issuance of permits to carry weapons that are not similar to this section. The list must be available on the

Internet. A person holding a carry permit from a state not on the list may use the license or permit in this state subject to the rights, privileges, and requirements of this section.

(b) Notwithstanding paragraph (a), no license or permit from another state is valid in this state if the holder is or becomes prohibited by law from possessing a firearm.

(c) Any sheriff or police chief may file a petition under subdivision 12 seeking an order suspending or revoking an out-of-state permit holder's authority to carry a pistol in this state on the grounds set forth in subdivision 6, paragraph (a), clause (3). * * *

(d) The commissioner must, when necessary, execute reciprocity agreements regarding carry permits with jurisdictions whose carry permits are recognized under paragraph (a).

Subd. 17. **Posting; trespass.** (a) A person carrying a firearm on or about his or her person or clothes under a permit or otherwise who remains at a private establishment knowing that the operator of the establishment or its agent has made a reasonable request that firearms not be brought into the establishment may be ordered to leave the premises. A person who fails to leave when so requested is guilty of a petty misdemeanor. The fine for a first offense must not exceed $25. Notwithstanding section 609.531, a firearm carried in violation of this subdivision is not subject to forfeiture.

(b) As used in this subdivision, the terms in this paragraph have the meanings given.

(1) "Reasonable request" means a request made under the following circumstances:

(i) the requester has prominently posted a conspicuous sign at every entrance to the establishment containing the following language: "(INDICATE IDENTITY OF OPERATOR) BANS GUNS IN THESE PREMISES."; or

(ii) the requester or the requester's agent personally informs the person that guns are prohibited in the premises and demands compliance.

(2) "Prominently" means readily visible and within four feet laterally of the entrance with the bottom of the sign at a height of four to six feet above the floor.

(3) "Conspicuous" means lettering in black arial typeface at least 1-1/2 inches in height against a bright contrasting background that is at least 187 square inches in area.

(4) "Private establishment" means a building, structure, or portion thereof that is owned, leased, controlled, or operated by a nongovernmental entity for a nongovernmental purpose.

(c) The owner or operator of a private establishment may not prohibit the lawful carry or possession of firearms in a parking facility or parking area.

(d) The owner or operator of a private establishment may not prohibit the lawful carry or possession of firearms by a peace officer * * * within the private establishment or deny the officer access thereto, except when specifically authorized by statute. * * *

(e) This subdivision does not apply to private residences. The lawful possessor of a private residence may prohibit firearms, and provide notice thereof, in any lawful manner.

(f) A landlord may not restrict the lawful carry or possession of firearms by tenants or their guests.

(g) Notwithstanding any inconsistent provisions in section 609.605, this subdivision sets forth the exclusive criteria to notify a permit holder when otherwise lawful firearm possession is not allowed in a private establishment and sets forth the exclusive penalty for such activity.

(h) This subdivision does not apply to a security guard acting in the course and scope of employment. * * *

Subd. 18. **Employers; public colleges and universities.** (a) An employer, whether public or private, may establish policies that restrict the carry or possession of firearms by its employees while acting in the course and scope of employment. * * *

(b) A public postsecondary institution * * * may establish policies that restrict the carry or possession of firearms by its students while on the institution's property. * * *

(c) Notwithstanding paragraphs (a) and (b), an employer or a postsecondary institution may not prohibit the lawful carry or possession of firearms in a parking facility or parking area.

Subd. 19. **Immunity.** Neither a sheriff, police chief, any employee of a sheriff or police chief involved in the permit issuing process, nor any certified instructor is liable for damages resulting or arising from acts with a firearm committed by a permit holder, unless the person had actual knowledge at the time the permit was issued or the instruction was given that the applicant was prohibited by law from possessing a firearm.

Subd. 20. **Monitoring.** (a) By March 1, 2004, and each year thereafter, the commissioner must report to the legislature on:

(1) the number of permits applied for, issued, suspended, revoked, and denied, further categorized by the age, sex, and zip code of the applicant or permit holder, since the previous submission, and in total;

(2) the number of permits currently valid;

(3) the specific reasons for each suspension, revocation, and denial and the number of reversed, canceled, or corrected actions; * * *

(5) the number of convictions and types of crimes committed since the previous submission, and in total, by individuals with permits including data as to whether a firearm lawfully carried solely by virtue of a permit was actually used in furtherance of the crime; [and]

(6) to the extent known or determinable, data on the lawful and justifiable use of firearms by permit holders[.] * * *

(b) Sheriffs and police chiefs must supply the Department of Public Safety with the basic data the department requires to complete the report under paragraph (a). Sheriffs and police chiefs may submit data classified as private to the Department of Public Safety under this paragraph. * * *

(d) Nothing contained in any provision of this section or any other law requires or authorizes the registration, documentation, collection, or providing of serial numbers or other data on firearms or on firearms' owners. * * *

Subd. 22. **Short title; construction; severability.** This section may be cited as the Minnesota Citizens' Personal Protection Act of 2003. * * *

Subd. 23. **Exclusivity.** This section sets forth the complete and exclusive criteria and procedures for the issuance of permits to carry and establishes their nature and scope. No sheriff, police chief, governmental unit, government official, government employee, or other person or body acting under color of law or governmental authority may change, modify, or supplement these criteria or procedures, or limit the exercise of a permit to carry.

Subd. 24. **Predatory offenders.** Except when acting under the authority of other law, it is a misdemeanor for a person required to register by section 243.166 to carry a pistol whether or not the carrier possesses a permit to carry issued under this section. * * *

HIST: 1975 c 378 s 4; * * * 2015 c 65 art 3 s 32; 2017 c 95 art 3 s 25

*Editors' Note: In February 2008, the Minnesota Court of Appeals declared certain provisions the Conceal & Carry legislation unconstitutional (e.g., the requirements concerning sign posting and the ability to exclude firearms from parking areas) as they apply to **churches** in violation of churches' "freedom-of-conscience rights."*

624.7142 CARRYING WHILE UNDER THE INFLUENCE OF ALCOHOL OR A CONTROLLED SUBSTANCE.

Subdivision 1. **Acts prohibited.** A person may not carry a pistol on or about the person's clothes or person in a public place:

(1) when the person is under the influence of a controlled substance, as defined in section 152.01, subdivision 4;

(2) when the person is under the influence of a combination of any two or more of the elements named in clauses (1) and (4);

(3) when the person is under the influence of an intoxicating substance as defined in section 169A.03, subdivision 11a, and the person knows or has reason to know that the substance has the capacity to cause impairment;

(4) when the person is under the influence of alcohol;

(5) when the person's alcohol concentration is 0.10 or more; or

(6) when the person's alcohol concentration is less than 0.10, but more than 0.04.

Subd. 2. **Arrest.** A peace officer may arrest a person for a violation under subdivision 1 without a warrant upon probable cause, without regard to whether the violation was committed in the officer's presence.

Subd. 3. **Preliminary screening test.** When an officer authorized under subdivision 2 to make arrests has reason to believe that the person may be violating or has violated subdivision 1, the officer may require the person to provide a breath sample for a preliminary screening test using a device approved by the commissioner for this purpose. The results of the preliminary screening test must be used for the purpose of deciding whether an arrest should be made under this section and whether to require the chemical tests authorized in section 624.7143, but may not be used in any court action except: (1) to prove that the test was properly required of a person under section 624.7143, or (2) in a civil action arising out of the use of the pistol. Following the preliminary screening test, additional tests may be required of the person as provided under section 624.7143. A person who refuses a breath sample is subject to the provisions of section 624.7143 unless, in compliance with that section, the person submits to a blood, breath, or urine test to determine the presence of alcohol or a controlled substance.

Subd. 4. **Evidence.** In a prosecution for a violation of subdivision 1, the admission of evidence of the amount of alcohol or a controlled substance in the person's blood, breath, or urine is governed by section 169A.45.

Subd. 5. **Suspension.** A person who is charged with a violation under this section may have their authority to carry a pistol in a public place on or about the person's clothes or person under the provisions of a permit or otherwise suspended by the court as a condition of release.

Subd. 6. **Penalties.** (a) A person who violates a prohibition under subdivision 1, clauses (1) to (5), is guilty of a misdemeanor. A second or subsequent violation is a gross misdemeanor.

(b) A person who violates subdivision 1, clause (6), is guilty of a misdemeanor.

(c) In addition to the penalty imposed under paragraph (a), if a person violates subdivision 1, clauses (1) to (5), the person's authority to carry a pistol in a public place on or about the person's clothes or person under the provisions of a permit or otherwise is revoked and the person may not reapply for a period of one year from the date of conviction.

(d) In addition to the penalty imposed under paragraph (b), if a person violates subdivision 1, clause (6), the person's authority to carry a pistol in a public place on or about the person's clothes or person under the provisions of a permit or otherwise is suspended for 180 days from the date of conviction.

(e) Notwithstanding section 609.531, a firearm carried in violation of subdivision 1, clause (6), is not subject to forfeiture.

Subd. 7. **Reporting.** Suspensions and revocations under this section must be reported in the same manner as in section 624.714, subdivision 12a.

HIST: 2003 c 28 art 2 s 29,34; * * * 2018 c 195 art 3 s 25

624.7143 CHEMICAL TESTING.

Subdivision 1. **Mandatory chemical testing.** (a) A person who carries a pistol in a public place on or about the person's clothes or person is required, subject to the provisions of this section, to take or submit to a test of the person's blood, breath, or urine for the purpose of determining the presence and amount of alcohol or a controlled substance. The test shall be administered at the direction of an officer authorized to make arrests under section 624.7142.

(b) Taking or submitting to a test of the person's breath is mandatory when requested by an officer who has probable cause to believe the person was carrying a pistol in violation of section 624.7142, and one of the following conditions exists:

(1) the person has been lawfully placed under arrest for violating section 624.7142;

(2) the person has been involved while carrying a firearm in a firearms-related accident resulting in property damage, personal injury, or death;

(3) the person has refused to take the preliminary screening test provided for in section 624.7142; or

(4) the screening test was administered and indicated an alcohol concentration of 0.04 or more.

(c) Taking or submitting to a test of the person's blood or urine is mandatory when requested by a peace officer under the conditions described in paragraph (b) if the officer is acting pursuant to a search warrant[.]

Subd. 1a. **Blood or urine test; search warrant required.** Notwithstanding any contrary provision in this section, a blood or urine test may be conducted only pursuant to a search warrant * * *, or a judicially recognized exception to the search warrant requirement. * * *

Subd. 2. **Penalties; refusal; revocation.** (a) If a person refuses to take a test required under subdivision 1, none must be given but the officer shall report the refusal to the sheriff and to the authority having responsibility for prosecution of misdemeanor offenses for the jurisdiction in which the incident occurred that gave rise to the test demand and refusal. On certification by the officer that probable cause existed to believe the person had been carrying a pistol on or about the person's clothes or person in a public place while under the influence of alcohol or a controlled substance, that in the case of a blood or urine test the officer was acting pursuant to a search warrant, and that the person refused to submit to testing, a court may impose a civil penalty of $500 and may revoke the person's authority to carry a pistol in a public place on or about the person's clothes or person under the provisions of a permit or otherwise for a period of one year from the date of the refusal. The person shall be accorded notice and an opportunity to be heard prior to imposition of the civil penalty or the revocation.

(b) Revocations under this subdivision must be reported in the same manner as in section 624.714, subdivision 12a.

Subd. 3. **Rights and obligations.** At the time a test is requested, the person must be informed that:

(1) Minnesota law requires a person to take a test to determine if the person is under the influence of alcohol or a controlled substance;

(2) if the person refuses to take the test, the person is subject to a civil penalty of $500 and is prohibited for a period of one year from carrying a pistol in a public place on or about the person's clothes or person, as provided under subdivision 2; and

(3) that, in the case of a breath test, the person has the right to consult with an attorney, but that this right is limited to the extent it cannot unreasonably delay administration of the test or the person will be deemed to have refused the test.

Subd. 4. **Type of test.** (a) A peace officer who directs a test pursuant to this section may direct a breath test.

(b) A peace officer, acting pursuant to a search warrant, may direct a blood or urine test as provided in the warrant. If the warrant authorizes either a blood or urine test, the officer may direct whether the test is of blood or urine. If the person to whom the test is directed objects to the test, the officer shall offer the person an alternative test of either blood or urine.

(c) If there is probable cause to believe there is impairment by a controlled substance that is not subject to testing by a breath test, a blood or urine test may be required pursuant to a search warrant even after a breath test has been administered.

(d) Action under this section may be taken against a person who refuses to take a blood test only if an alternative test was offered and action may be taken against a person who refuses to take a urine test only if an alternative test was offered.

Subd. 5. **Chemical tests.** Chemical tests administered under this section are governed by section 169A.51 in all aspects that are not inconsistent with this section.

HIST: 2003 c 28 art 2 s 30; 2005 c 83 s 1; 2017 c 83 art 3 s 13-17

624.7131 TRANSFEREE PERMIT; PENALTY.
* * *

Subd. 5. **Granting of permits.** The chief of police or sheriff shall issue a transferee permit or deny the application within seven days of application for the permit. The chief of police or sheriff shall provide an applicant with written notification of a denial and the specific reason for the denial. The permits and their renewal shall be granted free of charge.

Subd. 9. **Permit to carry.** A valid permit to carry issued pursuant to section 624.714 constitutes a transferee permit for the purposes of this section and section 624.7132.

HIST: 1977 c 349 s 4; * * * 2009 c 139 s 4

624.7132 REPORT OF TRANSFER.
* * *

Subd. 4. **Delivery.** Except as otherwise provided in subdivision 7 or 8, no person shall deliver a pistol or semiautomatic military-style assault weapon to a proposed transferee until five business days after the date the agreement to transfer is delivered to a chief of police or sheriff in accordance with subdivision 1 unless the chief of police or sheriff waives all or a portion of the seven day waiting period. The chief of police or sheriff may waive all or a portion of the five business day waiting period in writing if the chief of police or sheriff finds that the transferee requires access to a pistol or semiautomatic military-style assault weapon because of a threat to the life of the transferee or of any member of the household of the transferee.

No person shall deliver a pistol or semiautomatic military-style assault weapon to a proposed transferee after receiving a written notification that the chief of police or sheriff has determined that the proposed transferee is prohibited by section 624.713 from possessing a pistol or semiautomatic military-style assault weapon.

If the transferor makes a report of transfer and receives no written notification of disqualification of the proposed transferee within five business days after delivery of the agreement to transfer, the pistol or semiautomatic military-style assault weapon may be delivered to the transferee.
HIST: 1977 c 349 s 5; * * * 2009 c 139 s 5

624.7131 TRANSFEREE PERMIT; PENALTY.
* * *

Subd. 5. **Granting of permits.** The chief of police or sheriff shall issue a transferee permit or deny the application within seven days of application for the permit. The chief of police or sheriff shall provide an applicant with written notification of a denial and the specific reason for the denial. The permits and their renewal shall be granted free of charge.
HIST: 1977 c 349 s 4; * * * 2009 c 139 s 4

624.7132 REPORT OF TRANSFER.
* * *

Subd. 4. **Delivery.** Except as otherwise provided in subdivision 7 or 8, no person shall deliver a pistol or semiautomatic military-style assault weapon to a proposed transferee until five business days after the date the agreement to transfer is delivered to a chief of police or sheriff in accordance with subdivision 1 unless the chief of police or sheriff waives all or a portion of the seven day waiting period. The chief of police or sheriff may waive all or a portion of the five business day waiting period in writing if the chief of police or sheriff finds that the transferee requires access to a pistol or semiautomatic military-style assault weapon because of a threat to the life of the transferee or of any member of the household of the transferee.

No person shall deliver a pistol or semiautomatic military-style assault weapon to a proposed transferee after receiving a written notification that the chief of police or sheriff has determined that the proposed transferee is prohibited by section 624.713 from possessing a pistol or semiautomatic military-style assault weapon.

If the transferor makes a report of transfer and receives no written notification of disqualification of the proposed transferee within five business days after delivery of the agreement to transfer, the pistol or semiautomatic military-style assault weapon may be delivered to the transferee.
HIST: 1977 c 349 s 5; * * * 2009 c 139 s 5

624.7131 TRANSFEREE PERMIT; PENALTY.
* * *

Subd. 4. **Grounds for disqualification.** A determination by the chief of police or sheriff that the applicant is prohibited by section 624.713 from possessing a pistol or semiautomatic military-style assault weapon shall be the only basis for refusal to grant a transferee permit.
HIST: 1977 c 349 s 4; * * * 2009 c 139 s 4

624.7132 REPORT OF TRANSFER.
* * *

Subd. 15. **Penalties.** (a) Except as otherwise provided in paragraph (b), a person who does any of the following is guilty of a gross misdemeanor:

(1) transfers a pistol or semiautomatic military-style assault weapon in violation of subdivisions 1 to 13;

(2) transfers a pistol or semiautomatic military-style assault weapon to a person who has made a false statement in order to become a transferee, if the transferor knows or has reason to know the transferee has made the false statement;

(3) knowingly becomes a transferee in violation of subdivisions 1 to 13; or

(4) makes a false statement in order to become a transferee of a pistol or semiautomatic military-style assault weapon knowing or having reason to know the statement is false.

(b) A person who does either of the following is guilty of a felony:

(1) transfers a pistol or semiautomatic military-style assault weapon to a person under the age of 18 in violation of subdivisions 1 to 13; or

(2) transfers a pistol or semiautomatic military-style assault weapon to a person under the age of 18 who has made a false statement in order to become a transferee, if the transferor knows or has reason to know the transferee has made the false statement.
HIST: 1977 c 349 s 5; * * * 2009 c 139 s 5

624.7144 ALLOWING AN INELIGIBLE PERSON ACCESS TO FIREARMS.

A person who accepts a transferred firearm from an abusing party or offender pursuant to section 260C.201, subdivision 3; section 518B.01, subdivision 6, section 609.2242, subdivision 3; or section 609.749, subdivision 8, is guilty of a gross misdemeanor if the abusing party or offender obtains possession of the transferred firearm while the person is prohibited from possessing firearms. It is an affirmative defense to a violation of this section that the third party who accepted the transferred firearm exercised due care to ensure that the abusing party or offender could not access the firearm. The third party shall not return the firearm to the abusing party or offender until the prohibiting time period imposed * * * has expired and the abusing party or offender presents a current, valid transferee permit or passes a federal background check through the National Instant Criminal Background Check System. * * *
HIST: 2014 c 213 s 6

624.7132 REPORT OF TRANSFER.
* * *

Subd. 16. **Local regulation.** This section shall be construed to supersede municipal or county regulation of the transfer of pistols.
HIST: 1977 c 349 s 5; * * * 2009 c 139 s 5

624.717 LOCAL REGULATION.

Sections 624.711 to 624.716 shall be construed to supersede municipal or county regulation of the carrying or possessing of pistols and the regulation of Saturday Night Special Pistols.
HIST: 1975 c 378 s 7; 1985 c 144 s 3

624.719 POSSESSION OF FIREARM BY NONRESIDENT ALIEN.
A nonresident alien may not possess a firearm except to take game as a nonresident under the game and fish laws. A firearm possessed in violation of this section is contraband and may be confiscated.
HIST: 1986 c 386 art 4 s 32

624.72 INTERFERENCE WITH USE OF PUBLIC PROPERTY.
Subdivision 1. **Right to petition.** The state of Minnesota acknowledges and reaffirms the right of its citizens to petition, peacefully and in an orderly manner, all levels and units of government for the redress of grievances of whatever nature, but also affirms that functions and proceedings of governmental bodies and agencies must remain free from organized or calculated confusion, disturbance or delay, and that to this end rules and regulations for the governance of public property and business lawfully promulgated must be observed.
Subd. 2. **Public property.** As used in this section, "public property" means any building or other property owned by or in control of the state or any of its political subdivisions or of the board of regents of the University of Minnesota.
Subd. 3. **Rules.** For the purpose of protecting the free, proper and lawful access to, egress from and proper use of public property, and for the purpose of protecting the conduct of public business therein or thereon, free from interference, or disruption or the threat thereof, the legislature or any public officer, agency or board having the supervision thereof may to that end promulgate reasonable rules and regulations.
Subd. 4. **Rule violation.** Violation of a rule or regulation which has been published, posted, or announced in a reasonable manner at the time of such conduct shall be prima facie evidence of intent to violate this section.
Subd. 5. **Deny free access; penalty.** Whoever, intentionally, or through coercion, force or intimidation, denies or interferes with the lawful right of another to the free access to or egress from or to use or remain in or upon public property or in like manner interferes with the transaction of public business therein or thereon may be sentenced to imprisonment for not more than one year or a fine of not more than $3,000 or both.
Subd. 6. **No affect chapter 179.** Nothing contained herein shall in any way affect the provisions of chapter 179.
HIST: 1969 c 767 s 1-6; 1984 c 628 art 3 s 11

624.731 TEAR GAS AND TEAR GAS COMPOUNDS; ELECTRONIC INCAPACITATION DEVICES.
Subdivision 1. **Definitions.** For the purposes of this section:
(a) "authorized tear gas compound" means a lachrymator or any substance composed of a mixture of a lachrymator including chloroacetophenone, alpha-chloroacetophenone; phenylchloromethylketone, orthochlorobenzalmalononitrile or oleoresin capsicum, commonly known as tear gas; and
(b) "electronic incapacitation device" means a portable device which is designed or intended by the manufacturer to be used, offensively or defensively, to temporarily immobilize or incapacitate persons by means of electric pulse or current, including devices operating by means of carbon dioxide propellant. "Electronic incapacitation device" does not include cattle prods, electric fences, or other electric devices when used in agricultural, animal husbandry, or food production activities.
Subd. 2. **Authorized possession; use.** (a) A person may possess and use an authorized tear gas compound in the exercise of reasonable force in defense of the person or the person's property only if it is propelled from an aerosol container, labeled with or accompanied by clearly written instructions as to its use and the dangers involved in its use, and dated to indicate its anticipated useful life.
(b) A person may possess and use an electronic incapacitation device in the exercise of reasonable force in defense of the person or the person's property only if the electronic

incapacitation device is labeled with or accompanied by clearly written instructions as to its use and the dangers involved in its use.

Subd. 3. **Prohibited possession; use.** (a) No person under the age of 16 may possess or use an authorized tear gas compound except by written permission of a parent or guardian, and no person under the age of 18 may possess or use an electronic incapacitation device.

(b) No person prohibited from possessing a pistol pursuant to section 624.713, subdivision 1, clause (2), may possess or use an authorized tear gas compound or an electronic incapacitation device.

(c) No person prohibited from possessing a pistol pursuant to section 624.713, subdivision 1, clauses (3) to (5), may possess or use an authorized tear gas compound or an electronic incapacitation device, except that the certificate or other proof required for possession of a handgun shall not apply.

(d) No person shall possess or use tear gas or a tear gas compound other than an authorized tear gas compound.

Subd. 4. **Prohibited use.** (a) No person shall knowingly, or with reason to know, use tear gas, a tear gas compound, an authorized tear gas compound, or an electronic incapacitation device on or against a peace officer who is in the performance of duties.

(b) No person shall use tear gas, a tear gas compound, an authorized tear gas compound, or an electronic incapacitation device except as authorized in subdivision 2 or 6.

(c) Tear gas, a tear gas compound, or an electronic incapacitation device shall legally constitute a weapon when it is used in the commission of a crime.

(d) No person shall use tear gas or a tear gas compound in an immobilizing concentration against another person, except as otherwise permitted by subdivision 2.

Subd. 5. **Prohibited sale.** Except as permitted by subdivision 6, no person shall knowingly furnish or sell tear gas or a tear gas compound to another person. No person shall knowingly furnish or sell an authorized tear gas compound or an electronic incapacitation device to a person prohibited from possessing it by subdivision 3. No person shall knowingly furnish or sell an authorized tear gas compound or an electronic incapacitation device which fails to meet the requirements of subdivision 2. No tear gas, tear gas compound, authorized tear gas compound, or electronic incapacitation device shall be sold or furnished on premises where 3.2 percent malt liquor as defined in section 340A.101, subdivision 19, is sold on an on-sale basis or where intoxicating liquor as defined in section 340A.101, subdivision 13, is sold on an on-sale or off-sale basis. No person shall sell tear gas, a tear gas compound, authorized tear gas compound, or electronic incapacitation device in violation of local licensing requirements.

Subd. 6. **Exceptions.** Nothing in this section shall prohibit the possession or use of by, or the sale or furnishing of, tear gas, a tear gas compound, an authorized tear gas compound, or electronic incapacitation device to, a law enforcement agency, peace officer, the national guard or reserves, or a member of the national guard or reserves for use in their official duties, except that counties and municipalities may impose licensing requirements on sellers pursuant to subdivision 9.

Subd. 7. **Exemption.** Tear gas, tear gas compounds, and authorized tear gas compounds shall not be classified as an obnoxious or harmful gas, fluid, or substance under section 624.732.

Subd. 8. **Penalties.** (a) The following violations of this section shall be considered a felony:

(1) The possession or use of tear gas, a tear gas compound, an authorized tear gas compound, or an electronic incapacitation device by a person specified in subdivision 3, paragraph (b).

(2) Knowingly selling or furnishing of tear gas, a tear gas compound, an authorized tear gas compound, or an electronic incapacitation device to a person specified in subdivision 3, paragraph (b).

(3) The use of an electronic incapacitation device as prohibited in subdivision 4, paragraph (a).

(4) The use of tear gas or a tear gas compound as prohibited in subdivision 4, paragraph (d).

(b) The following violation of this section shall be considered a gross misdemeanor:

(1) The prohibited use of tear gas, a tear gas compound, or an authorized tear gas compound as specified in subdivision 4, paragraph (a);

(2) the use of an electronic incapacitation device except as allowed by subdivision 2 or 6.

(c) The following violations of this section shall be considered a misdemeanor:

(1) The possession or use of tear gas, a tear gas compound, an authorized tear gas compound, or an electronic incapacitation device which fails to meet the requirements of subdivision 2 by any person except as allowed by subdivision 6.

(2) The possession or use of an authorized tear gas compound or an electronic incapacitation device by a person specified in subdivision 3, paragraph (a) or (c).

(3) The use of tear gas, a tear gas compound, or an authorized tear gas compound except as allowed by subdivision 2 or 6.

(4) Knowingly selling or furnishing an authorized tear gas compound or an electronic incapacitation device to a person specified in subdivision 3, paragraph (a) or (c).

(5) Selling or furnishing of tear gas or a tear gas compound other than an authorized tear gas compound to any person except as allowed by subdivision 6.

(6) Selling or furnishing of an authorized tear gas compound or an electronic incapacitation device on premises where intoxicating liquor is sold on an on-sale or off-sale basis or where 3.2 percent malt liquor is sold on an on-sale basis.

(7) Selling an authorized tear gas compound or an electronic incapacitation device in violation of local licensing requirements.

Subd. 9. **Local licensing.** (a) For purposes of this section, "municipality" means statutory or home rule charter city or town.

(b) There is hereby conferred upon the governing body of each county, statutory or home rule charter city and town in the state the authority to license the business of vendors of tear gas, tear gas compounds, authorized tear gas compounds, or electronic incapacitation devices within their respective jurisdictions, to impose a license fee therefor, to impose qualifications for obtaining a license, the duration of licenses and to restrict the number of licenses the governing body will issue.

(c) Every person desiring a license from a local governing body shall file with the clerk of the municipality or the county board in the case of application to a county, a verified written application in the form to be prescribed by the local governing body.

(d) The local governing body may establish the grounds, notice and hearing procedures for revocation of licenses issued pursuant to this section. The local governing body may also establish penalties for sale of tear gas, tear gas compounds, authorized tear gas compounds, or electronic incapacitation devices in violation of its licensing requirements.

Subd. 10. **Local regulation.** This section shall be the exclusive regulation of the possession, use, and furnishing of tear gas, tear gas compounds, authorized tear gas compounds, and electronic incapacitation devices in Minnesota. This section shall supersede and preempt all regulation of the possession, use, and furnishing of tear gas, tear gas compounds, authorized tear gas compounds, and electronic incapacitation devices by political subdivisions.

HIST: 1981 c 283 s 1; * * * 2009 c 86 art 1 s 85

624.732 INTENTIONAL RELEASE OF HARMFUL SUBSTANCE.

Subdivision 1. **Misdemeanor.** A person is guilty of a misdemeanor if the person intentionally exposes another or the other's property to an obnoxious or harmful gas, fluid, or substance, with intent to injure, molest, or coerce.

Subd. 2. **Felony.** A person who violates subdivision 1 and knows that doing so creates a risk of death or bodily harm or serious property damage is guilty of a felony and may be sentenced to imprisonment for not more than five years or to payment of a fine of not more than $10,000, or both.

HIST: 1989 c 5 s 16

624.74 METAL-PENETRATING BULLETS.

Subdivision 1. **Intent.** This section is designed to give law enforcement officers performing their official duties a reasonable degree of protection from penetration of quality body armor. It is not the intent of this section to restrict the availability of ammunition for personal defense, sporting, or hunting purposes.

Subd. 2. **Definition.** For purposes of this section, "metal-penetrating bullet" means a handgun bullet of 9 mm, .25, .32, .357, .38, .41, .44, or .451 caliber which is comprised of a hardened core equal to the minimum of the maximum attainable hardness by solid red metal alloys which purposely reduces the normal expansion or mushrooming of the bullet's shape upon impact. "Metal-penetrating bullet" excludes any bullet composed of copper or brass jacket with lead or lead alloy cores and any bullet composed of lead or lead alloys.

Subd. 3. **Use or possession in commission of a crime.** Any person who uses or possesses a metal-penetrating bullet during the commission of a crime is guilty of a felony and may be sentenced to imprisonment for not more than three years or to payment of a fine of not more than $5,000, or both. Any imprisonment sentence imposed under this subdivision shall run consecutively to any sentence imposed for the other crime.

Subd. 4. **Local regulation.** This section shall be construed to supersede any municipal or county regulation of ammunition, including its component parts.

HIST: 1982 c 525 s 1; 1984 c 628 art 3 s 11

626.52 REPORTING OF SUSPICIOUS WOUNDS BY HEALTH PROFESSIONALS.

Subdivision 1. **Definition.** As used in this section, "health professional" means a physician, surgeon, person authorized to engage in the practice of healing, superintendent or manager of a hospital, nurse, or pharmacist.

Subd. 2. **Health professionals required to report.** A health professional shall immediately report, as provided under section 626.53, to the local police department or county sheriff all bullet wounds, gunshot wounds, powder burns, or any other injury arising from, or caused by the discharge of any gun, pistol, or any other firearm, which wound the health professional is called upon to treat, dress, or bandage.

A health professional shall report to the proper police authorities any wound that the reporter has reasonable cause to believe has been inflicted on a perpetrator of a crime by a dangerous weapon other than a firearm as defined under section 609.02, subdivision 6.

Subd. 3. **Reporting burns.** A health professional shall file a written report with the state fire marshal within 72 hours after being notified of a burn injury or wound that the professional is called upon to treat, dress, or bandage, if the victim has sustained second- or third-degree burns to five percent or more of the body, the victim has sustained burns to the upper respiratory tract or sustained laryngeal edema from inhaling superheated air, or the victim has sustained a burn injury or wound that may result in the victim's death. The state fire marshal shall provide the form for the report.

Subd. 4. **Immunity from liability.** Any person reporting in good faith and exercising due care shall have immunity from any liability, civil or criminal, that otherwise might result by reason of the person's actions pursuant to this section or section 626.53. No cause of action may be brought against any person for not making a report pursuant to this section or section 626.53.

HIST: (9950-22a) 1935 c 165 s 1; * * * 1Sp2001 c 8 art 12 s 17

626.53 REPORT BY TELEPHONE AND LETTER.

Subdivision 1. **Reports to sheriffs and police chiefs.** The report required by section 626.52, subdivision 2, shall be made forthwith by telephone or in person, and shall be promptly supplemented by letter, enclosed in a securely sealed, postpaid envelope, addressed to the sheriff of the county in which the wound is examined, dressed, or otherwise treated; except that, if the place in which the patient is treated for such injury or the patient's wound dressed or bandaged be in a city of the first, second, or third class, such report shall be made and transmitted as herein provided to the chief of police of such city instead of the sheriff. Except as otherwise provided in subdivision 2, the office of any such sheriff and of any such chief of police shall keep the report as a confidential communication and shall not disclose the name of the person making the same, and the party making the report shall not by reason thereof be subpoenaed, examined, or forced to testify in court as a consequence of having made such a report.

Subd. 2. **Reports to department of health.** Upon receiving a report of a wound caused by or arising from the discharge of a firearm, the sheriff or chief of police shall forward the information contained in the report to the commissioner of health. The commissioner of health shall keep the report as a confidential communication, as provided under subdivision 1. The commissioner shall maintain a statewide, computerized record system containing summary data, as defined in section 13.02, on information received under this subdivision.
HIST: (9950-23) 1935 c 165 s 2; 1986 c 444; 1988 c 548 s 3; 1995 c 244 s 38

626.54 APPLICATION OF SECTIONS 626.52 TO 626.55.

The requirements of sections 626.52 to 626.55 shall not apply to a nurse employed in a hospital nor to a nurse regularly employed by a physician, surgeon, or other person practicing healing, where the employer has made a proper report in compliance therewith.
HIST: (9950-24) 1935 c 165 s 3

626.55 PENALTY.

Subdivision 1. **Gross misdemeanor.** Any person who violates any provision of sections 626.52 to 626.55, other than section 626.52, subdivision 3, is guilty of a gross misdemeanor.
Subd. 2. [Repealed, 1Sp2001 c 8 art 12 s18]
HIST: (9950-25) 1935 c 165 s 4; 1985 c 288 s 2; 1986 c 444; 1988 c 548 s 4

626.553 GUNSHOT WOUNDS; PEACE OFFICERS, DISCHARGING FIREARMS; INVESTIGATIONS, REPORTS.

Subdivision 1. **Report; wounds; investigation.** Upon receipt of the report required in sections 626.52 and 626.53, the sheriff or chief of police receiving the report shall determine the general cause of the wound, and upon determining that the wound was caused by an action connected with the occupation or sport of hunting or shooting the sheriff or chief of police shall immediately conduct a detailed investigation into the facts surrounding the incident or occurrence which occasioned the injury or death reported. The investigating officer shall report the findings of the investigation to the commissioner of natural resources on forms provided by the commissioner for this purpose.

Subd. 2. **Discharge firearm; kill animal.** Whenever a peace officer discharges a firearm in the course of duty, other than for training purposes or the killing of an animal that is sick, injured, or dangerous, notification shall be filed within 30 days of the incident by the officer's department head with the commissioner of public safety. The commissioner of public safety shall forward a copy of the filing to the board of peace officer standards and training. The notification shall contain information concerning the reason for and circumstances surrounding discharge of the firearm. The commissioner of public safety shall file a report with the legislature by November 15 of each even-numbered year containing summary information concerning use of firearms by peace officers.
HIST: 1957 c 407 s 1; * * * 1991 c 141 s 1

626.5531 REPORTING OF CRIMES MOTIVATED BY BIAS.

Subdivision 1. **Reports required.** A peace officer must report to the head of the officer's department every violation of chapter 609 or a local criminal ordinance if the officer has reason to believe, or if the victim alleges, that the offender was motivated to commit the act by the victim's race, religion, national origin, sex, age, disability, or characteristics identified as sexual orientation. The superintendent of the bureau of criminal apprehension shall adopt a reporting form to be used by law enforcement agencies in making the reports required under this section. The reports must include for each incident all of the following:
(1) the date of the offense;

(2) the location of the offense;

(3) whether the target of the incident is a person, private property, or public property;

(4) the crime committed;

(5) the type of bias and information about the offender and the victim that is relevant to that bias;

(6) any organized group involved in the incident;

(7) the disposition of the case;

(8) whether the determination that the offense was motivated by bias was based on the officer's reasonable belief or on the victim's allegation; and

(9) any additional information the superintendent deems necessary for the acquisition of accurate and relevant data.

Subd. 2. **Use of information collected.** The head of a local law enforcement agency or state law enforcement department that employs peace officers licensed under section 626.843 must file a monthly report describing crimes reported under this section with the department of public safety, bureau of criminal apprehension. The commissioner of public safety must summarize and analyze the information received and file an annual report with the department of human rights and the legislature. The commissioner may include information in the annual report concerning any additional criminal activity motivated by bias that is not covered by this section.
HIST: 1988 c 643 s 1; 1989 c 261 s 9; 1992 c 571 art 15 s 12

626.5532 PURSUIT OF FLEEING SUSPECTS BY PEACE OFFICERS.

Subdivision 1. **Reports.** If a peace officer pursues a fleeing suspect, the officer's department head must file a notice of the incident with the commissioner of public safety within 30 days following the pursuit. A pursuit must be reported under this section if it is a pursuit by a peace officer of a motor vehicle being operated in violation of section 609.487. The notice must contain information concerning the reason for and circumstances surrounding the pursuit, including the alleged offense, the length of the pursuit in distance and time, the outcome of the pursuit, any charges filed against the suspect as a result of the pursuit, injuries and property damage resulting from the pursuit, and other information deemed relevant by the commissioner.

Subd. 2. Repealed, 1999 c 216 art 5 s 15
HIST: 1988 c 712 s 17; 1999 c 216 art 5 s 15

Editors' Note: Although the following statutes are not specifically described in these learning objectives, they have been included because of their close relationship to other mandatory reporting of events by peace officers.

626.5533 REPORTING POTENTIAL WELFARE FRAUD.

Subdivision 1. **Reports required.** A peace officer must report to the head of the officer's department every arrest where the person arrested possesses more than one welfare electronic benefit transfer card. Each report must include * * * the name of the suspect [and other detailed information.]

Subd. 2. **Use of information collected.** The head of a local law enforcement agency or state law enforcement department * * * must forward the report required under subdivision 1 to the commissioner of human services within 30 days of receiving the report. The commissioner * * * shall determine whether the suspect is authorized to possess any of the electronic benefit cards found in the suspect's possession. * * *
HIST: 2012 c 247 art 3 s 23

626.5534 USE OF FORCE REPORTING.

Subdivision 1. **Report required.** A chief law enforcement officer must provide the information requested by the Federal Bureau of Investigation about each incident of law enforcement use of force resulting in serious bodily injury or death, as those terms are defined in the Federal Bureau of Investigation's reporting requirements, to the superintendent of the Bureau of Criminal Apprehension. The superintendent shall adopt a reporting form for use by law enforcement agencies in making the report required under this section. The report must include for each incident all of the information requested by the Federal Bureau of Investigation.

Subd. 2. **Use of information collected.** A chief law enforcement officer must file the report under subdivision 1 once a month in the form required by the superintendent. The superintendent must summarize and analyze the information received and submit an annual written report to the chairs and ranking minority members of the house of representatives and senate committees with jurisdiction over public safety. The superintendent shall submit the information to the Federal Bureau of Investigation.

HIST: 2Sp2020 c 1 s 11

626.561 INTERVIEWS WITH CHILD ABUSE VICTIMS.

Subdivision 1. **Policy.** It is the policy of this state to encourage adequate and accurate documentation of the number and content of interviews conducted with alleged child abuse victims during the course of a child abuse assessment, criminal investigation, or prosecution, and to discourage interviews that are unnecessary, duplicative, or otherwise not in the best interests of the child.

Subd. 2. **Definitions.** As used in this section:

(a) "child abuse" means physical or sexual abuse as defined in section 626.556 subdivision 2;

(b) "government employee" means an employee of a state or local agency, and any person acting as an agent of a state or local agency;

(c) "interview" means a statement of an alleged child abuse victim which is given or made to a government employee during the course of a child abuse assessment, criminal investigation, or prosecution; and

(d) "record" means an audio or videotape recording of an interview, or a written record of an interview.

Subd. 3. **Record required.** Whenever an interview is conducted, the interviewer must make a record of the interview. The record must contain the following information:

(1) the date, time, place, and duration of the interview;

(2) the identity of the persons present at the interview; and

(3) if the record is in writing, a summary of the information obtained during the interview.

The records shall be maintained by the interviewer in accordance with applicable provisions of section 626.556, subdivision 11 and chapter 13.

Subd. 4. **Guidelines on tape recording of interviews.** Every county attorney's office shall be responsible for developing written guidelines on the tape recording of interviews by government employees who conduct child abuse assessments, criminal investigations, or prosecutions. The guidelines are public data as defined in section 13.02, subdivision 14.

HIST: 1985 c 286 s 21

626.8473 PORTABLE RECORDING SYSTEMS ADOPTION; WRITTEN POLICY REQUIRED.

Subdivision 1. **Definition.** As used in this section, "portable recording system" has the meaning provided in section 13.825, subdivision 1. * * *

Subd. 3. **Written policies and procedures required.** (a) The chief officer of every state and local law enforcement agency that uses or proposes to use a portable recording system must establish and enforce a written policy governing its use. * * * Use * * * without adoption of a written policy meeting the requirements of this section is prohibited. The written policy must be posted on the agency's Web site, if the agency has a Web site.

(b) At a minimum, the written policy must incorporate the following:

(1) the requirements of section 13.825 and other * * * safeguard * * * requirements of chapter 13[;]

(2) procedures for testing the portable recording system to ensure adequate functioning;

(3) procedures to address a system malfunction or failure, including requirements for documentation by the officer using the system at the time of a malfunction or failure;

(4) circumstances under which recording is mandatory, prohibited, or at the discretion of the officer using the system;

(5) circumstances under which a data subject must be given notice of a recording;

(6) circumstances under which a recording may be ended while an investigation, response or incident is ongoing;

(7) procedures for the secure storage of portable recording system data and the creation of backup copies of the data; and

(8) procedures to ensure compliance and address violations of the policy, which must include, at a minimum, supervisory or internal audits and reviews, and the employee discipline standards for unauthorized access to data contained in section 13.09.

HIST: 2016 c 171 s 6

299C.22 SECURITY GUARD; DISCHARGE OF FIREARMS; REPORT.

Subdivision 1. **Definitions.** For purposes of this section, "security guard" means any person who is paid a fee, wage or salary to perform one or more of the following functions:

(a) Prevention or detection of intrusion, unauthorized entry or activity, vandalism, or trespass on private property;

(b) Prevention or detection of theft, loss, embezzlement, misappropriation, or concealment of merchandise, money, bonds, stocks, notes, or other valuable documents or papers;

(c) Control, regulation, or direction of the flow or movements of the public, whether by vehicle or otherwise, to assure protection of private property;

(d) Protection of individuals from bodily harm; or

(e) Enforcement of policies and rules of the security guard's employer related to crime reduction insofar as such enforcement falls within the scope of the guard's duties.

The provisions of this subdivision are not intended to include within the definition of "security guard" auditors, accountants, and accounting personnel whether or not they are employees of a private firm, corporation or independent accounting firm.

Subd. 2. **Reports.** Each discharge of a firearm by a security guard in the course of employment, other than for training purposes, shall be reported to the chief of police of an organized full-time police department of the municipality in which the discharge occurred or to the county sheriff if there is no local chief of police. Reports required to be made under this subdivision shall be forwarded to the bureau of criminal apprehension upon forms as may be prescribed and furnished by the bureau. The superintendent shall cause a summary of the reports to be compiled and published annually.

HIST: 1979 c 196 s 1; 1986 c 444

299C.53 MISSING PERSONS REPORTS; DUTIES OF COMMISSIONER AND LAW ENFORCEMENT AGENCIES.

Subdivision 1. **Investigation and entry of information.** (a) A law enforcement agency shall accept without delay any report of a missing person. The law enforcement agency shall not refuse to accept a missing person report on the basis that:

(1) the missing person is an adult;

(2) circumstances do not indicate foul play;

(3) the person has been missing for a short amount of time;

(4) the person has been missing for a long amount of time;

(5) there is no indication that the missing person was in the jurisdiction served by the law enforcement agency at the time of the disappearance;

(6) the circumstances suggest that the disappearance may be voluntary;

(7) the reporting person does not have personal knowledge of the facts;

(8) the reporting person cannot provide all of the information requested by the law enforcement agency;

(9) the reporting person lacks a familial or other relationship with the missing person; or

(10) for any other reason, except in cases where the law enforcement agency has direct knowledge that the person is, in fact, not missing and the whereabouts and welfare of the person are known at the time the report is being made.

A law enforcement agency shall accept missing person reports in person. An agency may also accept reports by telephone or other electronic means to the extent the reporting is consistent with the agency's policies or practices.

(b) Upon receiving a report of a person believed to be missing, a law enforcement agency shall conduct a preliminary investigation to determine whether the person is missing, and if missing, whether the person is endangered. If the person is initially determined to be missing and endangered, the agency shall immediately consult the Bureau of Criminal Apprehension during the preliminary investigation, in recognition of the fact that the first two hours are critical. If the person is determined to be missing and endangered, the agency shall immediately enter identifying and descriptive information about the person through the CJIS into the NCIC computer. Law enforcement agencies having direct access to the CJIS and the NCIC computer shall enter and retrieve the data directly and shall cooperate in the entry and retrieval of data on behalf of law enforcement agencies which do not have direct access to the systems.

Subd. 2. **Location of missing person.** As soon as practically possible after a missing person is located, the law enforcement agency which located or returned the missing person shall notify the law enforcement agency having jurisdiction over the investigation, and that agency shall cancel the entry from the NCIC computer.

Subd. 3. **Missing and endangered persons.** If the Bureau of Criminal Apprehension receives a report from a law enforcement agency indicating that a person is missing and endangered, the superintendent may assist the law enforcement agency in conducting the preliminary investigation, offer resources, and assist the agency in helping implement the investigation policy with particular attention to the need for immediate action. The law enforcement agency shall promptly notify all appropriate law enforcement agencies in the state and, if deemed appropriate, law enforcement agencies in adjacent states or jurisdictions of any information that may aid in the prompt location and safe return of a missing and endangered person.

* * *

HIST: 1984 c 510 s 3; 1994 c 636 art 4 s 25,26; 2009 c 38 s 3

Chapter 23 -- MINNESOTA CONTROLLED SUBSTANCE LAWS

Category 2, Section 5:
2.5.1. Describe the basic organization, purpose, and definitions and principles of the Minnesota Criminal Code.
2.5.5. Given a variety of scenarios, identify indications a particular crime has been committed and identify the elements of that crime.

145.38 [Repealed, 1992 c 485 s 3]

145.406 INFORMATION ON THE SALE AND USE OF TOXIC SUBSTANCES.
The commissioner of health shall prepare and distribute materials designed to provide information to retail license businesses on the requirements of section 609.684.
HIST: 1989 c 28 2 s 31; 1992 c 485 s 1

609.684 ABUSE OF TOXIC SUBSTANCES.
Subdivision 1. **Toxic substances.** For purposes of this section, "toxic substance" means:
(1) glue, cement, or aerosol paint containing toluene, benzene, xylene, amyl nitrate, butyl nitrate, nitrous oxide, or containing other aromatic hydrocarbon solvents, but does not include glue, cement, or paint contained in a packaged kit for the construction of a model automobile, airplane, or similar item;
(2) butane or a butane lighter; or
(3) any similar substance declared to be toxic to the central nervous system and to have a potential for abuse, by a rule adopted by the commissioner of health under chapter 14.
Subd. 2. [Repealed 1997 c 239 art 3 s 25]
Subd. 3. **Use for intoxication prohibited.** A person is guilty of a misdemeanor who uses or possesses any toxic substance with the intent of inducing intoxication, excitement, or stupefaction of the central nervous system, except under the direction and supervision of a medical doctor. A person is guilty of a misdemeanor who intentionally aids another in violation of this subdivision.
Subd. 4. **Notice required.** (a) A business establishment that offers for sale at retail any toxic substance must display a conspicuous sign that contains the following, or substantially similar, language:
"NOTICE
It is a misdemeanor for a person to use or possess glue, cement, aerosol paint, with the intent of inducing intoxication, excitement, or stupefaction of the central nervous system. This use can be harmful or fatal." * * *
(c) A business establishment that does not sell any toxic substance listed in subdivision 1 other than butane or butane lighters is not required to post a notice under paragraph (a).
HIST: 1992 c 485 s 2; 1997 c 239 art 3 s 18; 1997 c 239 art 3 s 25

151.01 DEFINITIONS.
* * *
Subd. 5. **Drug.** "Drug" means all medicinal substances and preparations recognized by the United States Pharmacopoeia and National Formulary, or any revision thereof; biological products, other than blood or blood components; all substances and preparations intended for external and internal use in the diagnosis, cure, mitigation, treatment, or prevention of disease in humans or other animals; and all substances and preparations, other than food, intended to affect the structure or any function of the bodies of humans or other animals. The term drug shall also

mean any compound, substance, or derivative that is not approved for human consumption by the United States Food and Drug Administration or specifically permitted for human consumption under Minnesota law, and, when introduced into the body, induces an effect similar to that of a Schedule I or Schedule II controlled substance. * * *

Subd. 16a. **Prescription.** "Prescription" means a prescription drug order that is written or printed on paper, an oral order reduced to writing by a pharmacist, or an electronic order. To be valid, a prescription must be issued for an individual patient by a practitioner within the scope and usual course of the practitioner's practice. * * *

Subd. 17. **Legend drug.** "Legend drug" means a drug that is required by federal law to be dispensed only pursuant to the prescription of a licensed practitioner.

Subd. 18. **Label.** "Label" means a display of written, printed, or graphic matter upon the immediate container of any drug or medicine. Any word, statement, or other information required by or under the authority of this chapter to appear on the label shall also appear on the outside container or wrapper, if any there be, of the retail package of such drug or medicine, or be easily legible through the outside container or wrapper. * * *

HIST: (5808-1) 1937 c 354 s 1; * * * 2015 c 71 art 10 s 26,27; 2016 c 24 s 1,2; 2017 c 84 s 1-3; 2020 c 83, 115 art 1,2 s 19-21, 40-41

151.37 LEGEND DRUGS, WHO MAY PRESCRIBE, POSSESS.

Subdivision 1. **Prohibition.** Except as otherwise provided in this chapter, it shall be unlawful for any person to have in possession, or to sell, give away, barter, exchange, or distribute a legend drug.

Subd. 2. **Prescribing and filing.** (a) A licensed practitioner in the course of professional practice only, may prescribe, administer, and dispense a legend drug, and may cause the same to be administered by a nurse, a physician assistant, or medical student or resident under the practitioner's direction and supervision, and may cause a person who is an appropriately certified, registered, or licensed health care professional to prescribe and administer the same * * *. A licensed practitioner may prescribe a legend drug, without reference to a specific patient, by directing a licensed dietitian or licensed nutritionist * * *; a nurse * * *; physician assistant; or medical student or resident; or pharmacist * * *, to adhere to a particular practice guideline or protocol when treating patients whose condition falls within such guideline or protocol, and when such guideline or protocol specifies the circumstances under which the legend drug is to be prescribed and administered. An individual who verbally, electronically, or otherwise transmits a written, oral, or electronic order, as an agent of a prescriber, shall not be deemed to have prescribed the legend drug. This paragraph applies to a physician assistant only if the physician assistant meets the requirements of ~~section 147A.18~~ sections 147A.02 and 147A.09. * * *

Subd. 2a. **Delegation.** A supervising physician may delegate to a physician assistant * * * the authority to prescribe and administer legend drugs[.]

Subd. 3. **Veterinarians.** A licensed doctor of veterinary medicine, in the course of professional practice only and not for use by a human being, may personally prescribe, administer, and dispense a legend drug, and may cause the same to be administered or dispensed by an assistant under the doctor's direction and supervision.

Subd. 4. **Research.** (a) Any qualified person may use legend drugs in the course of a bona fide research project[.]

Subd. 5. **Exclusion for course of practice.** Nothing in this chapter shall prohibit the sale to, or the possession of, a legend drug by licensed drug wholesalers, licensed manufacturers, registered pharmacies, local detoxification centers, licensed hospitals, bona fide hospitals wherein animals are treated, or licensed pharmacists and licensed practitioners while acting within the course of their practice only.

Subd. 6. **Exclusion for course of employment.** (a) Nothing in this chapter shall prohibit the possession of a legend drug by an employee, agent, or sales representative of a registered drug manufacturer, or an employee or agent of a registered drug wholesaler, or registered pharmacy, while acting in the course of employment. * * *

Subd. 7. **Exclusion for prescriptions.** (a) Nothing in this chapter shall prohibit the possession of a legend drug by a person for that person's use when it has been dispensed to the person in accordance with a written or oral prescription by a practitioner.

(b) Nothing in this chapter shall prohibit a person, for whom a legend drug has been dispensed in accordance with a written or oral prescription by a practitioner, from designating a family member, caregiver, or other individual to handle the legend drug for the purpose of assisting the person in obtaining or administering the drug or sending the drug for destruction. * * *

Subd. 8. **Misrepresentation.** It is unlawful for a person to procure, attempt to procure, possess, or control a legend drug by any of the following means:

(1) deceit, misrepresentation, or subterfuge;

(2) using a false name; or

(3) falsely assuming the title of, or falsely representing a person to be a manufacturer, wholesaler, pharmacist, practitioner, or other authorized person for the purpose of obtaining a legend drug. * * *

Subd. 12. **Administration of opiate antagonists for drug overdose.** (a) A licensed physician, a licensed advanced practice registered nurse * * *, or a licensed physician's assistant * * *, may authorize the following individuals to administer opiate antagonists, as defined in section 604A.04, subdivision 1:

(1) an emergency medical responder[; and]

(2) a peace officer[.] * * *

HIST: 1969 c 933 s 18; * * *; 2016 c 158 art 1 s 69; 2019 c 63 art 2 s 4; 2020 c 115 art 2 s 24-25; 1Sp2021 c 7 art 6 s 3

151.40 POSSESSION AND SALE OF HYPODERMIC SYRINGES AND NEEDLES.

Subdivision 1. **Generally.** [I]t is unlawful for any person to possess, control, manufacture, sell, furnish, dispense, or otherwise dispose of hypodermic syringes or needles or any instrument or implement which can be adapted for subcutaneous injections, except for

(1) [T]he following persons when acting in the course of their practice or employment:

(i) licensed practitioners, and their employees, agents, or delegates;

(ii) licensed pharmacies and their employees or agents;

(iii) licensed pharmacists;

(iv) registered nurses and licensed practical nurses;

(v) registered medical technologists;

(vi) medical interns and residents;

(vii) licensed drug wholesalers and their employees or agents;

(viii) licensed hospitals;

(ix) bona fide hospitals where animals are treated;

(x) licensed nursing homes;

(xi) licensed morticians;

(xii) syringe and needle manufacturers; and their dealers and agents;

(xiii) persons engaged in animal husbandry;

(xiv) clinical laboratories and their employees;

(xv) persons engaged in bona fide research or education or industrial use of hypodermic syringes and needles provided such persons cannot use hypodermic syringes and needles for the administration of drugs to human beings unless such drugs are prescribed, dispensed, and administered by a person lawfully authorized to do so; and

(xvi) persons who administer drugs pursuant to an order or direction of a licensed practitioner;

(2) a person who self-administers drugs pursuant to either the prescription or the direction of a practitioner, or a family member, caregiver, or other individual who is designated by such

person to assist the person in obtaining and using needles and syringes for the administration of such drugs;

(3) a person who is disposing of hypodermic syringes and needles through an [approved] activity or program * * *; or

(4) a person who sells, possesses, or handles hypodermic syringes and needles pursuant to subdivision 2.

Subd. 2. **Sales of limited quantities of clean needles and syringes.** (a) A registered pharmacy or a licensed pharmacist may sell, without the prescription or direction of a practitioner, unused hypodermic needles and syringes in quantities of ten or fewer, provided the pharmacy or pharmacist complies with all of the requirements of this subdivision.

(b) At any location where hypodermic needles and syringes are kept for retail sale under this subdivision, the needles and syringes shall be stored in a manner that makes them available only to authorized personnel and not openly available to customers.
* * *

HIST: 1969 c 933 s 21; 1976 c 222 s 95; 1986 c 444; 1997 c 203 art s 17; 1Sp2019 c 9 art 10 s 41-42

152.01 DEFINITIONS.

Subdivision 1. **Words, terms, and phrases.** Unless the language or context clearly indicates that a different meaning is intended, the following words, terms, and phrases, for the purposes of this chapter, shall be given the meanings subjoined to them.

Subd. 2. **Drug.** The term "drug" includes all medicines and preparations recognized in the United States Pharmacopoeia or National Formulary and any substance or mixture of substances intended to be used for the cure, mitigation, or prevention of disease of either humans or other animals.

Subd. 3. **Administer.** "Administer" means to deliver by, or pursuant to the lawful order of a practitioner a single dose of a controlled substance to a patient or research subject by injection, inhalation, ingestion, or by any other immediate means.

Subd. 4. **Controlled substance.** "Controlled substance" means a drug, substance, or immediate precursor in Schedules I through V of section 152.02. The term shall not include distilled spirits, wine, malt beverages, intoxicating liquors or tobacco.

Subd. 5a. **Hallucinogen.** "Hallucinogen" means any hallucinogen listed in section 152.02, subdivision 2, paragraph (d), or Minnesota Rules, part 6800.4210, item C, except marijuana and Tetrahydrocannabinols.

Subd. 7. **Manufacture.** "Manufacture," in places other than a pharmacy, means and includes the production, cultivation, quality control, and standardization by mechanical, physical, chemical, or pharmaceutical means, packing, repacking, tableting, encapsulating, labeling, relabeling, filling, or by other process, of drugs.

Subd. 9. **Marijuana.** "Marijuana" means all parts the plant of any species of the genus Cannabis, including all agronomical varieties, whether growing or not; the seeds thereof; the resin extracted from any part of such plant; and every compound, manufacture, salt, derivative, mixture, or preparation of such plant, its seeds or resin, but shall not include the mature stalks of such plant, fiber from such stalks, oil or cake made from the seeds of such plant, any other compound, manufacture, salt, derivative, mixture, or preparation of such mature stalks, except the resin extracted therefrom, fiber, oil, or cake, or the sterilized seed of such plant which is incapable of germination. Marijuana does not include [commercially approved] hemp * * *

Subd. 10. **Narcotic drug.** "Narcotic drug" means any of the following, whether produced directly or indirectly by extraction from substances of vegetable origin, or independently by means of chemical synthesis, or by a combination of extraction and chemical synthesis:

(1) Opium, coca leaves, opiates, and methamphetamine;

(2) A compound, manufacture, salt, derivative, or preparation of opium, coca leaves, opiates, or methamphetamine;

(3) A substance, and any compound, manufacture, salt, derivative, or preparation thereof, which is chemically identical with any of the substances referred to in clauses (1) and (2), except that the words "narcotic drug" as used in this chapter shall not include decocainized coca leaves or extracts of coca leaves, which extracts do not contain cocaine or ecgonine.

Subd. 11. **Opiate.** "Opiate" means any dangerous substance having an addiction forming or addiction sustaining liability similar to morphine or being capable of conversion into a drug having such addiction forming or addiction sustaining liability.

Subd. 12a. **Park zone.** "Park zone" means an area designated as a public park by the federal government, the state, a local unit of government, a park district board, or a park and recreation board in a city of the first class. "Park zone" includes the area within 300 feet or one city block, whichever distance is greater, of the park boundary.

Subd. 14a. **School zone.** "School zone" means:

(1) any property owned, leased, or controlled by a school district or an organization operating a nonpublic school, as defined in section 123.932, subdivision 3, where an elementary, middle, secondary school, secondary vocational center or other school providing educational services in grade one through grade 12 is located, or used for educational purposes, or where extracurricular or cocurricular activities are regularly provided;

(2) the area surrounding school property as described in clause (1) to a distance of 300 feet or one city block, whichever distance is greater, beyond the school property; and

(3) the area within a school bus when that bus is being used to transport one or more elementary or secondary school students.

Subd. 15. **Immediate precursor.** "Immediate precursor" means a substance which the state board of pharmacy has found to be and by rule designates as being the principal compound commonly used or produced for use, and which is an immediate chemical intermediary used or likely to be used in the manufacture of a controlled substance, the control of which is necessary to prevent, curtail, or limit such manufacture.

Subd. 15a. **Sell.** "Sell" means:

(1) to sell, give away, barter, deliver, exchange, distribute or dispose of to another, or to manufacture; or

(2) to offer or agree to perform an act listed in clause (1); or

(3) to possess with intent to perform an act listed in clause (1).

Subd. 16. **Small amount.** "Small amount" as applied to marijuana means 42.5 grams or less. This provision shall not apply to the resinous form of marijuana. The weight of fluid used in a water pipe may not be considered in determining a small amount except in cases where the marijuana is mixed with four or more fluid ounces of fluid.

Subd. 18. **Drug paraphernalia.** (a) Except as otherwise provided in paragraph (b), "Drug paraphernalia" means all equipment, products, and materials of any kind, except those items used in conjunction with permitted uses of controlled substances under this chapter or the Uniform Controlled Substances Act, which are knowingly or intentionally used primarily in (1) manufacturing a controlled substance, (2) injecting, ingesting, inhaling, or otherwise introducing into the human body a controlled substance, (3) testing the strength effectiveness, or purity of a controlled substance, or (4) enhancing the effect of a controlled substance.

(b) "Drug paraphernalia" does not include the possession, manufacture, delivery, or sale of: (1) hypodermic needles or syringes in accordance with section 151.40, subdivision 2, or (2) products that detect the presence of fentanyl or a fentanyl analog in a controlled substance.

Subd. 23. **Analog.** * * * "[A]nalog" means a substance, the chemical structure of which is substantially similar to the chemical structure of a controlled substance in Schedule I or II:

(1) that has a stimulant, depressant, or hallucinogenic effect on the central nervous system that is substantially similar to or greater than the stimulant, depressant, or hallucinogenic effect on the central nervous system of a controlled substance in Schedule I or II; or

(2) with respect to a particular person, if the person represents or intends that the substance have a stimulant, depressant, or hallucinogenic effect on the central nervous system that is substantially similar to or greater than the stimulant, depressant, or hallucinogenic effect on the central nervous system of a controlled substance in Schedule I or II.

Subd. 24. **Aggravating factor.** Each of the following is an "aggravating factor":

(1) the defendant, within the previous ten years, has been convicted of a violent crime, as defined in section 609.1095, subdivision 1, paragraph (d), other than a violation of a provision under this chapter, including an attempt or conspiracy, or was convicted of a similar offense by the United States or another state;

(2) the offense was committed for the benefit of a gang under section 609.229;

(3) the offense involved separate acts of sale or possession of a controlled substance in three or more counties;

(4) the offense involved the transfer of controlled substances across a state or international border and into Minnesota;

(5) the offense involved at least three separate transactions in which controlled substances were sold, transferred, or possessed with intent to sell or transfer;

(6) the circumstances of the offense reveal the offender to have occupied a high position the drug distribution hierarchy;

(7) the defendant used a position or status to facilitate the commission of the offense, including positions of trust, confidence, or fiduciary relationships;

(8) the offense involved the sale of a controlled substance to a person under age of 18 or a vulnerable adult as defined in section 609.232, subdivision 11;

(9) the defendant or an accomplice manufactured, possessed, or sold a controlled substance in a school zone, park zone, correctional facility, or drug treatment facility; or

(10) the defendant or an accomplice possessed equipment, drug paraphernalia, documents, or money evidencing that offense involved the cultivation, manufacture, distribution, or possession of controlled substances in quantities substantially larger than the minimum threshold amount for the offense.

HIST: (3899-2, 3899-5, 3899-7, 3906-12) 1921 c 190 s 2, 5, 7; 1Sp2019 c 9 art 11 s 77; 1Sp2021 c 11 art 2 s 1

152.02 SCHEDULES OF CONTROLLED SUBSTANCES; ADMINISTRATION OF CHAPTER.

Subdivision 1. **Five Schedules.** There are established five schedules of controlled substances, to be known as Schedules I, II, III, IV, and V. The schedules consist of the substances listed in this section by whatever official name, common or usual name, chemical name, or trade name designated.

Subd. 7. **Board of Pharmacy; Regulation of Substances.** The board of pharmacy is authorized to regulate and define additional substances which contain quantities of a substance possessing abuse potential in accordance with the following criteria:

(1) The board of pharmacy shall place a substance in Schedule I if it finds that the substance has: A high potential for abuse, no currently accepted medical use in the United States, and a lack of accepted safety for use under medical supervision.

(2) The board of pharmacy shall place a substance in Schedule II if it finds that the substance has: A high potential for abuse, currently accepted medical use in the United States, or currently accepted medical use with severe restrictions, and that abuse may lead to severe psychological or physical dependence.

(3) The board of pharmacy shall place a substance in Schedule III if it finds that the substance has: A potential for abuse less than the substances listed in Schedules I and II, currently accepted medical use in treatment in the United States, and that abuse may lead to moderate or low physical dependence or high psychological dependence.

(4) The board of pharmacy shall place a substance in Schedule IV if it finds that the substance has: A low potential for abuse relative to the substances in Schedule III, currently accepted medical use in treatment in the United States, and that abuse may lead to limited physical dependence or psychological dependence relative to the substances in Schedule III.

(5) The board of pharmacy shall place a substance in Schedule V if it finds that the substance has: A low potential for abuse relative to the substances listed in Schedule IV, currently accepted medical use in treatment in the United States, and limited physical

dependence and/or psychological dependence liability relative to the substance listed in Schedule IV.
HIST: 1971 c 937 s 12; * * * 2015 c 65 art 8 s 1-5; 2016 c 182 s 1,2; 2017 c 95 art 5 s 1-3; 2020 c 115 art 2 s 1-3

152.021 CONTROLLED SUBSTANCE CRIME IN THE FIRST DEGREE.

Subdivision 1. **Sale crimes.** A person is guilty of controlled substance crime in the first degree if:

(1) on one or more occasions within a 90-day period the person unlawfully sells one or more mixtures of a total weight of 17 grams or more containing cocaine or methamphetamine;

(2) on one or more occasions within a 90-day period the person unlawfully sells one or more mixtures of a total weight of ten grams or more containing cocaine or methamphetamine and:

(i) the person or an accomplice possesses on their person or within immediate reach, or uses, whether by brandishing, displaying, threatening with, or otherwise employing, a firearm; or

(ii) the offense involves two aggravating factors;

(3) on one or more occasions within a 90-day period the person unlawfully sells one or more mixtures of a total weight of ten grams or more containing heroin;

(4) on one or more occasions within a 90-day period the person unlawfully sells one or more mixtures of a total weight of 50 grams or more containing a narcotic drug other than cocaine, heroin, or methamphetamine;

(5) on one or more occasions within a 90-day period the person unlawfully sells one or more mixtures of a total weight of 50 grams or more containing amphetamine, phencyclidine, or hallucinogen or, if the controlled substance is packaged in dosage units, equaling 200 or more dosage units, or

(6) on one or more occasions within a 90-day period the person unlawfully sells one or more mixtures of a total weight of 25 kilograms or more containing marijuana or Tetrahydrocannabinols.

Subd. 2. **Possession crimes.** (a) A person is guilty of a controlled substance crime in the first degree if:

(1) the person unlawfully possesses one or more mixtures of a total weight of 50 grams or more containing cocaine or methamphetamine;

(2) the person unlawfully possesses one or more mixtures of a total weight of 25 grams or more containing cocaine or methamphetamine and:

(i) the person or an accomplice possesses on their person or within immediate reach, or uses, whether by brandishing, displaying, threatening with, or otherwise employing, a firearm; or

(ii) the offense involves two aggravating factors;

(3) the person unlawfully possesses one or more mixtures of a total weight of 25 grams or more containing heroin;

(4) the person unlawfully possesses one or more mixtures of a total weight of 500 grams or more containing a narcotic drug other than cocaine, heroin, or methamphetamine;

(5) the person unlawfully possesses one or more mixtures of a total weight of 500 grams or more containing amphetamine, phencyclidine, or hallucinogen or, if the controlled substance is packaged in dosage units, equaling 500 or more dosage units; or

(6) the person unlawfully possesses one or more mixtures of a total weight of 50 kilograms or more containing marijuana or Tetrahydrocannabinols or possesses 500 or more marijuana plants.

(b) For the purposes of this subdivision, the weight of fluid used in a water pipe may not be considered in measuring the weight of a mixture except in cases where the mixture contains four or more fluid ounces of fluid.

Subd. 2a. **Methamphetamine manufacturing crime.** (a) Notwithstanding subdivision 1, sections 152.022, subdivision 1, 152.023, subdivision 1, and 152.024, subdivision 1, a person is guilty of controlled substance crime in the first degree if the person manufactures any amount of methamphetamine.

Editors' Note: The Revisor of Statutes, through a technical change, was directed to move Subd. 2a(b) into a separate statute found below as § 152.0262, Subdivision 1.

Subd. 2b. **Aggravated controlled substance crime in the first degree.** A person is guilty of aggravated controlled substance crime in the first degree if the person violates subdivision 1, clause (1), (2), (3), (4), or (5), or subdivision 2, paragraph (a), clause (1), (2), or (3), and the person or an accomplice sells or possesses 100 or more grams or 500 or more dosage units of a mixture containing the controlled substance at issue and:

(1) the person or an accomplice possesses on their person or within immediate reach, or uses, whether by brandishing, displaying, threatening with, or otherwise employing, a firearm; or

(2) the offense involves two aggravating factors.

Subd. 3. **Penalty.** (a) A person convicted under subdivisions 1 to 2a, paragraph (a), may be sentenced to imprisonment for not more than 30 years or to payment of a fine of not more than $1,000,000, or both.

(b) If the conviction is a subsequent controlled substance conviction, a person convicted under subdivisions 1 to 2a, paragraph (a), shall be committed to the commissioner of corrections for not less than four years nor more than 40 years and, in addition, may be sentenced to payment of a fine of not more than $1,000,000. * * *

(e) In a prosecution under subdivisions 1 to 2b involving sales by the same person in two or more counties within a 90-day period, the person may be prosecuted for all of the sales in any county in which one of the sales occurred.

HIST: 1989 c 290 art 3 s 8; * * * 2011 c 53 s 6; 2016 c 160 s 3

152.022 CONTROLLED SUBSTANCE CRIME IN THE SECOND DEGREE.

Subdivision 1. **Sale crimes.** A person is guilty of controlled substance crime in the second degree if:

(1) on one or more occasions within a 90-day period the person unlawfully sells one or more mixtures of a total weight of ten grams or more containing a narcotic drug other than heroin;

(2) on one or more occasions within a 90-day period the person unlawfully sells one or more mixtures of a total weight of three grams or more containing cocaine or methamphetamine and:

(i) the person or an accomplice possesses on their person or within immediate reach, or uses, whether by brandishing, displaying, threatening with, or otherwise employing, a firearm; or

(ii) the offense involves three aggravating factors.

(3) on one or more occasions within a 90-day period the person unlawfully sells one or more mixtures of a total weight of three grams or more containing heroin;

(4) on one or more occasions within a 90-day period the person unlawfully sells one or more mixtures of a total weight of ten grams or more containing amphetamine, phencyclidine, or hallucinogen or, if the controlled substance is packaged in dosage units, equaling 50 or more dosage units;

(5) on one or more occasions within a 90-day period the person unlawfully sells one or more mixtures of a total weight of ten kilograms or more containing marijuana or Tetrahydrocannabinols;

(6) the person unlawfully sells any amount of a schedule II or narcotic drug to a person under the age of 18, or conspires with or employs a person under the age of 18 to unlawfully sell the substance; or

(7) the person unlawfully sells any of the following in a school zone, a park zone, or a public housing zone, or a drug treatment facility:

(i) any amount of a schedule I or II narcotic drug, or lysergic acid diethylamide (LSD), 3,4-methylenedioxy amphetamine, or 3,4-methylenedioxymethamphetamine;

(ii) one or more mixtures containing methamphetamine or amphetamine; or

(iii) one or more mixtures of a total weight of five kilograms or more containing marijuana or Tetrahydrocannabinols.

Subd. 2. **Possession crimes.** (a) A person is guilty of controlled substance crime in the second degree if:

(1) the person unlawfully possesses one or more mixtures of a total weight of 25 grams or more containing cocaine or methamphetamine;

(2) the person unlawfully possesses one or more mixtures of a total weight of ten grams or more containing a narcotic drug other than cocaine or methamphetamine and:

(i) the person or an accomplice possesses on their person or within immediate reach, or uses, whether by brandishing, displaying, threatening with, or otherwise employing, a firearm; or

(ii) the offense involves three aggravating factors.

(3) the person unlawfully possesses one or more mixtures of a total weight of six grams or more containing heroin;

(4) the person unlawfully possesses one or more mixtures of a total weight of 50 grams or more containing a narcotic drug other than cocaine, heroin, or methamphetamine;

(5) the person unlawfully possesses one or more mixtures of a total weight of 50 grams or more containing amphetamine, phencyclidine, or hallucinogen or, if the controlled substance is packaged in dosage units, equaling 100 or more dosage units; or

(6) the person unlawfully possesses one or more mixtures of a total weight of 25 kilograms or more containing marijuana or Tetrahydrocannabinols, or possesses 100 or more marijuana plants.

(b) For the purposes of this subdivision, the weight of fluid used in a water pipe may not be considered in measuring the weight of a mixture except in cases where the mixture contains four or more fluid ounces of fluid.

Subd. 3. **Penalty.** (a) A person convicted under subdivision 1 or 2 may be sentenced to imprisonment for not more than 25 years or to payment of a fine of not more than $500,000, or both.

(b) If the conviction is a subsequent controlled substance conviction, a person convicted under subdivision 1 or 2 shall be committed to the commissioner of corrections for not less than three years nor more than 40 years and, in addition, may be sentenced to payment of a fine of not more than $500,000.

(c) In a prosecution under subdivision 1 involving sales by the same person in two or more counties within a 90-day period, the person may be prosecuted for all of the sales in any county in which one of the sales occurred.

HIST: 1989 c 290 art 3 s 9; * * * 2011 c 53 s 7; 2016 c 160 s 4

152.023 CONTROLLED SUBSTANCE CRIME IN THE THIRD DEGREE.

Subdivision 1. **Sale crimes.** A person is guilty of controlled substance crime in the third degree if:

(1) the person unlawfully sells one or more mixtures containing a narcotic drug;

(2) on one or more occasions within a 90-day period the person unlawfully sells one or more mixtures containing phencyclidine or hallucinogen, it is packaged in dosage units, and equals ten or more dosage units;

(3) the person unlawfully sells one or more mixtures containing a controlled substance classified in schedule I, II, or III, except a schedule I or II narcotic drug, to a person under the age of 18;

(4) the person conspires with or employs a person under the age of 18 to unlawfully sell one or more mixtures containing a controlled substance listed in schedule I, II, or III, except a schedule I or II narcotic drug; or

(5) on one or more occasions within a 90-day period the person unlawfully sells one or more mixtures of a total weight of five kilograms or more containing marijuana or Tetrahydrocannabinols.

Subd. 2. **Possession crimes.** (a) A person is guilty of controlled substance crime in the third degree if:

(1) on one or more occasions within a 90-day period the person unlawfully possesses one or more mixtures of a total weight of ten grams or more containing a narcotic drug other than heroin;

(2) on one or more occasions within a 90-day period the person unlawfully possesses one or more mixtures of a total weight of three grams or more containing heroin;

(3) on one or more occasions within a 90-day period the person unlawfully possesses one or more mixtures containing a narcotic drug, it is packaged in dosage units, and equals 50 or more dosage units:

(4) on one or more occasions within a 90-day period the person unlawfully possesses any amount of a schedule I or II narcotic drug or five or more dosage units of lysergic acid diethylamide (LSD), 3,4-methylenedioxy amphetamine, or 3,4-methylenedioxymethamphetamine in a school zone, a park zone, or a public housing zone, or a drug treatment facility;

(5) on one or more occasions within a 90-day period the person unlawfully possesses one or more mixtures of a total weight of ten kilograms or more containing marijuana or Tetrahydrocannabinols; or

(6) the person unlawfully possesses one or more mixtures containing methamphetamine or amphetamine in a school zone, a park zone, or a public housing zone, or a drug treatment facility.

(b) For the purposes of this subdivision, the weight of fluid used in a water pipe may not be considered in measuring the weight of a mixture except in cases where the mixture contains four or more fluid ounces of fluid.

Subd. 3. **Penalty.** (a) A person convicted under subdivision 1 or 2 may be sentenced to imprisonment for not more than 20 years or to payment of a fine of not more than $250,000, or both.

(b) In a prosecution under subdivision 1 or 2 involving sales or acts of possession by the same person in two or more counties within a 90-day period, the person may be prosecuted in any county in which one of the sales or acts of possession occurred.

HIST: 1989 c 290 art 3 s 10; * * * 2011 c 53 s 8; 2016 c 160 s 5

152.024 CONTROLLED SUBSTANCE CRIME IN THE FOURTH DEGREE.

Subdivision 1. **Sale crimes.** A person is guilty of controlled substance crime in the fourth degree if:

(1) the person unlawfully sells one or more mixtures containing a controlled substance classified in schedule I, II, or III, except marijuana or Tetrahydrocannabinols;

(2) the person unlawfully sells one or more mixtures containing a controlled substance classified in schedule IV or V to a person under the age of 18;

(3) the person conspires with or employs a person under the age of 18 to unlawfully sell a controlled substance classified in schedule IV or V; or

(4) the person unlawfully sells any amount of marijuana or Tetrahydrocannabinols in a school zone, a park zone, or a public housing zone, or a drug treatment facility, except a small amount for no remuneration.

Subd. 2. **Possession crimes.** A person is guilty of controlled substance crime in the fourth degree if:

(1) the person unlawfully possesses one or more mixtures containing phencyclidine or hallucinogen, it is packaged in dosage units, and equals ten or more dosage units; or

(2) the person unlawfully possesses one or more mixtures containing a controlled substance classified in schedule I, II, or III, except marijuana or Tetrahydrocannabinols, with the intent to sell it.

Subd. 3. **Penalty.** A person convicted under subdivision 1 or 2 may be sentenced to imprisonment for not more than 15 years or to payment of a fine of not more than $100,000, or both.

HIST: 1989 c 290 art 3 s 11; * * * 1997 c 239 art 4 s 12; 2016 c 160 s 6

152.025 CONTROLLED SUBSTANCE CRIME IN THE FIFTH DEGREE.

Subdivision 1. **Sale crimes.** A person is guilty of controlled substance crime in the fifth degree and upon conviction may be sentenced as provided in subdivision 3 if:

(1) the person unlawfully sells one or more mixtures containing marijuana or Tetrahydrocannabinols, except a small amount of marijuana for no remuneration; or

(2) the person unlawfully sells one or more mixtures containing a controlled substance classified in schedule IV.

Subd. 2. **Possession and other crimes.** A person is guilty of controlled substance crime in the fifth degree and upon conviction may be sentenced as provided in subdivision 3 if:

(1) the person unlawfully possesses one or more mixtures containing a controlled substance classified in schedule I, II, III, or IV, except a small amount of marijuana; or

(2) the person procures, attempts to procure, possesses, or has control over a controlled substance by any of the following means:

(i) fraud, deceit, misrepresentation, or subterfuge;

(ii) using a false name or giving false credit; or

(iii) falsely assuming the title of, or falsely representing any person to be, a manufacturer, wholesaler, pharmacist, physician, doctor of osteopathy licensed to practice medicine, dentist, podiatrist, veterinarian, or other authorized person for the purpose of obtaining a controlled substance.

Subd. 3. **Penalty.** (a) A person convicted under the provisions of subdivision 2, clause (1), who has not been previously convicted of a violation of this chapter or a similar offense in another jurisdiction, is guilty of a gross misdemeanor if: (1) the amount of the controlled substance possessed, other than heroin, is less than 0.25 grams or one dosage unit or less if the controlled substance was possessed in dosage units; or (2) the controlled substance possessed is heroin and the amount possessed is less than 0.05 grams.

(b) A person convicted under the provisions of subdivision 1; subdivision 2, clause (1), unless the conduct is described in paragraph (a); or subdivision 2, clause (2), may be sentenced to imprisonment of not more than five years or to payment of a fine of not more than $10,000, or both.

HIST: 1989 c 290 art 3 s 12; * * * 2010 c 382 s 35; 2016 c 160 s 7

152.097 SIMULATED CONTROLLED SUBSTANCES.

Subdivision 1. **Prohibition.** It is unlawful for any person knowingly to manufacture, sell, transfer or deliver or attempt to sell, transfer or deliver a noncontrolled substance upon:

(a) The express representation that the noncontrolled substance is a narcotic or nonnarcotic controlled substance or

(b) The express representation that the substance is of such nature or appearance that the recipient of the delivery will be able to sell, transfer or deliver the substance as a controlled substance; or

(c) Under circumstances which would lead a reasonable person to believe that the substance was a controlled substance. Any of the following factors shall constitute relevant evidence:

(i) The noncontrolled substance was packaged in a manner normally used for the illegal delivery of controlled substances; or

(ii) The delivery or attempted delivery included an exchange of or demand for money or other valuable property as consideration for delivery of the noncontrolled substance, and the amount of the consideration was substantially in excess of the reasonable value of the noncontrolled substance; or

(iii) The physical appearance of the noncontrolled substance is substantially identical to a specified controlled substance.

Subd. 2. **No defense.** In any prosecution under this section, it is no defense that the accused believed the noncontrolled substance to actually be a controlled substance.

Subd. 3. **Exemption.** This section does not apply to the prescribing and dispensing of placebos by licensed practitioners and licensed pharmacists.

Subd. 4. **Penalty.** A person who violates this section may be sentenced to imprisonment for not more than three years or to payment of a fine of not more than $20,000, or both. Sentencing for a conviction for attempting to sell, transfer, or deliver a noncontrolled substance in violation of this section is governed by section 609.17, subdivision 4

HIST: 1982 c 599 s 1; 1989 c 290 art 3 s 18

152.0261 IMPORTING CONTROLLED SUBSTANCES ACROSS STATE BORDERS.

Subdivision 1. **Felony.** A person who crosses a state or international border into Minnesota while in possession of an amount of a controlled substance that constitutes a first degree controlled substance crime under section 152.021, subdivision 2, is guilty of importing controlled substances and may be sentenced as provided in subdivision 3.

Subd. 1a. **Use of person under 18 to import.** A person who conspires with or employs a person under the age of 18 to cross a state or international border into Minnesota while that person or the person under the age of 18 is in possession of an amount of a controlled substance that constitutes a controlled substance crime under sections 152.021 to 152.025, with the intent to obstruct the criminal justice process, is guilty of importing controlled substances and may be sentenced as provided in subdivision 3.

Subd. 2. **Jurisdiction.** A violation of this section may be charged, indicted, and tried in any county, but not more than one county, into or through which the actor has brought the controlled substance.

Subd. 3. **Penalty.** A person convicted of violating this section is guilty of a felony and may be sentenced to imprisonment for not more than 35 years or to payment of a fine of not more than $1,250,000, or both.

HIST: 1990 c 602 art 7 s 7; 1998 c 367 art 4 s 4, 5

Editor's Note: The provisions of the following statute were previously found in §152.021 above.

152.0262 POSSESSION OF SUBSTANCES WITH INTENT TO MANUFACTURE METHAMPHETAMINE CRIME.

Subdivision 1. **Possession of precursors.** (a) A person is guilty of a crime if the person possesses any chemical reagents or precursors with the intent to manufacture methamphetamine and if convicted may be sentenced to imprisonment for not more than ten years or to payment of a fine of not more than $20,000, or both.

(b) A person is guilty of a crime if the person possesses any chemical reagents or precursors with the intent to manufacture methamphetamine and if convicted may be sentenced to imprisonment for not more than 15 years or to payment of a fine of not more than $30,000, or both, if the conviction is for a subsequent controlled substance conviction.

As used in this section and section 152.021, "chemical reagents or precursors" includes any of the following substances, or any similar substances that can be used to manufacture methamphetamine, or the salts, isomers, and salts of isomers of a listed or similar substance:

(1) ephedrine;
(2) pseudoephedrine;
(3) phenyl-2-propanone;
(4) phenylacetone;
(5) anhydrous ammonia;
(6) organic solvents;
(7) hydrochloric acid;
(8) lithium metal;
(9) sodium metal;
(10) ether;
(11) sulfuric acid;
(12) red phosphorus;

(13) iodine;
(14) sodium hydroxide;
(15) benzaldehyde;
(16) benzyl methyl ketone;
(17) benzyl cyanide;
(18) nitroethane;
(19) methylamine;
(20) phenylacetic acid;
(21) hydriodic acid; or
(22) hydriotic acid.

HIST: 1989 c 290 art 3 s 8 * * *

152.027 OTHER CONTROLLED SUBSTANCE OFFENSES.

Subdivision 1. **Sale of schedule V controlled substance.** Except as provided in section 152.02, subdivision 6, a person who unlawfully sells one or more mixtures containing a controlled substance classified in schedule V may be sentenced to imprisonment for not more than one year or to payment of a fine of not more than $3,000, or both.

Subd. 2. **Possession of schedule V controlled substance.** Except as provided in section 152.02, subdivision 6, a person who unlawfully possesses one or more mixtures containing a controlled substance classified in schedule V may be sentenced to imprisonment for not more than one year or to payment of a fine of not more than $3,000, or both. The court may order that a person who is convicted under this subdivision and placed on probation be required to take part in a drug education program as specified by the court.

Subd. 3. **Possession of marijuana in a motor vehicle.** A person is guilty of a misdemeanor if the person is the owner of a private motor vehicle, or is the driver of the motor vehicle if the owner is not present, and possesses on the person, or knowingly keeps or allows to be kept within the area of the vehicle normally occupied by the driver or passengers, more than 1.4 grams of marijuana. This area of the vehicle does not include the trunk of the motor vehicle if the vehicle is equipped with a trunk, or another area of the vehicle not normally occupied by the driver or passengers if the vehicle is not equipped with a trunk. A utility or glove compartment is deemed to be within the area occupied by the driver and passengers.

Subd. 4. **Possession or sale of small amounts of marijuana.** (a) A person who unlawfully sells a small amount of marijuana for no remuneration, or who unlawfully possesses a small amount of marijuana is guilty of a petty misdemeanor and shall be required to participate in a drug education program unless the court enters a written finding that a drug education program is inappropriate. The program must be approved by an area mental health board with a curriculum approved by the state alcohol and drug abuse authority.

(b) A person convicted of an unlawful sale under paragraph (a) who is subsequently convicted of an unlawful sale under paragraph (a) within two years is guilty of a misdemeanor and shall be required to participate in a chemical dependency evaluation and treatment if so indicated by the evaluation.

(c) A person who is convicted of a petty misdemeanor under paragraph (a) who willfully and intentionally fails to comply with the sentence imposed, is guilty of a misdemeanor. Compliance with the terms of the sentence imposed before conviction under this paragraph is an absolute defense.

Subd. 5. **Sale or possession of salvia divinorum.** (a) A person who unlawfully sells any amount of salvia divinorum or salvinorin A is guilty of a gross misdemeanor.

(b) A person who unlawfully possesses any amount of salvia divinorum or salvinorin A is guilty of a misdemeanor.

Subd. 6. **Sale or possession of synthetic cannabinoids.** (a) As used in this subdivision, "synthetic cannabinoid" includes any substance included in section 152.02, subdivision 2, paragraph (h), clause (3).

(b) A person who unlawfully sells any amount of a synthetic cannabinoid for no remuneration is guilty of a gross misdemeanor.

(c) A person who unlawfully sells a synthetic cannabinoid is guilty of a felony and if convicted may be sentenced to imprisonment or not more than five years or to payment of a fine of not more than $10,000, or both.

(d) A person who unlawfully possesses any amount of a synthetic cannabinoid is guilty of a misdemeanor.

(e) Notwithstanding any contrary provision in sections 152.021 to 152.025, this subdivision describes the exclusive penalties for the sale and possession of synthetic cannabinoid.

Subd. 7. **Sale or possession of kratom.** (a) A person who unlawfully sells any amount of kratom or a substance that contains mitragynine or 7-hydorxymitragynine to a person under the age of 18 is guilty of a gross misdemeanor.

(b) A person under the age of 18 who unlawfully possesses any amount of kratom or a substance that contains mitragynine or 7-hydorxymitragynine is guilty of a misdemeanor.
HIST: 1989 c 290 art 3 s 14; * * * 2018 c 195 art 2 s 2

152.0275 CERTAIN CONTROLLED SUBSTANCE OFFENSES; RESTITUTION; PROHIBITIONS ON PROPERTY USE; NOTICE PROVISIONS.

Subdivision 1. **Restitution.**
* * *

(b) A court may require a person convicted of a manufacturing or attempting to manufacture a controlled substance or of an illegal activity involving a precursor substance, where the response to the crime involved an emergency response, to pay restitution to all public entities that participated in the response. The restitution ordered may cover the reasonable costs of their participation in the response.

(c) In addition to the restitution authorized in paragraph (b), a court may require a person convicted of manufacturing or attempting to manufacture a controlled substance or of illegal activity involving a precursor substance to pay restitution to a property owner who incurred removal or remediation costs because of the crime.

Subd. 2. **Property-related prohibitions; notice; web site.**
* * *

(b) A peace officer who arrests a person at a clandestine lab site shall notify the appropriate county or local health department, state duty officer, and child protection services of the arrest and the location of the site.

(c) A county or local health department or sheriff shall order that any property or portion of a property that has been found to be a clandestine lab site and contaminated by substances, chemicals, or items of any kind used in the manufacture of methamphetamine or any part of the manufacturing process, or the by-products or degradates of manufacturing methamphetamine be prohibited from being occupied or used until it has been assessed and remediated as provided in the Department of Health's clandestine drug labs general cleanup guidelines.
HIST: 2005 c 136 art 7 s 9

152.028 PERMISSIVE INFERENCE OF KNOWING POSSESSION.

Subdivision 1. **Residences.** The presence of a controlled substance in open view in a room, other than a public place, under circumstances evincing an intent by one or more of the persons present to unlawfully mix, compound, package, or otherwise prepare for sale the controlled substance permits the factfinder to infer knowing possession of the controlled substance by each person in close proximity to the controlled substance when the controlled substance was found. The permissive inference does not apply to any person if:

(1) one of them legally possesses the controlled substance; or

(2) the controlled substance is on the person of one of the occupants.

Subd. 2. **Passenger automobiles.** The presence of a controlled substance in a passenger automobile permits the factfinder to infer knowing possession of the controlled substance by the driver or person in control of the automobile when the controlled substance was in the automobile. This inference may only be made if the defendant is charged with violating section 152.021, 152.022, 152.023, or 152.0261. The inference does not apply:

(1) to a duly licensed operator of an automobile who is at the time operating it for hire in the lawful and proper pursuit of the operator's trade;

(2) to any person in the automobile if one of them legally possesses a controlled substance; or

(3) when the controlled substance is concealed on the person of one of the occupants.

HIST: 1989 c 209 art 3 s 15; 1990 c 602 art 7 s 8

152.092 POSSESSION OF DRUG PARAPHERNALIA PROHIBITED.

(a) It is unlawful for any person knowingly or intentionally to use or to possess drug paraphernalia. Any violation of this section is a petty misdemeanor.

(b) A person who violates paragraph (a) and has previously violated paragraph (a) on two or more occasions has committed a crime and may be sentenced to imprisonment for up to 90 days or to payment of a fine up to $1,000, or both.

HIST: 1982 c 557 s 2; 2016 c 160 s 9

152.093 MANUFACTURE OR DELIVERY OF DRUG PARAPHERNALIA PROHIBITED.

It is unlawful for any person knowingly or intentionally to deliver drug paraphernalia or knowingly or intentionally to possess or manufacture drug paraphernalia for delivery. Any violation of this section is a misdemeanor.

HIST: 1982 c 557 s 3

152.094 DELIVERY OF DRUG PARAPHERNALIA TO A MINOR PROHIBITED.

Any person 18 years of age or older who violates section 152.093 by knowingly or intentionally delivering drug paraphernalia to a person under 18 years of age who is at least three years younger is guilty of a gross misdemeanor.

HIST: 1982 c 557 s 4; 1986 c 444

152.095 ADVERTISEMENT OF DRUG PARAPHERNALIA PROHIBITED.

It is unlawful for any person knowingly or intentionally to place in any newspaper, magazine, handbill, or other publication any advertisement or promotion for the sale of drug paraphernalia. A violation of this section is a misdemeanor.

HIST: 1982 c 557 s 5

152.0971 TERMS.

Subdivision 1. **Terms.** For purposes of sections 152.0971 to 152.0974, the following terms have the meanings given.

Subd. 2. **Furnish.** "Furnish" means to sell, transfer, deliver, send, or supply a precursor substance by any other means.

Subd. 3. **Supplier.** A "supplier" is a manufacturer, wholesaler, retailer, or any other person in this or any other state who furnishes a precursor substance to another person in this state.

HIST: 1990 c 565 s 22; 1993 c 326 art 3 s 306

152.0972 PRECURSORS OF CONTROLLED SUBSTANCES.

Subdivision 1. **Precursor substances.** The following precursors of controlled substances are "precursor substances":

* * *

(4)   d-lysergic acid;

* * *

(9)   barbituric acid;

* * *

(17) pseudoephedrine;
* * *
(25) benzyl cyanide;
* * *
(30) chloroephedrine;
(31) chloropseudophedrine; and
(32) any substance added to this list by rule adopted by the state board of pharmacy.
* * *
HIST: 1990 c 565 s 23; 1993 c 326 art 3 s 7

152.0973 REPORT OF TRANSACTION.

Subdivision 1. **Predelivery notice.** A supplier who furnishes a precursor substance to a person in this state shall, not less than 21 days before delivery of the substance, submit to the bureau of criminal apprehension a report of the transaction[.]

Subd. 1a. **Report of precursor substances received from out of state.** A purchaser of a precursor substance from outside of Minnesota shall, not less than 21 days before taking possession of the substance, submit to the bureau of criminal apprehension a report[.]

Subd. 2. **Regular reports.** The bureau may authorize a purchaser or supplier to submit the reports on a monthly basis with respect to repeated, regular transactions between the supplier and the purchaser involving the same substance[.]

Subd. 2a. **Report of missing precursor substance.** A supplier or purchaser who discovers a discrepancy between the quantity of precursor substance shipped and the quantity of precursor substance received shall report the discrepancy to the bureau of criminal apprehension within three days of knowledge of the discrepancy. * * *

Subd. 6. **Penalties.** (a) A person who does not submit a report as required by this section is guilty of a misdemeanor.

(b) A person who knowingly submits a report required by this section with false or fictitious information is guilty of a gross misdemeanor.

(c) A person who is convicted a second or subsequent time of violating paragraph (a) is guilty of a gross misdemeanor if the subsequent offense occurred after the earlier conviction.
HIST: 1990 c 565 s 24; 1993 c 326 art 3 s 8-14

152.0974 EXCEPTIONS.

Sections 152.0971 to 152.0974 do not apply to:

(1) a pharmacist or other authorized person who sells or furnishes a precursor substance on the prescription of a physician, dentist, podiatrist, or veterinarian;

(2) a physician, dentist, podiatrist, or veterinarian who administers or furnishes a precursor substance to patients;

(3) a manufacturer or wholesaler licensed by the state board of pharmacy who sells, transfers, or otherwise furnishes a precursor substance to a licensed pharmacy, physician, dentist, podiatrist, or veterinarian; or

(4) the furnishing or receipt of a drug that contains ephedrine, pseudoephedrine, norpseudoephedrine, or phenylpropanolamine and is lawfully furnished over the counter without a prescription under [federal law.]
HIST: 1990 c 565 s 25

152.10 SALES, PERSONS ELIGIBLE.

No person other than a licensed pharmacist, assistant pharmacist or pharmacist intern under the supervision of a pharmacist shall sell a stimulant or depressant drug[.]
HIST: (3906-13) 1939 c 102 s 3; 1967 c 408 s 5; 1991 c 199 art 2 s 1

152.136 ANHYDROUS AMMONIA; PROHIBITED CONDUCT; CRIMINAL PENALTIES; CIVIL LIABILITY.

* * *

Subd. 2. **Prohibited conduct.** (a) A person may not:

(1) steal or unlawfully take or carry away any amount of anhydrous ammonia;

(2) purchase, possess, transfer, or distribute any amount of anhydrous ammonia, knowing, or having reason to know, that it will be used to unlawfully manufacture a controlled substance;

(3) place, have placed, or possess anhydrous ammonia in a container that is not designed, constructed, maintained, and authorized to contain or transport anhydrous ammonia;

(4) transport anhydrous ammonia in a container that is not designed, constructed, maintained, and authorized to transport anhydrous ammonia;

(5) use, deliver, receive, sell, or transport a container designed and constructed to contain anhydrous ammonia without the express consent of the owner or authorized custodian of the container; or

(6) tamper with any equipment or facility used to contain, store, or transport anhydrous ammonia.

* * *

Subd. 4. **Criminal penalty.** A person who knowingly violates subdivision 2 is guilty of a felony and may be sentenced to imprisonment for not more than five years or to payment of a fine of not more than $50,000, or both.

HIST: 2005 c 136 art 7 s 11

152.137 METHAMPHETAMINE-RELATED CRIMES INVOLVING CHILDREN AND VULNERABLE ADULTS.

Subdivision 1. **Definitions.** (a) As used in this section, the following terms have the meanings given. * * *

(b) "Chemical substance" means a substance intended to be used as a precursor in the manufacture of methamphetamine or any other chemical intended to be used in the manufacture of methamphetamine.

(c) "Child" means any person under the age of 18 years. * * *

(f) "Vulnerable adult" has the meaning given in section 609.232, subdivision 11.

Subd. 2. **Prohibited conduct.** (a) No person may knowingly engage in any of the following activities in the presence of a child or vulnerable adult; in the residence of a child or a vulnerable adult; in a building, structure, conveyance, or outdoor location where a child or vulnerable adult might reasonably be expected to be present; in a room offered to the public for overnight accommodation; or in any multiple unit residential building:

(1) manufacturing or attempting to manufacture methamphetamine;

(2) storing any chemical substance;

(3) storing any methamphetamine waste products; or

(4) storing any methamphetamine paraphernalia.

(b) No person may knowingly cause or permit a child or vulnerable adult to inhale, be exposed to, have contact with, or ingest methamphetamine, a chemical substance, or methamphetamine paraphernalia.

Subd. 3. **Criminal penalty.** A person who violates subdivision 2 is guilty of a felony and may sentenced to imprisonment for not more than five years or to payment of a fine of not more than $10,000, or both. * * *

Subd. 5. **Protective custody.** A peace officer may take any child present in an area where any of the activities described in subdivision 2, paragraph (a), clauses (1) to (4), are taking place into protective custody[.] * * *

Subd. 6. **Reporting maltreatment of vulnerable adult.** (a) A peace officer shall make a report of suspected maltreatment of a vulnerable adult if the vulnerable is present in an area where any of the activities described in subdivision 2, paragraph (a), clauses (1) to (4), are taking place, and the peace officer has reason to believe the vulnerable adult inhaled, was exposed to,

had contact with, or ingested methamphetamine, a chemical substance, or methamphetamine paraphernalia. The peace officer shall immediately report to the county common entry point as described in section 626.557, subdivision 9b.
HIST: 2005 c 136 art 7 s 12

152.18 DISCHARGE AND DISMISSAL.

Subdivision 1. **Deferring prosecution for certain first time drug offenders.** (a) A court may defer prosecution as provided in paragraph (c) for any person found guilty, after trial or upon a plea of guilty, of a violation of section 152.023, subdivision 2, 152.024, subdivision 2, 152.025, subdivision 2, or 152.027, subdivision 2, 3, 4, or 6, paragraph (d), for possession of a controlled substance, who:

(1) who has not previously participated in or completed a diversion program authorized under section 401.065;

(2) has not previously been placed on probation without a judgment of guilty and thereafter been discharged from probation under this section; and

(3) has not been convicted of a felony violation of this chapter, including a felony-level attempt or conspiracy, or been convicted by the United States or another state of a similar offense that would have been a felony under this chapter if committed in Minnesota, unless ten years have elapsed since discharge from sentence. * * *
HIST: 1971 c 937 s 18; * * * 2012 c 240 s 3; 2016 c160 s 10

152.22 DEFINITIONS
* * *

Subd. 5c. **Hemp processor.** "Hemp processor" means a person or business licensed by the commissioner or agriculture under chapter 18K to convert raw hemp into a product.

Subd. 6. **Medical cannabis.** (a) "Medical cannabis" means any species of the genus cannabis plant, or any mixture or preparation of them, including whole plant extracts and resins, and is delivered in the form of:
* * *

(3) vaporized delivery method with use of liquid or oil ~~but which does not require the use of dried leaves or plant form; or~~;

(4) combustion with use of dried raw cannabis; or

~~(4)~~ (5) any other method, ~~excluding smoking,~~ approved by the commissioner.
EFFECTIVE DATE. This section is effective the earlier of (1) March 1, 2022, or (2) a date, as determined by the commissioner of health, by which (i) the rules adopted or amended under . . . section 152.26, paragraph (b) are in effect and (ii) independent laboratories under contract with the manufacturers have the necessary procedures and equipment in place to perform the required testing of dried raw cannabis. If this section is effective before March 1, 2022, the commissioner shall provide notice of that effective date to the public.
HIST: 2021 c 30 art 3 s 28, 29

Chapter 24 -- EMERGENCY MENTAL COMMITMENT

Category 2, Section 5:
2.5.7. Explain special Minnesota peace officer duties associated with specific statutes . . .

Editors' Note: In 2005, the descriptive term "mental retardation" and its variations appearing in Chapter 253B was replaced with the descriptive phrase "developmentally disabled" (and its variations).

253B.02 DEFINITIONS.
* * *

Subd. 2. **Chemically dependent person.** "Chemically dependent person" means any person (a) determined as being incapable of self-management or management of personal affairs by reason of the habitual and excessive use of alcohol or drugs, or other mind-altering substances; and (b) whose recent conduct as a result of habitual and excessive use of alcohol, drugs, or other mind-altering substances poses a substantial likelihood of physical harm to self or others as demonstrated by (i) a recent attempt or threat to physically harm self or others, (ii) evidence of recent serious physical problems, or (iii) a failure to obtain necessary food, clothing, shelter, or medical care. "Chemically dependent person" also means a pregnant woman who has engaged during the pregnancy in habitual or excessive use, for a nonmedical purpose, of any of the following controlled substances or their derivatives: cocaine, opium, heroin, phencyclidine, methamphetamine, amphetamine, tetrahydrocannabinol, or alcohol.
* * *

Subd. 6. [Repealed 1Sp2020 c 2 art 6 s 124]
Subd. 9. **Health officer.** "Health officer" means:
(1) a licensed physician;
(2) a licensed psychologist a mental health professional as defined in section 245.462, subdivision 18, clauses (1) to (6);
(3) a licensed social worker;
(4) a registered nurse working in an emergency room of a hospital;
(5) a psychiatric or public health nurse as defined in section 145A.02, subdivision 18;
(6) (5) an advanced practice registered nurse (APRN) as defined in section 148.171, subdivision 3;
(7) (6) a mental health professional practitioner as defined in section 245.462, subdivision 17, providing mental health mobile crisis intervention services as described under section 256B.0624 with the consultation and approval by a mental health professional; or
(8) (7) a formally designated member of a prepetition screening unit established by section 253B.07.
Subd. 10. **Interested person.** "Interested person" means:
(1) an adult who has a specific interest in the patient or proposed patient, including but not limited to, a public official, including a local welfare agency acting under section 626.5561, and 260E.31; a health care or mental health provider or the provider's employee or agent; the legal guardian, spouse, parent, legal counsel, adult child, or next of kin, ; or other person designated by a patient or proposed patient; or
(2) a health plan company that is providing coverage for a proposed patient.
Subd. 13. **Person who is mentally ill poses a risk of harm due to mental illness.** (a) A "person who is mentally ill poses a risk of harm due to mental illness" means any person who has an organic disorder of the brain or a substantial psychiatric disorder of thought, mood, perception, orientation, or memory which that grossly impairs judgment, behavior, capacity to recognize reality, or to reason or understand, which that is manifested by instances of grossly

disturbed behavior or faulty perceptions; and <u>who, due to this impairment,</u> poses a substantial likelihood of physical harm to self or others as demonstrated by:

(1) a failure to obtain necessary food, clothing, shelter, or medical care as a result of the impairment;

(2) an inability for reasons other than indigence to obtain necessary food, clothing, shelter, or medical care as a result of the impairment and it is more probable than not that the person will suffer substantial harm, significant psychiatric deterioration or debilitation, or serious illness, unless appropriate treatment and services are provided;

(3) a recent attempt or threat to physically harm self or others; or

(4) recent and volitional conduct involving significant damage to substantial property.

(b) A person is not mentally ill under section if the impairment is solely due to:

(1) epilepsy;

(2) developmental disability;

(3) brief periods of intoxication caused by alcohol, drugs, or other mind-altering substances; or

(4) dependence upon or addiction to any alcohol, drugs, or other mind-altering substances.

* * *

Subd. 14. **Developmentally disabled person.** "Developmentally disabled person" means any person: (a) who has been diagnosed as having significantly subaverage intellectual functioning existing concurrently with demonstrated deficits in adaptive behavior and who manifests these conditions prior to the person's 22nd birthday; and (b) whose recent conduct is a result of developmental disability and poses a substantial likelihood of physical harm to self or others in that there has been (i) a recent attempt or threat to physically harm self or others, or (ii) a failure and inability to obtain necessary food, clothing, shelter, safety, or medical care.

<u>Subd. 16. **Peace officer.** "Peace officer" means a sheriff or deputy sheriff; or municipal or other local police officer, or a State Patrol officer when engaged in the authorized duties of office.</u>

Subd. 17. **Person who** ~~is mentally ill~~ **<u>has a mental illness</u> and <u>is</u> dangerous to the public.** A "person who ~~is mentally ill~~ and <u>is</u> dangerous to the public" is a person<u>:</u>

<u>(1)</u> ~~(a)~~ who ~~is mentally ill~~; <u>has an organic disorder of the brain or a substantial psychiatric disorder of thought, mood, perception, orientation, or memory that grossly impairs judgment, behavior, capacity to recognize reality, or to reason or understand, and is manifested by instances of grossly disturbed behavior or faulty perceptions; and</u>

<u>(2)</u> ~~(b)~~ who as a result of that ~~mental illness~~ <u>impairment</u> presents a clear danger to the safety of others as demonstrated by the facts that (i) the person has engaged in an overt act causing or attempting to cause serious physical harm to another and (ii) there is a substantial likelihood that the person will engage in acts capable of inflicting serious physical harm on another. ~~A person committed as a psychopathic personality as defined in subdivision 18a and 18b is subject to the provisions of this chapter that apply to persons who are mentally ill and dangerous to the public.~~

Subd. 19. **Treatment facility.** "Treatment facility" means a <u>non-state-operated</u> hospital, ~~community mental health center, or other treatment provider~~ <u>residential treatment provider, crisis residential withdrawal management center, or corporate foster care home</u> qualified to provide care and treatment for persons ~~who are mentally ill, developmentally disabled, or chemically dependent~~ <u>who have a mental illness, developmental disability, or chemical dependency.</u>

HIST: 1981 c 37 s 2; * * * 2013 c 49 s 1,2<u>; 1Sp2020 c 2 art 6 s 5-9, 11, 123-24</u>

Category 2, Section 5:

2.5.7. Explain special Minnesota peace officer duties associated with specific statutes . . .

253B.05 EMERGENCY ADMISSION.
    Subdivision 1. [Repealed 1Sp2020 c 2 art 6 s 124]
    Subd. 2. [Repealed 1Sp2020 c 2 art 6 s 124]

    Subd. 2a. [Repealed 1997 c 217 art 2 s 118]
    Subd. 2b. [Repealed 1Sp2020 c 2 art 6 s 124]
    Subd. 3. [Repealed 1Sp2020 c 2 art 6 s 124]
    Subd. 4. [Repealed 1Sp2020 c 2 art 6 s 124]
    Subd. 5. [Repealed 1997 c 217 art 2 s 118]
HIST: 1982 c 581 s 5; * * * 2010 c 357 s 3; 2016 c 120 s 1-3; 2017 c 85 s 1; 1Sp2020 c 2 art 6 s 124

253B.051 EMERGENCY ADMISSION.
    Subdivision 1. **Peace officer or health officer authority.** (a) If a peace officer or health officer has reason to believe, either through direct observation of the person's behavior or upon reliable information of the person's recent behavior and, if available, knowledge or reliable information concerning the person's past behavior or treatment that the person:
    (1) has a mental illness or developmental disability and is in danger of harming self or others if the officer does not immediately detain the patient, the peace officer or health officer may take the person into custody and transport the person to an examiner or a treatment facility, state-operated treatment program, or community-based treatment program;
    (2) is chemically dependent or intoxicated in public and in danger of harming self or others if the officer does not immediately detain the patient, the peace officer or health officer may take the person into custody and transport the person to a treatment facility, state-operated treatment program, or community-based treatment program; or
    (3) is chemically dependent or intoxicated in public and not in danger of harming self, others, or property, the peace officer or health officer may take the person into custody and transport the person to the person's home.
    (b) An examiner's written statement or a health officer's written statement in compliance with the requirements of subdivision 2 is sufficient authority for a peace officer or health officer to take the person into custody and transport the person to a treatment facility, state-operated treatment program, or community-based treatment program.
    (c) A peace officer or health officer who takes a person into custody and transports the person to a treatment facility, state-operated treatment program, or community-based treatment program under this subdivision shall make written application for admission of the person containing:
    (1) the officer's statement specifying the reasons and circumstances under which the person was taken into custody;
    (2) identifying information on specific individuals to the extent practicable, if danger to those individuals is a basis for the emergency hold; and
    (3) the officer's name, the agency that employs the officer, and the telephone number or other contact information for purposes of receiving notice under subdivision 3.
    (d) A copy of the examiner's written statement and officer's application shall be made available to the person taken into custody.

    (e) The officer may provide the transportation personally or may arrange to have the person transported by a suitable medical or mental health transportation provider. As far as practicable, a peace officer who provides transportation for a person placed in a treatment facility, state-operated treatment program, or community-based treatment program under this subdivision must not be in uniform and must not use a vehicle visibly marked as a law enforcement vehicle.

Subd. 2. **Emergency hold.** (a) A treatment facility, state-operated treatment program, or community-based treatment program, other than a facility operated by the Minnesota sex offender program, may admit or hold a patient, including a patient transported under subdivision 1, for emergency care and treatment if the head of the facility or program consents to holding the patient and an examiner provides a written statement in support of holding the patient.

(b) The written statement must indicate that:

(1) the examiner examined the patient not more than 15 days prior to admission;

(2) the examiner interviewed the patient, or if not, the specific reasons why the examiner did not interview the patient;

(3) the examiner has the opinion that the patient has a mental illness or developmental disability, or is chemically dependent and is in danger of causing harm to self or others if a facility or program does not immediately detain the patient. The statement must include observations of the patient's behavior and avoid conclusory language. The statement must be specific enough to provide an adequate record for review. If danger to specific individuals is a basis for the emergency hold, the statement must identify those individuals to the extent practicable; and

(4) the facility or program cannot obtain a court order in time to prevent the anticipated injury.

(c) Prior to an examiner writing a statement, if another person brought the patient to the treatment facility, state-operated treatment program, or community-based treatment program, the examiner shall make a good-faith effort to obtain information from that person, which the examiner must consider in deciding whether to place the patient on an emergency hold. To the extent available, the statement must include direct observations of the patient's behaviors, reliable knowledge of the patient's recent and past behavior, and information regarding the patient's psychiatric history, past treatment, and current mental health providers. The examiner shall also inquire about health care directives under chapter 145C and advance psychiatric directives under section 253B.03, subdivision 6d.

(d) The facility or program must give a copy of the examiner's written statement to the patient immediately upon initiating the emergency hold. The treatment facility, state-operated treatment program, or community-based treatment program shall maintain a copy of the examiner's written statement. The program or facility must inform the patient in writing of the right to (1) leave after 72 hours, (2) have a medical examination within 48 hours, and (3) request a change to voluntary status. The facility or program shall assist the patient in exercising the rights granted in this subdivision.

(e) The facility or program must not allow the patient nor require the patient's consent to participate in a clinical drug trial during an emergency admission or hold under this subdivision. If a patient gives consent to participate in a drug trial during a period of an emergency admission or hold, it is void and unenforceable. This paragraph does not prohibit a patient from continuing participation in a clinical drug trial if the patient was participating in the clinical drug trial at the time of the emergency admission or hold.

Subd. 3. **Duration of hold, release procedures, and change of status**. (a) If a peace officer or health officer transports a person to a treatment facility, state-operated treatment program, or community-based treatment program under subdivision 1, an examiner at the facility or program must examine the patient and make a determination about the need for an emergency hold as soon as possible and within 12 hours of the person's arrival. The peace officer or health officer hold ends upon whichever occurs first: (1) initiation of an emergency hold on the person under subdivision 2; (2) the person's voluntary admission; (3) the examiner's decision not to admit the person; or (4) 12 hours after the person's arrival.

(b) Under this section, the facility or program may hold a patient up to 72 hours, exclusive of Saturdays, Sundays, and legal holidays, after the examiner signs the written statement for an emergency hold of the patient. The facility or program must release a patient when the emergency hold expires unless the facility or program obtains a court order to hold the patient. The facility or program may not place the patient on a consecutive emergency hold under this section.

(c) If the interested person files a petition to civilly commit the patient, the court may issue a judicial hold order pursuant to section 253B.07, subdivision 2b.

(d) During the 72-hour hold, a court must not release a patient under this section unless the court received a written petition for the patient's release and the court has held a summary hearing regarding the patient's release.

(e) The written petition for the patient's release must include the patient's name, the basis for the hold, the location of the hold, and a statement explaining why the hold is improper. The petition must also include copies of any written documentation under subdivision 1 or 2 that support the hold, unless the facility or program holding the patient refuses to supply the documentation. Upon receipt of a petition, the court must comply with the following:

(1) the court must hold the hearing as soon as practicable and the court may conduct the hearing by telephone conference call, interactive video conference, or similar method by which the participants are able to simultaneously hear each other;

(2) before deciding to release the patient, the court shall make every reasonable effort to provide notice of the proposed release and reasonable opportunity to be heard to:

(i) any specific individuals identified in a statement under subdivision 1 or 2 or individuals identified in the record who might be endangered if the person is not held;

(ii) the examiner whose written statement was the basis for the hold under subdivision 2; and

(iii) the peace officer or health officer who applied for a hold under subdivision 1; and

(3) if the court decides to release the patient, the court shall direct the patient's release and shall issue written findings supporting the decision. The facility or program must not delay the patient's release pending the written order.

(f) Notwithstanding section 144.293, subdivisions 2 and 4, if a treatment facility, state-operated treatment program, or community-based treatment program releases or discharges a patient during the 72-hour hold; the examiner refuses to admit the patient; or the patient leaves without the consent of the treating health care provider, the head of the treatment facility, state-operated treatment program, or community-based treatment program shall immediately notify the agency that employs the peace officer or health officer who initiated the transport hold. This paragraph does not apply to the extent that the notice would violate federal law governing the confidentiality of alcohol and drug abuse patient records under Code of Federal Regulations, title 42, part 2.

(g) If a patient is intoxicated in public and a facility or program holds the patient under this section for detoxification, a treatment facility, state-operated treatment program, or community-based treatment program may release the patient without providing notice under paragraph (f) as soon as the treatment facility, state-operated treatment program, or community-based treatment program determines that the person is no longer in danger of causing harm to self or others. The facility or program must provide notice to the peace officer or health officer who transported the person, or to the appropriate law enforcement agency, if the officer or agency requests notification.

(h) A treatment facility or state-operated treatment program must change a patient's status to voluntary status as provided in section 253B.04 upon the patient's request in writing if the head of the facility or program consents to the change.

HIST: 1Sp2020 c 2 art 6 s 33

253B.10 PROCEDURES UPON COMMITMENT.

Subdivision 1. **Administrative requirements.** (a) When a person is committed, the court shall issue a warrant or an order committing the patient to the custody of the head of the treatment facility. The warrant or order shall state that the patient meets the statutory criteria for civil commitment.

(b) The commissioner shall prioritize patients being admitted from jail or a correctional institution. * * *

(c) Upon the arrival of a patient at the designated treatment facility, state-operated treatment program, or community-based treatment program, the head of the facility or program shall retain the duplicate of the warrant and endorse receipt upon the original warrant, or acknowledge receipt of the order. The endorsed receipt or acknowledgment must be filed in the court of commitment. After arrival, the patient shall be under the control and custody of the head of the ~~treatment~~ facility or program.

(d) Copies of the petition for commitment, the court's findings of fact and conclusions of law, the court order committing the patient, the report of the court examiners, and the prepetition report, and any medical and behavioral information available shall be provided at the time of admission of a patient to the designated treatment facility or program to which the patient is committed. ~~This information shall also be provided by the head of the treatment facility to treatment facility staff.~~ Upon a patient's referral to the commissioner of human services for admission pursuant to subdivision 1, paragraph (b), any inpatient hospital, treatment facility, jail, or correctional facility that has provided care or supervision to the patient in the previous two years shall, when requested by the treatment facility or commissioner, provide copies of the patient's medical and behavioral records to the Department of Human Services for purposes of preadmission planning. This information shall be provided by the head of the treatment facility to treatment facility staff in a consistent and timely manner and pursuant to all applicable laws.

Subd. 2. **Transportation.** (a) When a ~~proposed~~ patient is about to be placed in a treatment facility, state-operated treatment program, or community-based treatment program, the court may order the designated agency, the treatment facility, state-operated treatment program, or community-based treatment program, or any responsible adult to transport the patient ~~to the treatment facility~~. A protected transport provider may transport the patient according to section 256B.0625, subdivision 17. Whenever possible, a peace officer who provides the transportation shall not be in uniform and shall not use a vehicle visibly marked as a ~~police~~ law enforcement vehicle. The proposed patient may be accompanied by one or more interested persons.

(b) When a patient who is at a ~~regional~~ state-operated treatment ~~center~~ program requests a hearing is to be held for adjudication of a patient's status pursuant to section 253B.17, the commissioner shall provide transportation.

Subd. 3. **Notice of admission.** Whenever a committed person has been admitted to a treatment facility, state-operated treatment program, or community-based treatment program, under the provisions of sections 253B.09 or 253B.18, the head of the ~~treatment~~ facility or program shall immediately notify the patient's spouse, health care agent, or parent and the county of financial responsibility if the county may be liable for a portion of the cost of treatment. If the committed person was admitted upon the petition of a spouse, health care agent, or parent the head of the treatment facility, state-operated treatment program, or community-based treatment program shall notify an interested person other than the petitioner.

Subd. 4. **Private treatment.** Patients or other responsible persons are required to pay the necessary charges for patients committed or transferred to ~~private~~ treatment facilities or community-based treatment programs. ~~Private~~ Treatment facilities or community-based treatment programs may not refuse to accept a committed person solely based on the person's court-ordered status. Insurers must provide treatment and services as ordered by the court under section 253B.045, subdivision 6, or as required under chapter 62M.

Subd. 5. **Transfer to voluntary status.** At any time prior to the expiration of the initial commitment period, a patient who has not been committed as ~~mentally ill~~ a person who has a mental illness and is dangerous to the public or ~~as~~ a sexually dangerous person or ~~as~~ a sexual psychopathic personality may be transferred to voluntary status upon the patient's application in writing with the consent of the head of the facility or program to which the person is committed. Upon transfer, the head of the treatment facility, state-operated treatment program, or community-based treatment program shall immediately notify the court in writing and the court shall terminate the proceedings.

HIST: 1982 c 581 s 10; * * * 2013 c 108 art 4 s 11; 1Sp2017 c 6 art 6 s 2; 1Sp2020 c 2 art 6 s 6

Chapter 25 -- MINNESOTA LIQUOR LAWS

Category 2, Section 5:
2.5.5. Given a variety of scenarios, identify indications a particular crime has been committed, and identify the elements of that crime.

340A.503 PERSONS UNDER 21; ILLEGAL ACTS.

Subdivision 1. **Consumption.** (a) It is unlawful for any:

(1) retail intoxicating liquor or nonintoxicating liquor licensee, municipal liquor store, or bottle club permit holder under section 340A.414, to permit any person under the age of 21 years to drink alcoholic beverages on the licensed premises or within the municipal liquor store; or

(2) person under the age of 21 years to consume any alcoholic beverages. If proven by a preponderance of the evidence, it is an affirmative defense to a violation of this clause that the defendant consumed the alcoholic beverage in the household of the defendant's parent or guardian and with the consent of the parent or guardian.

(b) An offense under paragraph (a), clause (2), may be prosecuted either in the jurisdiction where consumption occurs or the jurisdiction where evidence of consumption is observed.

(c) As used in this subdivision, "consume" includes the ingestion of an alcoholic beverage and the physical condition of having ingested an alcoholic beverage.

Subd. 2. **Purchasing.** It is unlawful for any person:

(1) to sell, barter, furnish, or give alcoholic beverages to a person under 21 years of age;

(2) under the age of 21 years to purchase or attempt to purchase any alcoholic beverage unless under the supervision of a responsible person over the age of 21 for training, education, or research purposes. Prior notification of the licensing authority is required unless the supervised alcohol purchase attempt is for professional research conducted by post-secondary educational institutions or state, county, or local health departments; or

(3) to induce a person under the age of 21 years to purchase or procure any alcoholic beverage, or to lend or knowingly permit the use of the person's driver's license, permit, Minnesota identification card, or other form of identification by a person under the age of 21 years for the purpose of purchasing or attempting to purchase an alcoholic beverage.

If proven by a preponderance of the evidence, it shall be an affirmative defense to a violation of clause (1) that the defendant is the parent or guardian of the person under 21 years of age and that the defendant gave or furnished the alcoholic beverage to that person solely for consumption in the defendant's household.

Subd. 3. **Possession.** It is unlawful for a person under the age of 21 years to possess any alcoholic beverage with the intent to consume it at a place other than the household of the person's parent or guardian. Possession at a place other than the household of the parent or guardian creates a rebuttable presumption of intent to consume it at a place other than the household of the parent or guardian. * * *

Subd. 4. **Entering licensed premises.** (a) It is unlawful for a person under the age of 21 years to enter an establishment licensed for the sale of alcoholic beverages or any municipal liquor store for the purpose of purchasing or having served or delivered any alcoholic beverage.

(b) Notwithstanding section 340A.509, no ordinance enacted by a statutory or home rule charter city may prohibit a person 18, 19, or 20 years old from entering an establishment licensed under this chapter to:

(1) perform work for the establishment, including the serving of alcoholic beverages, unless otherwise prohibited by section 340A.412, subdivision 10;

(2) consume meals; and

(3) attend social functions that are held in a portion of the establishment where liquor is not sold.

Subd. 5. **Misrepresentation of age.** It is unlawful for a person under the age of 21 years to claim to be 21 years old or older for the purpose of purchasing alcoholic beverages.

Subd. 5a. **Attainment of age.** With respect to purchasing, possessing, consuming, selling, furnishing, and serving alcoholic beverages, a person is not 21 years of age until 8:00 a.m. on the day of that person's 21st birthday.

Subd. 6. **Proof of age; defense; seizure of false identification.** (a) Proof of age for purchasing or consuming alcoholic beverages may be established only by one of the following:

(1) a valid driver's license or identification card issued by Minnesota, another state, or a province of Canada, and including the photograph and date of birth of the licensed person;

(2) a valid military identification card issued by the United States Department of Defense;

(3) a valid passport issued by the United States;

(4) a valid instructional permit issued * * * to a person * * *; or

(5) in the case of a foreign national, by a valid passport.

(b) In a prosecution under subdivision 2, clause (1), it is a defense for the defendant to prove by a preponderance of the evidence that the defendant reasonably and in good faith relied upon representations of proof of age authorized in paragraph (a) in selling, bartering, furnishing, or giving the alcoholic beverage.

(c) A licensed retailer or municipal liquor store may seize a form of identification listed under paragraph (a) if the retailer or municipal liquor store has reasonable grounds to believe that the form of identification has been altered or falsified or is being used to violate any law. A retailer or municipal liquor store that seizes a form of identification as authorized under this paragraph must deliver it to a law enforcement agency, within 24 hours of seizing it.
* * *

Subd. 8. **Prosecution; immunity.** (a) A person is not subject to prosecution under subdivision 1, paragraph (a), clause (2), or subdivision 3, if the person contacts a 911 operator to report that the person or another person is in need of medical assistance for an immediate health or safety concern, provided that the person who initiates contact is the first person to make such a report, provides a name and contact information, remains on the scene until assistance arrives, and cooperates with the authorities at the scene.

(b) The person who receives medical assistance shall also be immune from prosecution under paragraph (a).

(c) Paragraph (a) also applies to one or two persons acting in concert with the person initiating contact provided that all the requirements of paragraph (a) are met.
HIST: 1985 c 305 art 7 s 3; * * * 2015 c 9 art 2 s 6

340A.504 HOURS AND DAYS OF SALE.

Subdivision 1. **3.2 percent malt liquor.** No sale of 3.2 percent malt liquor may be made a.m. and 10:00 a.m. on Sunday, provided that an establishment between 2:00 a.m. and 8:00 a.m. on the days of Monday through Saturday, nor between 2:00 a.m. and 12:00 noon on Sunday.

Subd. 2. **Intoxicating liquor; on-sale.** No sale of intoxicating liquor for consumption on the licensed premises may be made:

(1) between 2:00 a.m. and 8:00 a.m. on the days of Monday through Saturday;

(2) after 2:00 a.m. on Sundays, except as provided by subdivision 3. * * *

Subd. 3. **Intoxicating liquor; Sunday sales; on-sale.** (a) A restaurant, club, bowling center, or hotel with a seating capacity for at least 30 persons and which holds an on-sale intoxicating liquor license may sell intoxicating liquor for consumption on the premises in conjunction with the sale of food between the hours of 8:00 a.m. on Sundays and 2:00 a.m. on Mondays.

(b) An establishment serving intoxicating liquor on Sundays must obtain a Sunday license. * * *

(c) A city may issue a Sunday intoxicating liquor license only if authorized to do so by the voters of the city voting on the question at a general or special election. A county may issue a Sunday intoxicating liquor license in a town [or unorganized territory] only if authorized to do so by the voters[.]

(e) Voter approval is not required for licenses issued by the metropolitan airports commission or common carrier licenses issued by the commissioner. Common carriers serving intoxicating liquor on Sunday must obtain a Sunday license.

Subd. 4. **Intoxicating liquor; off-sale.** (a) No sale of intoxicating liquor may be made by an off-sale licensee:

(1) on Sundays, except between the hours of 11:00 a.m. and 6:00 p.m.;

(2) before 8:00 a.m. or after 10:00 p.m. on Monday through Saturday;

(3) on Thanksgiving Day;

(4) on Christmas Day, December 25; or

(5) after 8:00 p.m. on Christmas Eve, December 24.

(b) No delivery of alcohol to an off-sale or on-sale licensee may be made by a wholesaler or accepted by an off-sale or on-sale licensee on a Sunday. No order solicitation or merchandising may be made by a wholesaler on a Sunday.

Subd. 5. **Bottle clubs.** No establishment licensed under section 340A.414, may permit a person to consume or display intoxicating liquor, and no person may consume or display intoxicating liquor between 1:00 a.m. and 12:00 noon on Sundays, and between 1:00 a.m. and 8:00 a.m. on Monday through Saturday.

Subd. 6. **Municipalities may limit hours.** A municipality may further limit the days or hours of on and off sales of alcoholic beverages, provided that further restricted on-sale hours for intoxicating liquor must apply equally to on-sale hours of 3.2 percent malt liquor. * * *

Subd. 7. **Sales after 1:00 a.m.; permit fee.** (a) No licensee may sell intoxicating liquor or 3.2 percent malt liquor on-sale between the hours of 1:00 a.m. and 2:00 a.m. unless the licensee has obtained a permit from the commissioner. * * *

HIST: 1985 c 139 s 1; * * *; 2017 c 6 s 1; 1Sp2017 c 4 art 5 s 9; 2020 c 103 s 3

340A.513 SALE OF BEER KEGS.

Subdivision 1. **Definitions.** For purposes of this section:

(a) "Beer keg" means any brewery-sealed, single container that contains not less than seven gallons of malt liquor.

(b) "Off-sale retailer" means a holder of a license under this chapter to sell alcoholic beverages at off-sale or a municipal liquor store.

Subd. 2. **Standards.** No off-sale retailer shall sell beer kegs unless that retailer affixes an identification label or tag to each beer keg. * * * The identification information contained on the label or tag shall include the licensed off-sale retailer's name, address, and telephone number; a unique beer keg number assigned by the retailer; and a prominently visible warning that intentional removal or defacement of the label or tag is a criminal offense. * * *

Subd. 3. **Identification required.** An off-sale retailer may not sell a beer keg unless the beer keg has attached an identification label or tag[.]

Subd. 4. **Retailers to keep records.** (a) An off-sale retailer who sells a beer keg must at the time of the sale record:

(1) the number of the purchaser's driver's license, Minnesota identification card, military identification card, or valid United States or foreign passport;

(2) the date and time of the purchase;

(3) the beer keg identification number required under subdivision 3; and

(4) the purchaser's signature.

(b) The record must be retained for not less than 90 days after the date of the sale.

Subd. 5. **Access to records.** An off-sale retailer required to retain records under subdivision 4 must make the records available during regular business hours for inspection by a peace officer, the commissioner, or an agent of the commissioner.

Subd. 6. **Violations.** (a) A person required to record information under subdivision 4 may not knowingly make a materially false entry in the book or register required under subdivision 4. In a prosecution under this subdivision, it is a defense for the defendant to prove by a preponderance of the evidence that the defendant reasonably and in good faith relied upon the identification provided by the purchaser of a beer keg.

(b) No person other than an off-sale retailer, a licensed wholesaler of malt beverages, a peace officer, the commissioner, or an agent of the commissioner may intentionally remove identification placed on a beer keg in compliance with subdivision 3. No person may intentionally deface or damage the identification on a beer keg to make it unreadable.
HIST: 2002 c 232 s 1

340A.502 SALES TO OBVIOUSLY INTOXICATED PERSONS.

No person may sell, give, furnish, or in any way procure for another alcoholic beverages for the use of an obviously intoxicated person.
HIST: 1985 c 305 art 7 s 2; 1987 c 152 art 1 s 1

340A.702 GROSS MISDEMEANORS.

It is a gross misdemeanor:

(1) to sell an alcoholic beverage without a license authorizing the sale;

(2) for a licensee to refuse or neglect to obey a lawful direction or order of the commissioner or the commissioner's agent, withhold information or a document the commissioner calls for examination, obstruct or mislead the commissioner in the execution of the commissioner's duties or swear falsely under oath;

(3) to violate the provisions of sections 340A.301 to 340A.312;

(4) to violate the provisions of section 340A.508;

(5) for any person, partnership, or corporation to knowingly have or possess direct or indirect interest in more than one off-sale intoxicating liquor license in a municipality in violation of section 340A.412, subdivision 3;

(6) to sell or otherwise dispose of intoxicating liquor within 1,000 feet of a state hospital, training school, reformatory, prison, or other institution under the supervision and control, in whole or in part, of the commissioner of human services or the commissioner of corrections;

(7) to violate the provisions of section 340A.502;

(8) except as otherwise provided in section 340A.701, to violate the provisions of section 340A.503, subdivision 2, clause (1) or (3);

(9) to withhold any information, book, paper, or other thing called for by the commissioner for the purpose of an examination;

(10) to obstruct or mislead the commissioner in the execution of the commissioner's duties;

(11) to swear falsely concerning any matter stated under oath; or

(12) to violate the provisions of section 340A.503, subdivision 5, after having been convicted previously of violating section 340A.503, subdivision 5.
HIST: 1985 c 305 art 9 s 2; * * * 2000 c 472 s 4

340A.703 MISDEMEANORS.

Where no other penalty is specified a violation of any provision of this chapter is a misdemeanor. A minimum fine of $100 must be assessed against a person under the age of 21 years who violates section 340A.503.
HIST: 1985 c 305 art 9 s 3; 1987 c 152 art 1 s 1; 1999 c 216 art 3 s 1

340A.704 SEARCH WARRANTS.

Search warrants may be issued in connection with violation of this chapter or other laws relating to sale, taxation, transportation, manufacture, or possession of alcoholic beverages in accordance with chapter 626.
HIST: 1985 c 305 art 9 s 4; 1987 c 152 art 1 s 1

340A.706 ALCOHOL WITHOUT LIQUID DEVICES PROHIBITED.

Subdivision 1. **Definition.** For purposes of this section, an "alcohol without liquid device" is a device, machine, apparatus, or appliance that mixes an alcoholic beverage with pure or diluted oxygen to produce an alcohol vapor that may be inhaled by an individual. An "alcohol without liquid device" does not include an inhaler, nebulizer, atomizer, or other device that is designed and intended specifically for medical purposes to dispense prescribed or over-the-counter medications.

Subd. 2. **Prohibition.** Except as provided in subdivision 3, it is unlawful for any person or business establishment to possess, purchase, sell, offer to sell, or use an alcohol without liquid device.

Subd. 3. **Research exception.** This section does not apply to a hospital that operates primarily for the purpose of conducting scientific research, a state institution conducting bona fide research, a private college or university conducting bona fide research, or a pharmaceutical company or biotechnology company conducting bona fide research.

Subd. 4. **Penalty.** Except as provided in subdivision 3, it is unlawful for any person or business establishment to utilize a nebulizer, inhaler, or atomizer or other device as described in subdivision 1, for the purposes of inhaling alcoholic beverages.
HIST: 2006 c 210 s 14; 2006 c 260 art 1 s 4

340A.801 CIVIL ACTIONS.

Subdivision 1. **Right of Action.** A spouse, child, parent, guardian, employer, or other person injured in person, property, or means of support, or who incurs other pecuniary loss by an intoxicated person or by the intoxication of another person has a right of action in the person's own name for all damages sustained against a person who caused the intoxication of that person by illegally selling alcoholic beverages. * * *

Subd. 3. **Comparative negligence.** Actions under this section are governed by section 604.01.

Subd. 3a. **Defense.** The defense described in section 340A.503, subdivision 6, applies to actions under this section.

Subd. 4. **Subrogation claims denied.** There shall be no recovery by any insurance company against any liquor vendor under subrogation clauses of the uninsured, underinsured, collision, or other first party coverages of a motor vehicle insurance policy as a result of payments made by the company to persons who have claims that arise in whole or part under this section. * * *

Subd. 6. **Common law claims.** Nothing in this chapter precludes common law tort claims against any person 21 years old or older who knowingly provides or furnishes alcoholic beverages to a person under the age of 21 years.
HIST: 1985 c 305 art 10 s 1; * * * 1990 c 555 s 10

340.90 CIVIL ACTION; INTOXICATION OF PERSON UNDER AGE 21.

Subdivision 1. **Right of action.** (a) A spouse, child, parent, guardian, employer, or other person injured in person, property, or means of support, or who incurs other pecuniary loss, by an intoxicated person under 21 years of age or by the intoxication of another person under 21 years of age, has for all damages sustained a right of action in the person's own name against a person who is 21 years or older who:

(1) had control over the premises and, being in a reasonable position to prevent the consumption of alcoholic beverages by that person, knowingly or recklessly permitted that consumption and the consumption caused the intoxication of that person; or

(2) sold, bartered, furnished or gave to, or purchased for a person under the age of 21 years alcoholic beverages that caused the intoxication of that person.

This paragraph does not apply to sales licensed under this chapter.

(b) All damages recovered by a minor under this section must be paid either to the minor or to the minor's parent, guardian, or next friend as the court directs.

(c) An intoxicated person under the age of 21 years who caused the injury has no right of action under this section.

Subd. 2. **Subrogation claims denied.** There shall be no recovery by any insurance company for any subrogation claim pursuant to any subrogation clause of the uninsured, underinsured, collision, or other first-party coverages of a motor vehicle insurance policy as a result of payments made by the company to persons who have claims that arise in whole or in part under this section.

* * *

HIST: 2000 c 423 s 1

340A.902 DRUNKENNESS NOT A CRIME.

No person may be charged with or convicted of the offense of drunkenness or public drunkenness. Nothing herein prevents the prosecution and conviction of an intoxicated person for offenses other than drunkenness or public drunkenness nor does this section relieve a person from civil liability for an injury to persons or property caused by the person while intoxicated.

HIST: 1985 c 305 art 11 s 2; 1987 c 152 art 1 s 1

Chapter 26 -- MISCELLANEOUS STATUTES (PART I)

Category 2, Section 5:
2.5.1 Describe the basic organization, purpose, and definitions and principles of the Minnesota Criminal Code.
2.5.3. Explain what is meant by elements of a crime and describe the connection between criminal conduct and criminal intent (mens rea).
2.5.5. Given a variety of scenarios, identify indications that a crime has been committed and identify the elements of that crime.

~~299F.811~~ [Repealed, 1994 c 636 art 5 s 18]

~~299F.815~~ [Repealed, 1994 c 636 art 5 s 18]

609.668 EXPLOSIVE AND INCENDIARY DEVICES.

Subdivision 1. **Definitions.** For purposes of this section, the following terms have the meanings given them.

(a) "Explosive device" means a device so articulated that an ignition by fire, friction, concussion, chemical reaction, or detonation of any part of the device may cause such sudden generation of highly heated gases that the resultant gaseous pressures are capable of producing destructive effects. Explosive devices include, but are not limited to, bombs, grenades, rockets having a propellant charge of more than four ounces, mines, and fireworks modified for other than their intended purpose. The term includes devices that produce a chemical reaction that produces gas capable of bursting its container and producing destructive effects. The term does not include firearms ammunition.

(b) "Incendiary device" means a device so articulated that an ignition by fire, friction, concussion, detonation, or other method may produce destructive effects primarily through combustion rather than explosion. The term does not include a manufactured device or article in common use by the general public that is designed to produce combustion for a lawful purpose, including but not limited to matches, lighters, flares, or devices commercially manufactured primarily for the purpose of illumination, heating, or cooking. The term does not include firearms ammunition.

(c) "Crime of violence" has the meaning given in section 624.12, subdivision 5, and also includes a domestic assault conviction when committed within the last three years or while an order for protection is active against the person, whichever period is longer.

Subd. 2. **Possession by certain persons prohibited.** The following persons are prohibited from possessing or reporting an explosive device or incendiary device:

(a) a person under the age of 18 years;

(b) a person who has been convicted in this state or elsewhere of a crime of violence unless ten years have elapsed since the person's civil rights have been restored or the sentence has expired, whichever occurs first, and during that time the person has not been convicted of any other crime of violence. For purposes of this section, crime of violence includes crimes in other states or jurisdictions that would have been crimes of violence if they had been committed in this state;

(c) a person who is or has ever been confined or committed in Minnesota or elsewhere as a person who is mentally ill, mentally retarded, or mentally ill and dangerous to the public, as defined in section 253B.02, to a treatment facility, unless the person possesses a certificate of a medical doctor or psychiatrist licensed in Minnesota, or other satisfactory proof, that the person is no longer suffering from this disability;

(d) a person who has been convicted in Minnesota or elsewhere for the unlawful use, possession, or sale of a controlled substance other than conviction for possession of a small amount of marijuana, as defined in section 152.01, subdivision 16, or who is or has ever been hospitalized or committed for treatment for the habitual use of a controlled substance or marijuana, as defined in sections 152.01 and 152.02, unless the person possesses a certificate of a medical doctor or psychiatrist licensed in Minnesota, or other satisfactory proof, that the person has not abused a controlled substance or marijuana during the previous two years;

(e) a person who has been confined or committed to a treatment facility in Minnesota or elsewhere as chemically dependent, as defined in section 253B.02, unless the person has completed treatment; and

(f) a peace officer who is informally admitted to a treatment facility under section 253B.04 for chemical dependency, unless the officer possesses a certificate from the head of the treatment facility discharging or provisionally discharging the officer from the treatment facility.
* * *

Subd. 3. **Uses permitted.** (a) The following persons may own or possess an explosive device or incendiary device provided that subdivision 4 is complied with:

(1) law enforcement officers for use in the course of their duties;

(2) fire department personnel for use in the course of their duties;

(3) corrections officers and other personnel at correctional facilities or institutions when used for the retention of persons convicted or accused of crime;

(4) persons possessing explosive devices or incendiary devices that although designed as devices have been determined by the commissioner of public safety or the commissioner's delegate, by reason of the date of manufacture, value, design, or other characteristics, to be a collector's item, relic, museum piece, or specifically used in a particular vocation or employment, such as the entertainment industry; and

(5) dealers and manufacturers who are federally licensed or registered.

(b) Persons listed in paragraph (a) shall also comply with the federal requirements for the registration and licensing of destructive devices.

Subd. 4. **Report required.** (a) Before owning or possessing an explosive device or incendiary device as authorized by subdivision 3, a person shall file a written report with the department of public safety[.]

Subd. 5. **Exceptions.** This section does not apply to:

(1) members of the armed forces of either the United States or the state of Minnesota when for use in the course of duties;

(2) educational institutions when the devices are manufactured or used in conjunction with an official education course or program;

(3) propellant-actuated devices, or propellant-actuated industrial tools manufactured, imported, or distributed for their intended purpose;

(4) items that are neither designed or redesigned for use as explosive devices or incendiary devices;

(5) governmental organizations using explosive devices or incendiary devices for agricultural purposes or control of wildlife;

(6) governmental organizations using explosive devices or incendiary devices for official training purposes or as items retained as evidence; or

(7) arsenals, navy yards, depots, or other establishments owned by, or operated by or on behalf of, the United States.

Subd. 6. **Acts prohibited; penalties.** (a) Except as otherwise provided in this section, whoever possesses, manufactures, transports, or stores an explosive device or incendiary device in violation of this section may be sentenced to imprisonment for not more than ten years or to payment of a fine of not more than $20,000, or both.

(b) Whoever legally possesses, manufactures, transports or stores an explosive device or incendiary device, with intent to use the device to damage property or cause injury, may be sentenced to imprisonment for not more than ten years or to payment of a fine of not more than $20,000, or both.

(c) Whoever, acting with gross disregard for human life or property, negligently causes an explosive device or incendiary device to be discharged, may be sentenced to imprisonment for not more than 20 years or to payment of a fine of not more than $100,000, or both.

Subd. 7. [Repealed, 2003 c 2 art 1 s 45]

HIST: 1994 c 636 art 5 s 15; 2002 c 221 s 47; 2003 c art 1 s 45

624.20 FIREWORKS.

Subdivision 1. **Regulation.** (a) As used in sections 624.20 to 624.25, the term "fireworks" means any substance or combination of substances or article prepared for the purpose of producing a visible or an audible effect by combustion, explosion, deflagration, or detonation, and includes blank cartridges, toy cannons, and toy canes in which explosives are used, the type of balloons which require fire underneath to propel them, firecrackers, torpedoes, skyrockets, Roman candles, daygo bombs, sparklers other than those specified in paragraph (c), or other fireworks of like construction, and any fireworks containing any explosive or inflammable compound, or any tablets or other device containing any explosive substance and commonly used as fireworks.

(b) The term "fireworks" shall not include toy pistols, toy guns, in which paper caps containing 25/100 grains or less of explosive compound are used and toy pistol caps which contain less than 20/100 grains of explosive mixture.

(c) The term also does not include wire or wood sparklers of not more than 100 grams of mixture per item, other sparkling items which are nonexplosive and nonaerial and contain 75 grams or less of chemical mixture per tube or a total of 500 grams or less for multiple tubes, snakes and glow worms, smoke devices, or trick noisemakers which include paper streamers, party poppers, string poppers, snappers, and drop pops, each consisting of not more than twenty-five hundredths grains of explosive mixture. The use of items listed in this paragraph is not permitted on public property. This paragraph does not authorize the purchase of items listed in it by persons younger than 18 years of age. The age of a purchaser of items listed in this paragraph must be verified by photographic identification.
* * *

Subd. 2. **Explosive fireworks.** As used in sections 624.20 to 624.25, the term "explosive fireworks" means any fireworks that contain pyrotechnic or flash powder, gunpowder, black powder, or any other explosive compound constructed to produce detonation or deflagration.

HIST:1941 c 125 s 1; 1988 c 584 s 2; 2002 c 350 s 1; 2003 c 128 art 15 s 6;2008 c 368 art 2 s 70

624.21 SALE, POSSESSION, AND USE OF FIREWORKS PROHIBITED.

Except as otherwise provided in sections 624.20 to 624.25, it shall be unlawful for any person to offer for sale, expose for sale, sell at retail or wholesale, possess, advertise, use, or explode any fireworks. * * *

HIST: 1941 c 125 s 2; 1963 c 818 s 1; 1982 c 440 s 1; 1988 c 584 s 3; 1994 c 636 art 5 s 17

624.22 FIREWORKS DISPLAYS; PERMIT; OPERATOR CERTIFICATION.

Subdivision 1. **General requirements; permit; investigation; fee.** (a) Sections 624.20 to 624.25 do not prohibit the supervised display of fireworks by a statutory or home rule charter city, fair association, amusement park, or other organization, except that:

(1) a fireworks display may be conducted only when supervised by an operator certified by the state fire marshal; and

(2) a fireworks display must either be given by a municipality or fair association within its own limits, or by any other organization, whether public or private, only after a permit for the display has first been secured.

(b) An application for a permit for an outdoor fireworks display must be made in writing to the municipal clerk at least 15 days in advance of the date of the display[.]

(c) When the supervised outdoor fireworks display for which a permit is sought is to be held outside the limits of an incorporated municipality, the application must be made to the county auditor[.]

(d) An application for an indoor fireworks display permit must be made in writing to the state fire marshal by the operator of the facility in which the display is to occur at least 15 days in advance of the date of any performance, show, or event which will include the discharge of fireworks inside a building or structure. * * *

Subd. 2. **Operator certification requirements.** (a) An applicant to be a supervising operator of a fireworks display shall meet the requirements of this subdivision before the applicant is certified by the state fire marshal. * * *

Subd. 5 . **Responsibilities of operator.** The operator is responsible for ensuring the fireworks display is organized and operated in accordance with the state fire marshal's guidelines described in subdivision 1.

Subd. 6. **Reports.** (a) The certified operator shall submit a written report to the state fire marshal within ten days following a fireworks display conducted by the operator if any of the following occurred:

(1) an injury to any person resulting from the display of fireworks;

(2) a fire or damage to property resulting from the display of fireworks; or

(3) an unsafe or defective pyrotechnic product or equipment was used or observed. * * *

Subd. 8. **Suspension, revocation, or refusal to renew certification.** (a) The state fire marshal may suspend, revoke, or refuse to renew certification of an operator if the operator has:

(1) submitted a fraudulent application;

(2) caused or permitted a fire or safety hazard to exist or occur during the storage, transportation, handling, preparation, or use of fireworks;

(3) conducted a display of fireworks without receipt of a permit required by the state or a political subdivision;

(4) conducted a display of fireworks with assistants who were not at least 18 years of age, properly instructed, and continually supervised; or

(5) otherwise failed to comply with any federal or state law or regulation, or the guidelines, relating to fireworks. * * *

HIST: 1941 c 125 s 3; * * * 2006 c 260 art 3 s 24

624.221 EXEMPTIONS FOR LICENSE OR PERMIT HOLDER.

Sections 624.20, 624.21, and 624.23 to 624.25 do not apply to:

(a) the holders of a federal explosives license or permit issued pursuant to United States Code, title 18, chapter 40, or their agents when the holder or agent is acting in compliance with the conditions of licensure; or

(b) the holders of permits issued pursuant to section 624.22 or their agents, from the date of issuance until 20 days after the date of exhibition authorized by the permit, when the holder or agent is acting in compliance with the conditions of the permit and section 624.22.

HIST: 1988 c 584 s 4

624.23 CONSTRUCTION OF SECTIONS 624.20 TO 624.25.

Nothing in sections 624.20 to 624.25 shall be construed to prohibit any resident wholesaler, dealer, or jobber, from possessing or selling at wholesale fireworks which are not prohibited; or the possession or sale of any kind of fireworks for shipment directly out of the

state; or the possession or use of fireworks by airplanes and railroads, or other transportation agencies for signal purposes or illumination; or the possession, sale, or use of blank cartridges for a show or theater, or for signal or ceremonial purposes in athletics or sports, or for use by military organizations or for use as a bird or animal repelling device.

HIST: 1941 c 125 s 4; 1971 c 710 s 1; 1988 c 584 s 5

624.24 OFFICERS MAY SEIZE ILLEGAL FIREWORKS.

The state fire marshal, or any sheriff, police officer, constable, or local fire marshal, shall seize, take, remove, or cause to be removed, at the expense of the owner, all stocks of fireworks

or combustibles offered or exposed for sale, stored, or held in violation of sections 624.20 to 624.25.
HIST: 1941 c 125 s 5

624.25 VIOLATION.
Any person violating the provisions of sections 624.20 to 624.24 may be sentenced as follows:
(1) if the violation involves explosive fireworks in an amount of 35 pounds gross container weight or more, to imprisonment for not more than one year, or to payment of a fine of not more than $3,000, or both;
(2) if the violation involves explosive fireworks in an amount of less than 35 pounds gross container weight, to imprisonment for not more than 90 days, or to payment of a fine of not more than $1,000, or both; and
(3) if the violation involves any amount of fireworks other than explosive fireworks, to imprisonment for not more than 90 days, or to payment of a fine of not more than $1,000, or both.
HIST: 1941 c 125 s 6; 1988 c 584 s 6; 2004 c 228 art 1 s 72

299C.37 POLICE COMMUNICATION EQUIPMENT; USE, SALE.
Subdivision 1. **Police communication equipment; use; sale.** (a) No person other than peace officers within the state, the members of the state patrol, and persons who hold an amateur radio license issued by the Federal Communications Commission, shall equip any motor vehicle with any radio equipment or combination of equipment, capable of receiving any radio signal, message, or information from any police emergency frequency, or install, use, or possess the equipment in a motor vehicle without permission from the superintendent of the bureau upon a form prescribed by the superintendent. * * * A person * * * issued a permit under subdivision 3 may use and possess radio equipment while in the course and scope of duties or employment without also having to obtain an individual permit.
(b) Except as provided in paragraph (c), any person who is convicted of a violation of this subdivision shall, upon conviction for the first offense, be guilty of a misdemeanor, and for the second and subsequent offenses shall be guilty of a gross misdemeanor.
(c) An amateur radio license holder who exercises the privilege granted by paragraph (a) shall carry the amateur radio license in the motor vehicle at all times and shall present the license to a peace officer on request. A violation of this paragraph is a petty misdemeanor. A second or subsequent violation is a misdemeanor. * * *
Subd. 3. **Permit.** (a)The superintendent of the bureau shall, upon written application, issue a written permit, which shall be nontransferable, to a person, firm, political subdivision, or corporation showing good cause to use radio equipment capable of receiving a police emergency frequency, as a necessity, in the lawful pursuit of a business, trade, or occupation.
(b) Notwithstanding paragraph (a), a permit is not required for emergency response personnel * * * who are members of a public safety agency * * * to use agency-issued radio equipment as described in subdivision 1, paragraph (a)[.] * * *
HIST: (9950-48) 1935 c 195 s 8; * * * 2008 c 224 s 1

299C.38 PRIORITY OF POLICE COMMUNICATIONS; MISDEMEANOR.
[A]ny person who willfully makes any false, misleading, or unfounded report to any public safety answering point for the purpose of interfering with the operation thereof, or with the intention of misleading any officer of this state, shall be guilty of a misdemeanor.
HIST: (9950-50) 1935 c 195 s 10; 1965 c 721 s 2; 2015 c 65 art 3 s 9

327.70 DEFINITIONS.
Subdivision 1. **Terms.** For the purposes of sections 327.70 to 327.76, the terms defined in this section have the meanings given them.

Subd. 2. **Guest.** "Guest" means a person who is registered at a hotel and to whom a bedroom is assigned. The term "guest" includes members of the guest's family who accompany the guest.

Subd. 3. **Hotel.** "Hotel" means a hotel, motel, resort, boarding house, bed and breakfast, furnished apartment house or other building, which is kept, used or advertised as, or held out to the public to be, a place where sleeping or housekeeping accommodations are supplied for pay to guests for transient occupancy.

Subd. 4. **Innkeeper.** "Innkeeper" means an owner or operator of a hotel.

Subd. 5. **Transient occupancy.** "Transient occupancy" means occupancy when it is the intention of the parties that the occupancy will be temporary. There is a rebuttable presumption that, if the unit occupied is the sole residence of the guest, the occupancy is not transient. There is a rebuttable presumption that, if the unit occupied is not the sole residence of the guest, the occupancy is transient.

Subd. 6. **Valuables.** "Valuables" includes money, bank notes, bonds, precious stones, jewelry, ornaments, watches, securities, transportation tickets, photographic cameras, checks, drafts, and other negotiable instruments, business papers, documents, and other papers, and other articles of value.
HIST: 1982 c 517 s 1; 1993 c 151 s 1

327.72 OVERSTAYING GUESTS.

A guest who intentionally continues to occupy an assigned room in a hotel beyond the scheduled departure date without the prior written approval of the innkeeper shall be deemed to be a trespasser.
HIST: 1982 c 517 s 3

327.73 UNDESIRABLE GUESTS; EJECTION OF, AND REFUSAL TO ADMIT.

Subdivision 1. **Innkeeper's right to eject.** An innkeeper may remove or cause to be removed from a hotel a guest or other person who:

(1) refuses or is unable to pay for accommodations or services;

(2) while on the premises of the hotel acts in an obviously intoxicated or disorderly manner, destroys or threatens to destroy hotel property, or causes or threatens to cause a disturbance;

(3) the innkeeper reasonably believes is using the premises for the unlawful possession or use of controlled substances * * *, or using the premises for the consumption of alcohol by a person under the age of 21 years * * *;

(4) the innkeeper reasonably believes has brought property into the hotel that may be dangerous to other persons, such as firearms or explosives;

(5) violates any federal, state, or local laws, ordinances, or rules relating to the hotel; or

(6) violates a rule of the hotel that is clearly and conspicuously posted at or near the front desk and on the inside of the entrance door of every guest room.

(b) If the guest has paid in advance, the innkeeper shall tender to the guest any unused portion of the advance payment at the time of removal.

Subd. 2. **Refusal of admission.** (a) An innkeeper may refuse to admit or refuse service or accommodations to a person who:

(1) while on the premises of the hotel acts in an obviously intoxicated or disorderly manner, destroys or threatens to destroy hotel property, or causes or threatens to cause a public disturbance;

(2) the innkeeper reasonably believes is seeking accommodations for the unlawful possession or use of controlled substances * * * or the use of the premises for the consumption of intoxicating liquor by a person under the age of 21 years * * *; or

(3) the innkeeper reasonably believes is bringing property into the hotel that may be dangerous to other persons, such as firearms or explosives.

(b) An innkeeper also may refuse to admit or refuse service or accommodations to a person who refuses or is unable to pay for the accommodations or services. An inn- keeper may require the prospective guest to demonstrate an ability to pay. An inn-keeper may require a parent or guardian of a minor to accept liability for the proper charges for the minor's accommodation, board, room, lodging, and any damages to the guest room or its furniture or furnishings caused by the minor, and provide a credit card to cover the charges. * * *

(c) An innkeeper may limit the number of persons who may occupy a particular guest room in the hotel.

Subd. 3. **Penalty.** A guest or person who remains or attempts to remain in a hotel after having been requested to leave for the reason or reasons specified in this section is guilty of a misdemeanor. * * *

HIST: 1982 c 517 s 4; 1993 c 151 s 2,3

327.731 LIABILITY NOTICE.

Subdivision 1. **Liability.** (a) A person who negligently or intentionally causes damage to the hotel or any furniture or furnishings within the hotel, is liable for damages sustained by the innkeeper, including the hotel's loss of revenue resulting from the inability to rent or lease rooms while the damage is being repaired.

(b) A person who negligently or intentionally causes injury to any person or damage to any personal property of the person on the hotel premises is liable for the injury or damage.

(c) A parent or guardian of a minor also is liable for acts of the minor described in paragraphs (a) and (b), if the parent or guardian provides a credit card or an advance cash deposit[.]

HIST: 1993 c 151 s 4

327.74 SETTING FIRE TO HOTEL BELONGINGS.

Subdivision 1. **Penalty.** A person in a hotel who, by smoking or attempting to light or smoke cigarettes, cigars, pipes, or other smoking material, in any manner in which lighters or matches are used, negligently sets fire to a part of the building, or any furniture or furnishings within the building, so as to endanger life or property in any way or to any extent, is guilty of a gross misdemeanor. * * *

HIST: 1982 c 517 s 5; 1993 c 151 s 5

327.742 SMOKING IN DESIGNATED NONSMOKING ROOMS.

Subdivision 1. **Smoking prohibited.** No person shall smoke cigarettes, cigars, pipes, or other smoking material in a hotel sleeping room designated nonsmoking.

Subd. 2. **Penalty.** A person who violates this section is guilty of a petty misdemeanor. Upon conviction, the court may require a person who violates this section to reimburse the innkeeper for actual cost incurred to restore the room to its previolation condition.

Subd. 2a. **Civil penalty and service charge.** Unless a court orders reimbursement under subdivision 2, a person who violates this section is liable to the innkeeper for the cost of restoring the damaged room to its previolation condition and a service charge of $30. * * *

HIST: 1993 c 66 s 1; 2008 c 355 s 1-6

327.75 FRAUD; PROOF OF FRAUD.

Subdivision 1. **Fraud.** A person who obtains food, lodging or other accommodations at any hotel or restaurant without paying therefor, with intent to defraud the owner or manager, or who obtains credit for food, lodging, or other accommodations at any hotel or restaurant, with intent to defraud the owner or manager, is guilty of a misdemeanor.

Subd. 2. **Proof of fraud.** Prima facie evidence of the fraudulent intent referred to in subdivision 1 includes:

(a) proof that the person obtained the services or credit for the services by false pretense, or by false or fictitious show or pretense of baggage or other property;

(b) proof that the person refused or neglected to pay for the services upon demand;

(c) proof that the person gave in payment of the services negotiable paper on which payment was refused;

(d) proof that the person absconded without offering to pay for the services; or

(e) proof that the person surreptitiously removed or attempted to remove baggage owned by that person.

HIST: 1982 c 517 s 6; 1986 c 444

327.76 INNKEEPER'S LIEN.

Subdivision 1. **Lien created.** An innkeeper shall have a lien upon the valuables, baggage or other property of a guest brought into the innkeeper's hotel, for the proper charges due on account of the guest's accommodation, board, room and lodging [and] for all money paid out for or advanced to the guest[.]

Subd. 2. **Possession prior to final judgment.** The lien created in subdivision 1 may be enforced only after final judgment in an action brought to recover the charges and moneys. During the pendency of the proceeding, the plaintiff may take possession of the valuables, baggage or other property upon an order issued by the court[.]

Subd. 3. **Final judgment; sale.** If final judgment is entered by the court for the defendant on the merits of the action, the plaintiff shall return possession of the valuables, baggage or other property to the defendant and pay to the defendant costs incurred by the defendant in defending against the plaintiff's claim. If final judgment is entered by the court in favor of the plaintiff, and if the judgment is not satisfied within 30 days, the valuables, baggage or other property subject to the innkeeper's lien may be sold at public auction to satisfy the lien, the costs of the action to enforce the lien, and the costs of sale. * * *

HIST: 1982 c 517 s 7; 1986 c 444

617.23 INDECENT EXPOSURE; PENALTIES.

Subdivision 1. **Misdemeanor.** A person who commits any of the following acts in any public place, or in any place where others are present, is guilty of a misdemeanor:

(1) willfully and lewdly exposes the person's body, or the private parts thereof;

(2) procures another to expose private parts; or

(3) engages in any open or gross lewdness or lascivious behavior, or any public indecency other than behavior specified in this subdivision.

Subd. 2. **Gross misdemeanor.** A person who commits any of the following acts is guilty of a gross misdemeanor:

(1) the person violates subdivision 1 in the presence of a minor under the age of 16; or

(2) the person violates subdivision 1 after having been previously convicted of violating subdivision 1, sections 609.342 to 609.3451, or a statute from another state in conformity with any of those sections.

Subd. 3. **Felony.** A person is guilty of a felony and may be sentenced to imprisonment for not more than five years or to payment of a fine of not more than $10,000, or both, if:

(1) the person violates subdivision 2, clause (1), after having been previously convicted of or adjudicated delinquent for violating subdivision 2, clause (1); section 609.3451, subdivision 1, clause (2); or a statute from another state in conformity with subdivision 2, clause (1), or section 609.3451, subdivision 1, clause (2); or

(2) the person commits a violation of subdivision 1, clause (1), in the presence of another person while intentionally confining that person or otherwise intentionally restricting that person's freedom to move.

Subd.4. **Exception.** It is not a violation of this section for a woman to breast feed.

HIST: (10186) RL s 4953; 1931 c 321; * * * 1998 c 369 s 2

617.246 USE OF MINORS IN SEXUAL PERFORMANCE PROHIBITED.

Subdivision 1. **Definitions.** (a) For the purpose of this section, the terms defined in this subdivision have the meanings given them.

(b) "Minor" means any person under the age of 18.

(c) "Promote" means to produce, direct, publish, manufacture, issue, or advertise.

(d) "Sexual performance" means any play, dance or other exhibition presented before an audience or for purposes of visual or mechanical reproduction that uses a minor to depict actual or simulated sexual conduct as defined by clause (e).

(e) "Sexual conduct" means any of the following:

(1) an act of sexual intercourse, normal or perverted, including genital-genital, anal-genital, or oral-genital intercourse, whether between human beings or between a human being and an animal;

(2) sadomasochistic abuse, meaning flagellation, torture, or similar demeaning acts inflicted by or upon a person who is nude or clad in undergarments or in a revealing costume, or the condition of being fettered, bound or otherwise physically restrained on the part of one so clothed;

(3) masturbation;

(4) lewd exhibitions of the genitals; or

(5) physical contact with the clothed or unclothed pubic areas or buttocks of a human male or female, or the breasts of the female, whether alone or between members of the same or opposite sex or between humans and animals in an act of apparent sexual stimulation or gratification.

(f) "Pornographic work" means:

(1) an original or reproduction of a picture, film, photograph, negative, slide, videotape, videodisc, or drawing of a sexual performance involving a minor; or

(2) any visual depiction, including any photograph, film, video, picture, drawing, negative, slide, or computer-generated image or picture, whether made or produced by electronic, mechanical, or other means that:

(i) uses a minor to depict actual or simulated sexual conduct;

(ii) has been created, adapted, or modified to appear that an identifiable minor is engaging in sexual conduct; or

(iii) is advertised, promoted, presented, described, or distributed in such a manner that conveys the impression that the material is or contains a visual depiction of a minor engaging in sexual conduct.

For purposes of this paragraph, an identifiable minor is a person who was a minor at the time the depiction was created or altered, whose image is used to create the visual depiction.

Subd. 2. **Use of minor.** (a) It is unlawful for a person to promote, employ, use or permit a minor to engage in or assist others to engage minors in posing or modeling alone or with others in any sexual performance or pornographic work if the person knows or has reason to know that the conduct intended is a sexual performance or pornographic work.

Any person who violates this paragraph is guilty of a felony and may be sentenced to imprisonment for not more than ten years or to payment of a fine of not more than $20,000, or both.

(b) A person who violates paragraph (a) is guilty of a felony and may be sentenced to imprisonment for not more than 15 years or to payment of a fine of not more than $40,000, or both, if:

(1) the person has a prior conviction or delinquency adjudication for violating this section or section 617.247;

(2) the violation occurs when the person is a registered predatory offender under section 243.166; or

(3) the violation involved a minor under the age of ~~13~~ 14 years.

Subd. 3. **Operation or ownership of business.** (a) A person who owns or operates a business in which a pornographic work, as defined in this section, is disseminated to an adult or a minor or is reproduced, and who knows the content and character of the pornographic work disseminated or reproduced, is guilty of a felony and may be sentenced to imprisonment for not more than ten years, or to payment of a fine of not more than $20,000, or both.

(b) A person who violates paragraph (a) is guilty of a felony and may be sentenced to imprisonment for not more than 15 years or to payment of a fine of not more than $40,000, or both, if:

(1) the person has a prior conviction or delinquency adjudication for violating this section or section 617.247;

(2) the violation occurs when the person is a registered predatory offender under section 243.166; or

(3) the violation involved a minor under the age of ~~13~~ 14 years.

Subd. 4. **Dissemination.** (a) A person who, knowing or with reason to know its content and character, disseminates for profit to an adult or a minor a pornographic work, as defined in this section, is guilty of a felony and may be sentenced to imprisonment for not more than ten years, or to payment of a fine of not more than $20,000, or both.

(b) A person who violates paragraph (a) is guilty of a felony and may be sentenced to imprisonment for not more than 15 years or to payment of a fine of not more than $40,000, or both, if:

(1) the person has a prior conviction or delinquency adjudication for violating this section or section 617.247;

(2) the violation occurs when the person is a registered predatory offender under section 243.166; or

(3) the violation involved a minor under the age of ~~13~~ 14 years.

Subd. 5. **Consent; mistake.** Neither consent to sexual performance by a minor or the minor's parent, guardian, or custodian nor mistake as to the minor's age is a defense to a charge of violation of this section.

Subd. 6. **Affirmative Defense.** It shall be an affirmative defense to a charge of violating this section that the sexual performance or pornographic work was produced using only persons who were 18 years or older.

EFFECTIVE DATE. This section is effective September 15, 2021, and applies to crimes committed on or after that date.

* * *

HIST: 1977 c 371 s 1; * * * 2013 c 96 s 6; 1Sp2019 c 5 art 4 s 12-15, 1Sp2021 c 11 art 4 s 25-27

617.247 POSSESSION OF PICTORIAL REPRESENTATIONS OF MINORS.

Subdivision 1. **Policy; purpose.** It is the policy of the legislature in enacting this section to protect minors from the physical and psychological damage caused by their being used in pornographic work depicting sexual conduct which involves minors. It is therefore the intent of the legislature to penalize possession of pornographic work depicting sexual conduct which involve minors or appears to involve minors in order to protect the identity of minors who are victimized by involvement in the pornographic work, and to protect minors from future involvement in pornographic work depicting sexual conduct.

Subd. 2. **Definitions.** For purposes of this section, the following terms have the meanings given them:

(a) "Pornographic work" has the meaning given to it in section 617.246.

(b) "Sexual conduct" has the meaning given to it in section 617.246.

Subd. 3. **Dissemination prohibited.** (a) A person who disseminates a pornographic work to an adult or a minor, knowing or with reason to know its content and character, is guilty of a felony and may be sentenced to imprisonment for not more than seven years or to payment of a fine of not more than $10,000, or both.

(b) A person who violates paragraph (a) is guilty of a felony and may be sentenced to imprisonment for not more than 15 years or to payment of a fine of not more than $20,000, or both, if:

(1) the person has a prior conviction or delinquency adjudication for violating this section or section 617.246;

(2) the violation occurs when the person is a registered predatory offender under section 243.166; or

(3) the violation involved a minor under the age of ~~13~~ 14 years.

(b) A person who violates paragraph (a) is guilty of a felony and may be sentenced to imprisonment for not more than 15 years if the violation occurs when the person is a registered predatory offender under section 243.166.

Subd. 4. **Possession prohibited.** (a) A person who possesses a pornographic work or a computer disk or computer or other electronic, magnetic, or optical storage system or a storage system of any other type, containing a pornographic work, knowing or with reason to know its content and character, is guilty of a felony and may be sentenced to imprisonment for not more than five years or to payment of a fine of not more than $5,000, or both.

(b) A person who violates paragraph (a) is guilty of a felony and may be sentenced to imprisonment for not more than ten years or to payment of a fine of not more than $10,000, or both, if:

(1) the person has a prior conviction or delinquency adjudication for violating this section or section 617.247;

(2) the violation occurs when the person is a registered predatory offender under section 243.166; or

(3) the violation involved a minor under the age of 13 14 years.

Subd. 5. **Exception.** This section does not apply to the performance of official duties by peace officers, court personnel, or attorneys, nor to licensed physicians, psychologists, or social workers or persons acting at the direction of a licensed physician, psychologist, or social worker in the course of a bona fide treatment or professional education program.

Subd. 6. **Consent.** Consent to sexual performance by a minor or the minor's parent, guardian, or custodian is not a defense to a charge of violation of this section.

Subd. 7. **Second offense.** If a person is convicted of a second or subsequent violation of this section within 15 years of the prior conviction, the court shall order a mental examination of the person. The examiner shall report to the court whether treatment of the person is necessary.

Subd. 8. **Affirmative Defense.** It shall be an affirmative defense to a charge of violating this section that the sexual performance or pornographic work was produced using only persons who were 18 years or older.
* * *

EFFECTIVE DATE. This section is effective September 15, 2021, and applies to crimes committed on or after that date.
HIST: 1982 c 604 s 3; * * * 2013 c 96 s 7; 1Sp2019 c 5 art 4 s 16-18; 1Sp2021 c 11 art 4 s 27-28

Editors' Note: Although the following statute is not specifically described in these learning objectives, it has been included because of its close relationship to other prohibited actions in Chapter 617 and, referenced since its passage in 2016, in other criminal statutes included elsewhere in these materials. The Minnesota Supreme Court recently held that the statute did not violate the First Amendment, concluding that the statute was narrowly tailored to meet a compelling government objective. State v. Casillas, 952 N.W.2d 629 (Minn. 2020).

617.261 NONCONSENSUAL DISSEMINATION OF PRIVATE SEXUAL IMAGES.

Subdivision 1. **Crime.** It is a crime to intentionally disseminate an image of another person who is depicted in a sexual act or whose intimate parts are exposed, in whole or in part, when:

(1) the person is identifiable:

(i) from the image itself, by the person depicted in the image or by another person; or

(ii) from the personal information displayed in connection with the image;

(2) the actor knows or reasonably should know that the person depicted in the image does not consent to the dissemination; and

(3) the image was obtained or created under circumstances in which the actor knew or reasonably should have known the person depicted had a reasonable expectation of privacy.

Subd. 2. **Penalties.** (a) Except as provided in paragraph (b), whoever violates subdivision 1 is guilty of a gross misdemeanor.

(b) Whoever violates subdivision 1 may be sentenced to imprisonment for not more than three years or to payment of a fine of $5,000, or both, if one of the following factors is present:

(1) the person depicted in the image suffers financial loss due to the dissemination of the image;

(2) the actor disseminates the image with intent to profit from the dissemination;

(3) the actor maintains an Internet Web site, online service, online application, or mobile application for the purpose of disseminating the image;

(4) the actor posts the image on a Web site;

(5) the actor disseminates the image with intent to harass the person depicted in the image;

(6) the actor obtained the image by committing a violation of section 609.52, 609.746, 609.89, or 609.891; or

(7) the actor has previously been convicted under this chapter.

Subd. 3. **No defense.** It is not a defense to a prosecution under this section that the person consented to the capture or possession of the image.
* * *

Subd. 5. **Exemptions.** Subdivision 1 does not apply when:

(1) the dissemination is made for the purpose of a criminal investigation or prosecution that is otherwise lawful;

(2) the dissemination is for the purpose of, or in connection with, the reporting of unlawful conduct;

(3) the dissemination is made in the course of seeking or receiving medical or mental health treatment and the image is protected from further dissemination;

(4) the image involves exposure in public or was obtained in a commercial setting for the purpose of the legal sale of goods or services, including the creation of artistic products for sale or display;

(5) the image relates to a matter of public interest and dissemination serves a lawful public purpose;

(6) the dissemination is for legitimate scientific research or educational purposes; or

(7) the dissemination is made for legal proceedings and is consistent with common practice in civil proceedings necessary for the proper functioning of the criminal justice system, or protected by court order which prohibits any further dissemination.
* * *
HIST: 2016 c 126 s 9

645.241 PUNISHMENT FOR PROHIBITED ACTS.

[W]hen the performance of any act is prohibited by a statute, and no penalty for the violation of the same shall be imposed in any statute, the doing of such act shall be a [petty] misdemeanor. * * *
HIST: (10047) RL s 4859; 2014 c 312 art 6 s 6; 2015 c 65 art 6 s 22

325G.01 EFFECT OF DELIVERY.

Unless otherwise agreed, where unsolicited goods are addressed to and sent to a person, the person has a right to refuse to accept delivery of the goods and is not bound to return such goods to the sender. The receipt of such unsolicited goods shall for all purposes be deemed an unconditional gift to the recipient who may use or dispose of the same in any manner the recipient sees fit without any obligation to the sender.
HIST: 1969 c 609 s 1; 1986 c 444
* * *

325G.03 UNSOLICITED FINANCIAL TRANSACTION CARDS.

No person in whose name a financial transaction card is issued shall be liable for any amount resulting from use of that card from which that person or a member of the person's

family or household derives no benefit unless the person has accepted the card by (1) signing or using the card, or (2) authorizing the use of the card by another. * * *
HIST: 1969 c 1004 s 2; 1985 c 243 s 3; 1986 c 444

325G.04 LOST OR STOLEN FINANCIAL TRANSACTION CARDS.

Subdivision 1. **Liability limited.** No person in whose name a financial transaction card has been issued which the person has accepted as provided in section 325G.03 shall be liable for any amount in excess of $50 resulting from the unauthorized use of the card from which the person or a member of the person's family or household derives no benefit; provided, however, that the limitation on liability of this subdivision shall be effective only if the issuer is notified of any unauthorized charges contained in a bill within 60 days of receipt of the bill by the person in whose name the card is issued.

Subd. 2. **Unauthorized use.** No person in whose name a financial transaction card is issued shall be liable for any amount resulting from the unauthorized use of the financial transaction card after receipt by the issuer of notice that the card has been lost or stolen and from which such person or a member of the person's family or household derives no benefit. * * *
HIST: 1969 c 1004 s 3; 1985 c 243 s 4; 1986 c 444; 1987 c 349 art 1 s 37

325G.041 MARRIED WOMAN; NAME ON CARD

If a financial transaction card issuer has determined in the normal course of business that it will issue a card to a married woman, the card shall be issued bearing either her current of former surname, as the woman may direct. * * *
HIST: 1984 c 533 s 1; 1985 c 243 s 5

325G.042 CONSUMER CREDIT; EQUAL TREATMENT OF SPOUSES.

Subdivision 1. **Consideration required; spousal credit history.** To the extent that a creditor considers credit history in evaluating the credit worthiness of similarly qualified applicants for a similar type and amount of credit, in evaluating an applicant's credit worthiness, a creditor shall consider:

(1) the credit history, when available, of accounts designated as accounts that the applicant and the applicant's spouse are permitted to use or for which both are contractually liable[.]

Subd. 2. **Credit reporting; equal treatment of spouses.** (a) A creditor that furnishes credit information shall designate:

(1) any new credit account to reflect the participation of both spouses if the applicant's spouse is contractually liable on the account, other than as a guarantor, surety, endorser, or similar party[.]
HIST: 1998 c 327 s 1

325G.05 DISPUTED ACCOUNTS.

Subdivision 1. **Billing information.** Every financial transaction card issuer shall include on each billing statement the name, address, and telephone number of the department designated by it to receive requests by the customer account holder to correct mistakes or make adjustments to the billing statement.

Subd. 2. **Required response.** Every financial transaction card issuer, within 30 days of receipt from a customer account holder, in writing at the address specified in subdivision 1, or a questioned or disputed charge, shall conduct an individual inquiry into the facts and send to the customer account holder an explanatory response in clear and definite terms. * * *
HIST: 1973 c 460 s 1; 1985 c 243 s 6

325G.051 SURCHARGES ON CREDIT CARDS.

Subdivision 1. **Limitation; prohibition.** (a) A seller of goods or services may impose a surcharge on a purchaser who elects to use a credit card in lieu of payment by cash, check, or similar means, provided (1) the seller informs the purchaser of the surcharge both orally at the time of sale and by a sign conspicuously posted on the seller's premises, and (2) the surcharge does not exceed five percent of the purchase price. * * *

Subd. 2. **Penalty.** A seller who violates this section is subject to a civil penalty of not more than $500 and shall refund the surcharge to each buyer.

HIST: 1987 c 172 s 1

325G.06 DEFINITIONS.

* * *

Subd. 2. **Home solicitation sale.** "Home solicitation sale" means a sale of goods, services, or improvements to real property by a seller who regularly engages in transactions of the same kind, purchased primarily for personal, family or household purposes, and not for agricultural purposes, with a purchase price of more than $25, in which the seller or a person acting for the seller personally solicits the sale, and when the buyer's agreement or offer to purchase is made at a place other than the place of business of the seller, except as otherwise provided in this subdivision. It does not include:

(a) a sale made pursuant to prior negotiations in the course of a visit by the buyer to a retail business establishment having a fixed permanent location where the goods are exhibited or the services are offered for sale on a continuing basis; or

(b) a sale in which the buyer has initiated the contact and the goods or services are needed to meet a bona fide immediate personal emergency of the buyer and the buyer furnishes the seller with a separate dated and signed statement not furnished by the seller describing the situation requiring immediate remedy and expressly acknowledging and waiving the right to cancel the sale. This exclusion shall only apply where (i) the seller in good faith makes a substantial beginning performance of the contract before the buyer gives notice of cancellation, and, (ii) in the case of goods, the goods cannot be returned to the seller in substantially as good condition as when received by the buyer; or

(c) a sale in which the buyer has initiated the contact and specifically requested the seller to visit the buyer's home for the purpose of repairing or performing maintenance upon the buyer's property[;] or

(d) a sale in which the buyer has initiated the contact either by oral, telephone, or written request (other than on a form provided by the seller), and requested the seller to visit the buyer's home for the purpose of negotiating the purchase of the specific good or service requested[;]or

(e) a sale of insurance, securities, or real property; or a sale by a public auction; or

(f) a sale of a motor vehicle, as defined in section 168.011, subdivision 4, when the buyer's agreement or offer to purchase is made at a place other than the buyer's place of residence. * * *

HIST: 1973 c 443 s 1; 1979 c 128 s 1; 1986 c 444; 2012 c 324 s 3

325G.07 BUYER'S RIGHT TO CANCEL.

In addition to any other rights the buyer may have, the buyer has the right to cancel a home solicitation sale until midnight of the third business day after the day on which the home solicitation sale occurs. * * *

HIST: 1973 c 443 s 2

325G.08 WRITING REQUIRED; NOTICE OF RIGHT TO CANCEL; NOTICE OF CANCELLATION.

Subdivision 1. **Seller's obligations.** In a home solicitation sale, at the time the sale occurs, the seller shall:

(a) inform the buyer orally of the right to cancel;

(b) furnish the buyer with a fully completed receipt or copy of a contract pertaining to the sale which shows the date of the transaction, contains the name and address of the seller, and [a "notice of cancellation" required by this subdivision".]

HIST: 1973 c 443 s 3; 1986 c 444

325G.09 RETURN OF PAYMENTS OR GOODS.

Subdivision 1. **Seller's obligations.** Within ten days after a home solicitation sale has been canceled or an offer to purchase revoked, the seller must tender to the buyer any payments made by the buyer and any note or other evidence of indebtedness. If the down payment includes goods traded in, the goods must also be tendered by the seller in as good condition as when received by the seller. If the seller fails to tender said goods, the buyer may elect to recover from the seller an amount equal to the trade-in allowance stated in the agreement.

Subd. 2. **Buyer's right to retain possession.** Until the seller has complied with the obligations imposed by this section, the buyer may retain possession of the goods delivered to the buyer by the seller.

Subd. 3. **Buyer's obligation to tender goods.** Except as provided in subdivision 2, within a reasonable time after a home solicitation sale has been canceled or an offer to purchase has been revoked, the buyer upon demand must tender to the seller any goods delivered by the seller pursuant to the sale. The buyer is not obligated to tender at any place other than the buyer's residence.

Subd. 4. **Seller's failure to demand possession.** If the seller fails to demand possession of goods within 20 days after cancellation or revocation, the goods become the property of the buyer without obligation to pay for them.

Subd. 5. **Buyer's duty of care.** The buyer has the duty to take reasonable care of the goods in the buyer's possession before cancellation or revocation and during the time provided in subdivision 4 for the seller to demand possession, during which time the goods are otherwise at the seller's risk.

Subd. 6. **Right to compensation limited.** If the seller has performed any services pursuant to a home solicitation sale prior to its cancellation, the seller is entitled to no compensation.

HIST: 1973 c 443 s 4; 1986 c 444
* * *

325G.13 DISCLOSURE OBLIGATION.

Before any personal solicitation every seller shall, at the time of initial contact or communication with the potential buyer, clearly and expressly disclose: the individual sellers name, the name of the business firm or organization the seller represents, the identity or kinds of goods or services the seller wishes to demonstrate or sell, and that the seller wishes to demonstrate or sell the identified goods or services. * * * Nonprofit organizations are exempt from the requirements of this section.

HIST: 1975 c 372 s 2; 1986 c 444
* * *

Category 2, Section 5:
2.5.5. Given a variety of scenarios, identify indications a particular crime has been committed and identify the elements of that crime.
2.5.7. Explain special Minnesota peace office duties associated with specific statutes . . .

343.12 DUTIES OF PEACE OFFICERS.

Upon application of any agent appointed by the federation or a county or district society, it shall be the duty of, any sheriff or the agent's deputy or any police officer to investigate any alleged violation of the law relative to cruelty to animals, and to arrest any person found violating those laws. It shall also be the duty of those officers to take possession of any animals

in their respective jurisdictions which have been cruelly treated, and deliver the same to the proper officers of the county or district for custody and care.
HIST: (7936) RL s 3128; 1975 c 369 s 9; 1977 c 332 s 15; 1986 c 444; 1987 c 394 s 7

343.20 DEFINITIONS.

Subdivision 1. **Application.** Except as otherwise indicated by the context, for purposes of sections 343.20 to 343.36, the terms defined in this section have the meanings given them.

Subd. 2. **Animal.** "Animal" means every living creature except members of the human race.

Subd. 3. **Torture; cruelty.** "Torture" or "cruelty" means every act, omission, or neglect which causes or permits unnecessary or unjustifiable pain, suffering, or death.

Subd. 4. **Impure milk.** "Impure and unwholesome milk" means all milk obtained from diseased or unhealthy animals, or from animals fed on any substance which is putrefied or fermented.

Subd. 5. **Animal control officer.** "Animal control officer" means an officer employed by or under contract with an agency of the state, county, municipality, or other governmental subdivision of the state which is responsible for animal control operations in its jurisdiction.

Subd. 6. **Pet or companion animal.** "Pet or companion animal" includes any animal owned, possessed by, cared for, or controlled by a person for the present or future enjoyment of that person or another as a pet or companion, or any stray pet or stray companion animal.

Subd. 7. **Service animal.** "Service animal" means an animal trained to assist a person with a disability.

Subd. 8. **Substantial bodily harm.** "Substantial bodily harm" means bodily injury which involves a temporary but substantial disfigurement, or which causes a temporary but substantial loss or impairment of the function of any bodily member or organ, or which causes a fracture of any bodily member to a service animal or a pet or companion animal.

Subd. 9. **Great bodily harm.** "Great bodily harm" means bodily injury which creates a high probability of death, or which causes serious permanent disfigurement, or which cause a permanent or protracted loss or impairment of the function of any bodily member or organ, or other serious bodily harm to a service animal or a pet or companion animal.
HIST: (10442) RL s 5151; 1981 c 53 s 1; 1989 c 37 s 1; 1Sp2001 c 8 art 8 s 5-8

343.21 OVERWORKING OR MISTREATING ANIMALS; PENALTY.

Subdivision 1. **Torture.** No person shall overdrive, overload, torture, cruelly beat, neglect, or unjustifiably injure, maim, mutilate, or kill any animal, or cruelly work any animal when it is unfit for labor, whether it belongs to that person or to another person.

Subd. 2. **Nourishment; shelter.** No person shall deprive any animal over which the person has charge or control of necessary food, water, or shelter.

Subd. 3. **Enclosure.** No person shall keep any cow or other animal in any enclosure without providing wholesome exercise and change of air.

Subd. 4. **Low feed.** No person shall feed any cow on food which produces impure or unwholesome milk.

Subd. 5. **Abandonment.** No person shall abandon any animal.

Subd. 6. **Temporary abandonment.** No person shall allow any maimed, sick, infirm, or disabled animal to lie in any street, road, or other public place for more than three hours after receiving notice of the animal's condition.

Subd. 7. **Cruelty.** No person shall willfully instigate or in any way further any act of cruelty to any animal or animals, or any act tending to produce cruelty to animals.

Subd. 8. **Caging.** No person shall cage any animal for public display purposes unless the display cage is constructed of solid material on three sides to protect the caged animal from the elements and unless the horizontal dimension of each side of the cage is at least four times the length of the caged animal. The provisions of this subdivision do not apply to the Minnesota state agricultural society, the Minnesota state fair, or to the county agricultural societies, county fairs, to any agricultural display of caged animals by any political subdivision of the state of

Minnesota, or to district, regional or national educational livestock or poultry exhibitions. The provisions of this subdivision do not apply to captive wildlife, the exhibition of which is regulated by section 97A.041.

Subd 8a. **Harming a service animal.** No person shall intentionally and without justification do either of the following to a service animal while it is providing service or while it is in the custody of the person it serves: (1) cause bodily harm to the animal; or (2) otherwise render the animal unable to perform its duties.

Subd. 9. **Penalty.** (a) Except as otherwise provided in this subdivision, a person who fails to comply with any provision of this section is guilty of a misdemeanor. A person convicted of a second or subsequent violation of subdivision 1 or 7 within five years of a previous violation of subdivision 1 or 7 is guilty of a gross misdemeanor.

(b) A person who intentionally violates subdivision 1 or 7 where the violation results in substantial bodily harm to a pet or companion animal may be sentenced to imprisonment for not more than one year or to payment of a fine of not more than $3,000, or both.

(c) A person convicted of violating paragraph (b) within five years of a previous gross misdemeanor or felony conviction for violating this section may be sentenced to imprisonment for not more than two years or to payment of a fine of not more than $5,000, or both.

(d) A person who intentionally violates subdivision 1 or 7 where the violation results in death or great bodily harm to a pet or companion animal may be sentenced to imprisonment for not more than two years or to payment of a fine of not more than $5,000, or both.

(e) A person who violates subdivision 8a where the violation renders the service animal unable to perform its duties is guilty of a gross misdemeanor.

(f) A person who violates subdivision 8a where the violation results in substantial bodily harm to a service animal may be sentenced to imprisonment for not more than two years or to payment of a fine of not more than $5,000, or both.

(g) A person who intentionally violates subdivision 1 or 7 where the violation results in substantial bodily harm to a pet or companion animal, and the act is done to threaten, intimidate, or terrorize another person, may be sentenced to imprisonment for not more than two years or to payment of a fine of not more than $5,000, or both.

(h) A person who violates subdivision 8a where the violation results in death or great bodily harm to a service animal may be sentenced to imprisonment of not more than four years or to payment of a fine of not more than $10,000, or both.

(i) A person who intentionally violates subdivision 1 or 7 where the violation results in death or great bodily harm to a pet or companion animal, and the act is done to threaten, intimidate, or terrorize another person, may be sentenced to imprisonment for not more than four years or to payment of a fine of not more than $10,000, or both. * * *

Subd. 10. **Restrictions.** If a person is convicted of violating this section, the court shall require that pet or companion animals that have not been seized by a peace officer or agent and are in the custody or control of the person must be turned over to a peace officer or other appropriate officer or agent unless the court determines that the person is able and fit to provide adequately for an animal. * * *
HIST: (10443) RL s 5152; * * * 2010 c 292 s 1-3

343.215 VETERINARIAN IMMUNITY.

A licensed veterinarian acting in good faith and in the normal course of business is immune from civil and criminal liability in any action arising in connection with the report of a suspected incident of animal cruelty.
HIST: 2020 c 89 art 4 s 33

343.22 INVESTIGATION OF CRUELTY COMPLAINTS.

Subdivision 1. **Reporting.** Any person who has reason to believe that a violation of this chapter has taken place or is taking place may apply to any court having jurisdiction over actions alleging violation of that section for a warrant and for investigation. * * * If the court is satisfied of the existence of the grounds of the application, or that there is probable cause to believe a violation exists, it shall issue a signed search warrant and order for investigation to a peace officer in the county. The order shall command the officer to proceed promptly to the location of the alleged violation. The order may command that a doctor of veterinary medicine accompany the officer.

Subd. 2. **Police investigation.** The peace officer shall search the place designated in the warrant and, together with the veterinary doctor, shall conduct an investigation of the facts surrounding the alleged violation. The peace officer may retain in custody, subject to the order of the court, any property or things which are specified in the warrant, including any animal if the warrant so specifies. * * * The officer executing the warrant shall promptly return the warrant to the court, and deliver to it a written inventory of the property or things taken, verified by the certificate of the officer. * * *

Subd. 3. **Disposal of animals.** Upon a proper determination by a licensed doctor of veterinary medicine, any animal taken into custody pursuant to subdivision 1 may be immediately disposed of when the animal is suffering and is beyond cure through reasonable care and treatment. All other animals shall be disposed of as provided in section 343.235. * * *
HIST: 1971 c 647 s 1; * * * 1991 c 122 s 1,2

343.23 EXPENSES OF INVESTIGATION.

The expenses of the investigation authorized by section 343.22, including the fee of the doctor of veterinary medicine, the expenses of keeping or disposing of any animal taken into custody pursuant to an investigation, and all other expenses reasonably incident to the investigation shall be paid by the county * * *. If the person alleged to have violated section 343.21 is found guilty of the violation, the county shall have judgment against the guilty person for the amount of the expenses.
HIST: 1971 c 647 s 2; 1977 c 332 s 16; 1981 c 53 s 4

343.235 DISPOSITION OF SEIZED ANIMALS.

Subdivision 1. **General rule.** An animal taken into custody under section 343.12, 343.22, 343.29, or 343.31 may be humanely disposed of at the discretion of the jurisdiction having custody of the animal ten days after the animal is taken into custody provided that the procedures in subdivision 3 are followed. An animal raised for food or fiber products may not be seized or disposed of without prior examination by a licensed veterinarian pursuant to a warrant issued by a judge.

Subd. 2. **Security.** A person claiming an interest in an animal in custody under subdivision 1 may prevent disposition of the animal by posting security in an amount sufficient to provide for the animal's actual costs of care and keeping. * * *

Subd. 3. **Notice right to hearing.** (a) The authority taking custody of an animal * * * shall give notice of this section by delivering or mailing it to a person claiming an interest in the animal or by posting a copy of it at the place where the animal is taken into custody or by delivering it to a person residing on the property, and telephoning, if possible. * * *

(b) Upon request of a person claiming an interest in the animal, which request must be made within ten days of the date of seizure, a hearing must be held within five business days of the request, to determine the validity of the seizure and impoundment. * * *

(c) The judge or hearing officer may authorize the return of the animal, if the judge or hearing officer finds that:

(1) the animal is physically fit; and

(2) the person claiming an interest in the animal can and will provide the care required by law for the animal.

(d) The person claiming an interest in the animal is liable for all actual costs of care, keeping, and disposal of the animal, except to the extent that a court or hearing officer finds that the seizure or impoundment was not substantially justified by law. * * *
HIST: 1991 c 122 s 4; 1995 c 244 s 7; 1Sp2001 c 8 art 8 s 12,13

343.24 CRUELTY IN TRANSPORTATION.

Subdivision 1. **Penalty.** Any person who does any of the following is guilty of a misdemeanor: (a) carries or causes to be carried, any live animals upon any vehicle or otherwise, without providing suitable racks, cars, crates, or cages in which the animals can both stand and lie down during transportation and while awaiting slaughter; (b) except as provided in subdivision 2, paragraph (a), carries or causes to be carried, upon a vehicle or otherwise, any live animal having feet or legs tied together, or in any other cruel or inhumane manner; (c) transports or detains livestock in cars or compartments for more than 28 consecutive hours without unloading the livestock in a humane manner into properly equipped pens for rest, water, and feeding for a period of at least five consecutive hours, unless requested to do so as provided in subdivision 2, paragraph (b), or unless prevented by storm or unavoidable causes which cannot be anticipated or avoided by the exercise of due diligence and foresight; or (d) permits livestock to be crowded together without sufficient space to stand, or so as to overlie, crush, wound, or kill each other.

Subd. 2. **Exceptions.** (a) A person may carry or cause to be carried, upon a vehicle or otherwise, a cloven-hoofed animal having legs tied together, if:

(1) the person transporting the animal is the animal's owner, or an employee or agent of the owner;

(2) the animal weighs 250 pounds or less;

(3) the tying is done in a humane manner and is necessary for the animal's safe transport; and

(4) the animal's legs are tied for no longer than one-half hour.

(b) A person or corporation engaged in transporting livestock may confine livestock for 36 consecutive hours if the owner or person with custody of that particular shipment of livestock requests in writing that an extension be allowed. * * *
HIST: (10444) RL s 5153; 1921 c 186 s 1; 1981 c 53 s 5; 1998 c 402 s 1

343.25 DOCKING HORSES; PENALTY.

A person who cuts the bony part of a horse's tail for the purpose of docking it, or who causes or knowingly permits the same to be done upon premises of which the person is owner, lessee, or user, or who assists in the cutting is guilty of a misdemeanor. * * *
HIST: (10445) RL s 5154; 1981 c 53 s 6; 1986 c 444

343.26 Repealed, 2010 c 333 art 1 s 40

343.27 POISONING ANIMALS.

Any person who unjustifiably administers any poisonous, or noxious drug or substance to any animal, or procures or permits it to be done, or unjustifiably exposes that drug or substance with intent that the drug be taken by any animal, whether the animal is the property of the person or another, is guilty of a gross misdemeanor.
HIST: (10448) RL s 5157; 1979 c 102 s 13; 1981 c 53 s 8; 1986 c 444

343.28 ANIMAL WITH INFECTIOUS DISEASE.

An owner or person having charge of any animal who knows the animal has any infectious or contagious disease, or knows the animal has recently been exposed to an infectious or contagious disease, who sells or barters the animal, or knowingly permits the animal to run at large or come into contact with any other animal, or with another person without that person's knowledge and permission shall be guilty of a misdemeanor.
HIST: (10450) RL s 5159; 1980 c 467 s 36; 1981 c 53 s 9

343.29 EXPOSURE OF ANIMALS; DUTY OF OFFICERS.
Subdivision 1. **Delivery to shelter.** Any peace officer, animal control officer, or agent of the federation or county or district societies for the prevention of cruelty, may remove, shelter, and care for any animal which is not properly sheltered from cold, hot, or inclement weather or any animal not properly fed and watered, or provided with suitable food and drink in circumstances that threaten the life of the animal. When necessary, a peace officer, animal control officer, or agent may deliver the animal to another person to be sheltered and cared for, and furnished with suitable food and drink. In all cases, the owner, if known, shall be immediately notified as provided in section 343.235, subdivision 3, and the person having possession of the animal, shall have a lien thereon for its actual costs of care and keeping and the expenses of the notice. If the owner or custodian is unknown and cannot by reasonable effort be ascertained, or does not, within ten days after notice, redeem the animal by paying the expenses authorized by this subdivision, the animal may be disposed of as provided in section 343.235.
Subd. 2. **Disposal of animals.** Upon a proper determination by a licensed doctor of veterinary medicine, any animal taken into custody pursuant to subdivision 1 may be immediately disposed of when the animal is suffering and is beyond cure through reasonable care and treatment. The expenses of disposal shall be subject to the provisions of section 343.23.
HIST: (10451) RL s 5160; * * * 1995 c 244 s 8

343.30 INJURY TO BIRDS.
A person who in any manner maliciously maims, kills, or destroys any bird designated as unprotected by section 97A.015, subdivision 52, or who maliciously destroys the nests or eggs of any such bird shall be guilty of a petty misdemeanor.
HIST: (10447) RL s 5156; 1981 c 53 s 11; 1986 c 386 art 4 s 25

343.31 ANIMAL FIGHTS AND POSSESSION OF FIGHTING ANIMALS.
Subdivision 1. **Penalty for animal fighting; attending animal fight.** (a) Whoever does any of the following is guilty of a felony:
(1) promotes, engages in, or is employed in the activity of cockfighting, dogfighting, or violent pitting of one pet or companion animal * * * against another of the same or a different kind;
(2) receives money for the admission of a person to a place used, or about to be used, for that activity;
(3) willfully permits a person to enter or use for that activity premises of which the permitter is the owner, agent, or occupant; or
(4) uses, trains, or possesses a dog or other animal for the purpose of participating in, engaging in, or promoting that activity.
(b) Whoever purchases a ticket of admission or otherwise gains admission to the activity of cockfighting, dogfighting, or violent pitting of one pet or companion animal * * * against another of the same or a different kind is guilty of a gross misdemeanor.
(c) Whoever possesses any device or substance with intent to use or permit the use of the device or substance to enhance an animal's ability to fight is guilty of a gross misdemeanor.
(d) This subdivision shall not apply to the taking of a wild animal by hunting.
Subd. 2. **Presumption of training a fighting dog.** There is a rebuttable presumption that a dog has been trained or is being trained to fight if:
(1) the dog exhibits fresh wounds, scarring, or other indications that the dog has been or will be used for fighting; and
(2) the person possesses training apparatus, paraphernalia, or drugs known to be used to prepare dogs to be fought. * * *
Subd. 3. **Presumption of training fighting birds.** There is a rebuttable presumption that a bird has been trained or is being trained to fight if:
(1) the bird exhibits fresh wounds, scarring, or other indications that the bird has been or will be used for fighting; or

(2) the person possesses training apparatus, paraphernalia, or drugs known to be used to prepare birds to be fought. * * *

Subd. 4. **Peace officer duties.** Animals described in subdivisions 2 and 3 are dangerous weapons and constitute an immediate danger to the safety of humans. A peace officer or animal control authority may remove, shelter, and care for an animal found in the circumstances described in subdivision 2 or 3. If necessary, a peace officer or animal control authority may deliver the animal to another person to be sheltered and cared for. In all cases, the peace officer or animal control authority must immediately notify the owner, if known. * * *

Subd. 5. **Disposition.** (a) An animal taken into custody under subdivision 4 may be humanely disposed of at the discretion of the jurisdiction having custody of the animal ten days after the animal is taken into custody, if the procedures [delineated in this subdivision are followed.] * * *

Subd. 6. **Photographs.** * * * A satisfactorily identified photographic record is as admissible in evidence as the animal itself.

Subd. 7. **Veterinary investigative report.** * * * A satisfactorily identified veterinary investigative report is as admissible in evidence as the animal itself. * * *

HIST: (10449) RL s 5158; * * * 2010 c 292 s 4

346.57 DOGS AND CATS IN MOTOR VEHICLES.

Subdivision 1. **Unattended dogs or cats.** A person may not leave a dog or a cat unattended in a standing or parked motor vehicle in a manner that endangers the dog's or cat's health or safety.

Subd. 2. **Removal of dogs or cats.** A peace officer, as defined in section 626.84, a humane agent a dog warden or a volunteer or professional member of a fire or rescue department of a political subdivision may use reasonable force to enter a motor vehicle and remove a dog or cat which has been left in the vehicle in violation of subdivision 1. A person removing a dog or a cat under this subdivision shall use reasonable means to contact the owner of the dog or cat to arrange for its return home. If the person is unable to contact the owner, the person may take the dog or cat to an animal shelter.

Subd. 3. **Petty misdemeanor.** A person who violates subdivision 1 is subject to a fine of $25.

HIST: 1988 c 711 s 6

347.17 ANY PERSON MAY KILL DOGS IN CERTAIN CASES.

Any person may kill any dog that the person knows is affected with the disease known as hydrophobia, or that may suddenly attack while the person is peacefully walking or riding and while being out of the enclosure of its owner or keeper, and may kill any dog found killing, wounding, or worrying any horses, cattle, sheep, lambs, or other domestic animals.

HIST: (7297-49) 1939 c 410 s 9; 1986 c 444

Chapter 27 -- MISCELLANEOUS STATUTES (PART II)

Category 2, Section 5:
2.5.1. Describe the basic organization, purpose, and definitions and principles of the Minnesota Criminal Code.
2.5.5. Given a variety of scenarios, identify indications that a particular crime has been committed and identify the elements of that crime.
2.5.7. Explain special Minnesota peace office duties associated with specific statutes including: . . . mandated reporter for child abuse and vulnerable adults.

Editors' Note: The following statutes reflect that the Legislature has substantially reorganized the statutes to create the Maltreatment of Minors Act (Chapter 203E).

626.556 REPORTING OF MALTREATMENT OF MINORS.
* * *

Subd. 2.	[Repealed, 1Sp2020 c 2 art 7 s 39]
Subd. 3.	[Repealed, 1Sp2020 c 2 art 7 s 39]
Subd. 3a.	[Repealed, 1Sp2020 c 2 art 7 s 39]
Subd. 3b.	[Repealed, 1Sp2020 c 2 art 7 s 39]
Subd. 3c.	[Repealed, 1Sp2020 c 2 art 7 s 39]
Subd. 3d.	[Repealed, 1Sp2020 c 2 art 7 s 39]
Subd. 3e.	[Repealed, 1Sp2020 c 2 art 7 s 39]
Subd. 3f.	[Repealed, 1Sp2020 c 2 art 7 s 39]
Subd. 4.	[Repealed, 1Sp2020 c 2 art 7 s 39]
Subd. 4a.	[Repealed, 1Sp2020 c 2 art 7 s 39]
Subd. 5.	[Repealed, 1Sp2020 c 2 art 7 s 39]
Subd. 6.	[Repealed, 1Sp2020 c 2 art 7 s 39]
Subd. 6a.	[Repealed, 1Sp2020 c 2 art 7 s 39]
Subd. 7.	[Repealed, 1Sp2020 c 2 art 7 s 39]
Subd. 7a.	[Repealed, 1Sp2020 c 2 art 7 s 39]
Subd. 8.	[Repealed, 1Sp2020 c 2 art 7 s 39]
Subd. 9.	[Repealed, 1Sp2020 c 2 art 7 s 39]
Subd. 10.	[Repealed, 1Sp2020 c 2 art 7 s 39]
Subd. 10a.	[Repealed, 1Sp2020 c 2 art 7 s 39]
Subd. 10b.	[Repealed, 1Sp2020 c 2 art 7 s 39]
Subd. 10c.	[Repealed, 1Sp2020 c 2 art 7 s 39]
Subd. 10d.	[Repealed, 1Sp2020 c 2 art 7 s 39]
Subd. 10e.	[Repealed, 1Sp2020 c 2 art 7 s 39]
Subd. 10f.	[Repealed, 1Sp2020 c 2 art 7 s 39]
Subd. 10g.	[Repealed, 1Sp2020 c 2 art 7 s 39]
Subd. 10h.	[Repealed, 1Sp2020 c 2 art 7 s 39]
Subd. 10i.	[Repealed, 1Sp2020 c 2 art 7 s 39]
Subd. 10j.	[Repealed, 1Sp2020 c 2 art 7 s 39]
Subd. 10k.	[Repealed, 1Sp2020 c 2 art 7 s 39]
Subd. 10l.	[Repealed, 1Sp2020 c 2 art 7 s 39]
Subd. 10m.	[Repealed, 1Sp2020 c 2 art 7 s 39]
Subd. 10n.	[Repealed, 1Sp2020 c 2 art 7 s 39]
§Subd. 11.	[Repealed, 1Sp2020 c 2 art 7 s 39]
Subd. 11a.	[Repealed, 1Sp2020 c 2 art 7 s 39]
Subd. 11b.	[Repealed, 1Sp2020 c 2 art 7 s 39]

Subd. 11c.   [Repealed, 1Sp2020 c 2 art 7 s 39]
Subd. 11d.   [Repealed, 1Sp2020 c 2 art 7 s 39]
Subd. 12.   [Repealed, 1Sp2020 c 2 art 7 s 39]
Subd. 13.   [Repealed, 1988 c 625 s 9]
Subd. 14.   [Repealed, 1Sp2020 c 2 art 7 s 39]
Subd. 15.   [Repealed, 1Sp2020 c 2 art 7 s 39]
Subd. 16.   [Repealed, 1Sp2020 c 2 art 7 s 39]

260E.01 POLICY.

(a) The legislature hereby declares that the public policy of this state is to protect children whose health or welfare may be jeopardized through maltreatment. While it is recognized that most parents want to keep their children safe, sometimes circumstances or conditions interfere with their ability to do so. When this occurs, the health and safety of the children must be of paramount concern. Intervention and prevention efforts must address immediate concerns for child safety and the ongoing risk of maltreatment and should engage the protective capacities of families. In furtherance of this public policy, it is the intent of the legislature under this chapter to:

(1) protect children and promote child safety;

(2) strengthen the family;

(3) make the home, school, and community safe for children by promoting responsible child care in all settings; and

(4) provide, when necessary, a safe temporary or permanent home environment for maltreated children.

(b) In addition, it is the policy of this state to:

(1) require the reporting of maltreatment of children in the home, school, and community settings;

(2) provide for the voluntary reporting of maltreatment of children;

(3) require an investigation when the report alleges sexual abuse or substantial child endangerment;

(4) provide a family assessment, if appropriate, when the report does not allege sexual abuse or substantial child endangerment; and

(5) provide protective, family support, and family preservation services when needed in appropriate cases.

260E.02 MULTIDISCIPLINARY CHILD PROTECTION TEAM.

Subdivision 1. **Establishment of team.** A county shall establish a multidisciplinary child protection team that may include, but not be limited to, the director of the local welfare agency or designees, the county attorney or designees, the county sheriff or designees, representatives of health and education, representatives of mental health or other appropriate human service or community-based agencies, and parent groups. As used in this section, a "community-based agency" may include, but is not limited to, schools, social service agencies, family service and mental health collaboratives, children's advocacy centers, early childhood and family education programs, Head Start, or other agencies serving children and families. A member of the team must be designated as the lead person of the team responsible for the planning process to develop standards for the team's activities with battered women's and domestic abuse programs and services.

Subd. 2. **Duties of team.** A multidisciplinary child protection team may provide public and professional education, develop resources for prevention, intervention, and treatment, and provide case consultation to the local welfare agency or other interested community-based agencies. The community-based agencies may request case consultation from the multidisciplinary child protection team regarding a child or family for whom the community-based agency is providing services. As used in this section, "case consultation" means a case review process in which recommendations are made concerning services to be provided to the identified children and family. Case consultation may be performed by a committee or subcommittee of members representing human services, including mental health and chemical dependency; law enforcement, including probation and parole; the county attorney; a children's advocacy center; health care; education; community-based agencies and other necessary agencies; and persons directly involved in an individual case as designated by other members performing case consultation.

Subd. 3. **Sexually exploited youth outreach program.** A multidisciplinary child protection team may assist the local welfare agency, local law enforcement agency, or an appropriate private organization in developing a program of outreach services for sexually exploited youth, including homeless, runaway, and truant youth who are at risk of sexual exploitation. For the purposes of this subdivision, at least one representative of a youth intervention program or, where this type of program is unavailable, one representative of a nonprofit agency serving youth in crisis shall be appointed to and serve on the multidisciplinary child protection team in addition to the standing members of the team. These services may include counseling, medical care, short-term shelter, alternative living arrangements, and drop-in centers. A juvenile's receipt of intervention services under this subdivision may not be conditioned upon the juvenile providing any evidence or testimony.

Subd. 4. **Information sharing.** (a) The local welfare agency may make available to the case consultation committee or subcommittee all records collected and maintained by the agency under this chapter and in connection with case consultation. A case consultation committee or subcommittee member may share information acquired in the member's professional capacity with the committee or subcommittee to assist in case consultation.

(b) Case consultation committee or subcommittee members must annually sign a data sharing agreement, approved by the commissioner of human services, assuring compliance with chapter 13. Not public data, as defined in section 13.02, subdivision 8a, may be shared with members appointed to the committee or subcommittee in connection with an individual case when the members have signed the data sharing agreement.

(c) All data acquired by the case consultation committee or subcommittee in exercising case consultation duties are confidential as defined in section 13.02, subdivision 3, and shall not be disclosed except to the extent necessary to perform case consultation, and shall not be subject to subpoena or discovery.

(d) No members of a case consultation committee or subcommittee meeting shall disclose what transpired at a case consultation meeting, except to the extent necessary to carry out the case consultation plan. The proceedings and records of the case consultation meeting are not subject to discovery, and may not be introduced into evidence in any civil or criminal action against a professional or local welfare agency arising out of the matter or matters which are the subject of consideration of the case consultation meeting. Information, documents, or records otherwise available from original sources are not immune from discovery or use in any civil or criminal action merely because they were presented during a case consultation meeting. Any person who presented information before the consultation committee or subcommittee or who is a member shall not be prevented from testifying as to matters within the person's knowledge. However, in a civil or criminal proceeding a person shall not be questioned about the person's presentation of information before the case consultation committee or subcommittee or about opinions formed as a result of the case consultation meetings.

(e) A person who violates this subdivision is subject to the civil remedies and penalties provided under chapter 13.

Subd. 5. **Children's advocacy center; definition.** (a) For purposes of this section, "children's advocacy center" means an organization using a multidisciplinary team approach whose primary purpose is to provide children who have been the victims of abuse and their nonoffending family members with:

(1) support and advocacy;

(2) specialized medical evaluation;

(3) trauma-focused mental health services; and

(4) forensic interviews.

(b) Children's advocacy centers provide multidisciplinary case review and the tracking and monitoring of case progress.

260E.03 DEFINITIONS.
Subdivision 1. **Scope.** As used in this chapter, the following terms have the meanings given them unless the specific content indicates otherwise.
Subd. 2. **Accidental.** "Accidental" means a sudden, not reasonably foreseeable, and unexpected occurrence or event that:
(1) is not likely to occur and could not have been prevented by exercise of due care; and
(2) if occurring while a child is receiving services from a facility, happens when the facility and the employee or person providing services in the facility are in compliance with the laws and rules relevant to the occurrence or event.
Subd. 3. **Child fatality.** "Child fatality" means the death of a child from maltreatment.
Subd. 4. **Commissioner.** "Commissioner" means the commissioner of human services unless otherwise indicated in this chapter.
Subd. 5. **Egregious harm.** "Egregious harm" means harm under section 260C.007, subdivision 14, or a similar law of another jurisdiction.
Subd. 6. **Facility.** "Facility" means:
(1) a licensed or unlicensed day care facility, certified license-exempt child care center, residential facility, agency, hospital, sanitarium, or other facility or institution required to be licensed under sections 144.50 to 144.58, 241.021, or 245A.01 to 245A.16, or chapter 144H, 245D, or 245H;
(2) a school as defined in section 120A.05, subdivisions 9, 11, and 13; and chapter 124E; or
(3) a nonlicensed personal care provider organization as defined in section 256B.0625, subdivision 19a.
Subd. 7. **Family assessment.** "Family assessment" means a comprehensive assessment of child safety, risk of subsequent maltreatment, and family strengths and needs that is applied to a maltreatment report that does not allege sexual abuse or substantial child endangerment. Family assessment does not include a determination as to whether maltreatment occurred but does determine the need for services to address the safety of family members and the risk of subsequent maltreatment.
Subd. 8. **Findings and information.** "Findings and information" means a written summary described in section 260E.35, subdivision 7, paragraph (b), of actions taken or services rendered by a local welfare agency following receipt of a report.
Subd. 9. **Immediately.** "Immediately" means as soon as possible but in no event longer than 24 hours.
Subd. 10. **Interested person acting on behalf of the child.** "Interested person acting on behalf of the child" means a parent or legal guardian; stepparent; grandparent; guardian ad litem; adult stepbrother, stepsister, or sibling; or adult aunt or uncle; unless the person has been determined to be the offender who committed the maltreatment.
Subd. 11. **Investigation.** "Investigation" means fact gathering conducted during:
(1) a family investigation related to the current safety of a child and the risk of subsequent maltreatment that determines whether maltreatment occurred and whether child protective services are needed; or
(2) a facility investigation related to duties under section 260E.28.
Subd. 12. **Maltreatment.** "Maltreatment" means any of the following acts or omissions:
(1) egregious harm under subdivision 5;
(2) neglect under subdivision 15;
(3) physical abuse under subdivision 18;
(4) sexual abuse under subdivision 20;
(5) substantial child endangerment under subdivision 22;
(6) threatened injury under subdivision 23;

(7) mental injury under subdivision 13; and

(8) maltreatment of a child in a facility.

Subd. 13. **Mental injury.** "Mental injury" means an injury to the psychological capacity or emotional stability of a child as evidenced by an observable or substantial impairment in the child's ability to function within a normal range of performance and behavior with due regard to the child's culture.

Subd. 14. **Near fatality.** "Near fatality" means a case in which a physician, advanced practice registered nurse, or physician assistant determines that a child is in serious or critical condition as the result of sickness or injury caused by maltreatment.

Subd. 15. **Neglect.** (a) "Neglect" means the commission or omission of any of the acts specified under clauses (1) to (8), other than by accidental means:

(1) failure by a person responsible for a child's care to supply a child with necessary food, clothing, shelter, health, medical, or other care required for the child's physical or mental health when reasonably able to do so;

(2) failure to protect a child from conditions or actions that seriously endanger the child's physical or mental health when reasonably able to do so, including a growth delay, which may be referred to as a failure to thrive, that has been diagnosed by a physician and is due to parental neglect;

(3) failure to provide for necessary supervision or child care arrangements appropriate for a child after considering factors as the child's age, mental ability, physical condition, length of absence, or environment, when the child is unable to care for the child's own basic needs or safety, or the basic needs or safety of another child in their care;

(4) failure to ensure that the child is educated as defined in sections 120A.22 and 260C.163, subdivision 11, which does not include a parent's refusal to provide the parent's child with sympathomimetic medications, consistent with section 125A.091, subdivision 5;

(5) prenatal exposure to a controlled substance, as defined in section 253B.02, subdivision 2, used by the mother for a nonmedical purpose, as evidenced by withdrawal symptoms in the child at birth, results of a toxicology test performed on the mother at delivery or the child at birth, medical effects or developmental delays during the child's first year of life that medically indicate prenatal exposure to a controlled substance, or the presence of a fetal alcohol spectrum disorder;

(6) medical neglect, as defined in section 260C.007, subdivision 6, clause (5);

(7) chronic and severe use of alcohol or a controlled substance by a person responsible for the child's care that adversely affects the child's basic needs and safety; or

(8) emotional harm from a pattern of behavior that contributes to impaired emotional functioning of the child, which may be demonstrated by a substantial and observable effect in the child's behavior, emotional response, or cognition that is not within the normal range for the child's age and stage of development, with due regard to the child's culture.

(b) Nothing in this chapter shall be construed to mean that a child is neglected solely because the child's parent, guardian, or other person responsible for the child's care in good faith selects and depends upon spiritual means or prayer for treatment or care of disease or remedial care of the child in lieu of medical care.

(c) This chapter does not impose upon persons not otherwise legally responsible for providing a child with necessary food, clothing, shelter, education, or medical care a duty to provide that care.

Subd. 16. **Person in a current or recent position of authority.** "Person in a current or recent position of authority" means an individual in a position of authority over a child and includes but is not limited to any person who is a parent or acting in the place of a parent and charged with any of a parent's rights, duties, or responsibilities to a child, or a person who is charged with any duty or responsibility for the health, welfare, or supervision of a child, either independently or through another, no matter how brief, within 120 days immediately preceding the act. Person in a position of authority includes a psychotherapist.

Subd. 17. **Person responsible for the child's care.** "Person responsible for the child's care" means (1) an individual functioning within the family unit and having responsibilities for the care of the child such as a parent, guardian, or other person having similar care responsibilities, or (2) an individual functioning outside the family unit and having responsibilities for the care of the child such as a teacher, school administrator, other school employee or agent, or other lawful custodian of a child having either full-time or short-term care responsibilities including, but not limited to, day care, babysitting whether paid or unpaid, counseling, teaching, and coaching.

Subd. 18. **Physical abuse.** (a) "Physical abuse" means any physical injury, mental injury under subdivision 13, or threatened injury under subdivision 23, inflicted by a person responsible for the child's care on a child other than by accidental means, or any physical or mental injury that cannot reasonably be explained by the child's history of injuries, or any aversive or deprivation procedures, or regulated interventions, that have not been authorized under section 125A.0942 or 245.825.

(b) Abuse does not include reasonable and moderate physical discipline of a child administered by a parent or legal guardian that does not result in an injury. Abuse does not include the use of reasonable force by a teacher, principal, or school employee as allowed by section 121A.582.

(c) For the purposes of this subdivision, actions that are not reasonable and moderate include, but are not limited to, any of the following:

(1) throwing, kicking, burning, biting, or cutting a child;

(2) striking a child with a closed fist;

(3) shaking a child under age three;

(4) striking or other actions that result in any nonaccidental injury to a child under 18 months of age;

(5) unreasonable interference with a child's breathing;

(6) threatening a child with a weapon, as defined in section 609.02, subdivision 6;

(7) striking a child under age one on the face or head;

(8) striking a child who is at least age one but under age four on the face or head, which results in an injury;

(9) purposely giving a child:

(i) poison, alcohol, or dangerous, harmful, or controlled substances that were not prescribed for the child by a practitioner in order to control or punish the child; or

(ii) other substances that substantially affect the child's behavior, motor coordination, or judgment; that result in sickness or internal injury; or that subject the child to medical procedures that would be unnecessary if the child were not exposed to the substances;

(10) unreasonable physical confinement or restraint not permitted under section 609.379, including but not limited to tying, caging, or chaining; or

(11) in a school facility or school zone, an act by a person responsible for the child's care that is a violation under section 121A.58.

Subd. 19. **Report.** "Report" means any communication received by the local welfare agency, police department, county sheriff, or agency responsible for child protection pursuant to this section that describes maltreatment of a child and contains sufficient content to identify the child and any person believed to be responsible for the maltreatment, if known.

Subd. 20. **Sexual abuse.** "Sexual abuse" means the subjection of a child by a person responsible for the child's care, by a person who has a significant relationship to the child, or by a person in a current or recent position of authority, to any act that constitutes a violation of section 609.342 (criminal sexual conduct in the first degree), 609.343 (criminal sexual conduct in the second degree), 609.344 (criminal sexual conduct in the third degree), 609.345 (criminal sexual conduct in the fourth degree), 609.3451 (criminal sexual conduct in the fifth degree), or 609.352 (solicitation of children to engage in sexual conduct; communication of sexually explicit materials to children). Sexual abuse also includes any act involving a child that constitutes a violation of prostitution offenses under sections 609.321 to 609.324 or 617.246. Sexual abuse includes all reports of known or suspected child sex trafficking involving a child who is identified as a victim of sex trafficking. Sexual abuse includes child sex trafficking as defined in section 609.321, subdivisions 7a and 7b. Sexual abuse includes threatened sexual abuse, which includes the status of a parent or household member who has committed a violation that requires registration as an offender under section 243.166, subdivision 1b, paragraph (a) or (b), or required registration under section 243.166, subdivision 1b, paragraph (a) or (b).

Subd. 21. **Significant relationship.** "Significant relationship" means a situation in which the alleged offender is:

(1) the child's parent, stepparent, or guardian;

(2) any of the following persons related to the child by blood, marriage, or adoption: brother, sister, stepbrother, stepsister, first cousin, aunt, uncle, nephew, niece, grandparent, great-grandparent, great-uncle, great-aunt; or

(3) an adult who jointly resides intermittently or regularly in the same dwelling as the child and who is not the child's spouse.

Subd. 22. **Substantial child endangerment.** "Substantial child endangerment" means that a person responsible for a child's care, by act or omission, commits or attempts to commit an act against a child under their care that constitutes any of the following:

(1) egregious harm under subdivision 5;

(2) abandonment under section 260C.301, subdivision 2;

(3) neglect under subdivision 15, paragraph (a), clause (2), that substantially endangers the child's physical or mental health, including a growth delay, which may be referred to as failure to thrive, that has been diagnosed by a physician and is due to parental neglect;

(4) murder in the first, second, or third degree under section 609.185, 609.19, or 609.195;

(5) manslaughter in the first or second degree under section 609.20 or 609.205;

(6) assault in the first, second, or third degree under section 609.221, 609.222, or 609.223;

(7) solicitation, inducement, and promotion of prostitution under section 609.322;

(8) criminal sexual conduct under sections 609.342 to 609.3451;

(9) solicitation of children to engage in sexual conduct under section 609.352;

(10) malicious punishment or neglect or endangerment of a child under section 609.377 or 609.378;

(11) use of a minor in sexual performance under section 617.246; or

(12) parental behavior, status, or condition that mandates that the county attorney file a termination of parental rights petition under section 260C.503, subdivision 2.

Subd. 23. **Threatened injury.** (a) "Threatened injury" means a statement, overt act, condition, or status that represents a substantial risk of physical or sexual abuse or mental injury.

(b) Threatened injury includes, but is not limited to, exposing a child to a person responsible for the child's care, as defined in subdivision 17, who has:

(1) subjected a child to, or failed to protect a child from, an overt act or condition that constitutes egregious harm under subdivision 5 or a similar law of another jurisdiction;

(2) been found to be palpably unfit under section 260C.301, subdivision 1, paragraph (b), clause (4), or a similar law of another jurisdiction;

(3) committed an act that resulted in an involuntary termination of parental rights under section 260C.301, or a similar law of another jurisdiction; or

(4) committed an act that resulted in the involuntary transfer of permanent legal and physical custody of a child to a relative under Minnesota Statutes 2010, section 260C.201, subdivision 11, paragraph (d), clause (1), section 260C.515, subdivision 4, or a similar law of another jurisdiction.

(c) A child is the subject of a report of threatened injury when the local welfare agency receives birth match data under section 260E.14, subdivision 4, from the Department of Human Services.

260E.04 EVIDENCE.

No evidence relating to the maltreatment of a child or to any prior incident of maltreatment involving any of the same persons accused of maltreatment shall be excluded in any proceeding arising out of the alleged maltreatment on the grounds of privilege set forth in section 595.02, subdivision 1, paragraph (a), (d), or (g).

260E.05 CULTURAL PRACTICES.

A person who conducts an assessment or investigation under this chapter shall take into account accepted child-rearing practices of the culture in which a child participates and accepted teacher discipline practices that are not injurious to the child's health, welfare, and safety.

260E.06 MALTREATMENT REPORTING.

Subdivision 1. **Mandatory reporters.** (a) A person who knows or has reason to believe a child is being maltreated, as defined in section 260E.03, or has been maltreated within the preceding three years, shall immediately report the information to the local welfare agency, agency responsible for assessing or investigating the report, police department, county sheriff, tribal social services agency, or tribal police department if the person is:

(1) a professional or professional's delegate who is engaged in the practice of the healing arts, social services, hospital administration, psychological or psychiatric treatment, child care, education, correctional supervision, probation and correctional services, or law enforcement; or

(2) employed as a member of the clergy and received the information while engaged in ministerial duties, provided that a member of the clergy is not required by this subdivision to report information that is otherwise privileged under section 595.02, subdivision 1, paragraph (c).

(b) "Practice of social services," for the purposes of this subdivision, includes but is not limited to employee assistance counseling and the provision of guardian ad litem and parenting time expeditor services.

Subd. 2. **Voluntary reporters.** Any person may voluntarily report to the local welfare agency, agency responsible for assessing or investigating the report, police department, county sheriff, tribal social services agency, or tribal police department if the person knows, has reason to believe, or suspects a child is being or has been maltreated.

Subd. 3. **Reporting in cases where selection of spiritual means or prayer for treatment or care may cause serious danger to child's health.** If the child's parent, guardian, or other person responsible for the child's care in good faith selects and depends upon spiritual means or prayer for treatment or care of disease or remedial care of the child in lieu of medical care, the parent, guardian, or caretaker, or a person mandated to report pursuant to subdivision 1, has a duty to report if a lack of medical care may cause serious danger to the child's health.

Subd. 4. **Licensing board duty to report.** A board or other entity whose licensees perform work within a school facility, upon receiving a complaint of alleged maltreatment, shall report the alleged maltreatment to the commissioner of education.

260E.07 RETALIATION PROHIBITED.

(a) An employer of any person required to make reports under section 260E.06, subdivision 1, or 260E.11, subdivision 1, shall not retaliate against the person for reporting in good faith maltreatment pursuant to this chapter or against a child with respect to whom a report is made, because of the report.

(b) The employer of any person required to report under section 260E.06, subdivision 1, or 260E.11, subdivision 1, who retaliates against the person because of a report of maltreatment is liable to that person for actual damages and, in addition, a penalty of up to $10,000.

(c) There shall be a rebuttable presumption that any adverse action within 90 days of a report is retaliatory. For purposes of this paragraph, the term "adverse action" refers to action taken by an employer of a person required to report under section 260E.06, subdivision 1, or 260E.11, subdivision 1, which is involved in a report against the person making the report or the child with respect to whom the report was made because of the report, and includes, but is not limited to:

(1) discharge, suspension, termination, or transfer from the facility, institution, school, or agency;

(2) discharge from or termination of employment;

(3) demotion or reduction in remuneration for services; or

(4) restriction or prohibition of access to the facility, institution, school, agency, or persons affiliated with it.

260E.08 CRIMINAL PENALTIES FOR FAILURE TO REPORT; CIVIL PENALTY FOR MAKING FALSE REPORT.

(a) A person mandated by section 260E.06, subdivision 1, to report who knows or has reason to believe that a child is maltreated, as defined in section 260E.03, or has been maltreated within the preceding three years, and fails to report is guilty of a misdemeanor.

(b) A person mandated by section 260E.06, subdivision 1, to report who knows or has reason to believe that two or more children not related to the offender have been maltreated, as defined in section 260E.03, by the same offender within the preceding ten years, and fails to report is guilty of a gross misdemeanor.

(c) A parent, guardian, or caretaker who knows or reasonably should know that the child's health is in serious danger and who fails to report as required by section 260E.06, subdivision 3, is guilty of a gross misdemeanor if the child suffers substantial or great bodily harm because of the lack of medical care. If the child dies because of the lack of medical care, the person is guilty of a felony and may be sentenced to imprisonment for not more than two years or to payment of a fine of not more than $4,000, or both. The provision in section 609.378, subdivision 1, paragraph (a), clause (1), providing that a parent, guardian, or caretaker may, in good faith, select and depend on spiritual means or prayer for treatment or care of a child, does not exempt a parent, guardian, or caretaker from the duty to report under this chapter.

(d) Any person who knowingly or recklessly makes a false report under the provisions of this chapter shall be liable in a civil suit for any actual damages suffered by the person or persons so reported and for any punitive damages set by the court or jury, plus costs and reasonable attorney fees.

260E.09 REPORTING REQUIREMENTS.

(a) An oral report shall be made immediately by telephone or otherwise. An oral report made by a person required under section 260E.06, subdivision 1, to report shall be followed within 72 hours, exclusive of weekends and holidays, by a report in writing to the appropriate police department, the county sheriff, the agency responsible for assessing or investigating the report, or the local welfare agency.

(b) Any report shall be of sufficient content to identify the child, any person believed to be responsible for the maltreatment of the child if the person is known, the nature and extent of the maltreatment, and the name and address of the reporter. The local welfare agency or agency responsible for assessing or investigating the report shall accept a report made under section 260E.06 notwithstanding refusal by a reporter to provide the reporter's name or address as long as the report is otherwise sufficient under this paragraph.

260E.10 NOTIFICATION TO REPORTERS.

Subdivision 1. **Screening notification.** If requested, the agency responsible for assessing or investigating a report shall inform the reporter within ten days after the report was made, either orally or in writing, whether the report was accepted or not. If the responsible agency determines the report does not constitute a report under this chapter, the agency shall advise the reporter that the report was screened out.

Subd. 2. **Final notification.** Any person mandated to report shall receive a summary of the disposition of any report made by that reporter, including whether the case has been opened for child protection or other services, or if a referral has been made to a community organization, unless release would be detrimental to the best interests of the child. Any person who is not mandated to report shall, upon request to the local welfare agency, receive a concise summary of the disposition of any report made by that reporter, unless release would be detrimental to the best interests of the child.

260E.11 AGENCY DESIGNATED TO RECEIVE REPORTS.

Subdivision 1. **Reports of maltreatment in facility.** A person mandated to report child maltreatment occurring within a licensed facility shall report the information to the agency responsible for licensing or certifying the facility under sections 144.50 to 144.58, 241.021, and 245A.01 to 245A.16; or chapter 144H, 245D, or 245H; or a nonlicensed personal care provider organization as defined in section 256B.0625, subdivision 19a.

Subd. 2. **Reporting deprivation of parental rights or kidnapping to law enforcement.** A person mandated to report under section 260E.06, subdivision 1, who knows or has reason to know of a violation of section 609.25 or 609.26 shall report the information to the local police department or the county sheriff.

Subd. 3. **Report to medical examiner or coroner; notification to local agency and law enforcement; report ombudsman.** (a) A person mandated to report maltreatment who knows or has reason to believe a child has died as a result of maltreatment shall report that information to the appropriate medical examiner or coroner instead of the local welfare agency, police department, or county sheriff.

(b) The medical examiner or coroner shall notify the local welfare agency, police department, or county sheriff in instances in which the medical examiner or coroner believes that the child has died as a result of maltreatment. The medical examiner or coroner shall complete an investigation as soon as feasible and report the findings to the police department or county sheriff and the local welfare agency.

(c) If the child was receiving services or treatment for mental illness, developmental disability, chemical dependency, or emotional disturbance from an agency, facility, or program as defined in section 245.91, the medical examiner or coroner shall also notify and report findings to the ombudsman established under sections 245.91 to 245.97.

260E.12 REQUIRED ACTIONS OF THE RESPONSIBLE AGENCY AND LAW ENFORCEMENT UPON RECEIVING REPORT.

Subdivision 1. **Police department or county sheriff.** (a) The police department or the county sheriff shall immediately notify the local welfare agency or agency responsible for child protection reports under this chapter orally and in writing when a report is received.

(b) Written reports received by a police department or the county sheriff shall be forwarded immediately to the local welfare agency or the agency responsible for assessing or investigating the report. The police department or the county sheriff may keep copies of reports received by them.

(c) The county sheriff and the head of each local welfare agency, agency responsible for child protection reports, and police department shall designate a person within the agency, department, or office who is responsible for ensuring that the notification duties of this section are carried out. If the alleged maltreatment occurs on tribal land, the local welfare agency or agency responsible for child protection reports and the local police department or county sheriff shall immediately notify the tribe's social services agency and tribal law enforcement orally and in writing when a report is received. When a police department or county determines that a child has been the subject of maltreatment by a person licensed by the Professional Educator Licensing and Standards Board or the Board of School Administrators, the department or sheriff shall, in addition to other duties under this section, immediately inform the licensing board.

(d) If a child is the victim of an alleged crime under subdivision 2, paragraph (c), the law enforcement agency shall immediately notify the local welfare agency, which shall offer appropriate social services for the purpose of safeguarding and enhancing the welfare of the maltreated child.

Subd. 2. **Local welfare agency or agency responsible for maltreatment report.** (a) The local welfare agency or agency responsible for child protection reports shall immediately notify the local police department or the county sheriff orally and in writing when a report is received.

(b) Copies of written reports received by a local welfare agency or the agency responsible for assessing or investigating the report shall be forwarded immediately to the local police department or the county sheriff.

(c) Receipt by a local welfare agency of a report or notification of a report of kidnapping under section 609.25 or depriving another of custodial or parental rights under section 609.26 shall not be construed to invoke the duties under this chapter except notification of law enforcement and the offer of services under section 260E.20, subdivision 1, paragraph (a), as appropriate.

Subd. 3. **Penalties for failure to cross notify.** (a) If a local welfare agency receives a report under section 260E.06 and fails to notify the local police department or county sheriff as required by subdivision 2, the person within the agency who is responsible for ensuring that notification is made shall be subject to disciplinary action in keeping with the agency's existing policy or collective bargaining agreement on discipline of employees.

(b) If a local police department or a county sheriff receives a report under section 260E.06 and fails to notify the local welfare agency as required by subdivision 1, the person within the police department or county sheriff's office who is responsible for ensuring that notification is made shall be subject to disciplinary action in keeping with the agency's existing policy or collective bargaining agreement on discipline of employees.

260E.13 REPORT TO OMBUDSMAN.

When a local welfare agency receives a report or otherwise has information indicating that a child who is a client, as defined in section 245.91, has been the subject of maltreatment at an agency, facility, or program, as defined in section 245.91, the local welfare agency shall, in addition to its other duties under this chapter, immediately inform the ombudsman established under sections 245.91 to 245.97. The commissioner of education shall inform the ombudsman established under sections 245.91 to 245.97 of reports regarding a child who is a client, as defined in section 245.91, that maltreatment occurred at a school as defined in section 120A.05, subdivisions 9, 11, and 13, and chapter 124E.

260E.14 AGENCY RESPONSIBLE FOR SCREENING AND ASSESSMENT OR INVESTIGATION.

Subdivision 1. **Facilities and schools.** (a) The local welfare agency is the agency responsible for investigating allegations of maltreatment in child foster care, family child care, legally nonlicensed child care, and reports involving children served by an unlicensed personal care provider organization under section 256B.0659. Copies of findings related to personal care provider organizations under section 256B.0659 must be forwarded to the Department of Human Services provider enrollment.

(b) The Department of Human Services is the agency responsible for screening and investigating allegations of maltreatment in juvenile correctional facilities listed under section 241.021 located in the local welfare agency's county and in facilities licensed or certified under chapters 245A, 245D, and 245H, except for child foster care and family child care.

(c) The Department of Health is the agency responsible for screening and investigating allegations of maltreatment in facilities licensed under sections 144.50 to 144.58 and 144A.43 to 144A.482 or chapter 144H.

(d) The Department of Education is the agency responsible for screening and investigating allegations of maltreatment in a school as defined in section 120A.05, subdivisions 9, 11, and 13, and chapter 124E. The Department of Education's responsibility to screen and investigate includes allegations of maltreatment involving students 18 to 21 years of age, including students receiving special education services, up to and including graduation and the issuance of a secondary or high school diploma.

(e) A health or corrections agency receiving a report may request the local welfare agency to provide assistance pursuant to this section and sections 260E.20 and 260E.22.

Subd. 2. **Sexual abuse.** (a) The local welfare agency is the agency responsible for investigating an allegation of sexual abuse if the alleged offender is the parent, guardian, sibling, or an individual functioning within the family unit as a person responsible for the child's care, or a person with a significant relationship to the child if that person resides in the child's household.

(b) The local welfare agency is also responsible for investigating when a child is identified as a victim of sex trafficking.

Subd. 3. **Neglect or physical abuse.** The local welfare agency is responsible for immediately conducting a family assessment or investigation if the report alleges neglect or physical abuse by a parent, guardian, or individual functioning within the family unit as a person responsible for the child's care.

Subd. 4. **Birth match.** (a) Upon receiving data under section 144.225, subdivision 2b, contained in a birth record or recognition of parentage identifying a child who is subject to threatened injury under section 260E.03, subdivision 23, the Department of Human Services shall send the data to the responsible local welfare agency. The data is known as "birth match data."

(b) Unless the responsible local welfare agency has already begun an investigation or assessment of the report due to the birth of the child or execution of the recognition of parentage and the parent's previous history with child protection, the agency shall accept the birth match data as a report under section 260E.03, subdivision 23.

Subd. 5. **Law enforcement.** (a) The local law enforcement agency is the agency responsible for investigating a report of maltreatment if a violation of a criminal statute is alleged.

(b) Law enforcement and the responsible agency must coordinate their investigations or assessments as required under this chapter when the report alleges maltreatment that is a violation of a criminal statute by a person who is a parent, guardian, sibling, person responsible for the child's care functioning within the family unit, or person who lives in the child's household and who has a significant relationship to the child, in a setting other than a facility as defined in section 260E.03.

260E.15 SCREENING GUIDELINES.

(a) Child protection staff, supervisors, and others involved in child protection screening shall follow the guidance provided in the maltreatment screening guidelines issued by the commissioner and, when notified by the commissioner, shall immediately implement updated procedures and protocols.

(b) Any modification to the screening guidelines must be preapproved by the commissioner and must not be less protective of children than is mandated by statute. The county agency must consult with the county attorney before proposing modifications to the commissioner. The guidelines may provide additional protection for children but must not limit reports that are screened in or provide additional limits on consideration of reports that were screened out in making a screening determination.

260E.16 TIMELINE FOR SCREENING.

(a) The local welfare agency shall determine if the report is to be screened in or out as soon as possible but in no event longer than 24 hours after the report is received.

(b) When determining whether a report will be screened in or out, the agency receiving the report must consider, when relevant, all previous history, including reports that were screened out. The agency may communicate with treating professionals and individuals specified under section 260E.35, subdivision 4, paragraph (b).

260E.17 RESPONSE PATH ASSIGNMENT.

Subdivision 1. **Local welfare agency.** (a) Upon receipt of a report, the local welfare agency shall determine whether to conduct a family assessment or an investigation as appropriate to prevent or provide a remedy for maltreatment.

(b) The local welfare agency shall conduct an investigation when the report involves sexual abuse or substantial child endangerment.

(c) The local welfare agency shall begin an immediate investigation if, at any time when the local welfare agency is using a family assessment response, the local welfare agency determines that there is reason to believe that sexual abuse or substantial child endangerment or a serious threat to the child's safety exists.

(d) The local welfare agency may conduct a family assessment for reports that do not allege sexual abuse or substantial child endangerment. In determining that a family assessment is appropriate, the local welfare agency may consider issues of child safety, parental cooperation, and the need for an immediate response.

(e) The local welfare agency may conduct a family assessment on a report that was initially screened and assigned for an investigation. In determining that a complete investigation is not required, the local welfare agency must document the reason for terminating the investigation and notify the local law enforcement agency if the local law enforcement agency is conducting a joint investigation.

Subd. 2. **Responsible social service agency.** The responsible agency shall conduct an investigation when the report alleges maltreatment in a facility required to be licensed or certified under chapter 144H, 245A, 245D, or 245H; under sections 144.50 to 144.58 and 241.021; in a school as defined in section 120A.05, subdivisions 9, 11, and 13, and chapter 124E; or in a nonlicensed personal care provider association as defined in section 256B.0625, subdivision 19a.

260E.18 NOTICE TO CHILD'S TRIBE.

The local welfare agency shall provide immediate notice, according to section 260.761, subdivision 2, to an Indian child's tribe when the agency has reason to believe the family assessment or investigation may involve an Indian child. For purposes of this section, "immediate notice" means notice provided within 24 hours.

260E.19 CONFLICT OF INTEREST.

(a) A potential conflict of interest related to assisting in an investigation or assessment under this chapter resulting in a direct or shared financial interest with a child maltreatment treatment provider or resulting from a personal or family relationship with a party in the investigation must be considered by the local welfare agency in an effort to prevent unethical relationships.

(b) A person who conducts an investigation or assessment under this chapter may not have:

(1) any direct or shared financial interest or referral relationship resulting in a direct shared financial gain with a child maltreatment treatment provider; or

(2) a personal or family relationship with a party in the assessment or investigation.

(c) If an independent assessor is not available, the person responsible for making the determination under this chapter may use the services of an assessor with a financial interest, referral, or personal or family relationship.

260E.20 AGENCY DUTIES REGARDING INVESTIGATION AND ASSESSMENT.

Subdivision 1. **General duties.** (a) The local welfare agency shall offer services to prevent future maltreatment, safeguarding and enhancing the welfare of the maltreated child, and supporting and preserving family life whenever possible.

(b) If the report alleges a violation of a criminal statute involving maltreatment or child endangerment under section 609.378, the local law enforcement agency and local welfare agency shall coordinate the planning and execution of their respective investigation and assessment efforts to avoid a duplication of fact-finding efforts and multiple interviews. Each agency shall prepare a separate report of the results of the agency's investigation or assessment.

(c) In cases of alleged child maltreatment resulting in death, the local agency may rely on the fact-finding efforts of a law enforcement investigation to make a determination of whether or not maltreatment occurred.

(d) When necessary, the local welfare agency shall seek authority to remove the child from the custody of a parent, guardian, or adult with whom the child is living.

(e) In performing any of these duties, the local welfare agency shall maintain an appropriate record.

(f) In conducting a family assessment or investigation, the local welfare agency shall gather information on the existence of substance abuse and domestic violence.

(g) If the family assessment or investigation indicates there is a potential for abuse of alcohol or other drugs by the parent, guardian, or person responsible for the child's care, the local welfare agency shall conduct a chemical use assessment pursuant to Minnesota Rules, part 9530.6615.

(h) The agency may use either a family assessment or investigation to determine whether the child is safe when responding to a report resulting from birth match data under section 260E.03, subdivision 23, paragraph (c). If the child subject of birth match data is determined to be safe, the agency shall consult with the county attorney to determine the appropriateness of filing a petition alleging the child is in need of protection or services under section 260C.007, subdivision 6, clause (16), in order to deliver needed services. If the child is determined not to be safe, the agency and the county attorney shall take appropriate action as required under section 260C.503, subdivision 2.

Subd. 2. **Face-to-face contact.** (a) Upon receipt of a screened in report, the local welfare agency shall conduct a face-to-face contact with the child reported to be maltreated and with the child's primary caregiver sufficient to complete a safety assessment and ensure the immediate safety of the child.

(b) The face-to-face contact with the child and primary caregiver shall occur immediately if sexual abuse or substantial child endangerment is alleged and within five calendar days for all other reports. If the alleged offender was not already interviewed as the primary caregiver, the local welfare agency shall also conduct a face-to-face interview with the alleged offender in the early stages of the assessment or investigation.

(c) At the initial contact with the alleged offender, the local welfare agency or the agency responsible for assessing or investigating the report must inform the alleged offender of the complaints or allegations made against the individual in a manner consistent with laws protecting the rights of the person who made the report. The interview with the alleged offender may be postponed if it would jeopardize an active law enforcement investigation.

(d) The local welfare agency or the agency responsible for assessing or investigating the report must provide the alleged offender with an opportunity to make a statement. The alleged offender may submit supporting documentation relevant to the assessment or investigation.

Subd. 3. **Collection of information.** (a) The local welfare agency responsible for conducting a family assessment or investigation shall collect available and relevant information to determine child safety, risk of subsequent maltreatment, and family strengths and needs and share not public information with an Indian's tribal social services agency without violating any law of the state that may otherwise impose a duty of confidentiality on the local welfare agency in order to implement the tribal state agreement.

(b) The local welfare agency or the agency responsible for investigating the report shall collect available and relevant information to ascertain whether maltreatment occurred and whether protective services are needed.

(c) Information collected includes, when relevant, information with regard to the person reporting the alleged maltreatment, including the nature of the reporter's relationship to the child and to the alleged offender, and the basis of the reporter's knowledge for the report; the child allegedly being maltreated; the alleged offender; the child's caretaker; and other collateral sources having relevant information related to the alleged maltreatment.

(d) Information relevant to the assessment or investigation must be asked for, and may include:

(1) the child's sex and age; prior reports of maltreatment, including any maltreatment reports that were screened out and not accepted for assessment or investigation; information relating to developmental functioning; credibility of the child's statement; and whether the

information provided under this clause is consistent with other information collected during the course of the assessment or investigation;

(2) the alleged offender's age, a record check for prior reports of maltreatment, and criminal charges and convictions;

(3) collateral source information regarding the alleged maltreatment and care of the child. Collateral information includes, when relevant: (i) a medical examination of the child; (ii) prior medical records relating to the alleged maltreatment or the care of the child maintained by any facility, clinic, or health care professional and an interview with the treating professionals; and (iii) interviews with the child's caretakers, including the child's parent, guardian, foster parent, child care provider, teachers, counselors, family members, relatives, and other persons who may have knowledge regarding the alleged maltreatment and the care of the child; and

(4) information on the existence of domestic abuse and violence in the home of the child, and substance abuse.

(e) Nothing in this subdivision precludes the local welfare agency, the local law enforcement agency, or the agency responsible for assessing or investigating the report from collecting other relevant information necessary to conduct the assessment or investigation.

(f) Notwithstanding section 13.384 or 144.291 to 144.298, the local welfare agency has access to medical data and records for purposes of paragraph (d), clause (3).

Subd. 4. **Consultation regarding alleged medical neglect.** If the report alleges medical neglect as defined in section 260C.007, subdivision 6, clause (5), the local welfare agency shall, in addition to its other duties under this section, immediately consult with designated hospital staff and with the parents of the infant to verify that appropriate nutrition, hydration, and medication are being provided; and shall immediately secure an independent medical review of the infant's medical charts and records and, if necessary, seek a court order for an independent medical examination of the infant.

Subd. 5. **Law enforcement fact finding.** If the report alleges maltreatment by a person who is not a parent, guardian, sibling, person responsible for the child's care functioning within the family unit, or a person who lives in the child's household and who has a significant relationship to the child, in a setting other than a facility as defined in section 260E.03, the local welfare agency may rely on the fact-finding efforts of the law enforcement investigation to make a determination whether or not threatened injury or other maltreatment has occurred under section 260E.03, subdivision 12, if an alleged offender has minor children or lives with minors.

260E.21 SCREENED OUT REPORTS.

Subdivision 1. **Records.** A report that is screened out must be maintained according to section 260E.35, subdivision 6, paragraph (b).

Subd. 2. **Offer of social services.** A local welfare agency or agency responsible for investigating or assessing a report may use a screened out report for making an offer of social services to the subjects of the screened out report.

260E.22 INTERVIEWS.

Subdivision 1. **Authority to interview.** (a) The agency responsible for assessing or investigating reports of maltreatment has the authority to interview the child, the person or persons responsible for the child's care, the alleged offender, and any other person with knowledge of the maltreatment for the purpose of gathering facts, assessing safety and risk to the child, and formulating a plan.

(b) Authority of the local welfare agency responsible for assessing or investigating the maltreatment report, the agency responsible for assessing or investigating the report, and the local law enforcement agency responsible for investigating the alleged maltreatment includes but is not limited to authority to interview, without parental consent, the alleged victim and any other children who currently reside with or who have resided with the alleged offender.

Subd. 2. **Interview procedure.** (a) The interview may take place at school or at any facility or other place where the alleged victim or other children might be found or the child may be transported to, and the interview may be conducted at a place appropriate for the interview of a child designated by the local welfare agency or law enforcement agency.

(b) The interview may take place outside the presence of the alleged offender or parent, legal custodian, guardian, or school official.

(c) For a family assessment, it is the preferred practice to request a parent or guardian's permission to interview the child before conducting the child interview, unless doing so would compromise the safety assessment.

Subd. 3. **Notification after interview.** (a) Except as provided in this subdivision, the parent, legal custodian, or guardian shall be notified by the responsible agency or local law enforcement agency no later than the conclusion of the investigation or assessment that this interview has occurred.

(b) Notwithstanding notice required under the Minnesota Rules of Juvenile Protection, the juvenile court may, after hearing on an ex parte motion by the local welfare agency, order that, where reasonable cause exists, the agency withhold notification of this interview from the parent, legal custodian, or guardian. If the interview took place or is to take place on school property, the order shall specify that school officials may not disclose to the parent, legal custodian, or guardian the contents of the notification of intent to interview the child on school property, as provided under this subdivision, and any other related information regarding the interview that may be a part of the child's school record. A copy of the order shall be sent by the local welfare or law enforcement agency to the appropriate school official.

Subd. 4. **Tennessen notice not required.** In conducting investigations and assessments pursuant to this chapter, the notice required by section 13.04, subdivision 2, need not be provided to a child under the age of ten who is the alleged victim of maltreatment.

Subd. 5. **Court order for interview.** (a) Where the alleged offender or a person responsible for the care of the alleged victim or other child prevents access to the victim or other child by the local welfare agency, the juvenile court may order the parent, legal custodian, or guardian to produce the alleged victim or other child for questioning by the local welfare agency or the local law enforcement agency outside the presence of the alleged offender or any person responsible for the child's care at reasonable places and times as specified by court order.

(b) Before making an order under paragraph (a), the court shall issue an order to show cause, either upon its own motion or upon a verified petition, specifying the basis for the requested interview and fixing the time and place of the hearing. The order to show cause shall be served personally and shall be heard in the same manner as provided in other cases in the juvenile court. The court shall consider the need for appointment of a guardian ad litem to protect the best interests of the child. If appointed, the guardian ad litem shall be present at the hearing on the order to show cause.

Subd. 6. **Interview format.** (a) When conducting an investigation, the local welfare agency shall use a question and answer interviewing format with questioning as nondirective as possible to elicit spontaneous responses.

(b) For investigations only, the following interviewing methods and procedures must be used whenever possible when collecting information:

(1) audio recording of all interviews with witnesses and collateral sources; and

(2) in a case of alleged sexual abuse, audio-video recording of each interview with the alleged victim and a child witness.

Subd. 7. **Interviews on school property.** (a) When the local welfare agency, local law enforcement agency, or the agency responsible for assessing or investigating a report of maltreatment determines that an interview should take place on school property, written notification of intent to interview the child on school property must be received by school officials before the interview. The notification shall include the name of the child to be interviewed, the purpose of the interview, and a reference to the statutory authority to conduct an interview on school property. For an interview conducted by the local welfare agency, the notification shall be signed by the chair of the local welfare agency or the chair's designee. The notification shall be private data on individuals subject to the provisions of this subdivision. School officials may not disclose to the parent, legal custodian, or guardian the contents of the notification or any other related information regarding the interview until notified in writing by the local welfare agency or local law enforcement agency that the investigation or assessment has been concluded, unless a school employee or agent is alleged to have maltreated the child. Until that time, the local welfare agency, local law enforcement agency, or the agency responsible for assessing or investigating a report of maltreatment shall be solely responsible for any disclosure regarding the nature of the assessment or investigation.

(b) Except where the alleged offender is believed to be a school official or employee, the time, place, and manner of the interview on school premises shall be within the discretion of school officials, but the local welfare agency or local law enforcement agency shall have the exclusive authority to determine who may attend the interview. The conditions as to time, place, and manner of the interview set by the school officials shall be reasonable, and the interview shall be conducted not more than 24 hours after the receipt of the notification unless another time is considered necessary by agreement between the school officials and the local welfare agency or local law enforcement agency. Where the school fails to comply with the provisions of this paragraph, the juvenile court may order the school to comply. Every effort must be made to reduce the disruption of the educational program of the child, other students, or school staff when an interview is conducted on school premises.

260E.23 DOCUMENTING INTERVIEWS WITH CHILD MALTREATMENT VICTIMS.

Subdivision 1. **Policy.** It is the policy of this state to encourage adequate and accurate documentation of the number and content of interviews conducted with alleged child maltreatment victims during the course of a child maltreatment assessment or investigation, criminal investigation, or prosecution, and to discourage interviews that are unnecessary, duplicative, or otherwise not in the best interests of the child.

Subd. 2. **Definitions.** As used in this section:

(1) "government employee" means an employee of a state or local agency, and any person acting as an agent of a state or local agency;

(2) "interview" means a statement of an alleged maltreatment victim which is given or made to a government employee during the course of a maltreatment assessment or investigation, criminal investigation, or prosecution; and

(3) "record" means an audio or video recording of an interview, or a written record of an interview.

Subd. 3. **Record required.** Whenever an interview is conducted, the interviewer must make a record of the interview. The record must contain the following information:

(1) the date, time, place, and duration of the interview;

(2) the identity of the persons present at the interview; and

(3) if the record is in writing, a summary of the information obtained during the interview.

Subd. 4. **Records maintained.** The records shall be maintained by the interviewer in accordance with applicable provisions of section 260E.35 and chapter 13.

Subd. 5. **Guidelines on tape recording of interviews.** Every county attorney's office shall be responsible for developing written guidelines on the tape recording of interviews by government employees who conduct child maltreatment assessments or investigations, criminal investigations, or prosecutions. The guidelines are public data as defined in section 13.02, subdivision 14.

260E.24 CONCLUSION OF FAMILY ASSESSMENT OR FAMILY INVESTIGATION BY LOCAL WELFARE AGENCY.

Subdivision 1. **Timing.** The local welfare agency shall conclude the family assessment or the investigation within 45 days of the receipt of a report. The conclusion of the assessment or investigation may be extended to permit the completion of a criminal investigation or the receipt of expert information requested within 45 days of the receipt of the report.

Subd. 2. **Determination after family assessment.** After conducting a family assessment, the local welfare agency shall determine whether child protective services are needed to address the safety of the child and other family members and the risk of subsequent maltreatment.

Subd. 3. **Determinations after family investigation.** (a) After conducting an investigation, the local welfare agency shall make two determinations: (1) whether maltreatment occurred; and (2) whether child protective services are needed.

(b) No determination of maltreatment shall be made when the alleged offender is a child under the age of ten.

(c) The local welfare agency or the agency responsible for investigating the report may make a determination of no maltreatment early in an investigation, and close the case and retain immunity, if the collected information shows no basis for a full investigation.

Subd. 4. **Child protective services.** For the purposes of this chapter, except for section 260E.37, a determination that child protective services are needed means that the local welfare agency documented conditions during the assessment or investigation sufficient to cause a child protection worker, as defined in section 260E.37, to conclude that a child is at significant risk of maltreatment if protective intervention is not provided and that the individual or individuals responsible for the child's care have not taken or are not likely to take action to protect the child from maltreatment or risk of maltreatment.

Subd. 5. **Notifications at conclusion of family investigation.** (a) Within ten working days of the conclusion of an investigation, the local welfare agency or agency responsible for investigating the report shall notify the parent or guardian of the child and the person determined to be maltreating the child, if not the parent or guardian of the child, of the determination and a summary of the specific reasons for the determination.

(b) The notice must include a certification that the information collection procedures under section 260E.20 were followed and a notice of the right of a data subject to obtain access to other private data on the subject collected, created, or maintained under this section.

(c) In addition, the notice shall include the length of time that the records will be kept under section 260E.35, subdivision 6. The investigating agency shall notify the parent or guardian of the child who is the subject of the report, and any person determined to have maltreated the child, of their appeal or review rights under this chapter.

(d) The notice must also state that a finding of maltreatment may result in denial of a license or certification application or background study disqualification under chapter 245C related to employment or services that are licensed or certified by the Department of Human Services under chapter 245A or 245H, the Department of Health under chapter 144 or 144A, the Department of Corrections under section 241.021, and from providing services related to an unlicensed personal care provider organization under chapter 256B.

Subd. 6. **Required referral to early intervention services.** A child under age three who is involved in a substantiated case of maltreatment shall be referred for screening under the Individuals with Disabilities Education Act, part C. Parents must be informed that the evaluation and acceptance of services are voluntary. The commissioner of human services shall monitor referral rates by county and annually report the information to the legislature. Refusal to have a child screened is not a basis for a child in need of protection or services petition under chapter 260C.

Subd. 7. **Notification at conclusion of family assessment.** Within ten working days of the conclusion of a family assessment, the local welfare agency shall notify the parent or guardian of the child of the need for services to address child safety concerns or significant risk of subsequent maltreatment. The local welfare agency and the family may also jointly agree that family support and family preservation services are needed.

260E.25 PROVISION OF MEDICAL CARE.

(a) If lack of medical care due to a parent's, guardian's, or caretaker's good faith selection and dependence upon spiritual means or prayer for treatment or care of disease or remedial care for the child in lieu of medical care may result in serious danger to the child's health, the local welfare agency may ensure that necessary medical services are provided to the child.

(b) If the review or examination required under section 260E.20, subdivision 4, leads to a conclusion of medical neglect, the agency shall intervene on behalf of the infant by initiating legal proceedings under section 260C.141 and by filing an expedited motion to prevent the withholding of medically indicated treatment.

260E.26 PROVISION OF CHILD PROTECTIVE SERVICES.

The local welfare agency shall create a written plan, in collaboration with the family whenever possible, within 30 days of the determination that child protective services are needed or upon joint agreement of the local welfare agency and the family that family support and preservation services are needed. Child protective services for a family are voluntary unless ordered by the court.

260E.27 CONSULTATION WITH THE COUNTY ATTORNEY.

The local welfare agency shall consult with the county attorney to determine the appropriateness of filing a petition alleging the child is in need of protection or services under section 260C.007, subdivision 6, if:

(1) the family does not accept or comply with a plan for child protective services;

(2) voluntary child protective services may not provide sufficient protection for the child; or

(3) the family is not cooperating with an investigation or assessment.

260E.28 CONDUCTING INVESTIGATION IN FACILITY OR SCHOOL.

Subdivision 1. **Immediate investigation for alleged maltreatment in a facility.** (a) The commissioner of human services, health, or education, whichever is responsible for investigating the report, shall immediately investigate if the report alleges that:

(1) a child who is in the care of a facility as defined in section 260E.03 is the victim of maltreatment in a facility by an individual in that facility or has been the victim of maltreatment in a facility by an individual in that facility within the three years preceding the report; or

(2) a child is the victim of maltreatment in a facility by an individual in a facility defined in section 260E.03, subdivision 6, while in the care of that facility within the three years preceding the report.

(b) The commissioner of the agency responsible for investigating the report shall arrange for the transmittal to the commissioner of reports received by local agencies and may delegate to a local welfare agency the duty to investigate reports. The commissioner of the agency responsible for investigating the report or local welfare agency may interview any children who are or have been in the care of a facility under investigation and the children's parents, guardians, or legal custodians.

(c) In conducting an investigation under this section, the commissioner has the powers and duties specified for a local welfare agency under this chapter.

Subd. 2. **Preinterview notification for facility investigation.** Before any interview related to maltreatment in a facility under the provisions of section 260E.22, the commissioner of the agency responsible for investigating the report or local welfare agency shall notify the parent, guardian, or legal custodian of a child who will be interviewed in the manner provided for in section 260E.22. If reasonable efforts to reach the parent, guardian, or legal custodian of a child in an out-of-home placement have failed, the child may be interviewed if there is reason to believe the interview is necessary to protect the child or other children in the facility. The commissioner of the agency responsible for assessing or investigating the report or local agency must provide the information required in this subdivision to the parent, guardian, or legal custodian of a child interviewed without parental notification as soon as possible after the interview. When the investigation is completed, any parent, guardian, or legal custodian notified under this subdivision shall receive the written memorandum provided for in section 260E.30, subdivision 5.

Subd. 3. **Facility records.** The commissioner of human services, the ombudsman for mental health and developmental disabilities, the local welfare agencies responsible for investigating reports, the commissioner of education, and the local law enforcement agencies have the right to enter a facility as defined in section 260E.03 and to inspect and copy the facility's records, including medical records, as part of the investigation. Notwithstanding the provisions of chapter 13, the commissioner of human services, the ombudsman for mental health and developmental disabilities, the local welfare agencies responsible for investigating reports, the commissioner of education, and the local law enforcement agencies also have the right to inform the facility under investigation that an investigation is being conducted, to disclose to the facility the names of the individuals under investigation for maltreating a child, and to provide the facility with a copy of the report and the investigative findings.

Subd. 4. **Access to information.** In conducting investigations under this chapter, the commissioner or local welfare agency shall obtain access to information consistent with section 260E.20, subdivision 3. In conducting investigations under this section, the commissioner of education shall obtain access to reports and investigative data that are relevant to a report of maltreatment and are in the possession of a school facility as defined in section 260E.03, subdivision 6, clause (2), notwithstanding the classification of the data as educational or personnel data under chapter 13. This includes but is not limited to school investigative reports, information concerning the conduct of school personnel alleged to have committed maltreatment of students, information about witnesses, and any protective or corrective action taken by the school facility regarding the school personnel alleged to have committed maltreatment.

Subd. 5. **Investigation involving school facility.** In conducting an investigation involving a school facility as defined in section 260E.03, subdivision 6, clause (2), the commissioner of education shall collect available and relevant information and use the procedures in sections 260E.20, subdivisions 2 and 3, and 260E.22, except that the requirement for face-to-face observation of the child and face-to-face interview of the alleged offender is to occur in the initial stages of the investigation provided that the commissioner may also base the investigation on investigative reports and data received from the school facility and local law enforcement agency, to the extent those investigations satisfy the requirements of sections 260E.20, subdivisions 2 and 3, and 260E.22.

260E.29 NOTIFICATION REQUIREMENTS FOR SCHOOLS AND FACILITIES.

Subdivision 1. **Notification requirements for school facility.** (a) Notwithstanding section 260E.09, the commissioner of education must inform the parent, guardian, or legal custodian of the child who is the subject of a report of alleged maltreatment in a school facility within ten days of receiving the report, either orally or in writing, whether the commissioner is investigating the report of alleged maltreatment.

(b) Regardless of whether a report is made under section 260E.09, as soon as practicable after a school receives information regarding an incident that may constitute maltreatment of a child in a school facility, the school shall inform the parent, legal guardian, or custodian of the child that an incident occurred that may constitute maltreatment of the child, when the incident occurred, and the nature of the conduct that may constitute maltreatment.

Subd. 2. **Notification requirements for other types of facilities.** When a report is received that alleges maltreatment of a child while in the care of a licensed or unlicensed day care facility, residential facility, agency, hospital, sanitarium, or other facility or institution required to be licensed or certified according to sections 144.50 to 144.58; 241.021; or 245A.01 to 245A.16; or chapter 144H, 245D, or 245H; or a school as defined in section 120A.05, subdivisions 9, 11, and 13; and chapter 124E; or a nonlicensed personal care provider organization as defined in section 256B.0625, subdivision 19a, the commissioner of the agency responsible for investigating the report or local welfare agency investigating the report shall provide the following information to the parent, guardian, or legal custodian of a child alleged to have been the victim of maltreatment in the facility; the name of the facility; the fact that a report alleging maltreatment in the facility has been received; the nature of the alleged maltreatment in the facility; that the agency is conducting an investigation; any protective or corrective measures being taken pending the outcome of the investigation; and that a written memorandum will be provided when the investigation is completed.

Subd. 3. **Discretionary notification.** The commissioner of the agency responsible for investigating the report or local welfare agency may also provide the information in subdivision 2 to the parent, guardian, or legal custodian of any other child in the facility if the investigative agency knows or has reason to believe the alleged maltreatment of a child in the facility occurred. In determining whether to exercise this authority, the commissioner of the agency responsible for investigating the report or local welfare agency shall consider the seriousness of the alleged maltreatment of a child in the facility; the number of alleged victims of maltreatment of a child in the facility; the number of alleged offenders; and the length of the investigation. The facility shall be notified whenever this discretion is exercised.

260E.30 CONCLUSION OF SCHOOL OR FACILITY INVESTIGATION.
Subdivision 1. **Investigation involving a school facility.** If the commissioner of education conducts an investigation, the commissioner shall determine whether maltreatment occurred and what corrective or protective action was taken by the school facility. If a determination is made that maltreatment occurred, the commissioner shall report to the employer, the school board, and any appropriate licensing entity the determination that maltreatment occurred and what corrective or protective action was taken by the school facility. In all other cases, the commissioner shall inform the school board or employer that a report was received; the subject of the report; the date of the initial report; the category of maltreatment alleged as defined in section 260E.03, subdivision 12; the fact that maltreatment was not determined; and a summary of the specific reasons for the determination.
Subd. 2. **Investigation involving a facility.** (a) When maltreatment is determined in an investigation involving a facility, the investigating agency shall also determine whether the facility or individual was responsible, or whether both the facility and the individual were responsible for the maltreatment using the mitigating factors in subdivision 4. Determinations under this subdivision must be made based on a preponderance of the evidence and are private data on individuals or nonpublic data as maintained by the commissioner of education.
(b) Any operator, employee, or volunteer worker at any facility who intentionally maltreats any child in the care of that facility may be charged with a violation of section 609.255, 609.377, or 609.378. Any operator of a facility who knowingly permits conditions to exist that result in maltreatment of a child in a facility while in the care of that facility may be charged with a violation of section 609.378. The facility operator shall inform all mandated reporters employed by or otherwise associated with the facility of the duties required of mandated reporters and shall inform all mandatory reporters of the prohibition against retaliation for reports made in good faith under this section.
Subd. 3. **Nonmaltreatment mistake.** (a) If paragraph (b) applies, rather than making a determination of substantiated maltreatment by the individual, the commissioner of human services shall determine that a nonmaltreatment mistake was made by the individual.
(b) A nonmaltreatment mistake occurs when:
(1) at the time of the incident, the individual was performing duties identified in the center's child care program plan required under Minnesota Rules, part 9503.0045;
(2) the individual has not been determined responsible for a similar incident that resulted in a finding of maltreatment for at least seven years;
(3) the individual has not been determined to have committed a similar nonmaltreatment mistake under this paragraph for at least four years;
(4) any injury to a child resulting from the incident, if treated, is treated only with remedies that are available over the counter, whether ordered by a medical professional or not; and
(5) except for the period when the incident occurred, the facility and the individual providing services were both in compliance with all licensing requirements relevant to the incident.
(c) This subdivision only applies to child care centers licensed under Minnesota Rules, chapter 9503.

Subd. 4. **Mitigating factors in investigating facilities.** (a) When determining whether the facility or individual is the responsible party, or whether both the facility and the individual are responsible for determined maltreatment in a facility, the investigating agency shall consider at least the following mitigating factors:

(1) whether the actions of the facility or the individual caregivers were according to, and followed the terms of, an erroneous physician order, prescription, individual care plan, or directive; however, this is not a mitigating factor when the facility or caregiver was responsible for the issuance of the erroneous order, prescription, individual care plan, or directive or knew or should have known of the errors and took no reasonable measures to correct the defect before administering care;

(2) comparative responsibility between the facility, other caregivers, and requirements placed upon an employee, including the facility's compliance with related regulatory standards and the adequacy of facility policies and procedures, facility training, an individual's participation in the training, the caregiver's supervision, and facility staffing levels and the scope of the individual employee's authority and discretion; and

(3) whether the facility or individual followed professional standards in exercising professional judgment.

(b) The evaluation of the facility's responsibility under paragraph (a), clause (2), must not be based on the completeness of the risk assessment or risk reduction plan required under section 245A.66, but must be based on the facility's compliance with the regulatory standards for policies and procedures, training, and supervision as cited in Minnesota Statutes and Minnesota Rules.

(c) Notwithstanding paragraphs (a) and (b), when maltreatment is determined to have been committed by an individual who is also the facility license holder, both the individual and the facility must be determined responsible for the maltreatment, and both the background study disqualification standards under section 245C.15, subdivision 4, and the licensing or certification actions under sections 245A.06, 245A.07, 245H.06, or 245H.07 apply.

Subd. 5. **Notification when school or facility investigation is completed.** (a) When the commissioner of the agency responsible for investigating the report or local welfare agency has completed its investigation, every parent, guardian, or legal custodian previously notified of the investigation by the commissioner or local welfare agency shall be provided with the following information in a written memorandum: the name of the facility investigated; the nature of the alleged maltreatment of a child in the facility; the investigator's name; a summary of the investigation findings; a statement of whether maltreatment was found; and the protective or corrective measures that are being or will be taken.

(b) The memorandum shall be written in a manner that protects the identity of the reporter and the child and shall not contain the name or, to the extent possible, reveal the identity of the alleged offender or the identity of individuals interviewed during the investigation.

(c) If maltreatment is determined to exist, the commissioner or local welfare agency shall also provide the written memorandum to the parent, guardian, or legal custodian of each child in the facility who had contact with the individual responsible for the maltreatment.

(d) When the facility is the responsible party for maltreatment, the commissioner or local welfare agency shall also provide the written memorandum to the parent, guardian, or legal custodian of each child who received services in the population of the facility where the maltreatment occurred.

(e) This notification must be provided to the parent, guardian, or legal custodian of each child receiving services from the time the maltreatment occurred until either the individual responsible for maltreatment is no longer in contact with a child or children in the facility or the conclusion of the investigation.

(f) In the case of maltreatment within a school facility, as defined in section 120A.05, subdivisions 9, 11, and 13, and chapter 124E, the commissioner of education need not provide notification to parents, guardians, or legal custodians of each child in the facility, but shall, within ten days after the investigation is completed, provide written notification to the parent, guardian, or legal custodian of any student alleged to have been maltreated.

(g) The commissioner of education may notify the parent, guardian, or legal custodian of any student involved as a witness to alleged maltreatment.

Subd. 6. **Notification to parent, child, or offender following investigation.** (a) Within ten working days of the conclusion of an investigation, the local welfare agency or agency responsible for investigating the report of maltreatment in a facility shall notify the parent or guardian of the child, the person determined to be maltreating the child, and the director of the facility of the determination and a summary of the specific reasons for the determination.

(b) When the investigation involves a child foster care setting that is monitored by a private licensing agency under section 245A.16, the local welfare agency responsible for investigating the report shall notify the private licensing agency of the determination and shall provide a summary of the specific reasons for the determination. The notice to the private licensing agency must include identifying private data, but not the identity of the reporter of maltreatment.

(c) The notice must also include a certification that the information collection procedures under section 260E.20, subdivision 3, were followed and a notice of the right of a data subject to obtain access to other private data on the subject collected, created, or maintained under this section.

(d) In addition, the notice shall include the length of time that the records will be kept under section 260E.35, subdivision 6.

(e) The investigating agency shall notify the parent or guardian of the child who is the subject of the report, and any person or facility determined to have maltreated a child, of their appeal or review rights under this section.

(f) The notice must also state that a finding of maltreatment may result in denial of a license or certification application or background study disqualification under chapter 245C related to employment or services that are licensed by the Department of Human Services under chapter 245A or 245H, the Department of Health under chapter 144 or 144A, the Department of Corrections under section 241.021, and from providing services related to an unlicensed personal care provider organization under chapter 256B.

260E.31 REPORTING OF PRENATAL EXPOSURE TO CONTROLLED SUBSTANCES.

Subdivision 1. **Reports required.** (a) Except as provided in paragraph (b), a person mandated to report under this chapter shall immediately report to the local welfare agency if the person knows or has reason to believe that a woman is pregnant and has used a controlled substance for a nonmedical purpose during the pregnancy, including but not limited to tetrahydrocannabinol, or has consumed alcoholic beverages during the pregnancy in any way that is habitual or excessive.

(b) A health care professional or a social service professional who is mandated to report under this chapter is exempt from reporting under paragraph (a) a woman's use or consumption of tetrahydrocannabinol or alcoholic beverages during pregnancy if the professional is providing the woman with prenatal care or other health care services.

(c) Any person may make a voluntary report if the person knows or has reason to believe that a woman is pregnant and has used a controlled substance for a nonmedical purpose during the pregnancy, including but not limited to tetrahydrocannabinol, or has consumed alcoholic beverages during the pregnancy in any way that is habitual or excessive.

(d) An oral report shall be made immediately by telephone or otherwise. An oral report made by a person required to report shall be followed within 72 hours, exclusive of weekends and holidays, by a report in writing to the local welfare agency. Any report shall be of sufficient content to identify the pregnant woman, the nature and extent of the use, if known, and the name and address of the reporter. The local welfare agency shall accept a report made under paragraph (c) notwithstanding refusal by a voluntary reporter to provide the reporter's name or address as long as the report is otherwise sufficient.

(e) For purposes of this section, "prenatal care" means the comprehensive package of medical and psychological support provided throughout the pregnancy.

Subd. 2. **Local welfare agency.** Upon receipt of a report of prenatal exposure to a controlled substance required under subdivision 1, the local welfare agency shall immediately conduct an appropriate assessment and offer services indicated under the circumstances. Services offered may include but are not limited to a referral for chemical dependency assessment, a referral for chemical dependency treatment if recommended, and a referral for prenatal care. The local welfare agency may also take any appropriate action under chapter 253B, including seeking an emergency admission under section 253B.051. The local welfare agency shall seek an emergency admission under section 253B.051 if the pregnant woman refuses recommended voluntary services or fails recommended treatment.

Subd. 3. **Related provisions.** Reports under this section are governed by sections 260E.05, 260E.06, 260E.34, and 260E.35.

Subd. 4. **Controlled substances.** For purposes of this section and section 260E.32, "controlled substance" means a controlled substance listed in section 253B.02, subdivision 2.
* * *

260E.34 IMMUNITY.

(a) The following persons are immune from any civil or criminal liability that otherwise might result from the person's actions, if the person is acting in good faith:

(1) a person making a voluntary or mandated report under this chapter or assisting in an assessment under this chapter;

(2) a person with responsibility for performing duties under this section or supervisor employed by a local welfare agency, the commissioner of an agency responsible for operating or supervising a licensed or unlicensed day care facility, residential facility, agency, hospital, sanitarium, or other facility or institution required to be licensed or certified under sections 144.50 to 144.58; 241.021; 245A.01 to 245A.16; or chapter 245B or 245H; or a school as defined in section 120A.05, subdivisions 9, 11, and 13; and chapter 124E; or a nonlicensed personal care provider organization as defined in section 256B.0625, subdivision 19a, complying with sections 260E.23, subdivisions 2 and 3, and 260E.30; and

(3) a public or private school, facility as defined in section 260E.03, or the employee of any public or private school or facility who permits access by a local welfare agency, the Department of Education, or a local law enforcement agency and assists in an investigation or assessment pursuant to this chapter.

(b) A person who is a supervisor or person with responsibility for performing duties under this chapter employed by a local welfare agency, the commissioner of human services, or the commissioner of education complying with this chapter or any related rule or provision of law is immune from any civil or criminal liability that might otherwise result from the person's actions, if the person is (1) acting in good faith and exercising due care, or (2) acting in good faith and following the information collection procedures established under section 260E.20, subdivision 3.

(c) Any physician or other medical personnel administering a toxicology test under section 260E.32 to determine the presence of a controlled substance in a pregnant woman, in a woman within eight hours after delivery, or in a child at birth or during the first month of life is immune from civil or criminal liability arising from administration of the test, if the physician ordering the test believes in good faith that the test is required under this section and the test is administered in accordance with an established protocol and reasonable medical practice.

(d) This section does not provide immunity to any person for failure to make a required report or for committing maltreatment.

(e) If a person who makes a voluntary or mandatory report under section 260E.06 prevails in a civil action from which the person has been granted immunity under this section, the court may award the person attorney fees and costs.

260E.35 DATA PRACTICES.

Subdivision 1. **Maintaining data.** Notwithstanding the data's classification in the possession of any other agency, data acquired by the local welfare agency or the agency responsible for assessing or investigating the report during the course of the assessment or investigation are private data on individuals and must be maintained according to this section.

Subd. 2. **Data collected during investigation of maltreatment in school.** (a) Data of the commissioner of education collected or maintained during and for the purpose of an investigation of alleged maltreatment in a school are governed by this chapter, notwithstanding the data's classification as educational, licensing, or personnel data under chapter 13.

(b) In conducting an investigation involving a school facility as defined in section 260E.03, subdivision 6, clause (2), the commissioner of education shall collect investigative reports and data that are relevant to a report of maltreatment from local law enforcement and the school facility.

Subd. 3. **Classification and release of data.** (a) A written copy of a report maintained by personnel of agencies, other than welfare or law enforcement agencies, which are subject to chapter 13 shall be confidential. An individual subject of the report may obtain access to the original report as provided by paragraphs (g) to (o).

(b) All reports and records created, collected, or maintained under this chapter by a local welfare agency or law enforcement agency may be disclosed to a local welfare or other child welfare agency of another state when the agency certifies that:

(1) the reports and records are necessary to conduct an investigation of actions that would qualify as maltreatment under this chapter; and

(2) the reports and records will be used only for purposes of a child protection assessment or investigation and will not be further disclosed to any other person or agency.

(c) The local social service agency or law enforcement agency in this state shall keep a record of all records or reports disclosed pursuant to this subdivision and of any agency to which the records or reports are disclosed. If in any case records or reports are disclosed before a determination is made under section 260E.24, subdivision 3, paragraph (a), or a disposition of a criminal proceeding is reached, the local social service agency or law enforcement agency in this state shall forward the determination or disposition to any agency that has received a report or record under this subdivision.

(d) The responsible authority of a local welfare agency or the responsible authority's designee may release private or confidential data on an active case involving assessment or investigation of actions that are defined as maltreatment under this chapter to a court services agency if:

(1) the court services agency has an active case involving a common client who is the subject of the data; and

(2) the data are necessary for the court services agency to effectively process the court services agency's case, including investigating or performing other duties relating to the case required by law.

(e) The data disclosed under paragraph (d) may be used only for purposes of the active court services case described in paragraph (d), clause (1), and may not be further disclosed to any other person or agency, except as authorized by law.

(f) Records maintained under subdivision 4, paragraph (b), may be shared with another local welfare agency that requests the information because it is conducting an assessment or investigation under this section of the subject of the records.

(g) Except as provided in paragraphs (b), (h), (i), (o), and (p); subdivision 1; and sections 260E.22, subdivision 2; and 260E.23, all records concerning individuals maintained by a local welfare agency or agency responsible for assessing or investigating the report under this chapter, including any written reports filed under sections 260E.06 and 260E.09, shall be private data on individuals, except insofar as copies of reports are required by section 260E.12, subdivision 1 or 2, to be sent to the local police department or the county sheriff.

(h) All records concerning determinations of maltreatment by a facility are nonpublic data as maintained by the Department of Education, except insofar as copies of reports are required by section 260E.12, subdivision 1 or 2, to be sent to the local police department or the county sheriff.

(i) Reports maintained by any police department or the county sheriff shall be private data on individuals, except the reports shall be made available to the investigating, petitioning, or prosecuting authority, including a county medical examiner or county coroner.

(j) Section 13.82, subdivisions 8, 9, and 14, apply to law enforcement data other than the reports.

(k) The local welfare agency or agency responsible for assessing or investigating the report shall make available to the investigating, petitioning, or prosecuting authority, including a county medical examiner or county coroner or a professional delegate, any records that contain information relating to a specific incident of maltreatment that is under investigation, petition, or prosecution and information relating to any prior incident of maltreatment involving any of the same persons. The records shall be collected and maintained according to chapter 13.

(l) An individual subject of a record shall have access to the record according to those sections, except that the name of the reporter shall be confidential while the report is under assessment or investigation except as otherwise permitted by this section.

(m) Any person conducting an investigation or assessment under this section who intentionally discloses the identity of a reporter before the completion of the investigation or assessment is guilty of a misdemeanor. After the assessment or investigation is completed, the name of the reporter shall be confidential. The subject of the report may compel disclosure of the name of the reporter only with the consent of the reporter or upon a written finding by the court that the report was false and that there is evidence that the report was made in bad faith. This subdivision does not alter disclosure responsibilities or obligations under the Rules of Criminal Procedure.

(n) Upon request of the legislative auditor, data on individuals maintained under this chapter must be released to the legislative auditor in order for the auditor to fulfill the auditor's duties under section 3.971. The auditor shall maintain the data according to chapter 13.

(o) Active law enforcement investigative data received by a local welfare agency or agency responsible for assessing or investigating the report under this chapter are confidential data on individuals. When this data become inactive in the law enforcement agency, the data are private data on individuals.

(p) Section 13.03, subdivision 4, applies to data received by the commissioner of education from a licensing entity.

Subd. 4. **Data disclosed to reporter.** (a) A local welfare or child protection agency, or the agency responsible for assessing or investigating the report of maltreatment, shall provide relevant private data on individuals obtained under this chapter to a mandated reporter who made the report and who has an ongoing responsibility for the health, education, or welfare of a child affected by the data, unless the agency determines that providing the data would not be in the best interests of the child.

(b) The agency may provide the data to other mandated reporters with ongoing responsibility for the health, education, or welfare of the child. Mandated reporters with ongoing responsibility for the health, education, or welfare of a child affected by the data include the child's teachers or other appropriate school personnel, foster parents, health care providers, respite care workers, therapists, social workers, child care providers, residential care staff, crisis nursery staff, probation officers, and court services personnel. Under this chapter, a mandated reporter need not have made the report to be considered a person with ongoing responsibility for the health, education, or welfare of a child affected by the data. Data provided under this chapter must be limited to data pertinent to the individual's responsibility for caring for the child.

(c) A reporter who receives private data on individuals under this subdivision must treat the data according to that classification, regardless of whether the reporter is an employee of a government entity. The remedies and penalties under sections 13.08 and 13.09 apply if a reporter releases data in violation of this chapter or other law.

Subd. 5. **Data provided to commissioner of education.** The commissioner of education must be provided with all requested data that are relevant to a report of maltreatment and are in possession of a school facility as defined in section 260E.03, subdivision 6, clause (2), when the data are requested pursuant to an assessment or investigation of a maltreatment report of a student in a school. If the commissioner of education makes a determination of maltreatment involving an individual performing work within a school facility who is licensed by a board or other agency, the commissioner shall provide a copy of its offender maltreatment determination report to the licensing entity with all student-identifying information removed. The offender maltreatment determination report shall include but is not limited to the following sections: report of alleged maltreatment; legal standard; investigation; summary of findings; determination; corrective action by a school; reconsideration process; and a listing of records related to the investigation. Notwithstanding section 13.03, subdivision 4, data received by a licensing entity under this paragraph are governed by section 13.41 or other applicable law governing data of the receiving entity, except that this section applies to the classification of and access to data on the reporter of the maltreatment.

Subd. 6. **Data retention.** (a) Notwithstanding sections 138.163 and 138.17, a record maintained or a record derived from a report of maltreatment by a local welfare agency, agency responsible for assessing or investigating the report, court services agency, or school under this chapter shall be destroyed as provided in paragraphs (b) to (e) by the responsible authority.

(b) For a report alleging maltreatment that was not accepted for assessment or investigation, a family assessment case, and a case where an investigation results in no determination of maltreatment or the need for child protective services, the record must be maintained for a period of five years after the date the report was not accepted for assessment or investigation or the date of the final entry in the case record. A record of a report that was not accepted must contain sufficient information to identify the subjects of the report, the nature of the alleged maltreatment, and the reasons as to why the report was not accepted. Records under this paragraph may not be used for employment, background checks, or purposes other than to assist in future screening decisions and risk and safety assessments.

(c) All records relating to reports that, upon investigation, indicate either maltreatment or a need for child protective services shall be maintained for ten years after the date of the final entry in the case record.

(d) All records regarding a report of maltreatment, including a notification of intent to interview that was received by a school under section 260E.22, subdivision 7, shall be destroyed by the school when ordered to do so by the agency conducting the assessment or investigation. The agency shall order the destruction of the notification when other records relating to the report under investigation or assessment are destroyed under this subdivision.

(e) Private or confidential data released to a court services agency under subdivision 3, paragraph (d), must be destroyed by the court services agency when ordered to do so by the local welfare agency that released the data. The local welfare agency or agency responsible for assessing or investigating the report shall order destruction of the data when other records relating to the assessment or investigation are destroyed under this subdivision.

Subd. 7. **Disclosure to public.** (a) Notwithstanding any other provision of law and subject to this subdivision, a public agency shall disclose to the public, upon request, the findings and information related to a child fatality or near fatality if:

(1) a person is criminally charged with having caused the child fatality or near fatality;

(2) a county attorney certifies that a person would have been charged with having caused the child fatality or near fatality but for that person's death; or

(3) a child protection investigation resulted in a determination of maltreatment.

(b) Findings and information disclosed under this subdivision consist of a written summary that includes any of the following information the agency is able to provide:

(1) the cause and circumstances regarding the child fatality or near fatality;

(2) the age and gender of the child;

(3) information on any previous reports of maltreatment that are pertinent to the maltreatment that led to the child fatality or near fatality;

(4) information on any previous investigations that are pertinent to the maltreatment that led to the child fatality or near fatality;

(5) the result of any investigations described in clause (4);

(6) actions of and services provided by the local welfare agency on behalf of a child that are pertinent to the maltreatment that led to the child fatality or near fatality; and

(7) the result of any review of the state child mortality review panel, a local child mortality review panel, a local community child protection team, or any public agency.

(c) Nothing in this subdivision authorizes access to the private data in the custody of a local welfare agency, or the disclosure to the public of the records or content of any psychiatric, psychological, or therapeutic evaluation, or the disclosure of information that would reveal the identities of persons who provided information related to maltreatment of the child.

(d) A person whose request is denied may apply to the appropriate court for an order compelling disclosure of all or part of the findings and information of the public agency. The application must set forth, with reasonable particularity, factors supporting the application. The court has jurisdiction to issue these orders. Actions under this chapter must be set down for immediate hearing, and subsequent proceedings in those actions must be given priority by the appellate courts.

(e) A public agency or its employees acting in good faith in disclosing or declining to disclose information under this chapter are immune from criminal or civil liability that might otherwise be incurred or imposed for that action.

Subd. 8. **Disclosure not required.** When interviewing a child under this chapter, an individual does not include the parent or guardian of the child for purposes of section 13.04, subdivision 2, when the parent or guardian is the alleged offender.

260E.36 SPECIALIZED TRAINING AND EDUCATION REQUIRED.

Subdivision 1. **Job classification; continuing education.** (a) The commissioner of human services, for employees subject to the Minnesota Merit System, and directors of county personnel systems, for counties not subject to the Minnesota Merit System, shall establish a job classification consisting exclusively of persons with the specialized knowledge, skills, and experience required to satisfactorily perform child protection duties pursuant to this chapter.
(b) All child protection workers or social services staff having responsibility for child protection duties under this chapter shall receive 15 hours of continuing education or in-service training each year relevant to providing child protective services. The local welfare agency shall maintain a record of training completed by each employee having responsibility for performing child protection duties.

Subd. 2. **Child protection worker foundation education.** An individual who seeks employment as a child protection worker after the commissioner of human services has implemented the foundation training program developed under section 260E.37 must complete competency-based foundation training during their first six months of employment as a child protection worker.

Subd. 3. **Background studies.** (a) County employees hired on or after July 1, 2015, who have responsibility for child protection duties or current county employees who are assigned new child protection duties on or after July 1, 2015, are required to undergo a background study. A county may complete these background studies by either:

(1) use of the Department of Human Services NETStudy 2.0 system according to sections 245C.03 and 245C.10; or

(2) an alternative process defined by the county.

(b) County social services agencies and local welfare agencies must initiate background studies before an individual begins a position allowing direct contact with persons served by the agency.

Subd. 4. **Joint training.** The commissioners of human services and public safety shall cooperate in the development of a joint program for training child maltreatment services professionals in the appropriate techniques for child maltreatment assessment and investigation. The program shall include but need not be limited to the following areas:

(1) the public policy goals of the state as set forth in section 260C.001 and the role of the assessment or investigation in meeting these goals;

(2) the special duties of child protection workers and law enforcement officers under this chapter;

(3) the appropriate methods for directing and managing affiliated professionals who may be utilized in providing protective services and strengthening family ties;

(4) the appropriate methods for interviewing alleged victims of child maltreatment and other children in the course of performing an assessment or an investigation;

(5) the dynamics of child maltreatment within family systems and the appropriate methods for interviewing parents in the course of the assessment or investigation, including training in recognizing cases in which one of the parents is a victim of domestic abuse and in need of special legal or medical services;

(6) the legal, evidentiary considerations that may be relevant to the conduct of an assessment or an investigation;

(7) the circumstances under which it is appropriate to remove the alleged offender or the alleged victim from the home;

(8) the protective social services that are available to protect alleged victims from further maltreatment, to prevent child maltreatment and domestic abuse, and to preserve the family unit; and training in the preparation of case plans to coordinate services for the alleged child victim with services for any parents who are victims of domestic abuse;

(9) the methods by which child protection workers and law enforcement workers cooperate in conducting assessments and investigations in order to avoid duplication of efforts; and

(10) appropriate methods for interviewing alleged victims and conducting investigations in cases where the alleged victim is developmentally, physically, or mentally disabled.

Subd. 5. **Priority training.** The commissioners of human services and public safety shall provide the program courses described in subdivision 2 at convenient times and locations in the state. The commissioners shall give training priority in the program areas cited in subdivision 2 to persons currently performing assessments and investigations pursuant to this chapter.
* * *

260E.37 CHILD PROTECTION WORKERS; TRAINING.

Subdivision 1. **Definitions.** (a) As used in this section, the following terms have the meanings given unless the specific context indicates otherwise.

(b) "Advanced training" means training provided to a local child protection worker after the person has performed an initial six months of employment as a child protection worker.

(c) "Child protection agency" means an agency authorized to receive reports, conduct assessments and investigations, and make determinations pursuant to this chapter.

(d) "Child protection services" means the receipt and assessment of reports of maltreatment and the provision of services to families and children when maltreatment has occurred or when there is risk of maltreatment. These services include:

(1) the assessment of risk to a child alleged to have been maltreated;

(2) interviews of any person alleged to have maltreated a child and the child or children involved in the report, and interviews with persons having facts or knowledge necessary to assess the level of risk to a child and the need for protective intervention;

(3) the gathering of written or evidentiary materials;

(4) the recording of case findings and determinations; and

(5) other actions required by this chapter, administrative rule, or agency policy.

(e) "Competency-based training" means a course of instruction that provides both information and skills practice, which is based upon clearly stated and measurable instructional objectives, and which requires demonstration of the achievement of a particular standard of skills and knowledge for satisfactory completion.

(f) "Foundation training" means training provided to a local child protection worker after the person has begun to perform child protection duties, but before the expiration of six months of employment as a child protection worker. This foundation training must occur during the performance of job duties and must include an evaluation of the employee's application of skills and knowledge.

Subd. 2. **Training program; development.** The commissioner of human services shall develop a program of competency-based foundation and advanced training for child protection workers if funds are appropriated to the commissioner for this purpose.

* * *

HIST: 1Sp2020 c 2 art 7 s 1-39

609.2335 FINANCIAL EXPLOITATION OF VULNERABLE ADULT.

Subdivision 1. **Crime.** Whoever does any of the following acts commits the crime of financial exploitation:

(1) in breach of a fiduciary obligation recognized elsewhere in law, including pertinent regulations, contractual obligations, documented consent by a competent person, or the obligations of a responsible party under section 144.6501 intentionally:

(i) fails to use the real or personal property or other financial resources of the vulnerable adult to provide food, clothing, shelter, health care, therapeutic conduct, or supervision for the vulnerable adult;

(ii) uses, manages, or takes either temporarily or permanently the real or personal property or other financial resources of the vulnerable adult, whether held in the name of the vulnerable adult or a third party, for the benefit of someone other than the vulnerable adult; or

(iii) deprives either temporarily or permanently a vulnerable adult of the vulnerable adult's real or personal property or other financial resources, whether held in the name of the vulnerable adult or a third party, for the benefit of someone other than the vulnerable adult; or

(2) in the absence of legal authority:

(i) acquires possession or control of an interest in real or personal property or other financial resources of a vulnerable adult, whether held in the name of the vulnerable adult or a third party, through the use of undue influence, harassment, or duress;

(ii) forces, compels, coerces, or entices a vulnerable adult against the vulnerable adult's will to perform services for the profit or advantage of another; or

(iii) establishes a relationship with a fiduciary obligation to a vulnerable adult by use of undue influence, harassment, duress, force, compulsion, coercion, or other enticement.

Subd. 2. **Defenses.** (a) Nothing in this section requires a facility or caregiver to provide financial management or supervise financial management for a vulnerable adult except as otherwise required by law.

(b) If the actor knew or had reason to know that the vulnerable adult lacked capacity to consent, consent is not a defense to a violation of this section.

Subd. 3. **Criminal penalties.** A person who violates subdivision 1, clause (1) or (2), item (i), may be sentenced as provided in section 609.52, subdivision 3. A person who violates subdivision 1, clause (2), item (ii) or (iii), may be sentenced to imprisonment for not more than one year or to payment of a fine of not more than $3,000, or both.

Subd. 4. **Aggregation.** In any prosecution under this section, the value of the money or property or services received by the defendant within any six-month period may be aggregated and the defendant charged accordingly in applying the provisions of subdivision 3; provided that when two or more offenses are committed by the same person in two or more counties, the accused may be prosecuted in any county in which one of the offenses was committed for all of the offenses aggregated under this subdivision.

Subd. 5. **Venue.** Notwithstanding anything to the contrary in section 627.01, an offense committed under this section may be prosecuted in: (1) the county where any part of the offense occurred; or (2) the county of residence of the victim or one of the victims.

History: 1995 c 229 art 2 s 5; 2009 c 119 s 8; 2013 c 5 s 1, 2

626.557 REPORTING OF MALTREATMENT OF VULNERABLE ADULTS.

Subdivision 1. **Public policy.** The legislature declares that the public policy of this state is to protect adults who, because of physical or mental disability or dependency on institutional services, are particularly vulnerable to maltreatment; to assist in providing safe environments for vulnerable adults; and to provide safe institutional or residential services, community-based services, or living environments for vulnerable adults who have been maltreated.

* * *

Subd. 2. Repealed, 1995 c 229 art s 24

Subd. 3. **Timing of report.** (a) A mandated reporter who has reason to believe that a vulnerable adult is being or has been maltreated, or who has knowledge that a vulnerable adult has sustained a physical injury which is not reasonably explained shall immediately report the information to the common entry point. If an individual is a vulnerable adult solely because the individual is admitted to a facility, a mandated reporter is not required to report suspected maltreatment of the individual that occurred prior to admission, unless:

(1) the individual was admitted to the facility from another facility and the reporter has reason to believe the vulnerable adult was maltreated in the previous facility; or

(2) the reporter knows or has reason to believe that the individual is a vulnerable adult as defined in section 626.5572, subdivision 21, clause (4).

(b) A person not required to report under the provisions of this section may voluntarily report as described above.

(c) Nothing in this section requires a report of known or suspected maltreatment, if the reporter knows or has reason to know that a report has been made to the common entry point.

(d) Nothing in this section shall preclude a reporter from also reporting to a law enforcement agency.

(e) A mandated reporter who knows or has reason to believe that an error under section 626.5572, subdivision 17, paragraph (c), clause (5), occurred must make a report under this subdivision. * * *

Subd. 3a. **Report not required.** The following events are not required to be reported under this section:

(a) A circumstance where federal law specifically prohibits a person from disclosing patient identifying information in connection with a report of maltreatment, unless the vulnerable adult, or the vulnerable adult's guardian, conservator, or legal representative, has consented to disclosure in a manner which conforms to federal requirements. Facilities whose patients or residents are covered by such a federal law shall seek consent to the disclosure of suspected maltreatment from each patient or resident, or a guardian, conservator, or legal representative, upon the patient's or resident's admission to the facility. Persons who are prohibited by federal law from reporting an incident of suspected maltreatment shall immediately seek consent to make a report.

(b) Verbal or physical aggression occurring between patients, residents, or clients of a facility, or self-abusive behavior by these persons does not constitute abuse unless the behavior causes serious harm. The operator of the facility or a designee shall record incidents of aggression and self-abusive behavior to facilitate review by licensing agencies and county and local welfare agencies.

(c) Accidents as defined in section 626.5572, subdivision 3.

(d) Events occurring in a facility that result from an individual's error in the provision of therapeutic conduct to a vulnerable adult, as provided in section 626.5572, subdivision 17, paragraph (c), clause (4).

(e) Nothing in this section shall be construed to require a report of financial exploitation, as defined in section 626.5572, subdivision 9, solely on the basis of the transfer of money or property by gift or as compensation for services rendered.

Subd. 4. **Reporting.** (a) A mandated reporter shall immediately make an oral report to the common entry point. * * * The common entry point may not require written reports. To the extent possible, the report must be of sufficient content to identify the vulnerable adult, the caregiver, the nature and extent of the suspected maltreatment, any evidence of previous maltreatment, the name and address of the reporter, the time, date, and location of the incident, and any other information that the reporter believes might be helpful in investigating the suspected maltreatment. * * *

Subd. 4a. **Internal reporting of maltreatment.** (a) Each facility shall establish and enforce an ongoing written procedure in compliance with applicable licensing rules to ensure that all cases of suspected maltreatment are reported. If a facility has an internal reporting procedure, a mandated reporter may meet the reporting requirements of this section by reporting internally. However, the facility remains responsible for complying with the immediate reporting requirements of this section.

(b) A facility with an internal reporting procedure that receives an internal report by a mandated reporter shall give the mandated reporter a written notice stating whether the facility has reported the incident to the common entry point. The written notice must be provided within two working days and in a manner that protects the confidentiality of the reporter.

(c) The written response to the mandated reporter shall note that if the mandated reporter is not satisfied with the action taken by the facility on whether to report the incident to the common entry point, then the mandated reporter may report externally.

(d) A facility may not prohibit a mandated reporter from reporting externally, and a facility is prohibited from retaliating against a mandated reporter who reports an incident to the common entry point in good faith. The written notice by the facility must inform the mandated reporter of this protection from retaliatory measure by the facility against the mandated reporter for reporting externally.

Subd. 5. **Immunity; protection for reporters.** (a) A person who makes a good faith report is immune from any civil or criminal liability that might otherwise result from making the report, or from participating in the investigation, or for failure to comply fully with the reporting obligation under section 609.234 or 626.557, subdivision 7.

(b) A person employed by a lead investigative agency or a state licensing agency who is conducting or supervising an investigation or enforcing the law in compliance with this section or any related rule or provision of law is immune from any civil or criminal liability that might otherwise result from the person's actions, if the person is acting in good faith and exercising due care.

(c) A person who knows or has reason to know a report has been made to a common entry point and who in good faith participates in an investigation of alleged maltreatment is immune from civil or criminal liability that otherwise might result from making the report, or from failure to comply with the reporting obligation or from participating in the investigation.

(d) The identity of any reporter may not be disclosed, except as provided in subdivision 12b. * * *

Subd. 6. **Falsified reports.** A person or facility who intentionally makes a false report under the provisions of this section shall be liable in a civil suit for any actual damages suffered by the reported facility, person or persons and for punitive damages up to $10,000 and attorney fees.

Subd. 7. **Failure to report.** A mandated reporter who negligently or intentionally fails to report is liable for damages caused by the failure. Nothing in this subdivision imposes vicarious liability for the acts or omissions of others.

Subd. 8. **Evidence not privileged.** No evidence regarding the maltreatment of the vulnerable adult shall be excluded in any proceeding arising out of the alleged maltreatment on the grounds of lack of competency under section 595.02.

Subd. 9. **The common entry point designation.** (a) * * * The commissioner of human services shall establish a common entry point effective July 1, 2015. The common entry point is the unit responsible for receiving the report of suspected maltreatment under this section.

(b) The common entry point must be available 24 hours per day to take calls from reporters of suspected maltreatment. The common entry point shall use a standard intake form[.]

(d) The common entry point shall immediately report to a law enforcement agency any incident in which there is reason to believe a crime has been committed.

(e) If a report is initially made to a law enforcement agency or a lead investigative agency, those agencies shall take the report on the appropriate common entry point intake forms and immediately forward a copy to the common entry point. * * *

Subd. 9a. **Evaluation and referral of reports made to a common entry point.** (a)The common entry point must screen the reports of alleged or suspected maltreatment for immediate risk and make all necessary referrals as follows:

(1) if the common entry point determines that there is an immediate need for emergency adult protective services, the common entry point agency shall immediately notify the appropriate county agency;

(2) if the report contains suspected criminal activity against a vulnerable adult, the common entry point shall immediately notify the appropriate law enforcement agency;

(3) the common entry point shall refer all reports of alleged or suspected maltreatment to the appropriate lead investigative agency as soon as possible, but in any event no longer than two working days; [and]

(4) if the report contains information about a suspicious death, the common entry point shall immediately notify the appropriate law enforcement agencies, the local medical examiner, and the ombudsman for mental and developmental disabilities established under section 245.92. Law enforcement agencies shall coordinate with the local medical examiner and the ombudsman as provided by law[.]

Subd. 9b. **Response to reports.** Law enforcement is the primary agency to conduct investigations of any incident in which there is reason to believe a crime has been committed. Law enforcement shall initiate a response immediately. If the common entry point notified a county agency for emergency adult protective services, law enforcement shall cooperate with that county agency when both agencies are involved and shall exchange data to the extent authorized in subdivision 12b, paragraph (g). County adult protection shall initiate a response immediately. Each lead investigative agency shall complete the investigative process for reports within its jurisdiction. * * * Each lead investigative agency shall develop guidelines for prioritizing reports for investigation.

Subd. 9c. **Lead investigative agency; notifications, dispositions, and determinations.** (a) Upon request of the reporter, the lead investigative agency shall notify the reporter that it has received the report, and provide information on the initial disposition of the report within five business days of receipt of the report, provided that the notification will not endanger the vulnerable adult or hamper the investigation.

　　　* * *

(e) The lead investigative agency shall complete its final disposition within 60 calendar days. If the lead investigative agency is unable to complete its final disposition within 60 calendar days, the lead investigative agency shall notify the following persons provided that the notification will not endanger the vulnerable adult or hamper the investigation: (1) the vulnerable adult or the vulnerable adult's guardian or health care agent, when known, if the lead investigative agency knows them to be aware of the investigation and (2) the facility, where applicable. The notice shall contain the reason for the delay and the projected completion date. If the lead investigative agency is unable to complete its final disposition by a subsequent projected completion date, the lead investigative agency shall again notify the vulnerable adult or the vulnerable adult's guardian or health care agent, when known if the lead investigative agency knows them to be aware of the investigation, and the where applicable, of the reason for the delay and the revised projected completion date provided that the notification will not endanger the vulnerable adult or hamper the investigation. * * *

(f) Within ten calendar days of completing the final disposition, the lead investigative agency shall provide a copy of the public investigation memorandum under subdivision 12b, paragraph (b), clause (1), when required to be completed under this section, to the following persons: (1) the vulnerable adult, or the vulnerable adult's guardian or health care agent, if known unless the lead investigative agency knows that the notification would endanger the well-being of the vulnerable adult; (2) the reporter, if the reporter requested notification when making the report, provided this notification would not endanger the well-being of the vulnerable adult; (3) the alleged perpetrator, if known; (4) the facility; and (5) the ombudsman for older Minnesotans, or the ombudsman for mental health and mental retardation, as appropriate. * * *

(h) The lead investigative agency shall notify the vulnerable adult who is the subject of the report or the vulnerable adult's guardian or health care agent, if known, and any person or facility determined to have maltreated a vulnerable adult, of their appeal or review rights under this section or section 2.

(i) The lead investigative agency shall routinely provide investigation memoranda for substantiated reports to the appropriate licensing boards. These reports must include the names of substantiated perpetrators. The lead investigative agency may not provide investigative memoranda for inconclusive or false reports to the appropriate licensing boards unless the lead investigative agency's investigation gives reason to believe that there may have been a violation of the applicable professional practice laws. If the investigation memorandum is provided to a licensing board, the subject of the investigation memorandum shall be notified and receive a summary of the investigative findings.
* * *

(k) The lead investigative agency must provide to the commissioner of human services its final dispositions, including the names of all substantiated perpetrators. The commissioner of human services shall establish records to retain the names of substantiated perpetrators.

Subd. 9d. **Administrative reconsideration; review panel.** (a) * * * [A]ny individual or facility which a lead investigative agency determines has maltreated a vulnerable adult, or the vulnerable adult or an interested person acting on behalf of the vulnerable adult, regardless of the lead investigative agency's determination, who contests the lead investigative agency's final disposition of an allegation of maltreatment, may request the lead investigative agency to reconsider its final disposition. * * *

(c) If, as a result of a reconsideration or review, the lead investigative agency changes the final disposition, it shall notify the parties specified in subdivision 9c, paragraph (d). * * *

Subd. 10. **Duties of the county social service agency.** (a) When the common entry point refers a report to the county social service agency as the lead investigative agency or makes a referral to the county social services agency for emergency adult protective services, or when another lead investigative agency requests assistance from the county social service agency for adult protective services, the county social service agency shall immediately assess and offer emergency and continuing protective social services for purposes of preventing further maltreatment and for safeguarding the welfare of the maltreated vulnerable adult. * * * In cases of suspected sexual abuse, the county social service agency shall immediately arrange for and make available to the vulnerable adult appropriate medical examination and treatment. When necessary in order to protect the vulnerable adult from further harm, the county social service agency shall seek authority to remove the vulnerable adult from the situation in which the maltreatment occurred. The county social service agency may also investigate to determine whether the conditions which resulted in the reported maltreatment place other vulnerable adults in jeopardy of being maltreated and offer protective social services that are called for by its determination.

(b) County social service agencies may enter facilities and inspect and copy records as part of an investigation. * * *

(c) When necessary in order to protect a vulnerable adult from serious harm, the county social service agency shall immediately intervene on behalf of that adult to help the family, vulnerable adult, or other interested person by seeking any of the following:

(1) a restraining order or a court order for removal of the perpetrator from the residence of the vulnerable adult pursuant to section 518B.01;

(2) the appointment of a guardian or conservator pursuant to sections 524.5-101 to 524.5-502, or guardianship or conservatorship pursuant to chapter 252A;

(3) replacement of a guardian or conservator suspected of maltreatment and appointment of a suitable person as guardian or conservator, pursuant to sections 524.5-101 to 524.5-502, or

(4) a referral to the prosecuting attorney for possible criminal prosecution of the perpetrator under chapter 609.

The expenses of legal intervention must be paid by the county in the case of indigent persons, under section 524.5-502 and chapter 563.

In proceedings under sections 524.5-101 to 524.5-502, if a suitable relative or other person is not available to petition for guardianship or conservatorship, a county employee shall present the petition with representation by the county attorney. * * * Any person retaliated against in violation of this subdivision shall have a cause of action against the county and shall be entitled to reasonable attorney fees and costs of the action if the action is upheld by the court. * * *

Subd. 12b. **Data management.** (a) In performing any of the duties of this section as a lead investigative agency, the county social service agency shall maintain appropriate records. * * *

Data maintained by the common entry point are confidential data on individuals or protected nonpublic data as defined in section 13.02. Notwithstanding section 138.163, the common entry point shall maintain data for three calendar years after date of receipt and thereafter destroy the data * * *.

(b) The commissioners of health and human services shall prepare an investigation memorandum for each report alleging maltreatment investigated under this section. * * * During an investigation by the commissioner of health or the commissioner of human services, data collected under this section are confidential data on individuals or protected nonpublic data as defined in section 13.02. Upon completion of the investigation, the data are classified as provided [elsewhere in this subdivision.]

The investigation memorandum must be written in a manner which protects the identity of the reporter and of the vulnerable adult and may not contain the names or, to the extent possible, data on individuals or private data listed in clause (2).

(2) Data on individuals collected and maintained in the investigation memorandum are private data, including:

(i) the name of the vulnerable adult;

(ii) the identity of the individual alleged to be the perpetrator;

(iii) the identity of the individual substantiated as the perpetrator; and

(iv) the identity of all individuals interviewed as part of the investigation.

(3) Other data on individuals maintained as part of an investigation under this section are private data on individuals upon completion of the investigation.

(c) After the assessment or investigation is completed, the name of the reporter must be confidential. The subject of the report may compel disclosure of the name of the reporter only with the consent of the reporter or upon a written finding by a court that the report was false and there is evidence that the report was made in bad faith. * * *

(e) The commissioners of health and human services shall annually publish on their Websites the number and type of reports of alleged maltreatment involving licensed facilities reported under this section, the number of those requiring investigation under this section, and the resolution of those investigations. On a biennial basis, the commissioners of health and human services shall jointly report * * * [detailed] information to the legislature and the governor[.] * * *

(g) Lead investigative agencies, prosecuting authorities, and law enforcement agencies may exchange not public data, defined in section 13.02, if the agency or authority requesting the data determines that the data are pertinent and necessary to the requesting agency in initiating, furthering, or completing an investigation under this section. Data collected under this section must be made available to prosecuting authorities and law enforcement officials, local county agencies, and licensing agencies investigating the alleged maltreatment under this section. * * *

(i) A lead investigative agency may notify other affected parties and their authorized representative if the lead investigative agency has reason to believe maltreatment has occurred and determines the information will safeguard the well-being of the affected parties or dispel wide-spread rumor or unrest in the affected facility.

(j) Under any notification provision of this section, where federal law specifically prohibits the disclosure of patient identifying information, lead investigative agency may not provide any notice unless the vulnerable adult has consented to disclosure in a manner which confirms to federal requirements. * * *

Subd. 14. **Abuse prevention plans.** (a) Each facility, except home health agencies and personal care attendant services providers, shall establish and enforce an ongoing written abuse prevention plan. The plan shall contain an assessment of the physical plant, its environment, and its population identifying factors which may encourage or permit abuse, and a statement of specific measures to be taken to minimize the risk of abuse. The plan shall comply with any rules governing the plan promulgated by the licensing agency.

(b) Each facility, including a home health care agency and personal care attendant services providers, shall develop an individual abuse prevention plan for each vulnerable adult residing there or receiving services from them. * * *

Subd. 17. **Retaliation prohibited.** (a) A facility or person shall not retaliate against any person who reports in good faith suspected maltreatment pursuant to this section, or against a vulnerable adult with respect to whom a report is made, because of the report.

(b) In addition to any remedies allowed under sections 181.931 to 181.935, any facility or person which retaliates against any person because of a report of suspected maltreatment is liable to that person for actual damages, punitive damages up to $10,000, and attorney's fees.

(c) There shall be a rebuttable presumption that any adverse action, as defined below, within 90 days of a report, is retaliatory. For purposes of this clause, the term "adverse action" refers to action taken by a facility or person involved in a report against the person making the report or the person with respect to whom the report was made because of the report, and includes, but is not limited to:

(1) Discharge or transfer from the facility;

(2) Discharge from or termination of employment;

(3) Demotion or reduction in remuneration for services;

(4) Restriction or prohibition of access to the facility or its residents; or

(5) Any restriction of rights set forth in section 144.651.
* * *

Subd. 20. **Cause of action for financial exploitation; damages.** (a) A vulnerable adult who is a victim of financial exploitation as defined in section 626.5572, subdivision 9, has a cause of action against the person who committed the financial exploitation. In an action under this subdivision, the vulnerable adult is entitled to recover damages equal to three times the amount of compensatory damages or $10,000, whichever is greater.

(b) In addition to damages under paragraph (a), the vulnerable adult is entitled to recover reasonable attorney fees and costs, including reasonable fees for the services of a guardian or conservator or guardian ad litem incurred in connection with a claim under this subdivision.

(c) An action may be brought under this subdivision regardless of whether there has been a report or final disposition under this section or a criminal complaint or conviction related to the financial exploitation. * * *
HIST: 1980 c 542 s 1; * * * 2015 c 78 art 6 s 23-25; 2019 c 50 art 1 s 128

626.5572 DEFINITIONS.

Subdivision 1. **Scope.** For purpose of section 626.557, the following terms have the meanings given them, unless otherwise specified.

Subd. 2. **Abuse.** "Abuse" means:

(a) An act against a vulnerable adult that constitutes a violation of, an attempt to violate, or aiding and abetting a violation of:

(1) assault in the first through fifth degrees as defined in sections 609.221 to 609.224;

(2) the use of drugs to injure or facilitate crime as defined in section 609.235;

(3) the solicitation, inducement, and promotion of prostitution as defined in section 609.322; and

(4) criminal sexual conduct in the first through fifth degrees as defined in sections 609.342 to 609.3451.

A violation includes any action that meets the elements of the crime, regardless of whether there is a criminal proceeding or conviction.

(b) Conduct which is not an accident or therapeutic conduct as defined in this section, which produces or could reasonably be expected to produce physical pain or injury or emotional distress including, but not limited to, the following:

(1) hitting, slapping, kicking, pinching, biting, or corporal punishment of a vulnerable adult;

(2) use of repeated or malicious oral, written, or gestured language toward a vulnerable adult or the treatment of a vulnerable adult which would be considered by a reasonable person to be disparaging, derogatory, humiliating, harassing, or threatening;

(3) use of any aversive or deprivation procedure, unreasonable confinement, or involuntary seclusion, including the forced separation of the vulnerable adult from other persons against the will of the vulnerable adult or the legal representative of the vulnerable adult; and

(4) use of any aversive or deprivation procedures for persons with developmental disabilities or related conditions not authorized under section 245.825.

(c) Any sexual contact or penetration as defined in section 609.341, between a facility staff person or a person providing services in the facility and a resident, patient, or client of that facility.

(d) The act of forcing, compelling, coercing, or enticing a vulnerable adult against the vulnerable adult's will to perform services for the advantage of another. * * *

Subd. 3. **Accident.** "Accident" means a sudden, unforeseen, and unexpected occurrence or event which:

(1) is not likely to occur and which could not have been prevented by exercise of due care; and

(2) if occurring while a vulnerable adult is receiving services from a facility, happens when the facility and the employee or person providing services in the facility are in compliance with the laws and rules relevant to the occurrence or event.

Subd. 4. **Caregiver.** "Caregiver" means an individual or facility who has responsibility for the care of a vulnerable adult as a result of a family relationship, or who has assumed responsibility for all or a portion of the care of a vulnerable adult voluntarily, by contract, or by agreement. * * *

Subd. 6. **Facility.** (a) "Facility" means a hospital or other entity required to be licensed under sections 144.50 to 144.58; a nursing home required to be licensed to serve adults under section 144A.02; a facility or service required to be licensed under chapter 245A; an assisted living facility required to be licensed under chapter 144I; a home care provider licensed or required to be licensed under sections 144A.43 to 144A.482; a hospice provider licensed under sections 144A.75 to 144A.755; or a person or organization that offers, provides, or arranges for personal care assistant services under the medical assistance program as authorized under section 256B.0625, subdivision 19a, sections 256B.0651 to 256B.0656, section 256B.0659, or section 256B.85.

(b) For services identified in paragraph (a) that are provided in the vulnerable adult's own home or in another unlicensed location, the term "facility" refers to the provider, person, or organization that offers, provides, or arranges for personal care services, and does not refer to the vulnerable adult's home or other location at which services are rendered.

Subd. 7. **False.** "False" means a preponderance of the evidence shows that an act that meets the definition of maltreatment did not occur.

Subd. 8. **Final disposition.** "Final disposition" is the determination of an investigation by a lead investigative agency that a report of maltreatment under Laws 1995, chapter 229, is substantiated, inconclusive, false, or that no determination will be made. When a lead investigative agency determination has substantiated maltreatment, the final disposition also identifies, if known, which individual or individuals were responsible for the substantiated maltreatment, and whether a facility was responsible for the substantiated maltreatment.

Subd. 9. **Financial exploitation.** "Financial exploitation" means:

(a) In breach of a fiduciary obligation recognized elsewhere in law, including pertinent regulations, contractual obligations, documented consent by a competent person, or the obligations of a responsible party under section 144.6501, a person:

(1) engages in unauthorized expenditure of funds entrusted to the actor by the vulnerable adult which results or is likely to result in detriment to the vulnerable adult; or

(2) fails to use the financial resources of the vulnerable adult to provide food, clothing, shelter, health care, therapeutic conduct or supervision for the vulnerable adult, and the failure results or is likely to result in detriment to the vulnerable adult.

(b) In the absence of legal authority a person:

(1) willfully uses, withholds, or disposes of funds or property of a vulnerable adult;

(2) obtains for the actor or another the performance of services by a third person for the wrongful profit or advantage of the actor or another to the detriment of the vulnerable adult;

(3) acquires possession or control of, or an interest in, funds or property of a vulnerable adult through the use of undue influence, harassment, duress, deception, or fraud; or

(4) forces, compels, coerces, or entices a vulnerable adult against the vulnerable adult's will to perform services for the profit or advantage of another. * * *

Subd. 11. **Inconclusive.** "Inconclusive" means there is less than a preponderance of evidence to show that maltreatment did or did not occur.

Subd. 13. **Lead investigative agency.** "Lead investigative agency" is the primary administrative agency responsible for investigating reports made under section 626.557.

(a) The department of health is the lead investigative agency for facilities or services licensed or required to be licensed as hospitals, home care providers, nursing homes, boarding care homes, hospice providers, [or] residential facilities that are also federally certified as intermediate care facilities that serve people with developmental disabilities[.] * * *

(b) The department of human services is the lead investigative agency for facilities or services licensed or required to be licensed as adult day care, adult foster care, community residential settings, programs for people with disabilities, family adult day services, mental health programs, mental health clinics, chemical dependency programs, [or] the Minnesota sex offender program[.] * * *

(c) The county social service agency or its designee is the lead investigative agency for all other reports[.] * * *

Subd. 15. **Maltreatment.** "Maltreatment" means abuse as defined in subdivision 2, neglect as defined in subdivision 17, or financial exploitation as defined in subdivision 9.

Subd. 16. **Mandated reporter.** "Mandated reporter" means a professional or professional's delegate while engaged in: (1) social services; (2) law enforcement; (3) education; (4) the care of vulnerable adults; (5) any of the occupations referred to in section 214.01, subdivision 2; (6) an employee of a rehabilitation facility certified by the commissioner of jobs and training for vocational rehabilitation; (7) an employee or person providing services in a facility as defined in subdivision 6; or (8) a person that performs the duties of the medical examiner or coroner.

Subd. 17. **Neglect.** "Neglect" means:

(a) The failure or omission by a caregiver to supply a vulnerable adult with care or services, including but not limited to, food, clothing, shelter, health care, or supervision which is:

(1) reasonable and necessary to obtain or maintain the vulnerable adult's physical or mental health or safety, considering the physical and mental capacity or dysfunction of the vulnerable adult; and

(2) which is not the result of an accident or therapeutic conduct.

(b) The absence or likelihood of absence of care or services, including but not limited to, food clothing, shelter, health care, or supervision necessary to maintain the physical and mental health of the vulnerable adult which a reasonable person would deem essential to obtain or maintain the vulnerable adult's health, safety, or comfort considering the physical or mental capacity or dysfunction of the vulnerable adult.

(c) For purposes of this section, a vulnerable adult is not neglected for the sole reason that: * * *

(4) an individual makes an error in the provision of therapeutic conduct to a vulnerable adult which does not result in injury or harm which reasonably requires medical or mental health care; or

(5) an individual makes an error in the provision of therapeutic conduct to a vulnerable adult that results in injury or harm, which reasonably requires the care of a physician; and:

(i) the necessary care is provided in a timely fashion as dictated by the condition of the vulnerable adult;

(ii) is after receiving care, the health status of the vulnerable adult can be reasonably expected, as determined by the attending physician, to be restored to the vulnerable adult's preexisting condition;

(iii) the error is not part of a pattern of errors by the individual;

(iv) if in a facility, the error is immediately reported as required under section 626.557, and recorded internally in the facility;

(v) if in a facility, the facility identifies and takes corrective action and implements measures designed to reduce the risk of further occurrence of this error and similar errors; and

(vi) if in a facility, the actions required under items (iv) and (v) are sufficiently documented for review and evaluation by the facility and any applicable licensing, certification, and ombudsman agency. * * *

Subd. 19. **Substantiated.** "Substantiated" means a preponderance of the evidence shows that an act that meets the definition of maltreatment occurred. * * *

Subd. 21. **Vulnerable adult.** (a) "Vulnerable adult" means any person 18 years of age or older who:

(1) is a resident or inpatient of a facility;

(2) receives services required to be licensed under chapter 245A, except that a person receiving outpatient services for treatment of chemical dependency or mental illness, or one who is served in the Minnesota sex offender program on a court-hold order for commitment, or is committed as a sexual psychopathic personality or as a sexually dangerous person under chapter 253B, is not considered a vulnerable adult unless the person meets the requirements of clause (4);

(3) receives services from a home care provider required to be licensed under sections 144A.43 to 144A.482; or from a person or organization that offers, provides, or arranges for personal care assistant services under [an authorized] medical assistance program * * *; or

(4) regardless of residence or whether any type of service is received, possesses a physical or mental infirmity or other physical, mental, or emotional dysfunction:

(i) that impairs the individual's ability to provide adequately for the individual's own care without assistance, including the provision of food, shelter, clothing, health care, or supervision; and

(ii) because of the dysfunction or infirmity and the need for care or services, the individual has an impaired ability to protect the individual's self from maltreatment.

(b) For purposes of this subdivision, "care or services" means care or services for the health, safety, welfare, or maintenance of an individual.

HIST: 1995 c 229 art 1 s 22; * * * 2016 c 158 art 1 s 210,211; 2019 c 60 art 4 s 33

609.234 FAILURE TO REPORT.

Subdivision 1. **Crime.** Any mandated reporter who is required to report under section 626.557, who knows or has reason to believe that vulnerable adult is being or has been maltreated, as defined in section 626.5572, subdivision 15, and who does any of the following is guilty of a misdemeanor:

(1) intentionally fails to make a report;

(2) knowingly provides information which is false, deceptive, or misleading; or

(3) intentionally fails to provide all of the material circumstances surrounding the incident which are known to the reporter when the report is made.

Subd. 2. **Increased penalty.** It is a gross misdemeanor for a person who is mandated to report under section 626.557, who knows or has reason to believe that a vulnerable adult is being or has been maltreated, as defined in section 626.5572, subdivision 15, to intentionally fail to make a report if:

(1) the person knows the maltreatment caused or contributed to the death or great bodily harm of a vulnerable adult; and

(2) the failure to report causes or contributes to the death or great bodily harm of a vulnerable adult or protects the mandated reporter's interests.

HIST: 1995 c 229 art 2 s 6

Chapter 28 -- MISCELLANEOUS STATUTES (PART III)

Category 2, Section 22:
2.22.1. Explain the Data Practices Act as it pertains to the gathering and release of information by law enforcement.
2.22.2. Discuss balancing the public's right to know with public safety needs and privacy issues with regard to data accessed by peace officers including:
- what and when information can be shared with the media or the public and by whom, and
- the repercussions of violating data practices.
2.22.3. Discuss the need for protection of data related to on-going investigations, crime victims, and juveniles.
2.22.4. Discuss ethical and responsible use of computers and databases by peace officers and the ramifications of misuse or unethical release of data.

Editors' Note: Selected portions of Chapter 13 concerning the Minnesota Government Data Practices Act have been edited to eliminate those provisions that have less importance to the duties of peace officers.

13.02 COLLECTION, SECURITY, AND DISSEMINATION OF RECORDS; DEFINITIONS.

Subdivision 1. **Applicability.** As used in this chapter, the terms defined in this section have the meanings given them.

Subd. 2. **Commissioner.** "Commissioner" means the commissioner of the department of administration.

Subd. 3. **Confidential data on individuals.** "Confidential data on individuals" are data made not public by statute or federal law applicable to the data and are inaccessible to the individual subject of those data.

Subd. 3a. **Criminal justice agencies.** "Criminal justice agencies" means all state and local prosecution authorities, all state and local law enforcement agencies, the sentencing guidelines commission, the bureau of criminal apprehension, the department of corrections, and all probation officers who are not part of the judiciary.

Subd. 4. **Data not on individuals.** "Data not on individuals" are all government data that are not data on individuals.

Subd. 5. **Data on individuals.** "Data on individuals" means all government data in which any individual is or can be identified as the subject of that data, unless the appearance of the name or other identifying data can be clearly demonstrated to be only incidental to the data and the data are not accessed by the name or other identifying data of any individual.
* * *

Subd. 7. **Government data.** "Government data" means all data collected, created, received, maintained or disseminated by any government entity regardless of its physical form, storage media or conditions of use.

Subd. 7a. **Government entity.** "Government entity" means a state agency, statewide system, or political subdivision.

Subd. 8. **Individual.** "Individual" means a natural person. In the case of a minor or an incapacitated person as defined in section 524.5—102, subdivision 6, "individual" includes a parent or guardian or an individual acting as a parent or guardian in the absence of a parent or guardian, except that the responsible authority shall withhold data from parents or guardians, or individuals acting as parents or guardians in the absence of parents or guardians, upon request by the minor if the responsible authority determines that withholding the data would be in the best interest of the minor.

Subd. 8a. **Not public data.** "Not public data" are any government data classified by statute, federal law, or temporary classification as confidential, private, nonpublic, or protected nonpublic.

Subd. 9. **Nonpublic data.** "Nonpublic data" are data not on individuals made by statute or federal law applicable to the data: (a) not accessible to the public; and (b) accessible to the subject, if any, of the data.

Subd. 10. **Person.** "Person" means any individual, partnership, corporation, association, business trust, or a legal representative of an organization.

Subd. 11. **Political subdivision.** "Political subdivision" means any county, statutory or home rule charter city, school district, special district, any town[,] * * * and any board, commission, district or authority created pursuant to law, local ordinance or charter provision. It includes * * * any nonprofit social service agency which performs services under contract to a governmental entity, to the extent that the nonprofit social service agency or nonprofit corporation collects, stores, disseminates, and uses data on individuals because of a contractual relationship with a governmental entity.

Subd. 12. **Private data on individuals.** "Private data on individuals" are data made by statute or federal law applicable to the data: (a) not public; and (b) accessible to the individual subject of those data.

Subd. 13. **Protected nonpublic data.** "Protected nonpublic data" are data not on individuals made by statute or federal law applicable to the data (a) not public and (b) not accessible to the subject of the data.

Subd. 14. **Public data not on individuals.** "Public data not on individuals" are data accessible to the public pursuant to section 13.03.

Subd. 15. **Public data on individuals.** "Public data on individuals" are data accessible to the public in accordance with the provisions of section 13.03.

Subd. 16. **Responsible authority.** (a) "Responsible authority" in a state agency or statewide system means the state official designated by law or by the commissioner as the individual responsible for the collection, use and dissemination of any set of data on individuals, government data, or summary data.

(b) "Responsible authority" in any political subdivision means the individual designated by the governing body of that political subdivision as the individual responsible for the collection, use, and dissemination of any set of data on individuals, government data, or summary data, unless otherwise provided by state law. * * *

Subd. 19. **Summary data.** "Summary data" means statistical records and reports derived from data on individuals but in which individuals are not identified and from which neither their identities nor any other characteristic that could uniquely identify an individual is ascertainable.
HIST: 1974 c 479 s 1; * * * 2012 c 290 s 1-9

13.03 ACCESS TO GOVERNMENT DATA.

Subdivision 1. **Public data.** All government data collected, created, received, maintained or disseminated by a government entity shall be public unless classified by statute, or temporary classification pursuant to section 13.06, or federal law, as nonpublic or protected nonpublic, or with respect to data on individuals, as private or confidential. * * *

Subd. 2. **Procedures.** (a) The responsible authority in every government entity shall establish procedures, consistent with this chapter, to insure that requests for government data are received and complied with in an appropriate and prompt manner. * * *

(b) Full convenience and comprehensive accessibility shall be allowed to researchers including historians, genealogists and other scholars to carry out extensive research and complete copying of all records containing government data except as otherwise expressly provided by law. * * *

Subd. 3. **Request for access to data.** (a) Upon request to a responsible authority or designee, a person shall be permitted to inspect and copy public government data at reasonable times and places, and, upon request, shall be informed of the data's meaning. If a person requests access for the purpose of inspection, the responsible authority may not assess a charge or require the requesting person to pay a fee to inspect data.

(b) For purposes of this section, "inspection" includes, but is not limited to, the visual inspection of paper and similar types of government data. Inspection does not include printing copies by the government entity, unless printing a copy is the only method to provide for inspection of the data. In the case of data stored in electronic form and made available in electronic form on a remote access basis to the public by the government entity, inspection includes remote access to the data by the public and the ability to print copies of or download the data on the public's own computer equipment. * * *

(c) The responsible authority or designee shall provide copies of public data upon request. If a person requests copies or electronic transmittal of the data to the person, the responsible authority may require the requesting person to pay the actual costs of searching for and retrieving government data, including the cost of employee time, and for making, certifying, compiling, and electronically transmitting the copies of the data or the data, but may not charge for separating public from not public data. * * *

(e) The responsible authority of a government entity that maintains public government data in a computer storage medium shall provide to any person making a request under this section a copy of any public data contained in that medium, in electronic form, if the government entity can reasonably make the copy or have a copy made. * * *

The entity may require the requesting person to pay the actual cost of providing the copy.

(f) If the responsible authority or designee determines that the requested data is classified so as to deny the requesting person access, the responsible authority or designee shall inform the requesting person of the determination either orally at the time of the request, or in writing as soon after that time as possible, and shall cite the specific statutory section, temporary classification, or specific provision of federal law on which the determination is based. Upon the request of any person denied access to data, the responsible authority or designee shall certify in writing that the request has been denied and cite the specific statutory section, temporary classification, or specific provision of federal law upon which the denial was based.

Subd. 4. **Change in classification of data; effect of dissemination among agencies.** (a) The classification of a government entity's data shall change if it is required to do so to comply with either judicial or administrative rules pertaining to the conduct of legal actions or with a specific statute applicable to the data in the possession of the disseminating or receiving entity.

(b) If data on individuals are classified as both private and confidential by this chapter, or any other statute or federal law, the data are private.

(c) To the extent that government data are disseminated to a government entity by another government entity, the data disseminated shall have the same classification at the entity receiving them as they had at the entity providing them.

(d) If a government entity disseminates data to another government entity, a classification provided for by law at the entity receiving the data does not affect the classification of the data at the entity that disseminates the data. * * *

Subd. 6. **Discoverability of not public data.** If a government entity opposes discovery of government data or release of data pursuant to court order on the grounds that the data are classified as not public, the party that seeks access to the data may bring before the appropriate presiding judicial officer, arbitrator, or administrative law judge an action to compel discovery or an action in the nature of an action to compel discovery. * * *

The presiding officer may fashion and issue any protective orders necessary to assure proper handling of the data by the parties. If the data are a videotape of a child victim or alleged victim alleging, explaining, denying, or describing an act of physical or sexual abuse, the presiding officer shall consider the provisions of section 611A.90[.]

Subd. 7. **Data transferred to archives.** When government data that is classified as not public by this chapter or any other statute, including private data on decedents, is physically transferred to the state archives, the data shall no longer be classified as not public and access to and use of the data shall be governed by section 138.17.

Subd. 8. **Change to classification of data not on individuals.** Except for security information, nonpublic and protected nonpublic data shall become public either ten years after the creation of the data by the government entity or ten years after the data was received or collected by any governmental entity unless the responsible authority for the originating or custodial entity for the data reasonably determines that, if the data were made available to the public or to the data subject, the harm to the public or to a data subject would outweigh the benefit to the public or to the data subject. If the responsible authority denies access to the data, the person denied access may challenge the denial by bringing an action in district court seeking release of the data. * * * The data in dispute shall be examined by the court in camera. * * * The court shall make a written statement of findings in support of its decision.

Subd. 9. **Effect of changes in classification of data.** Unless otherwise expressly provided by a particular statute, the classification of data is determined by the law applicable to the data at the time a request for access to the data is made, regardless of the data's classification at the time it was collected, created, or received.
* * *
HIST: 1979 c 328 s 7; * * * 2015 art 65 c 3 s 2

13.04 RIGHTS OF SUBJECTS OF DATA.
Subd. 3. **Access to data by individual.** Upon request to a responsible authority or designee, an individual shall be informed whether the individual is the subject of stored data on individuals, and whether it is classified as public, private or confidential. Upon further request, an individual who is the subject of stored private or public data on individuals shall be shown the data without any charge and, if desired, shall be informed of the content and meaning of that data. After an individual has been shown the private data and informed of its meaning, the data need not be disclosed to that individual for six months thereafter unless a dispute or action pursuant to this section is pending or additional data on the individual has been collected or created. The responsible authority or designee shall provide copies of the private or public data upon request by the individual subject of the data. The responsible authority or designee may require the requesting person to pay the actual costs of making and certifying the copies.

The responsible authority or designee shall comply immediately, if possible, with any request made pursuant to this subdivision, or within ten days of the date of the request, excluding Saturdays, Sundays and legal holidays, if immediate compliance is not possible.

Subd. 4. **Procedure when data is not accurate or complete.** (a) An individual subject of the data may contest the accuracy or completeness of public or private data. To exercise this right, an individual shall notify in writing the responsible authority describing the nature of the disagreement. The responsible authority shall within 30 days either: (1) correct the data found to be inaccurate or incomplete and attempt to notify past recipients of inaccurate or incomplete data, including recipients named by the individual; or (2) notify the individual that the authority believes the data to be correct. Data in dispute shall be disclosed only if the individual's statement of disagreement is included with the disclosed data.

The determination of the responsible authority may be appealed pursuant to the provisions of the administrative procedure act relating to contested cases. * * *

(b) Data on individuals that have been successfully challenged by an individual must be completed, corrected, or destroyed by a governmental entity without regard to the requirements of section 138.17.   * * *

HIST: 1974 c 479 s 4; * * * 2012 c 290 s 72

13.045 SAFE AT HOME PROGRAM PARTICIPANT DATA.

Subdivision 1. **Definitions.** As used in this section:
* * *

(2) "identity and location data" means any data that may be used to identify or physically locate a program participant, including, but not limited to the program participant's name, residential address, work address, and school address, and that is collected, received, or maintained by a government entity prior to the date a program participant's certification expires, or the date the entity receives notice that the program participant has withdrawn from the program, whichever is earlier.

Subd. 2. **Notification of certification.** A program participant may submit a notice, in writing, to the responsible authority of any government entity that the participant is certified in the Safe at Home address confidentiality program pursuant to chapter 5B. * * *

Subd. 3. **Classification of identity and location data; sharing and dissemination.** Identity and location data on a program participant that are not otherwise classified by law are private data on individuals. Notwithstanding any provision of law to the contrary, private or confidential identity and location data on a program participant who submits a notice under subdivision 2 may not be shared with any other government entity, or disseminated to any person[.] * * *

HIST: 2013 c 76 s 6

13.05 DUTIES OF RESPONSIBLE AUTHORITY.
* * *

Subd. 3. **General standards for collection and storage.** Collection and storage of all data on individuals and the use and dissemination of private and confidential data on individuals shall be limited to that necessary for the administration and management of programs specifically authorized by the legislature or local governing body or mandated by the federal government.

Subd. 4. **Limitations on collection and use of data.** Private or confidential data on an individual shall not be collected, stored, used, or disseminated by government entities for any purposes other than those stated to the individual at the time of collection in accordance with section 13.04, except as provided in this subdivision.

(a) Data collected prior to August 1, 1975, and which have not been treated as public data, may be used, stored, and disseminated for the purposes for which the data was originally collected or for purposed which are specifically approved by the commissioner as necessary to public health, safety, or welfare.

(b) Private or confidential data may be used and disseminated to individuals or entities specifically authorized access to that data by state, local, or federal law enacted or promulgated after the collection of the data. * * *

(d) Private data may be used by and disseminated to any person or entity if the individual subject or subjects of the data have given their informed consent. Whether a data subject has given informed consent shall be determined by rules of the commissioner.

The responsible authority may require a person requesting copies of data under this paragraph to pay the actual costs of making and certifying the copies.

(e) Private or confidential data on an individual may be discussed at a meeting open to the public to the extent provided in section 13D.05. * * *

Subd. 5. **Data protection.** (a) The responsible authority shall:
(1) establish procedures to assure that all data on individuals is accurate, complete, and current for the purposes for which it was collected; [and]
(2) establish appropriate security safeguards for all records containing data on individuals. * * *
Subd. 6. **Contracts.** Except as provided in section 13.46, subdivision 5, in any contract between a government entity subject to this chapter and any person, when the contract requires that data on individuals be made available to the contracting parties by the government entity, that data shall be administered consistent with this chapter. A contracting party shall maintain the data on individuals which it received according to the statutory provisions applicable to the data.
Subd. 7. **Preparation of summary data.** The use of summary data derived from private or confidential data on individuals under the jurisdiction of one or more responsible authorities is permitted. Unless classified pursuant to section 13.06, another statute, or federal law, summary data is public. The responsible authority shall prepare summary data from private or confidential data on individuals upon the request of any person if the request is in writing and the cost of preparing the summary data is borne by the requesting person. * * *
Subd. 8. **Publication of access procedures.** The responsible authority shall prepare a public document setting forth in writing the rights of the data subject pursuant to section 13.04 and the specific procedures in effect in the government entity for access by the data subject to public or private data on individuals.
Subd. 9. **Intergovernmental access of data.** A responsible authority shall allow another responsible authority access to data classified as not public only when the access is authorized or required by statute or federal law. * * *
Subd. 10. **International dissemination.** No governmental entity shall transfer or disseminate any private or confidential data on individuals to the private international organization known as Interpol, except through the Interpol-United States National Central Bureau, United States Department of Justice.
Subd. 11. **Privatization.** (a) If a government entity enters into a contract with a private person to perform any of its functions, all of the data created, collected, received, stored, used, maintained, or disseminated by the private person in performing those functions is subject to the requirements of this chapter and the private person must comply with those requirements as if it were a government entity. * * *
Subd. 12. **Identification or justification.** Unless specifically authorized by statute, government entities may not require persons to identify themselves, state a reason for, or justify a request to gain access to public government data. A person may be asked to provide certain identifying or clarifying information for the sole purpose of facilitating access to the data.
Subd. 13. **Data practices compliance official.** By December 1, 2000, each responsible authority or other appropriate authority in every government entity shall appoint or designate an employee of the government entity to act as the entity's data practices compliance official. * * *
HIST: 1974 c 479 s 2; * * * 2014 c 293 s 2

13.055 DISCLOSURE OF BREACH IN SECURITY; NOTIFICATION AND INVESTIGATION REPORT REQUIRED.

Subdivision 1. **Definitions.** For purposes of this section, the following terms have the meanings given to them.
(a) "Breach of the security of the data" means unauthorized acquisition of data maintained by a government agency that compromises the security and classification of the data. * * *
Subd. 2. **Notice to individuals; investigation report.** (a) A government agency that collects, creates, receives, maintains or disseminates private or confidential data on individuals must disclose any breach of the security of the data following discovery or notification of the breach. Written notification must be made to any individual who is the subject of the data and whose private or confidential data was, or is reasonably believed to have been, acquired by an unauthorized person[.] The disclosure must be made in the most expedient time possible and

without unreasonable delay, consistent with (1) the legitimate need of a law enforcement agency as provided in subdivision 3[.] * * *

 Subd. 3. **Delayed notice.** The notification required by this section may be delayed if a law enforcement agency determines that the notification will impede an active criminal investigation. The notification required by this section must be made after the law enforcement agency determines that it will not compromise the investigation. * * *
HIST: 2005 c 163 s 21; 2014 c 284 s 2

13.06 TEMPORARY CLASSIFICATION.

 Subdivision 1. **Application to commissioner.** (a) Notwithstanding the provisions of section 13.03, the responsible authority of a government entity may apply to the commissioner for permission to classify data or types of data on individuals as private or confidential, or data not on individuals as nonpublic or protected nonpublic, for its own use and for the use of other similar government entities on a temporary basis until a proposed statute can be acted upon by the legislature. * * *

 Subd. 5. **Determination.** (a) The commissioner shall either grant or disapprove the application for temporary classification within 45 days[.]   * * *
HIST: 1976 c 283 s 8; * * * 2010 c 365 art 1 s 12; 2010 c 365 art 2 s 1-7

13.07 DUTIES OF THE COMMISSIONER.

 The commissioner shall promulgate rules, in accordance with the rulemaking procedures in the administrative procedures act which shall apply to government entities to implement the enforcement and administration of this chapter. * * *
HIST: 1975 c 271 s 6; * * * 2005 c 163 s 26

13.072 OPINIONS BY THE COMMISSIONER.

 Subdivision 1. **Opinion; when required.** (a) Upon request of a government entity, the commissioner may give a written opinion on any question relating to public access to government data, rights of subjects of data, or classification of data under this chapter or other Minnesota statutes governing government data practices. * * *

 Subd. 2. **Effect.** Opinions issued by the commissioner under this section are not binding on the government entity or the members of a body subject to chapter 13D whose data or performance of duties is the subject of the opinion, but an opinion described in subdivision 1, paragraph (a), must be given deference by a court or other tribunal in a proceeding involving the data. * * *
HIST: 1993 c 192 s 38; * * * 2012 c 290 s 13

13.08 CIVIL REMEDIES.

 Subdivision 1. **Action for damages.** Notwithstanding section 466.03, a responsible authority or government entity which violates any provision of this chapter is liable to a person or representative of a decedent who suffers any damage as a result of the violation, and the person damaged or a representative in the case of private data on decedents or confidential data on decedents may bring an action against the responsible authority or government entity to cover any damages sustained, plus costs and reasonable attorney fees. In the case of a willful violation, the government entity shall, in addition, be liable to exemplary damages[.] * * *

 Subd. 4. **Action to compel compliance.** (a) * * * [A]ny aggrieved person seeking to enforce the person's rights under this chapter or obtain access to data may bring an action to district court to compel compliance with this chapter and may recover costs and disbursements, including reasonable attorney's fees, as determined by the court. If the court determines that an action brought under this subdivision is frivolous and without merit and a basis in fact, it may award reasonable costs and attorney fees to the responsible authority. If the court issues an order to compel compliance under this subdivision, the court may impose a civil penalty of up to $1,000 against the government entity. * * *
HIST: 1974 c 479 s 5; * * * 2013 c 125 art 1 s 1; 2016 c 158 art 1 s 6

13.09 PENALTIES.

(a) Any person who willfully violates the provisions of this chapter or any rules adopted under this chapter or whose conduct constitutes the knowing unauthorized acquisition of not public data, as defined in section 13.055, subdivision 1, is guilty of a misdemeanor.

(b) Willful violation of this chapter, including any action subject to a criminal penalty under paragraph (a), by any public employee constitutes just cause for suspension without pay or dismissal of the public employee.

HIST: 1974 c 479 s 6; * * * 2014 c 284 s 3

13.10 DATA ON DECEDENTS.

Subdivision 1. **Definitions.** As used in this chapter:

(a) "Confidential data on decedents" means data are, prior to the death of the data subject, were classified by statute, federal law, or temporary classification as confidential data.

(b) "Private data on decedents" are data which, prior to the death of the data subject, were classified by statute, federal law, or temporary classification as private data.

(c) "Representative of the decedent" are the personal representative of the estate of the decedent during the period of administration, or if no personal representative has been appointed or after discharge of the personal representative, the surviving spouse, any child of the decedent, or, if there is no surviving spouse or children, the parents of the decedent.

Subd. 2. **Classification of data on decedents.** Upon the death of the data subject, private data and confidential data shall become respectively, private data on decedents and confidential data on decedents. Private data on decedents and confidential data on decedents shall become public when ten years have elapsed from the actual or presumed death of the individual and 30 years have elapsed from the creation of the data. For purposes of this subdivision, an individual is presumed to be dead if either 90 years elapsed since the creation of the data or 90 years have elapsed since the individual's birth, whichever is earlier, except that an individual is not presumed to be dead if readily available data indicate that the individual is still living. * * *

Subd. 4. **Court review.** Any person may bring an action in the district court[.] * * * The responsible authority for the data being sought or any interested person may provide information regarding the possible harm or benefit from granting the request. The data in dispute shall be examined in the court in camera. * * * The court shall make a written statement of findings in support of its decision.
* * *

HIST: 1985 c 298 s 8; * * * 2012 c 290 s 14

13.69 PUBLIC SAFETY DATA.

Subdivision 1. **Classifications.** (a) The following government data of the department of public safety are private data:

(1) medical data on driving instructors, licensed drivers, and applicants for parking certificates and special license plates issued to physically handicapped persons; and

(2) other data on holders of a disability certificate under section 169.345, except that data that are not medical data may be released to law enforcement agencies * * *; and

(3) social security numbers in driver's license and motor vehicle registration records[.]
* * *

The department may release the social security number only as provided in clause (3) and must not sell or otherwise provide individual social security numbers or lists of social security numbers for any other purpose.

(b) The following government data of the department public safety are confidential data: data concerning an individual's driving ability when that data is received from a member of the individual's family.

Subd. 2. **Photographic negatives.** Photographic negatives obtained by the department of public safety in the process of issuing drivers licenses or Minnesota identification cards shall be private data on individuals pursuant to section 13.02, subdivision 12.
HIST: 1981 c 311 s 18,37,39; * * *; 2017 c 95 art 2 s 2; 1Sp2019 c 9 art 7 s 1

13.80 DOMESTIC ABUSE DATA.

All government data on individuals which is collected, created, received or maintained by police departments, sheriffs' offices or clerks of court pursuant to the domestic abuse act, section 518B.01, are classified as confidential data, pursuant to section 13.02, subdivision 3, until a temporary court order made pursuant to subdivision 5 or 7 of section 518B.01 is executed or served upon the data subject who is the respondent to the action.
HIST: 1981 c 311 s 23,39; 1982 c 545 s 24

13.82 COMPREHENSIVE LAW ENFORCEMENT DATA.

Subdivision 1. **Application.** This section shall apply to agencies which carry on a law enforcement function, including * * * fire departments, * * * the Department of Commerce, and county human service agency client and provider fraud investigation, prevention, and control units operated or supervised by the Department of Human Services.

Subd. 2. **Arrest data.** The following data created or collected by law enforcement agencies which documents any actions taken by them to cite, arrest, incarcerate or otherwise substantially deprive an adult individual of liberty shall be public at all times in the originating agency:

(a) Time, date and place of the action;

(b) Any resistance encountered by the agency;

(c) Any pursuit engaged in by the agency;

(d) Whether any weapons were used by the agency or other individual;

(e) The charge, arrest or search warrants, or other legal basis for the action;

(f) The identities of the agencies, units within the agencies and individual persons taking the action;

(g) Whether and where the individual is being held in custody or is being incarcerated by the agency;

(h) The date, time and legal basis for any transfer of custody and the identity of the agency or person who received custody;

(i) The date, time and legal basis for any release from custody or incarceration;

(j) The name, age, sex and last known address of an adult person or the age and sex of any juvenile person cited, arrested, incarcerated or otherwise substantially deprived of liberty;

(k) Whether the agency employed a portable recording system, automated license plate reader, wiretaps or other eavesdropping techniques, unless the release of this specific data would jeopardize an ongoing investigation;

(l) The manner in which the agencies received the information that led to the arrest and the names of individuals who supplied the information unless the identities of those individuals qualify for protection under subdivision 10; and

(m) response or incident report number;

Subd. 3. **Request for service data.** The following data created or collected by law enforcement agencies which document the agency's response to a request for service including, but not limited to, responses to traffic accidents, or which describes actions taken by the agency on its own initiative shall be public government data:

(a) The nature of the request or the activity complained of;

(b) The name and address of the individual making the request unless the identity of the individual qualifies for protection under subdivision 10;

(c) The time and date of the request or complaint; and

(d) The response initiated and the response or incident report number.

Subd. 4. **Audio recording of 911 call.** The audio recording of a call placed to a 911 system for the purpose of requesting service from a law enforcement, fire, or medical agency is private data on individuals with respect to the individual making the call, except that a written transcript of the audio recording is public, unless it reveals the identity of an individual otherwise protected under subdivision 10. A transcript shall be prepared upon request. The person requesting the transcript shall pay the actual cost of transcribing the call, in addition to any other applicable costs provided under section 13.03, subdivision 3. The audio recording may be disseminated to law enforcement agencies for investigative purposes. The audio recording may be used for public safety emergency medical services training purposes.

Subd. 5. **Domestic abuse data.** The written police report required by section 62.341, subdivision 4, of an alleged incident described in section 629.341, subdivision 1, and arrest data, request for service data, and response or incident data described in subdivision 2, 3, or 4 that arise out of this type of incident or out of an alleged violation of an order for protection must be released upon request at no cost to the victim of domestic violence, the victim's attorney, or an organization designated by the Office of Justice Programs in the Department of Corrections, or the Department of Public Safety as providing services to victims of domestic abuse. The executive director or the commissioner of the appropriate state agency shall develop written criteria for this designation.

Subd. 6. **Response or incident data.** The following data created or collected by law enforcement agencies which document the agency's response to a request for service including, but not limited to, responses to traffic accidents, or which describe actions taken by the agency on its own initiative shall be public government data:

(a) date, time and place of the action;

(b) agencies, units of agencies and individual agency personnel qualify for protection under subdivision 10;

(c) any resistance encountered by the agency;

(d) any pursuit engaged in by the agency;

(e) whether any weapons were used by the agency or other individuals;

(f) a brief factual reconstruction of events associated with the action;

(g) names and addresses of witnesses to the agency action or the incident unless the identity of any witness qualifies for protection under subdivision 10;

(h) names and addresses of any victims or casualties unless the identities of those individuals qualify for protection under subdivision 10;

(i) the name and location of the health care facility to which victims or casualties were taken;

(k) dates of birth of the parties involved in a traffic accident;

(l) whether the parties involved were wearing seat belts;

(m) the alcohol concentration of each driver; and

(n) whether the agency used a portable recording system to document the agency's response or actions.

Subd. 7. **Criminal investigative data.** Except for the data defined in subdivisions 2, 3, and 4, investigative data collected or created by a law enforcement agency in order to prepare a case against a person, whether known or unknown, for the commission of a crime or other offense for which the agency has primary investigative responsibility are confidential or protected nonpublic while the investigation is active. Inactive investigative data are public unless the release of the data would jeopardize another ongoing investigation or would reveal the identity of individuals protected under subdivision 17. Images and recordings, including photographs, video, and audio records, which are part of inactive investigative files and which are clearly offensive to common sensibilities are classified as private or nonpublic data, provided that the existence of the images and recordings shall be disclosed to any person requesting access to the inactive investigative file. An investigation becomes inactive upon the occurrence of any of following events:

(a) a decision by the agency or appropriate prosecutorial authority not to pursue the case;

(b) expiration of the time to bring a charge or file a complaint under the applicable statute of limitations, or 30 years after the commission of the offense, whichever comes earliest; or

(c) exhaustion of or expiration of all rights of appeal by a person convicted on the basis of the investigative data.

Any investigative data presented as evidence in court shall be public. Data determined to be inactive under clause (a) may become active if the agency or appropriate prosecutorial authority decides to renew the investigation.

During the time when an investigation is active, any person may bring an action in the district court. * * * The court may order that all or part of the data relating to a particular investigation be released to the public or to the person bringing the action. * * * [T]he court shall consider whether the benefit to the person bringing the action or to the public outweighs any harm to the public, to the agency or to any person identified in the data. The data in dispute shall be examined by the court in camera.

Subd. 8. **Child abuse identity data.** Active or inactive investigative data that identify a victim of child abuse or neglect reported under chapter 260E are private data on individuals. Active or inactive investigative data that identify a reporter of child abuse or neglect under section 626.556 are confidential data on individuals, unless the subject of the report compels disclosure under sections 260E.21, subdivision 4, or 260E.35.

Subd. 9. **Inactive child abuse data.** Investigative data that become inactive under subdivision 5, clause (a) or (b), and that relate to the alleged abuse or neglect of a child by a person responsible for the child's care, as defined in 260E.03, are private data.

Subd. 10. **Vulnerable adult identity data.** Active or inactive investigative data that identify a victim of vulnerable adult maltreatment under section 626.557 are private data on individuals. Active or inactive investigative data that identify a reporter of vulnerable adult maltreatment under section 626.557 are private data on individuals.

Subd. 11. **Inactive vulnerable adult maltreatment data.** Investigative data that becomes inactive under subdivision 5, paragraph (a) or (b), and that relate to the alleged maltreatment of a vulnerable adult by a caregiver or facility are private data on individuals.

Subd. 12. **Name change data.** Data on court records relating to name changes under section 259.10, subdivision 2, which is held by a law enforcement agency is confidential data on an individual while an investigation is active and is private data on an individual when the investigation becomes inactive.

Subd. 13. **Access to data for crime victims.** On receipt of a written request, the prosecuting authority shall release investigative data collected by a law enforcement agency to the victim of a criminal act or alleged criminal act or to the victim's legal representative unless the release to the individual subject of the data would be prohibited under section 13.391 or the prosecuting authority reasonably believes:

(a) that the release of that data will interfere with the investigation; or

(b) that the request is prompted by a desire on the part of the requester to engage in unlawful activities.

Subd. 14. **Withholding public data.** A law enforcement agency may temporarily withhold response or incident data from public access if the agency reasonably believes that public access would be likely to endanger the physical safety of an individual or cause a perpetrator to flee, evade detection or destroy evidence. In such instances, the agency shall, upon the request of any person, provide a statement which explains the necessity for its action. Any person may apply to a district court for an order requiring the agency to release the data being withheld. If the court determines that the agency's action is not reasonable, it shall order the release of the data and may award costs and attorney's fees to the person who sought the order. The data in dispute shall be examined by the court in camera.

Subd. 15. **Public benefit data.** Any law enforcement agency may make any data classified as confidential or protected nonpublic pursuant to subdivision 7 or as private or nonpublic under section 13.825 or 626.19 accessible to any person, agency, or the public if the agency determines that the access will aid the law enforcement process, promote public safety, or dispel widespread rumor or unrest.

Subd. 16. **Public access.** When data is classified as public under this section, a law enforcement agency shall not be required to make the actual physical data available to the public if it is not administratively feasible to segregate the public data from the not public. However, the agency must make the information described as public data available to the public in a reasonable manner. When investigative data becomes inactive, as described in subdivision 5, the actual physical data associated with that investigation, including the public data, shall be available for public access.

Subd. 17. **Protection of identities.** A law enforcement agency or a law enforcement dispatching agency working under direction of a law enforcement agency shall withhold public access to data on individuals to protect the identity of individuals in the following circumstances:

(a) when access to the data would reveal the identity of an undercover law enforcement officer, as provided in section 13.43, subdivision 5;

(b) when access to the data would reveal the identity of a victim or alleged victim of criminal sexual conduct or sex trafficking under section 609.322, 609.341 to 609.3451, or section 617.246, subdivision 2;

(c) when access to the data would reveal the identity of a paid or unpaid informant being used by the agency if the agency reasonably determines that revealing the identity of the informant would threaten the personal safety of the informant;

(d) when access to the data would reveal the identity of a victim of or witness to a crime if the victim or witness specifically requests not to be identified publicly, unless the agency reasonably determines that revealing the identity of the victim or witness would not threaten the personal safety or property of the individual;

(e) when access to the data would reveal the identity of a deceased person whose body was unlawfully removed from a cemetery in which it was interred;

(f) when access to the data would reveal the identity of a person who placed a call to a 911 system or the identity or telephone number of a service subscriber whose phone is used to place a call to the 911 system and: (1) the agency determines that revealing the identity may threaten the personal safety or property of any person; or (2) the object of the call is to receive help in a mental health emergency. For the purposes of this paragraph, a voice recording of a call placed to the 911 system is deemed to reveal the identity of the caller;

(g) when access to the data would reveal the identity of a juvenile witness and the agency reasonably determines that the subject matter of the investigation justifies protecting the identity of the witness; or

(h) when access to the data would reveal the identity of a mandated reporter under section 60A.952, subdivision 2, 609.456, or 626.557 or chapter 260E.

Data concerning individuals whose identities are protected by this subdivision are private data about those individuals. Law enforcement agencies shall establish procedures to acquire the data and make the decisions necessary to protect the identity of individuals described in clauses (c), (d), (f), and (g).

Subd. 18. **Data retention.** Nothing in this section shall require law enforcement agencies to create, collect or maintain data which is not required to be created, collected or maintained by any other applicable rule or statute.

Subd. 19. **Data in arrest warrant indices.** Data in arrest warrant indices are classified as confidential data until the defendant has been taken into custody, served with a warrant, or appears before the court, except when the law enforcement agency determines that the public purpose is served by making the information public.

Subd. 20. **Property data.** Data that uniquely describe stolen, lost, confiscated, or recovered property are classified as either private data on individuals or nonpublic data depending on the content of the not public data.

Subd. 21. **Reward program data.** To the extent that the release of program data would reveal the identity of an informant or adversely affect the integrity of the fund, financial records of a program that pays rewards to informants are protected nonpublic data in the case of data not on individuals or confidential data in the case of data on individuals.

Subd. 22. **Data on registered criminal offenders.** Data described in section 243.166 shall be classified as described in that section.

Subd. 23. **Data in missing children bulletins.** Data described in section 299C.54 shall be classified as described in that section.

Subd. 24. **Exchanges of information.** Nothing in this chapter prohibits the exchange of information by law enforcement agencies provided the exchanged information is pertinent and necessary to the requesting agency in initiating, furthering, or completing an investigation, except not public personnel data and the data governed by section 13.045.

Subd. 25. **Deliberative processes.** Data that reflect deliberative processes or investigative techniques of law enforcement agencies are confidential data on individuals or protected nonpublic data; provided that information, reports, or memoranda that have been adopted as the final opinion or justification for a decision of a law enforcement agency are public data.

Subd. 26. **Booking photographs.** (a) For purposes of this subdivision, "booking photograph" means a photograph or electronically produced image taken by law enforcement for identification purposes in connection with the arrest of a person.

(b) Except as otherwise provided in this subdivision, a booking photograph is public data. A law enforcement agency may temporarily withhold access to a booking photograph if the agency determines that access will adversely affect an active investigation.

Subd. 27. **Pawnshop data.** Data that would reveal the identity of persons who are customers of a licensed pawnbroker or secondhand goods dealer are private data on individuals. Data describing the property in a regulated transaction with a licensed pawnbroker or secondhand goods dealer are public. * * *

Subd. 29. **Juvenile offender photographs.** * * * [P]hotographs or electronically produced images of children adjudicated delinquent under chapter 260B shall not be expunged from law enforcement records or databases.

Subd. 29. **Inactive financial transaction investigative data.** Investigative data that become inactive under subdivision 7 that are a person's financial account number or transaction numbers are private or nonpublic data. * * *

Subd. 31. **Use of surveillance technology.** Notwithstanding subdivision 25 and section 13.37, subdivision 2, the existence of all technology maintained by a law enforcement agency that may be used to electronically capture an audio, video, photographic, or other record of the activities of the general public, or of an individual or group of individuals, for purposes of conducting an investigation, responding to an incident or request for service, monitoring or maintaining public order and safety, or engaging in any other law enforcement function authorized by law is public data.

Subd. 32 **Unmanned aerial vehicles.** Section 626.19 governs data collected, created, or maintained through the use of an unmanned aerial vehicle.
HIST: 1979 c 328 s 21; * * *; 2017 c 98 s 1; 2020 c 82 s 1, 2; 1Sp2020 c 2 art 8 s 6-8

13.824 AUTOMATED LICENSE PLATE READERS.

Subdivision 1. **Definitions.** As used in this section, "automated license plate reader" means an electronic device mounted on a law enforcement vehicle or positioned in a stationary location that is capable of recording data on, or taking a photograph of, a vehicle or its license plate and comparing the collected data and photographs to existing law enforcement databases for investigative purposes. Automated license plate reader includes a device that is owned or operated by a person who is not a government entity to the extent that data collected by the reader are shared with a law enforcement agency.

Subd. 2. **Data collection; classification; use restrictions.** (a) Data collected by an automated license plate reader must be limited to the following:

(1) license plate numbers;

(2) date, time, and location data on vehicles; and

(3) pictures of license plates, vehicles, and areas surrounding the vehicles. Collection of any data not authorized by this paragraph is prohibited.

(b) All data collected by an automated license plate reader are private data on individuals or nonpublic data unless the data are public under section 13.82, subdivision 2, 3, or 6, or are active criminal investigative data under section 13.82, subdivision 7.

(c) Data collected by an automated license plate reader may only be matched with data in the Minnesota license plate data file, provided that a law enforcement agency may use additional sources of data for matching if the additional data relate to an active criminal investigation. A central state repository of automated license plate reader data is prohibited unless explicitly authorized by law.

(d) Automated license plate readers must not be used to monitor or track an individual who is the subject of an active criminal investigation unless authorized by a warrant, issued upon probable cause, or exigent circumstances justify the use with obtaining a warrant.

Subd. 3. **Destruction of data required.** (a) Notwithstanding section 138.17, and except as otherwise provided in this subdivision, data collected by an automated license plate reader that are not related to an active criminal investigation must be destroyed no later than 60 days from the date of collection.

(b) Upon written request from an individual who is the subject of a pending criminal charge or complaint, along with the case or complaint number and a statement that the data may be used as exculpatory evidence, data otherwise subject to destruction under paragraph (a) must be preserved by the law enforcement agency until the criminal charge or complaint is resolved or dismissed.
* * *

(d) Data that are inactive criminal investigative data are subject to destruction * * * under section 138.17.

Subd. 4. **Sharing among law enforcement agencies.** (a) Automated license plate reader data that are not related to an active criminal investigation may only be shared with, or disseminated to, another law enforcement agency upon meeting the standards for requesting access to data as provided in subdivision 7.

(b) If data collected by an automated license plate reader are shared with another law enforcement agency under this subdivision, the agency that receives the data must comply with all data classification, destruction, and security requirements of this section.

(c) Automated license plate reader data that are not related to an active criminal investigation may not be shared with, disseminated to, sold to, or traded with any other individual or entity unless explicitly authorized by this subdivision or other law.

Subd. 5. **Log of use required.** (a) A law enforcement agency that installs or uses an automated license plate reader must maintain a public log of its use, including but not limited to:

(1) specific times of day that the reader actively collected data;

(2) the aggregate number of vehicles or license plates on which data are collected for each period of active use and a list of all state and federal databases with which the data were compared, unless the existence of the database itself is not public;

(3) for each period of active use, the number of vehicles or license plates in each of the following categories where the data identify a vehicle or license plate that has been stolen, a warrant for the arrest of the owner of the vehicle or an owner with a suspended or revoked driver's license or similar category, or are active investigative data; and

(4) for a reader at a stationary or fixed location, the location at which the reader actively collected data and is installed and used.

(b) The law enforcement agency must maintain a list of the current and previous locations, including dates at those locations, of any fixed stationary automated license plate readers or other surveillance devices with automated license plate reader capability used by the agency. The agency's list must be accessible to the public, unless the agency determines that the data are security information as provided in section 13.37, subdivision 2. A determination that these data are security information is subject to in-camera judicial review as provided in section 13.08, subdivision 4.

Subd. 6. **Biennial audit.** (a) In addition to the log required under subdivision 5, the law enforcement agency must maintain records showing the date and time automated license plate reader data were collected and the applicable classification of the data. The law enforcement agency shall arrange for an independent, biennial audit of the records to determine whether data currently in the records are classified, how the data are used, whether they are destroyed as required under this section, and to verify compliance with subdivision 7. * * *

(b) The results of the audit are public. The commissioner of administration shall review the results of the audit. If the commissioner determines that there is a pattern of substantial noncompliance with this section by the law enforcement agency, the agency must immediately suspend operation of all automated license plate reader devices until the commissioner has authorized the agency to reinstate their use. * * *

Subd. 7. **Authorization to access data.** (a) A law enforcement agency must comply with section 13.05, subdivision 5, and 13.055 in the operation of automated license plate readers, and in maintaining automated license plate reader data.

(b) The responsible authority for a law enforcement agency must establish written procedures to ensure that law enforcement personnel have access to the data only if authorized in writing by the chief of police, sheriff, or head of the law enforcement agency, or their designee, to obtain access to [collected data] for a legitimate, specified, and documented law enforcement purpose. [E]ach access must be based on a reasonable suspicion that the data are pertinent to an active criminal investigation and must include a record of the factual basis for the access and any associated case number, complaint, or incident that is the basis for the access.

(c) The ability of authorized individuals to enter, update, or access automated license plate reader data must be limited through the use of role-based access that corresponds to the official duties or training level of the individual and the statutory authorization that grants access for that purpose. All queries and responses, and all actions in which data are entered, updated, accessed, shared, or disseminated, must be recorded in a data audit trail. Data contained in the audit trail are public, to the extent that the data are not otherwise classified by law.

Subd. 8. **Notification to Bureau of Criminal Apprehension.** (a) Within ten days of the installation or current use of an automated license plate reader or the integration of automated license plate reader technology into another surveillance device, a law enforcement agency must notify the Bureau of Criminal Apprehension of that installation or use and of any fixed location of a stationary automated license plate reader.

(b) The Bureau of Criminal Apprehension must maintain a list of law enforcement agencies using automated license plate readers or other surveillance devices with automated license plate reader capability, including the locations of any fixed stationary automated license plate readers or other devices. Except to the extent that the law enforcement agency determines that the location of a specific reader or other device is security information, as defined in section 13.37, this list is accessible to the public and must be available on the bureau's Web site. A determination that the location of a reader or other device is security information is subject to in-camera judicial review, as provided in section 13.08, subdivision 5.
HIST: 2015 c 67 s 3

13.825 PORTABLE RECORDING SYSTEMS.

Subdivision 1. **Applications; definitions.** (a) This section applies to law enforcement agencies that maintain a portable recording system for use in investigations, or in response to emergencies, incidents, and requests for service.

(b) As used in this section:

(1) "portable recording system" means a device worn by a peace officer that is capable of both video and audio recording of the officer's activities and interactions with others or collecting digital multimedia evidence as part of an investigation; [and]

(2) "portable recording system data" means audio or video data collected by a portable recording system[.]

Subd. 2. **Data classification; court-authorized disclosure.** (a) [With some exceptions], data collected by a portable recording system are private data on individuals or nonpublic data[.]

Subd. 3. **Retention of data.** (a) Portable recording system data that are not active or inactive criminal investigative data and are not described in paragraph (b) must be maintained for at least 90 days and destroyed according to the agency's records retention schedule[.]

(b) Portable recording system data must be maintained for at least one year and destroyed according to the agency's records retention schedule * * * if:

(1) the data document (i) the discharge of a firearm by a peace officer in the course of duty if a notice is required under section 626.553, subdivision 2, or (ii) the use of force by a peace officer that results in substantial bodily harm; or

(2) a formal complaint is made against a peace officer related to the incident.

(c) If a subject of the data submits a written request to the law enforcement agency to retain the recording beyond the applicable retention period for possible evidentiary or exculpatory use * * * , the law enforcement agency shall retain the recording for an additional time period requested by the subject of up to 180 days and notify the requester that the recording will then be destroyed unless a new request is made under this paragraph.

(d) Notwithstanding paragraph (b) or (c), a government entity may retain a recording for as long as reasonably necessary for possible evidentiary or exculpatory use[.]

Subd. 4. **Access by data subjects.** (a) For purposes of this chapter, a portable recording system data subject includes the peace officer who collected the data, and any other individual or entity, including any other peace officer, regardless of whether the officer is or can be identified by the recording, whose image or voice is documented in the data.

(b) An individual who is the subject of portable recording system data has access to the data, including data on other individuals who are the subject of the recording. If the individual request a copy of the recording, data on other individuals who do not consent to its release must be redacted from the copy. The identity and activities of an on-duty peace officer engaged in an investigation or response to an emergency, incident, or request for service may not be redacted, unless the officer's identity is subject to protection under section 13.82, subdivision 17, clause (a).

Subd. 5. **Inventory of portable recording system technology.** A law enforcement agency that uses a portable recording system must maintain the following information, which is public data:

(1) the total number of recording devices owned or maintained by the agency;

(2) a daily record of the total number of recording devices actually deployed and used by officers and, if applicable, the precincts in which they were used;

(3) the policies and procedures for use of portable recording systems required by section 626.8473; and

(4) the total amount of recorded audio and video data collected * * * and maintained by the agency, the agency's retention schedule for the data, and the agency's procedures for destruction of the data.

Subd. 6. **Use of agency-issued portable recording systems.** While on duty, a peace officer may only use a portable recording system issued and maintained by the officer's agency in documenting the officer's activities.

Subd. 7. **Authorization to access data.** * * * (b) The responsible authority for a law enforcement agency must establish written procedures to ensure that law enforcement personnel have access to portable recording system data that are not public only if authorized in writing by the chief of police, sheriff, or head of the law enforcement agency, or their designee, to obtain access to the data for a legitimate, specified law enforcement purpose.

Subd. 8 **Sharing among agencies.** (a) Portable recording system data that are not public may only be shared with or disseminated to another law enforcement agency, a government entity, or a federal agency upon meeting the standards for requesting access to data as provided in subdivision 7.

(b) If data * * * are shared with another state or local law enforcement agency under this subdivision, the agency that receives the data must comply with all data classification, destruction, and security requirements of this section.

(c) Portable recording system data may not be shared with, disseminated to, sold to, or traded with any other individual or entity unless explicitly authorized by this section or other applicable law. * * *
HIST: 2016 c 171 s 5

13.83 MEDICAL EXAMINER DATA.

Subdivision 1. **Definition.** As used in this section, "medical examiner data" means data relating to deceased individuals and the manner and circumstances of their death which is created, collected, used or maintained by a county coroner or medical examiner[.]

Subd. 2. **Public data.** Unless specifically classified otherwise by state statute or federal law, the * * * data created or collected by a medical examiner or coroner on a deceased individual are public[.]

Subd. 3. **Unidentified individual; public data.** A county coroner or medical examiner unable during an investigation to identify a deceased individual, may release to the public any relevant data which would assist in ascertaining identity.

Subd. 4. **Investigative data.** Data created or collected by a county coroner or medical examiner which are part of an active investigation mandated by chapter 390, or any other general or local law relating to coroners or medical examiners are confidential data or protected nonpublic data, until the completion of the coroner's or medical examiner's final summary of findings but may be disclosed to a state or federal agency charged by law with investigating the death of the deceased individual about whom the medical examiner or coroner has medical examiner data. Upon completion of the coroner's or medical examiner's final summary of findings[.] * * *

Subd. 6. **Other data.** Unless a statute specifically provides a different classification, all other data created or collected by a county coroner or medical examiner that are not data on deceased individuals or the manner and circumstances of their death are public pursuant to section 13.03.

Subd. 7. **Court review.** Any person may petition the district court * * * to authorize disclosure of nonpublic, protected nonpublic, or confidential medical examiner data. * * * After examining the data in camera, the court may order disclosure of the data if it determines that disclosure would be in the public interest.

Subd. 8. **Access to nonpublic data.** The data made nonpublic by this section are accessible to the physician who attended the decedent at the time of death, the legal representative of the decedent's estate and to the decedent's surviving spouse, parents, children, and siblings and their legal representatives. * * *
HIST: 1981 c 311 s 24,39; * * * 2012 c 290 s 59-61

13.84 COURT SERVICES DATA.

Subdivision 1. **Definition.** As used in this section "court services data" means data that are created, collected, used or maintained by a court services department, parole or probation authority, correctional agency, or by an agent designated by the court to perform studies or other duties and that are on individuals who are or were defendants, parolees or probationers of a district court, participants in diversion programs, petitioners or respondents to a family court, or juveniles adjudicated delinquent and committed, detained prior to a court hearing or hearings, or found to be dependent or neglected and placed under the supervision of the court.

Subd. 2. **General.** Unless the data is summary data or a statute, including sections 609.115 and 257.70, specifically provides a different classification, the following court services data are classified as private pursuant to section 13.02, subdivision 12:

(a) Court services data on individuals gathered at the request of a district court to determine the need for any treatment, rehabilitation, counseling, or any other need of a defendant, parolee, probationer, or participant in a diversion program, and used by the court to assist in assigning an appropriate sentence or other disposition in a case;
* * *

(c) Court services data on individuals gathered by psychologists in the course of providing the court or its staff with psychological evaluations or in the course of counseling individual clients referred by the court for the purpose of assisting them with personal conflicts or difficulties.

Subd. 3. **Third party information.** Whenever, in the course of gathering the private data specified above, a psychologist, probation officer or other agent of the court is directed by the court to obtain data on individual defendants, parolees, probationers, or petitioners or respondents in a family court, and the source of that data provides the data only upon the condition of its being held confidential, that data and the identity of the source shall be confidential data on individuals, pursuant to section 13.02, subdivision 3.

Subd. 4. **Probation data.** Progress reports and other reports and recommendations provided at the request of the court by parole or probation officers for the purpose of determining the appropriate legal action or disposition regarding an individual on probation are confidential data on individuals.

Subd. 5. **Disclosure.** Private or confidential court services data shall not be disclosed except:

(a) pursuant to section 13.05;

(b) pursuant to a statute specifically authorizing disclosure of court services data;

(c) with the written permission of the source of confidential data;

(d) to the court services department, parole or probation authority or state or local correctional agency or facility having statutorily granted supervision over the individual subject of the data, or to county personnel within the welfare system;

(e) pursuant to subdivision 5a;

(f) pursuant to a valid court order; or

(g) pursuant to section 611A.06, subdivision 3a.

Subd. 6. **Public benefit data.** (a) The responsible authority or its designee of a parole or probation authority or correctional agency may release private or confidential court services data related to:

(1) criminal acts to any law enforcement agency, if necessary for law enforcement purposes; and

(2) criminal acts or delinquent acts to the victims of criminal or delinquent acts to the extent that the data are necessary for the victim to assert the victim's legal right to restitution.

(b) A parole or probation authority, a correctional agency, or agencies that provide correctional services under contract to a correctional agency may release to a law enforcement agency the following data on defendants, parolees, or probationers: current address, dates of entrance to and departure from agency programs, and dates and times of any absences, both authorized and unauthorized, from a correctional program.

(c) The responsible authority or its designee of a juvenile correctional agency may release private or confidential court services data to a victim of a delinquent act to the extent the data are necessary to enable the victim to assert the victim's right to request notice of release under section 611A.06. The data that may be released include only the name, home address, and placement site of a juvenile who has been placed in a juvenile correctional facility as a result of a delinquent act.

(d) [With certain restrictions, u]pon the victim's written or electronic request, if the victim and offender have been household or family members as defined in section 518B.01, subdivision 2, paragraph (b), the commissioner of corrections or the commissioner's designee may disclose to the victim of an offender convicted of a qualified domestic violence-related offense as defined in section 609.02, subdivision 16, notification of the city and five-digit zip code of the offender's residency upon or after release from a Department of Corrections facility[.] * * *

Subd. 7. **Public data.** The following court services data on adult individuals is public:

(a) name, age, date of birth, sex, occupation and the fact that an individual is a parolee, probationer or participant in a diversion program, and if so, at what location;

(b) the offense for which the individual was placed under supervision;

(c) the dates supervision began and ended and the duration of supervision;

(d) court services data which was public in a court or other agency which originated the data;

(e) arrest and detention orders, orders for parole or probation revocation and the reasons for revocation;

(f) the conditions of parole, probation or participation and the extent to which those conditions have been or are being met;

(g) identities of agencies, units within agencies and individuals providing supervision; and

(h) the legal basis for any change in supervision and the date, time and locations associated with the change. * * *

Subd. 9. **Child abuse data; release to child protective services.** [Under certain circumstances,] a court services agency may release private or confidential data on an active case involving assessment or investigation of actions that are defined as sexual abuse, physical abuse, or neglect under chapter 260E to a local welfare agency[.]

HIST: 1981 c 311 s 39; * * * 2014 c 312 art 6 s 1,2; 1Sp2017 c 6 art 7 s 4; 1Sp2020 c 2 art 8 s 10

13.85 CORRECTIONS AND DETENTION DATA.

Subdivision 1. **Definition.** As used in this section, "corrections and detention data" means data on individuals created, collected, used or maintained because of their lawful confinement or detainment in state reformatories, prisons and correctional facilities, municipal or county jails, lockups, work houses, work farms and all other correctional and detention facilities.

Subd. 2. **Private data.** Unless the data are summary data or arrest data, or a statute specifically provides a different classification, corrections and detention data on individuals are classified as private pursuant to section 13.02, subdivision 12, to the extent that the release of the data would either (a) disclose medical, psychological, or financial information, or personal information not related to their lawful confinement or detainment or (b) endanger an individual's life.

Subd. 3. **Confidential data.** Corrections and detention data are confidential, pursuant to section 13.02, subdivision 3, to the extent that release of the data would: (a) endanger an individual's life, (b) endanger the effectiveness of an investigation authorized by statute and relating to the enforcement of rules or law, (c) identify a confidential informant, or (d) clearly endanger the security of any institution or its population.

Subd. 4. **Public data.** After any presentation to a court, any data made private or confidential by this section shall be public to the extent reflected in court records.

Subd. 5. **Public benefit data.** The responsible authority or its designee of any agency that maintains corrections and detention data may release private or confidential corrections and detention data to any law enforcement agency, if necessary for law enforcement purposes, or to the victim of a criminal act where the data are necessary for the victim to assert the victim's legal right to restitution.

HIST: 1981 c 311 s 39; 1982 c 545 s 17, 24; 1988 c 670 s 7; 1998 c 371 s 5

13.854 RELEASE OF ARRESTED, DETAINED, OR CONFINED PERSON; AUTOMATED NOTIFICATION SERVICE.

For requests for notification of change in custody status of an arrested, detained or confined person from the Department of Corrections or other custodial authority made through an automated electronic notification system, all identifying information regarding the person requesting notification and that the notice was requested and provided to that person by the automated system is classified as private data on individuals * * * and is accessible only to that person.

HIST: 2013 c 34 s 1

13.86 INVESTIGATIVE DETENTION DATA.

Subdivision 1. **Definition.** As used in this section, "investigative detention data" means government data created, collected, used or maintained by the state correctional facilities, municipal or county jails, lockups, work houses, work farms and other correctional and detention facilities which: (a) if revealed, would disclose the identity of an informant who provided information about suspected illegal activities, and (b) if revealed, is likely to subject the informant to physical reprisals by others.

Subd. 2. **General.** Investigative detention data is confidential and shall not be disclosed except:

(a) pursuant to section 13.05 or any other statute;

(b) pursuant to a valid court order; or

(c) to a party named in a civil or criminal proceeding, whether administrative or judicial, to the extent required by the relevant rules of civil or criminal procedure.

HIST: 1979 c 102 s 13; 1980 c 603 s 22; 1981 c 3-1 s 39; 1982 c 545 s 24

* * *

13.87 CRIMINAL HISTORY DATA.

Subdivision 1. **Criminal history data.** (a) **Definition.** For purposes of this section, "criminal history data" means all data maintained in criminal history records compiled by the Bureau of Criminal Apprehension, including, but not limited to fingerprints, photographs, identification data, arrest data, prosecution data, criminal court data, custody and supervision data.

(b) **Classification.** Criminal history data maintained by agencies, political subdivisions and statewide systems are classified as private, pursuant to section 13.02, subdivision 12, except that data created, collected, or maintained by the bureau of criminal apprehension that identify an individual who was convicted of a crime and the offense of which the individual was convicted, associated court disposition and sentence information, controlling agency, and confinement information are public data for 15 years following the discharge of the sentence imposed for the offense.

The bureau of criminal apprehension shall provide to the public at the central office of the bureau the ability to inspect in person, at no charge, through a computer monitor the criminal conviction data classified as public under this subdivision. * * *

Subd. 2. **Firearms data.** All data pertaining to the purchase or transfer of firearms and applications for permits to carry firearms which are collected by state agencies, political subdivisions or statewide systems pursuant to sections 624.712 to 624.719 are private, pursuant to section 13.02, subdivision 12.

Subd. 3. **Internet access.** (a) Notwithstanding section 13.03, subdivision 3, paragraph (a), the bureau of criminal apprehension may charge a fee for Internet access to public criminal history data provided through August 1, 2003. The fee may not exceed $5 per inquiry or the amount needed to recoup the actual cost of implementing and providing Internet access, whichever is less.

(b) The Web site must include a notice to the subject of data of the right to contest the accuracy or completeness of data, as provided under section 13.04, subdivision 4, and provide a telephone number and address that the subject may contact for further information on this process. * * *

(d) The Web site must include a description of the types of criminal history data not available on the site, including arrest data, juvenile data, criminal history data from other states, federal data, data on convictions where 15 years have elapsed since discharge of the sentence, and other data that are not accessible to the public.

(e) A person who intends to access the Web site to obtain information regarding an applicant for employment, housing, or credit should disclose to the applicant the intention to do so. The Web site must include a notice that a person obtaining such access should notify the applicant that a background check using this Web site may be conducted. This paragraph does not create a civil cause of action on behalf of the data subject. * * *

Subd. 5. **Parole and probation authority access to records.** Parole and county probation authorities may access data identified in subdivision 2 on an applicant or permit holder who is subject to the supervision of that parole or county probation authority.
HIST: 1981 c 311 s 39; * * * 2012 c 290 s 62

13.88 COMMUNITY DISPUTE RESOLUTION CENTER DATA.

The guidelines shall provide that all files relating to a case in a community dispute resolution program are to be classified as private data on individuals, pursuant to section 13.02, subdivision 12, with the following exceptions:

(1) When a party to the case has been formally charged with a criminal offense, the data are to be classified as public data on individuals, pursuant to section 13.02, subdivision 15.

(2) Data relating to suspected neglect or physical or sexual abuse of children or maltreatment of vulnerable adults are to be subject to the reporting requirements of section 626.557 and chapter 260E.
HIST: 1984 c 654 art 2 s 39; 1995 c 229 art 4 s 2; 1Sp2020 c 2 art 8 s 12

299C.40 COMPREHENSIVE INCIDENT-BASED REPORTING SYSTEM.

Subdivision 1. **Definitions.** (a) The definitions in this subdivision apply to this section.

(b) "CIBRS" means the Comprehensive Incident-Based Reporting System, located in the Department of Public Safety and managed by the Bureau of Criminal Apprehension. A reference in this section to "CIBRS" includes the Bureau of Criminal Apprehension.
* * *

Subd. 2. **Purpose.** CIBRS is a statewide system containing data from law enforcement agencies. [Under certain circumstances,] data in CIBRS must be made available to law enforcement agencies[.] * * *

Subd. 5. **Access to CIBRS data by law enforcement agency personnel.** Only law enforcement agency personnel with certification from the Bureau of Criminal Apprehension may enter, update, or access CIBRS data[, and such ability] must be limited through the use of purpose codes that correspond to the official duties and training level of the personnel.

Subd. 6. **Access to CIBRS data by data subject.** (a) Upon request to the Bureau of Criminal Apprehension or to a law enforcement agency participating in CIBRS an individual shall be informed whether the individual is the subject of private or confidential data held by CIBRS. * * *
HIST: 2005 c 163 s 81; * * * 2014 c 284 s 4

299C.41 E-CHARGING.

Subdivision 1. **Definitions.** (a) The definitions in this subdivision apply to this section.

(b) "Auditing data" means data in [an] e-charging * * * document[.] * * *

(c) "Credentialed individual" means an individual who has provided credentialing data to a government entity or a court and has been authorized to use e-charging.

(d) "Credentialing data" means data in [an] e-charging * * * document for an individual who is or was authorized to use e-charging[.] * * *

(e) "E-charging" means a service operated by the Bureau of Criminal Apprehension to provide communication and workflow tools for law enforcement agencies, prosecutors, and the courts to use in apprehending, prosecuting, or adjudicating a person for an alleged delinquent act or an alleged criminal or petty misdemeanor offense [.] * * *

(h) "Workflow and routing data" means data in [an] e-charging * * * document[.] * * *

Subd. 2. **Data classification.** (a) Credentialing data held by a government entity are classified as private data on individuals * * * or nonpublic data[.] * * *

(b) Auditing data and workflow and routing data maintained by the Bureau of Criminal Apprehension are classified as confidential data on individuals * * * or protected nonpublic data

* * * until the investigation is inactive[.] * * * Once the investigation is inactive, and the recipient of the data authorizes release to the data subject, the auditing data and workflow and routing data maintained by the Bureau of Criminal Apprehension are classified as private data on individuals * * * or nonpublic data[.] * * *.

Subd. 3. **Data sharing authorized.** * * *

(b) Auditing, workflow and routing data, or credentialing data must be disclosed to a defendant in a pending criminal matter when the data are relevant to the individual's defense[.] The data may not be used outside the pending criminal matter and a recipient may not redisclose the data that are received. * * *

HIST: 2008 c 242 s 3; 2008 c 299 s 15; 2011 c 91 s 1

Editors' Note: Although the following statute is not specifically described in this performance objective, it has been included because of its close relationship to other Chapter 299C provisions.

299C.106 SEXUAL ASSAULT EXAMINATION KIT HANDLING.
* * *

Subd. 3. **Submission and storage of unrestricted sexual assault examination kits.** (a) Within 60 days of receiving an unrestricted sexual assault kit [collected by a health care professional with a release signed by the patient], a law enforcement agency shall submit the kit for testing to a forensic laboratory. The testing laboratory shall return unrestricted sexual assault examination kits to the submitting agency for storage after testing is complete. The submitting agency must store unrestricted sexual assault examination kits indefinitely.

(b) Within 60 days of a hospital preparing a restricted sexual assault examination kit [those not accompanied by a release by a patient] or a law enforcement agency receiving a restricted sexual assault examination kit from a hospital, the hospital or the agency shall submit the kit to the Bureau of Criminal Apprehension. The bureau shall store all restricted sexual assault examination kits collected by hospitals or law enforcement agencies in the state. The bureau shall retain a restricted sexual assault examination kit for at least 30 months from the date the bureau receives the kit.

Subd. 3a. **Uniform consent form.** The superintendent of the Bureau of Criminal Apprehension shall develop a uniform sexual assault examination kit consent form. The form must clearly explain the differences between designating a kit as unrestricted or restricted. In developing and designing the consent form, the superintendent must consult with hospital administrators, sexual assault nurse examiners, the Minnesota Coalition Against Sexual Assault, and other stakeholders. The uniform consent form shall be widely distributed to law enforcement agencies, medical providers, and other stakeholders. The superintendent must make the form available on the bureau's website.

Subd. 3b. **Web database requirement.** The commissioner, in consultation with the commissioner of administration, must maintain a website with a searchable database providing sexual assault victims with information on the status of their individual sexual assault examination kit. The superintendent must strictly control access to the database to protect the privacy of the victims' data.
* * *

HIST: 2018 c 160 s 2; 5Sp2020 c 3 art 9 s 1-3

Chapter 29 -- MISCELLANEOUS STATUTES (PART IV)

Editor's Note: While not specifically referred to in the learning objectives, the following statutes are included because they complement the Category 2 goal of a specialized body of knowledge for Minnesota's professional peace officer education. Selected portions of Chapter 326 concerning the licensing process for private detectives and protective agents have been edited to eliminate those provisions that have less importance to the duties of peace officers.

326.32 DEFINITIONS.

Subdivision 1. **Scope.** As used in sections 326.32 to 326.339, the terms defined in this section have the meanings given them.

Subd. 1a. **Armed with a firearm.** An individual is "armed with a firearm" if at any time in the performance of the individual's duties the individual wears, carries, possesses, or has access to a firearm.

Subd. 1b. **Armed with a weapon.** An individual is "armed with a weapon" if at any time in the performance of the individual's duties the individual wears, carries, possesses, or has access to:

(1) a weapon other than a firearm; or

(2) an immobilizing or restraining device.

Subd. 2. **Board.** "Board" means the board of private detective and protective agent services.

* * *

Subd. 8. **Applicant.** "Applicant" means any individual, partnership or corporation who has made application for a private detective or protective agent license.

Subd. 9. **License.** "License" means a private detective license or a protective agent license.

Subd. 10. **License holder.** "License holder" means any individual, partnership or corporation licensed to perform the duties of a private detective or a protective agent.

* * *

Subd. 10c. **Proprietary employer.** A "proprietary employer" means an individual, partnership, or corporation that is not engaged in the business of providing protective agents but employs individuals to serve as security guards solely on the employer's property and its curtilage.

* * *

Subd. 13. **Security guard.** (a) "Security guard" means a person who wears or carries any insignia that identifies the person to the public as security, who is paid a fee, wage, or salary to do one or more of the following:

(1) prevent or detect intrusion, unauthorized entry or activity, vandalism, or trespass on private property;

(2) prevent or detect theft, loss, embezzlement, misappropriation, or concealment of merchandise, money, bonds, stocks, notes, or other valuable documents or papers;

(3) control, regulate, or direct the flow or movements of the public, whether by vehicle or otherwise, to assure protection of private property;

(4) protect individuals from bodily harm; or

(5) enforce policies and rules of the security guard's employer related to crime reduction to the extent that the enforcement falls within the scope of the security guard's duties.

(b) The term "security guard" does not include:

* * *

(3) a person employed by a proprietary company to conduct plainclothes surveillance or investigation;

(4) a person temporarily employed under statute or ordinance by political subdivisions to provide protective services at social functions;

(5) an employee of an air or rail carrier; [or]

(6) a customer service representative or sales clerk employed in a retail establishment[.]
* * *

HIST: 1974 c 310 s 1; * * * 2001 c 168 s 1,2

* * *

326.33 BOARD OF PRIVATE DETECTIVE AND PROTECTIVE AGENT SERVICES.

Subdivision 1. **Members.** There is hereby created a board of private detective and protective agent services, consisting of the superintendent of the bureau of criminal apprehension or an assistant superintendent designated by the superintendent, and * * * members appointed by the commissioner of public safety[.] * * *

HIST: 1974 c 310 s 5; * * * 2000 c 445 art 1 s 3

* * *

326.3311 POWERS AND DUTIES.

The board has the following powers and duties:

(1) to receive and review all applications for private detective and protective agent licenses;

(2) to approve applications for private detective and protective agent licenses and issue, or reissue licenses as provided in sections 326.32 to 326.339;

(3) to deny applications for private detective and protective agent licenses[;]* * *

(4) to enforce all laws and rules governing private detectives and protective agents; and

(5) to suspend or revoke the license of a license holder or impose a civil penalty on a license holder for violations[.] * * *

HIST: 1987 c 360 s 9

* * *

326.3341 EXEMPTIONS.

Sections 326.32 to 326.339 do not apply to:

(1) an employee while providing security or conducting an investigation of a pending or potential claim against the employee's employer;

(2) a peace officer or employee of the United States, this state or one of its political subdivisions, while engaged in the discharge of official duties for the government employer;

(3) persons engaged exclusively in obtaining and furnishing information as to the financial standing, rating, and credit responsibility of persons or as to the personal habits and financial responsibility of applicants for insurance, indemnity bonds, or commercial credit;

(4) an attorney-at-law while performing the duties of an attorney-at-law or an investigator employed exclusively by an attorney or a law firm engaged in investigating legal matters;

(5) a collection agency or finance company licensed to do business under the laws of this state or an employee of one of those companies while acting within the scope of employment when making an investigation incidental to the business of the agency, including an investigation as to location of a debtor, of the debtor's assets or property, provided the client has a financial interest in or a lien upon the assets or property of the debtor;

(6) an insurance adjuster employed exclusively by an insurance company, or licensed as an adjuster with the state of Minnesota and engaged in the business of adjusting insurance claims;

(7) persons engaged in responding to alarm signals including, but not limited to, fire alarms, industrial process failure alarms and burglary alarms, for purposes of maintaining, repairing or resetting the alarm, or for opening the premises for law enforcement personnel or responding agents; or

(8) a certified public accountant or a CPA firm[.]

HIST: 1987 c 360 s 12; 2013 c 69 s 1

* * *

326.336 EMPLOYEES OF LICENSE HOLDERS.

Subdivision 1. **Background check.** A license holder may employ, in connection with the business of private detective or protective agent, as many unlicensed persons as may be necessary; provided that every license holder is at all times accountable for the good conduct of every person employed. When a license holder hires a person to perform services as a private detective or protective agent, the employer shall submit to the bureau of criminal apprehension a full set of fingerprints of each employee and the written consent of the employee to enable the bureau to determine whether that person has a criminal record. The employee is a conditional employee until the employer receives a report from the bureau that, based on a check of the criminal records maintained by the bureau, the prospective employee has not been convicted in Minnesota of a felony or any offense listed in section 326.3381, subdivision 3, other than a misdemeanor or gross misdemeanor assault. During the period of conditional employment, the person may not serve as a private detective or protective agent, but may be trained by the employer. The bureau shall immediately forward the fingerprints to the Federal Bureau of Investigation and request the Federal Bureau of Investigation to conduct a criminal history check of each conditional employee. The bureau shall determine if the Federal Bureau of Investigation report indicates that the employee was convicted of a disqualifying offense, and shall notify the employer accordingly. The employer shall immediately dismiss an employee who has been convicted of a disqualifying offense.

Subd. 2. **Identification card.** An identification card must be issued by the license holder to each employee. The card must be in the possession of the employee to whom it is issued at all times. * * *

Subd. 3. **Failure to return property.** Any person who shall be issued an identification card, badge, holster, weapon, shield, or any other equipment bearing the name, trademark or trade name, or any combination thereof, of any licensed agency, or indicating that such person is a private detective protective agent, or employee of same who does not return such badge, weapon, holster, identification card, uniform emblem or other equipment to the owner thereof within ten days of the termination of employment, or of receiving a written request to return same, made by certified mail to the person's last known address, whichever shall last occur, shall be guilty of a misdemeanor.

Subd. 4. **Confidentiality; false statements.** No employee of any license holder shall divulge to anyone other than the employer, or as the employer shall direct, except as may be required by law, any information acquired during such employment in respect of any matter or investigation undertaken or done by such employer. Any employee who shall make any false statement in an employment statement or who willfully makes a false report to the employer in respect to any matter in the course of the employer's business, or who shall otherwise violate the provisions of this subdivision is guilty of a misdemeanor.

HIST: 1945 c 130 s 7; * * * 2002 c 321 s 4

326.3361 TRAINING.

Subdivision 1. **Rules.** The board shall, by rule, prescribe the requirements, duration, contents, and standards for successful completion of certified training programs for license holders * * * and employees, including:

(1) for those individuals who are armed with a firearm, training in the proper use of, and the risks and dangers arising from the use of, firearms;

(2) for those individuals who are armed with a weapon, training in the proper use of, and the risks and dangers arising from the use of, weapons other than firearms, including, but not limited to, bludgeons, nightsticks, batons, chemical weapons, and electronic incapacitation devices, and restraint or immobilization techniques;

(3) for those individuals who are armed with a firearm or armed with a weapon, training in first aid and alternatives to the use of force, including advantages to not using force and specifically when force should not be used;

(4) for those individuals who are armed with a firearm or armed with a weapon, training in the legal limitations on the justifiable use of force and deadly force as specified in sections 609.06 and 609.065;

(5) standards for weapons and equipment issued to or carried or used by those individuals;

(6) preassignment or on-the-job training, or its equivalent, required before applicants may be certified as having completed training; and

(7) continuing training for license holders * * * and individuals armed with a weapon.

Subd. 2. **Required contents.** The rules adopted by the board must require:

(1) 12 hours of preassignment or on-the-job certified training within the first 21 days of employment, or evidence that the employee has successfully completed equivalent training before the start of employment;

(2) certification by the board of completion of certified training for a license holder, qualified representative, Minnesota manager, partner, and employee to carry or use a firearm, a weapon other than a firearm, or an immobilizing or restraint technique; and

(3) six hours a year of certified continuing training for all license holders, qualified representatives, Minnesota managers, partners, and employees, and an additional six hours a year for individuals who are armed with firearms or armed with weapons, which must include annual certification of the individual.

An individual may not carry or use a weapon while undergoing on-the-job training under this subdivision.

Subd. 3. **Use of weapons; certified training required.** The rules must provide that no license holder * * * or employee may carry or use a weapon or immobilizing or restraint technique without having successfully completed certified training as directed by the board.

Subd. 4. **Full-time peace officers.** A person licensed as a peace officer by the board of peace officer standards and training meets the training requirements of this section.

HIST: 1990 c 485 s 2; 1993 c 168 s 1-3; 2000 c 445 art 1 s 4; 2001 c 168 s 3,4

* * *

326.338 PERSONS ENGAGED AS PRIVATE DETECTIVES OR PROTECTIVE AGENTS.

Subdivision 1. **Private detective.** Persons who for a fee, reward, or other consideration, undertake any of the following acts for the purpose of obtaining information for others are considered to be engaged in the business of a private detective:

(1) investigating crimes or wrongs done or threatened against the government of the United States or of any state, county, or municipal subdivision thereof;

(2) investigating the identity, habits, conduct, movements, whereabouts, transactions, reputation, or character of any person or organization;

(3) investigating the credibility of witnesses or other persons;

(4) investigating the location or recovery of lost or stolen property;

(5) investigating the origin of and responsibility for libels, losses, accidents, or damage or injuries to persons or property;

(6) investigating the affiliation, connection, or relationship of any person, firm, or corporation with any organization, society, or association, or with any official, representative, or member thereof;

(7) investigating the conduct, honesty, efficiency, loyalty, or activities of employees, persons seeking employment, agents, or contractors and subcontractors;

(8) obtaining through investigation evidence to be used before any authorized investigating committee, board of award, board of arbitration, administrative body, or officer or in preparation for trial of civil or criminal cases; or

(9) investigating the identity or apprehension of persons suspected of crimes or misdemeanors.
* * *

Subd. 4. **Protective agent.** A person who for a fee, reward, or other valuable consideration undertakes any of the following acts is considered to be engaged in the business of protective agent:

(1) providing guards, private patrol, or other security personnel to protect persons or their property or to prevent the theft, unlawful taking of goods, merchandise, or money, or to prevent the misappropriation or concealment of goods, merchandise, money, or other valuable things, or to procure the return of those things;

(2) physically responding to any alarm signal device, burglar alarm, television camera, still camera, or a mechanical or electronic device installed or used to prevent or detect burglary, theft, shoplifting, pilferage, losses, or other security measures;

(3) providing armored car services for the protection of persons or property;

(4) controlling motor traffic on public streets, roads, and highways for the purpose of escorting a funeral procession and oversized loads; or

(5) providing management and control of crowds for the purpose of safety and protection.

A person covered by this subdivision may perform the traffic control duties in clause (4) in place of a police officer when a special permit is required, provided that the protective agent is first-aid qualified.
HIST: 1945 c 130 s 9; * * * 1996 c 387 s 6

326.3381 LICENSES.

Subdivision 1. Prohibition. No person shall engage in the business of private detective or protective agent, or advertise or indicate in any verbal statement or in written material that the person is so engaged or available to supply those services, without having first obtained a license as provided in sections 326.32 to 326.339.

Subd. 1a. **Proprietary employers.** A proprietary employer is not required to obtain a license, but must comply with section 326.336, subdivision 1, with respect to the hiring of security guards.

Subd. 2. **Application procedure.** The board shall issue a license upon application to any person qualified under sections 326.32 to 326.339 and under the rules of the board to engage in the business of private detective or protective agent. The license shall remain effective for two years as long as the license holder complies with sections 326.32 to 326.339, the laws of Minnesota, and the rules of the board. * * *

Subd. 3. **Disqualification.** No person is qualified to hold a license who has:

(1) been convicted of (i) a felony by the courts of this or any other state or of the United States; (ii) acts which, if done in Minnesota, would be criminal sexual conduct; assault; theft; larceny; burglary, robbery; unlawful entry, extortion; defamation; buying or receiving stolen property; using, possessing, manufacturing, or carrying weapons unlawfully; using, possessing, or carrying burglary tools unlawfully, escape; possession, production, sale, or distribution of narcotics unlawfully; or (iii) in any other country of acts which, if done in Minnesota, would be a felony or would be any of the other offenses provided in this clause and for which a full pardon or similar relief has not been granted;

(2) made any false statement in an application for a license or any document required to be submitted to the board; or

(3) failed to demonstrate to the board good character, honesty, and integrity.
* * *
HIST: 1987 c 360 s 16; 1989 c 171 s 4,5

326.3382 APPLICATION FOR LICENSE.
    Subdivision 1. **Application form.** (a) Application for a private detective or protective agent license shall be made on a form prescribed by the board. * * *
    Subd. 3. **Proof of insurance.** (a) No license may be issued to a private detective or protective agent applicant until the applicant has complied with the requirements in this subdivision.
    (b) The applicant shall execute a surety bond to the state of Minnesota in the penal sum of $10,000 and file it with the board. * * *
    (c) The applicant shall furnish proof, acceptable to the board, of the applicant's ability to respond in damages for liability on account of accidents or wrongdoings arising out of the ownership and operation of a private detective or protective agent business. * * *
    (d) The applicant may file with the board a certificate of insurance demonstrating coverage for general liability, completed operations, and personal injury. * * *
    (e) The applicant may file with the board an annual net worth statement[.] * * *
    (f) The applicant may file with the board an irrevocable letter of credit from a financial institution acceptable to the board[.] * * *
HIST: 1987 c 360 s 17; 2005 c 136 art 8 s 11; 2014 c 312 art 4 s 21

326.3383 LICENSE REISSUANCE.
    Subdivision 1. **Requirements.** The board shall reissue a private detective or protective agent license to a license holder without further board review, if the license holder who has complied with all applicable laws and rules:
    (1) submits to the board an application for license reissuance on a form prescribed by the board;
    (2) submits to the board a list of all current employees; and
    (3) remits the expired license to the board.
    * * *
    Subd. 3. **Bond and proof of financial responsibility.** Each applicant for license reissuance shall maintain a $10,000 surety bond, and show proof of financial responsibility as required in section 326.3382, subdivision 3.
HIST: 1987 c 360 s 18

326.3384 PROHIBITED ACTS.
    Subdivision 1. **Prohibition.** No license holder or employee of a license holder shall, in a manner that implies that the person is an employee or agent of a governmental agency, display on a badge, identification card, emblem, vehicle, uniform, stationery, or in advertising for private detective or protective agent services:
    (1) the words "public safety," "police," "constable," "highway patrol," "state patrol," "sheriff," "trooper," or "law enforcement"; or
    (2) the name of a municipality, county, state, or of the United States, or any governmental subdivision thereof.
    Subd. 1a. **Labor disputes.** No license holder, in the course of providing protective agent services, may provide armed protective personnel to labor disputes or strike locations. This subdivision does not apply to the use of armed security personnel services utilized in the usual course of business for the protection of persons, property, and payroll.
    Subd. 1b. **Acts prohibited during labor disputes, strikes, and lockouts.** (a) This subdivision applies to (1) a license holder or an employee of a license holder who is primarily performing the duties of a protective agent; or (2) a security guard who is primarily performing the duties of a security guard.
    (b) A person described in paragraph (a) is prohibited from doing any of the activities described in clauses (1) to (5) during a labor dispute, strike, or lockout as defined in section 179.01, subdivisions 7, 8, and 9;

(1) inciting, encouraging, or aiding in the incitement or encouragement of any participant to do unlawful acts against the person or property of anyone;

(2) photographing a participant when neither that person nor the photographer is on the premises being protected by the persons described in paragraph (a);

(3) stopping or detaining any vehicle unless the vehicle is on premises being protected by the persons described in paragraph (a);

(4) conducting surveillance of participants, when neither the participant nor the person conducting the surveillance is on the premises being protected by the person described in paragraph (a), or of their businesses, or homes; or

(5) any other activities that are outside of the scope of the duties described in sections 326.32, subdivision 13, and 326.338, subdivision 4, and have the purpose of intimidating or provoking a participant.

Subd. 2. **Penalty.** (a) A person violating this section is guilty of a gross misdemeanor.

(b) The board shall suspend the license of a license holder for the periods described in paragraph (c) if the license holder or an employee of the license holder is convicted of a violation of subdivision 1b. The board shall prohibit an employee of a license holder from working for any license holder for the periods described in paragraph (c) if the employee is convicted of a violation of subdivision 1b.

(c) The periods described in paragraph (b) are as follows:

(1) 60 days for the first violation;

(2) six months for the second violation; and

(3) one year for the third violation.

HIST: 1987 c 360 s 19; 1989 c 171 s 6,7; 1990 c 485 s 3,4; 2005 c 136 art 11 s 16

* * *

326.3387 DISCIPLINARY ACTION.

Subdivision 1 **Basis for action.** The board may revoke or suspend or refuse to issue or reissue a private detective or protective agent license if:

(a) the license holder violates a provision of sections 326.32 to 326.339 or a rule adopted under those sections;

(b) the license holder has engaged in fraud, deceit, or misrepresentation while in the business of private detective or protective agent;

(c) the license holder has made a false statement in an application submitted to the board or in a document required to be submitted to the board; or

(d) the license holder violates an order of the board.

* * *

HIST: 1987 c 360 s 22

326.3388 ADMINISTRATIVE PENALTIES.

* * * The board may impose a penalty from the schedule on a license holder for a violation of sections 326.32 to 326.339 or the rules of the board. The penalty is in addition to any criminal penalty imposed for the same violation. * * *

HIST: 1987 c 360 s 23

326.3389 LICENSES NONTRANSFERABLE.

A license issued under sections 326.32 to 326.339 may not be transferred.

HIST: 1987 c 360 s 24

326.339 VIOLATIONS; PENALTY.

Unless otherwise specifically provided any violation of any provision or requirement of sections 326.32 to 326.339 is a gross misdemeanor.

HIST: 1945 c 130 s 10; 1974 c 310 s 10; 1987 c 360 s 25

626.88 UNIFORMS; PEACE OFFICERS, SECURITY GUARDS; COLOR.

Subdivision 1. **Definitions.** (a) For the purposes of this section, the following terms have the meanings given them.

(b) "Peace officer" means an employee of a political subdivision or state law enforcement agency who is licensed pursuant to sections 626.84 to 626.855 charged with the prevention and detection of crime and the enforcement of the general criminal laws of the state and who has full power of arrest, and shall also include Minnesota state troopers, state conservation officers, park police, constables, and University of Minnesota police officers.

(c) "Security guard" means any person who is paid a fee, wage or salary to perform one or more of the following functions:

(1) prevention or detection of intrusion, unauthorized entry or activity, vandalism or trespass on private property;

(2) prevention or detection of theft, loss, embezzlement, misappropriation, or concealment of merchandise, money, bonds, stocks, notes, or other valuable documents or papers;

(3) control, regulation, or direction of the flow or movements of the public, whether by vehicle or otherwise, to assure protection of private property;

(4) protection of individuals from bodily harm;

(5) prevention or detection of intrusion, unauthorized entry or activity, vandalism, or trespass on Minnesota National Guard facilities, including, but not limited to, Camp Ripley and Air National Guard air bases; or

(6) enforcement of policies and rules of the security guard's employer related to crime reduction insofar as such enforcement falls within the scope of security guards duties.

The term "security guard" does not include: (i) auditors, accountants, and accounting personnel performing audits or accounting functions; (ii) employees of a firm licensed pursuant to section 326.3381 whose duties are primarily administrative or clerical in nature; (iii) unarmed security personnel; (iv) personnel temporarily employed pursuant to statute or ordinance by political subdivisions to provide protective services at social functions; (v) employees of air or rail carriers.

(d) "Bail bondsman" or "bail enforcement agent" means a surety acting as a bonding agent or any person who acts at the direction of a surety for the purpose of arresting a defendant that the surety believes:

(1) is about to flee;

(2) will not appear in court as required by the defendant's recognizance; or

(3) will otherwise not perform the conditions of the recognizance.

Subd. 2. **Uniforms.** (a) Uniforms for peace officers shall be of uniform colors throughout the state as provided herein.

(1) Municipal peace officers, including University of Minnesota peace officers, constables, and peace officers assigned to patrol duties in parks, shall be blue, brown or green;

(2) Peace officers who are members of the county sheriffs' office shall be blue, brown or green;

(3) State troopers shall be maroon;

(4) Conservation officers shall be green.

(b) The uniforms of security guards may be any color other than those specified for peace officers.

(c) The uniforms of a bail bondsman or bail enforcement agent or any person who acts at the direction of a surety may be any color other than those specified for peace officers. A violation of this paragraph is a petty misdemeanor.

(d) This subdivision shall apply to uniforms purchased subsequent to January 1, 1981.

Subd. 3. **Exception.** Security guards employed by the capitol complex security division of the department of public safety are not required to comply with subdivision 2.

HIST: 1980 c 578 s 9; * * * 2015 c 65 art 3 s 35

Chapter 30 -- MISCELLANEOUS STATUTES (PART V)

Category 2, Section 19: The Americans with Disabilities Act and Special Communications Situations

Editor's Note: While not specifically referred to in the learning objectives, the following statutes incorporated in Chapter 363A – the Minnesota Human Rights Act are included because they complement the Category 2 goal of a specialized body of knowledge for Minnesota's professional peace officer education. Please note that provisions of the Chapter 363A are arranged by topical area of coverage (as opposed to the numbering sequence of the various statutes themselves). Also, selected portions this Chapter 363A have been edited to exclude those provisions that have less importance to the duties of peace officers. Federal laws also concerning discrimination may be found in United States Code Title 42 Section 2000e (dealing with civil rights). The extensive nature of this latter material precludes its inclusion in this text.

363A.01 CITATION.
This chapter shall be known as the Minnesota Human Rights Act.
HIST: 1955 c 516 s 2; 1961 c 428 s 17; 1973 c 729 s 17

363A.02 PUBLIC POLICY.
Subdivision 1. **Freedom from discrimination.** (a) It is the public policy of this state to secure for persons in this state, freedom from discrimination:

(1) in employment because of race, color, creed, religion, national origin, sex, marital status, disability, status with regard to public assistance, sexual orientation, familial status, and age;

(2) in housing and real property because of race, color, creed, religion, national origin, sex, marital status, disability, status with regard to public assistance, sexual orientation, and familial status;

(3) in public accommodations because of race, color, creed, religion, national origin, sex, sexual orientation, and disability;

(4) in public services because of race, color, creed, religion, national origin, sex, marital status, disability, sexual orientation, and status with regard to public assistance; and

(5) in education because of race, color, creed, religion, national origin, sex, marital status, disability, status with regard to public assistance, sexual orientation, and age.

(b) Such discrimination threatens the rights and privileges of the inhabitants of this state and menaces the institutions and foundations of democracy. It is also the public policy of this state to protect all persons from wholly unfounded charges of discrimination. Nothing in this chapter shall be interpreted as restricting the implementation of positive action programs to combat discrimination.

Subd. 2. **Civil right.** The opportunity to obtain employment, housing, and other real estate, and full and equal utilization of public accommodations, public services, and educational institutions without such discrimination as is prohibited by this chapter is hereby recognized as and declared to be a civil right.

Subd. 3. **Severability.** If any provision of Laws 1967, chapter 897, or the application thereof to any person or circumstances is held invalid, the invalidity does not affect the other provisions or applications of Laws 1967, chapter 897, which can be given effect without the invalid provision or application, and to this end the provisions of Laws 1967, chapter 897, are severable.

HIST: 1955 c 516 s 1; 1961 c 428 s 16; 1967 c 897 s 26; 1969 c 975 s 15,16; 1973 c 729 s 14,15; 1977 c 351 s 11; 1980 c 531 s 8; 1993 c 22 s 19; 1Sp2021 c 11 art 3 s 12

363A.03 DEFINITIONS.

Subdivision 1. **Terms.** For the purposes of this chapter, the words defined in this section have the meanings ascribed to them.

* * *

Subd. 4. **Board.** "Board" means the state Board of Human Rights.

Subd. 5. **Business.** The term "business" includes any partnership, association, corporation, legal representative, trustee, trustee in bankruptcy, or receiver, but excludes the state and its departments, agencies, and political subdivisions.

* * *

Subd. 7. **Commissioner.** "Commissioner" means the commissioner of human rights.

Subd. 8. **Complainant.** "Complainant" means the commissioner of human rights after issuing a complaint[.]

* * *

Subd. 11. **Department.** "Department" means the department of human rights.

Subd. 12. **Disability.** "Disability" means any condition or characteristic that renders a person a disabled person. A disabled person is any person who (1) has a physical, sensory, or mental impairment which materially limits one or more major life activities; (2) has a record of such an impairment; or (3) is regarded as having such an impairment.

* * *

Subd. 24. **Marital status.** "Marital status" means whether a person is single, married, remarried, divorced, separated, or a surviving spouse and, in employment cases, includes protection against discrimination on the basis of the identity, situation, actions, or beliefs of a spouse or former spouse.

Subd. 25. **National origin.** "National origin" means the place of birth of an individual or of any of the individual's lineal ancestors.

* * *

Subd. 30. **Person.** "Person" includes partnership, association, corporation, legal representative, trustee, trustee in bankruptcy, receiver, and the state and its departments, agencies, and political subdivisions.

* * *

Subd. 36. **Qualified disabled person.** "Qualified disabled person" means:

(1) with respect to employment, a disabled person who, with reasonable accommodation, can perform the essential functions required of all applicants for the job in question; and

(2) with respect to public services, a person with a disability who, with or without reasonable modifications to rules, policies, or practices, removal of architectural, communications, or transportation barriers, or the provision of auxiliary aids and services, meets the essential eligibility requirements for receipt of services and for participation in programs and activities provided by the public service.

For the purposes of this subdivision, "disability" excludes any condition resulting from alcohol or drug abuse which prevents a person from performing the essential functions of the job in question or constitutes a direct threat to property or the safety of others.

If a respondent contends that the person is not a qualified disabled person, the burden is on the respondent to prove that it was reasonable to conclude the disabled person, with reasonable accommodation, could not have met the requirements of the job or that the selected person was demonstrably better able to perform the job.

* * *

Subd. 40. **Religious or denominational educational institutions.** "Religious or denominational educational institution" means an educational institution which is operated, supervised, controlled or sustained primarily by a religious or denominational organization, or is one which is stated by the parent church body to be and is, in fact, officially related to that church by being represented on the board of the institution, and by providing substantial financial assistance and which has certified, in writing, to the board that it is a religious or denominational educational institution.

Subd. 41. **Respondent.** "Respondent" means a person against whom a complaint has been filed or issued.

Subd. 42. **Sex.** "Sex" includes, but is not limited to, pregnancy, childbirth, and disabilities related to pregnancy or childbirth.

Subd. 43. **Sexual harassment.** "Sexual harassment" includes unwelcome sexual advances, requests for sexual favors, sexually motivated physical contact or other verbal or physical conduct or communication of a sexual nature when:

(1) submission to that conduct or communication is made a term or condition, either explicitly or implicitly, of obtaining employment, public accommodations or public services, education, or housing;

(2) submission to or rejection of that conduct or communication by an individual is used as a factor in decisions affecting that individual's employment, public accommodations or public services, education, or housing; or

(3) that conduct or communication has the purpose or effect of substantially interfering with an individual's employment, public accommodations or public services, education, or housing, or creating an intimidating, hostile, or offensive employment, public accommodations, public services, educational, or housing environment.
* * *

Subd. 44. **Sexual orientation.** "Sexual orientation" means having or being perceived as having an emotional, physical, or sexual attachment to another person without regard to the sex of that person or having or being perceived as having an orientation for such attachment, or having or being perceived as having a self-image or identity not traditionally associated with one's biological maleness or femaleness. "Sexual orientation" does not include a physical or sexual attachment to children by an adult.

Subd. 47. **Status with regard to public assistance.** "Status with regard to public assistance" means the condition of being a recipient of federal, state or local assistance, including medical assistance, or of being a tenant receiving federal, state or local subsidies, including rental assistance or rent supplements.

Subd. 48. **Unfair discriminatory practices.** "Unfair discriminatory practice" means any act described in sections 363A.08 to 363A.19, and 363A.38, subdivision 10.
* * *
HIST: 1955 c 516 s 3; * * * 2004 c 203 art 2 s 61

363A.20 EXEMPTION BASED ON EMPLOYMENT.

Subdivision 1. **Employment.** The provisions of section 363A.08 shall not apply to the employment of any individual:

(a) by the individual's parent, grandparent, spouse, child, or grandchild; or

(b) in the domestic service of any person.

Subd. 2. **Religious or fraternal organization.** The provisions of section 363A.08 shall not apply to a religious or fraternal corporation, association, or society, with respect to qualifications based on religion or sexual orientation, when religion or sexual orientation shall be a bona fide occupational qualification for employment.

Subd. 3. **Nonpublic service organization.** The provisions of section 363A.08 shall not apply to a nonpublic service organization whose primary function is providing occasional services to minors, such as youth sports organizations, scouting organizations, boys' or girls' clubs, programs providing friends, counselors, or role models for minors, youth theater, dance, music or artistic organizations, agricultural organizations for minors, including 4-H clubs, and other youth organizations, with respect to qualifications of employees or volunteers based on sexual orientation.

Subd. 4. **Employment selection.** The provisions of section 363A.08 do not apply to the employment of one person in place of another, standing by itself, shall not be evidence of an unfair discriminatory practice.
* * *

Subd. 8. **Physical exam.** (a) It is not an unfair employment practice for an employer, employment agency, or labor organization:

(1) to require or request a person to undergo physical examination, which may include a medical history, for the purpose of determining the person's capability to perform available employment, provided:

(i) that an offer of employment has been made on condition that the person meets the physical or mental requirements of the job, except that a law enforcement agency filling a peace officer position or part-time peace officer position may require or request an applicant to undergo psychological evaluation before a job offer is made provided that the psychological evaluation is for those job-related abilities set forth by the board of peace officer standards and training for psychological evaluations and is otherwise lawful;

(ii) that the examination tests only for essential job-related abilities;

(iii) that the examination * * * required of all persons conditionally offered employment for the same position regard less of disability; and

(iv) that the information obtained regarding the medical condition or history of the applicant is collected and maintained on separate forms and in separate medical files and is treated as a confidential medical record[; or] * * *

(2) with the consent of the employee, after employment has commenced, to obtain additional medical information for the purposes of assessing continuing ability to perform the job or employee health insurance eligibility; for purposes mandated by local, state, or federal law; for purposes of assessing the need to reasonably accommodate an employee or obtaining information to determine eligibility for the second injury fund under chapter 176; or pursuant to sections 181.950 to 181.957; or other legitimate business reason not otherwise prohibited by law;

(3) to administer preemployment tests provided that the tests (i) measure only essential job-related abilities, (ii) are required of all applicants for the same position regardless of disability except for tests authorized under chapter 176, and (iii) accurately measure the applicant's aptitude, achievement level, or whatever factors they purport to measure[; or] * * *

(5) to provide special safety considerations for pregnant women involved in tasks which are potentially hazardous to the health of the unborn child, as determined by medical criteria.
* * *

Subd. 9. **Mandatory retirement age.** By law or published retirement policy, a mandatory retirement age may be established without being a violation of this chapter if it is established consistent with section 181.81. * * *
HIST: 1955 c 516 s 4; * * * 2004 c 206 s 52

363A.21 EXEMPTION BASED ON REAL PROPERTY.

Subdivision 1. **Housing.** (1) The provisions of section 363A.09 shall not apply to:

(a) rooms in a temporary or permanent residence home run by a nonprofit organization, if the discrimination is by sex;

(b) the rental by a resident owner or occupier of a one-family accommodation of a room or rooms in the accommodation to another person or persons if the discrimination is by sex, marital status, status with regard to public assistance, sexual orientation, or disability[; or] * * *

(c) the rental by a resident owner of a unit in a dwelling containing not more than two units, if the discrimination is on the basis of sexual orientation. * * *

Subd. 2. **Familial status.** (a) The provisions of section 363A.09 prohibiting discrimination because of familial status shall not * * * apply to any owner occupied building containing four or fewer dwelling units or housing for elderly persons. * * *
HIST: 1955 c 516 s 4; * * * 2004 c 206 s 52

363A.22 EXEMPTION BASED ON FAMILIAL STATUS IN HOUSING.

The provisions of section 363.A.09 prohibiting discrimination because of familial status, do not apply to eviction from, or denial of continuing tenancy in, [exempt] dwelling units * * *, provided that: (1) one year has elapsed from the commencement of the familial status; and (2) six months prior written notice has been given to the tenant[.] * * *
HIST: 1955 c 516 s 4; * * * 1998 c 291 s 1; 1998 c 397 art 11 s 3

363A.23 EXEMPTION BASED ON EDUCATION.

Subdivision 1. **Religious or denominational institution.** It is not an unfair discriminatory practice for a religious or denominational institution to limit admission or give preference to applicants of the same religion. The provisions of section 363A.13 relating to sex, shall not apply to a private educational institution, or branch or level of a private educational institution, in which students of only one sex are permitted to enroll. * * *
HIST: 1955 c 516 s 4; * * * 1998 c 291 s 1; 1998 c 397 art 11 s 3

363A.24 EXEMPTION BASED ON PUBLIC ACCOMMODATIONS.

The provisions of section 363A.11 relating to sex, shall not apply to such facilities as restrooms, locker rooms, and other similar places. The provisions of section 363A.11 do not apply to employees or volunteers of a nonpublic service organization whose primary function is providing occasional services to minors, such as youth sports organizations, scouting organizations, boys' or girls' clubs, programs providing friends, counselors, or role models for minors, youth theater, dance, music or artistic organizations, agricultural organizations for minors, and other youth organizations, with respect to qualifications based on sexual orientation. * * *
HIST: 1955 c 516 s 4; * * * 1998 c 291 s 1; 1998 c 397 art 11 s 3

363A.25 EXEMPTION BASED ON DISABILITY. * * *

It is a defense to a complaint or action brought under the employment provisions of this chapter that the person bringing the complaint or action has a disability which in the circumstances and even with reasonable accommodation, as defined in section 363A.08, subdivision 6, poses a serious threat to the health or safety of the disabled person or others. The burden of proving this defense is upon the respondent.
HIST: 1955 c 516 s 4; * * * 1998 c 291 s 1; 1998 c 397 art 11 s 3

363A.26 EXEMPTION BASED ON RELIGIOUS ASSOCIATION.

Nothing in this chapter prohibits any religious association, religious corporation, or religious society that is not organized for private profit, or any institution organized for educational purposes that is operated, supervised, or controlled by a religious association, religious corporation, or religious society that is not organized for private profit, from:

(1) limiting admission to or giving preference to persons of the same religion or denomination;

(2) in matters relating to sexual orientation, taking any action with respect to education, employment, housing and real property, or use of facilities. This clause shall not apply to secular business activities engaged in by the religious association, religious corporation, or religious society, the conduct of which is unrelated to the religious and educational purposes for which it is organized[.] * * *
HIST: 1955 c 516 s 4; * * * 2013 c 74 s 1

363A.27 CONSTRUCTION OF LAW.

Nothing in this chapter shall be construed to:

(1) mean the state of Minnesota condones homosexuality or bisexuality or any equivalent lifestyle;

(2) authorize or permit the promotion of homosexuality or bisexuality in education institutions or require the teaching in education institutions of homosexuality or bisexuality as an acceptable lifestyle;

(3) authorize or permit the use of numerical goals or quotas, or other types of affirmative action programs, with respect to homosexuality or bisexuality in the administration or enforcement of the provisions of this chapter; or

(4) authorize the recognition of or the right of marriage between persons of the same sex.
HIST: 1993 c 22 s 7

363A.08 UNFAIR DISCRIMINATORY PRACTICES RELATING TO EMPLOYMENT OR UNFAIR EMPLOYMENT PRACTICE.
* * *

Subd. 2. **Employer.** Except when based on a bona fide occupational qualification, it is an unfair employment practice for an employer, because of race, color, creed, religion, national origin, sex, marital status, status with regard to public assistance, familial status, membership or activity in a local commission, disability, sexual orientation, or age to:

(a) refuse to hire or to maintain a system of employment which unreasonably excludes a person seeking employment; or

(b) discharge an employee; or

(c) discriminate against a person with respect to hiring, tenure, compensation, terms, upgrading, conditions, facilities, or privileges of employment.
* * *

Subd. 4. **Employer, employment agency or labor organization.** (a) Except when based on a bona fide occupational qualification, it is an unfair employment practice for an employer * * * to:

(1) require or request the person to furnish information that pertains to race, color, creed, religion, national origin, sex, marital status, status with regard to public assistance, familial status, disability, sexual orientation, or age; or, subject to section 363A.20, subdivisions 1 to 7, and 8, paragraph (a), clauses (1) to (5), to require or request a person to undergo physical examination; unless for the sole and exclusive purpose of national security, information pertaining to national origin is required by the United States, this state or a political subdivision or agency of the United States or this state, or for the sole and exclusive purpose of compliance with the Public Contracts Act or any rule, regulation, or laws of the United States or of this state requiring the information or examination. A law enforcement agency may, after notifying an applicant for a peace officer or part-time peace officer position that the law enforcement agency is commencing the background investigation on the applicant request the applicant's date of birth, gender, and race on a separate form for the sole and exclusive purpose of conducting a criminal history check, a driver's license check and fingerprint criminal history inquiry[; or] * * *

(2) seek and obtain for purposes of making a job decision, information from any source that pertains to the person's race, color, creed, religion, national origin, sex, marital status, status with regard to public assistance, familial status, disability, sexual orientation, or age, unless for the sole and exclusive purpose of compliance with the Public Contracts Act or any rule, regulation, or laws of the United States or of this state requiring the information; or

(3) cause to be printed or published a notice or advertisement that relates to employment or membership and discloses a preference, limitation, specification, or discrimination based on race, color, creed, religion, national origin, sex, marital status, status with regard to public assistance, familial status, disability, sexual orientation, or age.

(b) Any individual who is required to provide information that is prohibited by this subdivision is an aggrieved party under section 363A.06, subdivision 4, and 363A. 28, subdivisions 1 to 9.

Subd. 5. **Fringe benefits.** Except when based on a bona fide occupational qualification, it is an unfair employment practice for an employer * * * not to treat women affected by pregnancy, childbirth, or disabilities related to pregnancy or childbirth, the same as other persons who are not so affected but who are similar in their ability or inability to work, including a duty to make reasonable accommodations as provided by subdivision (6).

Subd. 6. **Reasonable accommodation.** Except when based on a bona fide occupational qualification, it is an unfair employment practice for an employer with a number of part-time or full-time employees * * * equal to or greater than 15 effective July 1, 1994 an employment agency, or a labor organization not to ~~make~~ provide a reasonable accommodation ~~to the known disability of a qualified disabled person or job applicant~~ for a job applicant or qualified employee with a disability unless the employer, agency, or organization can demonstrate that the accommodation would impose an undue hardship on the business, agency, or organization. "Reasonable accommodation" means steps which must be taken to accommodate the known physical or mental limitations of a qualified ~~disabled person~~ individual with a disability. To determine the appropriate reasonable accommodation the employer, agency, or organization shall initiate an informal, interactive process with the individual with a disability in need of the accommodation. This process should identify the limitations resulting from the disability and any potential reasonable accommodations that could overcome those limitations. "Reasonable accommodation" may include but is not limited to, nor does it necessarily require: (a) making facilities readily accessible to and usable by ~~disabled persons~~ individuals with disabilities; and (b) job restructuring, modified work schedules, reassignment to a vacant position, acquisition or modification of equipment or devices, and the provision of aides on a temporary or periodic basis.

In determining whether an accommodation would impose an undue hardship on the operation of a business or organization, factors to be considered include:

(a) the overall size of the business or organization with respect to number of employees or members and the number and type of facilities;

(b) the type of the operation, including the composition and structure of the workforce, and the number of employees at the location where the employment would occur;

(c) the nature and cost of the needed accommodation;

(d) the reasonable ability to finance the accommodation at each site of business; and

(e) documented good faith efforts to explore less restrictive or less expensive alternatives, including consultation with the disabled person or with knowledgeable disabled persons or organizations. * * *

HIST: l955 c 516 s 5; * * * 2014 c 239 art 4 s 6-9; 1Sp2021 c 11 art 3 s 13

363A.09 UNFAIR DISCRIMINATORY PRACTICES RELATING TO REAL PROPERTY.

Subdivision 1. **Real property interest; action by owner, lessee, and others.** It is an unfair discriminatory practice for an owner, lessee, sublessee, assignee, or managing agent of, or other person having the right to sell, rent or lease any real property, or any agent of any of these:

(a) to refuse to sell, rent, or lease or otherwise deny to or withhold from any person or group of persons any real property because of race, color, creed, religion, national origin, sex, marital status, status with regard to public assistance, disability, sexual orientation, or familial status; or

(b) to discriminate against any person or group of persons because of race, color, creed, religion, national origin, sex, marital status, status with regard to public assistance, disability, sexual orientation, or familial status in the terms, conditions or privileges of the sale, rental or lease of any real property or in the furnishing of facilities or services in connection therewith [; or] * * *

(c) in any transaction involving real property, to print, circulate or post or cause to be printed, circulated, or posted any advertisement or sign, or use any form of application for the purchase, rental or lease of real property, or make any record or inquiry in connection with the prospective purchase, rental, or lease of real property which expresses, directly or indirectly, any limitation, specification, or discrimination as to race, color, creed, religion, national origin, sex, marital status, status with regard to public assistance, disability, sexual orientation, or familial status, or any intent to make any such limitation, specification, or discrimination except that nothing in this clause shall be construed to prohibit the advertisement of a dwelling unit as available to adults-only if the person placing the advertisement reasonably believes that the provisions of this subdivision prohibiting discrimination because of familial status do not apply to the dwelling unit.

Subd. 2. **Real property interest; action by brokers, agents, and others.** It is an unfair discriminatory practice for a real estate broker, real estate salesperson, or employee, or agent thereof:

(a) to refuse to sell, rent, or lease or to offer for sale, rental, or lease any real property to any person or group of persons or to negotiate for the sale, rental, or lease of any real property to any person or group of persons because of race, color, creed, religion, national origin, sex, marital status, status with regard to public assistance, disability, sexual orientation, or familial status or represent that real property is not available for inspection, sale, rental, or lease when in fact it is so available, or otherwise deny or withhold any real property or any facilities of real property to or from any person or group of persons because of race, color, creed, religion, national origin, sex, marital status, status with regard to public assistance, disability, sexual orientation, or familial status; or

(b) to discriminate against any person because of race, color, creed, religion, national origin, sex, marital status, status with regard to public assistance, disability, sexual orientation, or familial status in the terms, conditions or privileges of the sale, rental or lease of real property or in the furnishing of facilities or services in connection therewith; or

(c) to print, circulate, or post or cause to be printed, circulated, or posted any advertisement or sign, or use any form of application for the purchase, rental, or lease of any real property or make any record or inquiry in connection with the prospective purchase, rental or lease of any real property, which expresses directly or indirectly, any limitation, specification or discrimination as to race, color, creed, religion, national origin, sex, marital status, status with regard to public assistance, disability, sexual orientation, or familial status or any intent to make any such limitation, specification, or discrimination except that nothing in this clause shall be construed to prohibit the advertisement of a dwelling unit as available to adults-only if the person placing the advertisement reasonably believes that the provisions of this subdivision prohibiting discrimination because of familial status do not apply to the dwelling unit.

Subd. 3. **Real property interest; action by financial institution.** It is an unfair discriminatory practice for a person, bank, banking organization, mortgage company, insurance company, or other financial institution or lender to whom application is made for financial assistance for the purchase, lease, acquisition, construction, rehabilitation, repair or maintenance of any real property or any agent or employee thereof:

(a) to discriminate against any person or group of persons because of race, color, creed religion, national origin, sex, marital status, status with regard to public assistance, disability, sexual orientation, or familial status of the person or group of persons or of the prospective occupants or tenants of the real property in the granting, withholding extending, modifying or renewing, or in the rates, terms, conditions, or privileges of the financial assistance or in the extension of services in connection therewith; or

(b) to use any form of application for the financial assistance or make any record or inquiry in connection with applications for the financial assistance which expresses, directly or indirectly, any limitation, specification, or discrimination as to race, color, creed, religion, national origin, sex, marital status, status with regard to public assistance, disability, sexual orientation, or familial status or any intent to make any such limitation, specification, or discrimination; or

(c) to discriminate against any person or group of persons who desire to purchase, lease acquire, construct, rehabilitate, repair, or maintain real property in a specific urban or rural area or any part thereof solely because of the social, economic, or environmental conditions of the area in the granting, withholding, extending, modifying, or renewing, or in the rates, terms, conditions, or privileges of the financial assistance or in the extension of services in connection therewith.

Subd. 4. **Real property transaction.** It is an unfair discriminatory practice for any real estate broker or real estate salesperson, for the purpose of inducing a real property transaction from which the person, the person's firm, or any of its members may benefit financially, to represent that a change has occurred or will or may occur in the composition with respect to race, creed, color, national origin, sex, marital status with regard to public assistance, sexual orientation, or disability of the owners or occupants in the block, neighborhood, or area in which the real property is located and to represent, directly or indirectly, that this change will or may result in undesirable consequences in the block, neighborhood, or area in which the real property is located, including but not limited to the lowering of property values, an increase in criminal or antisocial behavior, or a decline in the quality of schools or other public facilities.

Subd. 5. **Real property full and equal access.** It is an unfair discriminatory practice for a person to deny full and equal access to real property provided for in sections 363A.08 to 363A.19, and 363A.28, subdivision 10, to a person who ~~is totally or partially blind, deaf, or has a physical or sensory~~ has a disability and who uses a service animal~~, if the service animal can be properly identified as being from a recognized program which trains service animals to aid persons who are totally or partially blind or deaf or have physical or sensory disabilities.~~ The person may not be required to pay extra compensation for the service animal but is liable for damage done to the premises by the service animal.

Subd. 6. **Real property interest; interference with.** It is an unfair discriminatory practice for a person to coerce, intimidate, threaten, or interfere with a person in the exercise or enjoyment of, or on account of that person having exercised or enjoyed, or on account of that person having aided or encouraged a third person in the exercise or enjoyment of, any right granted or protected by this section.
HIST: 1955 c 516 s 4; * * * 1998 c 291 s 1; 1998 c 397 art 11 s 3; 1Sp2021 c 8 art 2 s 5

363A.10 REAL PROPERTY; DISABILITY DISCRIMINATION.

Subdivision 1. **Reasonable modifications/accommodations.** For purposes of section 363A.09, discrimination includes:

(1) a refusal to permit, at the expense of the disabled person, reasonable modifications of existing premises occupied or to be occupied by the disabled person if modifications may be necessary to afford the disabled person full enjoyment of the premises; a landlord may, where it is reasonable to do so, condition permission for a modification on the renter agreeing to restore the interior of the premises to the condition that existed before the modification, excluding reasonable wear and tear;[or]

(2) a refusal to make reasonable accommodations in rules, policies, practices, or services, when accommodations may be necessary to afford a disabled person equal opportunity to use and enjoy a dwelling[.] * * *
HIST: 1955 c 516 s 5; * * * 2001 c 186 s 1; 2001 c 194 s 2

363A.11 PUBLIC ACCOMMODATIONS.

Subdivision 1. **Full and equal enjoyment of public accommodations.** (a) It is an unfair discriminatory practice:

(1) to deny any person the full and equal enjoyment of the goods, services, facilities, privileges advantages, and accommodations of a place of public accommodation because of race, color, creed, religion, disability, national origin, marital status, sexual orientation, or sex, or for a taxicab company to discriminate in the access to, full utilization of, or benefit from service because of a person's disability; or

(2) for a place of public accommodation not to make reasonable accommodation to the known physical, sensory, or mental disability of a disabled person. * * *

Subd. 2. **General prohibitions.** * * * Goods, services, facilities, privileges advantages, and accommodations must be afforded to an individual with a disability in the most integrated setting appropriate to the needs of the individual. * * *

Subd. 5. **Private entity providing public transportation.** No individual may be discriminated against on the basis of disability in the full and equal enjoyment of specified public transportation services provided by a private entity that is primarily engaged in the business of transporting people and whose operations affect commerce. * * *

Subd. 6. **Construction of new facility or station; accessibility.** It is an unfair discriminatory practice to construct a new facility or station to be used in the provision of public transportation services, unless the facilities or stations are readily accessible to and usable by individuals with disabilities, including individuals who use wheelchairs. It is an unfair discriminatory practice for a facility or station currently used for the provision of public transportation services defined in this subdivision to fail to make alterations necessary in order, to the maximum extent feasible, to make the altered portions of facilities or stations readily accessible to and usable by individuals with disabilities[.] * * *
HIST: 1955 c 516 s 5; * * * 2001 c 186 s 1; 2001 c 194 s 2

363A.12 PUBLIC SERVICES.

Subdivision 1. **Access to public service.** It is an unfair discriminatory practice to discriminate against any person in the access to, admission to, full utilization of or benefit from any public service because of race, color, creed, religion, national origin, disability, sex, sexual orientation, or status with regard to public assistance or to fail to ensure physical and program access for disabled persons unless the public service can demonstrate that providing the access would impose an undue hardship on its operation. * * *

Subd. 2. **Access to public transit services.** It is an unfair discriminatory practice for public transit services to discriminate in the access to, full utilization of, or benefit from service because of a person's disability. Public transit services may use any of a variety of methods to provide transportation for disabled people, provided that persons who are disabled are offered transportation that, in relation to the transportation offered nondisabled persons, is:

(a) in a similar geographic area of operation. To the extent that the transportation provided disabled people is not provided in the same geographic area of operation as that provided nondisabled people[.] * * *

Subd. 3. **Public service operating a fixed route system.** It is an unfair discriminatory practice for a public service that operates a fixed route system to:

(a) purchase or lease a new bus or vehicle for use on the system if the bus or vehicle is not readily accessible to and usable by individuals with disabilities, including individuals who use wheelchairs;

(b) purchase or lease a used bus or vehicle for use on its system unless the public service makes a demonstrated good faith effort to purchase or lease a used bus or vehicle for use on the system that is accessible to and usable by individuals with disabilities, including individuals who use wheelchairs; or

(c) purchase or lease remanufactured buses or vehicles, or to remanufacture buses or vehicles for use on its system, if the bus or vehicle has been remanufactured to extend its usable life by five years or more, unless after the remanufacture, the bus or vehicle is, to the maximum extent feasible, readily accessible to and usable by persons with disabilities, including individuals who use wheelchairs. * * *

Subd. 4. **Public service operating a demand responsive system.** It is an unfair discriminatory practice for a public service operating a demand responsive system to purchase or lease new, used, or remanufactured vehicles that are not readily accessible to and usable by individuals with disabilities, including individuals who use wheelchairs[.] * * *

Subd. 5. **New facility or station; light and rapid rail transportation.** It is an unfair discriminatory practice to construct a new facility or station to be used in the provision of public transportation services, including intercity and commuter light and rapid rail transportation, unless the facility or station is readily accessible to and usable by individuals with disabilities including individuals who use wheelchairs, or for a facility or station currently used for the provision of public transportation services covered by this clause, to fail to make alterations necessary in order, to the maximum extent feasible, to make the altered portions of the facilities or stations, including restrooms, passenger platforms and waiting or ticketing areas, publicly

owned concessions areas, and drinking fountains and public telephones, accessible to and usable by individuals with disabilities, including individuals who use wheelchairs. * * *
HIST: 1955 c 516 s 5; * * * 2001 c 186 s 1; 2001 c 194 s 2

363A.13 EDUCATIONAL INSTITUTION.

Subdivision 1. **Utilization; benefit or services.** It is an unfair discriminatory practice to discriminate in any manner in the full utilization of or benefit from any educational institution, or the services rendered thereby to any person because of race, color, creed, religion, national origin, sex, age, marital status, status with regard to public assistance, sexual orientation, or disability, or to fail to ensure physical and program access for disabled persons. * * *

Subd. 2. **Exclude, expel, or selection.** It is an unfair discriminatory practice to exclude, expel, or otherwise discriminate against a person seeking admission as a student, or a person enrolled as a student because of race, color, creed, religion, national origin, sex, age, marital status, status with regard to public assistance, sexual orientation, or disability.

Subd. 3. **Admission form or inquiry.** It is an unfair discriminatory practice to make or use a written or oral inquiry, or form of application for admission that elicits or attempts to elicit information, or to make or keep a record, concerning the race, color, creed, religion, national origin, sex, age, marital status, sexual orientation, or disability of a person seeking admission, except as permitted by rules of the department.

Subd. 4. **Purpose for information and record.** It is an unfair discriminatory practice to make or use a written or oral inquiry or form of application that elicits or attempts to elicit information, or to keep a record concerning the race, color, national origin, sex, age, or marital status of a person seeking admission, unless the information is collected for purposes of evaluating the effectiveness of recruitment, admissions, and other educational policies, and is maintained separately from the application.
HIST: 1955 c 516 s 5; * * * 2001 c 186 s 1; 2001 c 194 s 2

363A.14 AIDING AND ABETTING AND OBSTRUCTION.

It is an unfair discriminatory practice for any person:

(1) Intentionally to aid, abet, incite, compel, or coerce a person to engage in any of the practices forbidden by this chapter;

(2) Intentionally to attempt to aid, abet, incite, compel, or coerce a person to engage in any of the practices forbidden by this chapter;

(3) To intentionally obstruct or prevent any person from complying with the provisions of this chapter, or any order issued thereunder, or to resist, prevent, impede, or interfere with the commissioner or any of the commissioner's employees or representatives in the performance of duty under this chapter.
HIST: 1955 c 516 s 5; * * * 2001 c 186 s 1; 2001 c 194 s 2

363A.15 REPRISALS.

It is an unfair discriminatory practice for any individual who participated in the alleged discrimination * * * to intentionally engage in any reprisal against any person because that person:

(1) Opposed a practice forbidden under this chapter or has filed a charge, testified, assisted, or participated in any manner in an investigation, proceeding, or hearing under this chapter; or

(2) Associated with a person or group of persons who are disabled or who are of different race, color, creed, religion, sexual orientation, or national origin.

A reprisal includes, but is not limited to, any form of intimidation, retaliation, or harassment. * * *
HIST: 1955 c 516 s 5; * * * 2001 c 194 s 2

363A.16 CREDIT; DISCRIMINATION.

Subdivision 1. **Personal or commercial credit.** It is an unfair discriminatory practice to discriminate in the extension of personal or commercial credit to a person, or in the requirements for obtaining credit, because of race, color, creed, religion, disability, national origin, sex, sexual orientation, or marital status, or due to the receipt of federal, state, or local public assistance including medical assistance.

Subd. 2. **Personal or commercial credit; tenant on assistance.** It is an unfair discriminatory practice to discriminate in the extension of personal or commercial credit against any person who is a tenant receiving federal, state, or local housing subsidies, including rental assistance or rent supplements because the person is a recipient of those subsidies or assistance.

Subd. 3. **Credit card issuer.** It is an unfair discriminatory practice for a credit card issuer to refuse to issue a credit card to a woman under her current or former surname unless there is an intent to defraud or mislead, except that a credit card issuer may require that a woman requesting a card under a former surname open a separate account in that name. * * *
HIST: 1955 c 516 s 5; * * * 2001 c 194 s 2

363A.17 BUSINESS DISCRIMINATION.

It is an unfair discriminatory practice for a person engaged in a trade or business or in the provision of a service:

(a) to refuse to do business with or provide a service to a woman based on her use of her current or former surname; or

(b) to impose, as a condition of doing business with or providing a service to a woman, that a woman use her current surname rather than a former surname; or

(c) to intentionally refuse to do business with, to refuse to contract with, or to discriminate in the basic terms, conditions, or performance of the contract because of a person's race, national origin, color, sex, sexual orientation, or disability, unless the alleged refusal or discrimination is because of a legitimate business purpose. * * *
HIST: 1955 c 516 s 5; * * * 2001 c 186 s 1; 2001 c 194 s 2

363A.19 DISCRIMINATION AGAINST BLIND, DEAF, OR OTHER PERSONS WITH PHYSICAL OR SENSORY DISABILITIES PROHIBITED.

(a) It is unfair discriminatory practice for an owner, operator, or manager of a hotel, restaurant, public conveyance, or other public place to prohibit a blind or deaf person or a person with a physical or sensory disability from taking a service animal into the public place or conveyance to aid blind or deaf persons or persons with physical or sensory disabilities, and if the service animal is properly harnessed or leashed so that the blind or deaf person or a person with a physical or sensory disability may maintain control of the service animal. * * *
HIST: 1955 c 516 s 5; * * * 2013 c 14 s 1

363A.40 RENTAL HOUSING PRIORITY; ACCESSIBLE UNITS.

Subdivision 1. **Definitions.** The definitions in this subdivision apply to this section.

(a) "Accessible unit" means an accessible rental housing unit that meets the persons with disabilities requirements of the State Building Code.

(b) "Landlord" has the meaning given it in section 505B.001, subdivision 7.

Subd. 2. **Priority requirement.** (a) A landlord of rental housing that contains accessible units must give priority for the rental of an accessible unit to a disabled person or a family with a disabled family member who will reside in the unit. The landlord must inform nondisabled persons and families that do not include a disabled family member of the possibility of being offered a non-handicapped-equipped unit as provided under this section before a rental agreement to rent an accessible unit is entered.

(b) If a nondisabled person or a family that does not include a disabled person is living in an accessible unit, the person or family must be offered a non-handicapped equipped unit if the following conditions occur:

(1) a disabled person or a family with a disabled family member who will reside in the unit has signed a rental agreement to rent the accessible unit; and

(2) a similar non-handicapped-equipped unit in the same rental housing complex is available at the same rent.

HIST: 1989 c 328 art 3 s 2; 1999 c 199 art 2 s 14; 2007 c 140 art 12 s 13

363A.05 DEPARTMENT OF HUMAN RIGHTS.

Subdivision 1. **Creation; commissioner.** There is established a department of human rights under the direction and supervision of a commissioner who shall be appointed by the governor under the provisions of section 15.06.

Subd. 2. **Deputy commissioner, duties.** There shall be in the department a deputy commissioner, who shall be appointed by the commissioner and shall serve at the pleasure of the commissioner. The deputy commissioner shall act for, and exercise the powers of the commissioner during the absence or disability of the commissioner or in the event of a vacancy in the office of commissioner. The deputy commissioner shall perform such functions, powers and duties as the commissioner shall prescribe from time to time. * * *

HIST: 1955 c 516 s 6; * * * 1983 c 260 s 60,61

363A.28 GRIEVANCES.

Subdivision 1. **Actions.** Any person aggrieved by a violation of this chapter may bring a civil action as provided in section 363A.33, subdivision 1, or may file a verified charge with the commissioner or the commissioner's designated agent. A charge filed with the commissioner must be in writing by hand, or electronically with an unsworn declaration under penalty of perjury, on a form provided by the commissioner and signed by the charging party.
* * *

HIST: 1955 c 516 s 5,8; * * * 2001 c 186 s 1; 2001 c 194 s 2,3; 2016 c 159 s 1; 2017 c 80 s 1; 1Sp2021 c 11 art 3 s 14

363A.29 HEARINGS.

Subdivision 1. **Conduct of hearings.** A complaint issued by the commissioner shall be heard as a contested case, except that the report of the administrative law judge shall be binding on all parties to the proceeding and if appropriate shall be implemented by an order as provided for in subdivision 3. The hearing shall be conducted at a place designated by the commissioner, within the county where the unfair discriminatory practice occurred or where the respondent resides or has a principal place of business. The hearing shall be conducted in accordance with sections 14.57 to 14.62, and is subject to appeal in accordance with sections 14.63 to 14.68.
* * *

Subd. 3. **Determination of discriminatory practice.** The administrative law judge shall make findings of fact and conclusions of law, and if the administrative law judge finds that the respondent has engaged in an unfair discriminatory practice, the administrative law judge shall issue an order directing the respondent to cease and desist from the unfair discriminatory practice found to exist and to take such affirmative action as in the judgment of the administrative law judge will effectuate the purposes of this chapter. The order shall be a final decision of the department.

Subd. 4. **Civil penalty; punitive damages.** (a) The administrative law judge shall order any respondent found to be in violation of any provision of sections 363A.08 to 363A.19, and 363A.28, subdivision 10, to pay a civil penalty to the state. This penalty is in addition to compensatory and punitive damages to be paid to an aggrieved party. The administrative law judge shall determine the amount of the civil penalty to be paid, taking into account the seriousness and extent of the violation, the public harm occasioned by the violation, whether the violation was intentional, and the financial resources of the respondent. Any penalties imposed under this provision shall be paid into the general fund of the state. In all cases where the administrative law judge finds that the respondent has engaged in an unfair discriminatory practice, the administrative law judge shall order the respondent to pay an aggrieved party, who has suffered discrimination, compensatory damages in an amount up to three times the actual damages sustained. In all cases, the administrative law judge may also order the respondent to pay an aggrieved party, who has suffered discrimination, damages for mental anguish or suffering and reasonable attorney's fees, in addition to punitive damages in an amount not more than $25,000 pursuant to section 549.20.

(b) In any case where a political subdivision is a respondent, the total of punitive damages awarded an aggrieved party may not exceed $25,000 and in that case if there are two or more respondents the punitive damages may be apportioned among them. Punitive damages may only be assessed against a political subdivision in its capacity as a corporate entity and no regular or ex officio member of a governing body of a political subdivision shall be personally liable for payment of punitive damages pursuant to subdivisions 3 to 6. * * *
HIST: 1967 c 897 s 21,22; * * * 2008 c 215 s 1

363A.30 DISTRICT COURT, REVIEW ORDERS OF PANEL OR EXAMINER; ENFORCEMENT; MISDEMEANOR.

Subdivision 1. **Appeal.** The commissioner or a person aggrieved by a final decision of the department reached after a hearing held pursuant to section 363A.29 may seek judicial review in accordance with chapter 14.
* * *
Subd. 3. **Enforcement.** When a respondent fails or refuses to comply with a final decision of the department, the commissioner may file with the court administrator of district court in the judicial district in which the hearing was held a petition requesting the court to order the respondent to comply with the order of the department. Thereupon the court shall issue an order to show cause directed to the respondent why an order directing compliance should not be issued. If the panel or examiner has ordered an award of damages pursuant to section 363A.30, the court shall enter judgment on the order or modified order in the same manner as in the case of an order of the district court, as provided in section 546.27.
* * *
Subd. 4. **Unfair discriminatory practice a misdemeanor.** In addition to all other remedies provided under this chapter, every person who commits an unfair discriminatory act as set forth in section 363A.11, or aids, abets, incites, compels, or coerces another to do so, shall be guilty of a misdemeanor.
HIST: 1967 c 897 s 21; * * * 1984 c 567 s 6

363A.04 CONSTRUCTION AND EXCLUSIVITY.

The provisions of this chapter shall be construed liberally for the accomplishment of the purposes thereof. Nothing contained in this chapter shall be deemed to repeal any of the provisions of the civil rights law or of any other law of this state relating to discrimination because of race, creed, color, religion, sex, age, disability, marital status, status with regard to public assistance, national origin, sexual orientation, or familial status; but, as to acts declared unfair by sections 363A.08 to 363A.19, and 363A.28, subdivision 10, the procedure herein provided shall, while pending, be exclusive.
HIST: 1955 c 516 s 13; * * * 1993 c 22 s 17

363A.33 COURT ACTIONS, SUITS BY PRIVATE PARTIES, INTERVENTION, DISTRICT COURT JURISDICTION, ATTORNEY'S FEES, AND COSTS.

Subdivision 1. **Court actions, suits by private parties, intervention.** The commissioner or a person may bring a civil action seeking redress for an unfair discriminatory practice directly to district court. In addition, a person may bring a civil action. * * *
Subd. 6. **District court jurisdiction.** Any action brought pursuant to this section shall be filed in the district court of the county wherein the unlawful discriminatory practice is alleged to have been committed or where the respondent resides or has a principal place of business.

A person bringing a civil action seeking redress for an unfair discriminatory practice or a respondent is entitled to a jury trial.

If the court or jury finds that the respondent has engaged in an unfair discriminatory practice, it shall issue an order or verdict directing appropriate relief as provided by section 363A.29, subdivisions 3 to 6.   * * *

Subd. 7. **Attorney's fees and costs.** In any action or proceeding brought pursuant to this section the court, in its discretion, may allow the prevailing party a reasonable attorney's fee as part of the costs. In any case brought by the department, the court shall order a respondent who is determined to have engaged in an unfair discriminatory practice to reimburse the department and the attorney general for all appropriate litigation and court costs expended in preparing for and conducting the hearing, unless payment of the costs would impose a financial hardship on the respondent. Appropriate costs include but are not limited to the costs of services rendered by the attorney general, private attorneys if engaged by the department, court costs, court reporters, and expert witnesses as well as the costs of transcripts and other necessary supplies and materials.
HIST: 1973 c 729 s 18; * * * 2014 c 233 s 1

363A.34 NOTICE OF APPEAL TO THE COMMISSIONER.

In any case that is appealed to the supreme court or the court of appeals in which an issue is raised under this chapter, the party raising the issue shall serve a copy of the notice of appeal on the commissioner. At the time of filing a notice of appeal or other papers, documents, or briefs in the case, a party shall file proof of service of the papers, documents, or briefs upon the commissioner.
HIST: 1988 c 660 s 14; 1989 c 280 s 20

363A.42 PUBIC RECORDS; ACCESSIBILITY.

Subdivision 1. **Definitions.** For purposes of this section, "records" means any publicly available recorded information that is collected, created, received, maintained or disseminated by the executive, judicial or legislative branches of the state, the Minnesota State Colleges and Universities, the University of Minnesota, cities, towns, counties, school districts and all other political subdivisions of the state, regardless of physical form or method of storage.

Subd. 2. **Accessibility.** Upon request by an individual, records must be available within a reasonable time period to persons with disabilities in a manner consistent with state and federal laws prohibiting discrimination against persons with disabilities. Reasonable modifications must be made in any policies, practices and procedures that might otherwise deny equal access to records to individuals with disabilities. * * *
HIST: 2010 c 271 s 2; 2010 c 347 art 1 s 22

363A.41 CRIMINAL CODE; EFFECT.

Nothing in this chapter alters the provisions of chapter 609 or other law relating to criminal penalties.
HIST: 1993 c 22 s 20

Category 2, Section 19:
2.19.15. Discuss methods for communicating with, assisting, or intervening in circumstances involving individuals who demonstrate indications of a variety of physical disabilities or mental impairments. (Minn. Stat. 626.8455)

626.8455 TRAINING IN COMMUNITY POLICING.

Subdivision 1. **Training course.** The board, in consultation with the Minnesota Institute of Community Policing, shall prepare a training course to instruct peace officers in the techniques of community policing. The course must include instruction on at least the following matters:

(1) techniques for expanding the training of peace officers to include problem-solving;

(2) techniques for organizing community members so that they are involved and trained in community policing activities;

(3) techniques for relating to diverse communities; and

(4) techniques for relating to individuals with physical or mental limitations.

The course also must include training on child development issues to enable officers to respond appropriately to perceived child protection situations. The board shall update the training course periodically as it deems appropriate.

Subd. 2. **Preservice training requirement.** An individual is not eligible to take the peace officer licensing examination after August 1, 1997, unless the individual has received the training described in subdivision 1.

Subd. 3. **Instructional materials.** The board shall provide to chief law enforcement officers instructional materials patterned after the materials developed by the board under subdivision 1. These materials must meet board requirements for continuing education credit.

HIST: 1996 c 411 s 1; 2013 c 62 s 30

Chapter 31 – PEACE OFFICER DUTIES ASSOCIATED WITH ARREST, DETENTION, SEARCHES, AND USE OF FORCE

Category 2, Section 3:

2.3.1. Define the following terms: search warrant, arrest warrant, subpoena, order for protection (OFP), ex-parte order for protection, qualified domestic violence-related order (QDVRO), Harassment Restraining Order (HRO), no-contact orders, night-capped warrant, no-knock warrant, and curtilage.

2.3.2. Explain and demonstrate search warrant preparation including establishing a factual basis for probable cause and identifying items to be searched for and seized.

2.3.3. Identify the legal requirements governing preparation and execution of the search warrant of a suspect's home or dwelling, vehicle, or person.

626.05 DEFINITIONS.

Subdivision 1. **Search warrant.** A "search warrant" is an order in writing, in the name of the state, signed by a court other than a court exercising probate jurisdiction, directed to a peace officer, commanding the peace officer to make a search as authorized by law and hold any item seized, subject to the order of a court.

Subd. 2. **Peace officer.** The term "peace officer," as used in sections 626.04 to 626.17, means a person who is licensed as a peace officer in accordance with section 626.84, subdivision 1, and who serves as a sheriff, deputy sheriff, police officer, conservation officer, agent of the Bureau of Criminal Apprehension, agent of the Division of Alcohol and Gambling Enforcement, peace officer of the Commerce Fraud Bureau, University of Minnesota peace officer, Metropolitan Transit police officer, Minnesota Department of Corrections Fugitive Apprehension Unit member, or State Patrol trooper as authorized by section 299D.03.

Subd. 3. **Crime.** The term "crime," as used in sections 626.04 to 626.17, includes (1) those offenses defined as crimes in section 609.02, subdivision 1, and (2) all violations of municipal ordinances for which a misdemeanor sentence may be imposed.

HIST: 1963 c 849 s 3; 1976 c 2 s 154; 1977 c 82 s 4; 1979 c 258 s 21; 1983 c 359 s 112; 1986 c 444; 1988 c 447 s 1; 1989 c 334 art 6 s 11; 1990 c 502 s 7; 1993 c 326 art 7 s 13; 1995 c 189 s 8; 1996 c 277 s 1; 1997 c 129 art 2 s 15; 2002 c 291 s 4; 2012 c 155 s 10; 2017 c 98 s 5

626.06 JURISDICTION TO ISSUE.

Search warrants may be issued by any court, other than a court exercising probate jurisdiction, having jurisdiction in the area where the place to be searched is located.

History: 1963 c 849 s 4; 1983 c 359 s 113; 1995 c 189 s 8; 1996 c 277 s 1

626.07 GROUNDS FOR ISSUANCE.

A search warrant may be issued upon any of the following grounds:

(1) the property or things were stolen or embezzled;

(2) the property or things were used as the means of committing a crime;

(3) the possession of the property or things constitutes a crime;

(4) the property or things are in the possession of any person with the intent to use them as a means of committing a crime, or the property or things so intended to be used are in the possession of another to whom they have been delivered for the purpose of concealing them or preventing their being discovered;

(5) the property or things to be seized consist of any item or constitute any evidence which tends to show a crime has been committed, or tends to show that a particular person has committed a crime.

The property or things described in this section may be taken pursuant to the warrant from any place, or from any person in whose possession they may be.
HIST: 1963 c 849 s 5

626.08 PROBABLE CAUSE.

A search warrant cannot be issued but upon probable cause, supported by affidavit, naming or describing the person, and particularly describing the property or thing to be seized, and particularly describing the place to be searched.
HIST: 1963 c 849 s 6

626.085 SEARCH WARRANT REQUIRED FOR ELECTRONIC COMMUNICATION INFORMATION.

Subdivision 1. **Definitions.** As used in this section, the following terms have the meanings given them:

(1) "electronic communication" means the transfer of signs, signals, writings, images, sounds, data, or intelligence of any nature in whole or in part by a wire, radio, electromagnetic, photoelectric, or photo-optical system;

(2) "electronic communication information" means any information about an electronic communication or the use of an electronic communication service, limited to the contents of electronic communications and precise or approximate location of the sender or recipients at any point during the communication;

(3) "electronic communication service" has the meaning given in section 626A.01, subdivision 17; and

(4) "government entity" has the meaning given in section 626A.42, subdivision 1, paragraph (d).

Subd. 2. **Warrant required; exceptions.** (a) Except as provided in paragraph (b), a government entity must obtain a search warrant to require disclosure of electronic communication information.

(b) A government entity may request disclosure of electronic communication information without a search warrant if the agency has valid consent from one authorized to give it, or exigent circumstances exist where there is a danger to the life or physical safety of an individual.

Subd. 3. **Notice to subject.** A government entity accessing electronic communication information under subdivision 2 must provide notice to the subject of the information consistent with the requirements of subdivision 4 and section 626.16.

Subd. 4. **Notice; temporary nondisclosure of search warrant.** (a) Within a reasonable time but not later than 90 days after the court unseals the search warrant under this subdivision, the issuing or denying judge shall cause to be served on the persons named in the warrant and the application an inventory which shall include notice of:

(1) the issuance of the warrant or the application;

(2) the date of issuance and the period of authorized, approved, or disapproved collection of electronic communication information, or the denial of the application; and

(3) whether electronic communication information was or was not collected during the period.

(b) A search warrant authorizing collection of electronic communication information must direct that:

(1) the warrant be sealed for a period of 90 days or until the objective of the warrant has been accomplished, whichever is shorter; and

(2) the warrant be filed with the court administrator within ten days of the expiration of the warrant.

(c) The prosecutor may request that the search warrant, supporting affidavits, and any order granting the request not be filed. An order must be issued granting the request in whole or in part if, from affidavits, sworn testimony, or other evidence, the court finds reasonable grounds exist to believe that filing the warrant may cause the search or a related search to be unsuccessful, create a substantial risk of injury to an innocent person, or severely hamper an ongoing investigation.

(d) The search warrant must direct that following the commencement of any criminal proceeding utilizing evidence obtained in or as a result of the search, the supporting application or affidavit must be filed either immediately or at any other time as the court directs. Until the filing, the documents and materials ordered withheld from filing must be retained by the judge or the judge's designee.

Subd. 5. **Reports.** (a) At the same time as notice is provided according to the requirements of subdivision 4, the issuing or denying judge shall report to the state court administrator:

(1) that a warrant was applied for under this section;

(2) whether the warrant was granted as applied for, was modified, or was denied;

(3) the period of collection of electronic communication information authorized by the warrant, and the number and duration of any extensions of the warrant;

(4) the offense specified in the warrant or application or extension of a warrant; and

(5) the identity of the applying investigative or peace officer and agency making the application and the person authorizing the application.

(b) On or before November 15 of each even-numbered year, the state court administrator shall transmit to the legislature a report concerning: (1) all warrants authorizing the collection of electronic communication information during the two previous calendar years; and (2) all applications that were denied during the two previous calendar years. Each report shall include a summary and analysis of the data required to be filed under this section. The report is public and must be available for public inspection at the Legislative Reference Library and the state court administrator's office and website.

(c) Nothing in this section prohibits or restricts a service provider from producing an annual report summarizing the demands or requests it receives under this section.
HIST: 2020 c 82 s 4

626.09 EXAMINATION OF PARTIES MAKING REQUEST.

The court may, before issuing the warrant, examine on oath the person seeking the warrant and any witnesses the person may produce. It shall take the affidavits in writing, and cause them to be subscribed to by the party or parties making them.
HIST: 1963 c 849 s 7; 1983 c 359 s 114; 1986 c 444

626.10 AFFIDAVIT; CONTENT.

The affidavit or affidavits must set forth the facts tending to establish the grounds of the application, or probable cause for believing that they exist.
HIST: 1963 c 849 s 8

626.11 ISSUANCE OF WARRANT.

(a) If the judge is satisfied of the existence of the grounds of the application, or that there is probable cause to believe their existence, the judge must issue a signed search warrant, naming the judge's judicial office, to a peace officer inside or outside the officer's jurisdiction. The warrant shall direct the officer to search the person or place named for the property or things specified, and to retain the property or things in the officer's custody subject to order of the court issuing the warrant.

(b) Nothing in sections 626.04 to 626.17 is meant to supersede another law or statute that limits a peace officer's authority to obtain, serve, or execute a search warrant.
HIST: 1963 c 849 s 9; 1979 c 258 s 22; 1983 c 359 s 115; 1986 c 444; 2000 c 325 s 1; 2001 c 78 s 2; 2002 c 291 s 5; 2003 c 86 s 1

626.12 APPLICANTS; NAMES ON WARRANT.

The warrant, in addition, shall contain the names of the persons presenting affidavits in support of the application, and the grounds for its issuance.
HIST: 1963 c 849 s 10

626.13 SERVICE; PERSONS MAKING.

A search warrant may in all cases be served anywhere within the issuing judge's jurisdiction by any of the officers mentioned in its directions, but by no other person, except in aid of the officer on the officer's requiring it, the officer being present and acting in its execution. An officer serving and executing a warrant shall notify the chief of police of an organized full-time police department of the municipality or, if there is no such local chief of police, the sheriff or a deputy sheriff of the county in which service is to be made prior to service and execution.
HIST: 1963 c 849 s 11; 1979 c 258 s 23; 1986 c 444; 1989 c 334 art 6 s 12; 1990 c 502 s 8; 1993 c 326 art 7 s 14; 1995 c 226 art 2 s 33; 1995 c 244 s 37; 1997 c 129 art 2 s 15; 2001 c 78 s 3; 2002 c 291 s 6; 2003 c 86 s 2

626.14 TIME AND MANNER OF SERVICE; NO-KNOCK WARRANTS.

Subdivision 1. **Time.** A search warrant may be served only between the hours of 7:00 a.m. and 8:00 p.m. unless the court determines on the basis of facts stated in the affidavits that a nighttime search outside those hours is necessary to prevent the loss, destruction, or removal of the objects of the search or to protect the searchers or the public. The search warrant shall state that it may be served only between the hours of 7:00 a.m. and 8:00 p.m. unless a nighttime search outside those hours is authorized.

Subd. 2. **Definition.** For the purposes of this section, "no-knock search warrant" means a search warrant authorizing peace officers to enter certain premises without first knocking and announcing the officer's presence or purpose prior to entering the premises. No-knock search warrants may also be referred to as dynamic entry warrants.

Subd. 3. **Requirements for a no-knock search warrant.** (a) No peace officer shall seek a no-knock search warrant unless the warrant application includes at a minimum:

(a) No peace officer shall seek a no-knock search warrant unless the warrant application includes at a minimum:

(1) all documentation and materials the issuing court requires;

(2) the information specified in paragraph (b); and

(3) a sworn affidavit as provided in section 626.08.

(b) Each warrant application seeking a no-knock entry must include, in detailed terms, the following:

(1) why peace officers are seeking the use of a no-knock entry and are unable to detain the suspect or search the residence through the use of a knock and announce warrant;

(2) what investigative activities have taken place to support issuance of the no-knock search warrant, or why no investigative activity is needed or able to be performed; and

(3) whether the warrant can be effectively executed during daylight hours according to subdivision 1.

(c) The chief law enforcement officer or designee and another superior officer must review and approve each warrant application. The agency must document the approval of both reviewing parties.

(d) A no-knock search warrant shall not be issued when the only crime alleged is possession of a controlled substance unless there is probable cause to believe that the controlled substance is for other than personal use.

Subd. 4. **Reporting requirements regarding no-knock search warrants.** (a) Law enforcement agencies shall report to the commissioner of public safety regarding the use of no-knock search warrants in a format prescribed by the commissioner. An agency must report the use of a no-knock search warrant to the commissioner no later than three months after the date the warrant was issued. The report shall include the following information:

(1) the number of no-knock search warrants requested;

(2) the number of no-knock search warrants the court issued;

(3) the number of no-knock search warrants executed;

(4) the number of injuries and fatalities suffered, if any, by peace officers and by civilians in the execution of no-knock search warrants; and

(5) any other information the commissioner requests.

(b) The commissioner of public safety shall report the information provided under paragraph (a) annually to the chairs and ranking minority members of the legislative committees with jurisdiction over public safety.

EFFECTIVE DATE. This section is effective September 1, 2021, and applies to warrants requested on or after that date.

HIST: 1963 c 849 s 12; 1983 c 359 s 116; 1992 c 569 s 29; 1Sp2021 c 11 art 9 s 23

626.15 EXECUTION AND RETURN OF WARRANT; TIME.

(a) Except as provided in paragraph (b), a search warrant must be executed and returned to the court which issued it within ten days after its date. After the expiration of this time, the warrant is void unless previously executed.

(b) A district court judge may grant an extension of a warrant on a financial institution for financial records upon an application under oath stating that the financial institution has not produced the requested financial records within ten days and that an extension is necessary to achieve the purposes for which the search warrant was granted. Each extension may not exceed 30 days.

For the purposes of this paragraph, "financial institution" has the meaning given in section 13A.01, subdivision 2, and "financial records" has the meaning given in section 13A.01, subdivision 3.

HIST: 1963 c 849 s 13; 1983 c 359 s 117; 1999 c 117 s 1

626.16 DELIVERY OF COPY OF WARRANT AND RECEIPT.

When the officer conducts the search the officer must give a copy of the warrant and, when property or things are taken, a receipt therefor (specifying it in detail) to the person in whose possession the premises or the property or things taken were found; or, in the absence of any person, the officer must leave such copy of the warrant and receipt in the place where the property or things were found. Such delivery of a copy of the warrant shall constitute service.
Hist: 1963 c 849 s 14; 1986 c 444

626.17 RETURN AND INVENTORY.

The officer must immediately return the warrant to the court and deliver to it a written inventory of the property or things taken, verified by the certificate of the officer at the foot of the inventory.
HIST: 1963 c 849 s 15; 1983 c 359 s 118

626.18 SEARCH WARRANTS RELATING TO ELECTRONIC COMMUNICATION SERVICES AND REMOTE COMPUTING SERVICES.

Subdivision 1. **Definitions.** The definitions in this subdivision apply to this section.

(a) The terms "electronic communication services" and "remote computing services" shall be construed in accordance with United States Code, title 18, sections 2701 to 2711, as amended through March 1, 2001. This section does not apply to corporations that do not provide those services to the general public.

(b) An "adverse result" occurs when notification of the existence of a search warrant results in:

(1) danger to the life or physical safety of an individual;

(2) a flight from prosecution;

(3) the destruction of or tampering with evidence;

(4) the intimidation of potential witnesses; or

(5) serious jeopardy to an investigation or undue delay of a trial.

(c) "Applicant" means a peace officer as defined in section 626.05, to whom a search warrant is issued pursuant to this chapter.

(d) "Minnesota corporation" refers to any corporation or other entity that is subject to section 5.25, excluding foreign corporations.

(e) A "foreign corporation" is considered to be doing business in Minnesota if it makes a contract or engages in a terms of service agreement with a resident of Minnesota to be performed in whole or in part by either party in Minnesota. The making of the contract or terms of service agreement is considered to be the agreement of the foreign corporation that any administrative subpoena or search warrant properly served on it has the same legal force and effect as if served personally on it within the state of Minnesota.

(f) "Properly served" means that a search warrant has been delivered by hand, or in a manner reasonably allowing for proof of delivery if delivered by United States mail, overnight delivery service, or facsimile to a person or entity listed in section 5.25 or covered by this statute.

Subd. 2. **Application.** (a) The following provisions shall apply to any search warrant issued under this chapter allowing a search for records that are in the actual or constructive possession of a foreign corporation that provides electronic communication services or remote computing services to the general public, where those records would reveal the identity of the customers using those services; data stored by, or on behalf of, the customer; the customer's usage of those services; the recipient or destination of communications sent to or from those customers; or the content of those communications.

(b) When properly served with a search warrant issued by the Minnesota court, a foreign corporation subject to this section shall provide to the applicant all records sought pursuant to that warrant within eight business days of receipt, including those records maintained or located outside this state.

(c) Where the applicant makes a showing and the judge finds that failure to produce records within less than eight business days would cause an adverse result, the warrant may require production of records within less than eight business days. A court may reasonably extend the time required for production of the records upon finding that the foreign corporation has shown good cause for that extension and that an extension of time would not cause an adverse result.

(d) A foreign corporation seeking to quash the warrant must seek relief from the court that issued the warrant within the time required for production of records under this section. The issuing court shall hear and decide that motion no later than eight court days after the motion is filed.

(e) The foreign corporation shall verify the authenticity of records that it produces by providing a written affidavit or statement to that effect.

Subd. 3. **Warrant of another state.** A Minnesota corporation that provides electronic communication services or remote computing services to the general public, when served with a warrant issued by another state to produce records that would reveal the identity of the customers using those services; data stored by, or on behalf of, the customer; the customer's usage of those services; the recipient or destination of communications sent to or from those customers; or the content of those communications, shall produce those records as if that warrant had been issued by a Minnesota court.

Subd. 4. **Immunity.** No cause of action shall lie against any foreign or Minnesota corporation subject to this section, its officers, employees, agents, or other specified persons for providing records, information, facilities, or assistance in accordance with the terms of a warrant issued pursuant to this chapter.
HIST: 2001 c 197 s 6

626.19 USE OF UNMANNED AERIAL VEHICLES.

Subdivision 1. **Application; definitions.** (a) This section applies to unmanned aerial vehicle data collected, created, or maintained by a law enforcement agency and to law enforcement agencies that maintain, use, or plan to use an unmanned aerial vehicle in investigations, training, or in response to emergencies, incidents, and requests for service. Unmanned aerial vehicle data collected, created, or maintained by a government entity is classified under chapter 13.

(b) For purposes of this section, the following terms have the meanings given:

(1) "government entity" has the meaning given in section 13.02, subdivision 7a, except that it does not include a law enforcement agency;

(2) "law enforcement agency" has the meaning given in section 626.84, subdivision 1;

(3) "unmanned aerial vehicle" or "UAV" means an aircraft that is operated without the possibility of direct human intervention from within or on the aircraft; and

(4) "terrorist attack" means a crime that furthers terrorism as defined in section 609.714, subdivision 1.

Subd. 2. **Use of unmanned aerial vehicles limited.** Except as provided in subdivision 3, a law enforcement agency must not use a UAV without a search warrant issued under this chapter.

Subd. 3. **Authorized use.** A law enforcement agency may use a UAV:

(1) during or in the aftermath of an emergency situation that involves the risk of death or bodily harm to a person;

(2) over a public event where there is a heightened risk to the safety of participants or bystanders;

(3) to counter the risk of a terrorist attack by a specific individual or organization if the agency determines that credible intelligence indicates a risk;

(4) to prevent the loss of life and property in natural or man-made disasters and to facilitate operational planning, rescue, and recovery operations in the aftermath of these disasters;

(5) to conduct a threat assessment in anticipation of a specific event;

(6) to collect information from a public area if there is reasonable suspicion of criminal activity;

(7) to collect information for crash reconstruction purposes after a serious or deadly collision occurring on a public road;

(8) over a public area for officer training or public relations purposes; and

(9) for purposes unrelated to law enforcement at the request of a government entity provided that the government entity makes the request in writing to the law enforcement agency and specifies the reason for the request and proposed period of use.

Subd. 4. **Limitations on use.** (a) A law enforcement agency using a UAV must comply with all Federal Aviation Administration requirements and guidelines.

(b) A law enforcement agency must not deploy a UAV with facial recognition or other biometric-matching technology unless expressly authorized by a warrant.

(c) A law enforcement agency must not equip a UAV with weapons.

(d) A law enforcement agency must not use a UAV to collect data on public protests or demonstrations unless expressly authorized by a warrant or an exception applies under subdivision 3.

Subd. 5. **Documentation required.** A law enforcement agency must document each use of a UAV, connect each deployment to a unique case number, provide a factual basis for the use of a UAV, and identify the applicable exception under subdivision 3 unless a warrant was obtained.

Subd. 6. **Data classification; retention.** (a) Data collected by a UAV are private data on individuals or nonpublic data, subject to the following:

(1) if the individual requests a copy of the recording, data on other individuals who do not consent to its release must be redacted from the copy;

(2) UAV data may be disclosed as necessary in an emergency situation under subdivision 3, clause (1);

(3) UAV data may be disclosed to the government entity making a request for UAV use under subdivision 3, clause (9);

(4) UAV data that are criminal investigative data are governed by section 13.82, subdivision 7; and

(5) UAV data that are not public data under other provisions of chapter 13 retain that classification.

(b) Section 13.04, subdivision 2, does not apply to data collected by a UAV.

(c) Notwithstanding section 138.17, a law enforcement agency must delete data collected by a UAV as soon as possible, and in no event later than seven days after collection unless the data is part of an active criminal investigation.

Subd. 7. **Evidence.** Information obtained or collected by a law enforcement agency in violation of this section is not admissible as evidence in a criminal, administrative, or civil proceeding against the data subject.

Subd. 8. **Remedies.** In addition to any other remedies provided by law, including remedies available under chapter 13, an aggrieved party may bring a civil action against a law enforcement agency to prevent or remedy a violation of this section.

Subd. 9. **Public comment.** A law enforcement agency must provide an opportunity for public comment before it purchases or uses a UAV. At a minimum, the agency must accept public comments submitted electronically or by mail. The governing body with jurisdiction over the budget of a local law enforcement agency must provide an opportunity for public comment at a regularly scheduled meeting.

Subd. 10. **Written policies and procedures required.** Prior to the operation of a UAV, the chief officer of every state and local law enforcement agency that uses or proposes to use a UAV must establish and enforce a written policy governing its use, including requests for use from government entities. In developing and adopting the policy, the law enforcement agency must provide for public comment and input as described in subdivision 9. The written policy must be posted on the agency's website, if the agency has a website.

Subd. 11. **Notice; disclosure of warrant.** (a) Within a reasonable time but not later than 90 days after the court unseals a warrant under this subdivision, the issuing or denying judge shall cause to be served on the persons named in the warrant and the application an inventory that shall include notice of:

(1) the issuance of the warrant or application;

(2) the date of issuance and the period of authorized, approved, or disapproved collection of information, or the denial of the application; and

(3) whether information was or was not collected during the period.

(b) A warrant authorizing collection of information with a UAV must direct that:

(1) the warrant be sealed for a period of 90 days or until the objective of the warrant has been accomplished, whichever is shorter; and

(2) the warrant be filed with the court administrator within ten days of the expiration of the warrant.

(c) The prosecutor may request that the warrant, supporting affidavits, and any order granting the request not be filed. An order must be issued granting the request in whole or in part if, from affidavits, sworn testimony, or other evidence, the court finds reasonable grounds exist to believe that filing the warrant may cause the search or a related search to be unsuccessful, create a substantial risk of injury to an innocent person, or severely hamper an ongoing investigation.

(d) The warrant must direct that, following the commencement of any criminal proceeding using evidence obtained in or as a result of the search, the supporting application or affidavit must be filed either immediately or at any other time as the court directs. Until the filing, the documents and materials ordered withheld from filing must be retained by the judge or the judge's designee.

Subd. 12. **Reporting.** (a) By January 15 of each year, each law enforcement agency that maintains or uses a UAV shall report to the commissioner of public safety the following information for the preceding calendar year:

(1) the number of times a UAV was deployed without a search warrant issued under this chapter, identifying the date of deployment and the authorized use of the UAV under subdivision 3; and

(2) the total cost of the agency's UAV program.

(b) By June 15 of each year, the commissioner of public safety shall compile the reports submitted to the commissioner under paragraph (a), organize the reports by law enforcement agency, submit the compiled report to the chairs and ranking minority members of the senate and house of representatives committees having jurisdiction over data practices and public safety, and make the compiled report public on the department's website.

(c) By January 15 of each year, a judge who has issued or denied approval of a warrant under this section that expired during the preceding year shall report to the state court administrator:

(1) that a warrant or extension was applied for;

(2) the type of warrant or extension applied for;

(3) whether the warrant or extension was granted as applied for, modified, or denied;

(4) the period of UAV use authorized by the warrant and the number and duration of any extensions of the warrant;

(5) the offense specified in the warrant or application or extension of a warrant; and

(6) the identity of the law enforcement agency making the application and the person authorizing the application.

(d) By June 15 of each year, the state court administrator shall submit to the chairs and ranking minority members of the senate and house of representatives committees or divisions having jurisdiction over data practices and public safety and post on the supreme court's website a full and complete report concerning the number of applications for warrants authorizing or approving use of UAVs or disclosure of information from the use of UAVs under this section and the number of warrants and extensions granted or denied under this section during the preceding calendar year. The report must include a summary and analysis of the data required to be filed with the state court administrator under paragraph (c).

History: 2020 c 82 s 5

NOTE: This section, as added by Laws 2020, chapter 82, section 5, is effective August 1, 2020, provided that the chief law enforcement officers adopt the written policy required under subdivision 10 no later than February 15, 2021. Laws 2020, chapter 82, section 5, the effective date.

626.21 RETURN OF PROPERTY AND SUPPRESSION OF EVIDENCE.

A person aggrieved by an unlawful search and seizure may move the district court for the district in which the property was seized or the district court having jurisdiction of the substantive offense for the return of the property and to suppress the use, as evidence, of

anything so obtained on the ground that (1) the property was illegally seized, or (2) the property was illegally seized without warrant, or (3) the warrant is insufficient on its face, or (4) the property seized is not that described in the warrant, or (5) there was not probable cause for believing the existence of the grounds on which the warrant was issued, or (6) the warrant was illegally executed, or (7) the warrant was improvidently issued. The judge shall receive evidence on any issue of fact necessary to the decision of the motion. If the motion is granted the property shall be restored unless otherwise subject to lawful detention, and it shall not be admissible in evidence at any hearing or trial. The motion to suppress evidence may also be made in the district where the trial is to be had. The motion shall be made before trial or hearing unless opportunity therefor did not exist or the defendant was not aware of the grounds for the motion, but the court in its discretion may entertain the motion at the trial or hearing.
HIST: 1963 c 850 s 1; 1998 c 254 art 2 s 71

626.22 MALICIOUSLY PROCURING SEARCH WARRANT; MISCONDUCT IN USE.

Every person who shall maliciously and without probable cause procure a search warrant to be issued and executed, and every officer who, in executing a search warrant, shall willfully exceed the officer's authority, or exercise it with unnecessary severity, shall be guilty of a misdemeanor.
HIST: (10031) RL s 4846; 1986 c 444

Category 2, Sections 4, 8:
2.4.1. Explain what constitutes an arrest and differences between a contact, a detention and an arrest.
2.4.3. Discuss protocols and terms associated with arrest including "reasonable suspicion" and "probable cause".
2.4.6. Describe when a citizen can make an arrest.
2.8.9. Explain when force may be used to make an arrest.

626.862 POWERS OF LAW ENFORCEMENT OFFICERS.

Except as specifically provided by statute, only a peace officer and part-time peace officer may:
(1) issue a citation in lieu of arrest or continued detention unless specifically authorized by ordinance;
(2) ask a person receiving a citation to give a written promise to appear in court; or
(3) take a person into custody as permitted by section 629.34.
HIST: 1987 c 334 s 5; 2005 c 10 art 2 s 4

629.30 ARRESTS; BY WHOM MADE; AIDING OFFICER.

Subdivision 1. **Definition.** Arrest means taking a person into custody that the person may be held to answer for a public offense. "Arrest" includes actually restraining a person or taking into custody a person who submits.
Subd. 2. **Who may arrest.** An arrest may be made:
(1) by a peace officer under a warrant;
(2) by a peace officer without a warrant;
(3) by an officer in the United States Customs and Border Protection or the United States Citizenship and Immigration Services without a warrant;
(4) by a private person.

A private person shall aid a peace officer in executing a warrant when requested to do so by the officer.
HIST: (10566) RL s 5225; 1981 c 108 s 1; 1985 c 265 art 10 s 1; 2007 c 13 art 1 s 25

629.31 TIME WHEN ARREST MAY BE MADE.

An arrest for a felony or gross misdemeanor may be made on any day and at any time of the day or night. An arrest for a misdemeanor may not be made on Sunday or between 10:00 p.m. and 8:00 a.m. on any other day except:

(1) when the judge orders in the warrant that the arrest may be made between those hours; or

(2) when the person named in the warrant is found on a public highway or street.
HIST: (10567) RL s 5226; Ex1971 c 27 s 46; 1983 c 359 s 128; 1984 c 433 s 1; 1985 c 265 art 10 s 1

629.32 MINIMUM RESTRAINT ALLOWED FOR ARREST; WARRANT SHOWN UPON REQUEST.

A peace officer making an arrest may not subject the person arrested to any more restraint than is necessary for the arrest and detention. The peace officer shall inform the defendant that the officer is acting under a warrant, and shall show the defendant the warrant if requested to do so. An arrest by a peace officer acting under a warrant is lawful even though the officer does not have the warrant in hand at the time of the arrest, but if the arrested person so requests the warrant must be shown to that person as soon as possible and practicable. A peace officer may lawfully arrest a person when advised by any other peace officer in the state that a warrant has been issued for that person.
HIST: (10568) RL s 5227; 1947 c 316 s 1; 1985 c 265 art 10 s 1

629.33 WHEN FORCE MAY BE USED TO MAKE ARREST.

If a peace officer has informed a defendant that the officer intends to arrest the defendant, and if the defendant then flees or forcibly resists arrest, the officer may use all necessary and lawful means to make the arrest but may not use deadly force unless authorized to do so under section 609.066. After giving notice of the authority and purpose of entry, a peace officer may break open an inner or outer door or window of a dwelling house to execute a warrant if:

(1) the officer is refused admittance;

(2) entry is necessary for the officer's own liberation; or

(3) entry is necessary for liberating another person who is being detained in the dwelling house after entering to make an arrest.
HIST: (10569) RL s 5228; 1978 c 736 s 3; 1985 c 265 art 10 s 1

629.34 WHEN ARREST MAY BE MADE WITHOUT A WARRANT.

Subdivision 1. **Peace officers.** (a) A peace officer, as defined in section 626.84, subdivision 1, clause (c), who is on or off duty within the jurisdiction of the appointing authority, or on duty outside the jurisdiction of the appointing authority pursuant to section 629.40, may arrest a person without a warrant as provided under paragraph (c).

(b) A part-time peace officer, as defined in section 626.84, subdivision 1, clause (f), who is on duty within the jurisdiction of the appointing authority, or on duty outside the jurisdiction of the appointing authority pursuant to section 629.40 may arrest a person without a warrant as provided under paragraph (c).

(c) A peace officer or part-time peace officer who is authorized under paragraph (a) or (b) to make an arrest without a warrant may do so under the following circumstances:

(1) when a public offense has been committed or attempted in the officer's presence;

(2) when the person arrested has committed a felony, although not in the officer's presence;

(3) when a felony has in fact been committed, and the officer has reasonable cause for believing the person arrested to have committed it;

(4) upon a charge based upon reasonable cause of the commission of a felony by the person arrested;

(5) under the circumstances described in clause (2), (3), or (4), when the offense is a gross misdemeanor violation of section 609.52, 609.595, 609.631, 609.749, or 609.821;

(6) under circumstances described in clause (2), (3), or (4), when the offense is a nonfelony violation of section 518B.01, subdivision 14; 609.748, subdivision 6; or 629.75, subdivision 2, or a nonfelony violation of any other restraining order or no contact order previously issued by a court;

(7) under the circumstances described in clause (2), (3), or (4), when the offense is a gross misdemeanor violation of section 609.485 and the person arrested is a juvenile committed to the custody of the commissioner of corrections; or

(8) if the peace officer has probable cause to believe that within the preceding 72 hours, exclusive of the day probable cause was established, the person has committed nonfelony domestic abuse, as defined in section 518B.01, subdivision 2, even though the assault did not take place in the presence of the peace officer.

(d) To make an arrest authorized under this subdivision, the officer may break open an outer or inner door or window of a dwelling house if, after notice of office and purpose, the officer is refused admittance.

Subd. 2. **United States Customs and Border Protection, United States Citizenship and Immigration Services officer.** An officer in the United States Customs and Border Protection or the United States Citizenship and Immigration Services may arrest a person without a warrant under the circumstances specified in clauses (1) and (2):

(1) when the officer is on duty within the scope of assignment and one or more of the following situations exist:

(i) the person commits an assault in the fifth degree, as defined in section 609.224, against the officer;

(ii) the person commits an assault in the fifth degree, as defined in section 609.224, on any other person in the presence of the officer, or commits any felony;

(iii) the officer has reasonable cause to believe that a felony has been committed and reasonable cause to believe that the person committed it; or

(iv) the officer has received positive information by written, teletypic, telephonic, radio, or other authoritative source that a peace officer holds a warrant for the person's arrest; or

(2) when the assistance of the officer has been requested by another Minnesota law enforcement agency.

HIST: (10570) RL s 5229; * * * 2009 c 59 art 4 s 7; 2014 c 177 s 1

629.341 ALLOWING PROBABLE CAUSE ARRESTS FOR DOMESTIC VIOLENCE; IMMUNITY FROM LIABILITY.

Subdivision 1. **Arrest.** Notwithstanding section 629.34 or any other law or rule, a peace officer may arrest a person anywhere without a warrant, including at the person's residence, if the peace officer has probable cause to believe that within the preceding 72 hours, exclusive of the day probable cause was established, the person has committed nonfelony domestic abuse, as defined in section 518B.01, subdivision 2. The arrest may be made even though the assault did not take place in the presence of the peace officer.

Subd. 2. **Immunity.** A peace officer acting in good faith and exercising due care in making an arrest pursuant to subdivision 1 is immune from civil liability that might result from the officer's action.

Subd. 3. **Notice of rights.** The peace officer shall tell the victim whether a shelter or other services are available in the community and give the victim immediate notice of the legal rights and remedies available. The notice must include furnishing the victim a copy of the following statement:

"IF YOU ARE THE VICTIM OF DOMESTIC VIOLENCE, you can ask the city or county attorney to file a criminal complaint. You also have the right to go to court and file a petition requesting an order for protection from domestic abuse. The order could include the following:

(1) an order restraining the abuser from further acts of abuse;

(2) an order directing the abuser to leave your household;

(3) an order preventing the abuser from entering your residence, school, business, or place of employment;

(4) an order awarding you or the other parent custody of or parenting time with your minor child or children; or

(5) an order directing the abuser to pay support to you and the minor children if the abuser has a legal obligation to do so."

The notice must include the resource listing, including telephone number, for the area battered women's shelter, to be designated by the Department of Corrections.

Subd. 4. **Report required.** Whenever a peace officer investigates an allegation that an incident described in subdivision 1 has occurred, whether or not an arrest is made, the officer shall make a written police report of the alleged incident. The report must contain at least the following information: the name, address and telephone number of the victim, if provided by the victim, a statement as to whether an arrest occurred, the name of the arrested person, and a brief summary of the incident. Data that identify a victim who has made a request under section 13.82, subdivision 17, paragraph (d), and that are private data under that subdivision, shall be private in the report required by this section. A copy of this report must be provided upon request, at no cost, to the victim of domestic abuse, the victim's attorney, or organizations designated by the Office of Justice Programs in the Department of Public Safety or the commissioner of corrections that are providing services to victims of domestic abuse. The officer shall submit the report to the officer's supervisor or other person to whom the employer's rules or policies require reports of similar allegations of criminal activity to be made.

Subd. 5. **Training.** The Board of Peace Officer Standards and Training shall provide a copy of this section to every law enforcement agency in this state on or before June 30, 1983. Upon request of the Board of Peace Officer Standards and Training to the Bureau of Criminal Apprehension, at least one training course must include instruction about domestic abuse. A basic skills course required for initial licensure as a peace officer must, after January 1, 1985, include at least three hours of training in handling domestic violence cases.

HIST: 1978 c 724 s 2; 1979 c 204 s 1; 1981 c 273 s 13; 1983 c 226 s 1; 1984 c 655 art 1 s 79; 1985 c 265 art 10 s 1; 1986 c 444; 1993 c 326 art 2 s 29; 1995 c 226 art 7 s 18; 1998 c 371 s 18; 1999 c 227 s 22; 2000 c 444 art 2 s 48; 2004 c 290 s 37; 2009 c 59 art 2 s 3; 2013 c 125 art 1 s 101; 2014 c 177 s 2

629.342 LAW ENFORCEMENT POLICIES; DOMESTIC ABUSE ARRESTS.

Subdivision 1. **Definition.** For purposes of this section, "domestic abuse" has the meaning given in section 518B.01, subdivision 2.

Subd. 2. **Policies required.** (a) Each law enforcement agency shall develop, adopt, and implement a written policy regarding arrest procedures for domestic abuse incidents. In the development of a policy, each law enforcement agency shall consult with domestic abuse advocates, community organizations, and other law enforcement agencies with expertise in the recognition and handling of domestic abuse incidents. The policy shall discourage dual arrests, include consideration of whether one of the parties acted in self defense, and provide guidance to officers concerning instances in which officers should remain at the scene of a domestic abuse incident until the likelihood of further imminent violence has been eliminated.

(b) The Bureau of Criminal Apprehension and the Board of Peace Officer Standards and Training, in consultation with the Minnesota Chiefs of Police Association, the Minnesota Sheriffs Association, the Minnesota Police and Peace Officers Association, and a domestic violence statewide coalition shall update the written policy regarding arrest procedures for domestic abuse incidents for use by local law enforcement agencies. Each law enforcement agency may adopt the model policy in lieu of developing its own policy under the provisions of paragraph (a).

Subd. 3. **Assistance to victim where no arrest.** If a law enforcement officer does not make an arrest when the officer has probable cause to believe that a person is committing or has committed domestic abuse or violated an order for protection, the officer shall provide immediate assistance to the victim. Assistance includes:

(1) assisting the victim in obtaining necessary medical treatment; and

(2) providing the victim with the notice of rights under section 629.341, subdivision 3.

Subd. 4. **Immunity.** A peace officer acting in good faith and exercising due care in providing assistance to a victim pursuant to subdivision 3 is immune from civil liability that might result from the officer's action.

History: 1992 c 571 art 6 s 22; 1993 c 326 art 2 s 30; 2000 c 445 art 2 s 28; 2014 c 212 art 1 s 12; 2014 c 286 art 6 s 7

629.343 ALLOWING PROBABLE CAUSE ARRESTS FOR OFFENSES ON SCHOOL PROPERTY.

Notwithstanding section 629.34, a peace officer, as defined in section 626.84, subdivision 1, paragraph (c), who is on or off duty within the jurisdiction of the appointing authority or on duty outside the jurisdiction of the appointing authority pursuant to section 629.40, may arrest a person without a warrant if the peace officer has probable cause to believe that the person within the preceding four hours has committed a fifth-degree assault, as defined in section 609.224, on school property, as defined in section 609.66, subdivision 1d. The arrest may be made even though the crimes were not committed in the presence of the peace officer.

HIST: 1995 c 55 s 1

629.344 CRIMINAL VEHICULAR OPERATION AND MANSLAUGHTER; CERTIFICATION OF PROBABLE CAUSE BY PEACE OFFICER.

If a peace officer determines that probable cause exists to believe that a person has violated section 609.2112, subdivision 1, paragraph (a), clause (2), (3), (4), (5), or (6); 609.2113, subdivision 1, clause (2), (3), (4), (5), or (6); subdivision 2, clause (2), (3), (4), (5), or (6); or subdivision 3, clause (2), (3), (4), (5), or (6); or 609.2114, subdivision 1, paragraph (a), clause (2), (3), (4), (5), or (6); or subdivision 2, clause (2), (3), (4), (5), or (6), the officer shall certify this determination and notify the commissioner of public safety.

HIST: 2013 c 117 art 3 s 35; 2014 c 180 s 9; 2020 c 83 art 1 s 98

629.35 ARREST AT NIGHT; WHEN PERMISSIBLE.

A peace officer may arrest a person at night without a warrant if the officer has reasonable cause to believe that person has committed a felony. An arrest under this section is lawful even if it appears after the arrest that no felony has been committed. When arresting a person at night without a warrant, a peace officer shall inform that person of the officer's authority and the cause of the arrest. This warning need not be given if the person is apprehended while committing a public offense or is pursued immediately after escape.

HIST: (10571) RL s 5230; 1985 c 265 art 10 s 1

629.355 PEACE OFFICER AUTHORITY TO DETAIN PERSON ON CONDITIONAL RELEASE.

(a) A peace officer may detain a person on conditional release upon probable cause that the person has violated a condition of release. "Conditional release" has the meaning given in section 401.01, subdivision 2.

(b) Except as provided in paragraph (c), no person may be detained longer than the period provided in rule 27.04 of the Rules of Criminal Procedure. The detaining peace officer shall provide a detention report to the agency supervising the person as soon as possible. The detention by the peace officer may not exceed eight hours without the approval of the supervising agency. The supervising agency may release the person without commencing revocation proceedings or commence revocation proceedings under rule 27.04 of the Rules of Criminal Procedure.

(c) A person detained under paragraph (a) who is on supervised release or parole may not be detained longer than 72 hours. The detaining peace officer shall provide a detention report to the commissioner of corrections as soon as possible. The detention by the peace officer may not exceed eight hours without the approval of the commissioner or a designee. The commissioner may release the person without commencing revocation proceedings or request a hearing before the hearings and release division.
HIST: 1998 c 367 art 7 s 12

629.36 PERMITTING BYSTANDER TO DELIVER ARRESTED PERSON TO PEACE OFFICER.

When a bystander arrests a person for breach of the peace, the bystander may deliver that person to a peace officer. The peace officer shall take the arrested person to a judge for criminal processing. When a public offense is committed in the presence of a judge, the judge may, by written or verbal order, command any person to arrest the offender, and then proceed as if the offender had been brought before the court on a warrant of arrest.
HIST: (10572) RL s 5231; 1983 c 359 s 129; 1985 c 265 art 10 s 1

629.361 PEACE OFFICERS RESPONSIBLE FOR CUSTODY OF STOLEN PROPERTY.

A peace officer arresting a person charged with committing or aiding in the committing of a robbery, aggravated robbery, or theft shall use reasonable diligence to secure the property alleged to have been stolen. After seizure of the property, the officer shall be answerable for it while it remains in the officer's custody. The officer shall annex a schedule of the property to the return of the warrant. Upon request of the county attorney, the law enforcement agency that has custody of the property alleged to have been stolen shall deliver the property to the custody of the county attorney for use as evidence at an omnibus hearing or at trial. The county attorney shall make a receipt for the property and be responsible for the property while it is in the county attorney's custody. When the offender is convicted, whoever has custody of the property shall turn it over to the owner.
HIST: (10376) RL s 5095; 1965 c 35 s 11; 1985 c 265 art 10 s 1; 1986 c 444

629.363 RAILWAY CONDUCTOR; AUTHORITY TO ARREST.

A conductor of a railway train may arrest a person committing an act upon the train prohibited by sections 609.681, 609.72, and 609.855, subdivision 1, with or without a warrant, and take that person to the proper law enforcement authorities, or to the station agent at the next railway station. The station agent shall take the arrested person to the law enforcement authorities. A conductor or station agent possesses the powers of a sheriff with a warrant in making arrests under this chapter.
HIST: (10297) RL s 5027; 1963 c 753 art 2 s 11; 1983 c 359 s 130; 1985 c 265 art 10 s 1; 1989 c 5 s 17

629.364 ARRESTS FOR SWINDLING.

(a) The following persons shall arrest, with or without a warrant, a person found committing an offense described in section 609.52, subdivision 2, paragraph (a), clause (4):
    (1) a conductor or other employee on a railway car or train;
    (2) a captain, clerk, or other employee on a boat;
    (3) a station agent at a depot;
    (4) an officer of a fair or fairground; or
    (5) a proprietor or employee of a public resort.
(b) A person not required to make an arrest under paragraph (a) may arrest, with or without a warrant, a person found committing an offense described in section 609.52, subdivision 2, paragraph (a), clause (4).
(c) A person making an arrest under paragraph (a) or (b) shall take the arrested person to the proper law enforcement authorities and have a written complaint issued against that person. A person making an arrest under paragraph (a) or (b) has the same authority in all respects as a

peace officer with a warrant, including the power to summon assistance. The person shall also arrest the person injured by reason of the offense, and take that person before a court, which shall require that person to give security for appearance as a witness on trial of the case.

(d) A victim of an offense described in section 609.52 who testifies at trial against the person arrested for the offense shall receive the fee for travel and attendance provided in section 357.24.

HIST: (10220) RL s 4970; 1965 c 51 s 84; 1983 c 359 s 131; 1985 c 265 art 10 s 1; 1986 c 444; 2020 c 83 art 1 s 99

629.365 DEFINITIONS.

Subdivision 1. **Applicability.** In this section and section 629.366, the terms defined in this section have the meanings given them.

Subd. 2. **Merchant.** "Merchant" means a person who owns, possesses, or controls personal property with authority to sell it in the regular course of business at retail or wholesale.

Subd. 3. **Person.** "Person" includes an individual, a partnership, corporation, or association.

HIST: 1957 c 805 s 1; 1985 c 265 art 10 s 1

629.366 THEFT IN BUSINESS ESTABLISHMENTS; DETAINING SUSPECTS.

Subdivision 1. **Circumstances justifying detention.** (a) A merchant or merchant's employee may detain a person if the merchant or employee has reasonable cause to believe:

(1) that the person has taken, or is taking, an article of value without paying for it, from the possession of the merchant in the merchant's place of business or from a vehicle or premises under the merchant's control;

(2) that the taking is done with the intent to wrongfully deprive the merchant of the property or the use or benefit of it; or

(3) that the taking is done with the intent to appropriate the use of the property to the taker or any other person.

(b) Subject to the limitations in paragraph (a), a merchant or merchant's employee may detain a person for any of the following purposes:

(1) to require the person to provide identification or verify identification;

(2) to inquire as to whether the person possesses unpurchased merchandise taken from the merchant and, if so, to receive the merchandise;

(3) to inform a peace officer; or

(4) to institute criminal proceedings against the person.

(c) The person detained shall be informed promptly of the purpose of the detention and may not be subjected to unnecessary or unreasonable force, nor to interrogation against the person's will. A merchant or merchant's employee may not detain a person for more than one hour unless:

(1) the merchant or employee is waiting to surrender the person to a peace officer, in which case the person may be detained until a peace officer has accepted custody of or released the person; or

(2) the person is a minor, or claims to be, and the merchant or employee is waiting to surrender the minor to a peace officer or the minor's parent, guardian, or custodian, in which case the minor may be detained until the peace officer, parent, guardian, or custodian has accepted custody of the minor.

(d) If at any time the person detained requests that a peace officer be summoned, the merchant or merchant's employee must notify a peace officer immediately.

Subd. 2. **Arrest.** Upon a charge being made by a merchant or merchant's employee, a peace officer may arrest a person without a warrant, if the officer has reasonable cause for believing that the person has committed or attempted to commit the offense described in subdivision 1.

Subd. 3. **Immunity.** No merchant, merchant's employee, or peace officer is criminally or civilly liable for any action authorized under subdivision 1 or 2 if the arresting person's action is based upon reasonable cause.

History: 1957 c 805 s 2; 1985 c 265 art 10 s 1; 1986 c 405 s 1,2; 1986 c 444

629.37 WHEN PRIVATE PERSON MAY MAKE ARREST.

A private person may arrest another:

(1) for a public offense committed or attempted in the arresting person's presence;

(2) when the person arrested has committed a felony, although not in the arresting person's presence; or

(3) when a felony has in fact been committed, and the arresting person has reasonable cause for believing the person arrested to have committed it.

HIST: (10573) RL s 5232; 1985 c 265 art 10 s 1

629.38 PRIVATE PERSON TO DISCLOSE CAUSE OF ARREST.

Before making an arrest a private person shall inform the person to be arrested of the cause of the arrest and require the person to submit. The warning required by this section need not be given if the person is arrested while committing the offense or when the person is arrested on pursuit immediately after committing the offense. If a person has committed a felony, a private person may break open an outer or inner door or window of a dwelling house to make the arrest if, before entering, the private person informs the person to be arrested of the intent to make the arrest and the private person is then refused admittance.

HIST: (10574) RL s 5233; 1985 c 265 art 10 s 1; 1986 c 444

629.39 PRIVATE PERSON MAKING ARREST TO DELIVER ARRESTEE TO JUDGE OR PEACE OFFICER.

A private person who arrests another for a public offense shall take the arrested person before a judge or to a peace officer without unnecessary delay. If a person arrested escapes, the person from whose custody the person has escaped may immediately pursue and retake the escapee, at any time and in any place in the state. For that purpose, the pursuer may break open any door or window of a dwelling house if the pursuer informs the escapee of the intent to arrest the escapee and the pursuer is refused admittance.

HIST: (10575) RL s 5234; 1983 c 359 s 132; 1985 c 265 art 10 s 1; 1986 c 444

629.40 ALLOWING ARRESTS ANYWHERE IN STATE.

Subdivision 1. **Definition.** In this section "peace officer" has the meaning given it in section 626.84, subdivision 1, paragraph (c).

Subd. 2. **Out of jurisdiction arrests.** In any case in which a person licensed under section 626.84, subdivision 1, may by law, either with or without a warrant, arrest a person for a criminal offense committed within the jurisdiction of the officer, and the person to be arrested escapes from or is out of the county, statutory or home rule charter city, or town, the officer may pursue and apprehend the person to be arrested anywhere in this state.

Subd. 3. **Authority for arrests outside jurisdiction.** When a person licensed under section 626.84, subdivision 1, in obedience to the order of a court or in the course and scope of employment or in fresh pursuit as provided in subdivision 2, is outside of the person's jurisdiction, the person is serving in the regular line of duty as fully as though the service was within the person's jurisdiction.

Subd. 4. **Off-duty arrests outside jurisdiction.** A peace officer, as defined in section 626.84, subdivision 1, paragraph (c), who is off duty and outside of the jurisdiction of the appointing authority but within this state may act pursuant to section 629.34 when and only when confronted with circumstances that would permit the use of deadly force under section 609.066. Nothing in this subdivision limits an officer's authority to arrest as a private person. Nothing in this subdivision shall be construed to restrict the authority of a political subdivision to limit the exercise of the power and authority conferred on its peace officers by this subdivision.

* * *

HIST: (10575-1) 1927 c 256 s 1; 1955 c 252 s 1; 1973 c 123 art 5 s 7; 1985 c 84 s 5; 1985 c 265 art 10 s 1; art 12 s 1; 1987 c 83 s 2

629.401 DELAYING TO TAKE PRISONER BEFORE JUDGE.

A peace officer or other person who willfully and wrongfully delays taking an arrested person before a judge having appropriate criminal jurisdiction is guilty of a gross misdemeanor.
HIST: (10029) RL s 4844; 1983 c 359 s 133; 1985 c 265 art 10 s 1

629.402 ARREST WITHOUT AUTHORITY.

It is a gross misdemeanor for a public officer, or one pretending to be a public officer, knowingly and under the pretense or color of any process (1) to arrest a person or detain a person against the person's will, (2) to seize or levy upon any property, or (3) to dispossess any one of lands or tenements, without a regular process for those actions.
HIST: (10030) RL s 4845; 1985 c 265 art 10 s 1; 1986 c 444

629.403 REFUSAL TO AID IN MAKING ARREST.

A person who willfully neglects or refuses to arrest another person after having been lawfully directed to do so by a judge is guilty of a misdemeanor.

A person who willfully neglects or refuses to aid a peace officer after being lawfully directed to aid the officer (1) in making an arrest, (2) in retaking a person who has escaped from custody, or (3) in executing a legal process is guilty of a misdemeanor.
HIST: (10032) RL s 4847; 1983 c 359 s 134; 1985 c 265 art 10 s 1

629.404 COUNTIES OR MUNICIPALITIES CAUSING ARREST; REQUIRING RETURN TRANSPORTATION.

Subdivision 1. **Return transportation.** A county or municipality which causes to be issued a warrant for arrest for a person under section 629.41 and rules 3.01 and 19.01 of the Rules of Criminal Procedure, shall furnish return transportation, upon request to the person arrested. The person must be transported to the municipality or township of residence in Minnesota after a trial or final hearing on the matter.

Subd. 2. **Exceptions.** This section does not apply:

(1) to arrests made outside the state pursuant to sections 629.01 to 629.291;

(2) if the person is convicted or pleads guilty to any offense; or

(3) if the arrest is made under section 629.61.
HIST: 1971 c 908 s 1,2; 1Sp1981 c 4 art 1 s 185; 1985 c 265 art 10 s 1; 1986 c 444

629.41 JUDGES TO ISSUE PROCESS FOR ARREST.

Judges, in vacation as well as in term time, may issue process to carry out law for the apprehension of persons charged with offenses.
HIST: (10576) RL s 5235; 1983 c 359 s 135; 1985 c 265 art 10 s 1

629.415 PROCEEDINGS ON SUMMONS TO APPEAR.

Subdivision 1. **Issuance of summons to appear.** A court may issue a summons in accordance with rule 3.01 of the Rules of Criminal Procedure to notify a person charged with a criminal offense of the need to appear at a certain time and place to answer the charge.

Subd. 2. **Service of summons.** A summons may be served in accordance with rule 3.03 of the Rules of Criminal Procedure. The court shall record the manner in which the summons was served and, if the summons was served by mailing it to the defendant's last known address, the court shall record whether the summons was returned as undeliverable.

Subd. 3. **Failure to appear; issuance of a sign and release warrant.** (a) Unless a prosecutor makes the showing described in subdivision 4, the court shall issue a sign and release warrant if:

(1) the court issued a summons;

(2) the summons was served by mailing it to the defendant's last known address and was returned as undeliverable;

(3) the defendant failed to appear at the time and place identified in the summons;

(4) the defendant had not previously failed to appear in the same case; and

(5) the defendant is charged with a misdemeanor offense other than a targeted misdemeanor, as defined in section 299C.10, subdivision 1, or a gross misdemeanor offense other than a violation of section 169A.20 (driving while impaired); 518B.01, subdivision 14 (violation of domestic abuse order for protection); 609.2231 (fourth-degree assault); 609.224 (fifth-degree assault); 609.2242 (domestic assault); 609.3451 (fifth-degree criminal sexual conduct); 609.377 (malicious punishment of a child); 609.378 (neglect or endangerment of a child); 609.748, subdivision 6 (violation of harassment restraining order); 609.749 (harassment or stalking); 609.78, subdivision 2 (interference with an emergency call); 617.261 (nonconsensual dissemination of private sexual images); or 629.75 (violation of domestic abuse no contact order).

(b) A sign and release warrant shall not require the defendant to post bail or comply with any other conditions of release. A sign and release warrant does not authorize the arrest of the defendant.

(c) Any court record provided or made available to a law enforcement agency shall indicate that the warrant is a sign and release warrant.

Subd. 4. **When bail may be required.** The court may issue a warrant that requires the defendant to post bail or comply with other conditions of release if a prosecutor shows, by a preponderance of the evidence, that bail is necessary:

(1) for the safety of a victim;

(2) because a defendant poses a risk to public safety; or

(3) because the defendant otherwise poses a danger to self or others.

Subd. 5. **Sign and release warrant; law enforcement duties.** (a) When a peace officer encounters a defendant who is the subject of a sign and release warrant, the officer shall inform the defendant of the missed court appearance and provide a new notice that includes a time to appear.

(b) Notice of the new time to appear shall be made in writing and must include the court file number or the warrant number. The defendant may be asked to sign a form acknowledging receipt of the notice. A defendant may not be required to sign the acknowledgment, but the peace officer or other employee may indicate that a notice was given and that the defendant refused to sign.

(c) After providing the notice, the peace officer shall release the defendant at the scene.

(d) As soon as practicable after providing the notice, the peace officer shall:

(1) inactivate the warrant or direct the appropriate office or department to inactivate the warrant; and

(2) submit a form or other notification that can be filed in the court's electronic filing system that includes the court case number, updates the defendant's personal contact information, and indicates that the defendant received notice of the new time to appear.

Subd. 6. **Exception; lawful arrest.** Nothing in this section prohibits a peace officer from arresting a defendant for any lawful reason.

Subd. 7. Procedure to notify peace officers; scheduling new court dates. (a) By January 1, 2024, the sheriff of every county, in coordination with the district court of that county, shall develop a procedure to inform peace officers about the type of warrant issued by the court and provide hearing dates for sign and release warrants.

(b) At a minimum, the procedure shall include:

(1) an office, department, or other entity that a peace officer can contact at any time to determine the type of warrant issued by a court;

(2) if the warrant is a sign and release warrant, the ability to obtain an updated time for a defendant to appear to answer the charge;

(3) the ability to inactivate a sign and release warrant after a defendant has been notified of the new time to appear; and

(4) the ability to submit a form or other notification to the court's electronic filing system updating the defendant's personal contact information and indicating that the defendant received notice of the new time.

(c) The sheriff may develop forms to provide defendants with notice of the new time to appear.

EFFECTIVE DATE. This section is effective July 1, 2021, and applies to warrants issued on or after January 1, 2024.

HIST: 1Sp2021 c 11 art 9 s 30

629.61 ARREST OF DEFAULTER.

When a defendant has been admitted to bail after verdict or trial, and neglects to appear at the time or place at which the defendant is bound to appear and submit to the jurisdiction of the proper court, the court may have that defendant arrested as provided in rule 6.03, subdivision 1, of the Rules of Criminal Procedure. In accordance with rules 6.02 and 6.03 of the Rules of Criminal Procedure, the court may continue the release upon the same conditions or impose different or additional conditions for the defendant's possible release.

HIST: (10597) RL s 5255; 1979 c 233 s 38; 1985 c 265 art 10 s 1; 1986 c 444

629.72 BAIL; DOMESTIC ABUSE; HARASSMENT; VIOLATION OF AN ORDER FOR PROTECTION; OR NO CONTACT ORDER.

Subdivision 1. **Definitions.** (a) For purposes of this section, the following terms have the meanings given them.

(b) "Domestic abuse" has the meaning given is section 518B.01, subdivision 2.

(c) "Stalking" has the meaning given in section 609.749.

(d) "Violation of a domestic abuse no contact order" has the meaning given in section 629.75, subdivision 1.

(e) "Violation of an order for protection" has the meaning given in section 629.75.

Subd. 1a. **Allowing detention in lieu of citation; release.** (a) Notwithstanding any other law or rule, an arresting officer may not issue a citation in lieu of arrest and detention to an individual charged with stalking, domestic abuse, violation of an order for protection, or violation of a domestic abuse no contact order.

(b) Notwithstanding any other law or rule, an individual who is arrested on a charge of stalking any person, domestic abuse, violation of an order for protection, or violation of a domestic abuse no contact order, must be brought to the police station or county jail. The officer in charge of the police station or the county sheriff in charge of the jail shall issue a citation in lieu of continued detention unless it reasonably appears to the officer or sheriff that release of the person (1) poses a threat to the alleged victim or another family or household member, (2) poses a threat to public safety, or (3) involves a substantial likelihood the arrested person will fail to appear at subsequent proceedings.

(c) If the arrested person is not issued a citation by the officer in charge of the police station or the county sheriff, the arrested person must be brought before the nearest available judge of the district court in the county in which the alleged stalking, domestic abuse, violation of an order for protection, or violation of a domestic abuse no contact order took place without unnecessary delay as provided by court rule.

Subd. 2. **Judicial review; release; bail.** (a) The judge before whom the arrested person is brought shall review the facts surrounding the arrest and detention of a person arrested for domestic abuse, stalking, violation of an order for protection, or violation of a domestic abuse no contact order. The prosecutor or prosecutor's designee shall present relevant information involving the victim's or the victim's family's account of the alleged crime to the judge to be considered in determining the arrested person's release. In making a decision concerning pretrial release conditions of a person arrested for domestic abuse, stalking, violation of an order for protection, or violation of a domestic abuse no contact order, the judge shall review the facts of the arrest and detention of the person and determine whether: (1) release of the person poses a threat to the alleged victim, another family or household member, or public safety; or (2) there is a substantial likelihood the person will fail to appear at subsequent proceedings. Before releasing a person arrested for or charged with a crime of domestic abuse, stalking, violation of an order for protection, or violation of a domestic abuse no contact order, the judge shall make findings on the record, to the extent possible, concerning the determination made in accordance with the factors specified in clauses (1) and (2).

(b) The judge may impose conditions of release or bail, or both, on the person to protect the alleged victim or other family or household members and to ensure the appearance of the person at subsequent proceedings. These conditions may include an order:

(1) enjoining the person from threatening to commit or committing acts of domestic abuse or stalking against the alleged victim or other family or household members or from violating an order for protection or a domestic abuse no contact order;

(2) prohibiting the person from harassing, annoying, telephoning, contacting, or otherwise communicating with the alleged victim, either directly or indirectly;

(3) directing the person to vacate or stay away from the home of the alleged victim and to stay away from any location where the alleged victim is likely to be;

(4) prohibiting the person from possessing a firearm or other weapon specified by the court;

(5) prohibiting the person from possessing or consuming alcohol or controlled substances; and

(6) specifying any other matter required to protect the safety of the alleged victim and to ensure the appearance of the person at subsequent proceedings.

(c) If conditions of release are imposed, the judge shall issue a written order for conditional release. The court administrator shall immediately distribute a copy of the order for conditional release to the agency having custody of the arrested person and shall provide the agency having custody of the arrested person with any available information on the location of the victim in a manner that protects the victim's safety. Either the court or its designee or the agency having custody of the arrested person shall serve upon the defendant a copy of the order. Failure to serve the arrested person with a copy of the order for conditional release does not invalidate the conditions of release.

(d) If the judge imposes as a condition of release a requirement that the person have no contact with the alleged victim, the judge may also, on its own motion or that of the prosecutor or on request of the victim, issue an ex parte temporary restraining order under section 609.748, subdivision 4, or an ex parte temporary order for protection under section 518B.01, subdivision 7. Notwithstanding section 518B.01, subdivision 7, paragraph (b), or 609.748, subdivision 4, paragraph (c), the temporary order is effective until the defendant is convicted or acquitted, or the charge is dismissed, provided that upon request the defendant is entitled to a full hearing on the restraining order under section 609.748, subdivision 5, or on the order for protection under section 518B.01. The hearing must be held within seven days of the defendant's request.

Subd. 2a. **Electronic monitoring as a condition of pretrial release; pilot project.** (a) Until a judicial district has adopted standards under paragraph (b) governing electronic monitoring devices used to protect victims of domestic abuse, a court within the judicial district, as a condition of release, may not order a person arrested for a crime described in section 609.135, subdivision 5a, paragraph (b), to use an electronic monitoring device to protect a victim's safety.

(b) The chief judge of a judicial district may appoint and convene an advisory group to develop and biennially update standards for the use of electronic monitoring and global positioning system devices to protect victims of domestic abuse. * * *

Subd. 3. **Release.** If the arrested person is not issued a citation by the officer in charge of the police station or the county sheriff pursuant to subdivision 1, and is not brought before a judge within the time limits prescribed by court rule, the arrested person shall be released by the arresting authorities, and a citation must be issued in lieu of continued detention.

Subd. 4. **Service of restraining order or order for protection.** If a restraining order is issued under section 609.748 or an order for protection is issued under section 518B.01 while the arrested person is still in detention, the order must be served upon the arrested person during detention if possible.

Subd. 5. **Violations of conditions of release.** The judge who released the arrested person shall issue a warrant directing that the person be arrested and taken immediately before the judge, if the judge:

(1) receives an application alleging that the arrested person has violated the conditions of release; and

(2) finds that probable cause exists to believe that the conditions of release have been violated.

Subd. 6. **Notice regarding release of arrested person.**

(a) Immediately after issuance of a citation in lieu of continued detention under subdivision 1, or the entry of an order for release under subdivision 2, but before the arrested person is released, the agency having custody of the arrested person or its designee must make a reasonable and good faith effort to inform orally the alleged victim, local law enforcement agencies known to be involved in the case, if different from the agency having custody, and, at the victim's request any local battered women's and domestic abuse programs established under section 611A.32 or sexual assault programs of:

(1) the conditions of release, if any;

(2) the time of release;

(3) the time, date, and place of the next scheduled court appearance of the arrested person and the victim's right to be present at the court appearance; and

(4) if the arrested person is charged with domestic abuse, the location and telephone number of the area battered women's shelter as designated by the Office of Justice Programs in the Department of Public Safety.

(b) As soon as practicable after an order for conditional release is entered, the agency having custody of the arrested person or its designee must personally deliver or mail to the alleged victim a copy of the written order and written notice of the information in clauses (2) and (3). * * *

Subd. 7. **Notice to victim regarding bail hearing.** When a person arrested for or a juvenile detained for domestic assault or stalking is scheduled to be reviewed under subdivision 2 for release from pretrial detention, the court shall make a reasonable good faith effort to notify: (1) the victim of the alleged crime; (2) if the victim is incapacitated or deceased, the victim's family; and (3) if the victim is a minor, the victim's parent or guardian. The notification must include:

(1) the date and appropriate time of the review;

(2) the location where the review will occur;

(3) the name and telephone number of a person that can be contacted for additional information; and

(4) a statement that the victim and the victim's family may attend the review.

HIST: 1978 c 724 s 3; * * * 2014 c 263 s 2

629.75 DOMESTIC ABUSE NO CONTACT ORDER.

Subdivision 1. **Establishment; description.** (a) A domestic abuse no contact order is an order issued by a court against a defendant in a criminal proceeding or a juvenile offender in a delinquency proceeding for:

(1) domestic abuse as defined in section 518B.01, subdivision 2;

(2) harassment or stalking charged under 609.749 when committed against a family or household member as defined in section 518B.01, subdivision 2;

(3) violation of an order for protection under section 518B.01, subdivision 14; or

(4) violation of a prior domestic abuse no contact order under this subdivision or section 518B.01, subdivision 22.

(b) A domestic abuse no contact order may be issued as a pretrial order before final disposition of the underlying criminal case or as a postconviction probationary order. A domestic abuse no contact order is independent of any condition of pretrial release or probation imposed on the defendant. A domestic abuse no contact order may be issued in addition to a similar restriction imposed as a condition of pretrial release or probation. In the context of a postconviction probationary order, a domestic abuse no contact order may be issued for an offense listed in paragraph (a) or for a conviction for any offense arising out of the same set of circumstances as an offense listed in paragraph (a).

(c) A no contact order under this section shall be issued in a proceeding that is separate from but held immediately following a proceeding in which any pretrial release or sentencing issues are decided.

* * *

Subd. 3. **Warrantless custodial arrest.** A peace officer shall arrest without a warrant and take into custody a person whom the peace officer has probable cause to believe has violated a domestic abuse no contact order, even if the violation of the order did not take place in the presence of the peace officer, if the existence of the order can be verified by the officer. The person shall be held in custody for at least 36 hours, excluding the day of arrest, Sundays, and holidays, unless the person is released earlier by a judge or judicial officer. A peace officer acting in good faith and exercising due care in making an arrest pursuant to this subdivision is immune from civil liability that might result from the officer's actions.
HIST: 2010 c 299 s 13; 2013 c 47 s 5,6

Category 2, Section 8:
2.8.1. Explain Minnesota statutes and relevant case law related to the application of force by peace officers.
2.8.2. Explain the following terms: objectively reasonable, totality of circumstances, situational factors, pre-assaultive indicators, and, escalation and de-escalation as related to peace officer use of force.
2.8.3. Discuss the term *reasonable* as it related to use of force.
2.8.6. Give Supreme Court case examples authorizing the use of deadly force.
2.8.8. Explain the Minnesota Statute that requires officers be trained in the use of those weapons and equipment the officer is issued or authorized to carry (Minn. Stat. 626.8452).
2.8.10. Discuss liabilities associated with the application of force by peace officers.

609.06 AUTHORIZED USE OF FORCE.
Subdivision 1. **When authorized.** Except as otherwise provided in subdivisions 2 and 3, reasonable force may be used upon or toward the person of another without the other's consent when the following circumstances exist or the actor reasonably believes them to exist:
(1) when used by a public officer or one assisting a public officer under the public officer's direction:
(i) in effecting a lawful arrest; or
(ii) in the execution of legal process; or
(iii) in enforcing an order of the court; or
(iv) in executing any other duty imposed upon the public officer by law; or
(2) when used by a person not a public officer in arresting another in the cases and in the manner provided by law and delivering the other to an officer competent to receive the other into custody; or
(3) when used by any person in resisting or aiding another to resist an offense against the person; or
(4) when used by any person in lawful possession of real or personal property, or by another assisting the person in lawful possession, in resisting a trespass upon or other unlawful interference with such property; or

(5) when used by any person to prevent the escape, or to retake following the escape, of a person lawfully held on a charge or conviction of a crime; or

(6) when used by a parent, guardian, teacher, or other lawful custodian of a child or pupil, in the exercise of lawful authority, to restrain or correct such child or pupil; or

(7) when used by a school employee or school bus driver, in the exercise of lawful authority, to restrain a child or pupil, or to prevent bodily harm or death to another; or

(8) when used by a common carrier in expelling a passenger who refuses to obey a lawful requirement for the conduct of passengers and reasonable care is exercised with regard to the passenger's personal safety; or

(9) when used to restrain a person with a mental illness or a person with a developmental disability from self-injury or injury to another or when used by one with authority to do so to compel compliance with reasonable requirements for the person's control, conduct, or treatment; or

(10) when used by a public or private institution providing custody or treatment against one lawfully committed to it to compel compliance with reasonable requirements for the control, conduct, or treatment of the committed person.

Subd. 2. **Deadly force used against peace officers.** Deadly force may not be used against peace officers who have announced their presence and are performing official duties at a location where a person is committing a crime or an act that would be a crime if committed by an adult.

Subd. 3. **Limitations on the use of certain restraints.** (a) A peace officer may not use any of the following restraints unless section 609.066 authorizes the use of deadly force to protect the peace officer or another from death or great bodily harm:

(1) a choke hold;

(2) tying all of a person's limbs together behind the person's back to render the person immobile; or

(3) securing a person in any way that results in transporting the person face down in a vehicle.

(b) For the purposes of this subdivision, "choke hold" means a method by which a person applies sufficient pressure to a person to make breathing difficult or impossible, and includes but is not limited to any pressure to the neck, throat, or windpipe that may prevent or hinder breathing, or reduce intake of air. Choke hold also means applying pressure to a person's neck on either side of the windpipe, but not to the windpipe itself, to stop the flow of blood to the brain via the carotid arteries.

HIST: 1963 c 753 art 1 s 609.06; 1986 c 444; 1993 c 326 art 1 s 4; 1996 c 408 art 3 s 12; 2002 c 221 s 46; 2013 c 59 art 3 s 16; 2013 c 62 s 28; 2Sp2020 c 1 s 7,8

609.065 JUSTIFIABLE TAKING OF LIFE.

The intentional taking of the life of another is not authorized by section 609.06, except when necessary in resisting or preventing an offense which the actor reasonably believes exposes the actor or another to great bodily harm or death, or preventing the commission of a felony in the actor's place of abode.

HIST: 1963 c 753 art 1 s 609.065; 1978 c 736 s 1; 1986 c 444

609.066 AUTHORIZED USE OF DEADLY FORCE BY PEACE OFFICERS.

Subdivision 1. **Deadly force defined.** For the purposes of this section, "deadly force" means force which the actor uses with the purpose of causing, or which the actor should reasonably know creates a substantial risk of causing, death or great bodily harm. The intentional discharge of a firearm, other than a firearm loaded with less lethal munitions and used by a peace officer within the scope of official duties, in the direction of another person, or at a vehicle in which another person is believed to be, constitutes deadly force. "Less lethal munitions" means projectiles which are designed to stun, temporarily incapacitate, or cause temporary discomfort to a person. "Peace officer" has the meaning given in section 626.84, subdivision 1.

Subd. 1a. **Legislative intent.** The legislature hereby finds and declares the following:

(1) that the authority to use deadly force, conferred on peace officers by this section, is a critical responsibility that shall be exercised judiciously and with respect for human rights and dignity and for the sanctity of every human life. The legislature further finds and declares that every person has a right to be free from excessive use of force by officers acting under color of law;

(2) as set forth below, it is the intent of the legislature that peace officers use deadly force only when necessary in defense of human life or to prevent great bodily harm. In determining whether deadly force is necessary, officers shall evaluate each situation in light of the particular circumstances of each case;

(3) that the decision by a peace officer to use deadly force shall be evaluated from the perspective of a reasonable officer in the same situation, based on the totality of the circumstances known to or perceived by the officer at the time, rather than with the benefit of hindsight, and that the totality of the circumstances shall account for occasions when officers may be forced to make quick judgments about using deadly force; and

(4) that peace officers should exercise special care when interacting with individuals with known physical, mental health, developmental, or intellectual disabilities as an individual's disability may affect the individual's ability to understand or comply with commands from peace officers.

[See Note.]

Subd. 2. **Use of deadly force.** (a) Notwithstanding the provisions of section 609.06 or 609.065, the use of deadly force by a peace officer in the line of duty is justified only if an objectively reasonable officer would believe, based on the totality of the circumstances known to the officer at the time and without the benefit of hindsight, that such force is necessary:

(1) to protect the peace officer or another from death or great bodily harm, provided that the threat:

(i) can be articulated with specificity by the law enforcement officer;

(ii) is reasonably likely to occur absent action by the law enforcement officer; and

(iii) must be addressed through the use of deadly force without unreasonable delay; or

(2) to effect the arrest or capture, or prevent the escape, of a person whom the peace officer knows or has reasonable grounds to believe has committed or attempted to commit a felony and the officer reasonably believes that the person will cause death or great bodily harm to another person under the threat criteria in clause (1), items (i) to (iii), unless immediately apprehended.

(b) A peace officer shall not use deadly force against a person based on the danger the person poses to self if an objectively reasonable officer would believe, based on the totality of the circumstances known to the officer at the time and without the benefit of hindsight, that the person does not pose a threat of death or great bodily harm to the peace officer or to another under the threat criteria in paragraph (a), clause (1), items (i) to (iii).

[See Note.]

Subd. 3. **No defense.** This section and sections 609.06, 609.065 and 629.33 may not be used as a defense in a civil action brought by an innocent third party.

HIST: 1978 c 736 s 2; 1986 c 444; 2001 c 127 s 1; 2Sp2020 c 1 s 9,10

NOTE: Subdivision 1a, as added by Laws 2020, Second Special Session chapter 1, section 9, is effective March 1, 2021. Laws 2020, Second Special Session chapter 1, section 9, the effective date. **NOTE:** The amendment to subdivision 2 by Laws 2020, Second Special Session chapter 1, section 10, is effective March 1, 2021. Laws 2020, Second Special Session chapter 1, section 10, the effective date.

626.553 GUNSHOT WOUNDS; PEACE OFFICERS, DISCHARGING FIREARMS; INVESTIGATIONS, REPORTS.

Subdivision 1. **Report; wounds; investigation.** Upon receipt of the report required in sections 626.52 and 626.53, the sheriff or chief of police receiving the report shall determine the general cause of the wound, and upon determining that the wound was caused by an action connected with the occupation or sport of hunting or shooting the sheriff or chief of police shall immediately conduct a detailed investigation into the facts surrounding the incident or occurrence which occasioned the injury or death reported. The investigating officer shall report the findings of the investigation to the commissioner of natural resources on forms provided by the commissioner for this purpose.

Subd. 2. **Discharge firearm; kill animal.** Whenever a peace officer discharges a firearm in the course of duty, other than for training purposes or the killing of an animal that is sick, injured, or dangerous, notification shall be filed within 30 days, of the incident by the officer's department head with the commissioner of public safety. The commissioner of public safety shall forward a copy of the filing to the board of peace officer standards and training. The notification shall contain information concerning the reason for and circumstances surrounding discharge of the firearm. The commissioner of public safety shall file a report with the legislature by November 15 of each even-numbered year containing summary information concerning use of firearms by peace officers.

HIST: 1957 c 407 s 1; * * * 1991 c 141 s 1

626.8452 DEADLY FORCE AND FIREARMS USE; POLICIES AND INSTRUCTION REQUIRED.

Subdivision 1. **Deadly force policy.** [T]he head of every local and state law enforcement agency shall establish and enforce a written policy governing the use of force, including deadly force, as defined in section 609.066, by peace officers and part-time peace officers employed by the agency. The policy must be consistent with the provisions of section 609.066, subdivision 2, and may not prohibit the use of deadly force under circumstances in which that force is justified under section 609.066, subdivision 2.

Subd. 2. **Deadly force and firearms use; initial instruction.** [T]he head of every local and state law enforcement agency shall provide instruction on the use of force, deadly force, and the use of firearms to every peace officer and part-time peace officer newly appointed by or beginning employment with the agency. This instruction must occur before the agency head issues a firearm to the officer or otherwise authorizes the officer to carry a firearm in the course of employment. The instruction must be based on the agency's written policy required in subdivision 1 and on the instructional materials require by the board of peace officer and part-time officer licensure.

Subd. 3. **Deadly force and firearms use; continuing instruction.** [T]he head of every local and state law enforcement agency shall provide the instruction described in subdivision 2 to every peace officer and part-time peace officer currently employed by the agency * * * at least once a year. * * *

HIST: 1991 c 141 s 2

626.8476 CONFIDENTIAL INFORMANTS; REQUIRED POLICY AND TRAINING

Subdivision 1. **Definitions.** (a) For the purposes of this section, the terms in this subdivision have the meanings given them.

(b) "Confidential informant" means a person who cooperates with a law enforcement agency confidentially in order to protect the person or the agency's intelligence gathering or investigative efforts and:

(1) seeks to avoid arrest or prosecution for a crime, mitigate punishment for a crime in which a sentence will be or has been imposed, or receive a monetary or other benefit; and

(2) is able, by reason of the person's familiarity or close association with suspected criminals, to:

(i) make a controlled buy or controlled sale of contraband, controlled substances, or other items that are material to a criminal investigation;

(ii) supply regular or constant information about suspected or actual criminal activities to a law enforcement agency; or

(iii) otherwise provide information important to ongoing criminal intelligence gathering or criminal investigative efforts.

(c) "Controlled buy" means the purchase of contraband, controlled substances, or other items that are material to a criminal investigation from a target offender that is initiated, managed, overseen, or participated in by law enforcement personnel with the knowledge of a confidential informant.

(d) "Controlled sale" means the sale of contraband, controlled substances, or other items that are material to a criminal investigation to a target offender that is initiated, managed, overseen, or participated in by law enforcement personnel with the knowledge of a confidential informant.

(e) "Mental harm" means a psychological injury that is not necessarily permanent but results in visibly demonstrable manifestations of a disorder of thought or mood that impairs a person's judgment or behavior.

(f) "Target offender" means the person suspected by law enforcement personnel to be implicated in criminal acts by the activities of a confidential informant.

Subd. 2. Model policy. (a) By January 1, 2022, the board shall adopt a model policy addressing the use of confidential informants by law enforcement. The model policy must establish policies and procedures for the recruitment, control, and use of confidential informants. In developing the policy, the board shall consult with representatives of the Bureau of Criminal Apprehension, Minnesota Police Chiefs Association, Minnesota Sheriff's Association, Minnesota Police and Peace Officers Association, Minnesota County Attorneys Association, treatment centers for substance abuse, and mental health organizations. The model policy must include, at a minimum, the following:

(1) information that the law enforcement agency shall maintain about each confidential informant that must include, at a minimum, an emergency contact for the informant in the event of the informant's physical or mental harm or death;

(2) a process to advise a confidential informant of conditions, restrictions, and procedures associated with participating in the agency's investigative or intelligence gathering activities;

(3) procedures for compensation to an informant that is commensurate with the value of the services and information provided and based on the level of the targeted offender, the amount of any seizure, and the significance of contributions made by the informant;

(4) designated supervisory or command-level review and oversight in the use of a confidential informant;

(5) limits or restrictions on off-duty association or social relationships by law enforcement agency personnel with a confidential informant;

(6) limits or restrictions on the potential exclusion of an informant from engaging in a controlled buy or sale of a controlled substance if the informant is known by the law enforcement agency to: (i) be receiving in-patient or out-patient treatment administered by a licensed service provider for substance abuse; (ii) be participating in a treatment-based drug court program; or (iii) have experienced a drug overdose within the past year;

(7) exclusion of an informant under the age of 18 years from participating in a controlled buy or sale of a controlled substance without the written consent of a parent or legal guardian, except that the informant may provide confidential information to a law enforcement agency;

(8) consideration of an informant's diagnosis of mental illness, substance abuse, or disability, and history of mental illness, substance abuse, or disability;

(9) guidelines for the law enforcement agency to consider if the agency decides to establish a procedure to request an advocate from the county social services agency for an informant if the informant is an addict in recovery or possesses a physical or mental infirmity or other physical, mental, or emotional dysfunction that impairs the informant's ability to understand instructions and make informed decisions, where the agency determines this process does not place the informant in any danger;

(10) guidelines for the law enforcement agency to use to encourage prospective and current confidential informants who are known to be substance abusers or to be at risk for substance abuse to seek prevention or treatment services;

(11) reasonable protective measures for a confidential informant when law enforcement knows or should have known of a risk or threat of harm to a person serving as a confidential

informant and the risk or threat of harm is a result of the informant's service to the law enforcement agency;

(12) guidelines for the training and briefing of a confidential informant;

(13) reasonable procedures to help protect the identity of a confidential informant during the time the person is acting as an informant;

(14) procedures to deactivate a confidential informant that maintain the safety and anonymity of the informant;

(15) optional procedures that the law enforcement agency may adopt relating to deactivated confidential informants to offer and provide assistance to them with physical, mental, or emotional health services;

(16) a process to evaluate and report the criminal history and propensity for violence of any target offenders; and

(17) guidelines for a written agreement between the confidential informant and the law enforcement agency that take into consideration, at a minimum, an informant's physical or mental infirmity or other physical, mental, or emotional dysfunction that impairs the informant's ability to knowingly contract or otherwise protect the informant's self-interest.

(b) The board shall annually review and, as necessary, revise the model confidential informant policy in collaboration with representatives from the organizations listed under paragraph (a).

Subd. 3. Agency policies required. (a) The chief law enforcement officer of every state and local law enforcement agency must establish and enforce a written policy governing the use of confidential informants. The policy must be identical or, at a minimum, substantially similar to the new or revised model policy adopted by the board under subdivision 2.

(b) Every state and local law enforcement agency must certify annually to the board that it has adopted a written policy in compliance with the board's model confidential informant policy.

(c) The board shall assist the chief law enforcement officer of each state and local law enforcement agency in developing and implementing confidential informant policies under this subdivision.

Subd. 4. Required in-service training. The chief law enforcement officer of every state and local law enforcement agency shall provide in-service training in the recruitment, control, and use of confidential informants to every peace officer and part-time peace officer employed by the agency who the chief law enforcement officer determines is involved in working with confidential informants given the officer's responsibilities. The training shall comply with learning objectives based on the policies and procedures of the model policy developed and approved by the board.

Subd. 5. Compliance reviews. The board has the authority to inspect state and local agency policies to ensure compliance with this section. The board may conduct the inspection based upon a complaint it receives about a particular agency or through a random selection process.

Subd. 6. Licensing sanctions; injunctive relief. The board may impose licensing sanctions and seek injunctive relief under section 214.11 for failure to comply with the requirements of this section.

EFFECTIVE DATE. This section is effective the day following final enactment.

HIST: 1Sp2021 c 11 art 9 s 29

Chapter 32 – DOMESTIC VIOLENCE

Category 2, Sections 5, 16:
2.5.7. Explain special Minnesota peace officer duties associated with specific statutes . . .
2.16.1. Explain what legally constitutes domestic abuse and assault.
2.16.6. Identify significant aspects of Minn. Stat. related to domestic abuse (Minn.Stat. 629.341 and 518.B01, 609.749, 609.2242) including what legally constitutes domestic assault, elements of various levels of domestic assault, and enhancement for prior domestic violence related offense convictions.
2.16.10. Explain the requirements for making an arrest and reporting in domestic assault situations.
2.16.11. Discuss when warrantless arrests may be made and when enhancements for previous assaults may be considered.

518B.01 DOMESTIC ABUSE ACT.

Subdivision 1. **Short title.** This section may be cited as the domestic abuse act.

Subd. 2. **Definitions.** As used in this section, the following terms shall have the meanings given them:

(a) "Domestic abuse" means the following, if committed against a family or household member by a family or household member:

(1) physical harm, bodily injury, or assault;

(2) the infliction of fear of imminent physical harm, bodily injury, or assault; or

(3) terroristic threats, within the meaning of section 609.713, subdivision 1; criminal sexual conduct, within the meaning of section 609.342, 609.343, 609.344, 609.345, or 609.3451; or interference with an emergency call within the meaning of section 609.78, subdivision 2.

(b) "Family or household members" means:

(1) spouses and former spouses;

(2) parents and children;

(3) persons related by blood;

(4) persons who are presently residing together or who have resided together in the past;

(5) persons who have a child in common regardless of whether they have been married or have lived together at any time;

(6) a man and woman if the woman is pregnant and the man is alleged to be the father regardless of whether they have been married or have lived together at any time; and

(7) persons involved in a significant romantic or sexual relationship.
Issuance of an order for protection on the ground in clause (6) does not affect a determination of paternity under sections 257.51 to 257.74. In determining whether persons are or have been involved in a significant romantic or sexual relationship under clause (7), the court shall consider the length of time of the relationship; type of relationship; frequency of interaction between the parties; and, if the relationship has terminated, length of time since the termination.

(c) "Qualified domestic violence-related offense" has the meaning given in section 609.02, subdivision 16.

Subd. 3. **Court jurisdiction.** An application for relief under this section may be filed in the court having jurisdiction over dissolution actions in the county of residence of either party, in the county in which a pending or completed family court proceeding involving the parties or their minor children was brought, or in the county in which the alleged domestic abuse occurred. There are no residency requirements that apply to a petition for an order for protection. In a jurisdiction which utilizes referees in dissolution actions, the court or judge may refer actions under this section to a referee to take and report the evidence in the action in the same manner and subject to the same limitations provided in section 518.13. Actions under this section shall be given docket priorities by the court.

Subd. 3a. **Filing fee.** The filing fees for an order for protection under this section are waived for the petitioner and respondent. The court administrator, the sheriff of any county in this state, and other law enforcement and corrections officers shall perform their duties relating to service of process without charge to the petitioner. The court shall direct payment of the reasonable costs of service of process if served by a private process server when the sheriff or other law enforcement or corrections officer is unavailable or if service is made by publication, without requiring the petitioner to make application under section 563.01.

Subd. 3b. **Information on petitioner's location or residence.** Upon the petitioner's request, information maintained by the court regarding the petitioner's location or residence is not accessible to the public and may be disclosed only to court personnel or law enforcement for purposes of service of process, conducting an investigation, or enforcing an order.

Subd. 4. **Order for protection**, There shall exist an action known as a petition for an order for protection in cases of domestic abuse.

(a) A petition for relief under this section may be made by any family or household member personally or by a family or household member, a guardian as defined in section 524.1-201, clause (26), or, if the court finds that it is in the best interests of the minor, by a reputable adult age 25 or older on behalf of minor family or household members. A minor age 16 or older may make a petition on the minor's own behalf against a spouse or former spouse, or a person with whom the minor has a child in common, if the court determines that the minor has sufficient maturity and judgment and that it is in the best interests of the minor.

(b) A petition for relief shall allege the existence of domestic abuse, and shall be accompanied by an affidavit made under oath stating the specific facts and circumstances from which relief is sought.

(c) A petition for relief must state whether the petitioner has ever had an order for protection in effect against the respondent.

(d) A petition for relief must state whether there is an existing order for protection in effect under this chapter governing both the parties and whether there is a pending lawsuit, complaint, petition or other action between the parties under chapter 257, 518, 518A, 518B, or 518C. The court administrator shall verify the terms of any existing order governing the parties. The court may not delay granting relief because of the existence of a pending action between the parties or the necessity of verifying the terms of an existing order. A subsequent order in a separate action under this chapter may modify only the provision of an existing order that grants relief authorized under subdivision 6, paragraph (a), clause (1). A petition for relief may be granted, regardless of whether there is a pending action between the parties.

(e)The court shall provide simplified forms and clerical assistance to help with the writing and filing of a petition under this section

(f)The court shall advise a petitioner under paragraph (e) of the right to file a motion and affidavit and to sue in forma pauperis pursuant to section 563.01 and shall assist with the writing and filing of the motion and affidavit

(g) The court shall advise a petitioner under paragraph (e) of the right to serve the respondent by published notice under subdivision 5, paragraph (b), if the respondent is avoiding personal service by concealment or otherwise, and shall assist with the writing and filing of the affidavit.

(h) The court shall advise the petitioner of the right to seek restitution under the petition for relief.

(i) The court shall advise the petitioner of the right to request a hearing under subdivision 7, paragraph (c). If the petitioner does not request a hearing, the court shall advise the petitioner that the respondent may request a hearing and that notice of the hearing date and time will be provided to the petitioner by mail at least five days before the hearing.

(j) The court shall advise the petitioner of the right to request supervised parenting time, as provided in section 518.175, subdivision 1a.

Subd. 5. **Hearing on application; notice.** (a) Upon receipt of the petition, the court shall order a hearing which shall be held not later than 14 days from the date of the order for hearing unless an ex parte order is issued.

(b) If an ex parte order has been issued under subdivision 7 and the petitioner seeks only the relief under subdivision 7, paragraph (a), a hearing is not required unless:

(1) the court declines to order the requested relief; or

(2) one of the parties requests a hearing.

(c) If an ex parte order has been issued under subdivision 7 and the petitioner seeks relief beyond that specified in subdivision 7, paragraph (a), or if the court declines to order relief requested by the petitioner, a hearing must be held within seven days. Personal service of the ex parte order may be made upon the respondent at any time up to 12 hours prior to the time set for the hearing, provided that the respondent at the hearing may request a continuance of up to five days if served fewer than five days prior to the hearing which continuance shall be granted unless there are compelling reasons not to.

(d) If an ex parte order has been issued only granting relief under subdivision 7, paragraph (a), and the respondent requests a hearing, the hearing shall be held within ten days of the court's receipt of the respondent's request. Service of the notice of hearing must be made upon the petitioner not less than five days prior to the hearing. The court shall serve the notice of hearing upon the petitioner by mail in the manner provided in the rules of civil procedure for pleadings subsequent to a complaint and motions and shall also mail notice of the date and time of the hearing to the respondent. In the event that service cannot be completed in time to give the respondent or petitioner the minimum notice required under this subdivision, the court may set a new hearing date no more than five days later.

(e) If for good cause shown either party is unable to proceed at the initial hearing and requests a continuance and the court finds that a continuance is appropriate, the hearing may be continued. Unless otherwise agreed by the parties and approved by the court, the continuance shall be for no more than five days. If the court grants the requested continuance, the court shall also issue a written order continuing all provisions of the ex parte order pending the issuance of an order after the hearing.

(f) Notwithstanding the preceding provisions of this subdivision, service on the respondent may be made by one week published notice, as provided under section 645.11, provided the petitioner files with the court an affidavit stating that an attempt at personal service made by a sheriff or other law enforcement or corrections officer was unsuccessful because the respondent is avoiding service by concealment or otherwise, and that a copy of the petition and notice of hearing has been mailed to the respondent at the respondent's residence or that the residence is not known to the petitioner. Service under this paragraph is complete seven days after publication. The court shall set a new hearing date if necessary to allow the respondent the five-day minimum notice required under paragraph (d)

Subd. 6. **Relief by the court.** (a) Upon notice and hearing, the court may provide relief as follows:

(1) restrain the abusing party from committing acts of domestic abuse;

(2) exclude the abusing party from the dwelling which the parties share or from the residence of the petitioner;

(3) exclude the abusing party from a reasonable area surrounding the dwelling or residence, which area shall be described specifically in the order;

(4) award temporary custody or establish temporary parenting time with regard to minor children of the parties on a basis which gives primary consideration to the safety of the victim and the children. * * * If the court finds that the safety of the victim or the children will be jeopardized by unsupervised or unrestricted parenting time, the court shall condition or restrict parenting time as to time, place, duration, or supervision, or deny parenting time entirely, as needed to guard the safety of the victim and the children. The court's decision on custody and parenting time shall in no way delay the issuance of an order for protection granting other relief

provided for in this section. The court must not enter a parenting plan under section 518.1705 as part of an action for an order for protection;

(5) on the same basis as is provided in chapter 518, establish temporary support for minor children or a spouse, and order the withholding of support from the income of the person obligated to pay the support according to chapter 518;

(6) provide upon request of the petitioner counseling or other social services for the parties, if married, or if there are minor children;

(7) order the abusing party to participate in treatment or counseling services, including requiring the abusing party to successfully complete a domestic abuse counseling program or educational program under section 518B.10;

(8) award temporary use and possession of property and restrain one or both parties from transferring, encumbering, concealing, or disposing of property except in the usual course of business or for the necessities of life, and to account to the court for all such transfers, encumbrances, dispositions, and expenditures made after the order is served or communicated to the party restrained in open court;

(9) exclude the abusing party from the place of employment of the petitioner, or otherwise limit access to the petitioner by the abusing party at the petitioner's place of employment;

(10) order the abusing party to have no contact with the petitioner whether in person, by telephone, mail, or electronic mail or messaging, through a third party, or by any other means;

(11) order the abusing party to pay restitution to the petitioner;

(12) order the continuance of all currently available insurance coverage without change in coverage or beneficiary designation;

(13) order, in its discretion, other relief as it deems necessary for the protection of a family or household member, including orders or directives to the sheriff or other law enforcement or corrections officer as provided by this section;

(14) directs the care, possession, or control of a pet or companion animal owned, possessed, or kept by the petitioner or respondent or a child of the petitioner or respondent; and

(15) direct the respondent to refrain from physically abusing or injuring any pet or companion animal, without legal justification, known to be owned, possessed, kept, or held by either party or a minor child residing in the residence or household of either party as an indirect means of intentionally threatening the safety of such person.

(b) Any relief granted by the order for protection shall be for a fixed period not to exceed two years, except when the court determines a longer fixed period is appropriate. When referee presides at the hearing on the petition, the order granting relief becomes effective upon the referee's signature.

(c) An order granting the relief authorized in paragraph (a), clause (1), may not be vacated or modified in a proceeding for dissolution of marriage or legal separation, except that the court may hear a motion for modification of an order for protection concurrently with a proceeding for dissolution of marriage upon notice of motion and motion. The notice required by court rule shall not be waived. If the proceedings are consolidated and the motion to modify is granted, a separate order for modification of an order for protection shall be issued.

(d) An order granting the relief authorized in paragraph (a), clause (2) or (3), is not voided by the admittance of the abusing party into the dwelling from which the abusing party is excluded.

(e) If a proceeding for dissolution of marriage or legal separation is pending between the parties, the court shall provide a copy of the order for protection to the court with jurisdiction over the dissolution or separation proceeding for inclusion in its file.

(f) An order for restitution issued under this subdivision is enforceable as civil judgment.

(g) An order granting relief shall prohibit the abusing party from possessing firearms for the length the order is in effect if the order (1) restrains the abusing party from harassing, stalking, or threatening the petitioner or restrains the abusing party from engaging in other conduct that would place the petitioner in reasonable fear of bodily injury, and (2) includes a finding that the abusing party represents a credible threat to the physical safety of the petitioner or prohibits the abusing party from using, attempting to use, or threatening to use physical force against the petitioner. The order shall inform the abusing party of that party's prohibited status. Except as provided in paragraph (i), the court shall order the abusing party to transfer any firearms that the person possesses, within three business days, to a federally licensed firearms dealer, a law enforcement agency, or a third party who may lawfully receive them. * * * [Such transferees] shall return the transferred firearms to the person upon request after the expiration of the prohibiting time period imposed under this subdivision, provided the person is not otherwise prohibited from possessing firearms under state or federal law. * * *

(h) An abusing party who is ordered to transfer firearms under paragraph (g) must file proof of transfer as provided for in this paragraph. If the transfer is made to a third party, the third party must sign an affidavit under oath before a notary public either acknowledging that the abusing party permanently transferred the abusing party's firearms to the third party or agreeing to temporarily store the abusing party's firearms until such time as the abusing party is legally permitted to possess firearms. * * * If the transfer is to a law enforcement agency or federally licensed firearms dealer, the law enforcement agency or federally licensed firearms dealer shall provide proof of transfer to the abusing party. * * *

(i) When a court issues an order containing a firearms restriction provided for in paragraph (g), the court shall determine by a preponderance of evidence if an abusing party poses an imminent risk of causing another person substantial bodily harm. Upon a finding of imminent risk, the court shall order that the local law enforcement agency take immediate possession of all firearms in the abusing party's possession. * * * [The agency] shall return the firearms to the person upon request after the expiration of the prohibiting time period, provided the person is not otherwise prohibited from possessing firearms under state or federal law. The local law enforcement agency shall, upon written notice from the abusing party, transfer the firearms to a federally licensed firearms dealer or a third party who may lawfully receive them. * * *

Subd. 6a. **Subsequent orders and extensions.** (a) Upon application, notice to all parties, and hearing, the court may extend the relief granted in an existing order for protection or, if a petitioner's order for protection is no longer in effect when an application for subsequent relief is made, grant a new order. * * *

(b) The court may extend the terms of an existing order or, if an order is no longer in effect, grant a new order upon a showing that:

(1) the respondent has violated a prior or existing order for protection;

(2) the petitioner is reasonably in fear of physical harm from the respondent;

(3) the respondent has engaged in acts of harassment or stalking within the meaning of section 609.749, subdivision 2; or

(4) the respondent is incarcerated and about to be released, or has recently been released from incarceration.

A petitioner does not need to show that physical harm is imminent to obtain an extension or a subsequent order under this subdivision.

(c) Relief granted by the order for protection may be for a period of up to 50 years, if the court finds:

(1) the respondent has violated a prior or existing order for protection on two or more occasions; or

(2) the petitioner has had two or more orders for protection in effect against the same respondent.

An order issued under this paragraph may restrain the abusing party from committing acts of domestic abuse; or prohibit the abusing party from having any contact with the petitioner, whether in person, by telephone, mail or electronic mail or messaging, through electronic devices, through a third party, or by any other means.

Subd. 7. **Ex parte order.** (a) Where an application under this section alleges an immediate and present danger of domestic abuse, the court may grant an ex parte order for protection and granting relief as the court deems proper, including an order:

(1) restraining the abusing party from committing acts of domestic abuse;

(2) excluding any party from the dwelling they share or from the residence of the other, including a reasonable area surrounding the dwelling or residence, which area shall be described specifically in the order, except by further order of the court;

(3) excluding the abusing party from the place of employment of the petitioner or otherwise limiting access to the petitioner by the abusing party at the petitioner's place of employment;

(4) order the abusing party to have no contact with the petitioner whether in person, by telephone, mail, e-mail, through electronic devices, or through a third party;

(5) continuing all currently available insurance coverage without change in coverage or beneficiary designation;

(6) directing the care, possession, or control of a pet or companion animal owned, possessed, or kept by a party or a child of a party; and

(7) directing the respondent to refrain from physically abusing or injuring any pet or companion animal, without legal justification, known to be owned, possessed, kept, or held by either party or a minor child residing in the residence or household of either party as an indirect means of intentionally threatening the safety of such person.

(b) A finding by the court that there is a basis for issuing an ex parte order for protection constitutes a finding that sufficient reasons exist not to require notice under applicable court rules governing applications for ex parte relief.

(c) Subject to paragraph (d), an ex parte order for protection shall be effective for a fixed period set by the court, as provided in subdivision 6, paragraph (b), or until modified or vacated by the court pursuant to a hearing. When signed by a referee, the ex parte order becomes effective upon the referee's signature. Upon request, a hearing, as provided by this section, shall be set. Except as provided in paragraph (d), the respondent shall be personally served forthwith a copy of the ex parte order along with a copy of the petition and, if requested by the petitioner, notice of the date set for the hearing. If the petitioner does not request a hearing, an order served on a respondent under this subdivision must include a notice advising the respondent of the right to request a hearing, must be accompanied by a form that can be used by the respondent to request a hearing and must include a conspicuous notice that a hearing will not be held unless requested by the respondent within five days of service of the order.

(d) Service of the ex parte order may be made by published notice, as provided under subdivision 5, provided that the petitioner files the affidavit required under that subdivision. If personal service is not made or the affidavit is not filed within 14 days of issuance of the ex parte order, the order expires. If the petitioner does not request a hearing, the petition mailed to the respondent's residence, if known, must be accompanied by the form for requesting a hearing and notice described in paragraph (c). Unless personal service is completed, if service by published notice is not completed within 28 days of issuance of the ex parte order, the order expires.

(e) If the petitioner seeks relief under subdivision 6 other than the relief described in paragraph (a), the petitioner must request a hearing to obtain the additional relief.

(f) Nothing in this subdivision affects the right of a party to seek modification of an order under subdivision 11.

Subd. 8. **Service; alternate service; publication; notice.** (a) The petition and any order issued under this section other than orders for dismissal shall be served on the respondent personally. Orders for dismissal may be served personally or by certified mail. In lieu of personal service of an order for protection, a law enforcement officer may serve a person with a short form notification as provided in subdivision 8a.

(b) When service is made out of this state and in the United States, it may be proved by the affidavit of the person making the service. When service is made outside the United States, it may be proved by the affidavit of the person making the service. taken before and certified by any United States minister, charge d'affaires, commissioner, consul, or commercial agent, or other consular or diplomatic officer of the United States appointed to reside in the other country, including all deputies or other representatives of the officer authorized to perform their duties; or before an office authorized to administer an oath with the certificate of an officer of a court of record of the country in which the affidavit is taken as to the identity and authority of the officer taking the affidavit.

(c) If personal service cannot be made, the court may order service of the petition and any order issued under this section by alternate means, or by publication, which publication must be made as in other actions. The application for alternate service must include the last known location of the respondent; the petitioner's most recent contacts with the respondent; the last known location of the respondent's employment; the names and location of the respondent's parents, siblings, children, and other close relatives; the names and locations of other persons who are likely to know the respondent's whereabouts; and a description of efforts to locate those persons.

The court shall consider the length of time the respondent's location has been unknown, the likelihood that the respondent's location will become known, the nature of the relief sought, and the nature of efforts made to locate the respondent. The court shall order service by first class mail, forwarding address requested, to any addresses where there is a reasonable possibility that mail or information will be forwarded or communicated to the respondent.

The court may also order publication, within or without the state, but only if it might reasonably succeed in notifying the respondent of the proceeding. Service shall be deemed complete 14 days after mailing or 14 days after court-ordered publication.

(d) A petition and any order issued under this section, including the short form notification, must include a notice to the respondent that if an order for protection is issued to protect the petitioner or a child of the parties, upon request of the petitioner in any parenting time proceeding, the court shall consider the order for protection in making a decision regarding parenting time.

Subd. 8a. **Short form notification.** (a) In lieu of personal service of an order for protection under subdivision 8, a law enforcement officer may serve a person with a short form notification. The short form notification must include the following clauses: the respondent's name; the respondent's date of birth, if known; the petitioner's name; the names of other protected parties; the date and county in which the ex parte order for protection or order for protection was filed; the court file number; the hearing date and time, if known; the conditions that apply to the respondent, either in checklist form or handwritten; and the name of the judge who signed the order.

The short form notification must be in bold print in the following form:

The order for protection is now enforceable. You must report to your nearest sheriff office or county court to obtain a copy of the order for protection. You are subject to arrest and may be charged with a misdemeanor, gross misdemeanor, or felony if you violate any of the terms of the order for protection or this short form notification.

(b) Upon verification of the identity of the respondent and the existence of an unserved order for protection against the respondent, a law enforcement officer may detain the respondent for a reasonable time necessary to complete and serve the short form notification.

(c) When service is made by short form notification, it may be proved by the affidavit of the law enforcement officer making the service.

(d) For service under this section only, service upon an individual may occur at any time, including Sundays, and legal holidays.

(e) The superintendent of the bureau of criminal apprehension shall provide the short form to law enforcement agencies.

Subd. 9. **Assistance of sheriff in service or execution.** When an order is issued under this section upon request of the petitioner, the court shall order the sheriff to accompany the petitioner and assist in placing the petitioner in possession of the dwelling or residence, or otherwise assist in execution or service of the order of protection. If the application for relief is brought in a county in which the respondent is not present, the sheriff shall forward the pleadings necessary for service upon the respondent to the sheriff of the county in which the respondent is present. This transmittal must be expedited to allow for timely service.

Subd. 9a. **Service by others.** Peace officers licensed by the state of Minnesota and corrections officers, including, but not limited to, probation officers, court services officers, parole officers, and employees of jails or correctional facilities, may serve an order for protection.

Subd. 10. **Right to apply for relief.** (a) A person's right to apply for relief shall not be affected by the person's leaving the residence or household to avoid abuse.

(b) The court shall not require security or bond of any party unless it deems necessary in exceptional cases.

Subd. 11. **Modification of order.** (a) Upon application, notice to all parties, and hearing, the court may modify the terms of an existing order for protection.

(b) If the court orders relief under subdivision 6a, paragraph (c), the respondent named in the order for protection may request to have the order vacated or modified if the order has been in effect for at least five years and the respondent has not violated the order during that time. * * * [T]he respondent named in the order for protection has the burden of proving by a preponderance of the evidence that there has been a material change in circumstances and that the reasons upon which the court relied in granting or extending the order for protection no longer apply and are unlikely to occur. If the court finds that the respondent named in the order for protection has met the burden of proof, the court may vacate or modify the order. If the court finds that the respondent named in the order for protection has not met the burden of proof, the court shall deny the request and no request may be made to vacate or modify the order for protection until five years have elapsed from the date of denial. * * *

Subd. 12. **Real estate.** Nothing in this section shall affect the title to real estate.

Subd. 13. **Copy to law enforcement agency.** (a) An order for protection and any continuance of an order for protection granted pursuant to this section shall be forwarded by the court administrator within 24 hours to the local law enforcement agency with jurisdiction over the residence of the applicant.

Each appropriate law enforcement agency shall make available to other law enforcement officers through a system for verification, information as to the existence and status of any order for protection issued pursuant to this section.

(b) If the applicant notifies the court administrator of change in the applicant's residence so that a different local law enforcement agency has jurisdiction over the residence, the order for protection and any continuance of an order for protection must be forwarded by the court administrator to the new law enforcement agency within 24 hours of the notice. If the applicant notifies the new law enforcement agency that an order for protection has been issued under this section and the applicant has established a new residence within that agency's jurisdiction, within 24 hours the local law enforcement agency shall request a copy of the order for protection from the court administrator in the county that issued the order.

(c) When an order for protection is granted, the applicant for an order for protection must be told by the court that:

(1) notification of a change in residence should be given immediately to the court administrator and to the local law enforcement agency having jurisdiction over the new residence of the applicant;

(2) the reason for notification of a change in residence is to forward an order for protection to the proper law enforcement agency; and

(3) the order for protection must be forwarded to the law enforcement agency having jurisdiction over the new residence within 24 hours of notification of a change in residence, whether notification is given to the court administrator or to the local law enforcement agency having jurisdiction over the applicant's new residence.

An order for protection is enforceable even if the applicant does not notify the court administrator or the appropriate law enforcement agency of a change in residence.

Subd. 14. **Violation of an order for protection.** (a) A person who violates an order for protection issued by a judge or referee is subject to the penalties provided in paragraphs (b) and (d).

(b) Except as otherwise provided in paragraphs (c) and (d), whenever an order for protection is granted by a judge or referee or pursuant to a similar law of another state, the United States, the District of Columbia, tribal lands, or United States territories, Canada, or a Canadian province, and the respondent or person to be restrained knows of the existence of the order, violation of the order for protection is a misdemeanor. Upon a misdemeanor conviction under this paragraph, the defendant must be sentenced to a minimum of three days imprisonment and must be ordered to participate in counseling or other appropriate programs selected by the court. If the court stays imposition or execution of the jail sentence and the defendant refuses or fails to comply with the count's treatment order, the court must impose and execute the stayed jail sentence. A violation of an order for protection shall also constitute contempt of court and be subject to the penalties provided in chapter 588.

(c) A person is guilty of a gross misdemeanor who violates this subdivision within ten years of a previous qualified domestic violence-related offense conviction or adjudication of delinquency. Upon a gross misdemeanor conviction under this paragraph, the defendant must be sentenced to a minimum of ten days imprisonment and must be ordered to participate in counseling or other appropriate programs selected by the court. Notwithstanding section 609.135, the court must impose and execute the minimum sentence provided in this paragraph for gross misdemeanor convictions.

(d) A person is guilty of a felony and may be sentenced to imprisonment for not more than five years or to payment of a fine of not more than $10,000, or both, if the person violates this subdivision:

(1) within ten years of the first of two or more previous qualified domestic violence-related offense convictions or adjudications of delinquency; or

(2) while possessing a dangerous weapon, as defined in section 609.02, subdivision 6. Upon a felony conviction under this paragraph in which the court stays imposition or execution of sentence, the court shall impose at least a 30-day period of incarceration as a condition of probation. The court also shall order that the defendant participates in counseling or other appropriate programs selected by the court. Notwithstanding section 609.135, the court must impose and execute the minimum sentence provided in this paragraph for felony convictions.

(e) A peace officer shall arrest without a warrant and take into custody a person whom the peace officer has probable cause to believe has violated an order granted pursuant to this section or a similar law of another state, the United States, the District of Columbia, tribal lands, or United States territories restraining the person or excluding the person from the residence or the petitioner's place of employment, even if the violation of the order did not take place in the presence of the peace officer, if the existence of the order can be verified by the officer. The probable cause required under this paragraph includes probable cause that the person knows of the existence of the order. If the order has not been served, the officer shall immediately serve the order whenever reasonably safe and possible to do so. An order for purposes of this subdivision, includes the short form order described in subdivision 8a. When the order is first served upon the person at a location at which, under the terms of the order, the person's presence constitutes a violation, the person shall not be arrested for violation of the order without first being given a reasonable opportunity to leave the location in the presence of the peace officer. A person arrested under this paragraph shall be held in custody for at least 36 hours, excluding the day of arrest, Sundays, and holidays, unless the person is released earlier by a judge or judicial officer. A peace officer acting in good faith and exercising due care in making an arrest pursuant to this paragraph is immune from civil liability that might result from the officer's actions.

(f) If the court finds that the respondent has violated an order for protection and that there is reason to believe that the respondent will commit a further violation of the provisions of the order restraining the respondent from committing acts of domestic abuse or excluding the respondent from the petitioner's residence, the court may require the respondent to acknowledge an obligation to comply with the order on the record. The court may require a bond sufficient to deter the respondent from committing further violations of the order for protection, considering the financial resources of the respondent, and not to exceed $10,000. If the respondent refuses to comply with an order to acknowledge the obligation or post a bond under this paragraph, the court shall commit the respondent to the county jail during the term of the order for protection or until the respondent complies with the order under this paragraph. The warrant must state the cause of commitment, with the sum and time for which any bond is required. If an order is issued under this paragraph, the court may order the costs of the contempt action, or any part of them, to be paid by the respondent. An order under this paragraph is appealable.

(g) Upon the filing of an affidavit by the petitioner, any peace officer, or an interested party designated by the court, alleging that the respondent has violated any order for protection granted pursuant to this section or a similar law of another state, the United States, the District of Columbia, tribal lands, or united States territories, the court may issue an order to the respondent, requiring the respondent to appear and show cause within 14 days why the respondent should not be found in contempt of court and punished therefor. The hearing may be held by the court in any county in which the petitioner or respondent temporarily or permanently resides at the time of the alleged violation, or in the county in which the alleged violation occurred, if the petitioner and respondent do not reside in this state. The court also shall refer the violation of the order for protection to the appropriate prosecuting authority for possible prosecution under paragraph (b), (c), or (d).

(h) If it is alleged that the respondent has violated an order for protection issued under subdivision 6 or a similar law of another state, the United States, the District of Columbia, tribal lands, or United States territories, and the court finds that the order has expired between the time of the alleged violation and the court's hearing on the violation, the court may grant a new order for protection under subdivision 6 based solely on the respondent's alleged violation of the prior order, to be effective until the hearing on the alleged violation of the prior order. If the court finds that the respondent has violated the prior order, the relief granted in the new order for protection shall be extended for a fixed period, not to exceed one year, except when the court determines a longer fixed period is appropriate.

(i) The admittance into petitioner's dwelling of an abusing party excluded from the dwelling under an order for protection is not a violation by the petitioner of the order for protection.

A peace officer is not liable under section 609.43, clause (1), for a failure to perform a duty required by paragraph (c).

(j) When a person is convicted under paragraph (a) of violating an order for protection under this section and the court determines that the person used a firearm in any way during commission of the violation, the court may order that the person is prohibited from possessing any type of firearm for any period longer than three years or for the remainder of the person's life. A person who violates this paragraph is guilty of a gross misdemeanor. At the time of the conviction, the court shall inform the defendant whether and for how long the defendant is prohibited from possessing a firearm and that it is a gross misdemeanor to violate this paragraph. The failure of the court to provide this information to a defendant does not affect the applicability of the firearm possession prohibition or the gross misdemeanor penalty to that defendant.

(k) Except as otherwise provided in paragraph (j), when a person is convicted under paragraph (a) of violating an order for protection under this section, the court shall inform the defendant that the defendant is prohibited from possessing a pistol for three years from the date of conviction and that it is a gross misdemeanor offense to violate this prohibition. The failure of the court to provide this information to a defendant does not affect the applicability of the pistol possession prohibition or the gross misdemeanor penalty to that defendant.

(l) Except as otherwise provided in paragraph (j), a person is not entitled to possess a pistol if the person has been convicted under paragraph (a) after August 1, 1996, of violating an order for protection under this section, unless three years have elapsed from the date of conviction and, during that time, the person has not been convicted of any other violation of this section. Property rights may not be abated but access may be restricted by the courts. A person who possesses a pistol in violation of this paragraph is guilty of a gross misdemeanor.

(m) If the court determines that a person convicted under paragraph (a) of violating an order for protection own or possesses a firearm and used it in any way during the commission of the violation, it shall order that the firearm be summarily forfeited under section 609.5316, subdivision 3.

Subd. 14a. **Venue.** A person may be prosecuted under subdivision 14 at the place where any call is made or received or, in the case of wireless or electronic communication or any communication made through any available technologies, where the actor or victim resides, or in the jurisdiction of the victim's designated address if the victim participates in the address confidentiality program established under chapter 5B.

Subd. 15. **Admissibility of testimony in criminal proceeding.** Any testimony offered by a respondent in a hearing pursuant to this section is inadmissible in a criminal proceeding.

Subd. 16. **Other remedies available.** Any proceeding under this section shall be in addition to other civil or criminal remedies.

Subd. 17. **Effect on custody proceedings.** In a subsequent custody proceeding the court must consider a finding in a proceeding under this chapter or under a similar law of another state that domestic abuse has occurred between the parties.

Subd. 18. **Notices.** (a) Each order for protection granted under this chapter must contain a conspicuous notice to the respondent or person to be restrained that:

(1) violation of an order for protection is either (i) a misdemeanor punishable by imprisonment for up to 90 days or a fine of up $1,000, or both, (ii) a gross misdemeanor punishable by imprisonment of up to one year or a fine of up to $3,000, or both, or (iii) a felony punishable by imprisonment of up to five years or a fine of up to $10,000, or both;

(2) the respondent is forbidden to enter or stay at the petitioner's residence, even if invited to do so by the petitioner or any other person; in no event is the order for protection voided; and

(3) a peace officer must arrest without warrant and take into custody a person whom the peace officer has probable cause to believe has violated an order for protection restraining the person or excluding the person from a residence; and

(4) pursuant to the Violence Against Women Act of 1994, United States Code, title 18, section 2265, the order is enforceable in all 50 states, the District of Columbia, tribal lands, and United States territories, that violation of the order may also subject the respondent to federal charges and punishment under United States Code, title 18, sections 2261 and 2262, and that if a final order is entered against the respondent after the hearing, the respondent may be prohibited from possessing, transporting, or accepting a firearm under the 1994 amendment of the Gun Control Act, United States Code, title 18, section 922(g)(8).

(b) If the court grants relief under subdivision 6a, paragraph (c), the order for protection must also contain a conspicuous notice to the respondent or person to be restrained that the respondent must wait five years to seek a modification of the order.

Subd. 19. **Recording required.** Proceedings under this section must be recorded.

Subd. 19a. **Entry and enforcement of foreign protective orders.** (a) As used in this subdivision, "foreign protective order" means an order for protection entered by a court of another state; an order by an Indian tribe or United States territory that would be a protective order entered under this chapter; a Canadian order for protection as defined in section 518F.02; a temporary or permanent order or protective order to exclude a respondent from a dwelling; or an order that establishes conditions of release or is a protective order or sentencing order in a criminal prosecution arising from a domestic abuse assault if it had been entered in Minnesota.

(b) A person for whom a foreign protection order has been issued or the issuing court or tribunal may provide a certified or authenticated copy of a foreign protective order to the court administrator in any county that would have venue if the original action was being commenced in this state or in which the person in whose favor the order was entered may be present, for filing and entering of the same into the state order for protection database.

(c) The court administrator shall file and enter foreign protective orders that are not certified or authenticated, if supported by an affidavit of a person with personal knowledge, subject to the penalties for perjury. The person protected by the order may provide this affidavit.

(d) The court administrator shall provide copies of the order as required by this section.

(e) A valid foreign protective order has the same effect and shall be enforced in the same manner as an order for protection issued in this state whether or not filed with a court administrator or otherwise entered in the state order for protection database.
* * *

(h) A peace officer shall treat a foreign protective order as a valid legal document and shall make an arrest for a violation of the foreign protective order in the same manner that a peace officer would make an arrest for a violation of a protective order issued within this state.

(i) The fact that foreign protective order has not been filed with the court administrator or otherwise entered into the state order for protection database shall not be grounds to refuse to enforce the terms of the order unless it is apparent to the officer that the order is invalid on its face.

(j) A peace officer acting reasonably and in good faith in connection with the enforcement of a foreign protective order is immune from civil and criminal liability in any action arising in connection the enforcement. * * *

Subd. 20. **Statewide application.** An order for protection granted under this section applies throughout this state.

Subd. 21. **Order for protection forms.** The state court administrator, in consultation with city and county attorneys, and legal advocates who work with victims, shall update the uniform order for protection form that facilitates the consistent enforcement of orders for protection throughout the state.

Subd. 22. Repealed, 2010 c 299 s 15

Subd. 23. **Prohibition against employer retaliation.** (a) An employer shall not discharge, discipline, threaten, otherwise discriminate against, or penalize an employee regarding the employee's compensation, terms, conditions, location, or privileges of employment, because the employee took reasonable time off from work to obtain or attempt to obtain relief under this chapter. * * * Upon request of the employer, the employee shall provide verification that supports the employee's reason for being absent from the workplace. All information related to the employee's leave pursuant to this section shall be kept confidential by the employer.

(b) An employer who violates paragraph (a) is guilty of a misdemeanor and may be punished for contempt of court. In addition, the court shall order the employer to pay back wages and offer job reinstatement to any employee discharged from employment in violation of paragraph (a).

HIST: 1979 c 214 s 1; * * * 2015 c 21 art 1 s 95; 2016 c 141 s 1-3; 2016 c 176 s 1; 2021 c 6 art 2, s 1-2

Editors' Note: Although the following statute is not specifically described in this performance objective, it has been included because it outlines the requirements of domestic abuse counseling and educational programming where an offender is placed on probation and as a condition of a stayed sentence, is ordered to successfully complete such programming. This statute also includes a number of victim-related protections and notices that law enforcement officers might wish to be aware of.

518B.02 DOMESTIC ABUSE COUNSELING PROGRAM OR EDUCATIONAL PROGRAM REQUIRED.

Subdivision 1. **Court-ordered domestic abuse counseling program or educational program.** If the court stays imposition or execution of a sentence for a domestic abuse offense and places the offender on probation, the court shall order that, as a condition of the stayed sentence, the offender participate in and successfully complete a domestic abuse counseling program or educational program.

Subd. 2. **Standards for domestic abuse counseling programs and domestic abuse educational programs.** (a) Domestic abuse counseling or educational programs that provide group or class sessions for court-ordered domestic abuse offenders must provide documentation to the probation department or the court on program policies and how the program meets the criteria contained in paragraphs (b) to (l).

(b) Programs shall require offenders and abusing parties to attend a minimum of 24 sessions or 36 hours of programming, unless a probation agent has recommended fewer sessions. The documentation provided to the probation department or the court must specify the length of the program that offenders are required to complete.

(c) Programs must have a written policy requiring that counselors and facilitators report to the court and to the offender's probation or corrections officer any threats of violence made by the offender or abusing party, acts of violence by the offender or abusing party, violation of court orders by the offender or abusing party, and violation of program rules that resulted in the offender's or abusing party's termination from the program. Programs shall have written policies requiring that counselors and facilitators hold offenders and abusing parties solely responsible for their behavior.

Programs shall have written policies requiring that counselors and facilitators be violence free in their own lives.

(d) * * * If the offender or abusing party poses a risk to self or others, the program shall report this information to the court, the probation or corrections officer, and the victim.

(e) If the offender or abusing party is reported back to the court or is terminated from the program, the program shall notify the victim of the circumstances unless the victim requests otherwise.

* * *

(g) If a counselor or facilitator contacts the victim, the counselor or facilitator must not elicit any information that the victim does not want to provide. A counselor or facilitator who contacts a victim shall (1) notify the victim of the right not to provide any information, (2) notify the victim of how any information provided will be used and with whom it will be shared, and (3) obtain the victim's permission before eliciting information from the victim or sharing information with anyone other than staff of the counseling program.

Programs shall have written policies requiring that counselors and facilitators inform victims of the confidentiality of information as provided by this subdivision. Programs must maintain separate files for information pertaining to the offender or abusing party and to the victim.

If a counselor or facilitator contacts a victim, the counselor or facilitator shall provide the victim with referral information for support services.

(h) Programs shall have written policies forbidding program staff from disclosing any confidential communication made by the offender or abusing party without the consent of the offender or abusing party, except that programs must warn a potential victim of imminent danger based upon information provided by an offender or abusing party.

* * *

(j) Programs shall have written policies forbidding program staff from offering or referring marriage or couples counseling until the offender or abusing party has completed a domestic abuse counseling program or educational program for the minimum number of court-ordered sessions and the counselor or facilitator reasonably believes that the violence, intimidation, and coercion has ceased and the victim feels safe to participate.

* * *

(l) Programs must have written policies to coordinate with the court, probation and corrections officers, battered women's and domestic abuse programs, child protection services, and other providers on promotion of victim safety and offender accountability.

Subd. 3. **Program accountability.** The Office of Justice Programs in the Department of Public Safety will consult with domestic abuse counseling and educational programs, the court, probation departments, and the interagency task force on the prevention of domestic and sexual

abuse on acceptable measures to ensure program accountability. By December 30, 2001, the center shall make recommendations to the house and senate committees and divisions with jurisdiction over criminal justice policy and funding on agreed upon accountability measures including outcome studies.
HIST: 1Sp2001 c 8 art 10 s 6; 2013 c 125 art 1 s 82

518F.02 DEFINITIONS
 Subdivision 1. **Terms.** For the purposes of this chapter, the following terms have the meanings given them.
 Subd. 2. Canadian order for protection. "Canadian order for protection" means a civil protection order, judgment or part of a judgment, or other order issued in a civil proceeding by a court of Canada under law of the issuing jurisdiction that relates to domestic abuse, would be a protective order under this chapter, and prohibits a respondent from:
 (1) committing acts of domestic abuse;
 (2) being in physical proximity to a protected individual or following a protected individual;
 (3) having contact with the petitioner whether in person, by telephone, mail, or e-mail or messaging, through a third party, or by any other means;
 (4) being within a certain distance of a specified place or location associated with a protected individual; or
 (5) molesting, annoying, harassing, or engaging in threatening conduct directed at a protected individual.
 Subd. 3. Domestic abuse. "Domestic abuse" has the meaning given in section 518B.01, subdivision 2, paragraph (a).
 Subd. 4. Issuing court. "Issuing court" means the court that issues a Canadian order for protection.
 Subd. 5. Order for protection. "Order for protection" means an order issued under section 518B.01.
 Subd. 6. Peace officer. "Peace officer" has the meaning given in section 626.84, subdivision 1, paragraph (c).
 Subd. 7. Person. "Person" means an individual, estate, business or nonprofit entity, public corporation, government or governmental subdivision, agency, or instrumentality, or other legal entity.
 Subd. 8. Protected individual. "Protected individual" means an individual protected by a Canadian order for protection.
 Subd. 9. Record. "Record" means information that is inscribed on a tangible medium or that is stored in an electronic or other medium and is retrievable in perceivable form.
 Subd. 10. Respondent. "Respondent" means an individual against whom a Canadian order for protection is issued.

518F.03 ENFORCEMENT OF CANADIAN ORDERS FOR PROTECTION BY PEACE OFFICER
 (a) If a peace officer determines under paragraph (b) or (c) that there is probable cause to believe that a valid Canadian order for protection exists and that the order has been violated, the officer shall enforce the terms of the Canadian order for protection as if the terms were in an order issued by a court in this state. Presentation to a peace officer of a certified copy of a Canadian order for protection is not required for enforcement. A peace officer who has probable cause to believe that an order exists and has been violated shall make an arrest for a violation of the order in the same manner that a peace officer would make an arrest for a violation of a protective order issued within this state.
 (b) Presentation to a peace officer of a record of a Canadian order for protection that identifies both a protected individual and a respondent and on its face is in effect constitutes probable cause to believe that a valid order exists.

(c) If a record of a Canadian order for protection is not presented as provided in paragraph (b), a peace officer may consider other information in determining whether there is probable cause to believe that a valid Canadian order for protection exists.

(d) If a peace officer determines that an otherwise valid Canadian order for protection cannot be enforced because the respondent has not been notified of or served with the order, the officer shall notify the protected individual that the officer will make reasonable efforts to contact the respondent, consistent with the safety of the protected individual. After notice to the protected individual and consistent with the safety of the individual, the officer shall make a reasonable effort to inform the respondent of the order, notify the respondent of the terms of the order, provide a record of the order, if available, to the respondent, and allow the respondent a reasonable opportunity to comply with the order before the officer enforces the order. The provisions of section 518B.01, subdivisions 8 and 9a, apply to service of a Canadian order for protection by a peace officer.

(e) If a peace officer determines that an individual is a protected individual, the officer shall inform the individual of available local victim services.

518F.06 IMMUNITY.

The state, state agency, local governmental agency, peace officer, prosecuting attorney, court administrator, and state or local governmental official acting in an official capacity are immune from civil and criminal liability for an act or omission arising out of the registration or enforcement of a Canadian order for protection or the detention or arrest of an alleged violator of a Canadian order for protection if the act or omission was a good faith effort to comply with this chapter.

HIST: 2021 c 6 art 1 s 1-6

609.2242 DOMESTIC ASSAULT.

Subdivision 1. **Misdemeanor.** Whoever does any of the following against a family or household member as defined in section 518B.01, subdivision 2, commits an assault and is guilty of a misdemeanor:

(1) commits an act with intent to cause fear in another of immediate bodily harm or death; or

(2) intentionally inflicts or attempts to inflict bodily harm upon another.

Subd. 2. **Gross misdemeanor.** Whoever violates subdivision 1 within ten years of a previous qualified domestic violence-related offense conviction or an adjudication of delinquency is guilty of a gross misdemeanor and may be sentenced to imprisonment for not more than one year or to payment of a fine of not more than $3,000, or both.

§Subd. 3.Domestic assaults; firearms. (a) When a person is convicted of a violation of this section or section 609.221, 609.222, 609.223, 609.224, or 609.2247, the court shall determine and make written findings on the record as to whether:

(1) the assault was committed against a family or household member, as defined in section 518B.01, subdivision 2;

(2) the defendant owns or possesses a firearm; and

(3) the firearm was used in any way during the commission of the assault.

(b) If the court determines that the assault was of a family or household member, and that the offender owns or possesses a firearm and used it in any way during the commission of the assault, it shall order that the firearm be summarily forfeited under section 609.5316, subdivision 3.

(c) When a person is convicted of assaulting a family or household member and is determined by the court to have used a firearm in any way during commission of the assault, the court may order that the person is prohibited from possessing any type of firearm for any period longer than three years or for the remainder of the person's life. A person who violates this paragraph is guilty of a gross misdemeanor. At the time of the conviction, the court shall inform the defendant for how long the defendant is prohibited from possessing a firearm and that it is a gross misdemeanor to violate this paragraph. The failure of the court to provide this information to a defendant does not affect the applicability of the firearm possession prohibition or the gross misdemeanor penalty to that defendant.

(d) Except as otherwise provided in paragraph (c), when a person is convicted of a violation of this section or section 609.224 and the court determines that the victim was a family or household member, the court shall inform the defendant that the defendant is prohibited from possessing a firearm for three years from the date of conviction and that it is a gross misdemeanor offense to violate this prohibition. The failure of the court to provide this information to a defendant does not affect the applicability of the firearm possession prohibition or the gross misdemeanor penalty to that defendant.

(e) Except as otherwise provided in paragraph (c), a person is not entitled to possess a pistol if the person has been convicted after August 1, 1992, or a firearm if a person has been convicted on or after August 1, 2014, of domestic assault under this section or assault in the fifth degree under section 609.224 and the assault victim was a family or household member as defined in section 518B.01, subdivision 2, unless three years have elapsed from the date of conviction and, during that time, the person has not been convicted of any other violation of this section or section 609.224. Property rights may not be abated but access may be restricted by the courts. A person who possesses a firearm in violation of this paragraph is guilty of a gross misdemeanor.

(f) Except as otherwise provided in paragraphs (b) and (h), when a person is convicted of a violation of this section or section 609.221, 609.222, 609.223, 609.224, or 609.2247 and the court determines that the assault was against a family or household member, the court shall order the defendant to transfer any firearms that the person possesses, within three business days, to a federally licensed firearms dealer, a law enforcement agency, or a third party who may lawfully receive them. The transfer may be permanent or temporary, unless the court prohibits the person from possessing a firearm for the remainder of the person's life under paragraph (c). A temporary firearm transfer only entitles the receiving party to possess the firearm. A temporary transfer does not transfer ownership or title. A defendant may not transfer firearms to a third party who resides with the defendant. If a defendant makes a temporary transfer, a federally licensed firearms dealer or law enforcement agency may charge the defendant a reasonable fee to store the person's firearms and may establish policies for disposal of abandoned firearms, provided such policies require that the person be notified by certified mail prior to disposal of abandoned firearms. For temporary firearms transfers under this paragraph, a law enforcement agency, federally licensed firearms dealer, or third party shall exercise due care to preserve the quality and function of the transferred firearms and shall return the transferred firearms to the person upon request after the expiration of the prohibiting time period imposed under this subdivision, provided the person is not otherwise prohibited from possessing firearms under state or federal law. The return of temporarily transferred firearms to a person shall comply with state and federal law. If a defendant permanently transfers the defendant's firearms to a law enforcement agency, the agency is not required to compensate the defendant and may charge the defendant a reasonable processing fee. A law enforcement agency is not required to accept a person's firearm under this paragraph. The court shall order that the person surrender all permits to carry and purchase firearms to the sheriff.

(g) A defendant who is ordered to transfer firearms under paragraph (f) must file proof of transfer as provided for in this paragraph. If the transfer is made to a third party, the third party must sign an affidavit under oath before a notary public either acknowledging that the defendant permanently transferred the defendant's firearms to the third party or agreeing to temporarily store the defendant's firearms until such time as the defendant is legally permitted to possess firearms. The affidavit shall indicate the serial number, make, and model of all firearms transferred by the defendant to the third party. The third party shall acknowledge in the affidavit that the third party may be held criminally and civilly responsible under section 624.7144 if the defendant gains access to a transferred firearm while the firearm is in the custody of the third party. If the transfer is to a law enforcement agency or federally licensed firearms dealer, the law enforcement agency or federally licensed firearms dealer shall provide proof of transfer to the defendant. The proof of transfer must specify whether the firearms were permanently or temporarily transferred and include the name of the defendant, date of transfer, and the serial number, make, and model of all transferred firearms. The defendant shall provide the court with a signed and notarized affidavit or proof of transfer as described in this section within two business days of the firearms transfer. The court shall seal affidavits and proofs of transfer filed pursuant to this paragraph.

(h) When a person is convicted of a violation of this section or section 609.221, 609.222, 609.223, 609.224, or 609.2247, and the court determines that the assault was against a family or household member, the court shall determine by a preponderance of the evidence if the person poses an imminent risk of causing another person substantial bodily harm. Upon a finding of imminent risk, the court shall order that the local law enforcement agency take immediate possession of all firearms in the person's possession. The local law enforcement agency shall exercise due care to preserve the quality and function of the defendant's firearms and shall return the firearms to the person upon request after the expiration of the prohibiting time period, provided the person is not otherwise prohibited from possessing firearms under state or federal law. The local law enforcement agency shall, upon written notice from the person, transfer the firearms to a federally licensed firearms dealer or a third party who may lawfully receive them. Before a local law enforcement agency transfers a firearm under this paragraph, the agency shall require the third party or federally licensed firearms dealer receiving the firearm to submit an affidavit or proof of transfer that complies with the requirements for affidavits or proofs of transfer established in paragraph (g). The agency shall file all affidavits or proofs of transfer received with the court within two business days of the transfer. The court shall seal all affidavits or proofs of transfer filed pursuant to this paragraph. A federally licensed firearms dealer or third party who accepts a firearm transfer pursuant to this paragraph shall comply with paragraphs (f) and (g) as if accepting transfer from the defendant. If the law enforcement agency does not receive written notice from the defendant within three business days, the agency may charge a reasonable fee to store the defendant's firearms. A law enforcement agency may establish policies for disposal of abandoned firearms, provided such policies require that the person be notified via certified mail prior to disposal of abandoned firearms.

Subd. 4. **Felony.** Whoever violates the provisions of this section or section 609.224, subdivision 1, within ten years of the first of any combination of two or more previous qualified domestic violence-related offense convictions or adjudications of delinquency is guilty of a felony and may be sentenced to imprisonment for not more than five years or payment of a fine of not more than $10,000, or both.

HIST: 1995 c 259 art 3 s 15; 2000 c 437 s 8,9; 1Sp2001 c 8 art 10 s 10,11; 2005 c 136 art 17 s 12; 2006 c 260 art 1 s 18,19; 2013 c 47 s 3; 2014 c 213 s 3

609.2247 DOMESTIC ASSAULT BY STRANGULATION.

Subdivision 1. **Definitions.** (a) As used in this section, the following terms have the meanings given.

(b) "Family or household members" has the meaning given in section 518B.01, subdivision 2.

(c) "Strangulation" means intentionally impeding normal breathing or circulation of the blood by applying pressure on the throat or neck or by blocking the nose or mouth of another person.

Subd. 2. **Crime.** Unless a greater penalty is provided elsewhere, whoever assaults a family or household member by strangulation is guilty of a felony and may be sentenced to imprisonment for not more than three years or to payment of a fine of not more than $5,000, or both.

HIST: 2005 c 136 art 17 s 13

609.749 HARASSMENT; STALKING; PENALTIES.

Subdivision 1. Repealed, 2020 c 96 s 6

Subd. 1a. Repealed, 2020 c 96 s 6

* * *

Subd. 1c. **Arrest.** For all violations under this section, except a violation of subdivision 2, clause (7), a peace officer may make an arrest under the provisions of section 629.34. A peace officer may not make a warrantless, custodial arrest of any person for a violation of subdivision 2, clause (7).

Subd. 2. **Harassment crimes.** (a) As used in this subdivision, the following terms have the meanings given:

(1) "family or household members" has the meaning given in section 518B.01, subdivision 2, paragraph (b);

(2) "personal information" has the meaning given in section 617.261, subdivision 7, paragraph (f);

(3) "sexual act" has the meaning given in section 617, subdivision 7, paragraph (g); and

(4) "substantial emotional distress" means mental distress, mental suffering, or mental anguish as demonstrated by a victim's response to an act including but not limited to seeking psychotherapy as defined in section 604.20, losing sleep or appetite, being diagnosed with a mental-health condition, experiencing suicidal ideation, or having difficulty concentrating on tasks resulting in lack of productivity.

(b) A person who harasses another by committing commits any of the following acts listed in paragraph (c) is guilty of a gross misdemeanor if the person, with the intent to kill, injure, harass, or intimidate another person:

(1) places the other person in reasonable fear of substantial bodily harm;

(2) places the person in reasonable fear that the person's family or household members will be subject to substantial bodily harm; or

(3) causes or would reasonably be expected to cause substantial emotional distress to the other person:

(c) A person commits harassment under this section if the person:

(1) directly or indirectly, or through third parties, manifests a purpose or intent to injure the person, property, or rights of another by the commission of an unlawful act;

(2) follows, monitors, or pursues another, whether in person or through any available technological or other means;

(3) returns to the property of another if the actor is without claim of right to the property or consent of one with authority to consent;

(4) repeatedly makes telephone calls, sends text messages, or induces a victim to make telephone calls to the actor, whether or not conversation ensues;

(5) makes or causes the telephone of another repeatedly or continuously to ring;

(6) repeatedly mails or delivers or causes the delivery by any means, including, electronically, of letters, telegrams, messages, packages, through assistive devices for people with vision impairments or hearing loss, or any communication made through any available technologies or other objects;

(7) knowingly makes false allegations against a peace officer concerning the officer's performance of official duties with intent to influence or tamper with the officer's performance of official duties; or

(8) uses another's personal information, without consent, to invite, encourage, or solicit a third party to engage in a sexual act with the person.

For purposes of this clause, "personal information" and "sexual act" have the meanings given in section 617.261, subdivision 7.

Subd. 3. **Aggravated violations.** (a) A person who commits any of the following acts is guilty of a felony and may be sentenced to imprisonment for not more than five years or to payment of a fine of not more than $10,000, or both:

(1) commits any offense described in subdivision 2 because of the victim's or another's actual or perceived race, color, religion, sex, sexual orientation, disability as defined in section 363.01, age, or national origin;

(2) commits any offense described in subdivision 2 by falsely impersonating another;

(3) commits any offense described in subdivision 2 and possesses a dangerous weapon at the time was used in any way in the commission of the offense;

(4) harasses another, as defined in subdivision 1,_commits any offense described in subdivision 2 with intent to influence or otherwise tamper with a juror or a judicial proceeding or with intent to retaliate against a judicial officer, as defined in section 609.415, or a prosecutor, defense attorney, or officer of the court, because of that person's performance of official duties in connection with a judicial proceeding; or

(5) commits any offense described in subdivision 2 against a victim under the age of 18, if the actor is more than 36 months older than the victim.

(b) A person who commits any offense described in subdivision 2 against a victim under the age of 18, if the actor is more than 36 months older than the victim, and the act is committed with sexual or aggressive intent, is guilty of a felony and may be sentenced to imprisonment for not more than ten years or to payment of a fine of not more than $20,000, or both.

Subd. 4. **Second or subsequent violations; felony.** (a) A person is guilty of a felony who violates any provision of subdivision 2 within ten years of a previous qualified domestic violence-related offense conviction or adjudication of delinquency, and may be sentenced to imprisonment for not more than five years or to payment of a fine of not more than $10,000, or both.

(b) A person is guilty of a felony who violates any provision of subdivision 2 within ten years of the first of two or more previous qualified domestic violence-related offense convictions or adjudications of delinquency, and may be sentenced to imprisonment for not more than ten years or to payment of a fine of not more than $20,000, or both.

Subd. 5. **Stalking.** (a) A person who engages in stalking with respect to a single victim or one or more members of a single household which the actor knows or has reason to know would cause the victim under the circumstances to feel terrorized or to fear bodily harm and which does cause this reaction on the part of the victim, is guilty of a felony and may be sentenced to imprisonment for not more than ten years or to payment of a fine of not more than $20,000, or both.

(b) For purposes of this subdivision, "stalking " means two or more acts within a five-year period that violate or attempt to violate the provisions of any of the following or a similar law of another state, the United States, the District of Columbia, tribe, or United States territories:

(1) this section;

(2) sections 609.185 to 609.205 (first- to third-degree murder and first- and second-degree manslaughter);

(3) section 609.713 (terroristic threats);

(4) section 609.224 (fifth-degree assault);

(5) section 609.2242 (domestic assault);

(6) section 518B.01, subdivision 14 (violations of domestic abuse orders for protection);

(7) section 609.748, subdivision 6 (violations of harassment restraining orders);

(8) section 609.605, subdivision 1, paragraph (b), clauses (3), (4), and (7) (certain trespass offenses);

(9) sections 609.78, subdivision 2 (interference with an emergency call);

(10) section 609.79 (obscene or harassing telephone calls);

(11) section 609.795 (letter, telegram, or package; opening; harassment);

(12) section 609.582 (burglary);

(13) section 609.595 (damage to property);

(14) section 609.765 (criminal defamation);

(15) sections 609.342 to 609.3451 (first- to fifth-degree criminal sexual conduct); or

(16) section 629.75, subdivision 2 (violations of domestic abuse no contact orders).
* * *

Subd. 6. **Mental health assessment and treatment.** (a) When a person is convicted of a felony offense under this section, or another felony offense arising out of a charge based on this section, the court shall order an independent professional mental health assessment of the offender's need for mental health treatment. The court may waive the assessment if an adequate assessment was conducted prior to the conviction.

(b) Notwithstanding section 13.42, 13.85, 144.335, or 260.161, the assessor has access to the following private or confidential data on the person if access is relevant and necessary for the assessment:

(1) medical data under section 13.42;

(2) welfare data under section 13.46;

(3) corrections and detention data under section 13.85;

(4) health records under section 144.335; and

(5) juvenile court records under section 260.161.

Data disclosed under this section may be used only for purposes of the assessment and may not be further disclosed to any other person, except as authorized by law.

(c) If the assessment indicates that the offender is in need of and amenable to mental health treatment, the court shall include in the sentence a requirement that the offender undergo treatment.

(d) The court shall order the offender to pay the costs of assessment under this subdivision unless the offender is indigent under section 563.01.

Subd. 7. **Exception.** Conduct is not a crime under this section if it is performed under terms of a valid license, to ensure compliance with a court order, or to carry out a specific lawful commercial purpose or employment duty, is authorized or required by a valid contract, or is authorized, required, or protected by state, federal, or tribal law or the state, federal, or tribal constitutions. Subdivision 2, clause (2), does not impair the right of any individual or group to engage in speech protected by the federal, state, or tribal constitutions, or federal, state, or tribal law, including peaceful and lawful handbilling and picketing.

Subd. 8. **Harassment; stalking; firearms.** (a) When a person is convicted of harassment or stalking under this section and the court determines that the person used a firearm in any way during commission of the crime, the court may order that the person is prohibited from possessing any type of firearm for any period longer than three years or for the remainder of the person's life. A person who violates this paragraph is guilty of a gross misdemeanor. At the time of the conviction, the court shall inform the defendant for how long the defendant is prohibited from possessing a firearm and that it is a gross misdemeanor to violate this paragraph. The failure of the court to provide this information to a defendant does not affect the applicability of the firearm possession prohibition or the gross misdemeanor penalty to that defendant.

(b) Except as otherwise provided in paragraph (a), when a person in convicted of harassment or stalking under this section, the court shall inform the defendant that the defendant is prohibited from possessing a firearm from three years from the date of conviction and that it is a gross misdemeanor offense to violate this prohibition. The failure of the court to provide this information to a defendant does not affect the applicability of the firearm possession prohibition or the gross misdemeanor penalty to that defendant.

(c) Except as otherwise provided in paragraph (a), a person is not entitled to possess a pistol if the person has been convicted after August 1, 1996, of harassment or stalking under this section, or to possess a firearm if the person has been convicted on or after the effective of a stalking crime under this section, unless three years have elapsed from the date of conviction and, during that time, the person has not been convicted of any other violation of this section. Property rights may not be abated but access may be restricted by the courts. A person who possesses a firearm in violation of this paragraph is guilty of a gross misdemeanor.

(d) If the court determines that a person convicted of harassment or stalking under this section owns or possesses a firearm and used it in any way during the commission of the crime, it shall order that the firearm be summarily forfeited under section 609.5316, subdivision 3.

(e) Except as otherwise provided in paragraphs (d) and (g), when a person is convicted of harassment or stalking under this section, the court shall order the defendant to transfer any firearms that the person possesses, within three business days, to a federally licensed firearms dealer, a law enforcement agency, or a third party who may lawfully receive them. * * * [Such transferees] shall return the transferred firearms to the person upon request after the expiration of the prohibiting time period imposed under this subdivision, provided the person is not otherwise prohibited from possessing firearms under state or federal law. * * * The court shall order that the person surrender all permits to carry and purchase firearms to the sheriff.

(f) A defendant who is ordered to transfer firearms under paragraph (e) must file proof of transfer as provided for in this paragraph. If the transfer is made to a third party, the third party must sign an affidavit under oath before a notary public either acknowledging that the defendant permanently transferred the defendant's firearms to the third party or agreeing to temporarily store the defendant's firearms until such time as the defendant is legally permitted to possess firearms. * * * If the transfer is to a law enforcement agency or federally licensed firearms dealer, the law enforcement agency or federally licensed firearms dealer shall provide proof of transfer to the defendant. * * *

(g) When a person is convicted of harassment or stalking under this section, the court shall determine by a preponderance of evidence if the person poses an imminent risk of causing another person substantial bodily harm [, and] shall order that the local law enforcement agency take immediate possession of all firearms in the person's possession. * * * [The agency] shall return the firearms to the person upon request after the expiration of the prohibiting time period, provided the person is not otherwise prohibited from possessing firearms under state or federal law. The local law enforcement agency shall, upon written notice from the person, transfer the firearms to a federally licensed firearms dealer or a third party who may lawfully receive them. * * *

HIST: 1993 c 326 art 2 s 22; * * * 1Sp2019 c 5 art 2 s 17-21; 2020 c 96 s 2-3

611A.0311 DOMESTIC ABUSE PROSECUTIONS PLAN AND PROCEDURES; PILOT PROGRAM.

Subdivision 1. **Definitions.** (a) "Domestic abuse" has the meaning given in section 518B.01, subdivision 2.

(b) "Domestic abuse case" means a prosecution for:

(1) a crime that involves domestic abuse;

(2) violation of a condition of release following an arrest for a crime that involves domestic abuse; or

(3) violation of a domestic abuse order for protection.

Subd. 2. **Contents of plan.** Each county and city attorney shall develop and implement a written plan to expedite and improve the efficiency and just disposition of domestic abuse cases brought to the prosecuting authority. Domestic abuse advocates, law enforcement officials, and other interested members of the public must have an opportunity to assist in the development or adaptation of the plans in each jurisdiction. The commissioner shall make the plan and related training and technical assistance available to all city and county attorneys. All plans must state goals and contain policies and procedures to address the following matters:

(1) early assignment of a trial prosecutor who has the responsibility of handling the domestic abuse case through disposition, whenever feasible, or, where applicable, probation revocation; and early contact between the trial prosecutor and the victim;

(2) procedures to facilitate the earliest possible contact between the prosecutor's office and the victim for the purpose of acquainting the victim with the criminal justice process, the use of subpoenas, the victim's role as a witness in the prosecution, and the domestic abuse or victim services that are available;

(3) procedures to coordinate the trial prosecutor's efforts with those of the domestic abuse advocate or victim advocate, where available, and to facilitate the early provision of advocacy services to the victim;

(4) procedures to encourage the prosecution of all domestic abuse cases where a crime can be proven;

(5) methods that will be used to identify, gather, and preserve evidence in addition to the victim's in-court testimony that will enhance the ability to prosecute a case when a victim is reluctant to assist, including but not limited to physical evidence of the victim's injury, evidence relating to the scene of the crime, eyewitness testimony, and statements of the victim made at or near the time of the injury;

(6) procedures for educating local law enforcement agencies about the contents of the plan and their role in assisting with its implementation;

(7) the use for subpoenas to victims and witnesses, where appropriate;

(8) procedures for annual review of the plan to evaluate whether it is meeting its goals effectively and whether improvements are needed; and

(9) a timetable for implementation.

* * *

HIST: 1990 c 583 s 5; 1992 c 571 art 6 s 18,19; 2014 c 212 art 1 s 7

611A.201 DIRECTOR OF PREVENTION OF DOMESTIC VIOLENCE AND SEXUAL ASSAULT.

Subdivision 1. **Appointment of director.** The executive director of the Office of Justice Programs in the Department of Public Safety shall appoint a person to serve as director of domestic violence and sexual assault prevention in the office. The director must have experience in domestic violence and sexual assault prevention issues. The director serves at the executive director's pleasure in the unclassified service. The executive director may appoint, supervise, discipline, and discharge employees to assist the director in carrying out the director's responsibilities under this section.

Subd. 2. **Director's responsibilities.** The director shall have the following duties:

(1) advocate for the rights of victims of domestic violence and sexual assault;

(2) increase public education and visibility about the prevention of domestic violence and sexual assault;

(3) encourage accountability regarding domestic violence and sexual assault at all levels of the system, and develop recommendations to improve accountability when the system fails;

(4) support prosecution and civil litigation efforts regarding domestic violence and sexual assault at the federal and state levels;

(5) study issues involving domestic violence and sexual assault as they pertain to both men and women and present findings and recommendations resulting from these studies to all branches of government;

(6) initiate policy changes regarding domestic violence and sexual assault at all levels of government;

(7) coordinate existing resources and promote coordinated and immediate community responses to better serve victims of domestic violence and sexual assault;

(8) build partnerships among law enforcement, prosecutors, defenders, advocates, and courts to reduce the occurrence of domestic violence and sexual assault;

(9) encourage and support the efforts of health care providers, mental health experts, employers, educators, clergy members, and others, in raising awareness of and addressing how to prevent domestic violence and sexual assault;

(10) coordinate and maximize the use of federal, state, and local resources available to prevent domestic violence and sexual assault and leverage more resources through grants and private funding; and

(11) serve as a liaison between the executive director of the Office of Justice Programs in the Department of Public Safety and the commissioner of health with regard to the Department of Health's sexual violence prevention program funded by federal block grants, and oversee how this money is spent.

* * *

HIST: 2000 c 368 s 1; 1Sp2001 c 8 art 10 s 17; 2013 c 125 art 1 s 89-91

611A.203 DOMESTIC FATALITY REVIEW TEAMS.

Subdivision 1. **Domestic fatality review teams; purpose.** A judicial district may establish a domestic fatality review team to review domestic violence deaths that have occurred in the district. The team may review cases in which prosecution has been completed or the prosecutorial authority has decided not to pursue the case. The purpose of the review team is to assess domestic violence deaths in order to develop recommendations for policies and protocols for community prevention and intervention initiatives to reduce and eliminate the incidence of domestic violence and resulting fatalities.

Subd. 2. **Definition of domestic violence death.** "Domestic violence death" means a homicide or suicide under any of the following circumstances:

(1) the alleged perpetrator and victim resided together at any time;

(2) the alleged perpetrator and victim have a child in common, regardless of whether they were married or lived together at any time;

(3) the alleged perpetrator and victim were married, separated, or divorced;

(4) the alleged perpetrator and victim had a sexual relationship or a significant romantic relationship;

(5) the alleged perpetrator had been harassing or stalking the victim;

(6) the homicide victim lived in the same household, was present in the workplace of, was in proximity of, or was related by blood or affinity to a victim who experienced or was threatened with domestic abuse by the alleged perpetrator;

(7) the victim or the perpetrator was a child of a person in a relationship that is described within this definition; or

(8) any other circumstances that the domestic fatality review team decides fall within the parameters of its mission.

"Domestic violence death" must be interpreted broadly to give the domestic fatality review team discretion to review fatalities that have occurred both directly and peripherally to domestic relationships.

Subd. 3. **Membership.** (a) The chief judge, in consultation with the family violence coordinating council, shall appoint the members of the domestic fatality review team. Membership must reflect a commitment to diversity and relevant professional experience. The review team members must include:

(1) the medical examiner;

(2) a judicial court officer (judge or referee);

(3) a county and city attorney and a public defender;

(4) the county sheriff and a peace officer;

(5) a representative from family court services and the Department of Corrections;

(6) a physician familiar with domestic violence issues;

(7) a representative from district court administration and the domestic abuse service center;

(8) a public citizen representative or a representative from a civic organization;

(9) a mental health professional; and

(10) domestic violence advocates or shelter workers.

(b) There must be at least three domestic violence advocates or shelter workers on the domestic fatality review team. No two members may represent the same agency. Members representing advocates or shelters must be selected by the advocacy community. At least one position must be designated for a minority representative and one position must rotate in order to include an advocate from the community in which the fatality under review took place.

(c) The domestic fatality review team may also invite other relevant persons to serve on an ad hoc basis and participate as full members of the review team for a particular review. These persons may include, but are not limited to:

(1) individuals with particular expertise that would be helpful to the review panel; or

(2) representatives of organizations or agencies that had contact with or provided services to the homicide victim, or to the alleged perpetrator, a victim who experienced or was threatened with domestic abuse by the alleged perpetrator, or a family member of one of those individuals.

Subd. 4. **Duties; access to data.** (a) The domestic fatality review team shall collect, review, and analyze death certificates and death data, including investigative reports, medical and counseling records, victim service records, employment records, child abuse reports, or other information concerning domestic violence deaths, survivor interviews and surveys, and other information deemed by the team as necessary and appropriate concerning the causes and manner of domestic violence deaths.

(b) The review team has access to the following not public data, as defined in section 13.02, subdivision 8a, relating to a case being reviewed by the team: inactive law enforcement investigative data under section 13.82; autopsy records and coroner or medical examiner investigative data under section 13.83; hospital, public health, or other medical records of the victim under section 13.384; records under section 13.46, created by social service agencies that provided services to the victim, the alleged perpetrator, or another victim who experienced or was threatened with domestic abuse by the perpetrator; and child maltreatment records under chapter 260E, relating to the victim or a family or household member of the victim. Access to medical records under this paragraph also includes records governed by sections 144.291 to 144.298. The review team has access to corrections and detention data as provided in section 13.85.

(c) As part of any review, the domestic fatality review team may compel the production of other records by applying to the district court for a subpoena, which will be effective throughout the state according to the Rules of Civil Procedure.

Subd. 5. **Confidentiality; data privacy.** A person attending a domestic fatality review team meeting may not disclose what transpired at the meeting, except to carry out the purposes of the review team or as otherwise provided in this subdivision. The review team may disclose the names of the victims in the cases it reviewed. The proceedings and records of the review team are confidential data as defined in section 13.02, subdivision 3, or protected nonpublic data as defined in section 13.02, subdivision 13, regardless of their classification in the hands of the person who provided the data, and are not subject to discovery or introduction into evidence in a civil or criminal action against a professional, the state, or a county agency, arising out of the matters the team is reviewing. Information, documents, and records otherwise available from other sources are not immune from discovery or use in a civil or criminal action solely because they were presented during proceedings of the review team. This section does not limit a person who presented information before the review team or who is a member of the panel from testifying about matters within the person's knowledge. However, in a civil or criminal proceeding, a person may not be questioned about the person's good faith presentation of information to the review team or opinions formed by the person as a result of the review team meetings.

Subd. 6. **Immunity.** Members of the domestic fatality advisory board, members of the domestic fatality review team, and members of each review panel, as well as their agents or employees, are immune from claims and are not subject to any suits, liability, damages, or any other recourse, civil or criminal, arising from any act, proceeding, decision, or determination undertaken or performed or recommendation made by the domestic fatality review team, provided they acted in good faith and without malice in carrying out their responsibilities. Good faith is presumed until proven otherwise and the complainant has the burden of proving malice or a lack of good faith. No organization, institution, or person furnishing information, data, testimony, reports, or records to the domestic fatality review team as part of an investigation is civilly or criminally liable or subject to any other recourse for providing the information.

Subd. 7. **Evaluation and report.** (a) Each domestic fatality review team shall develop a system for evaluating the effectiveness of its program and shall focus on identifiable goals and outcomes. An evaluation must include data components as well as input from individuals involved in the review process.

(b) Each fatality review team shall issue an annual report to the chairs and ranking minority members of the senate and house of representatives committees with jurisdiction over public safety issues. The report must consist of the written aggregate recommendations of the domestic fatality review team without reference to specific cases. The report must be available upon request and distributed to the governor, attorney general, supreme court, county board, and district court.

HIST: 2009 c 59 art 2 s 2; 2013 c 82 s 37; 1Sp2019 c 5 art 2 s 29; 1Sp2020 c 2 art 8 s 142

611A.31 DEFINITIONS.

Subdivision 1. **Scope.** For the purposes of sections 611A.31 to 611A.35, the following terms have the meanings given.

Subd. 2. **Battered woman.** "Battered woman" means a woman who is being or has been victimized by domestic abuse as defined in section 518B.01, subdivision 2.

Subd. 3. **Emergency shelter services.** "Emergency shelter services" include, but are not limited to, secure crisis shelters for battered women and housing networks for battered women.

Subd. 4. **Support services.** "Support services" include, but are not limited to, advocacy services, legal services, counseling services, transportation services, child care services, and 24 hour information and referral services.

Subd. 5. **Commissioner.** "Commissioner" means the commissioner of the Department of Corrections or a designee.

HIST: 1977 c 428 s 1; 1983 c 262 art 1 s 6; 1986 c 444; 1991 c 272 s 8; 1995 c 226 art 7 s 11; 2015 c 65 art 3 s 21

611A.32 BATTERED WOMEN PROGRAMS.

Subdivision 1. **Grants awarded.** The commissioner shall award grants to programs which provide emergency shelter services to battered women and support services to battered women and domestic abuse victims and their children. The commissioner shall also award grants for training, technical assistance, and for the development and implementation of education programs to increase public awareness of the causes of battering, the solutions to preventing and ending domestic violence, and the problems faced by battered women and domestic abuse victims. Grants shall be awarded in a manner that ensures that they are equitably distributed to programs serving metropolitan and nonmetropolitan populations. By July 1, 1995, community-based domestic abuse advocacy and support services programs must be established in every judicial assignment district.

Subd. 1a. **Program for American Indian women.** The commissioner shall establish at least one program under this section to provide emergency shelter services and support services to battered American Indian women. The commissioner shall grant continuing operating expenses to the program established under this subdivision in the same manner as operating expenses are granted to programs established under subdivision 1.

Subd. 2. **Applications.** Any public or private nonprofit agency may apply to the commissioner for a grant to provide emergency shelter services to battered women, support services to domestic abuse victims, or both, to battered women and their children. The application shall be submitted in a form approved by the commissioner by rule adopted under chapter 14 and shall include:

(1) a proposal for the provision of emergency shelter services for battered women, support services for domestic abuse victims, or both, for battered women and their children;

(2) a proposed budget;

(3) the agency's overall operating budget, including documentation on the retention of financial reserves and availability of additional funding sources;

(4) evidence of an ability to integrate into the proposed program the uniform method of data collection and program evaluation established under section 611A.33;

(5) evidence of an ability to represent the interests of battered women and domestic abuse victims and their children to local law enforcement agencies and courts, county welfare agencies, and local boards or departments of health;

(6) evidence of an ability to do outreach to unserved and underserved populations and to provide culturally and linguistically appropriate services; and

(7) any other content the commissioner may require by rule adopted under chapter 14, after considering the recommendations of the advisory council.

Programs which have been approved for grants in prior years may submit materials which indicate changes in items listed in clauses (1) to (7), in order to qualify for renewal funding. Nothing in this subdivision may be construed to require programs to submit complete applications for each year of renewal funding.

Subd. 3. **Duties of grantees.** Every public or private nonprofit agency which receives a grant to provide emergency shelter services to battered women and support services to battered women and domestic abuse victims shall comply with all rules of the commissioner related to the administration of the pilot programs.

* * *

Subd. 5. **Classification of data collected by grantees.** Personal history information and other information collected, used or maintained by a grantee from which the identity or location of any victim of domestic abuse may be determined is private data on individuals, as defined in section 13.02, subdivision 12, and the grantee shall maintain the data in accordance with the provisions of chapter 13.

HIST: 1977 c 428 s 2; 1978 c 732 s 1-3; 1981 c 311 s 39; 1Sp1981 c 4 art 1 s 14; 1982 c 545 s 24; 1983 c 262 art 1 s 6; 1988 c 689 art 2 s 237; 1991 c 272 s 9,10; 1992 c 571 art 6 s 21; 2000 c 445 art 2 s 10-13; 2010 c 215 art 11 s 17; 2014 c 286 art 6 s 3

611A.35 DOMESTIC ABUSE PROGRAM DIRECTOR.

The commissioner shall appoint a program director. The program director shall administer the funds appropriated for sections 611A.31 to 611A.35 and perform other duties related to battered women's and domestic abuse programs as the commissioner may assign. The program director shall serve at the pleasure of the commissioner in the unclassified service.

HIST: 1977 c 428 s 5; 1983 c 262 art 1 s 6; 1986 c 444; 1991 c 272 s 14; 2000 c 445 art 2 s 19; 2014 c 286 art 6 s 6; 2015 c 65 art 3 s 23

629.341 ALLOWING PROBABLE CAUSE ARRESTS FOR DOMESTIC VIOLENCE; IMMUNITY FROM LIABILITY.

Subdivision 1. **Arrest.** Notwithstanding section 629.34 or any other law or rule, a peace officer may arrest a person anywhere without a warrant, including at the person's residence if the peace officer has probable cause to believe that the person within the preceding 72 hours, exclusive of the day probable cause was established, the person has committed nonfelony domestic abuse, as defined in section 518B.01, subdivision 2. The arrest may be made even though the assault did not take place in the presence of the peace officer.

Subd. 2. **Immunity.** A peace officer acting in good faith and exercising due care in making an arrest pursuant to subdivision 1 is immune from civil liability that might result from the officer's action.

Subd. 3. **Notice of rights.** The peace officer shall tell the victim whether a shelter or other services are available in the community and give the victim immediate notice of the legal rights and remedies available. The notice must include furnishing the victim a copy of the following statement:

"IF YOU ARE THE VICTIM OF DOMESTIC VIOLENCE, you can ask the city or county attorney to file a criminal complaint. You also have the right to go to court and file a petition requesting an order for protection from domestic abuse. The order could include the following:

(1) an order restraining the abuser from further acts of abuse;

(2) an order directing the abuser to leave your household;

(3) an order preventing the abuser from entering your residence, school, business, or place of employment;

(4) an order awarding you or the other parent custody of or parenting time with your minor child or children; or

(5) an order directing the abuser to pay support to you and the minor children if the abuser has a legal obligation to do so."

The notice must include the resource listing, including telephone number, for the area battered women's shelter, to be designated by the department of corrections.

Subd. 4. **Report required.** Whenever a peace officer investigates an allegation that an incident described in subdivision 1 has occurred, whether or not an arrest is made, the officer shall make a written police report of the alleged incident. The report must contain at least the following information: the name, address and telephone number of the victim, if provided by the victim, a statement as to whether an arrest occurred, the name of the arrested person, and a brief summary of the incident. Data that identify a victim who has made a request under section 13.82, subdivision 10, paragraph (d), and that are private data under that subdivision, shall be private in the report required by this section. A copy of this report must be provided upon request, at no cost, to the victim of domestic abuse, the victim's attorney, or organizations designated by the Office of Justice Programs in the Department of Public Safety, or the commissioner of corrections that are providing services to victims of domestic abuse. The officer shall submit the report to the officer's supervisor or other person to whom the employer's rules or policies require reports of similar allegations of criminal activity to be made.

Subd. 5. **Training.** The board of peace officer standards and training shall provide a copy of this section to every law enforcement agency in this state on or before June 30, 1983.

Upon request of the board of peace officer standards and training to the bureau of criminal apprehension, at least one training course must include instruction about domestic abuse. A basic skills course required for initial licensure as a peace officer must, after January 1, 1985, include at least three hours of training in handling domestic violence cases.

HIST: 1978 c 724 s 2; * * * 2014 c 177 s 2

629.342 LAW ENFORCEMENT POLICIES; DOMESTIC ABUSE ARRESTS.

Subdivision 1. **Definition.** For purposes of this section, "domestic abuse" has the meaning given in section 518B.01, subdivision 2.

Subd. 2. **Policies required.** (a) Each law enforcement agency shall develop, adopt, and implement a written policy regarding arrest procedures for domestic abuse incidents. In the development of a policy, each law enforcement agency shall consult with domestic abuse advocates, community organizations, and other law enforcement agencies with expertise in the recognition and handling of domestic abuse incidents. The policy shall discourage dual arrests, include consideration of whether one of the parties acted in self defense, and provide guidance to officers concerning instances in which officers should remain at the scene of a domestic abuse incident until the likelihood of further imminent violence has been eliminated.

(b) The Bureau of Criminal Apprehension and the Board of Peace Officer Standards and Training, in consultation with the Minnesota Chiefs of Police Association, the Minnesota Sheriffs Association, the Minnesota Police and Peace Officers Association, and a domestic violence statewide coalition shall update the written policy regarding arrest procedures for domestic abuse incidents for use by local law enforcement agencies. Each law enforcement agency may adopt the model policy in lieu of developing its own policy under the provisions of paragraph (a).

Subd. 3. **Assistance to victim where no arrest.** If a law enforcement officer does not make an arrest when the officer has probable cause to believe that a person is committing or has committed domestic abuse or violated an order for protection, the officer shall provide immediate assistance to the victim. Assistance includes:

(1) assisting the victim in obtaining necessary medical treatment; and

(2) providing the victim with the notice of rights under section 629.341, subdivision 3.

Subd. 4. **Immunity.** A peace officer acting in good faith and exercising due care in providing assistance to a victim pursuant to subdivision 3 is immune from civil liability that might result from the officer's action.

HIST: 1992 c 571 art 6 s 22; 1993 c 326 art 2 s 30; 2000 c 445 art 2 s 28; 2014 c 212 art 1 s 12; 2014 c 286 art 6 s 7

629.75 DOMESTIC ABUSE NO CONTACT ORDER.

Subdivision 1. **Establishment; description.** (a) A domestic abuse no contact order is an order issued by a court against a defendant in a criminal proceeding or a juvenile offender in a delinquency proceeding for:

(1) domestic abuse as defined in section 518B.01, subdivision 2;

(2) harassment or stalking charged under 609.749 when committed against a family or household member as defined in section 518B.01, subdivision 2;

(3) violation of an order for protection under section 518B.01, subdivision 14; or

(4) violation of a prior domestic abuse no contact order under this subdivision or section 518B.01, subdivision 22.

(b) A domestic abuse no contact order may be issued as a pretrial order before final disposition of the underlying criminal case or as a postconviction probationary order. A domestic abuse no contact order is independent of any condition of pretrial release or probation imposed on the defendant. A domestic abuse no contact order may be issued in addition to a similar restriction imposed as a condition of pretrial release or probation. In the context of a postconviction probationary order, a domestic abuse no contact order may be issued for an offense listed in paragraph (a) or for a conviction for any offense arising out of the same set of circumstances as an offense listed in paragraph (a).

(c) A no contact order under this section shall be issued in a proceeding that is separate from but held immediately following a proceeding in which any pretrial release or sentencing issues are decided.

Subd. 2. **Criminal penalties.** (a) As used in the subdivision "qualified domestic violence-related offense" has the meaning given in section 609.02, subdivision 16.

(b) Except as otherwise provided in paragraphs (c) and (d), a person who knows of the existence of a domestic abuse no contact order issued against the person and violates the order is guilty of a misdemeanor.

(c) A person is guilty of a gross misdemeanor who violates this subdivision within ten years of a previous qualified domestic violence-related offense conviction or adjudication of delinquency. Upon a gross misdemeanor conviction under this paragraph, the defendant must be sentenced to a minimum of ten days' imprisonment and must be ordered to participate in counseling or other appropriate programs selected by the court as provided in section 518B.02. Notwithstanding section 609.135, the court must impose and execute the minimum sentence provided in this paragraph for gross misdemeanor convictions.

(d) A person is guilty of a felony and may be sentenced to imprisonment for not more than five years or to payment of a fine of not more than $10,000, or both, if the person violates this subdivision:

(1) within ten years of the first of two or more previous qualified domestic violence-related offense convictions or adjudications of delinquency; or

(2) while possessing a dangerous weapon, as defined in section 609.02, subdivision 6. Upon a felony conviction under this paragraph in which the court stays imposition or execution of sentence, the court shall impose at least a 30-day period of incarceration as a condition of probation. The court also shall order that the defendant participate in counseling or other appropriate programs selected by the court. Notwithstanding section 609.135, the court must impose and execute the minimum sentence provided in this paragraph for felony convictions.

Subd. 2a. **Venue.** A person may be prosecuted under subdivision 2 at the place where any call is made or received or, in the case of wireless or electronic communication or any communication made through any available technologies, where the actor or victim resides, or in the jurisdiction of the victim's designated address if the victim participates in the address confidentiality program established under chapter 5B.

Subd. 3. **Warrantless custodial arrest.** A peace officer shall arrest without a warrant and take into custody a person whom the peace officer has probable cause to believe has violated a domestic abuse no contact order, even if the violation of the order did not take place in the presence of the peace officer, if the existence of the order can be verified by the officer. The person shall be held in custody for at least 36 hours, excluding the day of arrest, Sundays, and holidays, unless the person is released earlier by a judge or judicial officer. A peace officer acting in good faith and exercising due care in making an arrest pursuant to this subdivision is immune from civil liability that might result from the officer's actions.
HIST: 2010 c 299 s 13; 2013 c 47 s 5,6

Chapter 33 – VICTIMS AND VICTIM'S RIGHTS

Category 2, Sections 5, 18:
2.5.7. Explain special Minnesota peace officer duties associated with specific statutes including: informing crime victims of their rights . . .
2.18.2. Describe the current state of victim's rights in the criminal justice system. (Minn. Stat. 611A)

609.3471 RECORDS PERTAINING TO VICTIM IDENTITY CONFIDENTIAL.

Notwithstanding any provision of law to the contrary, no data contained in records or reports relating to petitions, complaints, or indictments issued pursuant to section 609.322, 609.342, 609.343, 609.344, 609.345, or 609.3453, which specifically identifies a victim who is a minor shall be accessible to the public, except by order of the court. Nothing in this section authorizes denial of access to any other data contained in the records or reports, including the identity of the defendant.
HIST: 1984 c 573 s 9; * * * 2015 c 65 art 6 s 15

611A.01 DEFINITIONS.

For the purposes of sections 611A.01 to 611A.06:
(a) "Crime" means conduct that is prohibited by local ordinance and results in bodily harm to an individual; or conduct that is included within the definition of "crime" in section 609.02, subdivision 1, or would be included within that definition but for the fact that (1) the person engaging in the conduct lacked capacity to commit the crime under the laws of this state, or (2) the act was alleged or found to have been committed by a juvenile.
(b) "Victim" means a natural person who incurs loss or harm as a result of a crime, including a good faith effort to prevent a crime, and for purposes of sections 611A.04 and 611A.045, also includes (1) a corporation that incurs loss or harm as a result of a crime, (2) a government entity that incurs loss or harm as a result of a crime, and (3) any other entity authorized to receive restitution under section 609.10 or 609.125. The term "victim" includes the family members, guardian, conservator, or custodian of a minor, incompetent, incapacitated, or deceased person. In a case where the prosecutor finds that the number of family members makes it impracticable to accord all of the family members the rights described in sections 611A.02 to 611A.0395, the prosecutor shall establish a reasonable procedure to give effect to those rights. The procedure may not limit the number of victim impact statements submitted to the court under section 611A.038. The term "victim" does not include the person charged with or alleged to have committed the crime.
(c) "Juvenile" has the same meaning as given to the term "child" in section 260B.007, subdivision 3.
HIST: 1983 c 262 art 1 s 1; 1987 c 254 s 10; 1988 c 649 s 1; 1995 c 226 art 7 s 8; 1996 c 408 art 7 s 5; 1997 c 239 art 7 s 19; 1999 c 139 art 4 s 2; 2005 c 136 art 8 s 22; 2020 c 86 art 1 s 40

611A.015 SCOPE OF VICTIMS' RIGHTS.

The rights afforded to crime victims in sections 611A.01 to 611A.06 are applicable to adult criminal cases, juvenile delinquency proceedings, juvenile traffic proceedings involving driving under the influence of alcohol or drugs, and proceedings involving any other act committed by a juvenile that would be a crime as defined in section 609.02, if committed by an adult.
HIST: 1993 c 326 art 6 s 6

611A.02 NOTIFICATION OF VICTIM SERVICES AND VICTIMS' RIGHTS.
* * *

Subd. 2. **Victims' rights.** (a) The Office of Justice Programs in the Department of Public Safety shall update the two model notices of the rights of crime victims.

(b) The initial notice of the rights of crime victims must be distributed by a peace officer to each victim, as defined in section 611A.01, at the time of initial contact with the victim. The notice must inform a victim of:

(1) the victim's right to apply for reparations to cover losses, not including property losses, resulting from a violent crime and the telephone number to call to request an application;

(2) the victim's right to request that the law enforcement agency withhold public access to data revealing the victim's identity under section 13.82, subdivision 17, paragraph (d);

(3) the additional rights of domestic abuse victims as described in section 629.341;

(4) information on the nearest crime victim assistance program or resource;

(5) the victim's rights, if an offender is charged, to be informed of and participate in the prosecution process, including the right to request restitution; and

(6) in homicide cases, information on rights and procedures available under sections 524.2-803, 524.3-614, and 524.3-615.

(c) A supplemental notice of the rights of crime victims must be distributed by the city or county attorney's office to each victim, within a reasonable time after the offender is charged or petitioned. This notice must inform a victim of all the rights of crime victims under this chapter.

Subd. 3. **Notice of rights of victims in juvenile court.** (a) The Office of Justice Programs in the Department of Public Safety shall update the notice of the rights of victims in juvenile court that explains:

(1) the rights of victims in the juvenile court;

(2) when a juvenile matter is public;

(3) the procedures to be followed in juvenile court proceedings; and

(4) other relevant matters.

(b) The juvenile court shall distribute a copy of the notice to each victim of juvenile crime who attends a juvenile court proceeding, along with a notice of services for victims available in that judicial district.
HIST: 1983 c 262 art 1 s 2; 1988 c 649 s 2; 1991 c 170 s 3; 1992 c 464 art 1 s 50; 1993 c 326 art 6 s 7; 1994 c 576 s 53; 1999 c 227 s 22; 2013 c 94 s 4; 2013 c 125 art 1 s 88; 2014 c 212 art 1 s 5,6

611A.03 PLEA AGREEMENTS; NOTIFICATION.

Subdivision 1. **Plea agreements; notification of victim.** Prior to the entry of the factual basis for a plea pursuant to a plea agreement recommendation, a prosecuting attorney shall make a reasonable and good faith effort to inform the victim of:

(1) the contents of the plea agreement recommendation, including the amount of time recommended for the defendant to serve in jail or prison if the court accepts the agreement; and

(2) the right to be present at the sentencing hearing and at the hearing during which the plea is presented to the court and to express orally or in writing, at the victim's option, any objection to the agreement or to the proposed disposition. If the victim is not present when the court considers the recommendation, but has communicated objections to the prosecuting attorney, the prosecuting attorney shall make these objections known to the court.

Subd. 2. **Notification duties.** A prosecuting attorney satisfies the requirements of subdivision 1 by notifying:

(1) the victim's legal guardian or guardian ad litem; or

(2) the three victims the prosecuting attorney believes to have suffered the most, if there are more than three victims of the offense.
* * *
HIST: 1983 c 262 art 1 s 3; 1986 c 351 s 18; 1986 c 444; 1Sp1986 c 3 art 1 s 76; 1989 c 190 s 3; 1992 c 571 art 5 s 4; 2003 c 116 s 4

611A.0301 RIGHT TO SUBMIT STATEMENT AT PLEA PRESENTATION HEARING.
A victim has the rights described in section 611A.03, subdivision 1, clause (2), at a plea presentation hearing.
HIST: 2003 c 116 s 5

611A.0311 DOMESTIC ABUSE PROSECUTIONS PLAN AND PROCEDURES; PILOT PROGRAM.
Subdivision 1. Definitions. (a) "Domestic abuse" has the meaning given in section 518B.01, subdivision 2.

(b) "Domestic abuse case" means a prosecution for:

(1) a crime that involves domestic abuse;

(2) violation of a condition of release following an arrest for a crime that involves domestic abuse; or

(3) violation of a domestic abuse order for protection.

Subd. 2. **Contents of plan.** Each county and city attorney shall develop and implement a written plan to expedite and improve the efficiency and just disposition of domestic abuse cases brought to the prosecuting authority. Domestic abuse advocates, law enforcement officials, and other interested members of the public must have an opportunity to assist in the development or adaptation of the plans in each jurisdiction. The commissioner shall make the plan and related training and technical assistance available to all city and county attorneys. All plans must state goals and contain policies and procedures to address the following matters:

(1) early assignment of a trial prosecutor who has the responsibility of handling the domestic abuse case through disposition, whenever feasible, or, where applicable, probation revocation; and early contact between the trial prosecutor and the victim;

(2) procedures to facilitate the earliest possible contact between the prosecutor's office and the victim for the purpose of acquainting the victim with the criminal justice process, the use of subpoenas, the victim's role as a witness in the prosecution, and the domestic abuse or victim services that are available;

(3) procedures to coordinate the trial prosecutor's efforts with those of the domestic abuse advocate or victim advocate, where available, and to facilitate the early provision of advocacy services to the victim;

(4) procedures to encourage the prosecution of all domestic abuse cases where a crime can be proven;

(5) methods that will be used to identify, gather, and preserve evidence in addition to the victim's in-court testimony that will enhance the ability to prosecute a case when a victim is reluctant to assist, including but not limited to physical evidence of the victim's injury, evidence relating to the scene of the crime, eyewitness testimony, and statements of the victim made at or near the time of the injury;

(6) procedures for educating local law enforcement agencies about the contents of the plan and their role in assisting with its implementation;

(7) the use for subpoenas to victims and witnesses, where appropriate;

(8) procedures for annual review of the plan to evaluate whether it is meeting its goals effectively and whether improvements are needed; and

(9) a timetable for implementation.
* * *
HIST: 1990 c 583 s 5; 1992 c 571 art 6 s 18,19; 2014 c 212 art 1 s 7

611A.0392 NOTICE TO COMMUNITY CRIME PREVENTION GROUP.
Subdivision 1. **Definitions.** (a) As used in this section, the following terms have the meanings given them.

(b) "Cities of the first class" has the meaning given in section 410.01.

(c) "Community crime prevention group" means a community group focused on community safety and crime prevention that:

(1) meets regularly for the purpose of discussing community safety and patrolling community neighborhoods for criminal activity;

(2) is previously designated by the local law enforcement agency as a community crime prevention group; and

(3) interacts regularly with the police regarding community safety issues.

Subd. 2. **Notice.** (a) A law enforcement agency that is responsible for arresting individuals who commit crimes within cities of the first class shall make reasonable efforts to disclose certain information in a timely manner to the designated leader of a community crime prevention group that has reported criminal activity, excluding petty misdemeanors, to law enforcement. The law enforcement agency shall make reasonable efforts to disclose information on the final outcome of the investigation into the criminal activity including, but not limited to, where appropriate, the decision to arrest or not arrest the person and whether the matter was referred to a prosecuting authority. If the matter is referred to a prosecuting authority, the law enforcement agency must notify the prosecuting authority of the community crime prevention group's request for notice under this subdivision.
* * *

(c) A community crime prevention group that would like to receive written or Internet notice under this subdivision must request the law enforcement agency and the prosecuting authority where the specific alleged criminal conduct occurred to provide notice to the community crime prevention group leader. The community crime prevention group must provide the law enforcement agency with the name, address, and telephone number of the community crime prevention group leader and the preferred method of communication.
HIST: 1Sp2003 c 2 art 8 s 17

611A.0393 CRIME ALERTS; VIOLENT CRIMES; DISABLED ACCESS.

If a law enforcement agency provides a crime alert to citizens within its jurisdiction, the alerts and any accompanying documents must be in a form that a disabled person can access with commercially available text-based screen reader software. Any contact information provided by a citizen requesting a crime alert is private data on individuals as defined in section 13.02.
HIST: 2009 c 22 s 2

611A.04 ORDER OF RESTITUTION.

Subdivision 1. **Request; decision.** (a) A victim of a crime has the right to receive restitution as part of the disposition of a criminal charge or juvenile delinquency proceeding against the offender if the offender is convicted or found delinquent. The court, or a person or agency designated by the court, shall request information from the victim to determine the amount of restitution owed. The court or its designee shall obtain the information from the victim in affidavit form or by other competent evidence. Information submitted relating to restitution must describe the items or elements of loss, itemize the total dollar amounts of restitution claimed, and specify the reasons justifying these amounts, if restitution is in the form of money or property. A request for restitution may include, but is not limited to, any out-of-pocket losses resulting from the crime, including medical and therapy costs, replacement of wages and services, expenses incurred to return a child who was a victim of a crime under section 609.26 to the child's parents or lawful custodian, and funeral expenses. An actual or prospective civil action involving the alleged crime shall not be used by the court as a basis to deny a victim's right to obtain court-ordered restitution under this section. In order to be considered at the sentencing or dispositional hearing, all information regarding restitution must be received by the court administrator of the appropriate court at least three business days before the sentencing or dispositional hearing. The court administrator shall provide copies of this request to the prosecutor and the offender or the offender's attorney at least 24 hours before the sentencing or dispositional hearing. The issue of restitution is reserved or the sentencing or dispositional hearing or hearing on the restitution request may be continued if the victim's affidavit or other competent evidence submitted by the victim is not received in time. At the sentencing or dispositional hearing, the court shall give the offender an opportunity to respond to specific items of restitution and their dollar amounts in accordance with the procedures established in section 611A.045, subdivision 3.

(b) The court may amend or issue an order of restitution after the sentencing or dispositional hearing if:

(1) the offender is on probation, committed to the commissioner of corrections, or on supervised release;

(2) sufficient evidence of a right to restitution has been submitted; and

(3) the true extent of the victim's loss or the loss of the Crime Victims Reparations Board was not known at the time of the sentencing or dispositional hearing, or hearing on the restitution request.

If the court holds a hearing on the restitution request, the court must notify the offender, the offender's attorney, the victim, the prosecutor, and the Crime Victims Reparations Board at least five business days before the hearing. The court's restitution decision is governed by this section and section 611A.045.

(c) The court shall grant or deny restitution or partial restitution and shall state on the record its reasons for its decision on restitution if information relating to restitution has been presented. If the court grants partial restitution it shall also specify the full amount of restitution that may be docketed as a civil judgment under subdivision 3. The court may not require that the victim waive or otherwise forfeit any rights or causes of action as a condition of granting restitution or partial restitution. In the case of a defendant who is on probation, the court may not refuse to enforce an order for restitution solely on the grounds that the order has been docketed as a civil judgment.

Subd. 1a. **Crime board request.** The Crime Victims Reparations Board may request restitution on behalf of a victim by filing a copy of orders of the board, if any, which detail any amounts paid by the board to the victim. The board may file the payment order with the court administrator or with the person or agency the court has designated to obtain information relating to restitution. The board shall submit the payment order not less than three business days after it is issued by the board. The court administrator shall provide copies of the payment order to the prosecutor and the offender or the offender's attorney within 48 hours of receiving it from the board or at least 24 hours before the sentencing or dispositional hearing, whichever is earlier. By operation of law, the issue of restitution is reserved if the payment order is not received at least three days before the sentencing or dispositional hearing. The filing of a payment order for reparations with the court administrator shall also serve as a request for restitution by the victim. The restitution requested by the board may be considered to be both on its own behalf and on behalf of the victim. If the board has not paid reparations to the victim or on the victim's behalf, restitution may be made directly to the victim. If the board has paid reparations to the victim or on the victim's behalf, the court shall order restitution payments to be made directly to the board.

Subd. 1b. **Affidavit of disclosure.** An offender who has been ordered by the court to make restitution in an amount of $500 or more shall file an affidavit of financial disclosure with the correctional agency responsible for investigating the financial resources of the offender on request of the agency. The commissioner of corrections shall prescribe what financial information the affidavit must contain.

Subd. 2. **Procedures.** The offender shall make restitution payments to the court administrator of the county, municipal, or district court of the county in which the restitution is to be paid. The court administrator shall disburse restitution in incremental payments and may not keep a restitution payment for longer than 30 days; except that the court administrator is not required to disburse a restitution payment that is under $10 unless the payment would fulfill the offender's restitution obligation. The court administrator shall keep records of the amount of restitution ordered in each case, any change made to the restitution order, and the amount of restitution actually paid by the offender. The court administrator shall forward the data collected to the state court administrator who shall compile the data and make it available to the supreme court and the legislature upon request.

Subd. 3. **Effect of order for restitution.** An order of restitution may be enforced by any person named in the order to receive the restitution, or by the Crime Victims Reparations Board in the same manner as a judgment in a civil action. Any order for restitution in favor of a victim shall also operate as an order for restitution in favor of the Crime Victims Reparations Board, if the board has paid reparations to the victim or on the victim's behalf. Filing fees for docketing an order of restitution as a civil judgment are waived for any victim named in the restitution order. An order of restitution shall be docketed as a civil judgment, in the name of any person named in the order and in the name of the crime victims reparations board, by the court administrator of the district court in the county in which the order of restitution was entered. The court administrator also shall notify the commissioner of revenue of the restitution debt in the manner provided in chapter 270A, the Revenue Recapture Act. A juvenile court is not required to appoint a guardian ad litem for a juvenile offender before docketing a restitution order. Interest shall accrue on the unpaid balance of the judgment as provided in section 549.09. Whether the order of restitution has been docketed or not, it is a debt that is not dischargeable in bankruptcy. A decision for or against restitution in any criminal or juvenile proceeding is not a bar to any civil action by the victim or by the state pursuant to section 611A.61 against the offender. The offender shall be given credit, in any order for judgment in favor of a victim in a civil action, for any restitution paid to the victim for the same injuries for which the judgment is awarded.

Subd. 4. **Payment of restitution.** When the court orders the payment of restitution and the payment of a fine, fees, surcharges, or other financial obligations, the court administrator shall apply any payments to the restitution obligation before applying payments to the fine, fees, surcharges, or other financial obligations, unless otherwise ordered by the court.

Subd. 5. **Unclaimed restitution payments.** Restitution payments held by the court for a victim that remain unclaimed by the victim for more than three years shall be deposited in the crime victims account created in section 611A.612.
At the time the deposit is made, the court shall record the name and last known address of the victim and the amount being deposited, and shall forward the data to the Crime Victims Reparations Board.

Subd. 6. **Estate of victim.** If a victim dies before or after a request for restitution is made or an order for restitution is issued, the personal representative of the victim's estate may request or enforce an order for restitution on behalf of the victim. If a personal representative is not appointed and no application is pending, an heir of the victim may file an affidavit to request or enforce an order for restitution pursuant to this subdivision. Appointment of a personal representative does not affect the right of other victims, as defined in section 611A.01, to request an order for restitution on their behalf.

HIST: 1983 c 262 art 1 s 4,6; 1985 c 110 s 1; 1986 c 463 s 10; 1Sp1986 c 3 art 1 s 82; 1987 c 244 s 2; 1987 c 254 s 11; 1989 c 21 s 4-6; 1990 c 579 s 8; 1991 c 211 s 1; 1992 c 571 art 5 s 6,7; 1993 c 326 art 6 s 8-10; 1994 c 636 art 7 s 3; 1995 c 226 art 7 s 9; 1996 c 408 art 7 s 6-8; 1997 c 239 art 7 s 24; 1999 c 136 s 1; 2013 c 39 s 1; 2014 c 204 s 11

611A.046 VICTIM'S RIGHT TO REQUEST PROBATION REVIEW HEARING.

A victim has the right to ask the offender's probation officer to request a probation review hearing if the offender fails to pay restitution as required in a restitution order.
HIST: 1989 c 21 s 8

611A.06 RIGHT TO NOTICE OF RELEASE.

Subdivision 1. **Notice of release required.** The commissioner of corrections or other custodial authority shall make a good faith effort to notify the victim that the offender is to be released from imprisonment or incarceration, including release on extended furlough and for work release; released from a juvenile correctional facility; released from a facility in which the offender was confined due to incompetency, mental illness, or mental deficiency, or commitment under section 253B.18 or chapter 253D; or if the offender's custody status is reduced, if the victim has mailed to the commissioner of corrections or to the head of the facility in which the offender is confined a written request for this notice, or the victim has made a request for this notice to the commissioner of corrections through the Department of Corrections electronic victim notification system. The good faith effort to notify the victim must occur prior to the offender's release or when the offender's custody status is reduced. For a victim of a felony crime against the person for which the offender was sentenced to imprisonment for more than 18 months, the good faith effort to notify the victim must occur 60 days before the offender's release.

Subd. 1a. **Notice of expungement required.** The prosecuting authority with jurisdiction over an offense for which expungement is being sought shall make a good faith effort to notify a victim that the expungement is being sought if: (1) the victim has mailed to the prosecuting authority with jurisdiction over an offense for which expungement is being sought a written request for this notice, or (2) the victim has indicated on a request for notice of expungement submitted under subdivision 1 a desire to be notified in the event the offender seeks an expungement for the offense.

A copy of any written request for a notice of expungement request received by the commissioner of corrections or other custodial authority shall be forwarded to the prosecutorial authority with jurisdiction over the offense to which the notice relates. The prosecutorial authority complies with this section upon mailing a copy of an expungement petition relating to the notice to the address which the victim has most recently provided in writing.

Subd. 2. **Contents of notice.** The notice given to a victim of a crime against a person must include the conditions governing the offender's release, and either the identity of the corrections agent who will be supervising the offender's release or a means to identify the court services agency that will be supervising the offender's release. The commissioner or other custodial authority complies with this section upon mailing the notice of impending release to the victim at the address which the victim has most recently provided to the commissioner or authority in writing, or by providing electronic notice to the victim who requested this notice through the Department of Corrections electronic victim notification system.

Subd. 3. **Notice of escape.** If an offender escapes from imprisonment or incarceration, including from release on extended furlough or work release, or from any facility described in subdivision 1, the commissioner or other custodial authority shall make all reasonable efforts to notify a victim who has requested notice of the offender's release under subdivision 1 within six hours after discovering the escape and shall also make reasonable efforts to notify the victim within 24 hours after the offender is apprehended.

Subd. 3a. **Offender location.** (a) Upon the victim's written or electronic request and if the victim and offender have been household or family members as defined in section 518B.01, subdivision 2, paragraph (b), the commissioner of corrections or the commissioner's designee shall disclose to the victim of an offender convicted of a qualified domestic violence-related offense as defined in section 609.02, subdivision 16, notification of the city and five-digit zip code of the offender's residency upon release from a Department of Corrections facility, unless:

(1) the offender is not under correctional supervision at the time of the victim's request;

(2) the commissioner or the commissioner's designee does not have the city or zip code; or

(3) the commissioner or the commissioner's designee reasonably believes that disclosure of the city or zip code of the offender's residency creates a risk to the victim, offender, or public safety.

(b) All identifying information regarding the victim including, but not limited to, the notification provided by the commissioner or the commissioner's designee is classified as private data on individuals as defined in section 13.02, subdivision 12, and is accessible only to the victim.

(c) This subdivision applies only where the offender is serving a prison term for a qualified domestic violence-related offense committed against the victim seeking notification.

Subd. 4. **Private data.** All identifying information regarding the victim, including the victim's request and the notice provided by the commissioner or custodial authority, is classified as private data on individuals as defined in section 13.02, subdivision 12, and is accessible only to the victim.

Subd. 5. **Definition.** As used in this section, "crime against the person" means a crime listed in section 611A.031.

HIST: 1983 c 262 art 1 s 5; 1986 c 444; 1986 c 445 s 4; 1986 c 463 s 11; 1987 c 224 s 3; 1988 c 649 s 4; 1989 c 190 s 4; 1990 c 579 s 9; 1991 c 170 s 5; 1993 c 326 art 6 s 11; art 13 s 35; 1994 c 636 art 7 s 5; 1Sp1994 c 1 art 2 s 33; 2001 c 209 s 7; 2012 c 155 s 8,9; 2013 c 49 s 22; 2014 c 312 art 6 s 5

611A.07 ELECTRONIC MONITORING TO PROTECT DOMESTIC ABUSE VICTIMS; STANDARDS.

Subdivision 1. **Generally.** The commissioner of corrections, after considering the recommendations of the Advisory Council on Battered Women and Domestic Abuse and the Sexual Assault Advisory Council, and in collaboration with the commissioner of public safety, shall adopt standards governing electronic monitoring devices used to protect victims of domestic abuse. In developing proposed standards, the commissioner shall consider the experience of the courts in the Tenth Judicial District in the use of the devices to protect victims of domestic abuse. These standards shall promote the safety of the victim and shall include measures to avoid the disparate use of the device with communities of color, product standards, monitoring agency standards, and victim disclosure standards.
* * *
HIST: 1992 c 571 art 6 s 20; 2000 c 445 art 2 s 9

611A.08 BARRING PERPETRATORS OF CRIMES FROM RECOVERING FOR INJURIES SUSTAINED DURING CRIMINAL CONDUCT.

Subdivision 1. **Definitions.** As used in this section:

(1) "perpetrator" means a person who has engaged in criminal conduct and includes a person convicted of a crime;

(2) "victim" means a person who was the object of another's criminal conduct and includes a person at the scene of an emergency who gives reasonable assistance to another person who is exposed to or has suffered grave physical harm;

(3) "course of criminal conduct" includes the acts or omissions of a victim in resisting criminal conduct; and

(4) "convicted" includes a finding of guilt, whether or not the adjudication of guilt is stayed or executed, an unwithdrawn judicial admission of guilt or guilty plea, a no contest plea, a judgment of conviction, an adjudication as a delinquent child, an admission to a juvenile delinquency petition, or a disposition as an extended jurisdiction juvenile.

Subd. 2. **Perpetrator's assumption of risk.** A perpetrator assumes the risk of loss, injury, or death resulting from or arising out of a course of criminal conduct involving a violent crime, as defined in this section, engaged in by the perpetrator or an accomplice, as defined in section 609.05, and the crime victim is immune from and not liable for any civil damages as a result of acts or omissions of the victim if the victim used reasonable force as authorized in section 609.06 or 609.065.

Subd. 3. **Evidence.** Notwithstanding other evidence which the victim may adduce relating to the perpetrator's conviction of the violent crime involving the parties to the civil action, a certified copy of: a guilty plea; a court judgment of guilt; a court record of conviction as specified in section 599.24, 599.25, or 609.041; an adjudication as a delinquent child; or a disposition as an extended jurisdiction juvenile pursuant to section 260B.130 is conclusive proof of the perpetrator's assumption of the risk.

Subd. 4. **Attorney fees to victim.** If the perpetrator does not prevail in a civil action that is subject to this section, the court may award reasonable expenses, including attorney's fees and disbursements, to the victim.
* * *

Subd. 6. **Violent crime; definition.** For purposes of this section, "violent crime" means an offense named in sections 609.185; 609.19; 609.195; 609.20; 609.205; 609.221; 609.222; 609.223; 609.2231; 609.24; 609.245; 609.25; 609.255; 609.342; 609.343; 609.344; 609.345; 609.561; 609.562; 609.563; and 609.582, or an attempt to commit any of these offenses. "Violent

crime" includes crimes in other states or jurisdictions which would have been within the definition set forth in this subdivision if they had been committed in this state.
HIST: 1995 c 226 art 6 s 15; 1999 c 139 art 4 s 2

611A.19 TESTING SEX OFFENDER FOR HUMAN IMMUNODEFICIENCY VIRUS.

Subdivision 1. **Testing on request of victim.** (a) Upon the request or with the consent of the victim, the prosecutor shall make a motion in camera and the sentencing court shall issue an order requiring an adult convicted of or a juvenile adjudicated delinquent for violating section 609.342 (criminal sexual conduct in the first degree), 609.343 (criminal sexual conduct in the second degree), 609.344 (criminal sexual conduct in the third degree), 609.345 (criminal sexual conduct in the fourth degree), or any other violent crime, as defined in section 609.1095, to submit to testing to determine the presence of human immunodeficiency virus (HIV) antibody if:

(1) the crime involved sexual penetration, however slight, as defined in section 609.341, subdivision 12; or

(2) evidence exists that the broken skin or mucous membrane of the victim was exposed to or had contact with the offender's semen or blood during the commission of the crime in a manner which has been demonstrated epidemiologically to transmit the human immunodeficiency virus (HIV).

(b) When the court orders an offender to submit to testing under paragraph (a), the court shall order that the test be performed by an appropriate health professional who is trained to provide the counseling described in section 144.7414, and that no reference to the test, the motion requesting the test, the test order, or the test results may appear in the criminal record or be maintained in any record of the court or court services, except in the medical record maintained by the Department of Corrections.

(c) The order shall include the name and contact information of the victim's choice of health care provider.

Subd. 2. **Disclosure of test results.** The date and results of a test performed under subdivision 1 are private data as defined in section 13.02, subdivision 12, when maintained by a person subject to chapter 13, or may be released only with the subject's consent, if maintained by a person not subject to chapter 13. The results are available, on request, to the victim or, if the victim is a minor, to the victim's parent or guardian and positive test results shall be reported to the commissioner of health. Unless the subject of the test is an inmate at a state correctional facility, any test results given to a victim or victim's parent or guardian shall be provided by a health professional who is trained to provide the counseling described in section 144.7414. If the subject of the test is an inmate at a state correctional facility, test results shall be given by the Department of Corrections' medical director to the victim's health care provider who shall give the results to the victim or victim's parent or guardian. Data regarding administration and results of the test are not accessible to any other person for any purpose and shall not be maintained in any record of the court or court services or any other record. After the test results are given to the victim or the victim's parent or guardian, data on the test must be removed from any medical data or health records maintained under sections 13.384 or 144.291 to 144.298 and destroyed, except for those medical records maintained by the Department of Corrections.
HIST: 1992 c 569 s 27; 1994 c 636 art 7 s 6; 1995 c 226 art 7 s 10; 1998 c 367 art 6 s 15; 1999 c 227 s 22; 2000 c 422 s 53,54; 2001 c 202 s 16; 2001 c 210 s 27; 2005 c 136 art 8 s 24; 2007 c 147 art 10 s 15

611A.20 NOTICE OF RISK OF SEXUALLY TRANSMITTED DISEASE.

Subdivision 1. **Notice required.** A hospital shall give a written notice about sexually transmitted diseases to a person receiving medical services in the hospital who reports or evidences a sexual assault or other unwanted sexual contact or sexual penetration. When appropriate, the notice must be given to the parent or guardian of the victim.
§Subd. 2.Contents of notice. The commissioners of public safety and corrections, in consultation with sexual assault victim advocates and health care professionals, shall develop the notice required by subdivision 1. The notice must inform the victim of:

(1) the risk of contracting sexually transmitted diseases as a result of a sexual assault;

(2) the symptoms of sexually transmitted diseases;

(3) recommendations for periodic testing for the diseases, where appropriate;

(4) locations where confidential testing is done and the extent of the confidentiality provided;

(5) information necessary to make an informed decision whether to request a test of the offender under section 611A.19; and

(6) other medically relevant information.

HIST: 1990 c 436 s 1; 1992 c 569 s 28

611A.201 DIRECTOR OF PREVENTION OF DOMESTIC VIOLENCE AND SEXUAL ASSAULT.

Subdivision 1. **Appointment of director.** The executive director of the Office of Justice Programs in the Department of Public Safety shall appoint a person to serve as director of domestic violence and sexual assault prevention in the office. The director must have experience in domestic violence and sexual assault prevention issues. The director serves at the executive director's pleasure in the unclassified service. The executive director may appoint, supervise, discipline, and discharge employees to assist the director in carrying out the director's responsibilities under this section.

Subd. 2. **Director's responsibilities.** The director shall have the following duties:

(1) advocate for the rights of victims of domestic violence and sexual assault;

(2) increase public education and visibility about the prevention of domestic violence and sexual assault;

(3) encourage accountability regarding domestic violence and sexual assault at all levels of the system, and develop recommendations to improve accountability when the system fails;

(4) support prosecution and civil litigation efforts regarding domestic violence and sexual assault at the federal and state levels;

(5) study issues involving domestic violence and sexual assault as they pertain to both men and women and present findings and recommendations resulting from these studies to all branches of government;

(6) initiate policy changes regarding domestic violence and sexual assault at all levels of government;

(7) coordinate existing resources and promote coordinated and immediate community responses to better serve victims of domestic violence and sexual assault;

(8) build partnerships among law enforcement, prosecutors, defenders, advocates, and courts to reduce the occurrence of domestic violence and sexual assault;

(9) encourage and support the efforts of health care providers, mental health experts, employers, educators, clergy members, and others, in raising awareness of and addressing how to prevent domestic violence and sexual assault;

(10) coordinate and maximize the use of federal, state, and local resources available to prevent domestic violence and sexual assault and leverage more resources through grants and private funding; and

(11) serve as a liaison between the executive director of the Office of Justice Programs in the Department of Public Safety and the commissioner of health with regard to the Department of Health's sexual violence prevention program funded by federal block grants, and oversee how this money is spent.

* * *

HIST: 2000 c 368 s 1; 1Sp2001 c 8 art 10 s 17; 2013 c 125 art 1 s 89-91

611A.203 DOMESTIC FATALITY REVIEW TEAMS.

Subdivision 1. **Domestic fatality review teams; purpose.** A judicial district may establish a domestic fatality review team to review domestic violence deaths that have occurred in the district. The team may review cases in which prosecution has been completed or the prosecutorial authority has decided not to pursue the case. The purpose of the review team is to assess domestic violence deaths in order to develop recommendations for policies and protocols for community prevention and intervention initiatives to reduce and eliminate the incidence of domestic violence and resulting fatalities.

Subd. 2. **Definition of domestic violence death.** "Domestic violence death" means a homicide or suicide under any of the following circumstances:

(1) the alleged perpetrator and victim resided together at any time;

(2) the alleged perpetrator and victim have a child in common, regardless of whether they were married or lived together at any time;

(3) the alleged perpetrator and victim were married, separated, or divorced;

(4) the alleged perpetrator and victim had a sexual relationship or a significant romantic relationship;

(5) the alleged perpetrator had been harassing or stalking the victim;

(6) the homicide victim lived in the same household, was present in the workplace of, was in proximity of, or was related by blood or affinity to a victim who experienced or was threatened with domestic abuse by the alleged perpetrator;

(7) the victim or the perpetrator was a child of a person in a relationship that is described within this definition; or

(8) any other circumstances that the domestic fatality review team decides fall within the parameters of its mission.

"Domestic violence death" must be interpreted broadly to give the domestic fatality review team discretion to review fatalities that have occurred both directly and peripherally to domestic relationships.

Subd. 3. **Membership.** (a) The chief judge, in consultation with the family violence coordinating council, shall appoint the members of the domestic fatality review team. Membership must reflect a commitment to diversity and relevant professional experience. The review team members must include:

(1) the medical examiner;

(2) a judicial court officer (judge or referee);

(3) a county and city attorney and a public defender;

(4) the county sheriff and a peace officer;

(5) a representative from family court services and the Department of Corrections;

(6) a physician familiar with domestic violence issues;

(7) a representative from district court administration and the domestic abuse service center;

(8) a public citizen representative or a representative from a civic organization;

(9) a mental health professional; and

(10) domestic violence advocates or shelter workers.

(b) There must be at least three domestic violence advocates or shelter workers on the domestic fatality review team. No two members may represent the same agency. Members representing advocates or shelters must be selected by the advocacy community. At least one position must be designated for a minority representative and one position must rotate in order to include an advocate from the community in which the fatality under review took place.

(c) The domestic fatality review team may also invite other relevant persons to serve on an ad hoc basis and participate as full members of the review team for a particular review. These persons may include, but are not limited to:

(1) individuals with particular expertise that would be helpful to the review panel; or

(2) representatives of organizations or agencies that had contact with or provided services to the homicide victim, or to the alleged perpetrator, a victim who experienced or was threatened with domestic abuse by the alleged perpetrator, or a family member of one of those individuals.

Subd. 4. **Duties; access to data.** (a) The domestic fatality review team shall collect, review, and analyze death certificates and death data, including investigative reports, medical and counseling records, victim service records, employment records, child abuse reports, or other information concerning domestic violence deaths, survivor interviews and surveys, and other information deemed by the team as necessary and appropriate concerning the causes and manner of domestic violence deaths.

(b) The review team has access to the following not public data, as defined in section 13.02, subdivision 8a, relating to a case being reviewed by the team: inactive law enforcement investigative data under section 13.82; autopsy records and coroner or medical examiner investigative data under section 13.83; hospital, public health, or other medical records of the victim under section 13.384; records under section 13.46, created by social service agencies that provided services to the victim, the alleged perpetrator, or another victim who experienced or was threatened with domestic abuse by the perpetrator; and child maltreatment records under chapter 260E, relating to the victim or a family or household member of the victim. Access to medical records under this paragraph also includes records governed by sections 144.291 to 144.298. The review team has access to corrections and detention data as provided in section 13.85.

(c) As part of any review, the domestic fatality review team may compel the production of other records by applying to the district court for a subpoena, which will be effective throughout the state according to the Rules of Civil Procedure.

Subd. 5. **Confidentiality; data privacy.** A person attending a domestic fatality review team meeting may not disclose what transpired at the meeting, except to carry out the purposes of the review team or as otherwise provided in this subdivision. The review team may disclose the names of the victims in the cases it reviewed. The proceedings and records of the review team are confidential data as defined in section 13.02, subdivision 3, or protected nonpublic data as defined in section 13.02, subdivision 13, regardless of their classification in the hands of the person who provided the data, and are not subject to discovery or introduction into evidence in a civil or criminal action against a professional, the state, or a county agency, arising out of the matters the team is reviewing. Information, documents, and records otherwise available from other sources are not immune from discovery or use in a civil or criminal action solely because they were presented during proceedings of the review team. This section does not limit a person who presented information before the review team or who is a member of the panel from testifying about matters within the person's knowledge. However, in a civil or criminal proceeding, a person may not be questioned about the person's good faith presentation of information to the review team or opinions formed by the person as a result of the review team meetings.

Subd. 6. **Immunity.** Members of the domestic fatality advisory board, members of the domestic fatality review team, and members of each review panel, as well as their agents or employees, are immune from claims and are not subject to any suits, liability, damages, or any other recourse, civil or criminal, arising from any act, proceeding, decision, or determination undertaken or performed or recommendation made by the domestic fatality review team, provided they acted in good faith and without malice in carrying out their responsibilities. Good faith is presumed until proven otherwise and the complainant has the burden of proving malice or a lack of good faith. No organization, institution, or person furnishing information, data, testimony, reports, or records to the domestic fatality review team as part of an investigation is civilly or criminally liable or subject to any other recourse for providing the information.

Subd. 7. **Evaluation and report.** (a) Each domestic fatality review team shall develop a system for evaluating the effectiveness of its program and shall focus on identifiable goals and outcomes. An evaluation must include data components as well as input from individuals involved in the review process.

(b) Each fatality review team shall issue an annual report to the chairs and ranking minority members of the senate and house of representatives committees with jurisdiction over public safety issues. The report must consist of the written aggregate recommendations of the domestic fatality review team without reference to specific cases. The report must be available upon request and distributed to the governor, attorney general, supreme court, county board, and district court.

HIST: 2009 c 59 art 2 s 2; 2013 c 82 s 37; 1Sp2019 c 5 art 2 s 29; 1Sp2020 c 2 art 8 s 142

611A.211 PROGRAMS FOR VICTIMS OF SEXUAL ASSAULT.
Subdivision 1. **Grants.** The commissioner of public safety shall award grants to programs which provide support services to victims of sexual assault. The commissioner shall also award grants for training, technical assistance, and the development and implementation of education programs to increase public awareness of the causes of sexual assault, the solutions to preventing and ending sexual assault, and the problems faced by sexual assault victims.
Subd. 2. **Applications.** Any public or private nonprofit agency may apply to the commissioner for a grant to provide services to victims of sexual assault. The application shall be submitted in a form approved by the commissioner.
Subd. 3. **Duties of grantees.** Every public or private nonprofit agency which receives a grant to provide services to victims of sexual assault shall comply with rules of the commissioner related to the administration of the grant programs.
Subd. 4. **Sexual assault.** For the purposes of this section, "sexual assault" means any violation of sections 609.342 to 609.3453.
HIST: 2014 c 212 art 1 s 8

611A.212 PROGRAMS FOR SEXUAL ASSAULT PRIMARY PREVENTION.
Subdivision 1. **Grants.** The commissioner of public safety shall award grants to programs that provide sexual assault primary prevention services to prevent initial perpetration or victimization of sexual assault.
Subd. 2. **Applications.** Any public or private nonprofit agency may apply to the commissioner for a grant. The commissioner may give preference to applications from an agency receiving a grant from the programs for victims of sexual assault under section 611A.211. The application shall be submitted in a form approved by the commissioner.
Subd. 3. **Duties of grantees.** Every public or private nonprofit agency that receives a grant to provide sexual assault primary prevention services shall comply with rules of the commissioner related to the administration of the grant programs.
Subd. 4. **Sexual assault.** For the purpose of this section, "sexual assault" means a violation of sections 609.342 to 609.3453.
HIST: 2015 c 65 art 1 s 20

611A.26 POLYGRAPH EXAMINATIONS; CRIMINAL SEXUAL CONDUCT COMPLAINTS; LIMITATIONS.
Subdivision 1. **Polygraph prohibition.** No law enforcement agency or prosecutor shall require that a complainant of a criminal sexual conduct or sex trafficking offense submit to a polygraph examination as part of or a condition to proceeding with the investigation, charging, or prosecution of such offense.
Subd. 2. **Law enforcement inquiry.** A law enforcement agency or prosecutor may not ask that a complainant of a criminal sexual conduct offense submit to a polygraph examination as part of the investigation, charging, or prosecution of such offense unless the complainant has been referred to, and had the opportunity to exercise the option of consulting with a sexual assault counselor as defined in section 595.02, subdivision 1, paragraph (k).
Subd. 3. **Informed consent requirement.** At the request of the complainant, a law enforcement agency may conduct a polygraph examination of the complainant only with the complainant's written, informed consent as provided in this subdivision.
§Subd. 4.Informed consent. To consent to a polygraph, a complainant must be informed in writing that:
(1) the taking of the polygraph examination is voluntary and solely at the victim's request;
(2) a law enforcement agency or prosecutor may not ask or require that the complainant submit to a polygraph examination;
(3) the results of the examination are not admissible in court; and

(4) the complainant's refusal to take a polygraph examination may not be used as a basis by the law enforcement agency or prosecutor not to investigate, charge, or prosecute the offender.

Subd. 5. **Polygraph refusal.** A complainant's refusal to submit to a polygraph examination shall not prevent the investigation, charging, or prosecution of the offense.

Subd. 6. **Definitions.** For the purposes of this section, the following terms have the meanings given.

(a) "Criminal sexual conduct" means a violation of section 609.342, 609.343, 609.344, 609.345, or 609.3451.

(b) "Sex trafficking" means a violation of section 609.322.

(c) "Complainant" means a person reporting to have been subjected to criminal sexual conduct or sex trafficking.

(d) "Polygraph examination" means any mechanical or electrical instrument or device of any type used or allegedly used to examine, test, or question individuals for the purpose of determining truthfulness.
HIST: 2007 c 54 art 4 s 7; 2015 c 65 art 6 s 18,19

611A.27 VICTIM RIGHTS TO SEXUAL ASSAULT EVIDENCE INFORMATION.

Subdivision 1. Access to law enforcement data. (a) Upon written request from the victim or victim's designee as described in subdivision 2, the investigating law enforcement agency shall release the following active investigative data, as defined in section 13.82, subdivision 7, to a victim of sexual assault about a submitted sexual assault examination kit, as defined in section 299C.106, subdivision 1, paragraph (g):

(1) the date that a sexual assault examination kit was submitted to a forensic laboratory, as defined in section 299C.157, subdivision 1, clause (2), and the date that the agency received notice of the results of that testing; and

(2) whether a DNA profile was obtained from the testing.

(b) The agency may refuse the request under paragraph (a) if the release of that data will interfere with the investigation.

Subd. 2. **Responding to a victim request for data.** No later than January 1, 2019, each law enforcement agency shall adopt policies and procedures subject to section 13.82, subdivision 7, to provide investigative data under this section that includes but is not limited to the following requirements:

(1) agency identification of a representative or representatives to respond to requests for data from sexual assault victims and to serve as a liaison between the agency and the forensic laboratory;

(2) agency response to inquiries within 30 days of receipt, unless the agency declines to provide the information under subdivision 1, paragraph (b);

(3) the sexual assault victim can designate another person to request information on the victim's behalf by providing written authorization to the agency except that an agency can decline to provide the information under subdivision 1, paragraph (b); and

(4) agency development of a procedure that allows a sexual assault victim to contact the agency representative to request that a restricted kit as defined in section 299C.106, subdivision 1, paragraph (e), be reclassified as an unrestricted kit as defined in section 299C.106, subdivision 1, paragraph (h), if the restricted kit is in the possession of the agency.
HIST: 2018 c 160 s 3

611A.31 DEFINITIONS.

Subdivision 1. **Scope.** For the purposes of sections 611A.31 to 611A.35, the following terms have the meanings given.

Subd. 2. **Battered woman.** "Battered woman" means a woman who is being or has been victimized by domestic abuse as defined in section 518B.01, subdivision 2.

Subd. 3. **Emergency shelter services.** "Emergency shelter services" include, but are not limited to, secure crisis shelters for battered women and housing networks for battered women.

Subd. 4. **Support services.** "Support services" include, but are not limited to, advocacy services, legal services, counseling services, transportation services, child care services, and 24 hour information and referral services.

Subd. 5. **Commissioner.** "Commissioner" means the commissioner of the Department of Corrections or a designee.

HIST: 1977 c 428 s 1; 1983 c 262 art 1 s 6; 1986 c 444; 1991 c 272 s 8; 1995 c 226 art 7 s 11; 2015 c 65 art 3 s 21

611A.32 BATTERED WOMEN PROGRAMS.

Subdivision 1. **Grants awarded.** The commissioner shall award grants to programs which provide emergency shelter services to battered women and support services to battered women and domestic abuse victims and their children. The commissioner shall also award grants for training, technical assistance, and for the development and implementation of education programs to increase public awareness of the causes of battering, the solutions to preventing and ending domestic violence, and the problems faced by battered women and domestic abuse victims. Grants shall be awarded in a manner that ensures that they are equitably distributed to programs serving metropolitan and nonmetropolitan populations. By July 1, 1995, community-based domestic abuse advocacy and support services programs must be established in every judicial assignment district.

Subd. 1a. **Program for American Indian women.** The commissioner shall establish at least one program under this section to provide emergency shelter services and support services to battered American Indian women. The commissioner shall grant continuing operating expenses to the program established under this subdivision in the same manner as operating expenses are granted to programs established under subdivision 1.

Subd. 2. **Applications.** Any public or private nonprofit agency may apply to the commissioner for a grant to provide emergency shelter services to battered women, support services to domestic abuse victims, or both, to battered women and their children. The application shall be submitted in a form approved by the commissioner by rule adopted under chapter 14 and shall include:

(1) a proposal for the provision of emergency shelter services for battered women, support services for domestic abuse victims, or both, for battered women and their children;

(2) a proposed budget;

(3) the agency's overall operating budget, including documentation on the retention of financial reserves and availability of additional funding sources;

(4) evidence of an ability to integrate into the proposed program the uniform method of data collection and program evaluation established under section 611A.33;

(5) evidence of an ability to represent the interests of battered women and domestic abuse victims and their children to local law enforcement agencies and courts, county welfare agencies, and local boards or departments of health;

(6) evidence of an ability to do outreach to unserved and underserved populations and to provide culturally and linguistically appropriate services; and

(7) any other content the commissioner may require by rule adopted under chapter 14, after considering the recommendations of the advisory council.

Programs which have been approved for grants in prior years may submit materials which indicate changes in items listed in clauses (1) to (7), in order to qualify for renewal funding. Nothing in this subdivision may be construed to require programs to submit complete applications for each year of renewal funding.

Subd. 3. **Duties of grantees.** Every public or private nonprofit agency which receives a grant to provide emergency shelter services to battered women and support services to battered women and domestic abuse victims shall comply with all rules of the commissioner related to the administration of the pilot programs.
* * *

Subd. 5. **Classification of data collected by grantees.** Personal history information and other information collected, used or maintained by a grantee from which the identity or location

of any victim of domestic abuse may be determined is private data on individuals, as defined in section 13.02, subdivision 12, and the grantee shall maintain the data in accordance with the provisions of chapter 13.
HIST: 1977 c 428 s 2; 1978 c 732 s 1-3; 1981 c 311 s 39; 1Sp1981 c 4 art 1 s 14; 1982 c 545 s 24; 1983 c 262 art 1 s 6; 1988 c 689 art 2 s 237; 1991 c 272 s 9,10; 1992 c 571 art 6 s 21; 2000 c 445 art 2 s 10-13; 2010 c 215 art 11 s 17; 2014 c 286 art 6 s 3

611A.35 DOMESTIC ABUSE PROGRAM DIRECTOR.

The commissioner shall appoint a program director. The program director shall administer the funds appropriated for sections 611A.31 to 611A.35 and perform other duties related to battered women's and domestic abuse programs as the commissioner may assign. The program director shall serve at the pleasure of the commissioner in the unclassified service.
HIST: 1977 c 428 s 5; 1983 c 262 art 1 s 6; 1986 c 444; 1991 c 272 s 14; 2000 c 445 art 2 s 19; 2014 c 286 art 6 s 6; 2015 c 65 art 3 s 23

611A.45 PROGRAMS FOR VICTIMS OF CRIME.

Subdivision 1. **Grants.** The commissioner of public safety shall award grants to programs which provide support services to victims of crime.

Subd. 2. **Applications.** Any public or private nonprofit agency may apply to the commissioner for a grant to provide services to victims of crime. The application shall be submitted in a form approved by the commissioner.

Subd. 3. **Duties of grantees.** Every public or private nonprofit agency which receives a grant to provide services to victims of crime shall comply with rules of the commissioner related to the administration of the grant programs.
HIST: 2014 c 212 art 1 s 10

Editors' Note: Selected portions of Chapter 611A concerning the Minnesota Crime Victims Reparations Board have been edited to eliminate those provisions that have less importance to the duties of peace officers.

611A.51 TITLE.

Sections 611A.51 to 611A.68 shall be known as the Minnesota crime victims reparations act.
HIST: 1974 c 463 s 1; 1983 c 262 art 1 s 6

611A.52 DEFINITIONS.

Subdivision 1. **Terms.** For the purposes of sections 611A.51 to 611A.68 the following terms shall have the meanings given them.

Subd. 2. **Accomplice.** "Accomplice" means any person who would be held criminally liable for the crime of another pursuant to section 609.05.

Subd. 3. **Board.** "Board" means the crime victims reparations board established by section 611A.55.

Subd. 4. **Claimant.** "Claimant" means a person entitled to apply for reparations pursuant to sections 611A.51 to 611A.68.

Subd. 5. **Collateral source.** "Collateral source" means a source of benefits or advantages for economic loss otherwise reparable under sections 611A.51 to 611A.67 which the victim or claimant has received, or which is readily available to the victim, from:

(1) the offender;

(2) the government of the United States or any agency thereof, a state or any of its political subdivisions, or an instrumentality of two or more states, unless the law providing for the benefits or advantages makes them excess or secondary to benefits under sections 611A.51 to 611A.68;

(3) social security, Medicare, and Medicaid;

(4) state required temporary nonoccupational disability insurance;

(5) workers' compensation;

(6) wage continuation programs of any employer;

(7) proceeds of a contract of insurance payable to the victim for economic loss sustained because of the crime;

(8) a contract providing prepaid hospital and other health care services, or benefits for disability; or

(9) any private source as a voluntary donation or gift;

(10) proceeds of a lawsuit brought as a result of the crime.

The term does not include a life insurance contract.

Subd. 6. **Crime.** (a) "Crime" means conduct that:

(1) occurs or is attempted anywhere within the geographical boundaries of this state, including Indian reservations and other trust lands;

(2) poses a substantial threat of personal injury or death; and

(3) is included within the definition of "crime" in section 609.02, subdivision 1, or would be included within that definition but for the fact that (i) the person engaging in the conduct lacked capacity to commit the crime under the laws of this state; or (ii) the act was alleged or found to have been committed by a juvenile.

(b) A crime occurs whether or not any person is prosecuted or convicted but the conviction of a person whose acts give rise to the claim is conclusive evidence that a crime was committed unless an application for rehearing, appeal, or petition for certiorari is pending or a new trial or rehearing has been ordered.

(c) "Crime" does not include an act involving the operation of a motor vehicle, aircraft, or watercraft that results in injury or death, except that a crime includes any of the following:

(1) injury or death intentionally inflicted through the use of a motor vehicle, aircraft, or watercraft;

(2) injury or death caused by a driver in violation of section 169.09, subdivision 1; 169A.20; or 609.21; and

(3) injury or death caused by a driver of a motor vehicle in the immediate act of fleeing the scene of a crime in which the driver knowingly and willingly participated.

(d) Notwithstanding paragraph (a), "crime" includes an act of international terrorism as defined in United States Code, title 18, section 2331, committed outside of the United States against a resident of this state.

Subd. 7. **Dependent.** "Dependent" means any person who was dependent upon a deceased victim for support at the time of the crime.

Subd. 8. **Economic loss.** "Economic loss" means actual economic detriment incurred as a direct result of injury or death.

(a) In the case of injury the term is limited to:

(1) reasonable expenses incurred for necessary medical, chiropractic, hospital, rehabilitative, and dental products, services, or accommodations, including ambulance services, drugs, appliances, and prosthetic devices;

(2) reasonable expenses associated with recreational therapy where a claimant has suffered amputation of a limb;

(3) reasonable expenses incurred for psychological or psychiatric products, services, or accommodations, not to exceed an amount to be set by the board, where the nature of the injury or the circumstances of the crime are such that the treatment is necessary to the rehabilitation of the victim;

(4) loss of income that the victim would have earned had the victim not been injured;

(5) reasonable expenses incurred for substitute child care or household services to replace those the victim or claimant would have performed had the victim or the claimant's child not been injured. As used in this clause, "child care services" means services provided by facilities licensed under and in compliance with either Minnesota Rules, _* * *_ or exempted from licensing requirements pursuant to section 245A.03. Licensed facilities must be paid at a rate not to exceed $3 an hour per child for daytime child care or $4 an hour per child for evening child care;

(6) reasonable expenses actually incurred to return a child who was a victim of a crime under section 609.25 or 609.26 to the child's parents or lawful custodian. These expenses are limited to transportation costs, meals, and lodging from the time the child was located until the child was returned home; and

(7) the claimant's moving expenses, storage fees, and phone and utility installation fees, up to a maximum of $1,000 per claim, if the move is necessary due to a reasonable fear of danger related to the crime for which the claim was filed.

(b) In the case of death the term is limited to:

(1) reasonable expenses actually incurred for funeral, burial, or cremation, not to exceed an amount to be determined by the board on the first day of each fiscal year;

(2) reasonable expenses for medical, chiropractic, hospital, rehabilitative, psychological and psychiatric services, products or accommodations which were incurred prior to the victim's death and for which the victim's survivors or estate are liable;

(3) loss of support, including contributions of money, products or goods, but excluding services which the victim would have supplied to dependents if the victim had lived; and

(4) reasonable expenses incurred for substitute child care and household services to replace those which the victim or claimant would have performed for the benefit of dependents if the victim or the claimant's child had lived.

Claims for loss of support for minor children made under clause (3) must be paid for three years or until the child reaches 18 years old, whichever is the shorter period. After three years, if the child is less than 18 years old a claim for loss of support may be resubmitted to the board, and the board staff shall evaluate the claim giving consideration to the child's financial need and to the availability of funds to the board. Claims for loss of support for a spouse made under clause (3) shall also be reviewed at least once every three years. The board shall evaluate the claim giving consideration to the spouse's financial need and to the availability of funds to the board.

Claims for substitute child care services made under clause (4) must be limited to the actual care that the deceased victim would have provided to enable surviving family members to pursue economic, educational, and other activities other than recreational activities.

Subd. 9. **Injury.** "Injury" means actual bodily harm including pregnancy and emotional trauma.

Subd. 10. **Victim.** "Victim" means a person who suffers personal injury or death as a direct result of:

(1) a crime;

(2) the good faith effort of any person to prevent a crime; or

(3) the good faith effort of any person to apprehend a person suspected of engaging in a crime.

HIST: 1974 c 463 s 2; * * *; 2016 c 158 art 1 s 207

611A.53 ELIGIBILITY FOR REPARATIONS.

Subdivision 1. **Generally.** Except as provided in subdivisions 1a and 2, the following persons shall be entitled to reparations upon a showing by a preponderance of the evidence that the requirements for reparations have been met:

(a) a victim who has incurred economic loss;

(b) a dependent who has incurred economic loss;

(c) the estate of a deceased victim it the estate has incurred economic loss;

(d) any other person who has incurred economic loss by purchasing any of the products, services, and accommodations described in section 611A.52, subdivision 8, for a victim;

(e) the guardian, guardian ad litem, conservator or authorized agent of any of these persons.

Subd. 1a. **Providers; limitations.** No hospital, medical organization, health care provider, or other entity that is not an individual may qualify for reparations under subdivision 1, clause (d). * * *

Subd. 2. **Limitations on awards.** No reparations shall be awarded to a claimant otherwise eligible if:

(a) the crime was not reported to the police within 30 days of its occurrence or, if it could not reasonably have been reported within that period, within 30 days of the time when a report could reasonably have been made. A victim of criminal sexual conduct in the first, second, third, or fourth degree who does not report the crime within 30 days of its occurrence is deemed to have been unable to have reported it within that period;

(b) the victim or claimant failed or refused to cooperate fully with the police and other law enforcement officials;

(c) the victim or claimant was the offender or an accomplice of the offender or an award to the claimant would unjustly benefit the offender or an accomplice;

(d) the victim or claimant was in the act of committing a crime at the time the injury occurred;

(e) no claim was filed with the board within two years of victim's injury or death; except that (1) if the claimant was unable to file a claim within that period, then the claim can be made within three years of the time when a claim could have been filed; and (2) if the victim's injury or death was not reasonably discoverable within three years of the injury or death, then the claim can be made within three years of the time when the injury or death is reasonably discoverable [; or] * * *

(f) the claim is less than $50.

The limitations contained in clauses (a) and (e) do not apply to victims of domestic child abuse. In those cases the three year limitation period commences running with the report of the crime to the police.

HIST: 1974 c 463 s 3; * * * 2005 c 136 art 8 s 25

611A.54 AMOUNT OF REPARATIONS.

Reparations shall equal economic loss except that:

(1) reparations shall be reduced to the extent that economic loss is recouped from a collateral source or collateral sources. Where compensation is readily available to a claimant from a collateral source, the claimant must take reasonable steps to recoup from the collateral source before claiming reparations;

(2) reparations shall be denied or reduced to the extent, if any, that the board deems reasonable because of the contributory misconduct of the claimant or of a victim through whom the claimant claims; and

(3) reparations paid to all claimants suffering economic loss as the result of the injury or death of any one victim shall not exceed $50,000.

No employer may deny an employee an award of benefits based on the employee's eligibility or potential eligibility for reparations.

HIST: 1974 c 463 s 4; * * * 1989 c 264 s 5

611A.55 CRIME VICTIMS REPARATIONS BOARD.

Subdivision 1. Creation of board. There is created in the department of public safety, for budgetary and administrative purposes, the crime victims reparations board, which shall consist of five members appointed by the commissioner of public safety. * * *

HIST: 1974 c 463 s 5; * * * 2007 c 13 art 1 s 17,18

611A.56 POWERS AND DUTIES OF THE BOARD.

Subdivision 1. Duties. In addition to carrying out any duties specified elsewhere in sections 611A.51 to 611A.68 or in other law, the board shall:

(a) provide all claimants with an opportunity for hearings pursuant to chapter 14;

(b) adopt rules to implement and administer sections 611A.51 to 611A.68, including rules governing the method of practice and procedure before the board, prescribing the manner in which applications for reparations shall be made, and providing for discovery proceedings; [and]

(c) publicize widely the availability of reparations and the method of making claims[.]
* * *

Subd. 2. **Powers.** In addition to exercising any powers specified elsewhere in sections 611A.51 to 611A.68 or other law, the board upon its own motion or the motion of a claimant or the attorney general may:

(a) issue subpoenas for the appearance of witnesses and the production of books, records, and other documents; * * *

(d) order a mental or physical examination of a victim or an autopsy of a deceased victim provided that notice is given to the person to be examined and that the claimant and the attorney general receive copies of any resulting report;

(e) suspend or postpone the proceedings on a claim if a criminal prosecution arising out of the incident which is the basis of the claim has been commenced or is imminent;

(f) request from prosecuting attorneys and law enforcement officers investigations and data to enable the board to perform its duties under sections 611A.51 to 611A.68; [and] * * *

(h) reconsider any decision granting or denying reparations or determining their amount.
HIST: 1974 c 463 s 6; * * * 1997 c 7 art 2 s 64

611A.57 DETERMINATION OF CLAIMS.

Subdivision 1. [Repealed, 1993 c 326 art 6 s 26]

Subd. 2. **Investigation.** The board staff shall examine the papers filed in support of the claim and cause an investigation to be conducted into the validity of the claim to the extent that an investigation is necessary. * * *

Subd. 4. **Written decision.** The written decision granting or denying a claim shall be filed with the board, and a copy shall be provided to the claimant.

Subd. 5. **Reconsideration.** The claimant may, within 30 days after receiving the decision of the board, apply for reconsideration before the entire board. Upon request for reconsideration, the board shall reexamine all information filed by the claimant, including any new information the claimant provides, and all information obtained by investigation. The board may also conduct additional examination into the validity of the claim. Upon reconsideration, the board may affirm, modify, or reverse its prior ruling. A claimant denied reparations upon reconsideration is entitled to a contested case hearing within the meaning of chapter 14.

Subd. 6. **Data.** Claims for reparations and supporting documents and reports are investigative data and subject to the provisions of section 13.39 until the claim is paid, denied, withdrawn, or abandoned. Following the payment, denial, withdrawal, or abandonment of a claim, the claim and supporting documents and reports are private data on individuals as defined in section 13.02, subdivision 12; provided that the board may forward any reparations claim forms, supporting documents, and reports to local law enforcement authorities for purposes of implementing section 611A.67.
HIST: 1974 c 463 s 7; * * * 1993 c 326 art 6 s 15-17
* * *

611A.61 SUBROGATION.

Subdivision 1. **Subrogation rights of state.** The state shall be subrogated, to the extent of reparations awarded, to all the claimant's rights to recover benefits or advantages for economic loss from a source which is or, if readily available to the victim or claimant would be, a collateral source. Nothing in this section shall limit the claimant's right to bring a cause of action to recover for other damages.

Subd. 2. **Duty of claimant to assist.** A claimant who receives reparations must agree to assist the state in pursuing any subrogation rights arising out of the claim. The board may require a claimant to agree to represent the state's subrogation interests if the claimant brings a cause of action for damages arising out of the crime or occurrence for which the board has awarded reparations. An attorney who represents the state's subrogation interests pursuant to the client's agreement with the board is entitled to reasonable attorney's fees not to exceed one-third of the amount recovered on behalf of the state.

Subd. 3. Repealed, 1995 c 226 art 7 s 26

HIST: 1974 c 463 s 10; * * *1989 c 335 art 4 s 101

611A.62 MEDICAL PRIVILEGE.

There is no privilege as to communication or records relevant to an issue of the physical, mental, or emotional condition of the claimant or victim in a proceeding under sections 611A.51 to 611A.56 in which that condition is an issue. Nothing contained in this section shall be interpreted to abridge the attorney-client privilege.
HIST: 1974 c 463 s 11; 1983 c 262 art 1 s 6

611A.63 ENFORCEMENT OF BOARD'S ORDERS.

If a person refuses to comply with an order of the board or asserts a privilege to withhold or suppress evidence relevant to a claim, the board may make any just order including denial of the claim, but may not find the person in contempt. If necessary to carry out any of its powers and duties, the board may petition the district court for an appropriate order, but the court may not find a person in contempt for refusal to submit to a mental or physical examination.
HIST: 1974 c 463 s 12; 1983 c 262 art 1 s 6

611A.64 DEPARTMENT OF CORRECTIONS; RESTITUTION.

The department of corrections may, as a means to assist in the rehabilitation of persons committed to their care, establish programs and procedures whereby such persons may contribute toward restitution of those persons injured as a consequence of their criminal acts.
HIST: 1974 c 463 s 13; 1983 c 262 art 1 s 6

611A.65 USE OF RECORD OF CLAIM; EVIDENCE.

Neither a record of the proceedings on a claim, a decision of the board, nor the fact that an award has been made or denied shall be admissible as evidence in any criminal or civil action against the alleged offender, except an action by the state on its subrogation claim.
HIST: 1974 c 463 s 14; 1979 c 173 s 2; 1983 c 262 art 1 s 6

611A.66 LAW ENFORCEMENT AGENCIES; DUTY TO INFORM VICTIMS OF RIGHT TO FILE CLAIM.

All law enforcement agencies investigating crimes shall provide victims with notice of their right to apply for reparations with the telephone number to call to request an application form.

Law enforcement agencies shall assist the board in performing its duties under sections 611A.51 to 611A.68. Law enforcement agencies within ten days after receiving a request from the board shall supply the board with requested reports, notwithstanding any provisions to the contrary in chapter 13, and including reports otherwise maintained as confidential or not open to inspection under section 260.161. All data released to the board retains the data classification that it had in the possession of the law enforcement agency.
HIST: 1974 c 463 s 15; * * * 1995 c 266 art 7 s 25

611A.67 FRAUDULENT CLAIMS; PENALTY.

Any person who knowingly makes a false claim under sections 611A.51 to 611A.68 is guilty of a gross misdemeanor.
HIST: 1974 c 463 s 16; 1983 c 262 art 1 s 6; 1988 c 638 s 7

611A.68 LIMITING COMMERCIAL EXPLOITATION OF CRIMES; PAYMENT OF VICTIMS.

Subdivision 1. **Definition.** For purposes of this section, the following terms have the meanings given them in this subdivision.

(a) "Contract" means an agreement regarding, in whole or in part, (1) the reenactment of an offender's crime by way of a movie, book, newspaper or magazine article, radio or television presentation, or live or recorded entertainment of any kind, or (2) the expression of the offender's thoughts, feelings, opinions, or emotions about the crime.

(b) "Crime" means an offense which is a felony under the laws of Minnesota or that would have been a felony if committed in Minnesota, and includes an offense committed or attempted on an Indian reservation or other trust land.

(c) "Offender" means a person convicted of a crime or found not guilty of a crime by reason of insanity.

(d) "Person" includes persons, corporations, partnerships, and other legal entities.

Subd. 2. Repealed, 1988 c 638 s 17

Subd. 2a. **Notice and payment of proceeds to board required.** A person that enters into a contract with an offender convicted in this state, and a person that enters into a contract in this state with an offender convicted in this state or elsewhere within the United States, must comply with this section if the person enters into the contract during the ten years after the offender is convicted of a crime or found not guilty by reason of insanity. If an offender is imprisoned or committed to an institution following the conviction or finding of not guilty by reason of insanity, the ten-year period begins on the date of the offender's release. A person subject to this section must notify the crime victims reparations board of the existence of the contract immediately upon its formation, and pay over to the board money owed to the offender or the offender's representatives by virtue of the contract according to the following proportions:

(a) if the crime occurred in this state, the person shall pay to the board 100 percent of the money owed under the contract;

(b) if the crime occurred in another jurisdiction having a law applicable to the contract which is substantially similar to this section, this section does not apply, and the person must not pay to the board any of the money owed under the contract; and

(c) in all other cases, the person shall pay to the board that percentage of money owed under the contract which can fairly be attributed to commerce in this state with respect to the subject matter of the contract.

Subd. 3. **Victim notification.** When the board receives a payment pursuant to this section, it shall attempt to notify any known victims of the crime and shall publish a notice of that fact in a newspaper having general circulation in the county where the crime was committed. The expenses of notification shall be paid from the amount received for that case.

Subd. 4. **Deductions.** When the board has made reparations payments to or on behalf of a victim of the offender's crime pursuant to sections 611A.51 to 611A.68, it shall deduct the amount of the reparations award from any payment received under this section by virtue of the offender's contract unless the board has already been reimbursed for the reparations award from another collateral source.

Subd. 4a. **Offender's minor dependent claims.** Immediately after money is deposited with the board under this section, the board may allocate up to ten percent of any money remaining after a deduction is made under subdivision 4 for the benefit of the offender's dependent minor children. The board shall then retain the funds allocated until a claim is made by the dependent minor children or their representative. Upon receiving a claim, the board shall disburse the allocated funds to the dependent minor children if it is shown by clear and convincing evidence that the funds will not be used in a way that benefits the offender.

Subd. 4b. **Claims by victims of offender's crime.** A victim of a crime committed by the offender and the estate of a deceased victim of a crime committed by the offender may submit the following claims for reparations and damages to the board to be paid from money received by virtue of the offender's contract:

(1) claims for reparations to which the victim is entitled under sections 611A.51 to 611A.68 and for which the victim has not yet received an award from the board;

(2) claims for reparations to which the victim would have been entitled under sections 611A.51 to 611A.68, but for the $50,000 maximum limit contained in section 611A.54, clause (3); and

(3) claims for other uncompensated damages suffered by the victim as a result of the offender's crime including, but not limited to, damages for pain and suffering.

The victim must file the claim within five years of the date on which the board received payment under this section. The board shall determine the victim's claim in accordance with the procedures contained in sections 611A.57 to 611A.63. An award made by the board under this subdivision must be paid from the money received by virtue of the offender's contract that remains after a deduction or allocation, if any, has been made under subdivision 4 or 4a.

Subd. 4c. **Claims by other crime victims.** The board may use money received by virtue of an offender's contract for the purpose of paying reparations awarded to victims of other crimes pursuant to sections 611A.51 to 611A.68 under the following circumstances:

(1) moneys remain after deductions and allocations have been made under subdivisions 4 and 4a, and claims have been paid under subdivision 4b; or

(2) no claim is filed under subdivision 4b within five years of the date on which the board received payment under this section.

None of these moneys may be used for purposes other than the payment of reparations.

Subd. 5. [Repealed, 1988 c 638 s 17]

Subd. 6. **Payments for costs of defense.** Notwithstanding any other provision of this section, the board shall make payments to an offender from the account of amounts received with reference to that offender upon the order of a court of competent jurisdiction after a showing by that offender that the money shall be used for the reasonable costs of defense in the appeal of a criminal conviction or in proceedings pursuant to this section.

    * * *

Subd. 8. **Penalty.** (a) A person who willfully fails to notify the board of the existence of a contract as required by this section is guilty of a gross misdemeanor.

(b) Except as otherwise provided in paragraph (a), any person or offender who takes any action, whether by way of execution of a power of attorney, creation of corporate or trust entities or otherwise, to defeat the purpose of this section is guilty of a misdemeanor.

HIST: 1979 c 234 s 1; * * * 1995 c 226 art 7 s 25

611A.74 CRIME VICTIM OMBUDSMAN; CREATION.

Subdivision 1. **Authority under this act.** The commissioner shall have the authority under sections 611A.72 to 611A.74 to investigate decisions, acts, and other matters of the criminal justice system so as to promote the highest attainable standards of competence, efficiency, and justice for crime victims in the criminal justice system.

Subd. 1a. [Repealed, 2002 c 220 art 7 s 33]

Subd. 2. **Duties.** The commissioner investigate complaints concerning possible violation of the rights of crime victims or witnesses provided under this chapter, the delivery of victim services by victim assistance programs, the administration of the crime victims reparations act, and other complaints of mistreatment by elements of the criminal justice system or victim assistance programs. The commissioner shall act as a liaison, when the commissioner deems necessary, between agencies, either in the criminal justice system or in victim assistance programs, and victims and witnesses. The commissioner may be concerned with activities that strengthen procedures and practices which lessen the risk that objectionable administrative acts will occur. The commissioner must answer questions concerning the criminal justice system and victim services put to the commissioner by victims and witnesses in accordance with the commissioner's knowledge of the facts or law, unless the information is otherwise restricted. The commissioner shall establish a procedure for referral to the crime victim crisis centers, the crime victims reparations board, and other victim assistance programs when services are requested by crime victims or deemed necessary by the commissioner.

The commissioner's files are confidential data as defined in section 13.02, subdivision 3, during the course of an investigation or while the files are active. Upon completion of the investigation or when the files are placed on inactive status, they are private data on individuals as defined in section 13.02, subdivision 12.

Subd. 3. **Powers.** The commissioner has those powers necessary to carry out the duties set out in subdivision 2, including:

(a) The commissioner may investigate, with or without a complaint, any action of an element of the criminal justice system or a victim assistance program included in subdivision 2.

(b) The commissioner may request and shall be given access to information and assistance the commissioner considers necessary for the discharge of responsibilities. The commissioner may inspect, examine, and be provided copies of records and documents of all elements of the criminal justice system and victim assistance programs. The commissioner may request and shall be given access to police reports pertaining to juveniles and juvenile delinquency petitions, notwithstanding section 260.161. Any information received by the commissioner retains its data classification under chapter 13 while in the commissioner's possession. Juvenile records obtained under this subdivision may not be released to any person.
* * *

(d) After completing investigation of a complaint, the commissioner shall inform in writing the complainant, the investigated person or entity, and other appropriate authorities, including the attorney general, of the action taken. If the complaint involved the conduct of an element of the criminal justice system in relation to a criminal or civil proceeding, the commissioner's findings shall be forwarded to the court in which the proceeding occurred.
* * *

Subd. 4. **No compelled testimony.** Neither the ombudsman nor any member of the ombudsman's staff may be compelled to testify in any court with respect to matters involving the exercise of official duties except as may be necessary to enforce the provisions of this section.

Subd. 5. **Recommendations.** (a) On finding a complaint valid after duly considering the complaint and whatever material the commissioner deems pertinent, the commissioner may recommend action to the appropriate authority.

(b) If the commissioner makes a recommendation to an appropriate authority for action, the authority shall, within a reasonable time period, inform the commissioner about the action taken or the reasons for not complying with the recommendation.
* * *

HIST: 1Sp1985 c 4 s 20; * * * 2002 c 220 art 7 s 22-27,33

611A.90 RELEASE OF VIDEOTAPES OF CHILD ABUSE VICTIMS.

Subdivision 1. **Definition.** For purposes of this section, "physical abuse" and "sexual abuse" have the meanings given in section 260E.03, except that abuse is not limited to acts by a person responsible for the child's care or in a significant relationship with the child or position of authority.

Subd. 2. **Court order required.** (a) A custodian of a videotape of a child victim or alleged victim alleging, explaining, denying, or describing an act of physical or sexual abuse as part of an investigation or evaluation of the abuse may not release a copy of the videotape without a court order, notwithstanding that the subject has consented to the release of the videotape or that the release is authorized under law.
(b) The court order may govern the purposes for which the videotape may be used, reproduction, release to other persons, retention and return of copies, and other requirements reasonably necessary for protection of the privacy and best interests of the child.

Subd. 3. **Petition.** An individual subject of data, as defined in section 13.02, or a patient, as defined in sections 144.291 to 144.298, who is seeking a copy of a videotape governed by this section may petition the district court in the county where the alleged abuse took place or where the custodian of the videotape resides for an order releasing a copy of the videotape under subdivision 2. Nothing in this section establishes a right to obtain access to a videotape by any other person nor limits a right of a person to obtain access if access is otherwise authorized by law or pursuant to discovery in a court proceeding.
History: 1995 c 259 art 4 s 6; 2007 c 147 art 10 s 15; 1Sp2020 c 2 art 8 s 143

611A.95 CERTIFICATION FOR VICTIMS OF CRIMES.

Subdivision 1. **Definitions.** For purposes of this section, the following terms have the meanings given:

(1) "certifying entity" means a state or local law enforcement agency;

(2) "criminal activity" means qualifying criminal activity pursuant to section 101(a)(15)(U)(iii) of the Immigration and Nationality Act, as amended through June 1, 2021, and includes the attempt, conspiracy, or solicitation to commit such crimes; and

(3) "certification" means any certification or statement required by federal immigration law, as amended through June 1, 2021, including, but not limited to, the information required by United States Code, title 8, section 1184(p), and United States Code, title 8, section 1184(o), including current United States Citizenship and Immigration Services Form I-918, Supplement B, and United States Citizenship and Immigration Services Form I-914, Supplement B, and any substantively similar successor forms.

Subd. 2. Certification process. (a) A certifying entity shall process a certification requested by a victim of criminal activity or a representative of the victim, including the victim's attorney, family member, or domestic violence or sexual assault violence advocate, within the time period prescribed in paragraph (b).

(b) A certifying entity shall process the certification within 90 days of request, unless the victim is in removal proceedings, in which case the certification shall be processed within 14 days of request. Requests for expedited certification must be affirmatively raised at the time of the request.

(c) An active investigation, the filing of charges, or a prosecution or conviction are not required for the victim of criminal activity to request and obtain the certification, provided that the certifying entity initiated an investigation and the victim cooperated in it.

Subd. 3. Certifying entity; designate agent. (a) The head of a certifying entity shall designate an agent to perform the following responsibilities:

(1) timely process requests for certification;

(2) provide outreach to victims of criminal activity to inform them of the entity's certification process; and

(3) keep a written or electronic record of all certification requests and responses.

(b) All certifying entities shall implement a language access protocol for non-English-speaking victims of criminal activity.

Subd. 4. Disclosure prohibited; data classification. (a) A certifying entity is prohibited from disclosing the immigration status of a victim of criminal activity, except to comply with federal law or legal process, or if authorized by the victim of criminal activity or representative requesting the certification.

(b) Data provided to a certifying entity under this section is classified as private data pursuant to section 13.02, subdivision 12.

EFFECTIVE DATE. Subdivisions 1, 2, and 4 are effective the day following final enactment. Subdivision 3 is effective July 1, 2021.

HIST: 1Sp2021 c 11 art 3 s 34

629.341 ALLOWING PROBABLE CAUSE ARRESTS FOR DOMESTIC VIOLENCE; IMMUNITY FROM LIABILITY.

* * *

Subd. 3. **Notice of rights.** The peace officer shall tell the victim whether a shelter or other services are available in the community and give the victim immediate notice of the legal rights and remedies available. The notice must include furnishing the victim a copy of the following statement:

"IF YOU ARE THE VICTIM OF DOMESTIC VIOLENCE, you can ask the city or county attorney to file a criminal complaint. You also have the right to go to court and file a petition requesting an order for protection from domestic abuse. The order could include the following:

(1) an order restraining the abuser from further acts of abuse;

(2) an order directing the abuser to leave your household;

(3) an order preventing the abuser from entering your residence, school, business, or place of employment;

(4) an order awarding you or the other parent custody of or parenting time with your minor child or children; or

(5) an order directing the abuser to pay support to you and the minor children if the abuser has a legal obligation to do so."

The notice must include the resource listing, including telephone number, for the area battered women's shelter, to be designated by the Department of Corrections.

* * *

HIST: 1978 c 724 s 2; 1979 c 204 s 1; 1981 c 273 s 13; 1983 c 226 s 1; 1984 c 655 art 1 s 79; 1985 c 265 art 10 s 1; 1986 c 444; 1993 c 326 art 2 s 29; 1995 c 226 art 7 s 18; 1998 c 371 s 18; 1999 c 227 s 22; 2000 c 444 art 2 s 48; 2004 c 290 s 37; 2009 c 59 art 2 s 3; 2013 c 125 art 1 s 101; 2014 c 177 s 2

629.342 LAW ENFORCEMENT POLICIES; DOMESTIC ABUSE ARRESTS.

* * *

Subd. 3. **Assistance to victim where no arrest.** If a law enforcement officer does not make an arrest when the officer has probable cause to believe that a person is committing or has committed domestic abuse or violated an order for protection, the officer shall provide immediate assistance to the victim. Assistance includes:

(1) assisting the victim in obtaining necessary medical treatment; and

(2) providing the victim with the notice of rights under section 629.341, subdivision 3.

Subd. 4. **Immunity.** A peace officer acting in good faith and exercising due care in providing assistance to a victim pursuant to subdivision 3 is immune from civil liability that might result from the officer's action.

HIST: 1992 c 571 art 6 s 22; 1993 c 326 art 2 s 30; 2000 c 445 art 2 s 28; 2014 c 212 art 1 s 12; 2014 c 286 art 6 s 7

634.045 JAILHOUSE WITNESSES.

Subdivision 1. **Definitions.** (a) As used in this section, the following terms have the meanings given.

(b) "Benefit" means any plea bargain, bail consideration, reduction or modification of sentence, or any other leniency, immunity, financial payment, reward, or amelioration of current or future conditions of incarceration offered or provided in connection with, or in exchange for, testimony that is offered or provided by a jailhouse witness.

(c) "Jailhouse witness" means a person who (1) while incarcerated, claims to have obtained information from a defendant in a criminal case or a person suspected to be the perpetrator of an offense, and (2) offers or provides testimony concerning statements made by that defendant or person suspected to be the perpetrator of an offense. It does not mean a codefendant or confidential informant who does not provide testimony against a suspect or defendant.

(d) "Commissioner" means the commissioner of corrections.

* * *

Subd. 5. **Victim notification.** (a) A prosecutor shall make every reasonable effort to notify a victim if the prosecutor has decided to offer or provide any of the following to a jailhouse witness in exchange for, or as the result of, a jailhouse witness offering or providing testimony against a suspect or defendant:

(1) reduction or dismissal of charges;

(2) a plea bargain;

(3) support for a modification of the amount or conditions of bail; or

(4) support for a motion to reduce or modify a sentence.

(b) Efforts to notify the victim should include, in order of priority: (1) contacting the victim or a person designated by the victim by telephone; and (2) contacting the victim by mail. If a jailhouse witness is still in custody, the notification attempt shall be made before the jailhouse witness is released from custody.

(c) Whenever a prosecutor notifies a victim of domestic assault, criminal sexual conduct, or harassment or stalking under this section, the prosecutor shall also inform the victim of the method and benefits of seeking an order for protection under section 518B.01 or a restraining order under section 609.748 and that the victim may seek an order without paying a fee.

(d) The notification required under this subdivision is in addition to the notification requirements and rights described in sections 611A.03, 611A.0315, 611A.039, and 611A.06.
EFFECTIVE DATE. This section is effective August 1, 2021.
HIST: 1Sp2021 c 11 art 3 s 35

APPENDIX - GLOSSARY OF TERMS

Editors' Note: In addition to statutory terms specifically identified in the Learning Objectives, this glossary includes terms that are closely related to them or which complement the foundational goal of a specialized body of knowledge for Minnesota's professional peace officer education. Where primary legal authority is cited for a particular term, that term should be read in conjunction with the cited legal authority. Terms that are defined separately in the Glossary are identified in **bold.** *The definitions cited below from Black's Law Dictionary (11th ed. 2019, Bryan A. Garner editor in chief) are copyrighted by Thomson Reuters and used by permission.*

Affirmative Defense: A defendant's assertion of facts and arguments that, if true, will defeat the plaintiff's or prosecution's claim, even if all the allegations in the complaint are true. The defendant bears the burden of proving an affirmative defense. *Black's Law Dictionary*, 11th ed. (2019).

Ammunition: Ammunition or cartridge cases, primers, bullets, or propellant powder designed for use in any firearm. Ammunition does not include ornaments, curiosities, or souvenirs constructed from or resembling ammunition or ammunition components that are not operable as ammunition. Minn. Stat. § 609.02, subd. 17 (2021).

Arraignment: A hearing conducted in open court where, except in cases involving homicide where the case will be presented to a grand jury or offenses punishable by life imprisonment, the court must ask the defendant to enter a plea. If the defendant pleads guilty, the case proceeds to pre-sentencing and sentencing. If the defendant does not wish to plead guilty, the arraignment must be continued until the **Omnibus Hearing**. Minn. R. Crim. P. 8.02, subd. 1.

Arrest: Taking a person into **custody** that the person may be held to answer for a public offense. "Arrest" includes actually restraining a person or taking into **custody** a person who submits. Minn. Stat. § 629.30 (2021).

Arrest Warrant: A **warrant** issued by a disinterested magistrate after a showing of probable cause, directing a law-enforcement officer to arrest and take a person into **custody**. *Black's Law Dictionary*, 11th ed. (2019).

Assault: (1) An act done with intent to cause fear in another of immediate bodily harm or death; or (2) the intentional infliction of or attempt to inflict **bodily harm** upon another. Minn. Stat. § 609.02, subd. 10 (2021).

Bodily Harm: Physical pain or injury, illness, or any impairment of physical condition. Minn. Stat. § 609.02, subd. 7 (2021).

Circumstantial Evidence: Indirect evidence used to prove an issue by implication or inference. Circumstantial evidence, <u>even if</u> believed, does <u>not</u> necessarily resolve a question or issue. *Cf.* **direct evidence.**

Conviction: Any of the following accepted and recorded by the court: (1) a plea of guilty; or (2) a verdict of guilty by a jury or a finding of guilty by the court. Minn. Stat. § 609.02, subd. 5 (2021).

Crime: Conduct which is prohibited by statute and for which the actor may be sentenced to imprisonment, with or without a fine. Minn. Stat. § 609.02, subd. 1 (2021).

Crime of Violence: A violation of, or an attempt or conspiracy to violate, certain enumerated laws of Minnesota or any similar laws of the United States or any other state. Minn. Stat. § 609.1095, subd. 1(d) (2021).

Criminal Gang: Any ongoing organization, association, or group of three or more persons, whether formal or informal, that: (1) has, as one of its primary activities, the commission of one or more of the offenses listed in section 609.11, subdivision 9; (2) has a common name or common identifying sign or symbol; and (3) includes members who individually or collectively engage in or have engaged in a pattern of criminal activity. Minn. Stat. § 609.229, subd. 1 (2021).

Curtilage: The land or yard adjoining a house, usually within an enclosure. Under the Fourth Amendment, the curtilage is an area usually protected from **warrantless searches.** *Black's Law Dictionary*, 11th ed. (2019).

Custody: To be in custody means that a reasonable person in the suspect's situation would have understood that he was in custody. If a suspect has not yet been arrested, a district court must examine all of the surrounding circumstances and evaluate whether a reasonable person in the suspect's position would have believed he was in custody to the degree associated with **arrest.** *State v. Staats*, 658 N.W.2d 207, 211 (Minn. 2003).

Dangerous Weapon: Any firearm, whether loaded or unloaded, or any device designed as a weapon and capable of producing death or great bodily harm, any combustible or flammable liquid or other device or instrumentality that, in the manner it is used or intended to be used, is calculated or likely to produce death or great bodily harm, or any fire that is used to produce death or great bodily harm. "Flammable liquid" means any liquid having a flash point below 100 degrees Fahrenheit and having a vapor pressure not exceeding 40 pounds per square inch (absolute) at 100 degrees Fahrenheit but does not include intoxicating liquor. "Combustible liquid" is a liquid having a flash point at or above 100 degrees Fahrenheit. Minn. Stat. § 609.02, subd. 6 (2021).

De-escalation: The strategic slowing down of an incident in a manner that allows officers more time, distance, space and tactical flexibility during dynamic situations on the street. *Press Release, U.S. Dept. of Justice, Justice Department Applauds Adoption of Police Department-Wide Tactical De-escalation Training Program in Seattle (Apr. 16, 2015).*

Direct Evidence: Evidence that directly and necessarily proves a point. Evidence which, <u>if believed</u>, resolves a question or issue. *Cf.* **circumstantial evidence.**

Domestic Abuse: Any of the following, if committed against a **family or household member** by a family or household member: (1) physical harm, bodily injury, or **assault**; (2) the infliction of fear of imminent physical harm, bodily injury, or **assault**; or (3) **terroristic threats**, within the meaning of section 609.713, subdivision 1; criminal sexual conduct, within the meaning of section 609.342, 609.343, 609.344, 609.345, or 609.3451; or interference with an emergency call within the meaning of section 609.78, subdivision 2. Minn. Stat. § 518B.01, subd. 2(a) (2021).

Double Jeopardy: The fact of being prosecuted or sentenced twice for substantially the same offense. Double jeopardy is prohibited by the Fifth Amendment. *Black's Law Dictionary*, 11th ed. (2019).

Drug Endangered Child: A child in circumstances where a parent, legal guardian, or caretaker who endangers the child's person or health by knowingly causing or permitting the child to be present where any person is selling, manufacturing, possessing immediate precursors or chemical substances with intent to manufacture, or possessing a controlled substance, as defined in section 152.01, subdivision 4. Minn. Stat. § 609.378, subd. 2(b)(2) (2021). *See also* 32 U.S.C. § 10663 (authorizing grants to States, territories, and Indian tribes (as defined in section 10554 for the purpose of carrying out programs to provide comprehensive services to aid children who are living in a home in which methamphetamine or other controlled substances are unlawfully manufactured, distributed, dispensed, or used.

Entrapment: An **affirmative defense** to a criminal charge in which the defendant must show by a fair preponderance of the evidence that the government induced the defendant to commit the crime. Inducement must involve something in the nature of persuasion, badgering, or pressure by the state. The defense will bar a conviction unless the state can show beyond a reasonable doubt that the defendant was predisposed to commit the crime. The prosecution may prove predisposition by evidence that the accused readily responded to the state's solicitation to commit a crime. *State v. Abraham*, 345 N.W.2d 745, 747 (Minn. 1983).

Escalation: An increase in the extent, volume, number, amount, intensity, or scope of a situation.

Exclusionary Rule: A rule that excludes or suppresses evidence obtained in violation of an accused person's constitutional rights. *Black's Law Dictionary*, 11th ed. (2019).

Exigent Circumstances: A situation in which a police officer must take immediate action to effectively make an arrest, search, or seizure for which probable cause exists, and thus may do so without first obtaining a warrant. Exigent circumstances may exist if (1) a person's life or safety is threatened, (2) a suspect's escape is imminent, or (3) evidence is about to be removed or destroyed. *Black's Law Dictionary*, 11th ed. (2019).

Ex-Parte: Done or made at the instance and for the benefit of one party only, and without notice to, or argument by, anyone having an adverse interest; of, relating to, or involving court action taken or received by one party without notice to the other, usually for temporary or emergency relief [e.g.,] an ex parte hearing [or] an ex parte injunction. *Black's Law Dictionary*, 11th ed. (2019).

Family or Household Member: (1) spouses and former spouses; (2) parents and children; (3) persons related by blood; (4) persons who are presently residing together or who have resided together in the past; (5) persons who have a child in common regardless of whether they have been married or have lived together at any time; (6) a man and woman if the woman is pregnant and the man is alleged to be the father, regardless of whether they have been married or have lived together at any time; and (7) persons involved in a significant romantic or sexual relationship. Minn. Stat. § 518B.01, subd. 2(b) (2021).

Felony: A crime for which a sentence of imprisonment for more than one year may be imposed. Minn. Stat. § 609.02, subd. 2 (2021).

Forfeiture: A governmental proceeding brought against a person to **seize** property as punishment for the person's criminal behavior. *Black's Law Dictionary*, 11th ed. (2019). The court may order a person convicted of certain crimes, e.g., **racketeering**, to forfeit to the prosecuting authority any real or personal property that was used in the course of, intended for use in the course of, derived from, or realized through criminal conduct. Minn. Stat. § 609.905 (2021).

Fruit-of-the-Poisonous Tree Doctrine: The rule that evidence derived from an illegal search, arrest, or interrogation is inadmissible because the evidence (the "fruit") was tainted by the illegality (the "poisonous tree"). *Black's Law Dictionary*, 11th ed. (2019). *Cf.* **inevitable discovery.**

Good Faith Exception: An exception to the **exclusionary rule** adopted by the U.S. Supreme Court in *U.S. v. Leon*, 468 U.S. 897, 913 (1984) (holding that the exclusionary rule should not be applied so as to bar the use in the prosecution's case in chief of evidence obtained by officers acting in **reasonable** reliance on a **search warrant** issued by a detached and neutral magistrate but ultimately found to be invalid).

Great Bodily Harm: Bodily injury which creates a high probability of death, or which causes serious permanent disfigurement, or which causes a permanent or protracted loss or impairment of the function of any bodily member or organ or other serious bodily harm. Minn. Stat. § 609.02, subd. 8 (2021).

Gross Misdemeanor: Any **crime** which is not a **felony** or **misdemeanor**. The maximum fine which may be imposed for a gross misdemeanor is $3,000. Minn. Stat. § 609.02, subd. 4 (2020).

Guardian ad Litem: An independent person, not necessarily an attorney, whom the court appoints to represent the interests of a minor or incapacitated person and advise the court. In all child custody, marriage dissolution, or legal separation proceedings where custody or parenting time is an issue, and the court as reason to believe that the minor is a victim of domestic child abuse or neglect, the court must appoint a guardian ad litem. Minn. Stat. § 518.165, subd. 2 (2021).

Harassment Restraining Order: A restraining order that a court may issue on behalf of a person who is a victim of harassment. Minn. Stat. § 609.748 (2021).

***In Loco Parentis*:** Of, relating to, or acting as a temporary guardian or caretaker of a child, taking on all or some of the responsibilities of a parent. The Supreme Court has recognized that during the school day, a teacher or administrator may act *in loco parentis*. *Black's Law Dictionary*, 11th ed. (2019).

Indictment: 1. The formal written accusation of a crime, made by a grand jury and presented to a court for prosecution against the accused person. 2. The act or process of preparing or bringing forward such a formal written accusation. *Black's Law Dictionary*, 11th ed. (2019).

Inevitable Discovery: The rule that evidence obtained indirectly from an illegal search is admissible, and the illegality of the search is harmless, if the evidence would have been obtained nevertheless in the ordinary course of police work. The rule is an exception to the **fruit-of-the-poisonous-tree** doctrine. The prosecution bears the burden of establishing the inevitability of the discovery. *Black's Law Dictionary*, 11th ed. (2019).

***Mens Rea*:** The state of mind that the prosecution, to secure a conviction, must prove that a defendant had when committing a **crime**, [e.g.,] the mens rea for theft is the intent to deprive the rightful owner of the property. Under the Model Penal Code, the required levels of mens rea — expressed by the adverbs *purposely*, *knowingly*, *recklessly*, and *negligently* — are termed "culpability requirements." *Black's Law Dictionary*, 11th ed. (2019).

Mental State: When criminal intent is an element of a **crime**, such intent is indicated by term "intentionally," the phrase "with intent to," the phrase "with intent that," or some form of the verbs "know" or "believe." "Know" requires only that the actor believes that a specified fact exists. "Intentionally" means that the actor either has a purpose to do the thing or cause the result specified or believes that the act performed by the actor, if successful, will cause that result. In addition, the actor must know those facts which are necessary to make the actor's conduct criminal and which are set forth after the word "intentionally." "With intent to" or "with intent that" means that the actor either has a purpose to do the thing or cause the result specified or believes that the act, if successful, will cause the result. Criminal intent does not require proof of knowledge of the existence or constitutionality of the statute under which the actor is prosecuted or the scope or meaning of the terms used in the statute. Criminal intent does not require proof of knowledge of a minor's age even though age is a material element in the crime in question. Minn. Stat. § 609.02, subd. 9 (2021).

***Miranda* Warning:** A constitutional requirement that police inform individuals in **custody** and subject to interrogation that they have the right to remain silent, that any statements they make may subsequently be used against them at trial, and they have the right to be assisted by an attorney. *Miranda v. Arizona*, 348 U.S. 436 (1966).

Misdemeanor: A **crime** for which a sentence of not more than 90 days or a fine of not more than $1,000, or both, may be imposed. Minn. Stat. § 609.02, subd. 3 (2020).

Night-Capped Warrant: A **warrant** issued pursuant to statute authorizing law enforcement to make an **arrest** at any time. Minn. Stat. § 609.31 (2021).

No-Contact Order: An order issued by a court against a defendant in a criminal proceeding or a juvenile offender in a delinquency proceeding for **domestic abuse**, harassment or stalking, violation of an **order for protection**, or violation of a prior domestic abuse no contact order. Minn. Stat. § 629.75, subd. 1 (2021).

Objectively Reasonable: A test applied in e.g., Fourth Amendment cases, to judge whether a police officer's actions are lawful, and which does not depend on the officer's subjective intentions; *Terry v. Ohio*, 392 U.S. 1, 21-22 (1968) (holding that facts must be judged against an objective standard: would the facts available to the officer at the moment of the **seizure** or the search 'warrant a man of reasonable caution in the belief' that the action taken was appropriate?).

Omnibus Hearing: An evidentiary hearing which must be held in **felony** and **gross misdemeanor** cases where the defendant has pleaded not guilty and which deals with motions relating to, inter alia, probable cause, evidentiary issues, discovery, constitutional issues, and any other issues related to a fair and expeditious trial. Minn. R. Crim. P. 11.02.

Order for Protection: Relief for which a party alleging **domestic abuse** may petition the court and which may include, but is not limited to, restraining the abusing party from committing acts of domestic abuse and excluding the abusing party from a shared dwelling. Minn. Stat. § 518B.01, subds., 4, 6(a) (2021).

Organized Crime: Widespread criminal activities that are coordinated and controlled through a central syndicate. *Black's Law Dictionary*, 11th ed. (2019).

Parole: The conditional release of a prisoner from imprisonment before the full sentence has been served. Although not available under some sentences, parole is usually granted for good behavior on the condition that the parolee regularly report to a supervising officer for a specified period. *Black's Law Dictionary*, 11th ed. (2019).

Petty Misdemeanor: A petty offense, which is prohibited by statute, which does not constitute a **crime** and for which a sentence of a fine of not more than $300 may be imposed. Minn. Stat. § 609.02, subd. 4a (2020).

Pre-Assaultive Indicators: Verbal or non-verbal behaviors or cues suggesting that contact or engagement may **escalate** to assault.

Predatory Offender: A person was charged with or petitioned for a **felony** violation of or attempt to violate, or aiding, abetting, or conspiracy to commit certain enumerated statutes and convicted of or adjudicated delinquent for that offense or another offense arising out of the same set of circumstances. Minn. Stat. § 243.166 (2021).

Probable Cause: A **reasonable** ground to suspect that a person has committed or is committing a **crime** or that a place contains specific items connected with a crime. Under the Fourth Amendment, probable cause — which amounts to more than a bare suspicion but less than evidence that would justify a conviction — must be shown before an arrest warrant or **search warrant** may be issued. *Black's Law Dictionary*, 11th ed. (2019).

Probation: A court-ordered sanction imposed upon an offender for a period of supervision no greater than that set by statute. It is imposed as an alternative to confinement or in conjunction with confinement or intermediate sanctions. The purpose of probation is to deter further criminal behavior, punish the offender, help provide reparation to **crime** victims and their communities, and provide offenders with opportunities for rehabilitation. Minn. Stat. § 609.02, subd. 15 (2021).

Qualified Domestic Violence Related Offense: A violation of certain enumerated Minnesota statutes and similar laws of other states, the United States, the District of Columbia, and United States territories. Minn. Stat. § 609.02, subd. 16 (2021).

Qualified Domestic Violence-Related Order: An order that a court may issue in connection with certain offenses. Minn. Stat. § 609.02, subd. 16 (2021).

Racketeering: A person is guilty of racketeering if the person: (1) is employed by or associated with an enterprise and intentionally conducts or participates in the affairs of the enterprise by participating in a pattern of criminal activity; (2) acquires or maintains an interest in or control of an enterprise, or an interest in real property, by participating in a pattern of criminal activity; or (3) participates in a pattern of criminal activity and knowingly invests any proceeds derived from that conduct, or any proceeds derived from the investment or use of those proceeds, in an enterprise or in real property. Minn. Stat. § 609.903, subd. 1 (2021).

Reasonable: 1. Fair, proper, or moderate under the circumstances; sensible; 2. According to reason. 3. (Of a person) having the faculty of reason. *Black's Law Dictionary*, 11th ed. (2019); *Graham v. Connor*, 490 U.S. 386, 396 (1990) (holding that the test or reasonableness under the Fourth Amendment is not capable of precise definition or mechanical application and requires careful attention to the facts and circumstances of each particular case, including the severity of the **crime** at issue, whether the suspect poses an immediate threat to the safety of the officers or others, and whether he is actively resisting arrest or attempting to evade arrest by flight).

Reasonable Force: A peace officer may not subject the person arrested to any more restraint than is necessary for the **arrest** and detention. Minn. Stat. § 629.32 (2021); *Johnson v. Morris*, 453 N.W.2d 31, 40 (Minn. 1990) (noting that courts have refused to classify the pointing of a gun at a suspect during the course of an arrest as being "unreasonable" because permitting police to use such threats may actually decrease the potentiality of violence).

Reasonable Suspicion: A particularized and objective basis for suspecting criminal activity. Reasonable suspicion requires something more than an unarticulated hunch, and the officer must be able to point to something that objectively supports the suspicion at issue. An assessment of reasonable suspicion must be based on the **totality of the circumstances**—the whole picture. *State v. Lugo*, 887 N.W.2d 476, 486-87 (Minn. 2016).

Search Warrant: A judge's written order authorizing a law-enforcement officer to conduct a search of a specified place and to **seize** evidence. *Black's Law Dictionary*, 11ᵗʰ ed. (2019). Search **warrant** applications must be supported by a written affidavit signed under oath, a signed statement attested to under oath, or by a written statement signed under penalty of perjury. Minn. R. Crim. P. 37.01.

Second or Subsequent Violation or Offense: Prior to the commission of the violation or offense, the actor has been adjudicated guilty of a specified similar violation or offense. (Minn. Stat. § 609.02, subd. 11 (2021).

Seizure: The act or an instance of taking possession of a person or property by legal right or process; esp., in constitutional law, a confiscation or arrest that may interfere with a person's reasonable expectation of privacy. *Black's Law Dictionary*, 11ᵗʰ ed. (2019). Property that is contraband may be seized by the commissioner of revenue or the director of alcohol and gambling enforcement or their authorized agents or by any sheriff or other police officer, with or without process, and is subject to **forfeiture.** Minn. Stat. § 349.2125, subd. 2 (2021).

Situational Factors: The characteristics of police-citizen encounters that may influence how an officer acts during that situation. Such factors are external in that they apply to the suspect or the victim, for example.

Status Offense: 1. A **crime** of which a person is guilty by being in a certain condition or of a specific character. 2. A minor's violation of the juvenile code by doing some act that would not be considered illegal if an adult did it, but that indicates that the minor is beyond parental control. 3. An offense that only a certain category of people can be charged with, such as felon in possession of a firearm. 4. An offense in which motive is not a consideration in determining guilt, such as a traffic violation. *Black's Law Dictionary*, 11ᵗʰ ed. (2019).

Subpoena: A writ or order commanding a person to appear before a court or other tribunal, subject to a penalty for failing to comply. *Black's Law Dictionary*, 11ᵗʰ ed. (2019).

Substantial Bodily Harm: Bodily injury which involves a temporary but substantial disfigurement, or which causes a temporary but substantial loss or impairment of the function of any bodily member or organ, or which causes a fracture of any bodily member. Minn. Stat. § 609.02, subd. 7a (2021).

Summons: 1. A writ or process commencing the plaintiff's action and requiring the defendant to appear and answer. 2. A notice requiring a person to appear in court as a juror or witness. *Black's Law Dictionary*, 11ᵗʰ ed. (2019).

Terroristic Threats: Threatening, directly or indirectly, to commit any **crime of violence** with purpose to terrorize another or to cause evacuation of a building, place of assembly, vehicle or facility of public transportation or otherwise to cause serious public inconvenience, or in a reckless disregard of the risk of causing such terror or inconvenience. Minn. Stat. § 609.713, subd. 1 (2021).

Totality of Circumstances: A standard for determining whether evidence (such as an informant's tip) is sufficiently reliable to establish probable cause for an **arrest** or **search warrant**. Under this test, the reliability of the evidence is weighed by focusing on the entire situation as described in the **probable-cause** affidavit, and not on any one specific factor. *Black's Law Dictionary*, 11th ed. (2019).

Vice Crime: A **crime** of immoral conduct, such as gambling or prostitution. *Black's Law Dictionary*, 11th ed. (2019).

Warrant: A writ directing or authorizing someone to do an act, especially one directing a law enforcer to make an **arrest**, a **search**, or a **seizure**. *Black's Law Dictionary*, 11th ed. (2019). If the facts in the complaint and any supporting documents or supplemental sworn testimony establish probable cause to believe an offense has been committed and the defendant committed it, a **summons** or warrant must issue. A summons rather than a warrant must issue unless a substantial likelihood exists that the defendant will fail to respond to a summons, the defendant's location is not reasonably discoverable, or the defendant's arrest is necessary to prevent imminent harm to anyone. A warrant for the defendant's arrest must be issued to any person authorized by law to execute it. The warrant or summons must be issued by a judge of the district court. If the offense is punishable by fine only, a court administrator may issue the summons when authorized by court order. A summons must issue in lieu of a warrant if the offense is punishable by fine only in misdemeanor cases. A judge must issue a summons whenever requested to do so by the prosecutor. If a defendant fails to appear in response to a summons, a warrant must issue. Minn. R. Crim. P. 3.01.

Warrantless Searches: A search conducted absent a **warrant**. Warrantless searches and **seizures** are per se unreasonable unless permitted by one of a limited number of exceptions, including the presence of **probable cause** that an individual has committed a **crime** and **exigent circumstances** related to its investigation. The state bears the burden of showing that at least one of the exceptions applies in order to avoid suppression of the evidence acquired from the warrantless search. *State v. Johnson*, 698 N.W.2d 247, 251 (Minn. 2004). Other exceptions to the warrant requirement involve *Terry* stops, searches incident to **arrest**, consent, public schools, drug testing, prisons, and probation and **parole** regulation.